THE BRIEF

AMERICAN PAGEANT

THE BRIEF

AMERICAN PAGEANT

A HISTORY OF THE REPUBLIC

Seventh Edition

VOLUME I

TO 1877

David M. Kennedy
Stanford University

Lizabeth Cohen
Harvard University

Mel Piehl
Valparaiso University

Houghton Mifflin Company Boston New York

Publisher: Suzanne Jeans
Senior Marketing Manager: Katherine Bates
Marketing Assistant: Lauren Bussard
Senior Development Editor: Jeffrey Greene
Senior Project Editor: Bob Greiner
Editorial Assistant: Emily Meyer
Senior Art and Design Coordinator: Jill Haber
Cover Design Director: Anthony F. Saizon
Senior Photo Editor: Jennifer Meyer Dare
Composition Buyer: Chuck Dutton
New Title Project Manager: James Lonergan

Cover Image: *Goddess of Liberty Weathervane.* American. Gilded and molded copper, third quarter of the 19th c. Courtesy of Sotheby's Inc.

Printed in the U.S.A.

Library of Congress Control Number: 2006924976

Instructor's Exam Copy
ISBN-10: 0-618-83408-7
ISBN-13: 978-0-618-83408-2

For orders, use student text ISBNs:
ISBN-10: 0-618-77613-3
ISBN-13: 978-0-618-77613-9

2 3 4 5 6 7 8 9-CRK-10 09 08 07

CONTENTS

PART TWO

Building the New Nation

1776–1860

112

PART THREE

Testing the New Nation

1820–1877

MAPS

CHARTS AND TABLES

PREFACE

This new edition of *The Brief American Pageant,* a concise version of *The American Pageant,* Thirteenth Edition, includes significant innovations. As always, this Brief Edition presents the core content of *The American Pageant* in an efficient and attractive fashion. For the first time in the Brief Edition, we have included numerous additional features designed to enhance core academic skills and foundational knowledge essential to serious academic work in history, as well as closely related areas of the social sciences and humanities. This Brief Edition aims not only to teach students American history, but also to teach them how to learn history and other subjects more effectively.

The text incorporates these features while preserving the liveliness and readability that have long been *The American Pageant*'s hallmark. We are often told that the *Pageant* is the sole American history text that has a distinctive personality—defined by clarity, concreteness, a consistent chronological narrative, strong emphasis on major themes, avoidance of clutter, access to a variety of interpretive perspectives, and a colorful writing style leavened, as appropriate, with wit. That personality, we strongly believe, is what has made the Pageant both appealing and useful to countless students for more than four decades. In *The Brief American Pageant,* Seventh Edition, David M. Kennedy, Lizabeth Cohen, and Mel Piehl have preserved the parent text's essential character, while making this edition far more useful to students and instructors alike.

Changes in this Edition

Like *The American Pageant,* the Brief Edition provides overview essays designed to encourage students to think coherently about six eras in American history. Those essays, revised for this edition, demonstrate that the study of history is not just a matter of piling up mountains of facts, but is principally concerned with discovering complex patterns of change over time and organizing seemingly disparate events, actions, and ideas into meaningful chains of cause and consequence.

The Brief Edition includes for the first time the feature "Examining the Evidence." This feature is intended to deepen students' understanding of the historical craft in another way, by conveying how historians develop interpretations of the past through research in many kinds of primary sources. Students will learn about the insights historians derive from a wide range of historical artifacts: what a letter from a black freedman to his former master in 1865 reveals about his family's enslavement as well as their hopes for a new life; how a song popular during World War I contains clues to soldiers' experiences in the military; why the *Gettysburg Address* sheds light not only on President Lincoln's brilliant oratory but also on his vision of the American nation; what the manuscript census teaches us about immigrant households on the Lower East Side of New York in 1900; and how a new kind of architectural structure—the shopping mall—changed both consumers' behavior and politicians' campaign tactics after World War II. Other featured sources include maps, furniture, clothing, private correspondence, travelogues, paintings and photographs, court decisions, political broadsides and cartoons, novels, motion pictures, newspapers, public opinion polling, and transcripts of important diplomatic conferences and political meetings.

The popular "Makers of America" feature shows how Americans have forged their group identities through shared experiences, intellectual interests, and technical skills as well as through ethnicity and neighborhoods. The twenty-nine essays constitute a comprehensive mosaic of the diverse peoples and groups that have composed our strikingly pluralistic society.

Readers will also find in this edition of *The Brief American Pageant* enriched discussion of the experiences and contributions of women, the Seven Years' War, the election of 1800, law and the national economy in the antebellum period, the Compromise of 1850, the rise of colleges and universities, American involvement in Asia, the Spanish-American War, and the Cold War.

Our greatest attention in this revision has gone to expanding two areas of inquiry that are often overlooked in U.S. history textbooks: the cultural innovations and ideas that have engaged Americans and the international context in which U.S. history has unfolded. We hope to give readers a greater appreciation for the contributions of American writers, artists, and thinkers, while also conveying how extensively the American experience has been shaped by interaction with other peoples on the world stage.

In addition, this Brief Edition introduces for the first time boxed quotations that provide more varied perspectives to the events chronicled in the *Pageant's* historical narrative. We have also compressed and reorganized the material concerning United States foreign involvements from 1890–1909 into a single Chapter 27. Treatment of the post-World War II period has expanded to include an additional chapter, as that era lengthens in time. The final chapter has been thoroughly revised, to portray the present state of the nation in historical perspective. Updated "Varying Viewpoints" essays reflect new interpretations of significant trends and events. Selecting visual material that illuminates complex and important historical ideas continues to be a high priority, and readers will find many new and revised maps and charts, as well as fresh documentary images. Completely updated bibliographies are located at the end of the book. "An American Profile: The United States and Its People," containing abundant statistical data on many aspects of the American historical experience is located on the companion web site.

New Pedagogical Features

In this edition of *The Brief American Pageant,* we are introducing a new four-color design, many new pedagogical features, and a larger format to display these features most effectively. This is all part of our effort to help students become more effective and efficient learners. The special pedagogical features of the Brief Edition are many and varied, and may be used in different ways by students and instructors.

- **"What if . . . ?"** questions at the end of each overview essay prompt students to consider how history might have changed if certain events had turned out differently. These questions illustrate the contingent nature of history.
- **Chapter Outlines** begin each chapter to provide a roadmap for the student.
- **Focus Questions** come at the beginning of each chapter, pointing to the key issues and ideas in the account that follows, and guiding the student's reading and understanding.
- The **Chronology** has been moved to the beginning of the chapter, so that students will have an idea of the succession of important events as they start to read the chapter.
- The **Marginal Glossary** highlights and defines key words to expand students' general historical and social science vocabulary.
- **Icons** in the margins direct students to primary sources and interactive maps on the companion web site.
- **Examining the Evidence,** the feature that acquaints students with historical evidence, offers questions to develop historical and critical thinking skills.
- **Map-Reading Skill Builders** are questions designed to improve students' map-reading ability.
- **Chapter Summaries** provide a handy review that highlights the chapter's main points.

Goals of *The Brief American Pageant*

Like its predecessors, this seventh edition of *The Brief American Pageant* cultivates its readers' capacity for balanced judgment and informed understanding about American society by holding up to the present the mirror and measuring rod that is the past. The book's goal is not to teach the art of prophecy but the much subtler and more difficult arts of seeing things in context, of understanding the roots and direction and pace of change, and of distinguishing what is truly new under the sun from what is not. The study of history, it has been rightly said, does not make one smart for the next time, but wise forever.

We hope that *The Brief American Pageant* will develop those intellectual assets in its readers, and that those who use the book will take from it both a fresh appreciation of what has gone before and a seasoned perspective on what is to come. And we hope, too, that readers will take as much pleasure in reading *The Brief American Pageant* as we have had in writing it.

Teaching and Learning Aids

These supplements have been created with the diverse needs of today's students and instructors in mind.

For the Instructor

- The **Online Teaching Center** (http://college.hmco.com/pic/kennedybrief7e) includes PowerPoint slides of hundreds of maps, images, and other media that are related to each chapter in the book as well as web links and questions for use with Personal Response Systems. Instructors have access to 100 interactive maps and over 500 primary sources to use for assignments. In addition, there is an Instructor's Resource Guide that can aid in encouraging classroom discussions or constructively enhance a class presentation.

• **HM Testing** is a new program with improved functionality that provides instructors all the tools they will need to create, write, customize, and deliver multiple types of tests. Instructors can import questions directly from the test bank, create their own questions, or edit existing questions, all within Diploma's powerful electronic platform.

• **Blackboard/WebCT** provides instructors who want to offer all or part of their entire course online with much of the fundamental material for their course. From this base, instructors can customize the course to meet their needs including program-level, graded homework questions organized by topic.

• **Eduspace** provides the ability for instructors to create part or all of their courses online, using the widely recognized tools of Blackboard Learning System and content from Houghton Mifflin. Instructors can quickly and easily assign homework exercises, quizzes and tests, tutorials, and supplementary study materials, and can modify or add content of their own. A powerful grade book in Eduspace allows instructors to monitor student progress and easily tabulate grades.

• **The Houghton Mifflin U.S. History Transparency Set, Volumes I and II,** is a set of standard U.S. history transparencies, taken from illustrations and maps in the Houghton Mifflin survey texts. It includes 150 full-color maps.

• **BiblioBase for U.S. History** is a database of hundreds of primary source documents—including speeches, essays, travel accounts, government documents, and memoirs—covering U.S. history from the fifteenth century to the present. This comprehensive database enables you to create a customized course pack of primary sources to complement any U.S. history text. You can search for documents by period, region, approach, theme, and type and then view the documents in their entirety before choosing your course pack selections.

• The **Rand McNally Atlas of American History** is offered for packaging with the textbook. Please contact your sales representative for additional information.

For the Student

• The **Online Study Center** (http://college.hmco.com/pic/kennedybrief7e) is a student web site that includes a wide array of interactive study content such as preclass quizzes, ACE Practice Tests, vocabulary-building exercises, identification exercises, and interactive map activities, among many others. This web site also contains the same primary sources and interactive maps that are on the Online Teaching Center.

• **Icons** in the text direct students to interactive maps, primary sources, and ACE practice test questions.

Acknowledgments

Many people contributed to the seventh edition of *The Brief American Pageant*. Foremost among them are the countless students and teachers who have written unsolicited letters of comment or inquiry. We also offer thanks to the following colleagues for their particular contributions to improving the text:

Carol Bender, *Saddleback College*
Wesley B. Borucki, *Palm Beach Atlantic University*
Janet Newlan Bower, *San Diego Mesa College*
Linzy Brekke-Aloise, *Harvard University*
Jon L. Brudvig, *University of Mary*
Scott Buchanan, *South Plains College*
Andrea J. DeKoter, *SUNY Cortland*
Yonatan Eyal, *Harvard University*
Ronald H. Fritze, *Athens State University*
Frederick B. Gates, *Southwestern Oklahoma State University*
Robert Gudmestad, *University of Memphis*
David Holland, *Stanford University*
David Hollinger, *University of California, Berkeley*
David Hunter, *San Bernardino City Unified Schools*
Timothy K. Kinsella, *Ursuline College*
Robert MacDougall, *Harvard University*
Frank Ninkovich, *St. John's University*
Selina Pearson, *Northwest-Shoals Community College*
Kimberly Sims, *Harvard University*
Ann Engram Smith, *Darton College*
Richard A. Straw, *Radford University*
Ruth Suyama, *Los Angeles Mission College*
F. Walter VanderHeijden, *Hempfield High School*
Gerald R. Virgilio, *New Mexico State University at Alamogordo*
Larry Wade, *Darton College*
Daniel Wewers, *Harvard University*

D.M.K.
L.C.
M.P.

Sail, sail thy best, ship of Democracy,
Of value is thy freight, 'tis not the Present only,
The Past is also stored in thee,
Thou holdest not the venture of thyself alone, not
of the Western continent alone,
Earth's résumé entire floats on thy keel, O ship, is
steadied by thy spars,
With thee Time voyages in trust, the antecedent
nations sink or swim with thee,
With all their ancient struggles, martyrs, heroes,
epics, wars, thou bear'st the other continents,
Theirs, theirs as much as thine, the destination-port
triumphant. . . .

Walt Whitman
Thou Mother with Thy Equal Brood, 1872

FOR STUDENTS

A Guide to Your Textbook

Welcome to U.S. History! What follows is a guide to how to use the features of your textbook, *The Brief American Pageant*. Spending a few minutes on these next few pages will help you get the most out of your book, and do well in your class.

PART ONE

Founding the New Nation

c. 33,000 B.C.–A.D. 1783

The European explorers who followed Christopher Columbus to North America in the sixteenth century had no notion of founding a new nation. Neither did the first European settlers who peopled the thirteen English colonies on the eastern shores of the continent in the seven-

individual liberty, self-government, religious tolerance, and economic opportunity. They also commonly displayed a willingness to subjugate outsiders—first Indians, who were nearly annihilated through war and disease, and then Africans, who were

■ The chapters in this book are grouped into six parts, representing six distinct eras in American history. Each part opens with an essay that identifies the major themes and events of the era. Reading the essay will help you understand the larger patterns and trends discussed in the chapters to follow.

■ Following the part essay is a list of **"What if..."** questions. These questions ask what our country would look like if certain events had turned out differently. They prompt you to consider that history is not a story of inevitable events; there are always other possibilities.

What if . . . ?

■ **What if some sort of compromise between the North and South had prevented the Civil War?**

What might such a compromise have looked like?

What might have been its consequences for the future of slavery, and for American nationhood?

Was *any* such compromise politically possible—or morally defensible?

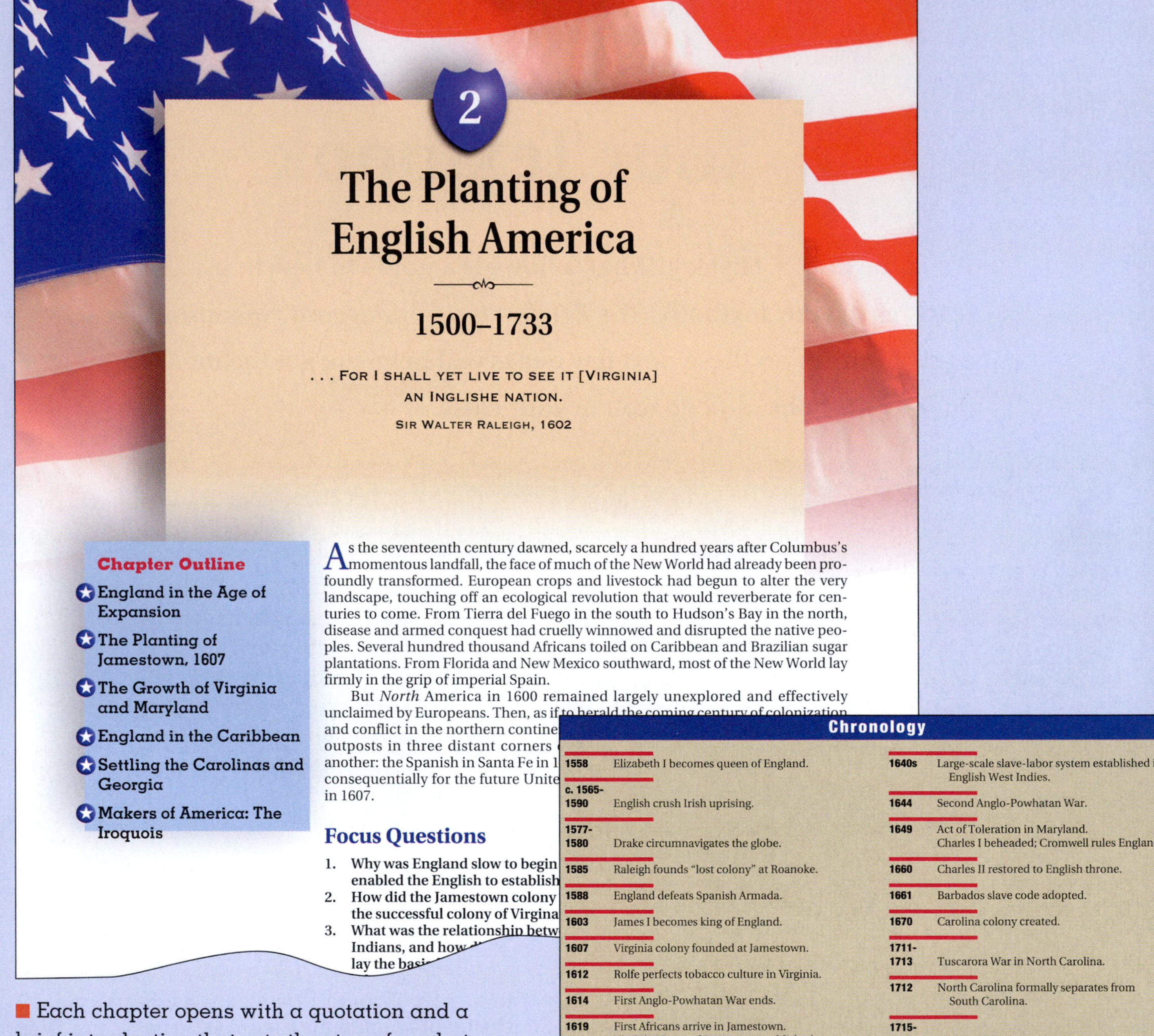

2

The Planting of English America

1500–1733

. . . FOR I SHALL YET LIVE TO SEE IT [VIRGINIA] AN INGLISHE NATION.

SIR WALTER RALEIGH, 1602

Chapter Outline

- England in the Age of Expansion
- The Planting of Jamestown, 1607
- The Growth of Virginia and Maryland
- England in the Caribbean
- Settling the Carolinas and Georgia
- Makers of America: The Iroquois

As the seventeenth century dawned, scarcely a hundred years after Columbus's momentous landfall, the face of much of the New World had already been profoundly transformed. European crops and livestock had begun to alter the very landscape, touching off an ecological revolution that would reverberate for centuries to come. From Tierra del Fuego in the south to Hudson's Bay in the north, disease and armed conquest had cruelly winnowed and disrupted the native peoples. Several hundred thousand Africans toiled on Caribbean and Brazilian sugar plantations. From Florida and New Mexico southward, most of the New World lay firmly in the grip of imperial Spain.

But *North* America in 1600 remained largely unexplored and effectively unclaimed by Europeans. Then, as if
and conflict in the northern contine
outposts in three distant corners
another: the Spanish in Santa Fe in 1
consequentially for the future Unite
in 1607.

Focus Questions

1. Why was England slow to begin
enabled the English to establish
2. How did the Jamestown colony
the successful colony of Virgina
3. What was the relationship betw
Indians, and how
lay the basi

■ Each chapter opens with a quotation and a brief introduction that sets the stage for what is to come in the chapter. The opening page also includes a **Chapter Outline** and **Focus Questions**. The outline shows the major topics that will be discussed and the focus questions introduce you to the issues you should be thinking about as you read the chapter.

Chronology

1558	Elizabeth I becomes queen of England.
c. 1565–1590	English crush Irish uprising.
1577–1580	Drake circumnavigates the globe.
1585	Raleigh founds "lost colony" at Roanoke.
1588	England defeats Spanish Armada.
1603	James I becomes king of England.
1607	Virginia colony founded at Jamestown.
1612	Rolfe perfects tobacco culture in Virginia.
1614	First Anglo-Powhatan War ends.
1619	First Africans arrive in Jamestown. Virginia House of Burgesses established.
1624	Virginia becomes royal colony.
1640s	Large-scale slave-labor system established in English West Indies.
1644	Second Anglo-Powhatan War.
1649	Act of Toleration in Maryland. Charles I beheaded; Cromwell rules England.
1660	Charles II restored to English throne.
1661	Barbados slave code adopted.
1670	Carolina colony created.
1711–1713	Tuscarora War in North Carolina.
1712	North Carolina formally separates from South Carolina.
1715–1716	Yamasee War in South Carolina.
1733	Georgia colony founded.

■ The **Chronology** lists the important events that are discussed in the chapter. It is a convenient reminder of what happened when. When you are done reading the chapter, you can use it to review the major events.

oyed farmers took to the
like Bristol and London.
at only eldest sons were el-
ous younger sons, among
eir fortunes elsewhere. By
f such courtiers were re-
onsiderable number of in-

unity for English coloniza-
oyment, as well as a thirst
ovided the motives. Joint-
tage was set for a historic
ncharted North American

primogeniture *The legal principle that the oldest son inherits all family property or land.*

joint-stock company *An economic arrangement by which a number of investors pool their capital for investment.*

charter *A legal document granted by a government to some group or agency to implement a stated purpose, and spelling out the attending rights and obligations.*

Seedling

destiny beckoned toward
ny of London, received a
orld. The main attractions
ge through America to the
Virginia Company was in-
ockholders hoped to liqui-
e on the luckless colonists,

■ The **On-Page Glossary** provides definitions of important terms and concepts in the margin of the page on which the term appears. This makes it easy to review these important terms. Also they appear in boldface type so you can find them quickly.

■ The **Boxed Quotations** give you a feeling for the era being discussed by presenting the perspectives of the people who participated in and were affected by the historical events under discussion.

In the years immediately following the defeat of the Spanish Armada, the English writer Richard Hakluyt (1552?–1616) extravagantly exhorted his countrymen to cast off their "sluggish security" and undertake the colonization of the New World:

"There is under our noses the great and ample country of Virginia; the inland whereof is found of late to be so sweet and wholesome a climate, so rich and abundant in silver mines, a better and richer country than Mexico itself. If it shall please the Almighty to stir up Her Majesty's heart to continue with transporting one or two thousand of her people, she shall by God's assistance, in short space, increase her dominions, enrich her coffers, and reduce many pagans to the faith of Christ."

The charter of the Virginia Company is a significant document in American history. It guaranteed to the overseas settlers the same rights of Englishmen that they would have enjoyed if they had stayed at home. This precious boon was gradually extended to the other English colonies, helping to reinforce the colonists' sense that even on the far shore of the Atlantic they remained comfortably within the embrace of traditional English institutions. But ironically, a century and a half later, the colonists' insistence on the "rights of Englishmen" fed their hot resentment against an increasingly meddlesome mother country and nourished their appetite for independence.

Setting sail in late 1606, the Virginia Company's tiny band of colonists eventually arrived at a site on the wooded and malarial banks of a swampy river. There, on May 24, 1607, about a hundred English settlers, all men, disembarked. They called the place Jamestown and the river the James in honor of King James I.

The early years of Jamestown proved to be a nightmare for all concerned—except the buzzards. Once ashore, the settlers died by the dozens from disease, malnutrition, and starvation. The woods rustled with game, and the rivers flopped with fish, but the greenhorn settlers, many of them self-styled "gentlemen" unaccustomed to fending for themselves, wasted valuable time grubbing for nonexistent gold when they should have been gathering provisions.

Chapter Summary

The defeat of the Spanish Armada and the exuberant spirit of Elizabethan nationalism finally drew England into the colonial race. After some early failures, the first permanent English colony was established at Jamestown, Virginia. Harsh conditions, gentlemanly aversion to work, and Indian hostility nearly caused it to fail, but stern leadership and tobacco cultivation finally brought prosperity and population growth.

The early encounters of English settlers with the Powhatan Indians in Virginia established many of the patterns that characterized later Indian-white relations in North America, including disease, warfare, and removal. Indian societies underwent their own substantial changes as a result of warfare, disease, and trade. For a time after the Atlantic coastal tribes were nearly wiped out, the larger Indian peoples of the Appalachian area formed a formidable barrier to white expansion.

Maryland and South Carolina were founded by aristocratic proprietors. Maryland was originally a Catholic refuge. South Carolina flourished by establishing close ties with the British sugar colonies in the West Indies, and brought the West Indian pattern of harsh slave codes and large plantation agriculture to North America. North Carolina was a less hierarchical settlement of largely poor white colonists who owned small farms and disdained authority. Latecomer Georgia served initially as a buffer against the Spanish and a haven for debtors.

Despite some differences, all the southern colonies depended on staple plantation agriculture for their survival and on the institutions of indentured servitude and African slavery for their labor. With widely scattered rural settlements, they had relatively weak religious and social institutions and tended to develop hierarchical economic and social orders.

■ At the end of every chapter is a **Chapter Summary**. It's a convenient place to review quickly the major themes of the chapter.

EXAMINING THE EVIDENCE

A Seventeenth-Century Valuables Cabinet In 1999 a boatyard worker on Cape Cod and his sister, a New Hampshire teacher, inherited a small (20-pound, 16–1/2 inch-high) chest that had always stood on their grandmother's hall table, known in the family as the "Franklin chest." Eager to learn more about it, they set out to discover the original owner, tracing their family genealogy and consulting with furniture experts. In January 2000 this rare seventeenth-century cabinet, its full provenance now known, appeared on the auction block and sold for a record $2.4 million to the Peabody Essex Museum in Salem, Massachusetts. No less extraordinary than the price was the history of its creator and its owners embodied in the piece. Salem cabinetmaker James Symonds (1636–1726) had made the chest for his relatives Joseph Pope (1650–1712) and Bathsheba Folger (1652–1726) to commemorate their 1679 marriage. Symonds carved the Popes' initials and the date on the door of the cabinet. He also put elaborate S curves on the sides remarkably similar to the Mannerist carved oak paneling produced in Norfolk, England, from where his own cabinetmaker father had emigrated. Behind the chest's door are ten drawers where the Popes would have kept jewelry, money, deeds, and writing materials. Surely they prized the chest as a sign of refinement to be shown off in their best room, a sentiment passed down through the next thirteen generations even as the Popes' identities were lost. The chest may have become known as the "Franklin chest" because Bathsheba was Benjamin Franklin's aunt, but also because that identification appealed more to descendants ashamed that the Quaker Popes, whose own parents had been persecuted for their faith, were virulent accusers during the Salem witch trials of 1692.

1. What significant features of this seventeenth-century chest could be determined simply by careful examination of the material object itself, and which could be learned only by historical research?
2. After studying the chest itself, which elements of the construction and carving might provide significant clues about what historical inquiries to pursue?
3. What does the nature of the chest and its original function as a storage place for valuables tell you about the economic status of the original owners, Joseph and Bathsheba Pope? Why might this chest have been handed down through their descendants for over 300 years, when most other material arti-

■ **Examining the Evidence** shows how historians might interpret primary sources, the original material of history. Official documents, letters, song lyrics, polls, and photographs are some of the sources examined. See if you can answer the questions that follow the description of each source.

The Iroqu

Well before the crowned heads of Europe turned their eyes and their dreams of empire toward North America, a great military power had emerged in

■ **Makers of America** introduces you to the wide diversity of people who compose our pluralistic society. The achievements of scientists, philosophers, soldiers, and ordinary people are highlighted to show how Americans have forged their group identities through shared experiences.

VARYING VIEWPOINTS

Europeanizing America or Americanizing Europe?

The history of discovery and the earliest colonization raises perhaps the single most fundamental question about all American history. Should it be understood as the extension of European civilization into the New World or as the gradual development of a uniquely "American" culture? One school of thought tended to emphasize the Europeanization of America. Historians of that persuasion paid close attention to the situation in Europe, particularly in England and Spain, in the fifteenth and sixteenth centuries. They also focused on the various means by which the values and institutions of the mother continent were exported to the new lands in the western sea. Some European writers varied this general question by asking what transforming effect the discovery of America had on Europe itself. Both of these approaches are Eurocentric. More recently, historians have concentrated on the distinctiveness of America. The concern with European origins has evolved into a comparative treatment of English, Spanish, Dutch, and French settlements in the New World. The newest trend to emerge is a transatlantic history that views European empires and their American

ropean, African, and Native American ways of life. Scholars including Richard White, Alfred W. Crosby, William Cronon, Karen Kupperman, and Timothy Silver have enhanced understanding of the cultural as well as physical transformations that resulted from contact.

The variety of American societies that emerged out of the interaction of Europeans, Africans, and Native Americans has also become better appreciated. Studies such as Richard S. Dunn's *Sugar and Slaves* (1972) emphasize the importance of the Caribbean in early English colonization efforts. Similarly, Edmund S. Morgan's *American Slavery, American Freedom* (1975) stresses the role of economic ambition in explaining the English peopling of the Chesapeake and the eventual importation of African slaves to that region. Studies by Bernard Bailyn and David Hackett Fischer demonstrate that there was scarcely a "typical" English migrant to the New World. English colonists migrated both singly and in families, and for economic, social, political, and religious reasons.

The picture of colonial America that is emerging

■ **Varying Viewpoints** raises questions about events, people, and movements that might cause you to rethink common conceptions about these trends and events. This feature demonstrates that the interpretation of historical events is never fixed, that new ideas are always possible.

■ **The *Brief American Pageant* Website** offers students, through the Online Study Center, and instructors, through the Online Teaching Center, a wide array of teaching and learning resources.

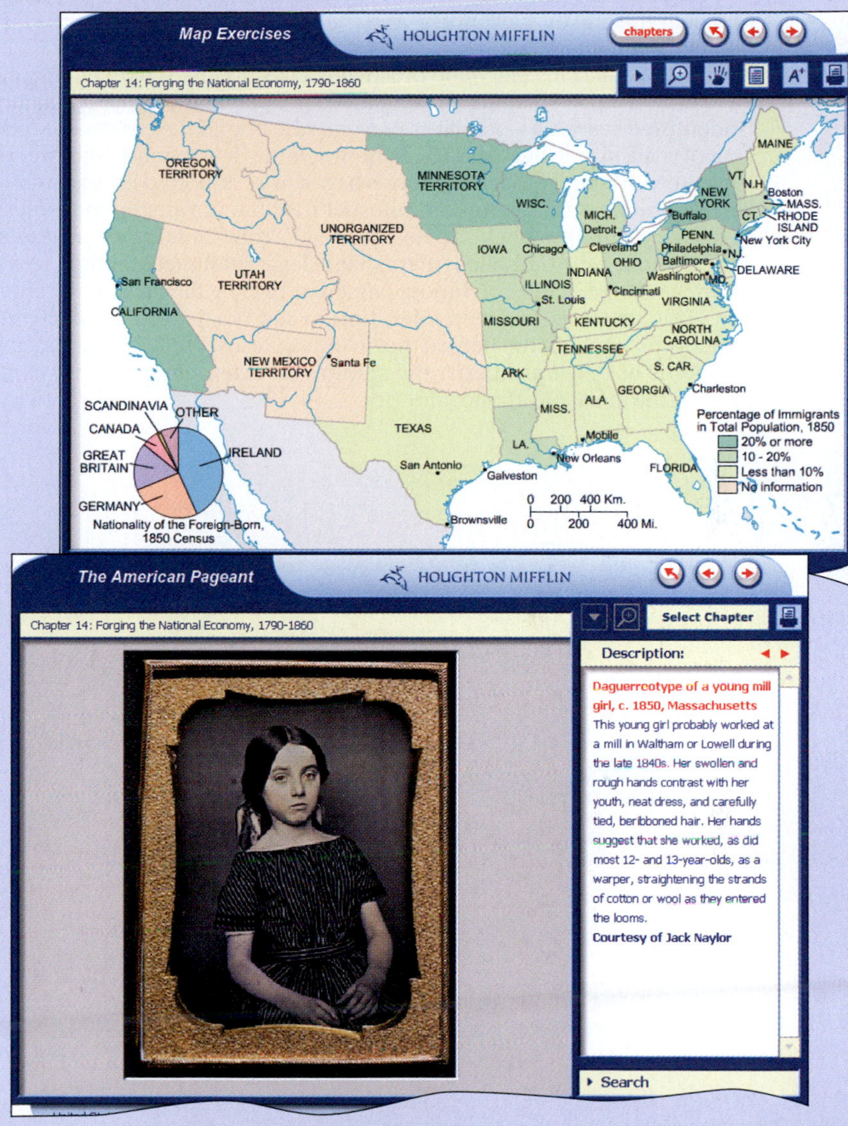

■ **For Students:**

- ACE practice test questions
- Chapter themes and a summary
- Flashcards for testing your vocabulary
- Chronology exercises
- Examining the Evidence activities
- Primary sources with pedagogy and questions
- Interactive maps with questions

■ **For Instructors:**

- Historical images in PowerPoint
- Maps in PowerPoint
- Primary sources with pedagogy and questions
- Interactive maps with questions
- Test Items and HM Testing (available on a CD-ROM)
- Instructors Resource Manual

organized and
conomic func-
ods to offer in
s' desire for a

Primary source
European Settlements and Indian Tribes in North America
college.hmco.com/pic/kennedybrief7e

enous peoples
went forward.

■ Throughout the book, you will see icons for the **Online Study Center** in the margin that direct you to **primary sources** and **interactive maps** on the website. The interactive maps provide a dynamic way to improve your knowledge of geography and the primary sources offer another opportunity to engage the raw material of history.

cracy, were intended to arise amidst the fertile forests. As in Virginia, ists proved willing to come only if offered the opportunity to acquire land ir own. Soon they were dispersed around the Chesapeake region on mod- rms, and the haughty land barons, mostly Catholic, were surrounded by tful backcountry planters, mostly Protestant. Resentment flared into open lion near the end of the century, and the Baltimore family for a time lost its ietary rights.

espite these tensions Maryland prospered. Like Virginia, it blossomed forth in of tobacco. Also like Virginia, it depended for labor in its early years mainly on **indentured servants**—penniless persons who bound themselves to work for nber of years to pay their passage. In both colonies it was only in the later years seventeenth century that black slaves began to be imported in large numbers.

ord Baltimore at first permitted unusual freedom of worship for Protestant rs in Maryland. But when the heavy tide of Protestants threatened to sub- e the Catholics, the Catholic settlers sought legal guarantees for their religious ice in the famed Act of Toleration, passed in 1649 by the local representative nbly. This statute guaranteed **toleration** to all Christians, but it decreed the penalty for anyone who denied the divinity of Jesus. While falling far short of standards of religious liberty, the statute did extend a temporary cloak of ction to the uneasy Catholic minority.

feudal *Concerning the decentralized medieval social system of personal obligations between rulers and ruled.*

indentured servants *Poor persons obligated to a fixed term of unpaid labor, often in exchange for a benefit such as transportation, protection, or training.*

toleration *Originally, religious freedom granted by an established church to a religious minority.*

■ Early Maryland and Virginia

Map Skill-Builder: Understanding Political Maps

1. Where did the original land grant to Lord Baltimore follow natural geographical features, and where did it follow certain "artificial" straight lines of latitude or longitude on the map?
2. Did the eventual *political* boundary of Maryland mostly follow the natural features, or did it add more artificially drawn boundaries?

■ The **Map-Reading Skill Builders** are questions that appear adjacent to selected maps and are designed to help you better understand the information conveyed by the map.

THE BRIEF AMERICAN PAGEANT

PART ONE

Founding the New Nation

c. 33,000 B.C.–A.D. 1783

The European explorers who followed Christopher Columbus to North America in the sixteenth century had no notion of founding a new nation. Neither did the first European settlers who peopled the thirteen English colonies on the eastern shores of the continent in the seventeenth and eighteenth centuries. These original colonists may have fled poverty or religious persecution in the Old World, but they continued to view themselves as Europeans, and as subjects of the English king. They regarded America as but the western rim of a transatlantic European world.

Yet life in the New World made the colonists different from their European cousins, and eventually, during the American Revolution, the Americans came to embrace a vision of their country as an independent nation. How did this epochal transformation come about? How did the colonists overcome the conflicts that divided them, unite against Britain, and declare themselves at great cost to be an "American" people?

They had much in common to begin with. Most were English-speaking. Most came determined to create an agricultural society modeled on English customs. Conditions in the New World deepened their common bonds. Most colonists strove to live lives unfettered by the tyrannies of royal authority, official religion, and social hierarchies that they had left behind. They grew to cherish ideals that became synonymous with American life—individual liberty, self-government, religious tolerance, and economic opportunity. They also commonly displayed a willingness to subjugate outsiders—first Indians, who were nearly annihilated through war and disease, and then Africans, who were brought in chains to serve as slave labor, especially on the tobacco, rice, and indigo plantations of the southern colonies.

But if the settlement experience gave people a common stock of values, both good and bad, it also divided them. The thirteen colonies were quite different from one another. Puritans carved tight, pious, and relatively democratic communities of small family farms out of rocky-soiled New England. Theirs was a homogeneous world in comparison with most of the southern colonies, where large landholders, mostly Anglicans, built plantations along the coast from which they lorded over a labor force of black slaves and looked down upon the poor white farmers who settled the backcountry. Different still were the middle colonies stretching from New York to Delaware. There diversity reigned. Well-to-do merchants put their stamp on New York City, as Quakers did on Philadelphia, while out in the countryside sprawling estates were interspersed with modest homesteads. Within individual colonies, conflicts festered over economic interests, ethnic rivalries, and religious practices. All those clashes made it difficult for colonists to imagine that they were a single people with a common destiny, much less that they ought to break free from Britain.

The American colonists in fact had little reason to complain about Britain. Each of the thirteen colonies enjoyed a good deal of self-rule. Many colonists profited from trade within the British Empire. But by the 1760s this stable arrangement began to crumble, a victim of the imperial rivalry between France and Britain. Their struggle for supremacy in North America began in the late seventeenth century and finally dragged in the colonists during the French and Indian War from 1756 to 1763. That war in one sense strengthened ties with Britain, since colonial militias fought triumphantly alongside the British army against their mutual French and Indian enemies. But once the French were driven from the North American continent, the colonists no longer needed Britain for protection. More important still, after 1763 a financially overstretched British government made the fateful choice of imposing taxes on colonies that had been accustomed to answering mainly to their own colonial assemblies. By the 1770s issues of taxation, self-rule, and trade restrictions brought the crisis of imperial authority to a head. Although as late as 1775 most people in the colonies clung to the hope of some kind of accommodation short of outright independence, royal intransigence soon thrust the colonists into a war of independence that neither antagonist could have anticipated just a few years before.

Eight years of revolutionary war did more than anything in the colonial past to bring Americans together as a nation. Comradeship in arms and the struggle to shape a national government forced Americans to subdue their differences as best they could. But the spirit of national unity was hardly universal. One in five colonists sided with the British as "Loyalists," and a generation would pass before the wounds of this first American "civil war" fully healed. Yet in the end, Americans won the Revolution, with no small measure of help from the French, because in every colony people shared a firm belief that they were fighting for the "unalienable rights" of "life, liberty, and the pursuit of happiness," in the words of Thomas Jefferson's magnificent Declaration of Independence. Almost two hundred years of living a new life had prepared Americans to found a new nation.

What if...?

- **What if France had won the French and Indian War and maintained its colonial power in Canada and west of the Appalachians?**

  Would Britain's American colonies still have protested taxes and declared their independence?

New World Beginnings

33,000 B.C.–A.D. 1769

I HAVE COME TO BELIEVE THAT THIS IS A MIGHTY CONTINENT WHICH WAS HITHERTO UNKNOWN. . . . YOUR HIGHNESSES HAVE AN OTHER WORLD HERE.

CHRISTOPHER COLUMBUS, 1498

Chapter Outline

- The Geology of the New World
- Native Americans Before Columbus
- Europeans and Africans
- The Ecological Consequences of Columbus's Discovery
- Spain Builds a New World Empire
- Makers of America: The Spanish *Conquistadores*

About six thousand years ago—only a minute in geological time—recorded history began among certain peoples of the ancient Middle East who developed a written culture. Just five hundred years ago—only a few seconds figuratively speaking—European explorers stumbled on the Americas. This dramatic accident forever altered the future of both the Old World and the New, and of Africa and Asia as well.

Focus Questions

1. **What geological, geographical, and climatic conditions set the stage for human history in America?**
2. **What were the primary features of the diverse Indian cultures of the Americas, and how did they change over time?**
3. **What developments in European and global history paved the way for Columbus's voyage and the subsequent collision of two worlds?**
4. **How did the mutual relations of Indians, Europeans, and Africans shape a genuinely new biological, cultural, and economic world in the Americas?**
5. **How did Spain's conquest of the Indian civilizations of Mexico and South America shape the essential features of its vast New World empire?**

The Shaping of North America

Planet earth took on its present form slowly. Some 225 million years ago, a single supercontinent contained all the world's dry land. Then enormous chunks of terrain began to drift away from this colossal continent, opening the Atlantic and Indian Oceans, narrowing the Pacific Ocean, and forming the great landmasses of Eurasia, Africa, Australia, Antarctica, and the Americas.

Continued shifting and folding of the earth's crust thrust up mountain ranges. The Appalachians were probably formed even before continental separation, perhaps 350 million years ago. The majestic ranges of western North America—the Rockies, the Sierra Nevada, the Cascades, and the Coast Ranges—arose much more recently, geologically speaking, some 135 million to 25 million years ago.

Chronology

c. 33,000–8000 B.C.	First humans cross over to the Americas from Asia.
c. 5000 B.C.	Corn is developed as a staple crop in highland Mexico.
c. 4000 B.C.	First civilized societies develop in the Middle East.
c. 1200 b.c.	Corn planting reaches present-day American Southwest.
c. A.D. 1000	Norse voyagers discover and briefly settle in North America. Corn cultivation reaches Midwest and southeastern Atlantic seaboard.
c. A.D. 1100	Height of Mississippian settlement at Cahokia.
c. A.D. 1100–1300	Christian crusades arouse European interest in Asia.
1295	Marco Polo returns to Europe.
late 1400s	Spain becomes united.
1488	Díaz rounds southern tip of Africa.
1492	Columbus lands in the Bahamas.
1494	Treaty of Tordesillas between Spain and Portugal.
1498	Da Gama reaches India. Cabot explores northeastern coast of North America for England.
1513, 1521	Ponce de León explores Florida.
1519–1521	Cortés conquers Mexico for Spain.
1532	Pizarro crushes Incas.
1540–1542	Coronado explores present-day Southwest.
1542	Cabrillo explores California coast for Spain.
1565	Spanish build fortress at St. Augustine.
late 1500s	Iroquois Confederacy founded, according to Iroquois legend.
1609	Spanish found New Mexico.
1680	Popé's Rebellion in New Mexico.
1680s	French expedition down Mississippi River under La Salle.
1769	Serra founds first California mission, at San Diego.

By about 10 million years ago, nature had sculpted the basic geological shape of North America. The continent was anchored in its northeastern corner by the massive Canadian Shield—a zone undergirded by ancient rock, probably the first part of what became the North American landmass to have emerged above sea level. A narrow eastern coastal plain, or "tidewater" region, creased by many valleys, sloped gently upward to the timeworn ridges of the Appalachians. Those ancient mountains slanted away on their western side into the huge midcontinental basin that rolled downward to the Mississippi Valley bottom and then rose relentlessly to the towering peaks of the Rockies. From the Rocky Mountain crest—the "roof of America"—the land fell off jaggedly into the intermountain Great Basin, bounded by the Rockies on the east and the Sierra and Cascade ranges on the west. The valleys of the Sacramento and San Joaquin rivers and the Willamette–Puget Sound trough seamed the interiors of present-day California, Oregon, and Washington. The land at last met the foaming Pacific, where the Coast Ranges rose steeply from the sea.

Primary source
Routes of the First Americans
college.hmco.com/pic/kennedybrief7e

Beginning about 2 million years ago, two-mile-thick ice sheets crept across much of northern Europe, Asia, and the Americas. In North America, the glaciers spread as far southward as a line stretching from Pennsylvania through the Ohio country and the Dakotas to the Pacific Northwest.

When the glaciers finally retreated about 10,000 years ago, they left the North American landscape transformed, and much as we know it today. The grinding and flushing action of the moving and melting ice pitted the rocky surface of the Canadian Shield with thousands of shallow depressions, into which the melting glaciers flowed to form lakes. The same glacial action scooped out and filled the Great Lakes. When the Great Lakes eventually found an outlet to the Atlantic Ocean through the St. Lawrence River, they left the Missouri-Mississippi-Ohio river system to drain the enormous midcontinental basin between the Appalachians and the Rockies.

Similarly, in the West, water from the melting glaciers filled sprawling Lake Bonneville, covering much of present-day Utah, Nevada, and Idaho. Eventually deprived of both inflow and drainage as the glaciers retreated, the giant lake became a shrinking inland sea. It grew increasingly saline, slowly evaporated, and left an arid, mineral-rich desert, with only the Great Salt Lake as a relic of its former vastness. Today Lake Bonneville's ancient beaches are visible on mountainsides up to 1,000 feet above the dry floor of the Great Basin.

Map Skill-Builder: Using Map Distance Scales
When the first migrants crossed the Bering Land Bridge from Siberia to North America, approximately how many miles did they have to walk before they were south of the large ice caps to either side of the only open route?
a) 200 miles b) 500 miles
c) 2,000 miles d) 3,000 miles

SIBERIA
Bering Land Bridge
ARCTIC OCEAN
GREENLAND
ALASKA
Hudson Bay
CANADA
PACIFIC OCEAN
UNITED STATES
ATLANTIC OCEAN
MEXICO
0 500 Miles
0 500 Kilometers
Area of land bridge, c.35,000–10,000 years ago
Maximum extent of glaciers
Possible migratory paths
Earliest discovered Indian sites

The First Discoverers of America The origins of the first Americans remain something of a mystery. According to the most plausible theory of how the Americas were populated, for some 25,000 years, people crossed the Bering Strait land bridge from Eurasia to North America. Gradually, they dispersed southward down ice-free valleys, populating both of the American continents.

Interactive map
First Americans Enter the New World
college.hmco.com/pic/kennedybrief7e

Peopling the Americas

The Great Ice Age shaped more than the geological history of North America. It also contributed to the origins of the continent's human history. Some 35,000 years ago, the Ice Age congealed much of the world's oceans into massive ice-pack glaciers, lowering the level of the sea. As the sea level dropped, it exposed a land bridge connecting Eurasia with North America. Across that bridge spanning the present-day Bering Sea between Siberia and Alaska ventured small bands of nomadic Asian hunters—the "immigrant" ancestors of the Native Americans. They continued to trek across the Bering isthmus for some 250 centuries, slowly peopling the American continents.

As the Ice Age ended and the glaciers melted, the sea level rose again, inundating the land bridge about 10,000 years ago. Nature thus barred the door to further immigration for many thousands of years, leaving this part of the human family to develop its separate existence on the American continents.

Time did not stand still for these original Americans. Roaming slowly through this awesome wilderness, they eventually reached the far tip of South America, some 15,000 miles from Siberia. By the time the Europeans arrived in America in 1492, perhaps 54 million people inhabited the two American continents. Over the centuries they split into countless tribes, evolved more than 2,000 separate languages, and developed many diverse religions, cultures, and ways of life.

Incas in Peru, Mayans in Central America, and Aztecs in Mexico shaped stunningly sophisticated civilizations. Their advanced agricultural practices, based primarily on the cultivation of maize (Indian corn), fed large populations, perhaps as many as 20 million in Mexico alone. Though lacking technologies such as the wheel, these peoples built elaborate cities and carried on far-flung commerce. Talented mathematicians, they made strikingly accurate astronomical observations. The Aztecs also sought the favor of their gods by offering human sacrifices, cutting the hearts out of the chests of living victims, who were often captives conquered in battle.

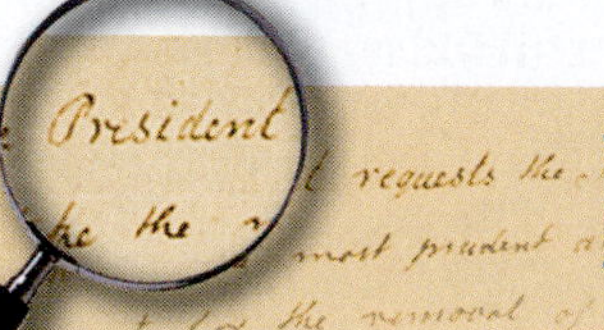

Examining the Evidence

Making Sense of the New World This map from 1546 by Sebastian Münster represents one of the earliest efforts to make geographic sense out of the New World (*Nouus Orbis* and *Die Nüw Welt* on the map). The very phrase *New World* suggests just how staggering a blow to the European imagination was the discovery of the Americas. Europeans reached instinctively for the most expansive of all possible terms—*world,* not simply *places,* or even *continents*—to comprehend Columbus's startling report that lands and peoples previously unimagined lay beyond the horizon of Europe's western sea.

Gradually the immense implications of the New World's existence began to impress themselves on Europe, with consequences for literature, art, politics, the economy, and, of course, cartography. Maps can only be *representations* of reality and are therefore necessarily distortions. This map bears a recognizable resemblance to modern mapmakers' renderings of the American continents, but it also contains gross geographic inaccuracies (note the location of Japan—*Zipangri*—relative to the North American west coast) as well as telling commentaries on what sixteenth-century Europeans found remarkable (note the Land of Giants—*Regio Gigantum*—and the indication of cannibals—*Canibali*—in present-day Argentina and Brazil, respectively).

1. What further clues to the European mentality of the time does the map offer? In what ways might misconceptions about the geography of the Americas have influenced further exploration and settlement patterns?
2. Which portions of "New World" geography were more accurately mapped by European cartographers in 1546? Which were most distorted? Why?
3. Notice the closeness of *Zipangri* (Japan) and India to the West Coast of North America on the map. What does this tell you about Europeans' continuing belief in a "western route to the Indies" a half century after Columbus stumbled upon the Americas?
4. Look closely at the very small illustration of *Canibali* (cannibals) located on the map in today's South America. What does it reveal about Europeans' views of Native Americans?

■ A Rocky Mountain Lake near Aspen, Colorado The geologically young Rockies form the rugged backbone of the North American Continent.

The Earliest Americans

Agriculture, especially corn growing, accounted for the size and sophistication of the Native American civilizations in Mexico and South America. About 5000 B.C. hunter-gatherers in highland Mexico developed a wild grass into the staple of corn, which became the foundation of the complex, large-scale, centralized Aztec and Incan **nation-states**. As cultivation of corn spread across the Americas from the Mexican heartland, it transformed some nomadic hunting bands into settled agricultural villagers.

nation-states *The form of political society that traditionally combines centralized government with a high degree of ethnic and cultural unity.*

Corn planting reached the present-day American Southwest by about 1200 B.C. and powerfully molded Pueblo culture. The Pueblo peoples in the Rio Grande Valley constructed intricate irrigation systems to water their cornfields, and they built villages of terraced, multistory buildings. Corn cultivation reached other parts of North America considerably later, and the timing of its arrival explains much about the relative rates of development of different Native American peoples. North and east of the Pueblos, elaborately developed "societies" in the modern sense of the word scarcely existed. The lack of dense concentrations of population or complex nation-states was one reason for the relative ease with which the European colonizers subdued the native North Americans.

✪ Map Skill-Builder:
Understanding Demographic-Topographic Maps
(See map, p. 9)
List five Indian tribes that lived in each of the following regions of North America:
(a) Southwest (b) Great Plains
(c) Northeast (d) Southeast

The Mound Builders of the Ohio River valley, the Mississippian culture of the lower Midwest, and the desert-dwelling Anasazi peoples of the Southwest did sustain some large settlements after the incorporation of corn-planting into their way of life during the first millennium A.D. The Mississippian settlement at Cahokia, near present-day East St. Louis, was at one time home to as many as 25,000 people. The Anasazis built an elaborate pueblo of more than six hundred inter-connected rooms in Chaco Canyon in modern-day New Mexico. But mysteriously, perhaps due to prolonged drought, all those ancient cultures fell into decline by about 1300.

Maize cultivation, as well as high-yielding strains of beans and squash, reached the southeastern Atlantic seaboard region of North America about A.D. 1000. The rich diet provided by these three crops produced some of the highest population densities on the continent, among them the Creek, Choctaw, and Cherokee peoples. In the northeastern woodlands, the Iroquois, inspired by their

North American Indian Peoples at the Time of First Contact with Europeans Because this map depicts the location of various Indian peoples *at the time of their first contact with Europeans*, and because initial contacts ranged from the sixteenth to the nineteenth centuries, it is necessarily subject to considerable chronological skewing and is only a crude approximation of the "original" territory of any given group. The map also cannot capture the fluidity and dynamism of Native American life even before Columbus's "discovery." For example, the Navajo and Apache peoples had migrated from present-day northern Canada only shortly before the Spanish first encountered them in the present-day American Southwest in the 1500s. The map also places the Sioux on the Great Plains, where Europeans met up with them in the early nineteenth century—but the Sioux had spilled onto the Plains not long before then from the forests surrounding the Great Lakes. The indigenous populations of the southeastern and mid-Atlantic regions are especially difficult to represent accurately in a map like this because pre-Columbian intertribal conflicts had so scrambled the native inhabitants that it is virtually impossible to determine which groups were originally where.

■ Cahokia This artist's rendering of Cahokia, based on archaeological excavations, shows the huge central square and the imposing Monk's Mound, which rivaled in size the pyramids of Egypt.

Interactive map
Indian Economies in North America
college.hmco.com/pic/kennedybrief7e

Primary source
Cahokia
college.hmco.com/pic/kennedybrief7e

confederacy *An alliance or league of nations or peoples looser than a federation.*

matrilinear *The form of society in which family line, power, and wealth are passed primarily through the female side.*

primeval *Concerning the earliest origin of things; of ancient age.*

saga *A lengthy story or poem recounting the great deeds and adventures of a people and their heroes.*

legendary leader Hiawatha, created in the sixteenth century perhaps the closest North American approximation to the great nation-states of Mexico and Peru. The Iroquois **Confederacy** developed the political and organizational skills to sustain a robust military alliance that menaced its neighbors, Native American and European alike, for well over a century (see "Makers of America: The Iroquois," pp. 28–29).

But for the most part, the native peoples of North America were living in scattered and impermanent settlements on the eve of the Europeans' arrival. In more settled agricultural groups, women tended the crops while men hunted, fished, gathered fuel, and cleared fields for planting. This pattern of life frequently conferred substantial authority on women, and many North American native peoples, including the Iroquois, developed **matrilinear** cultures, in which power and possessions passed down the female side of the family line.

Unlike the Europeans, who would soon arrive with the presumption that humans had dominion over the earth and with the technologies to alter the very face of the land, Native Americans had neither the desire nor the means to manipulate nature aggressively. They revered the physical world and endowed nature with spiritual properties. Yet they did sometimes ignite massive forest fires, deliberately torching trees to create better hunting habitats, especially for deer. This practice accounted for the open, park-like appearance of the eastern woodlands that so amazed early European explorers.

But in a broad sense, the land did not feel the hand of the Native Americans heavy upon it, partly because they were so few in number. In the fateful year 1492, probably no more than 4 million Native Americans padded through the whispering, **primeval** forests and paddled across the sparkling, virgin waters of North America. They were blissfully unaware that the historic isolation of the Americas was about to end forever, as both the land and the native peoples alike felt the full shock of the European "discovery."

Indirect Discoverers of the New World

Europeans were equally unaware of the existence of the Americas. Blond-bearded Norse seafarers from Scandinavia chanced upon northeastern North America about 1000 A.D., and briefly settled in a place they called Vinland, near L'Anse aux Meadows in present-day Newfoundland. But no strong nation-state, yearning to expand, supported these venturesome voyagers. Their flimsy settlements consequently were soon abandoned, and their discovery was forgotten, except in Scandinavian **saga** and song.

For several centuries thereafter, other restless Europeans, with the growing power of ambitious governments behind them, sought contact with a wider world, whether for conquest or trade. They thus set in motion the chain of events that led to a drive toward Asia, the exploitation of Africa, and the completely accidental discovery of the New World.

Christian crusaders of the eleventh to the fourteenth centuries rank high among America's indirect discoverers. Though ultimately foiled in their attempts to wrest the Holy Land from Muslim control, the crusaders nevertheless acquired a taste for the exotic delights of Asia—silk for clothing, drugs for aching flesh, perfumes for unbathed bodies, colorful draperies for gloomy castles, and sugar and spices for preserving and flavoring food. The Italian adventurer Marco Polo further whetted European appetites for Asian luxury goods when he returned from China in 1295 telling tales of its golden pagodas and rose-tinted pearls.

But the distance and difficulties of transportation, for which Muslim and Italian **middlemen** charged dearly, made European consumers and distributors eager to find a less expensive route to the riches of Asia. Their hopes for an ocean route to Asia were long frustrated. Before the mid-fifteenth century, European sailors refused to sail southward along the coast of West Africa because they could not beat their way home again against the prevailing northerly winds and south-flowing currents.

Primary source
European Explorations in America
college.hmco.com/pic/kennedybrief7e

middlemen *In trading systems, those dealers who operate between the original producers of goods and the retail merchants who sell to consumers.*

caravel *A small vessel with a high deck and three triangular sails.*

plantation(s) *A large-scale agricultural enterprise growing commercial crops and usually employing coerced or slave labor.*

Europeans Enter Africa

About 1450, Portuguese mariners overcame these obstacles by developing the **caravel**, a ship that could sail more closely into the wind. They also learned that they could return to Europe by sailing northwesterly from the African coast toward the Azores islands, where the prevailing westward breezes would carry them home.

The new world of sub-Saharan Africa, previously remote and mysterious to Europeans, now came within their questing grasp. African gold, perhaps two-thirds of Europe's supply, crossed the Sahara on camelback, and tales may have reached Europe about the flourishing West African kingdom of Mali in the Niger River valley, with its impressive Islamic university at Timbuktu. But Europeans had no direct access to sub-Saharan Africa until the Portuguese mariners began to creep down the West African coast in the mid-fifteenth century.

The Portuguese promptly set up trading posts along the African shore for the purchase of gold—and slaves. Arab and African merchants had traded slaves for centuries before the Europeans arrived. They routinely charged higher prices for slaves from distant sources, who could not flee to their native villages. Slave brokers also deliberately separated persons from the same tribes to frustrate organized resistance.

The Portuguese adopted these Arab and African practices in the sugar **plantations** that they, and later the Spanish, established on the African coastal islands of Madeira, the Canaries, São Tomé, and Principe. The Portuguese appetite for slaves was enormous, and slave trading became big business. Some forty thousand Africans were carried away to the Atlantic sugar islands in the last half of the fifteenth century. Millions more would be wrenched from their home continent after the discovery of the Americas. These fifteenth-century Portuguese adventures in Africa contained the origins of the modern plantation system, based on large-scale commercial agriculture and the wholesale exploitation of slave labor. This kind of plantation economy would shape the destiny of much of the New World.

After years of cautious exploration down the African coast, the Portuguese mariner Bartholomeu Días rounded the southernmost tip of Africa in 1488. Ten years later Vasco da Gama reached India and returned home with a small but tantalizing cargo of jewels and spices.

Meanwhile, the kingdom of Spain was united as a result of the marriage of two sovereigns, Ferdinand of Aragon and Isabella of Castile. After the brutal expulsion of the Muslim Moors from Spain, the new Spanish nation was eager to outstrip its Portuguese rivals in the race to tap the wealth of the Indies. Because Portugal controlled the round-Africa water route to India, Spain of necessity looked westward.

Columbus Comes upon a New World

The stage was now set for a cataclysmic shift in the course of history—the history not only of Europe but of all the world. Europeans clamored for more and cheaper products from the lands beyond the Mediterranean. Africa had been established as a source of cheap slave labor for plantation agriculture. The Portuguese voyages had demonstrated the feasibility of long-range ocean navigation. In Spain a modern national state was taking shape, with the unity, wealth, and power to shoulder the formidable tasks of discovery, conquest, and colonization. The dawn of the Renaissance in the fourteenth century nurtured an ambitious spirit of optimism and adventure. Printing presses, introduced about 1450, facilitated the spread of scientific knowledge. The mariner's compass, possibly borrowed from the Arabs, eliminated some of the uncertainties of sea travel.

Onto this stage stepped Christopher Columbus. This skilled Italian seafarer persuaded the Spanish monarchs to outfit him with three tiny but seaworthy ships. Columbus sailed westward into the oceanic unknown, and after six weeks at sea his fearful sailors grew increasingly mutinous. But on October 12, 1492, the crew sighted an island in the Bahamas. A new world thus swam within the vision of Europeans.

Only gradually did Europeans realize that Columbus had in fact bumped into enormous new continents. For decades explorers tried to get through or around the "islands" that, they assumed, blocked the ocean pathway to Asia. Columbus himself was at first so certain that he had skirted the rim of the "Indies" that he called the native peoples Indians, a gross geographical misnomer that somehow stuck.

Columbus's discovery would eventually convulse four continents—Europe, Africa, and the two Americas. Thanks to his epochal voyage, an interdependent global economic system emerged on a scale undreamed-of before he set sail. Its workings touched every shore washed by the Atlantic Ocean. Europe provided the markets, the capital, and the technology; Africa furnished the labor; and the New World offered its raw materials—especially its precious metals and its soil for the cultivation of sugar cane. For Europeans, as well as for Africans and Native Americans, the world after 1492 would never be the same, for better or worse.

When Worlds Collide

ecosystems *A naturally evolved network of relations among organisms in a stable environment.*

Two **ecosystems**—the fragile, naturally evolved networks of relations among organisms in a stable environment—commingled and clashed when Columbus waded ashore. The flora and fauna of the Old and New Worlds had been separated for thousands of years. European explorers marveled at the strange sights that greeted them, including exotic beasts such as iguanas and "snakes with castanets" (rattlesnakes). Native New World plants such as tobacco, maize, beans, tomatoes, and especially the lowly potato eventually revolutionized the international economy and fed the rapid population growth of the Old World. These foodstuffs were among the most important Indian gifts to the Europeans and the rest of the world. Ironically, the introduction into Africa of New World foodstuffs like maize, manioc, and sweet potatoes may have fed an African population boom that numerically, though not morally, more than offset the losses inflicted by the slave trade.

In exchange the Europeans introduced Old World crops and animals, such as cattle and horses, to the Americas. Horses reached the North American mainland through Mexico. North American tribes like the Apaches, Sioux, and Blackfoot swiftly adopted the horse, transforming their cultures into highly mobile, wide-ranging hunter societies that pursued the shaggy buffalo across the Great Plains. Columbus also brought sugar cane to the Americas. Thriving in the warm Caribbean climate, it prompted a "sugar revolution" in the European diet that fueled the forced migration of millions of Africans to work the canefields and sugar mills of the New World.

Online Study Center
Primary source
Plant Exchange: The New World and Old World Crops
college.hmco.com/pic/kennedybrief7e

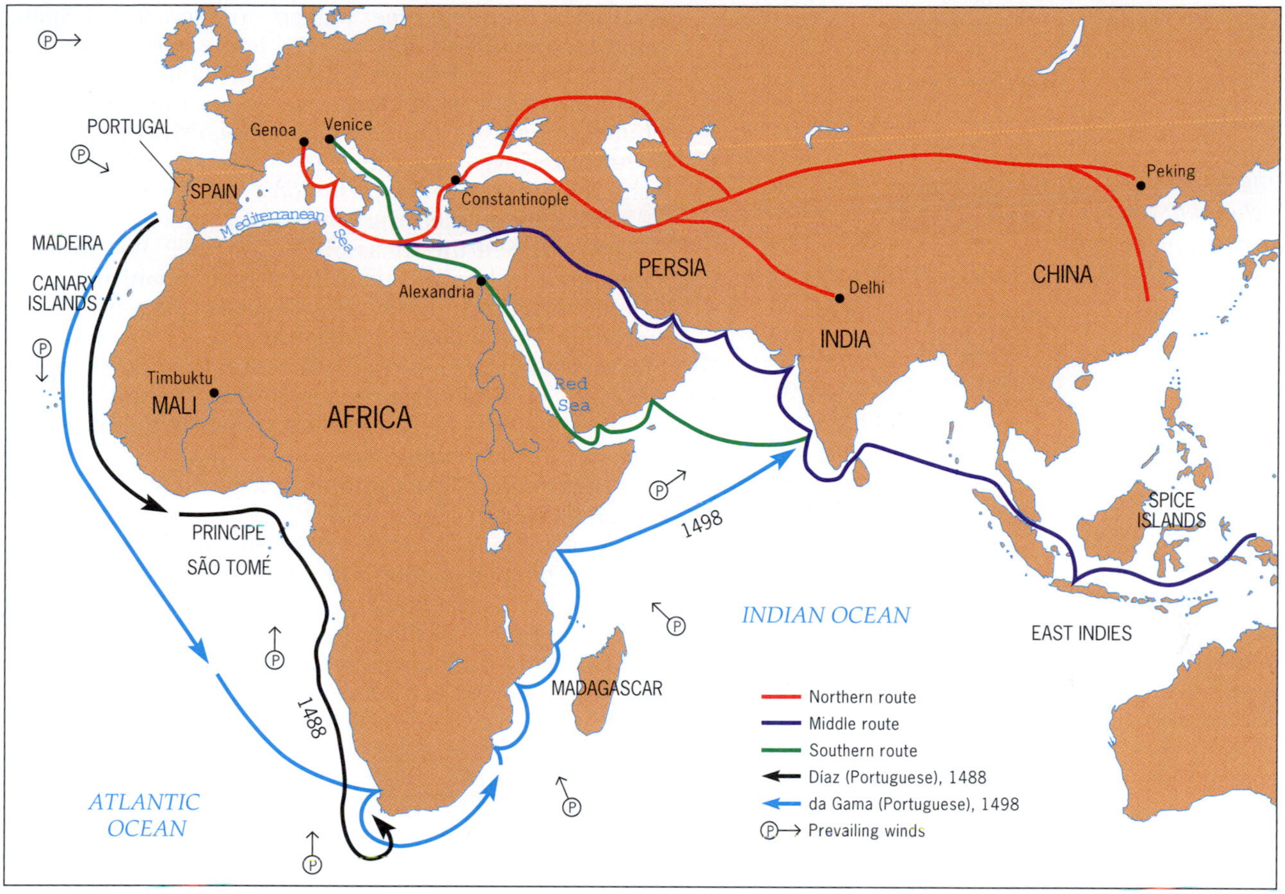

Trade Routes with the East Goods on the early routes passed through so many hands along the way that their ultimate source remained mysterious to Europeans.

Unwittingly, the Europeans also brought in their bodies the germs that caused smallpox, yellow fever, and malaria—diseases that quickly devastated the Native Americans. During the Indians' millennia of separate existence in the Americas, most of the Old World's killer maladies had disappeared from among them. But generations of freedom from those illnesses had also wiped out protective antibodies. Devoid of natural resistance to Old World sicknesses, Indians died in droves. Within fifty years of the Spanish arrival, the population of the Taino natives in Hispaniola dwindled from some 1 million people to about 200. The lethal germs spread among New World peoples with the speed and force of a hurricane, swiftly sweeping far ahead of the human invaders; most of those afflicted never laid eyes on a European. In the centuries after Columbus's landfall, as many as 90 percent of Native Americans perished, a **demographic** catastrophe without parallel in human history. Depopulation was so severe that entire cultures and ancient ways of life were extinguished forever. The Indians, by contrast, unintentionally infected the early explorers with syphilis, injecting that lethal sexually transmitted disease for the first time into Europe.

Map Skill-Builder: Understanding Economic Maps

In the early European trading routes with Asia and the East Indies, what one common destination could be reached by the Middle route, the Southern route, and da Gama's ocean route?
a) Constantinople b) Persia
c) China d) India

The Spanish *Conquistadores*

Gradually, Europeans realized that the American continents held rich prizes, especially the gold and silver of the advanced civilizations in Mexico and Peru. Spain secured its claim to Columbus's discoveries in the Treaty of Tordesillas (1494), dividing with Portugal the "heathen lands" of the New World.

Spain became the dominant exploring and colonizing power of the 1500s. Seeking both the glitter of gold and the glory of God, Spanish ***conquistadores*** (conquerors) fanned out across the Caribbean and eventually onto the mainland of the

Interactive map
Africa and Its Peoples, c. 1400
college.hmco.com/pic/kennedybrief7e

demographic *Concerning the general characteristics of a given population, including such factors as numbers, age, gender, birth and death rates, and so on.*

Bartolomé de Las Casas (1474–1566), a reform-minded Dominican friar, wrote The Destruction of the Indies *in 1542 to chronicle the awful fate of the Native Americans and to protest Spanish policies in the New World. He was especially horrified at the catastrophic effects of disease on the native peoples:*

"Who of those in future centuries will believe this? I myself who am writing this and saw it and know the most about it can hardly believe that such was possible."

American continents (see "Makers of America: The Spanish *Conquistadores*," pp. 16–17). Some early explorers, among them Ponce de León, Coronado, and de Soto, ventured into territory that eventually became part of the United States. But the permanent Spanish conquests of Peru and Mexico were by far the most consequential achievements of the *conquistadores.*

In South America, the ironfisted conqueror Francisco Pizarro crushed the Incas of Peru in 1532 and added a huge horde of booty, especially silver, to Spanish coffers. This flood of precious metal touched off a price revolution in Europe that increased consumer costs by as much as 500 percent in the hundred years after the mid-sixteenth century. Some scholars see in this ballooning European money supply the fuel that fed the growth of the economic system known as **capitalism**.

The islands of the Caribbean Sea—the West Indies—served as offshore bases where supplies could be stored and men and horses rested for the Spanish invasion of the mainland Americas. The vulnerable native communities of the West Indies also provided laboratories for testing the techniques that would eventually subdue Mexico and Peru. Most important was the institution of the ***encomienda***, which allowed the government to give Indians to certain colonists in return for the promise to try to Christianize them. It was slavery in all but name, and the Spanish missionary Bartolome de Las Casas called it "a moral pestilence invented by Satan."

Online Study Center
Primary source
Spanish Monk Pleads for Better Treatment of the Indians
college.hmco.com/pic/kennedybrief7e

conquistadores *Spanish conquerors or adventurers in the Americas.*

capitalism *An economic system characterized by private property, generally free trade, and open and accessible markets.*

encomienda *The Spanish labor system in which persons were held to unpaid service under the permanent control of their masters, though not legally owned by them.*

The Conquest of Mexico

The conquest of Mexico was engineered by Hernán Cortés, who set sail from Cuba in 1519 with sixteen horses and several hundred men. From an island near the coast of Mexico, he picked up a female Indian slave named Malinche, who knew both Mayan and Nahuatl, the language of the powerful Aztecs. Aided by Malinche and another interpreter, Cortés learned of the unrest among subordinate peoples within the Aztec empire, and of the gold and other wealth in its capital of Tenochtitlán. "We Spanish suffer from a strange disease of the heart,"

Conquistadores, c. 1534
This illustration for a book called the Köhler Codex of Nuremberg may be the earliest depiction of the *conquistadores* in the Americas. It portrays men and horses alike as steadfast and self-assured in their work of conquest.

Cortés allegedly informed emissaries of the Aztec ruler Moctezuma, "for which the only known remedy is gold." The ambassadors reported this comment to Moctezuma, along with the astonishing fact that the newcomers rode on the backs of "deer" (horses). Believing that Cortés was the god Quetzalcoatl, whose return from the eastern sea was predicted in Aztec legends, Moctezuma allowed the *conquistadores* to approach his capital unopposed.

The Spaniards were amazed by the beauty and wealth of Tenochtitlán, with its 300,000 inhabitants and marvelous temples, aqueducts, and floating gardens. Moctezuma treated Cortés hospitably at first, but soon the Spanish were unable to contain their lust for gold. After warfare broke out on the *noche triste* (sad night) of June 30, 1520, Cortés laid siege to the city. It capitulated on August 13, 1521.

The Aztec empire thus gave way to three centuries of Spanish rule. Its people suffered not only from the armed conquest but from smallpox and other epidemics that burned through the Valley of Mexico. The native population of Mexico shrank from more than 20 million to fewer than 2 million people in less than a century. The temples of Tenochtitlán were destroyed to make way for the Christian cathedrals of Mexico City, built on the site of the ruined Aztec capital.

Yet the invader brought more than conquest and death. He brought his language, laws, customs, and religion, all of which proved adaptable to the peoples of Mexico. He intermarried with the surviving Indians, creating a distinctive culture of ***mestizos***, people of mixed Indian and European heritage. To this day Mexican civilization remains a unique blend of the Old World and the New, producing both ambivalence and pride among people of Mexican heritage. Cortés's translator Malinche, for example, has given her name to the Mexican language in the word *malinchista*, or "traitor." But Mexicans also celebrate Columbus Day as the *Dia de la Raza*—the birthday of a wholly new race of people.

mestizo(s) *A person of mixed Native American and European ancestry.*

province *A medium-sized subunit of territory and governmental administration within a larger nation or empire.*

The Spread of Spanish America

Spain's colonial empire grew swiftly and impressively. Within about half a century of Columbus's landfall, hundreds of Spanish cities and towns flourished in the Americas. Majestic cathedrals dotted the land, printing presses turned out books, and scholars studied at distinguished universities, including those at Mexico City and Lima, Peru, both founded in 1551, eighty-five years before Harvard, the first college established in the English colonies.

But how secure were these imperial possessions? Other powers were already sniffing around the edges of the Spanish domain, eager to bite off their share of the promised wealth of the new lands. The upstart English sent Giovanni Caboto (known in English as John Cabot) to explore the northeastern coast of North America in 1497 and 1498. The French king dispatched Giovanni da Verrazano to probe the eastern seaboard in 1524 and Jacques Cartier to explore the St. Lawrence River in 1534. To protect sea lanes and secure their northern borderlands against such encroachments, the Spanish erected a fortress at St. Augustine, Florida, in 1565, thus founding the oldest continually inhabited European settlement in the future United States.

In Mexico, the tales of Francisco Coronado's expedition of the 1540s beckoned *conquistadores* northward from Mexico into the Rio Grande and Colorado River regions. A Spanish expedition led by Don Juan de Oñate entered the Rio Grande Valley in 1598 and cruelly abused the Pueblo peoples they encountered. In the battle of Acoma in 1599, the Spanish severed one foot of each survivor. They proclaimed the area to be the **province** of New Mexico in 1609 and founded its capital at Santa Fe the following year. The Spanish settlers found precious little gold, but missionaries did discover a wealth of souls to be harvested for the Christian religion. Their efforts to suppress Pueblo religious customs provoked an uprising called Popé's Rebellion in 1680. The Pueblo rebels destroyed every Catholic church in the province and killed a score of priests and hundreds of Spanish settlers. It took nearly half a century for the Spanish to reclaim New Mexico from the insurrectionary Indians.

Meanwhile, as a further hedge against the ever-threatening French, who had sent an expedition under Robert La Salle down the Mississippi River in the 1680s,

The Spanish *Conquistadores*

In 1492, the same year that Columbus sighted America, the great Moorish city of Grenada fell after a ten-year siege. For five centuries, the Christian kingdoms of Spain had tried to drive the North African Muslim Moors off the Iberian peninsula, and with the fall of Grenada this "Reconquista" succeeded. Centuries of religious war nurtured an obsession with status and honor, bred religious zealotry and intolerance, and created a large class of men who regarded manual labor and commerce contemptuously. With the Reconquista ended, some of these men turned their restless gaze to Spain's New World frontier.

Between 1519 and 1540, Spanish *conquistadores* swept across the Americas in two wide arcs of conquest—one driving from Cuba through Mexico into what is now the southwestern United States, the other starting from Panama, previously conquered by Vasco Balboa, and pushing south into Peru. The military conquest of this vast region was achieved by just ten thousand men, organized in a series of private expeditions. Hernán Cortés, Francisco Pizarro, and other aspiring conquerors signed contracts with the Spanish monarch, raised money from investors, and then proceeded to recruit private armies. Only a minority of the *conquistadores* were nobles. About half were professional soldiers or sailors; the rest comprised peasants, artisans, and members of the middling classes. Most were in their twenties and early thirties.

Some of these motley adventurers hoped to win royal titles or favors. Others sought to ensure God's favor by spreading Christianity to the pagans. Some men aspired to escape dubious pasts, while others sought the kind of historical adventure experienced by heroes of classical antiquity. Nearly all shared a lust for gold.

An Aztec View of the Conquest, 1531 Produced just a dozen years after Cortés's arrival in 1519, this drawing by an Aztec artist pictures the Indians rendering tribute to their conquerors. The inclusion of the banner showing Madonna and child also illustrates the early incorporation of Christian beliefs by the Indians.

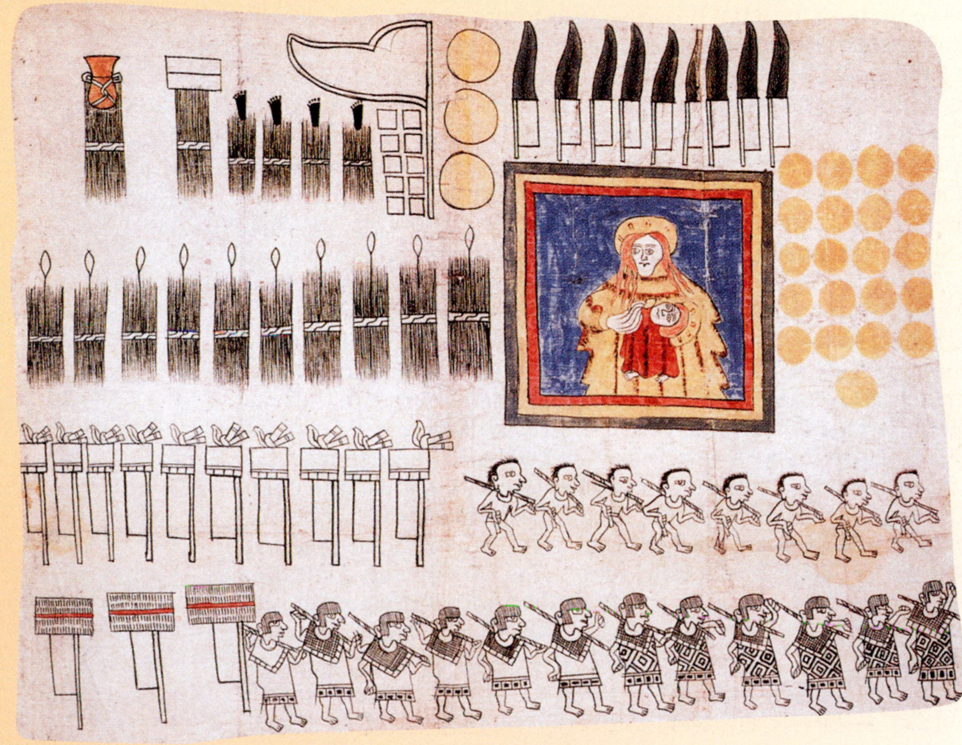

But most never achieved their dreams of glory or riches. Even when an expedition captured exceptionally rich booty, the spoils were unevenly divided: men from the commander's home region often received more, and men on horseback generally got two shares to the infantryman's one. The *conquistadores* lost still more power as the crown tightened its control in the New World. By the 1550s, the day of the *conquistador* had ended.

Nevertheless, the *conquistadores* achieved a kind of immortality. Because of a scarcity of Spanish women in the early days of the conquest, many *conquistadores* married Indian women. Their offspring, the "new race" of *mestizos*, formed a cultural and biological bridge between Latin America's European and Indian races.

the Spanish began around 1716 to establish a few settlements and missions in Texas, including the one at San Antonio later known as the Alamo. To the west, in California, no serious foreign threat loomed, and Spain directed its attention there only belatedly. Juan Rodriguez Cabrillo had explored the California coast in 1542, but for some two centuries thereafter California slumbered undisturbed by European intruders.

Then in 1769, Spanish missionaries led by Father Junipero Serra founded at San Diego the first of a chain of twenty-one missions that wound up the coast as far as Sonoma, north of San Francisco Bay. Father Serra's brown-robed Franciscan friars toiled with zealous devotion to Christianize three hundred thousand native Californians and teach them horticulture and crafts. These "mission Indians" did adopt Christianity, but they lost their native cultures and often lost their lives as well, as the white man's diseases doomed these biologically vulnerable peoples.

The misdeeds of the Spanish in the New World obscured their substantial achievements and helped give birth to the "Black Legend." This false concept held that the conquerors merely tortured and butchered the Indians, stole their gold, infected them with smallpox, and left little but misery behind. The Spanish invaders did indeed kill, enslave, and infect countless natives, but they also grafted their culture, laws, religion, and language onto a vast array of native societies, laying the foundations for a score of Spanish-speaking nations.

■ The Devastation of Disease This engraving of a burial service records the horrendous impact of Old World diseases on the vulnerable Native Americans.

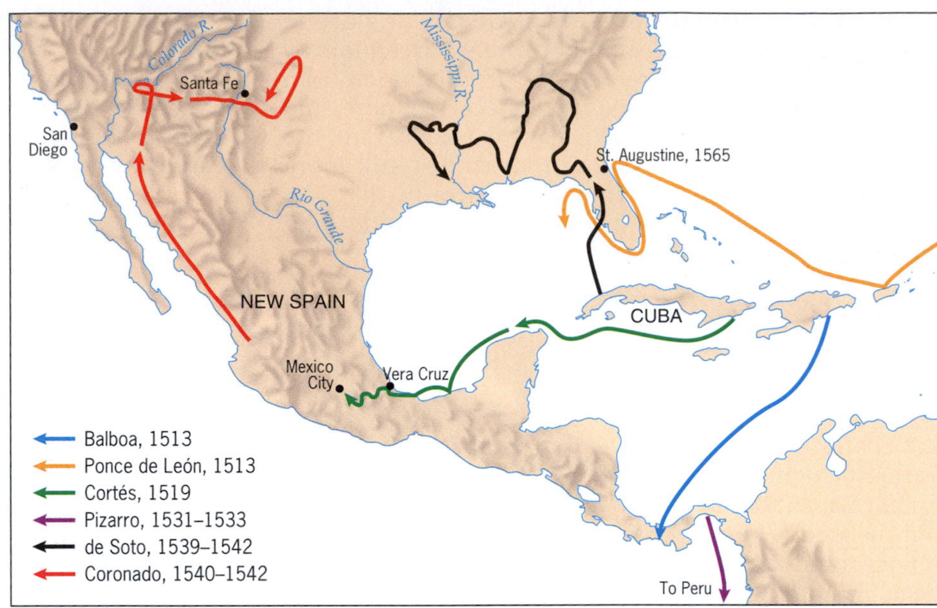

Principal Early Spanish Explorations and Conquests Notice that Coronado traversed northern Texas and Oklahoma. In present-day eastern Kansas, he found, instead of the great golden city he sought, a drab encampment, probably of Wichita Indians.

Clearly, the Spanish, who had more than a century's head start over the English, were genuine empire builders and cultural innovators in the New World. Compared with their Anglo-Saxon rivals, their colonial establishment was larger and richer, and it was destined to endure more than a quarter of a century longer. And in the last analysis, the Spanish paid the Native Americans the high compliment of fusing with them through marriage and incorporating indigenous culture into their own, rather than shunning and eventually isolating the Indians as their English adversaries would do.

Chapter Summary 

Millions of years ago, the two American continents became geologically separated from the Eastern Hemisphere landmasses where humanity originated. The first people to enter these continents came across a temporary land bridge from Siberia about 35,000 years ago. Spreading across the two continents, they developed a great variety of societies based largely on corn agriculture and hunting. In North America, some ancient Indian peoples like the Pueblos, the Anasazi, and the Mississippian culture developed elaborate settlements. But on the whole, North American Indian societies were less numerous and urbanized than those in Central and South America, though equally diverse in culture and social organization.

The impetus for European exploration came from the desire for new trade routes to Asia, the spirit and technological discoveries of the Renaissance, and the power of the new European national monarchies. The European encounters with America and Africa, beginning with the Portuguese and Spanish explorers, convulsed the entire world. Biological change, disease, population loss, conquest, African slavery, cultural change, and economic expansion were just some of the consequences of the commingling of two ecosystems.

After they conquered and then intermarried with Indians of the great civilizations of South America and Mexico, the Spanish *conquistadores* expanded northward into the northern border territories of Florida, New Mexico, Texas, and California. There they established small but permanent settlements in competition with the French and English explorers who also were venturing into North America.

2

The Planting of English America

1500–1733

. . . For I shall yet live to see it [Virginia] an Inglishe nation.

Sir Walter Raleigh, 1602

Chapter Outline

- England in the Age of Expansion
- The Planting of Jamestown, 1607
- The Growth of Virginia and Maryland
- England in the Caribbean
- Settling the Carolinas and Georgia
- Makers of America: The Iroquois

As the seventeenth century dawned, scarcely a hundred years after Columbus's momentous landfall, the face of much of the New World had already been profoundly transformed. European crops and livestock had begun to alter the very landscape, touching off an ecological revolution that would reverberate for centuries to come. From Tierra del Fuego in the south to Hudson's Bay in the north, disease and armed conquest had cruelly winnowed and disrupted the native peoples. Several hundred thousand Africans toiled on Caribbean and Brazilian sugar plantations. From Florida and New Mexico southward, most of the New World lay firmly in the grip of imperial Spain.

But *North* America in 1600 remained largely unexplored and effectively unclaimed by Europeans. Then, as if to herald the coming century of colonization and conflict in the northern continent, three European powers planted primitive outposts in three distant corners of the continent within three years of one another: the Spanish in Santa Fe in 1610, the French at Quebec in 1608, and, most consequentially for the future United States, the English at Jamestown, Virginia, in 1607.

Focus Questions

1. **Why was England slow to begin colonization, and what factors finally enabled the English to establish successful colonies?**
2. **How did the Jamestown colony evolve from its disastrous beginnings into the successful colony of Virgina?**
3. **What was the relationship between early Virginia settlers and the Powhatan Indians, and how did Indian policies in the southern colonies eventually lay the basis for forced removal and reservations?**
4. **What was the basis for the economic and labor systems of Virginia and the other southern colonies?**
5. **What were the fundamental similarities and lesser differences among the five southern colonies of Virginia, Maryland, North Carolina, South Carolina, and Georgia?**

England's Imperial Stirrings

Feeble indeed were England's efforts in the 1500s to compete with the sprawling Spanish Empire. As Spain's ally in the first half of the century, England took little interest in establishing its own overseas colonies. But in 1558 the Protestant Elizabeth ascended to the English throne and solidified her father King Henry VIII's break with the Roman Catholic Church. Protestantism became dominant in England, and rivalry with Catholic Spain intensified.

An early scene of that rivalry was Ireland, where the Catholic Irish sought help from Catholic Spain to throw off the yoke of the new Protestant English queen. In crushing the Irish uprising of the 1570s and 1580s with terrible ferocity, many English soldiers developed a sneering contempt for the "savage" natives, an attitude they brought with them to the New World.

Encouraged by the ambitious Queen Elizabeth, hardy English buccaneers now swarmed out upon the shipping lanes to plunder Spanish treasure ships and raid Spanish settlements. The most famous of these semipiratical "sea dogs" was the courtly Francis Drake, who plundered his way around the planet and returned in 1580 laden with Spanish gold.

■ **Elizabeth I (1533–1603), by Marcus Gheeraets the Younger, c. 1592** Although accused of being vain, fickle, prejudiced, and miserly, she proved to be an unusually successful ruler. She never married (hence, the "Virgin Queen"), although various royal matches were projected.

nationalism *Fervent belief and loyalty devoted to the political unit of the nation-state.*

The first English attempt at colonization, in bleak Newfoundland, collapsed when its promoter, Sir Humphrey Gilbert, lost his life at sea in 1583. Inspired by Gilbert's ill-starred dream, his gallant half-brother, Sir Walter Raleigh, organized another group of settlers, who went ashore in 1585 on North Carolina's Roanoke Island. But the hapless Roanoke colony mysteriously vanished, swallowed up by the wilderness.

These pathetic English failures at colonization contrasted embarrassingly with the glories of the Spanish Empire, whose profits were fabulously enriching Spain. Philip II of Spain, self-anointed foe of the Protestant Reformation, used part of his imperial gains to amass an "Invincible Armada" of ships for an invasion of England in 1588. But the skillful English sea dogs inflicted heavy damage on the armada, and a devastating storm (the "Protestant wind") scattered the crippled Spanish ships.

The rout of the Spanish Armada marked the beginning of the end of Spanish imperial dreams, though Spain's New World empire would not fully collapse for three more centuries. England's victory also started that country on its way to becoming master of the world oceans—a fact of enormous importance to the American people. Indeed England now possessed many of the strengths that Spain displayed on the eve of its colonizing adventure a century earlier: a strong, unified national state under a popular monarch; a measure of religious unity after a protracted struggle between Protestants and Catholics; and a vibrant sense of **nationalism** and national destiny.

This new sense of national pride and patriotism blossomed in the Elizabethan golden age of culture and politics. William Shakespeare, who made occasional poetic references to England's American colonies, was only one of many contemporary poets and writers who expressed boundless faith in the future of the English nation.

But England's scepter'd isle, as Shakespeare called it, also throbbed with social and economic tensions as the seventeenth century opened. Its population was mushrooming, from some 3 million people in 1550 to about 4 million in 1600. In the ever-green English countryside, landlords were "enclosing" croplands for sheep grazing, forcing many small farmers into precarious tenancy or off the land altogether. It was no accident that the woolen districts of eastern and western England—where Puritanism had taken strong root—supplied many of the earliest immigrants to America. When economic depression hit the

Chronology

1558	Elizabeth I becomes queen of England.
c. 1565-1590	English crush Irish uprising.
1577-1580	Drake circumnavigates the globe.
1585	Raleigh founds "lost colony" at Roanoke.
1588	England defeats Spanish Armada.
1603	James I becomes king of England.
1607	Virginia colony founded at Jamestown.
1612	Rolfe perfects tobacco culture in Virginia.
1614	First Anglo-Powhatan War ends.
1619	First Africans arrive in Jamestown. Virginia House of Burgesses established.
1624	Virginia becomes royal colony.
1634	Maryland colony founded.
1640s	Large-scale slave-labor system established in English West Indies.
1644	Second Anglo-Powhatan War.
1649	Act of Toleration in Maryland. Charles I beheaded; Cromwell rules England.
1660	Charles II restored to English throne.
1661	Barbados slave code adopted.
1670	Carolina colony created.
1711-1713	Tuscarora War in North Carolina.
1712	North Carolina formally separates from South Carolina.
1715-1716	Yamasee War in South Carolina.
1733	Georgia colony founded.

woolen trade in the late 1500s, thousands of unemployed farmers took to the roads, often ending up as beggars and paupers in cities like Bristol and London.

At the same time, laws of **primogeniture** decreed that only eldest sons were eligible to inherit landed estates. Landholders' ambitious younger sons, among them Gilbert, Raleigh, and Drake, were forced to seek their fortunes elsewhere. By the early 1600s the unsuccessful lone-wolf ventures of such courtiers were replaced by the **joint-stock company,** which enabled a considerable number of investors to pool their capital.

Peace with a chastened Spain provided the opportunity for English colonization. Population growth provided the workers. Unemployment, as well as a thirst for adventure, for markets, and for religious freedom, provided the motives. Joint-stock companies provided the financial means. The stage was set for a historic effort to establish an English beachhead in the still uncharted North American wilderness.

primogeniture *The legal principle that the oldest son inherits all family property or land.*

joint-stock company *An economic arrangement by which a number of investors pool their capital for investment.*

charter *A legal document granted by a government to some group or agency to implement a stated purpose, and spelling out the attending rights and obligations.*

England Plants the Jamestown Seedling

In 1606, two years after peace with Spain, the hand of destiny beckoned toward Virginia. A joint-stock company, the Virginia Company of London, received a **charter** from King James I for a settlement in the New World. The main attractions were the promise of gold and the desire to find a passage through America to the Indies. Like most joint-stock companies of the day, the Virginia Company was intended to endure for only a few years, after which its stockholders hoped to liquidate it for a profit. This arrangement put severe pressure on the luckless colonists, who were threatened with abandonment in the wilderness if they did not quickly strike it rich on the company's behalf. Few of the investors thought in terms of long-term colonization. Apparently no one even faintly suspected that the seeds of a mighty nation were being planted.

In the years immediately following the defeat of the Spanish Armada, the English writer Richard Hakluyt (1552?–1616) extravagantly exhorted his countrymen to cast off their "sluggish security" and undertake the colonization of the New World:

"There is under our noses the great and ample country of Virginia; the inland whereof is found of late to be so sweet and wholesome a climate, so rich and abundant in silver mines, a better and richer country than Mexico itself. If it shall please the Almighty to stir up Her Majesty's heart to continue with transporting one or two thousand of her people, she shall by God's assistance, in short space, increase her dominions, enrich her coffers, and reduce many pagans to the faith of Christ."

The charter of the Virginia Company is a significant document in American history. It guaranteed to the overseas settlers the same rights of Englishmen that they would have enjoyed if they had stayed at home. This precious boon was gradually extended to the other English colonies, helping to reinforce the colonists' sense that even on the far shore of the Atlantic they remained comfortably within the embrace of traditional English institutions. But ironically, a century and a half later, the colonists' insistence on the "rights of Englishmen" fed their hot resentment against an increasingly meddlesome mother country and nourished their appetite for independence.

Setting sail in late 1606, the Virginia Company's tiny band of colonists eventually arrived at a site on the wooded and malarial banks of a swampy river. There, on May 24, 1607, about a hundred English settlers, all men, disembarked. They called the place Jamestown and the river the James in honor of King James I.

The early years of Jamestown proved to be a nightmare for all concerned—except the buzzards. Once ashore, the settlers died by the dozens from disease, malnutrition, and starvation. The woods rustled with game, and the rivers flopped with fish, but the greenhorn settlers, many of them self-styled "gentlemen" unaccustomed to fending for themselves, wasted valuable time grubbing for nonexistent gold when they should have been gathering provisions.

The authorities meted out harsh discipline in the young Virginia colony. One Jamestown settler who publicly criticized the governor was sentenced to

"be disarmed [and] have his arms broken and his tongue bored through with an awl [and] shall pass through a guard of 40 men and shall be butted [with muskets] by every one of them and at the head of the troop kicked down and footed out of the fort."

Virginia was saved from utter collapse at the start largely by the leadership and resourcefulness of an intrepid young adventurer, Captain John Smith. Taking over in 1608, he whipped the gold-hungry colonists into line with the rule "He who shall not work shall not eat." He had been kidnapped in December 1607 and subjected to a mock execution by the Indian chieftain Powhatan, whose daughter Pocahontas "saved" Smith by dramatically interposing her head between his and the war clubs of his captors. Pocahontas became an intermediary between the Indians and the settlers, helping to preserve a shaky peace and provide needed food.

Still, the colonists died in droves, and living skeletons were driven to desperate acts. They were reduced to eating "dogges, Catts, Ratts, and Myce" and even to digging up corpses for food. One hungry man killed, salted, and ate his wife, for which misbehavior he was executed. Of the four hundred settlers who managed to make it to Virginia by 1609, only sixty survived the "starving time" winter of 1609–1610. Diseased and despairing, the remaining colonists were ready to return to England in the spring of 1610 when a relief party suddenly arrived, headed by a new governor, Lord De La Warr.

De La Warr ordered the settlers to stay in Jamestown, imposed a harsh military regime on the colony, and soon undertook aggressive military action against the Indians. But disease continued to reap a gruesome harvest. By 1625 Virginia contained only some twelve hundred hard-bitten survivors of the nearly eight thousand adventurers who had tried to start life anew in the ill-fated colony.

Cultural Clash in the Chesapeake

When the English landed in 1607, the chieftain Powhatan dominated the few dozen small tribes in the James River area. Powhatan at first may have considered the English potential allies in his struggle to extend his power over his Indian rivals, and he tried to be conciliatory. But relations between the Indians and the English remained tense, especially as the starving colonists took to raiding Indian food supplies.

The atmosphere grew even more strained after Lord De La Warr arrived in 1610. He carried orders from the Virginia Company that amounted to a declaration of war against the Indians in the Jamestown region. A veteran of the vicious campaigns against the Irish, De La Warr introduced "Irish tactics" against the Indians. His troops raided Indian villages, burned houses, confiscated provisions, and torched cornfields. A peace settlement ended this First Anglo-Powhatan War in 1614, sealed by the marriage of Pocahontas to the colonist John Rolfe—the first known interracial union in Virginia.

A fragile peace prevailed for eight years. But the Indians, pressed by the land-hungry whites and ravaged by European diseases, struck back in 1622. A series of Indian attacks left 347 settlers dead, including John Rolfe. Pushed westward by retaliatory settler raids, the Indians made one last effort to dislodge the Virginians in the Second Anglo-Powhatan War in 1644. They were again defeated. The peace treaty of 1646 repudiated any hope of assimilating the native peoples into Virginian society or of peacefully coexisting with them. Instead it effectively banished the Chesapeake Indians from their ancestral lands and formally separated Indian from white areas of settlement—the origins of the later reservation system. By 1669 an official **census** revealed that only about two thousand Indians remained in Virginia, perhaps 10 percent of the population the original English settlers had encountered in 1607. By 1685 the English considered the Powhatan peoples extinct.

Pocahontas (c. 1595–1617) Taken to England by her husband, she was received as a princess. She died when preparing to return to Virginia. Her infant son ultimately reached Virginia, where hundreds of his descendants have lived, including the second Mrs. Woodrow Wilson.

It had been the Powhatans' calamitous misfortune to fall victim to three Ds: disease, disorganization, and disposability. Like native peoples throughout the New World, they were struck down by European epidemics of smallpox and measles. They also lacked the unity to oppose the relatively well-organized and militarily disciplined whites. Finally, the Powhatans served no economic function for the Virginia colonists, having no gold, labor, or valuable goods to offer in commerce. Indeed the Indian presence frustrated the colonists' desire for a local commodity the Europeans desperately wanted: land.

census *An official count of population, often also including other information about the population.*

Primary source
European Settlements and Indian Tribes in North America
college.hmco.com/pic/kennedybrief7e

The Indians' New World

The fate of the Powhatans foreshadowed the destinies of indigenous peoples throughout the continent as the process of European settlement went forward. Native Americans, of course, were no strangers to change, adaptation, and even catastrophe throughout their history, well before Columbus's arrival. But the shock of large-scale European colonization disrupted Native American life on a vast scale, inducing unprecedented demographic and cultural transformations.

Some changes were fairly benign. Horses acquired from the Spanish catalyzed a substantial migration of previously sedentary forest-dwelling peoples such as the Lakotas (Sioux) onto the Great Plains in the eighteenth century. There they thrived impressively, adopting an entirely new way of life as mounted nomadic hunters. But the effects of contact with Europeans proved less salutary for most other native peoples.

Disease was by far the biggest disrupter, as Old World pathogens licked lethally through biologically defenseless Indian populations. Disease took more than human life; it extinguished entire cultures and occasionally helped to shape new ones. Epidemics often robbed native peoples of the elders who preserved their oral traditions, and the survivors then faced the daunting task of literally re-inventing themselves without benefit of accumulated wisdom or kin networks. The decimation and forced migration of native peoples sometimes scrambled them together in wholly new ways. The Catawba nation of the southern Piedmont region, for example, was formed from the remnants of several different groups uprooted by the Europeans.

Trade also transformed Indian life, as traditional barter-and-exchange networks gave way to the temptations of European commerce. The drive to acquire European firearms in exchange for fur pelts fueled competition among the tribes for prime hunting grounds and led to an escalating cycle of Indian-on-Indian violence.

Indians along the Atlantic seaboard felt the most ferocious effects of European contact. Further inland, native peoples had the advantages of time, space, and numbers as they sought to adapt to the European incursion. The Algonquians in the Great Lakes area, for instance, became a substantial regional power, able to deal from a position of strength with the few Europeans who managed to penetrate the interior. As a result, a British or French trader wanting to do business with the inland tribes had little choice but to conform to Indian ways, often taking an Indian wife. Thus was created a middle ground, a zone where both Europeans and Native Americans were compelled to accommodate one another—at least until the Europeans arrived in large numbers.

Primary source
Origins of Ottawa Society, as Related by N. Perrot
college.hmco.com/pic/kennedybrief7e

Virginia: Child of Tobacco

John Rolfe, the husband of Pocahontas, became the father of the tobacco industry and an economic savior of the Virginia colony. By 1612 he had perfected methods of raising and curing the pungent weed. A tobacco rush swept over Virginia, as crops were planted in the streets of Jamestown and even between the numerous graves. Colonists who had once hungered for food now hungered for ever more land on which to plant ever more tobacco. Relentlessly, they pressed the frontier of settlement up the river valleys to the west, abrasively edging against the Indians.

Virginia's prosperity was finally built on tobacco smoke. This "bewitching weed" played a vital role in putting the colony on firm economic foundations. But tobacco—King Nicotine—was something of a tyrant. It was ruinous to the soil when greedily planted in successive years, and it chained Virginia's fortunes to the fluctuating price of a single crop. Tobacco also promoted the broad-acred plantation system and with it a brisk demand for slave labor.

In 1619, the year before the Plymouth Pilgrims landed in New England, what was described as a Dutch warship appeared off Jamestown and sold some twenty Africans. The scanty record does not reveal whether they were purchased as lifelong slaves or as servants committed to limited years of servitude. This commercial transaction planted the seeds of the North American slave system. Yet blacks were too costly for most of the hard-pinched white colonists to acquire, and for decades few were brought to Virginia. In 1650 Virginia counted but three hundred blacks, although by the end of the century blacks, most of them enslaved, made up approximately 14 percent of the colony's population.

Representative self-government was also born in primitive Virginia, in the same cradle with slavery and in the same year—1619. The London Company authorized the settlers to summon an assembly, known as the House of Burgesses. A momentous precedent was thus feebly established, for this assemblage was the first of many miniature parliaments to flourish in the soil of America.

As time passed, James I grew increasingly hostile to Virginia. He detested tobacco, and he distrusted the representative House of Burgesses, which he branded a "seminary of sedition." In 1624 he revoked the charter of the bankrupt Virginia Company, thus making Virginia a royal colony directly under his control.

Maryland: Catholic Haven

Maryland—the second plantation colony but the fourth English colony to be planted—was founded in 1634 by Lord Baltimore, of a prominent English Catholic family. He embarked on the venture partly to reap financial profits and partly to create a refuge for his fellow Catholics, who were harshly persecuted in Protestant England.

Absentee proprietor Lord Baltimore hoped that the two hundred settlers who founded Maryland at St. Marys, on Chesapeake Bay, would be the vanguard of a vast new **feudal** domain. Huge estates were to be awarded to his largely Catholic relatives, and gracious manor houses, modeled on those of England's aristocracy, were intended to arise amidst the fertile forests. As in Virginia, colonists proved willing to come only if offered the opportunity to acquire land of their own. Soon they were dispersed around the Chesapeake region on modest farms, and the haughty land barons, mostly Catholic, were surrounded by resentful backcountry planters, mostly Protestant. Resentment flared into open rebellion near the end of the century, and the Baltimore family for a time lost its proprietary rights.

Despite these tensions Maryland prospered. Like Virginia, it blossomed forth in acres of tobacco. Also like Virginia, it depended for labor in its early years mainly on white **indentured servants**—penniless persons who bound themselves to work for a number of years to pay their passage. In both colonies it was only in the later years of the seventeenth century that black slaves began to be imported in large numbers.

Lord Baltimore at first permitted unusual freedom of worship for Protestant settlers in Maryland. But when the heavy tide of Protestants threatened to submerge the Catholics, the Catholic settlers sought legal guarantees for their religious practice in the famed Act of Toleration, passed in 1649 by the local representative assembly. This statute guaranteed **toleration** to all Christians, but it decreed the death penalty for anyone who denied the divinity of Jesus. While falling far short of later standards of religious liberty, the statute did extend a temporary cloak of protection to the uneasy Catholic minority.

Online Study Center
Primary source
Divorce in Maryland
college.hmco.com/pic/kennedybrief7e

Online Study Center
Interactive map
European Settlements and Indian Tribes in Eastern North America, 1650
college.hmco.com/pic/kennedybrief7e

feudal *Concerning the decentralized medieval social system of personal obligations between rulers and ruled.*

indentured servants *Poor persons obligated to a fixed term of unpaid labor, often in exchange for a benefit such as transportation, protection, or training.*

toleration *Originally, religious freedom granted by an established church to a religious minority.*

Early Maryland and Virginia

Map Skill-Builder: Understanding Political Maps

1. Where did the original land grant to Lord Baltimore follow natural geographical features, and where did it follow certain "artificial" straight lines of latitude or longitude on the map?
2. Did the eventual *political* boundary of Maryland mostly follow the natural features, or did it add more artificially drawn boundaries?

African slaves destined for the West Indian sugar plantations were bound and branded on West African beaches and ferried out in canoes to the waiting slave ships. An English sailor described the scene:

"The Negroes are so wilful and loth to leave their own country, that they have often leap'd out of the canoes, boat and ship, into the sea, and kept under water till they were drowned, to avoid being taken up and saved by our boats, which pursued them; they having a more dreadful apprehension of Barbadoes than we can have of hell."

The West Indies: Way Station to Mainland America

While the English were nursing the first frail colonial shoots in the Chesapeake, they were also busily colonizing the West Indies. By the mid-seventeenth century, England had secured its claim to several West Indian islands, including the large prize of Jamaica in 1655.

Sugar formed the foundation of the West Indian economy. What tobacco was to the Chesapeake, sugar cane was to the Caribbean—with one crucial difference. Tobacco was a poor man's crop that could be planted and processed easily. Sugar cane was a rich man's crop, requiring extensive planting and an elaborate refining process in a mill. Because of the need for land, and for the labor to clear it and to run the mills, sugar cultivation was a capital-intense business. Only wealthy growers with abundant resources to invest could succeed in sugar.

The sugar lords extended their dominion over the West Indies in the seventeenth century. To work their sprawling plantations, they imported enormous numbers of African slaves—more than a quarter of a million in the five decades after 1640. By about 1700, black slaves outnumbered white settlers in the English West Indies by nearly four to one, and the region's population has remained predominantly black ever since. West Indians thus take their place among the numerous children of the African diaspora—the vast scattering of African peoples throughout the New World in the three and a half centuries following Columbus's discovery.

Primary source
Estimated Slave Imports to the New World
college.hmco.com/pic/kennedybrief7e

To control this large and potentially restive population of slaves, English authorities devised formal "codes" that defined the slaves' legal status and the masters' prerogatives. The notorious Barbados slave code of 1661 denied even the most fundamental rights to slaves and gave masters virtually complete control over their laborers.

A group of English settlers from Barbados arrived in Carolina in 1670, bringing with them a few African slaves, as well as the model of the Barbados code. In 1696 Carolina officially adopted a version of the code, which eventually inspired statutes governing slavery throughout the mainland colonies. The Caribbean islands thus served as a staging area for the slave system that would take root elsewhere in British North America.

Colonizing the Carolinas

Civil war convulsed England in the 1640s. King Charles I had dismissed Parliament in 1629, and when he recalled it in 1640, the members were mutinous. Finding their great champion in the Puritan soldier Oliver Cromwell, they ultimately beheaded Charles in 1649, and Cromwell ruled England for nearly a decade. Finally, Charles II, son of the decapitated king, was restored to the throne in 1660.

Colonization had been interrupted during this period of bloody unrest. Now, in the so-called Restoration period, empire building resumed with even greater intensity—and royal involvement. Carolina was formally created in 1670, after King Charles II granted to eight of his court favorites, the Lords Proprietors, an expanse of wilderness ribboning across the continent to the Pacific. These aristocratic founders hoped to grow foodstuffs to provision the sugar plantations in Barbados and to export non-English products like wine, silk, and olive oil.

Carolina prospered by developing close economic ties with the flourishing sugar islands of the English West Indies. Among the colonists' ventures was the capture and sale of inland Indians, which they turned into a thriving export business. As many as ten thousand Indians were dispatched to lifelong labor in the

West Indies, and others were sold to New England. A war with the Savannah Indians that began in 1707 ended this deplorable commerce. By 1710 the Indian tribes of coastal Carolina were all but annihilated.

After much experimentation, rice emerged as the principal export crop in Carolina. Since rice was grown in Africa, the Carolinians were soon paying premium prices for West African slaves experienced in rice cultivation. The Africans' agricultural skill and their relative immunity to malaria made them ideal laborers on the hot and swampy rice plantations. By 1710 they constituted a majority of Carolinians.

Moss-festooned Charles Town—named for King Charles II—rapidly became the busiest seaport in the South. Many high-spirited sons of English landed families, deprived of an inheritance, came to the Charleston area and gave it a rich aristocratic flavor. The village became a colorfully diverse community, to which French Protestant refugees and others were attracted by religious toleration.

Nearby, in Florida, the Catholic Spaniards abhorred the intrusion of these Protestant heretics. Carolina's frontier was often aflame. Armor-clad Spanish soldiers, often aided by their Indian allies, attacked English settlements during the successive Anglo-Spanish wars. But by 1700 Carolina was too strong to be wiped out.

The wild northern expanse of the huge Carolina grant bordered on Virginia. From the older colony drifted down a ragtag group of poverty-stricken outcasts and religious dissenters, many of them repelled by the wealthy plantation gentry of Virginia, who belonged to the established Church of England. These small farmers, who frequently were "**squatters**" without legal right to the soil, raised their tobacco and other crops with little need for slaves. Regarded as riffraff by their snobbish neighbors, the North Carolinians earned a reputation for being resistant to authority, hostile to religion, and hospitable to pirates. Their location between aristocratic Virginia and aristocratic South Carolina caused the area to be dubbed "a vale of humility between two mountains of conceit." North Carolina was officially separated from South Carolina in 1712, and subsequently each segment became a royal colony.

squatter *A frontier farmer who illegally occupied land owned by others or not yet officially opened for settlement.*

buffer *In politics, a small territory or state between two larger, antagonistic powers and intended to minimize the possibility of conflict between them.*

North Carolina, unlike its sister colony, did not at first import large numbers of African slaves. But both Carolinas shared in the ongoing tragedy of bloody relations between Indians and Europeans. After Tuscarora Indians fell upon the fledgling settlement of Newbern in 1711, North and South Carolinians retaliated by crushing the Tuscaroras in battle and selling hundreds of them into slavery. In another ferocious encounter four years later, the South Carolinians defeated and scattered the Yamasees, thereby devastating the last of the coastal Indian tribes in the southern colonies. In the interior Appalachian Mountains, however, the powerful Cherokees, Creeks, and Iroquois remained (see "Makers of America: The Iroquois," pp. 28–29). Stronger and more numerous than their coastal cousins, they managed for half a century more to contain British settlement on the coastal plain east of the mountains.

Late-Coming Georgia: The Buffer Colony

Pine-forested Georgia, with the harbor of Savannah nourishing its chief settlement, was formally founded in 1733. It proved to be the last of the thirteen colonies to be planted—126 years after the first, Virginia, and 52 years after the twelfth, Pennsylvania.

The British crown intended Georgia to serve chiefly as a **buffer**. It would protect the more valuable Carolinas against vengeful Spaniards from Florida and hostile French from Louisiana. Georgia indeed suffered much buffeting, especially when wars broke out between Spain and Britain in the European arena.

Named in honor of King George II of Britain, Georgia was launched by a high-minded group of philanthropists. Besides protecting their neighboring northern colonies and producing silk and wine, they were also determined to carve out a haven for wretched souls imprisoned for debt. The ablest of the founders was the dynamic soldier-statesman James Oglethorpe, who became keenly interested in prison reform after one of his friends died in a debtors' jail. As an able military

The Iroquois

Well before the crowned heads of Europe turned their eyes and their dreams of empire toward North America, a great military power had emerged in the Mohawk Valley of what is now New York State. The Iroquois Confederacy, dubbed by whites the "League of the Iroquois," bound together five Indian nations—the Mohawks, the Oneidas, the Onondagas, the Cayugas, and the Senecas. According to Iroquois legend, the alliance was founded in the late 1500s by two leaders, Deganawidah and Hiawatha. This proud and potent league vied with neighboring Indians for territorial supremacy, then with invading Europeans for control of the fur trade. Ultimately, decimated by the white man's diseases, whiskey, and muskets, the Iroquois struggled for their very survival as a people.

Online Study Center

Primary source
Dekanawida Myth and the Achievement of Iroquois Unity
college.hmco.com/pic/kennedybrief7e

■ **The Longhouse (reconstruction)** The photo shows a modern-day reconstruction of a Delaware Indian longhouse (almost identical in design and building materials to the Iroquois longhouses), at Historic Waterloo Village on Winakung Island in New Jersey. (The Iroquois conquered the Delawares in the late 1600s.) Bent saplings and sheets of elm bark made for sturdy, weathertight shelters. Longhouses were typically furnished with deerskin-covered bunks and shelves for storing baskets, pots, fur pelts, and corn.

The building block of Iroquois society was the longhouse. Twenty-five feet wide and up to two hundred feet long, these wooden structures sheltered several closely related nuclear families, their connections of blood running exclusively through the maternal line. The oldest woman in a clan was the honored matriarch. Men dominated the society, but they owed their positions of prominence to their mothers' families.

As if sharing one great longhouse, the five nations joined in the Iroquois Confederacy but kept their own separate fires. Although they celebrated together and shared a common policy toward outsiders, they remained essentially independent of one another. On the eastern flank, the Mohawks, known as the Keepers of the Eastern Fire, specialized as middlemen with European traders, whereas the outlying Senecas, the Keepers of the Western Fire, became fur suppliers. In the early 1700s, the Tuscaroras from the Carolina region gained affiliation with the Iroquois Confederacy.

Throughout the seventeenth and eighteenth centuries the Iroquois allied alternately with the British against the French and vice versa, for a time successfully working this perpetual rivalry to their advantage. But the confederacy divided during the American Revolution, with most tribes siding with the British. Their ultimate defeat left the Iroquois Confederacy in tatters. Most Iroquois moved to British Canada or were relegated to reservations in western New York.

Reservation life proved unbearable to the proud Iroquois, who fell into feuding and alcoholism. But in 1799 an Iroquois prophet named Handsome Lake arose, warning his people to mend their ways, affirm family values, and revive their old Iroquois customs. Handsome Lake died in 1813, but his teachings, in the form of the Longhouse religion, survive to this day.

leader, Oglethorpe repelled Spanish attacks. As an imperialist and a philanthropist, he saved "the Charity Colony" by his energetic leadership and by heavily mortgaging his own personal fortunes.

The hamlet of Savannah, like Charleston, was a **melting-pot** community that included German Lutherans and kilted Scottish Highlanders, among others. All Christian worshipers except Catholics enjoyed religious toleration. Many Bible-carrying missionaries arrived to work among debtors and Indians, including young John Wesley, who later returned to Britain and founded the Methodist church.

Georgia grew with painful slowness and at the end of the colonial era was perhaps the least populous of the colonies. The development of a plantation economy was thwarted by an unhealthful climate, by early restrictions on black slavery, and by demoralizing Spanish attacks.

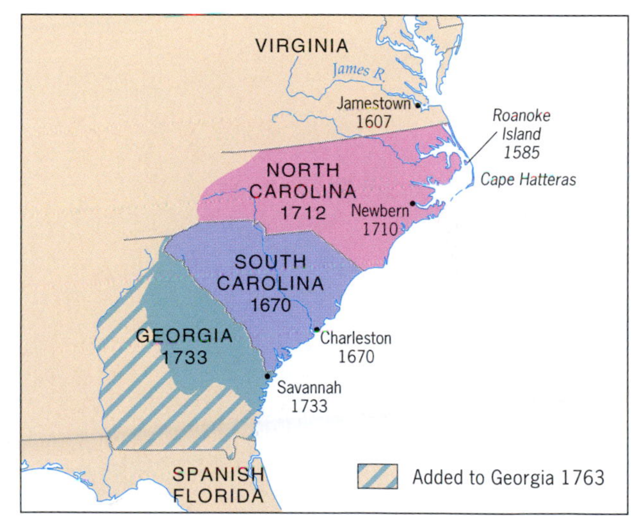

■ Early Carolina and Georgia Settlements

The Plantation Colonies

Certain distinctive features were shared by all of Britain's southern mainland colonies: Maryland, Virginia, North Carolina, South Carolina, and Georgia. Broad-acred, these outposts of empire were all to some degree devoted to exporting commercial agricultural crops like tobacco, rice, and indigo. Slavery was found in all the plantation colonies, though only after 1750 in reform-minded Georgia. Immense acreage in the hands of a favored few fostered a strong aristocratic atmosphere, except in North Carolina and to some extent in debtor-tinged Georgia. The wide scattering of plantations and farms, often along stately rivers, retarded the growth of cities and made the establishment of churches and schools both difficult and expensive.

Although the tax-supported Church of England became the dominant faith, all the plantation colonies permitted some religious toleration. The plantation colonies were to some degree expansionary. "Soil butchery" by excessive tobacco growing drove settlers westward, and the long, lazy rivers invited penetration of the continent—and continuing confrontation with Native Americans.

melting pot *Popular American term for an ethnically diverse population that is presumed to be "melting" toward some eventual commonality.*

Interactive map
The Settlements of the Lower South
college.hmco.com/pic/kennedybrief7e

Chapter Summary

The defeat of the Spanish Armada and the exuberant spirit of Elizabethan nationalism finally drew England into the colonial race. After some early failures, the first permanent English colony was established at Jamestown, Virginia. Harsh conditions, gentlemanly aversion to work, and Indian hostility nearly caused it to fail, but stern leadership and tobacco cultivation finally brought prosperity and population growth.

The early encounters of English settlers with the Powhatan Indians in Virginia established many of the patterns that characterized later Indian-white relations in North America, including disease, warfare, and removal. Indian societies underwent their own substantial changes as a result of warfare, disease, and trade. For a time after the Atlantic coastal tribes were nearly wiped out, the larger Indian peoples of the Appalachian area formed a formidable barrier to white expansion.

Maryland and South Carolina were founded by aristocratic proprietors. Maryland was originally a Catholic refuge. South Carolina flourished by establishing close ties with the British sugar colonies in the West Indies, and brought the West Indian pattern of harsh slave codes and large plantation agriculture to North America. North Carolina was a less hierarchical settlement of largely poor white colonists who owned small farms and disdained authority. Latecomer Georgia served initially as a buffer against the Spanish and a haven for debtors.

Despite some differences, all the southern colonies depended on staple plantation agriculture for their survival and on the institutions of indentured servitude and African slavery for their labor. With widely scattered rural settlements, they had relatively weak religious and social institutions and tended to develop hierarchical economic and social orders.

Settling the Northern Colonies

1619–1700

GOD HATH SIFTED A NATION THAT HE MIGHT SEND CHOICE GRAIN INTO THIS WILDERNESS.

WILLIAM STOUGHTON [OF MASSACHUSETTS BAY], 1669

Chapter Outline

- The Puritan Faith
- Plymouth Colony, 1620
- The Puritan Commonwealth of Massachusetts Bay Colony, 1630
- The Expansion of New England
- New Netherland Becomes New York
- Pennsylvania and the Middle Colonies
- Makers of America: The English
- Examining the Evidence: A Seventeenth-Century Valuables Cabinet
- Varying Viewpoints: Europeanizing America or Americanizing Europe?

Although colonists both north and south were bound together by a common language and a common allegiance to Mother England, they established different patterns of settlements, different economies, different political systems, and even different sets of values—defining distinctive regional characteristics that would persist for generations. The promise of riches—especially from golden-leafed tobacco—drew the first settlers to the southern colonies. But to the north, in the fertile valleys of the middle Atlantic region and especially along the rocky shores of New England, it was not worldly wealth but religious devotion that principally shaped the earliest settlements.

Focus Questions

1. What motivated English Pilgrims and Puritans to emigrate to the New World, and how did their religious beliefs affect the character and organization of the Plymouth and Massachusetts Bay Colonies?
2. How did religious dissent, economic circumstances, and Indian relations shape the founding and development of the other New England colonies?
3. What were the early efforts to promote intercolonial unity in New England, and why did they generally fail?
4. What were the original motives for the founding of New York and Pennsylvania? In what ways were the two colonies different, and in what ways were they similar?
5. What were the central features of the four middle colonies, and how did they differ from the New England colonies?

The Protestant Reformation Produces Puritanism

Little did the German monk Martin Luther suspect, when he nailed his protests against Catholic doctrines to the door of Wittenberg's castle church in 1517, that he was shaping the destiny of a yet unknown nation. Denouncing the authority of priests and popes, Luther declared that the Bible alone was the source of God's word. He ignited a fire of religious reform (the "Protestant Reformation") that licked its way across Europe for more than a century, dividing people, toppling sovereigns, and kindling the spiritual fervor of millions of men and women—some of whom helped to found America.

The reforming flame burned especially brightly in the bosom of John Calvin of Geneva. This somber and severe religious leader elaborated Martin Luther's ideas in ways that profoundly affected the thought and character of generations of Americans yet unborn. Calvinism became the dominant theological credo not only of the New England Puritans but of other American settlers as well, including Scottish Presbyterians, French Huguenots, and Dutch Reformed.

Calvin argued in the *Institutes of the Christian Religion* (1536) that God was all-powerful and all-good. Humans, because of the corrupting effect of original sin, were weak and wicked. God was also all-knowing, and since the first moment of creation had destined some souls—the elect—for eternal bliss and others for eternal torment. Good works could not save those whom **predestination** had marked for the infernal fires.

predestination *The Calvinist doctrine that God has foreordained some people to be saved and some to be damned.*

elect *In Calvinist doctrine, those people who have been chosen by God for salvation.*

conversion *A religious turn to God, thought by Calvinists to involve an intense, identifiable personal experience of grace.*

visible saints *In Calvinism, those who publicly proclaimed their experience of conversion and were expected to lead godly lives.*

But neither could the **elect** count on their determined salvation and lead lives of wild, immoral abandon. For one thing, no one could be certain of his or her status in the heavenly ledger. Gnawing doubts about their eternal fate caused Calvinists constantly to seek signs of "**conversion,**" or the receipt of God's free gift of saving grace, in themselves and others. Those who had the intense personal experience of conversion were expected to lead "sanctified" lives, demonstrating by their holy behavior that they were among the "**visible saints.**"

These doctrines swept into England just as King Henry VIII was breaking his ties with the Roman Catholic Church in the 1530s, making himself the head of the Church of England. Henry would have been content to retain Roman rituals and creeds, but some English religious reformers sought a total purification of English Christianity. As they grew increasingly unhappy with the snail-like progress of the Protestant Reformation in England, these "Puritans" burned with pious zeal to see the Church of England wholly de-Catholicized.

The most devout Puritans, including those who eventually settled New England, believed that only "visible saints" (that is, persons who felt the stirrings of grace in their souls and could demonstrate its presence to their fellow Puritans) should be admitted to church membership. But the Church of England enrolled all the king's subjects, which meant that the "saints" had to share pews and communion rails with the "damned." Appalled by this unholy fraternizing, a tiny group of dedicated Puritans, known as Separatists, vowed to break away entirely from the Church of England. King James I, who was head of both the church and the state in England from 1603 to 1625, threatened to harass the more bothersome Separatists out of the land.

The Pilgrims End Their Pilgrimage at Plymouth

The most famous congregation of Separatists, fleeing royal wrath, departed for Holland in 1608. During the ensuing twelve years of toil and poverty, they were increasingly distressed by the "Dutchification" of their children. They longed to find a haven where they could live and die as English men and women—and as purified Protestants. America was the logical refuge.

A group of the Separatists in Holland, after negotiating with the Virginia Company, at length secured rights to settle under its jurisdiction. But their crowded *Mayflower*, sixty-five days at sea, missed its destination and arrived off the rocky coast of New England in 1620, with a total of 102 persons. Because their settlement at inhospitable Plymouth Bay was outside the domain of the Virginia Company,

Chronology

1517	Martin Luther begins Protestant Reformation.
1536	John Calvin of Geneva publishes *Institutes of the Christian Religion.*
1620	Pilgrims sail on the *Mayflower* to Plymouth Bay.
1624	Dutch found New Netherland.
1629	Charles I dismisses Parliament and persecutes Puritans.
1630	Puritans found Massachusetts Bay Colony.
1635-1636	Roger Williams convicted of heresy and founds Rhode Island colony.
1635-1638	Connecticut and New Haven colonies founded.
1637	Pequot War.
1638	Anne Hutchinson banished from Massachusetts colony.
1639	Connecticut's Fundamental Orders drafted.
1642-1648	English Civil War.
1643	New England Confederation formed.
1655	New Netherland conquers New Sweden.
1664	England seizes New Netherland from Dutch. East and West Jersey colonies founded.
1675-1676	King Philip's War.
1681	William Penn founds Pennsylvania colony.
1686	Royal authority creates Dominion of New England.
1688-1689	Glorious Revolution overthrows Stuarts and Dominion of New England.

the Pilgrims became squatters without legal right to the land or specific authority to establish a government.

Before disembarking, the Pilgrim leaders drew up and signed the brief Mayflower Compact. Although setting an invaluable precedent for later written constitutions, this document was not a constitution at all. It was a simple agreement to form a crude government and to submit to the will of the majority under the regulations agreed upon. The compact was signed by forty-one adult males, eleven of them with the exalted rank of "mister," though not by the servants and two seamen. The pact was a promising step toward genuine self-government, for

Plymouth Plantation Carefully restored, the modest village at Plymouth looks today much as it did nearly four hundred years ago.

Primary source
Mortality at Plymouth Plantation
college.hmco.com/pic/kennedybrief7e

soon the adult male settlers were assembling to make their own laws in open-discussion town meetings—a great laboratory of liberty.

The Pilgrims' first winter of 1620–1621 took a grisly toll. Only 44 out of the 102 survived. Yet when the *Mayflower* sailed back to England in the spring, not a single one of the courageous band of Separatists left. As one of them wrote, "It is not with us as with other men, whom small things can discourage."

God made his children to prosper, so the Pilgrims believed. The next autumn, that of 1621, brought bountiful harvests and with them the first Thanksgiving Day in New England. In time the frail colony found sound economic legs in fur, fish, and lumber. The beaver and the Bible were the early mainstays: the one for the sustenance of the body, the other for the sustenance of the soul. The Pilgrims were also extremely fortunate in their leaders, especially William Bradford, a self-taught scholar who read Hebrew, Greek, Latin, French, and Dutch and was elected governor thirty times.

Quiet and quaint, the little colony of Plymouth was never important economically or numerically. Its population numbered only seven thousand by 1691, when, still charterless, it merged with its giant neighbor, the Massachusetts Bay Colony. But the tiny settlement of Pilgrims was big both morally and spiritually.

Primary source
The Great Puritan Migration
college.hmco.com/pic/kennedybrief7e

The Bay Colony Bible Commonwealth

The Separatist Pilgrims were dedicated extremists—the purest Puritans. More moderate Puritans sought to reform the Church of England from within. But their efforts faced catastrophe when Charles I dismissed Parliament in 1629 and sanctioned the anti-Puritan persecutions of the reactionary Archbishop William Laud.

In 1629 an energetic group of non-Separatist Puritans, fearing for their faith and for England's future, secured a royal charter to form the Massachusetts Bay Company. Stealing a march on both king and church, the newcomers brought their charter with them when they emigrated to Massachusetts. For many years they used it as a kind of constitution, out of easy reach of royal authority.

The Massachusetts Bay enterprise was singularly blessed. The well-equipped expedition of 1630, with eleven vessels carrying nearly a thousand immigrants, started the colony off on a larger scale than any of the other English settlements. Continuing turmoil in England tossed up additional enriching waves of Puritans on the shores of Massachusetts in the following decade (see "Makers of America: The English," p. 36). During the "Great Migration" of the 1630s, about seventy thousand refugees left England. But not all of them were Puritans, and only about twenty thousand came to Massachusetts. Many were more attracted to the warm and fertile West Indies, especially Barbados.

Interactive map
English Migration, 1610–1660
college.hmco.com/pic/kennedybrief7e

Many fairly prosperous, educated persons emigrated to the Bay Colony, including John Winthrop, a well-to-do pillar of English society. A successful attorney and manor lord in England, Winthrop eagerly accepted the offer to become the first governor of the Massachusetts Bay Colony, believing that he had a "**calling**" from God to lead the new religious experiment. He served as governor or deputy governor for nineteen years. The resources and skills of talented settlers like Winthrop helped Massachusetts prosper, and the Bay Colony rapidly shot to the fore as the biggest and the most influential of the New England outposts.

calling *In Protestantism, the belief that saved individuals have a religious obligation to engage in worldly work.*

Massachusetts also benefited from a shared sense of purpose among most of the first settlers. "We shall be as a city upon a hill," a beacon to humanity, declared Governor Winthrop. The Puritan bay colonists believed that they had a covenant with God, an agreement to build a holy society that would be a model for humankind.

Building the Bay Colony

These common convictions deeply shaped the infant colony's life. Soon after arrival the settlers extended the franchise to all "freemen"—adult males who belonged to the Puritan congregations, which in time came to be called collectively the Congregational Church. On this basis about two-fifths of adult males enjoyed the franchise in provincial affairs, a far larger proportion than in contemporary England. Town governments, which conducted much important business, were even more inclusive. There all male property holders, and in some cases other residents as well, discussed and voted on public issues.

Yet the provincial government, liberal by the standards of the time, was not a democracy. "If the people be governors," asked one Puritan clergyman, "who shall be the governed?" True, the freemen annually elected the governor and his assistants, as well as a representative assembly called the General Court. But only Puritans—the "visible saints" who were alone eligible for church membership—could be freemen. And according to the doctrine of the covenant, the whole purpose of government was to enforce God's laws—which applied to believers and nonbelievers alike. Moreover, nonbelievers as well as believers paid taxes for the government-supported church.

> *William Bradford (1590–1657) wrote in* Of Plymouth Plantation,
>
> "Thus out of small beginnings greater things have been produced by His hand that made all things of nothing, and gives being to all things that are; and, as one small candle may light a thousand, so the light here kindled hath shone unto many, yea in some sort to our whole nation."

Religious leaders thus wielded enormous influence in the Massachusetts "Bible commonwealth." They powerfully influenced admission to church membership, by conducting public interrogations of persons claiming to have experienced conversions. But the power of preachers, such as the eminent and learned John Cotton, was not absolute. Because Puritans had suffered so much at the hands of a "political" Anglican clergy, they barred clergymen from holding formal political office. In a limited way, the bay colonists thus endorsed the idea of the separation of church and state.

Primary source
Land Division for a Typical Puritan Town
college.hmco.com/pic/kennedybrief7e

The Puritans were a worldly lot, despite—or even because of—their spiritual intensity. Like John Winthrop, they believed in the doctrine of a "calling" to do God's work on this earth. They shared in what was later called the "Protestant ethic," which involved serious commitment to work and to engagement in worldly pursuits. Legend to the contrary, they also enjoyed simple pleasures; they ate plentifully, drank heartily, sang songs occasionally, and made love monogamously.

Yet to the Puritans life was serious business, and hellfire was real—a hell where sinners shriveled and shrieked in vain and forever for divine mercy. Puritan clergyman Michael Wigglesworth's poem "Day of Doom" (1662) described the horrifying fate of the damned:

> They cry, they roar for anguish sore,
> and gnaw their tongues for horrour,
> But get away without delay,
> Christ pitties not your cry:
> Depart to hell, there may you yell,
> and roar Eternally.

Trouble in the Bible Commonwealth

The Bay Colony enjoyed a high degree of social harmony, stemming from common beliefs, in its early years. But even in this tightly knit community, dissension soon appeared. Quakers, who flouted the authority of the Puritan clergy, were persecuted with fines, floggings, and banishment. In one extreme case, four Quakers were hanged on Boston Common for their beliefs.

A sharp challenge to Puritan orthodoxy came from Anne Hutchinson. An exceptionally intelligent, strong-willed, and talkative woman, she claimed that the truly saved need not bother to obey the law of either God or man. This assertion, known as *antinomianism* (from the Greek, "against the law"), was high **heresy.** Brought to trial in 1638, the quick-witted Hutchinson bamboozled her clerical inquisitors for days, until she eventually boasted that she had come by her beliefs through a direct revelation from God. This was even higher heresy. After the Puritan magistrates banished her, she traveled on foot to Rhode Island, and finally moved to New York, where she and all but one of her household were killed by Indians.

heresy *Departure from correct or officially defined belief.*

More threatening to the Puritan leaders was a personable and popular Salem minister, Roger Williams. An extreme Separatist with an unrestrained tongue, Williams demanded a clean break with the corrupt Church of England and challenged the legality of the Bay Colony's charter, which he condemned for its unfairness to the Indians. As if all this were not enough, he went on to deny the

The English

During the late Middle Ages, the Black Death and other epidemics that ravaged England kept the island's population in check. But by 1500 increased resistance to such diseases allowed the population to soar; and a century later the island nation was bursting at the seams. This population explosion, combined with economic depression and religious repression, sparked the first major European migration to England's New World colonies.

Some of those who voyaged to Virginia and Maryland in the seventeenth century were independent artisans or younger members of English gentry families. But roughly three-quarters of the English migrants to the Chesapeake during this period came as servants, signed to "indentures" ranging from four to seven years. One English observer described such indentured servants as "idle, lazie, simple people," and another complained that many of those taking ship for the colonies "have been pursued by hue-and-cry for robberies, burglaries, or breaking prison."

Whereas English immigration to the Chesapeake was spread over nearly a century, most English voyagers to New England arrived within a single decade. In the twelve years between 1629 and 1642, some twenty thousand Puritans swarmed to the Massachusetts Bay Colony. Fleeing a sustained economic depression and the cruel religious repression of Charles I, the Puritans came to plant a godly commonwealth in New England's rocky soil.

In contrast to the single indentured servants of the Chesapeake, the New England Puritans migrated in family groups, and in many cases whole communities were transplanted from England to America. Although they remained united by the common language and common Puritan faith they carried to New England, their English baggage was by no means uniform. Most New Englanders were farmers, but some towns recreated the specialized economies of particular localities in England. Marblehead, Massachusetts, for example, became a fishing village because most of its settlers had been fishermen in Old England. The townsfolk of Rowley, Massachusetts, brought from Yorkshire their distinctive way of life revolving around textile manufacturing.

Political practices, too, reflected the towns' variegated English roots. In Ipswich, Massachusetts, settled by East Anglian Puritans, the ruling selectmen served long terms and ruled with an iron hand. By contrast, local politics in the town of Newbury was often contentious and turnovers among officeholders high; the town's founders were from western England, a region with little tradition of local government. Although the Puritans' imperial masters in London eventually circumscribed such precious local autonomy, this diverse heritage of fiercely independent New England towns endured, reasserting itself during the American Revolution.

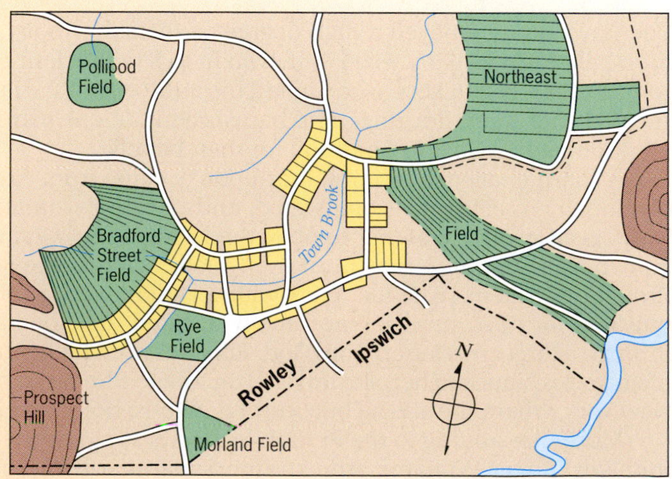

Land Use in Rowley, Massachusetts, c. 1650 The settlers of Rowley brought from their native Yorkshire the practice of granting families very small farming plots and reserving large common fields for use by the entire community. On the map, the yellow areas show private land; the green areas show land held in common.

authority of civil government to regulate religious behavior—a **seditious** blow at the Puritan idea of government's very purpose. Their patience exhausted by 1635, the Bay Colony authorities found Williams guilty of disseminating "newe & dangerous opinions" and ordered him banished.

seditious *Concerning resistance to or rebellion against the government.*

New England Spreads Out

Aided by friendly Indians, Roger Williams fled to the Rhode Island area in 1636, where he built a Baptist church. He established complete freedom of religion, even for Jews and Catholics, a degree of toleration far ahead of the other English settlements in the New World. He demanded no oaths regarding religious beliefs, no compulsory attendance at worship, and no taxes to support a state church. He even sheltered the abused Quakers, although disagreeing sharply with their views.

Those outcasts who clustered about Roger Williams also enjoyed additional blessings. They exercised simple manhood suffrage from the start, though this broadminded practice was later narrowed by a property qualification. Opposed to special privilege of any sort, the malcontents and exiles who largely populated "Rogues' Island" had little in common with Roger Williams—except being unwelcome anywhere else. The Puritan clergy back in Boston sneered at Rhode Island as "that sewer" in which the "Lord's debris" had collected and rotted. Stubbornly individualistic, the squatters in "Little Rhody" finally established rights to the soil when they secured a charter from Parliament in 1644. A huge bronze statue of the "Independent Man" appropriately stands today on the dome of the state house in Providence.

Anne Hutchinson, Dissenter
Mistress Hutchinson (1591–1643) held unorthodox views that challenged the authority of the clergy and the very integrity of the Puritan experiment in the Massachusetts Bay Colony.

The fertile valley of the Connecticut River had meanwhile attracted a different type of Dutch and English settlers. Hartford was founded in 1635, and the next year an energetic group of Boston Puritans, led by the Reverend Thomas Hooker, swarmed into the area. In 1639 the settlers of the new Connecticut River colony drafted a trailblazing document known as the Fundamental Orders, which established a regime controlled by the "substantial" citizens.

Another flourishing Connecticut settlement began to spring up at New Haven in 1638. It was a prosperous community, founded by Puritans who contrived to set up an even closer church-government alliance than in Massachusetts. The colonists dreamed of making New Haven a bustling seaport, but they fell into disfavor with Charles II because they sheltered two of the judges who had condemned his father, Charles I, to death. In 1662 the crown granted a charter that merged New Haven with the more democratic settlements in the Connecticut Valley.

Two smaller settlements grew up north of Massachusetts Bay. The fishermen and fur traders who had been active along the coast of Maine even before the founding of Plymouth were absorbed by Massachusetts Bay in 1677. The Maine territory remained part of Massachusetts for nearly a century and a half before becoming a separate state. In 1641 the Bay Colony also annexed its immediate northern neighbor, New Hampshire, under a strained interpretation of the Massachusetts charter. The king, annoyed by this display of greed, separated New Hampshire from Massachusetts in 1679 and made it a royal colony.

Interactive map
Pattern of Settlement in Surry County, Virginia, 1620–1660
college.hmco.com/pic/kennedybrief7e

Puritans Versus Indians

The spread of English settlements inevitably led to clashes with the Indians, who were particularly weak in New England. Shortly before the Pilgrims arrived at Plymouth in 1620, an epidemic, probably triggered by contact with English fishermen, had swept through the coastal tribes and killed more than three-fourths of the native people. The deserted fields that greeted the Plymouth settlers provided grim evidence of the impact of the disease.

In no position to resist the English incursion, the local Wampanoag Indians at first befriended the settlers. Cultural accommodation was facilitated by Squanto, a Wampanoag who had learned English from a ship's captain who had kidnapped him some years earlier. The Wampanoag chieftain Massasoit signed a treaty with

Seventeenth-Century New England Settlements The Massachusetts Bay Colony was the hub of New England. All earlier colonies grew into it; all later colonies grew out of it.

the Plymouth Pilgrims in 1621 and helped them celebrate the first Thanksgiving after the autumn harvests that same year.

As more English settlers arrived and pushed inland into the Connecticut River valley, confrontations between Indians and whites ruptured these peaceful relations. Hostilities exploded in 1637 between the settlers and the powerful Pequot tribe. In a brutal war the English militiamen and their Naragansett Indian allies virtually annihilated the Pequots.

During the ensuing four decades of tense peace, the Puritans made some feeble efforts to convert the remaining Indians to Christianity. But their missionary zeal never equaled that of the Spanish and French Catholics, and a mere handful of Indians were gathered into Puritan "praying towns."

The Indians' only hope for resisting English encroachment lay in intertribal unity—a pan-Indian alliance against the swiftly spreading settlements. In 1675 Massasoit's son Metacom, called King Philip by the English, forged such an alliance and mounted a series of coordinated assaults on English villages throughout New England. When the war ended in 1676, fifty-two Puritan towns had been attacked, and twelve destroyed entirely. Hundreds of colonists and many more Indians lay dead. Metacom was captured, beheaded, and drawn and quartered. His head was carried on a pike back to Plymouth, where it was displayed for years.

King Philip's War slowed the westward march of English settlement in New England for several decades. But the war inflicted a lasting defeat on New England's Indians. Drastically reduced in numbers, dispirited, and disbanded, they thereafter posed only sporadic threats to the New England colonists.

Online Study Center

Primary source
Timucuan Shows Frenchmen How His People Respect a . . .
college.hmco.com/pic/kennedybrief7e

commonwealth(s) *An organized civil government or social order united for a shared purpose.*

autocratic *Absolute or dictatorial rule.*

Primary source
Narragansett Leader Complains of English Encroachment
college.hmco.com/pic/kennedybrief7e

Primary source
How the Savages Roast Their Enemies
college.hmco.com/pic/kennedybrief7e

Seeds of Colonial Unity and Revolt

A path-breaking experiment in union was launched in 1643, when four colonies banded together to form the New England Confederation. The confederation was intended to provide defense against foes like the Indians, French, and Dutch, as well as to solve intercolonial problems like runaway servants and criminals. Each member colony, regardless of size, wielded two votes.

Weak though it was, the confederation was the first notable milestone on the long and rocky road toward colonial unity. The delegates took tottering but long-overdue steps toward acting together on matters of intercolonial importance.

English monarchs had paid little attention to the American colonies during the early years of settlement. This era of benign neglect allowed the colonies, in effect, to become semiautonomous **commonwealths.** But when Charles II was restored to the throne in 1660, the royalists and their Church of England allies determined to take an aggressive hand in the management of the colonies. The king's agents took particular aim at proud and stubborn Massachusetts by extending rival Connecticut's charter in 1662 and granting a charter to the outcasts in Rhode Island in 1663. A final and crushing blow fell on the stiff-necked Bay Colony in 1684, when its precious charter was revoked by royal authorities. Massachusetts suffered further humiliation in 1686, when the royal government created the Dominion of New England, which was soon expanded to include New York and East and West Jersey. Unlike the homegrown New England Confederation, the Dominion was imposed from London and designed primarily to stitch England's overseas possessions more tightly to the motherland by throttling American trade with countries not ruled by the British crown.

The new Dominion's governor was **autocratic** Sir Edmund Andros, an able but tactless English military man who established his headquarters in Puritan Boston and promptly outraged the colonials with his profane soldiers and iron-handed tactics. Andros ruthlessly curbed the cherished town meetings, restricted the courts, and taxed the people without the consent of their duly elected representatives in the assemblies.

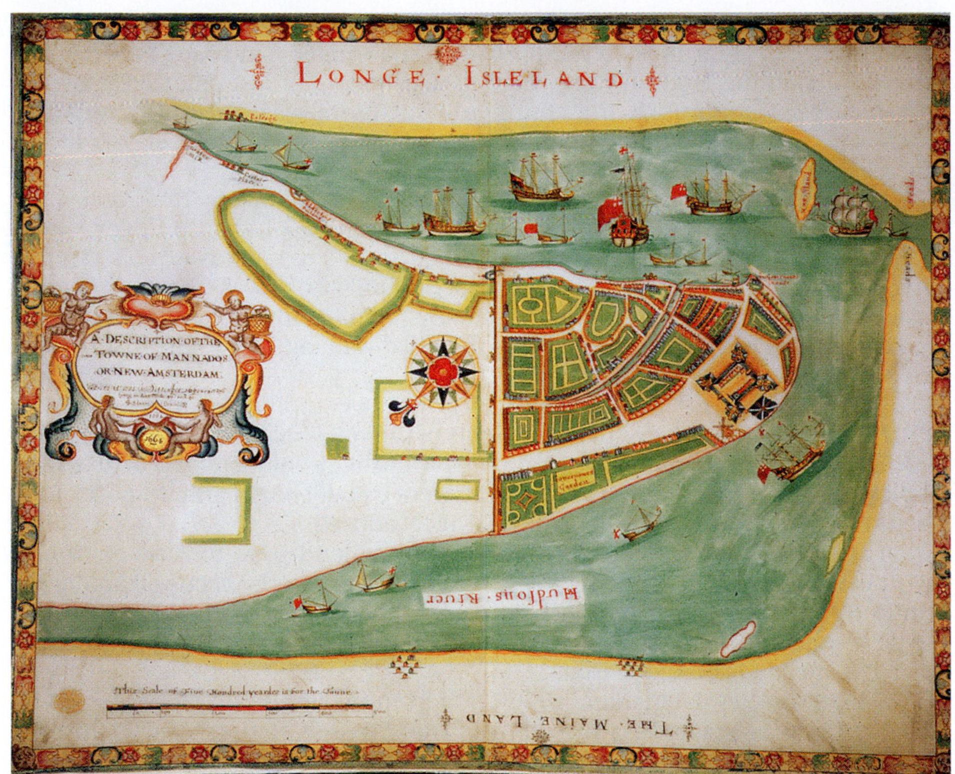

New York (then New Amsterdam), 1664 This drawing clearly shows the tip of Manhattan Island protected by the wall after which Wall Street was named.

On the verge of revolt, the New Englanders were beaten to the punch by the people of old England. In the Glorious Revolution of 1688–1689 they overthrew the despotic Catholic King James II and then invited the Dutch Protestant rulers William III and Mary to assume the English throne. When news of the Glorious Revolution reached America, a Boston mob rose against the existing regime, and the ramshackle Dominion of New England collapsed like a house of cards. Sir Edmund Andros attempted to flee in women's clothing but was betrayed by boots protruding beneath his dress. He was hastily shipped off to England. Though rid of the despotic Andros, Massachusetts did not gain as much from the upheaval as it had hoped. In 1691 it was arbitrarily made a royal colony, and the proud Puritans were forced to yield the privilege of voting—once a monopoly of church members—to all qualified male property holders.

The new English monarchs relaxed the royal grip on colonial trade and inaugurated a period of "salutary neglect" in which the much-resented Navigation Laws were only weakly enforced. Yet residues remained of Charles II's effort to assert tighter administrative control over his empire. More English officials—judges, clerks, customs officials—staffed the courts and strolled the wharves of English America. Many were incompetent, corrupt hacks who knew little and cared less about American affairs. Aggrieved Americans viewed them with mounting contempt and resentment as the eighteenth century wore on.

New Netherland Becomes New York

Late in the sixteenth century, the oppressed people of the Netherlands unfurled the standard of rebellion against Catholic Spain. After bloody and protracted fighting, they finally succeeded, with the aid of Protestant England, in winning their independence. This vigorous little lowland nation quickly emerged as a major commercial and naval power that ungratefully challenged the supremacy of its former benefactor, England.

The Dutch Republic also became a leading colonial power through the activities of the enterprising Dutch East India Company. The company's vast riches came mostly from the East Indies, where it maintained an enormous and profitable empire for over three hundred years. In 1609 it employed an English explorer, Henry Hudson, who ventured into Delaware Bay and New York Bay and then ascended the Hudson River, hoping that he had at last chanced upon the coveted shortcut through the continent. But there was no transcontinental waterway, so Hudson merely filed a Dutch claim to the magnificently watered and wooded area.

Primary source
English Trade with Indians, as Seen by Theodore de Bry
college.hmco.com/pic/kennedybrief7e

New Netherland was permanently planted in 1623–1624 by the Dutch West India Company, the less wealthy counterpart of the East India Company. Never more than a secondary interest of the founders, the colony was exploited for its quick-profit fur trade. The company's most brilliant stroke was to buy Manhattan Island from the Indians (who did not actually "own" it) for trinkets— twenty-two thousand acres of what is now perhaps the most valuable real estate in the world for pennies per acre.

New Amsterdam—later New York City—was a company town. It was run by and for the Dutch company, in the interests of the stockholders. The investors had no enthusiasm for religious toleration, free speech, or democratic practices; and the governors appointed by the company were usually harsh and despotic. Religious dissenters like the Quakers were savagely abused.

The picturesque Dutch colony of New Netherland soon took on a strongly aristocratic tinge and retained it for generations. Vast feudal estates fronting the Hudson River, known as patroonships, were granted to promoters who agreed to settle fifty people on them. One patroonship in the Albany area was slightly larger than the later state of Rhode Island.

A threat to New Netherland soon came from the Swedes, who trespassed on Dutch preserves by planting the colony of New Sweden on the Delaware River in 1638. Resenting the Swedish intrusion, the Dutch dispatched a small military expedition in 1655, led by the able but despotic director-general Peter Stuyvesant. The main fort fell after a bloodless siege, and Swedish rule came to an abrupt end, leaving behind in later Delaware only a sprinkling of Swedish place-names and Swedish log cabins (the first in America), as well as an admixture of Swedish blood.

Just as New Netherland absorbed New Sweden, it was soon the turn of the Dutch to be swallowed up by the English. In 1664, after the imperially ambitious King Charles II granted the area to his brother, the Duke of York, a strong English squadron appeared off the decrepit defenses of New Amsterdam. A fuming Peter Stuyvesant, short of all munitions except courage, was forced to surrender without firing a shot. New Amsterdam was thereupon renamed New York, in honor of the Duke of York. England won a splendid harbor, strategically located in the middle of the mainland colonies, with the stately Hudson River penetrating the interior. With the removal of this foreign wedge, the English banner waved triumphantly over a solid stretch of territory from Maine to the Carolinas.

The conquered Dutch province tenaciously retained many of the illiberal features of earlier days. An autocratic spirit survived, and the aristocratic element gained strength when certain corrupt English governors granted immense acreage to their favorites. Influential landowning families—such as the Livingstons and the De Lanceys—wielded disproportionate power in the affairs of colonial New York. These monopolistic land policies, combined with the lordly atmosphere, discouraged many European immigrants from coming. The physical growth of New York was correspondingly retarded.

Penn's Holy Experiment in Pennsylvania

A remarkable group of dissenters, commonly known as Quakers, arose in England during the mid-1600s. Their name derived from the report that they "quaked" when touched by deep religious emotion. Officially they were known as the Religious Society of Friends.

Quakers were especially offensive to the authorities, both religious and civil. They refused to support the established Church of England with taxes. They built simple meetinghouses, without a paid clergy, and "spoke up" themselves in meetings when moved. Believing that all were equal as children in the sight of God, Quakers kept their broad-brimmed hats on in the presence of their "betters" and addressed others with simple "thee's" and "thou's," rather than with conventional titles. They would take no oaths because Jesus had commanded, "Swear not at all." This peculiarity often embroiled them with government officials, for "test oaths" were still required to establish the fact that a person was not a Roman Catholic.

The Quakers, beyond a doubt, were a people of deep conviction. They abhorred strife and warfare and refused military service. As advocates of **passive resistance,** they would turn the other cheek and rebuild their meetinghouse on the sites where their enemies had torn it down. Their courage and devotion to principle finally triumphed. Although at times they seemed stubborn and unreasonable, they were a simple, devoted, democratic people, contending in their own way for religious and civic freedom.

passive resistance *Nonviolent action in opposition to authority or laws, often in accord with religious or moral beliefs.*

asylum *A place of refuge and security, especially for the persecuted or unfortunate.*

William Penn, a well-born and athletic young Englishman, was attracted to the Quaker faith in 1660, when only sixteen years old. His father, disapproving, administered a sound flogging. After various adventures in the army (the best portrait of the peaceful Quaker has him in armor), the youth firmly embraced the despised faith and suffered much persecution.

Penn felt keenly the plight of his fellow Quakers, thousands of whom were executed, flogged, or cast into dank prisons. Penn's thoughts naturally turned to the New World, where a sprinkling of Quakers had already fled, notably to Rhode Island, North Carolina, and New Jersey. Eager to establish an **asylum** for his people, he also hoped to experiment with liberal ideas in government and at the same time make a profit. Finally, in 1681, he managed to secure from the king an immense grant of fertile land, in consideration of a monetary debt that the crown owed to his deceased father. The king called the area Pennsylvania ("Penn's Woodland") in honor of the father.

Pennsylvania was by far the best advertised of all the colonies. Its founder sent out paid agents and distributed countless pamphlets printed in English, Dutch, French, and German. Unlike the lures of many an American real estate promoter, then and later, Penn's inducements were generally truthful. He especially welcomed substantial citizens, including industrious carpenters, masons, and shoemakers. His liberal land policy, which encouraged substantial holdings, was instrumental in attracting a heavy inflow of immigrants.

Penn formally launched his colony in 1681. He farsightedly bought land along the Delaware River from the Indians for his town of Philadelphia ("brotherly love" in Greek). His treatment of the native people was so fair that the Quaker "broad brims" went among them unarmed and even employed them as babysitters. For a brief period, Pennsylvania seemed the promised land of amicable Indian-white relations. Some southern tribes even migrated there, seeking the Quaker haven. But ironically, Quaker tolerance proved the undoing of Quaker Indian policy. As

Penn's Treaty, by Edward Hicks The peace-loving Quaker founder of Pennsylvania made a serious effort to live in harmony with the Indians, as this treaty-signing scene illustrates. But the westward thrust of white settlement eventually caused friction between the two groups, as in other colonies.

> *In a Boston lecture in 1869, Ralph Waldo Emerson (1803–1882) declared,*
> "The sect of the Quakers in their best representatives appear to me to have come nearer to the sublime history and genius of Christ than any other of the sects."

non-Quaker European immigrants flooded into the welcoming province, they undermined the Quakers' own benevolent policy toward the Indians. The feisty Scots-Irish were particularly unpersuaded by Quaker idealism.

Among other noteworthy features, no provision was made by the Quakers of Pennsylvania for a military defense. No restrictions were placed on immigration, and **naturalization** was made easy. The humane Quakers early developed a strong dislike of black slavery, and in the genial glow of Pennsylvania some progress was made toward social reform.

With its many liberal features, Pennsylvania attracted a rich mix of **ethnic** groups. They included numerous religious misfits who were repelled by the harsh practices of neighboring colonies. This Quaker refuge boasted a surprisingly modern atmosphere in an unmodern age, and to an unusual degree it afforded economic opportunity, civil liberty, and religious freedom. Even so, "**blue laws**" prohibited "ungodly revelers," stage plays, playing cards, dice, games, and excessive hilarity.

naturalization *The granting of citizenship to foreigners or immigrants.*

ethnic *Concerning diverse peoples or cultures, specifically—in America—those of non-Anglo-Saxon background.*

blue laws *Laws designed to restrict personal behavior in accord with a strict code of morality.*

Under such generally happy auspices, Penn's brainchild grew lustily. The Quakers were shrewd businesspeople, and in a short time the settlers were exporting grain and other foodstuffs. Within two years Philadelphia claimed three hundred houses and twenty-five hundred people. Within nineteen years—by 1700—the colony was surpassed in population and wealth only by long-established Virginia and Massachusetts.

William Penn spent only about four years in the colony and eventually died full of sorrows back in England. But Pennsylvania, his enduring monument, was not only a noble experiment in government but also a new commonwealth. Based on civil and religious liberty, and dedicated to freedom of conscience and worship, it held aloft a hopeful torch in a world of semidarkness.

Small Quaker settlements flourished next door to Pennsylvania. New Jersey was started in 1664, when two noble proprietors received the area from the Duke of York. One of the proprietors sold West New Jersey in 1674 to a group of Quakers, and Quakers also acquired East New Jersey a few years later. In 1702, the crown clipped the Quakers' wings and combined the two Jerseys in a royal colony.

Swedish-tinged Delaware consisted of only three counties—two at high tide, the witticism goes—and was named after Lord De La Warr, the harsh military governor who had arrived in Virginia in 1610. Harboring some Quakers, and closely associated with Penn's flourishing colony, Delaware was granted its own assembly in 1703. But until the American Revolution it remained under the governor of Pennsylvania.

The Middle Way in the Middle Colonies

The middle colonies—New York, New Jersey, Delaware, and Pennsylvania—enjoyed certain features in common. In general, the soil was fertile and the expanse of land was broad, unlike rock-strewn New England. Pennsylvania, New York, and New Jersey came to be known as the "bread colonies" because of their heavy exports of grain.

Rivers also played a vital role. Broad, languid streams—notably the Susquehanna, the Delaware, and the Hudson—tapped the fur trade of the interior and beckoned adventuresome spirits into the backcountry. The rivers, unlike New England's, had few cascading waterfalls and hence presented little inducement to manufacturing with water-wheel power.

A surprising amount of industry nonetheless hummed in the middle colonies. Virginal forests abounded for lumbering and shipbuilding. The presence of deep river estuaries and landlocked harbors stimulated both commerce and the growth of seaports, such as New York and Philadelphia. Even Albany, more than a hundred miles up the Hudson, was a port of some consequence in colonial days.

The middle colonies stood midway between New England and the southern plantation group in many respects besides geography. Except in aristocratic New

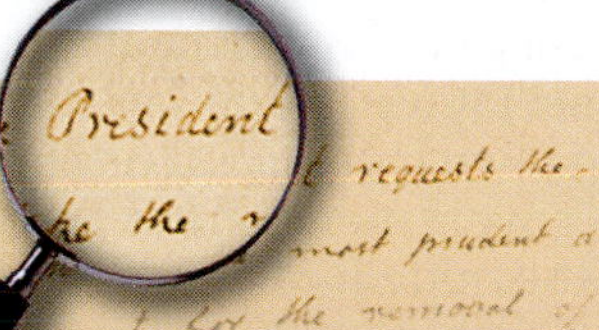

EXAMINING THE EVIDENCE

A Seventeenth-Century Valuables Cabinet In 1999 a boatyard worker on Cape Cod and his sister, a New Hampshire teacher, inherited a small (20-pound, 16–1/2 inch-high) chest that had always stood on their grandmother's hall table, known in the family as the "Franklin chest." Eager to learn more about it, they set out to discover the original owner, tracing their family genealogy and consulting with furniture experts. In January 2000 this rare seventeenth-century cabinet, its full provenance now known, appeared on the auction block and sold for a record $2.4 million to the Peabody Essex Museum in Salem, Massachusetts. No less extraordinary than the price was the history of its creator and its owners embodied in the piece. Salem cabinetmaker James Symonds (1636–1726) had made the chest for his relatives Joseph Pope (1650–1712) and Bathsheba Folger (1652–1726) to commemorate their 1679 marriage. Symonds carved the Popes' initials and the date on the door of the cabinet. He also put elaborate S curves on the sides remarkably similar to the Mannerist carved oak paneling produced in Norfolk, England, from where his own cabinetmaker father had emigrated. Behind the chest's door are ten drawers where the Popes would have kept jewelry, money, deeds, and writing materials. Surely they prized the chest as a sign of refinement to be shown off in their best room, a sentiment passed down through the next thirteen generations even as the Popes' identities were lost. The chest may have become known as the "Franklin chest" because Bathsheba was Benjamin Franklin's aunt, but also because that identification appealed more to descendants ashamed that the Quaker Popes, whose own parents had been persecuted for their faith, were virulent accusers during the Salem witch trials of 1692.

1. What significant features of this seventeenth-century chest could be determined simply by careful examination of the material object itself, and which could be learned only by historical research?
2. After studying the chest itself, which elements of the construction and carving might provide significant clues about what historical inquiries to pursue?
3. What does the nature of the chest and its original function as a storage place for valuables tell you about the economic status of the original owners, Joseph and Bathsheba Pope? Why might this chest have been handed down through their descendants for over 300 years, when most other material artifacts disappeared?

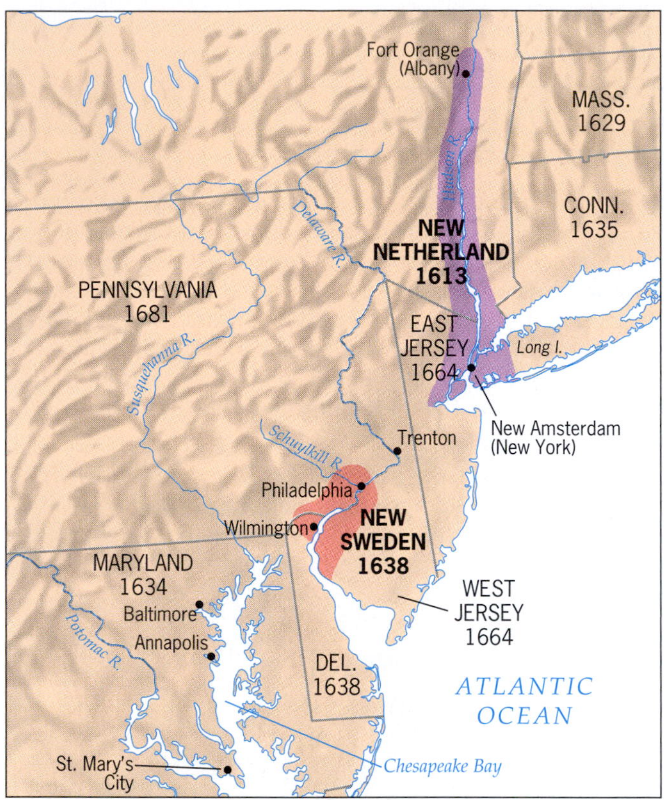

Early Settlements in the Middle Colonies, with Founding Dates

York, the landholdings were generally intermediate in size—smaller than in the big-acreage South but larger than in small-farm New England. Local government lay somewhere between the personalized town meeting of New England and the diffused county government of the South. There were fewer industries in the middle colonies than in New England, more than in the South.

Yet the middle colonies could claim certain distinctions in their own right. Generally speaking, the population was more ethnically mixed than that of other settlements. The people were blessed with an unusual degree of religious toleration and democratic control. Earnest and devout Quakers, in particular, made a contribution to human freedom out of all proportion to their numbers. Desirable land was more easily acquired in the middle colonies than in New England or in the tidewater South. One result was that a considerable amount of economic and social democracy prevailed, though less so in aristocratic New York.

Modern-minded Benjamin Franklin, often regarded as the most representative American personality of this era, was a child of the middle colonies. Although it is true that Franklin was born a Yankee in puritanical Boston, he entered Philadelphia as a seventeen-year-old in 1720 with a loaf of bread under each arm and immediately found a congenial home in the urbane, open atmosphere of what was then North America's biggest city. One Pennsylvanian later boasted that Franklin "came to life, at seventeen, in Philadelphia."

By the time Franklin arrived in the City of Brotherly Love, the American colonies themselves were "coming to life." Population was growing robustly. Transportation and communication were improving. The British, for the most part, left the colonists to fashion their own local governments, run their own churches, and develop networks of intercolonial trade. As people and products crisscrossed the colonies with increasing frequency and increasing volume, Americans began to realize that—far removed from Mother England—they were not merely surviving, but truly thriving.

Chapter Summary

The New England colonies were founded primarily by English Calvinist religious dissenters called Puritans. While most Puritans sought to "purify" the Church of England from within, and not to break away from it, a small group of Separatists—the Pilgrims—founded the first small, pious Plymouth Colony in New England. More important was the larger group of nonseparating Puritans, led by John Winthrop, who founded the Massachusetts Bay Colony as part of a "great migration" of Puritans fleeing persecution in England in the 1630s.

A strong sense of common religious and moral purpose shaped the Massachusetts Bay Colony. Because of the close alignment of religion and politics in the colony, those who challenged religious orthodoxy, among them Anne Hutchinson and Roger Williams, were considered guilty of sedition as well, and driven out of Massachusetts. The banished Williams founded Rhode Island, by far the most religiously and politically tolerant of the colonies. Other New England settlements, all originating in Massachusetts Bay, were established in Connecticut, Maine, and New Hampshire. Although they shared a common way of life, and occasionally engaged in common action (for instance, against the Indians), each of the New England colonies developed with a substantial degree of independence.

The middle colonies took shape quite differently. New York, founded as New Netherland by the Dutch and later conquered by England, was economically and ethnically diverse, socially hierarchical, and politically quarrelsome. Pennsylvania, founded as a Quaker haven by William Penn, attracted an economically ambitious and religiously tolerant but politically troublesome population of diverse ethnic groups.

With their economic variety, ethnic and religious diversity, and political factionalism, the middle colonies were the most typically "American" of England's thirteen Atlantic seaboard colonies.

VARYING VIEWPOINTS

Europeanizing America or Americanizing Europe?

The history of discovery and the earliest colonization raises perhaps the single most fundamental question about all American history. Should it be understood as the extension of European civilization into the New World or as the gradual development of a uniquely "American" culture? One school of thought tended to emphasize the Europeanization of America. Historians of that persuasion paid close attention to the situation in Europe, particularly in England and Spain, in the fifteenth and sixteenth centuries. They also focused on the various means by which the values and institutions of the mother continent were exported to the new lands in the western sea. Some European writers varied this general question by asking what transforming effect the discovery of America had on Europe itself. Both of these approaches are Eurocentric. More recently, historians have concentrated on the distinctiveness of America. The concern with European origins has evolved into a comparative treatment of English, Spanish, Dutch, and French settlements in the New World. The newest trend to emerge is a transatlantic history that views European empires and their American colonies as players in a process of cultural cross-fertilization affecting not only the colonies but Europe and Africa as well.

This less Eurocentric approach has changed the way historians explain the colonial development of America. Historians increasingly view the colonial period as one of "contact" and "adaptation" between European, African, and Native American ways of life. Scholars including Richard White, Alfred W. Crosby, William Cronon, Karen Kupperman, and Timothy Silver have enhanced understanding of the cultural as well as physical transformations that resulted from contact.

The variety of American societies that emerged out of the interaction of Europeans, Africans, and Native Americans has also become better appreciated. Studies such as Richard S. Dunn's *Sugar and Slaves* (1972) emphasize the importance of the Caribbean in early English colonization efforts. Similarly, Edmund S. Morgan's *American Slavery, American Freedom* (1975) stresses the role of economic ambition in explaining the English peopling of the Chesapeake and the eventual importation of African slaves to that region. Studies by Bernard Bailyn and David Hackett Fischer demonstrate that there was scarcely a "typical" English migrant to the New World. English colonists migrated both singly and in families, and for economic, social, political, and religious reasons.

The picture of colonial America that is emerging from all this new scholarship is of a society unique—and diverse—from its inception. No longer simply Europe transplanted, American colonial society by 1700 is now viewed as an outgrowth of many intertwining roots—of different European and African heritages, of varied encounters with native peoples, and of complicated mixtures of settler populations, each with its own distinctive set of ambitions.

4

American Life in the Seventeenth Century

1607–1692

BEING THUS PASSED THE VAST OCEAN, AND A SEA OF TROUBLES BEFORE IN THEIR PREPARATION . . ., THEY HAD NOW NO FRIENDS TO WELLCOME THEM, NOR INNS TO ENTERTAINE OR REFRESH THEIR WEATHERBEATEN BODYS, NO HOUSES OR MUCH LESS TOWNS TO REPAIRE TOO, TO SEEKE FOR SUCCORE.

WILLIAM BRADFORD, *OF PLYMOUTH PLANTATION*, C. 1630

Chapter Outline

- Life and Labor in the Chesapeake Region
- Indentured Servants and Bacon's Rebellion in Virginia, 1676
- Slavery and African American Culture
- Families in New England
- The Salem Witchcraft Trials, 1692
- The Changing New England Way of Life
- Examining the Evidence: An Indentured Servant's Contract, 1746
- Makers of America: From African to African American

As the seventeenth century wore on, the crude encampments of the first colonists slowly gave way to permanent settlements. Durable and distinctive ways of life emerged, as Europeans and Africans adapted to the New World and as Native Americans adapted to the newcomers. Even the rigid doctrines of Puritanism softened somewhat in response to the circumstances of life in America. And though all the colonies remained tied to England and stitched tightly into the fabric of an Atlantic economy, regional differences continued to crystallize, notably the increasing importance of slavery to the southern way of life.

Focus Questions

1. **What were the major features of the economy, population, and social structure of England's North American colonies in the seventeenth century?**
2. **How did the social order and ways of life differ between the southern and northern colonies?**
3. **How did the labor system of white indentured servitude work, and why did plantation owners eventually replace it with African slavery?**
4. **How did the African slave trade develop, and how did African slaves develop their own culture and practices in America?**
5. **What were the major features of the "New England way of life," and how did religion, family life, and women's roles change in the later seventeenth century?**

The Unhealthy Chesapeake

Life in the American wilderness was nasty, brutish, and short for the earliest Chesapeake settlers. Malaria, dysentery, and typhoid took a cruel toll, cutting ten years off the life expectancy of newcomers from England. Half the people born in early Virginia and Maryland did not survive to celebrate their twentieth birthdays. Few of the remaining half lived to see their fiftieth—or even their fortieth, if they were women.

Chronology

1619	First Africans arrive in Virginia.
1625	Population of English colonies in America about 2,000.
1636	Harvard College founded.
1662	Half-Way Covenant for Congregational Church membership established.
1670	Virginia assembly disfranchises landless freemen.
1676	Bacon's Rebellion in Virginia.
1680s	Mass expansion of slavery in colonies.
1689–1691	Leisler's Rebellion in New York.
1692	Salem witch trials in Massachusetts.
1693	College of William and Mary founded.
1698	Royal African Company slave trade monopoly ended.
1700	Population of English colonies in America about 250,000.
1712	New York City slave revolt.
1739	South Carolina slave revolt.

The disease-ravaged settlements of the Chesapeake grew only slowly in the seventeenth century, mostly through fresh immigration from England. The great majority of immigrants were single men in their late teens and early twenties, and most perished soon after arrival. Surviving males competed for the affections of the extremely scarce women, whom they outnumbered nearly six to one in 1650 and still outnumbered by three to two at the end of the century. Eligible women did not remain single for long.

Families were few and fragile in this ferocious environment. Most men could not find mates. Most marriages were destroyed by the death of a partner within seven years. Scarcely any children reached adulthood under the care of two parents, and almost no one knew a grandparent. Weak family ties were reflected in the many pregnancies among unmarried young girls. In one Maryland county, more than a third of all brides were already pregnant when they wed.

Yet despite these hardships, the Chesapeake colonies struggled on. The native-born inhabitants eventually acquired immunity to the killer diseases that had ravaged the original immigrants. The presence of more women allowed more families to form, and by the end of the seventeenth century the white population of the Chesapeake was growing on the basis of its own birthrate. As the eighteenth century opened, Virginia, with some fifty-nine thousand people, was the most populous colony. Maryland, with about thirty thousand, was the third largest (after Massachusetts).

The Tobacco Economy

Although unhealthy for human life, the Chesapeake was immensely hospitable to tobacco cultivation. Profit-hungry settlers often planted tobacco to sell before they planted corn to eat. But intense tobacco cultivation quickly exhausted the soil, creating a nearly insatiable demand for new land. Relentlessly seeking fresh fields to plant in tobacco, commercial growers plunged ever farther up the river valleys, provoking ever more Indian attacks.

This continual expansion created tobacco yields that reached almost 40 million pounds a year by the end of the seventeenth century. This enormous production depressed prices, but colonial Chesapeake tobacco growers responded to falling prices by planting still more acres in tobacco and bringing still more product to market.

More tobacco meant more labor, but where was it to come from? Families procreated too slowly to provide it by natural population increase. Indians died too quickly on contact with whites, and African slaves cost too much money. But England still had a "surplus" of displaced farmers desperate for employment. Many of them, as indentured servants, voluntarily mortgaged the sweat of their bodies for

Primary source
Excerpts of Virginia Law on Indentured Servitude
college.hmco.com/pic/kennedybrief7e

An agent for the Virginia Company in London submitted the following description of the Virginia colony in 1622:

"I found the plantations generally seated upon mere salt marshes full of infectious bogs and muddy creeks and lakes, and thereby subjected to all those inconveniences and diseases which are so commonly found in the most unsound and most unhealthy parts of England."

several years to Chesapeake masters. In exchange they received transatlantic passage and eventual "freedom dues," including a few barrels of corn, a suit of clothes, and perhaps a small parcel of land.

Both Virginia and Maryland employed the "**headright**" system to encourage the importation of servant workers. Under its terms, whoever paid the passage of a laborer received the right to acquire fifty acres of land. Taking advantage of this system, some masters soon parlayed their investments in servants into vast holdings in real estate. They became the great merchant-planters who came to dominate the agriculture and commerce of the southern colonies. Chesapeake planters had brought some 100,000 indentured servants to the region by 1700. These "white slaves" represented more than three-quarters of all European immigrants to Virginia and Maryland in the seventeenth century.

Indentured servants led a hard but hopeful life in the early days of the Chesapeake settlements. They looked forward to becoming free and acquiring land of their own after completing their term of servitude. But as prime land became scarcer toward the end of the seventeenth century, masters became increasingly resistant to including land grants in "freedom dues." Even after formal freedom was granted, penniless freed workers often had little choice but to hire themselves out for pitifully low wages to their former masters.

Primary source
Indentured Servant's Confession
college.hmco.com/pic/kennedybrief7e

Frustrated Freemen and Bacon's Rebellion

An accumulating mass of footloose, impoverished freemen was drifting discontentedly about the Chesapeake region by the late seventeenth century. Mostly single young men, they were frustrated by their broken hopes of acquiring land as well as by their gnawing failure to find single women to marry.

The swelling number of these wretched bachelors rattled the established planters. Encouraged by Governor William Berkeley, the Virginia assembly in 1670 **disenfranchised** most of the landless knockabouts. About a thousand poverty-stricken Virginians then broke out of control in 1676, led by a twenty-nine-year-old planter, Nathaniel Bacon. Angered by Berkeley's mild Indian policies as well as economic grievances, Bacon and his followers first mercilessly attacked Indians on the frontier. They then chased Berkeley from Jamestown and put the torch to the capital. Chaos swept the raw colony as frustrated freemen and resentful servants—described as "a rabble of the basest sort of people"—went on a rampage of plundering and pilfering.

As this **civil war** in Virginia ground on, Bacon suddenly died of disease. Berkeley thereupon crushed the uprising with brutal cruelty, hanging more than twenty rebels. Back in England King Charles II complained, "That old fool has put to death more people in that naked country than I did here for the murder of my father."

The distant English king could scarcely imagine the depths of passion and fear that Bacon's Rebellion excited in Virginia. Bacon had ignited the smoldering unhappiness of landless former servants, and he had pitted the hardscrabble backcountry frontiersmen against the haughty gentry of the **tidewater** plantations. The rebellion was suppressed, but these tensions remained. Lordly planters, surrounded by a still-seething sea of malcontents, anxiously looked about for less troublesome laborers to toil in their restless tobacco kingdom. Their eyes soon lit on Africa.

headright *The right to acquire a certain amount of land that was granted to the person who financed the passage of an indentured servant or laborer.*

disenfranchise *To take away the right to vote.*

civil war *Any significant conflict between rival forces of the same country, both claiming to be the sovereign government of the territory in whole or in part.*

tidewater *The territory adjoining water affected by tides—that is, near the seacoast or coastal estuaries and rivers.*

Interactive map
African Origins of North American Slaves 1690–1807
college.hmco.com/pic/kennedybrief7e

Colonial Slavery

Perhaps 10 million Africans were carried in chains to the New World in the three centuries or so following Columbus's landing. Only about 400,000 of them ended up in North America. Most were hauled to Spanish and Portuguese South America or the sugar-rich West Indies. Africans had been brought to Jamestown as early as 1619, but

Examining the Evidence

An Indentured Servant's Contract, 1746 Legal documents, such as this contract signed in Virginia in 1746, not only provide evidence about the ever-changing rules by which societies have regulated their affairs, but also furnish rich information about the conditions of life and the terms of human relationships in the past. This agreement between Thomas Clayton and James Griffin provides a reminder that not all indentured servants in early America came from abroad. Indentured servitude could be equivalent to an apprenticeship, in which a young person traded several years of service to a master in exchange for instruction in the master's craft. Here Clayton pledges himself to five years in Griffin's employ in return for a promise to initiate the young man into the "Mystery" of the master's craft.

1. Why might the master's trade be described as a "mystery"?
2. From the evidence of this contract, what are the principal objectives of each of the parties to it?
3. What problems do the master and the servant/apprentice each anticipate? What obligations does each assume?

4. What does the consent of Clayton's mother to the contract suggest about the young man's situation?
5. The first sentence of the contract says that Clayton "doth voluntarily and of his own free will and accord, and with the consent and approbation of his mother, put himself apprentice to James Griffin. . . ." Why was it legally important that Clayton affirm that he had *voluntarily* made himself an unpaid servant/laborer for a term of five years?
6. The contract also declares that Griffin may not, among other things, "commit fornication," marry, or play cards or dice during his term of servitude. What does this provision reveal about the relationship of master to servant? Should this document be considered an "employment contract" or something else?

Primary source
Early Evidence of Sexual Tensions Within Slavery
college.hmco.com/pic/kennedybrief7e

middle passage *That portion of a slave ship's journey in which slaves were carried from Africa to slave markets in the Americas. (The slave-carrying shipments from Africa to American slave markets were the "middle" leg of a round-trip voyage from Europe or New England and back.)*

as late as 1670 they numbered only about 7 percent of the 50,000 people in the southern plantation colonies as a whole. For hard-pinched colonists, white servants were far less costly than high-priced slaves who might die soon after arrival.

Drastic change came in the 1680s. Rising wages in England shrank the pool of potential indentured servants, while large planters grew increasingly fearful of the potentially mutinous former servants in their midst. By the mid-1680s, for the first time, black slaves outnumbered white servants among the plantation colonies' new arrivals. In 1698 the Royal African Company, first chartered in 1672, lost its crown-granted monopoly on carrying slaves to the colonies. Enterprising Americans, especially Rhode Islanders, rushed to cash in on the lucrative slave trade, and the supply of slaves rose steeply. By 1750 blacks accounted for nearly half the population of Virginia, and in South Carolina they outnumbered whites two to one.

Most of the slaves who reached North America came from the west coast of Africa, especially the area stretching from present-day Senegal to Angola. They were originally captured by African coastal tribes, who traded them in crude markets to itinerant European—and American—flesh merchants. Usually branded and bound, the captives were herded aboard sweltering ships for the gruesome "**middle passage,**" on which death rates ran as high as 20 percent. Terrified survivors were eventually shoved onto auction blocks in New World ports like Newport, Rhode Island, or Charleston, South Carolina, where a giant slave market traded in human misery for more than a century.

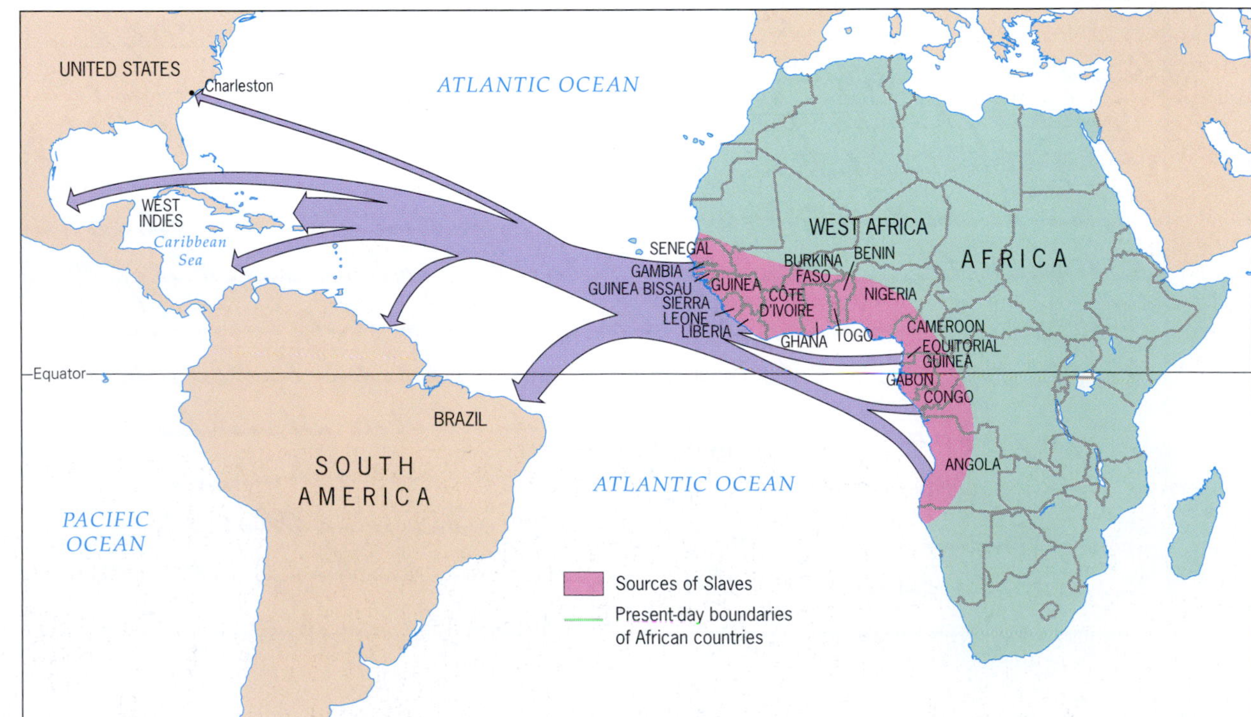

Main Sources of African Slaves, c. 1500 to c. 1800 The three centuries of the African diaspora scattered blacks all over the New World, with about 400,000 coming to North America. Boundaries shown are those of modern African states.

A few of the earliest African immigrants gained their freedom, and some even became slaveowners themselves. But as the number of Africans in their midst increased dramatically toward the end of the seventeenth century, white colonists reacted remorselessly to this supposed racial threat. Beginning in Virginia in 1662, the iron conditions of bondage were spelled out in slave codes that made blacks *and their children* the property (or "chattels") for life of their white masters. Not even conversion to Christianity could qualify a slave for freedom. Slavery might have begun in America for economic reasons, but by the end of the seventeenth century, it was clear that racial discrimination also powerfully molded the American slave system.

The Mennonites of Germantown, Pennsylvania, recorded the earliest known protest against slavery in America in 1688:

"There is a saying, that we should do to all men like as we will be done ourselves. . . . But to bring men hither, or to rob and sell them against their will, we stand against. . . . Pray, what thing in the world can be done worse towards us, than if men should rob or steal us away, and sell us for slaves to strange countries, separating husbands from their wives and children?"

Africans in America

In the deepest South, slave life was especially severe. The climate was hostile to health, and the labor was life draining. The widely scattered South Carolina rice and indigo plantations were lonely hells on earth where gangs of mostly male Africans toiled and perished. Only fresh imports could sustain the slave population under these loathsome conditions.

Blacks in the tobacco-growing Chesapeake region had a somewhat easier lot. Tobacco was less physically demanding than the crops of the deeper South. Tobacco plantations were smaller and closer to one another than rice plantations. By about 1720 the proportion of females in the Chesapeake slave population had begun to rise, making family life possible. The captive black population of the Chesapeake area soon began to grow not only through new imports but also through its own **fertility**—making it one of the few slave societies in history to perpetuate itself by its own natural reproduction.

Native-born African Americans contributed to the growth of a stable and distinctive slave culture, a mixture of African and American elements of speech, religion, and folkways (see "Makers of America: From African to African American," pp. 52–53). On the sea islands off South Carolina's coast, blacks evolved a unique language, Gullah, that blended English with several African languages, including Yoruba, Ibo, and Hausa. The ringshout, a West African religious dance performed by shuffling in a circle while answering a preacher's shouts, was brought to colonial America by slaves and eventually contributed to the development of jazz.

Slaves also helped mightily to build the country with their labor. A few became skilled artisans—carpenters, bricklayers, and tanners. But chiefly they performed the sweaty toil of clearing swamps, grubbing out trees, and other **menial** tasks. Condemned to life under the lash, slaves naturally pined for freedom. Slave revolts erupted in New York City in 1712, and again in South Carolina in 1739. But in the end the slaves in the South proved to be a more manageable labor force than the white indentured servants they gradually replaced. No slave uprising in American history matched the scale of Bacon's Rebellion.

Interactive map
West Africa and the Atlantic Slave Trade
college.hmco.com/pic/kennedybrief7e

fertility *The ability to mate and produce abundant young.*

menial *Fit for servants; humble or low.*

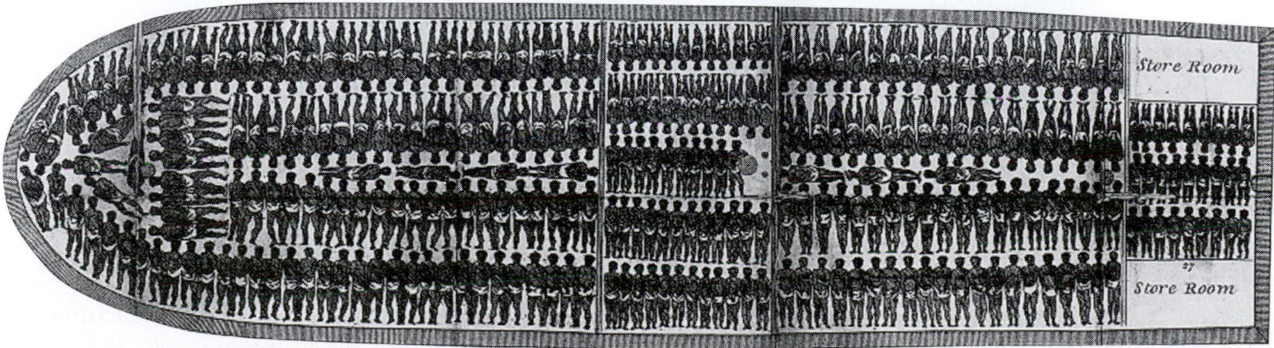

The "Middle Passage" Human cargo in the hold of a slave ship.

From African to African American

Dragged in chains from West African shores, the first African Americans struggled to preserve their diverse heritages from the ravages of slavery. Their children, the first generation of American-born slaves, melded these various traditions—Guinean, Ibo, Yoruba, Angolan—into a distinctive African American culture. Their achievement sustained them during the cruelties of enslavement and has endured to this day to enrich American life.

With the arrival of the first Africans in the seventeenth century, a cornucopia of African traditions poured into the New World: handicrafts and skills in numerous trades; a plethora of languages, musics, and cuisines; even rice-planting techniques that conquered the inhospitable soil

■ **Yarrow Mamout, by Charles Willson Peale, 1819** When Peale painted this portrait, Mamout was over 100 years old. A devout Muslim brought to Maryland as a slave, he eventually bought his freedom and settled in Georgetown.

The Emergence of an African American Culture In this scene from the mid-nineteenth century, African Americans play musical instruments of European derivation, like the fiddle, as well as instruments of African origin, like the bones and banjo—a vivid illustration of the blending of the two cultures in the crucible of the New World.

of South Carolina. It was North America's rice paddies, tilled by experienced West Africans, that introduced the staple rice into the English diet.

These first American slaves were mostly males who lived and worked on small, isolated farms. But by the beginning of the eighteenth century, a settled slave society was emerging in the southern colonies. Laws tightened; slave traders stepped up their deliveries of human cargo; large plantations formed. Most significantly, a new generation of American-born slaves joined their forebears at labor in the fields. By 1740 large groups of slaves lived together on sprawling plantations, the American-born outnumbered the African-born, and the importation of African slaves slowed.

Plantation life was an endless cycle of miserable toil for the slaves. After a day's backbreaking work, women were expected to sit up for hours spinning, weaving, or sewing clothes for themselves and their families. Enslaved women also lived in constant fear of sexual exploitation by conscienceless masters.

Slave religion illustrates how new ideas were combined with a traditional heritage. Most slaves became Christians but fused elements of African and Western traditions and drew their own conclusions from Scripture. White Christians might encourage slaves to "stay in their place," but black Christians emphasized God's role in freeing the Hebrews from slavery and saw Jesus as the Messiah who would deliver them from bondage.

At their Sunday and evening prayer meetings, slaves also patched African remnants onto conventional Christian ritual. Black Methodists, for example, evaded the traditional Methodist ban on dancing by practicing the "ringshout." Some worshipers clapped their hands and beat time in a circle while others walked around the ring, singing in unison. Christian slaves also often used outwardly religious songs as encoded messages about escape or rebellion. The hymn "Wade in the Water," for instance, taught fleeing slaves one way of covering their trails. The "Negro spirituals" that took shape as a distinctive form of American music thus had their origins in both Christianity and slavery. Indeed, much American music was born in the slave quarters from African importations. But this rich cultural harvest came at the cost of generations of human agony.

Southern Society

hierarchy *A social group arranged in ranks or classes.*

As slavery spread, the gaps in the South's social structure widened. The rough equality of poverty and disease of the early days was giving way to a defined **hierarchy** of wealth and status in the early eighteenth century. At the top of this southern social ladder perched a small but powerful covey of great planters. Owning gangs of slaves and vast domains of land, the planters ruled the region's economy and virtually monopolized political power. Yet, legend to the contrary, these great seventeenth-century merchant-planters were not silk-swathed cavaliers gallantly imitating the ways of English country gentlemen. For the most part they were a hard-working, businesslike lot, laboring long hours over the problems of plantation management.

Far beneath the planters in wealth, prestige, and political power were the small farmers, the largest social group. They might or might not own one or two slaves, but they lived a ragged, hand-to-mouth existence on their modest plots. Still lower on the social scale were landless whites and, below them, indentured servants still serving out their terms. The oppressed black slaves, of course, remained enchained in society's basement.

Few cities sprouted in the colonial South, and consequently an urban professional class, including lawyers and financiers, was slow to emerge. Southern life revolved around the great plantations, distantly isolated from one another. Waterways, rather than the wretched roads, provided the principal means of transportation from one plantation to another.

The New England Family

Nature smiled more benignly on pioneer New Englanders than on their disease-plagued fellow colonists to the south. Clean water and cool temperatures, which retarded the spread of microbes, created healthier living conditions that enabled settlers in seventeenth-century New England to *add* ten years to their life spans by migrating from the Old World, in stark contrast to the fate of Chesapeake immigrants. The first generations of Puritan colonists enjoyed, on the average, about seventy years on this earth—not very different from the life expectancy of present-day Americans.

In further contrast with the Chesapeake, New Englanders tended to migrate not as single individuals but as families, and the family remained at the center of New England life. Early marriage and prolific childbearing enabled New England's population to grow from natural reproductive increase almost from the outset. Women typically wed by their early twenties and produced babies about every two years thereafter until menopause. A married woman could expect to experience up to ten pregnancies and rear as many as eight surviving children. A New England woman might well have dependent children living in her household from the earliest days of her marriage until the day of her death, and child raising became virtually her full-time occupation.

Primary source
Puritan Prescription for Marital Concord
college.hmco.com/pic/kennedybrief7e

Primary source
Family Ties: A Puritan Woman's Advice on Dealing . . .
college.hmco.com/pic/kennedybrief7e

Primary source
Early Prenuptial Agreement
college.hmco.com/pic/kennedybrief7e

The longevity of the New Englanders contributed to family stability. Children received nurturing love and guidance not only from their parents but from their grandparents as well. Family stability was reflected in low premarital pregnancy rates (again in contrast with the Chesapeake) and in the generally strong, tranquil social structure characteristic of colonial New England.

Oddly enough, the strength of New England families actually weakened the economic independence of women in that region compared with women in the South. Because southern men frequently died young, leaving widows with small children to support, the southern colonies allowed married women to retain separate titles to their property and gave widows the right to inherit their husband's estates. But in New England, Puritan lawmakers worried that recognizing women's separate property rights would undercut the unity of husband and wife. New England women, therefore, usually gave up their property rights when they married.

"A true wife accounts subjection her honor," one Massachusetts Puritan leader declared, expressing a sentiment then common in Europe as well as America. But in the New World, a rudimentary conception of women's rights as individuals was beginning to appear in the seventeenth century. Women still could not vote, and the popular attitude persisted that they were morally weaker than men. But a husband's power over his wife was not absolute. The New England authorities could and did intervene to restrain abusive spouses, and women had some spheres of autonomy. Midwifery—assisting with childbirths—was a virtual female monopoly, and midwives often fostered networks of women bonded by the common travails of motherhood.

Above all, the laws of Puritan New England sought to defend the integrity of marriages. Divorce was exceedingly rare: outright abandonment and adultery were among the few permissible grounds for divorce. Convicted adulterers—especially if they were women—were whipped in public and forced forever after to wear the capital letter "A" cut out in cloth and sewn on their outer garments—the basis for Nathaniel Hawthorne's famous 1850 tale, *The Scarlet Letter*.

Life in the New England Towns

Sturdy New Englanders evolved a tightly knit society, the basis of which was small villages and farms. Puritanism especially made for unity of purpose—and for concern about the moral health of the whole community.

Even territorial expansion occurred in orderly, communal fashion, in contrast to the Chesapeake's normal mode of expansion by lone-wolf planters on their own initiative. New towns were legally chartered by the colonial authorities, and the distribution of land was entrusted to the steady hands of sober-minded town fathers, or

Mrs. Elizabeth Freake and Baby Mary This portrait of a Boston mother and child in about 1674 suggests the strong family ties that characterized early New England society.

militia *An armed force of citizens called out only in emergencies.*

jeremiad *A sermon or prophecy recounting wrongdoing, warning of doom, and calling for repentance.*

hinterland *An inland region set back from a port, river, or seacoast.*

Primary source
Mr. John Freake
college.hmco.com/pic/kennedybrief7e

"proprietors." After receiving a grant of land from the colonial legislature, the proprietors usually laid out their town around a meetinghouse, which served as both the place of worship and the town hall. Also marked out was a village green, where the **militia** could drill. Each family received several parcels of land.

Towns of more than fifty families were required to provide elementary education, and roughly half of the adults knew how to read and write. As early as 1636, just six years after the colony's founding, the Massachusetts Puritans established Harvard College to train local boys for the ministry. Only in 1693, eighty-six years after the founding of Jamestown, did the Virginians establish their first college, William and Mary.

Puritans ran their own churches, and democracy in Congregational Church government led logically to democracy in political government. The town meeting, in which the adult males met together and each man voted, was a showcase and a classroom for democracy. The New England town meeting, observed Thomas Jefferson, was "the best school of political liberty the world ever saw."

The Changing New England Way of Life

Yet worries plagued the God-fearing pioneers of these tidy New England settlements. The pressure of a growing population was gradually dispersing the Puritans onto outlying farms, far from the control of church and neighbors. And although the core of Puritan belief still burned brightly, the passage of time was dampening the first generation's religious zeal. About the middle of the seventeenth century, earnest preachers began scolding parishioners for their waning piety in a new form of sermon—the "**jeremiad.**" In response to the apparent decline in conversions, troubled ministers in 1662 announced a new formula for church membership, the "Half-Way Covenant." This new arrangement admitted to baptism, but not to "full communion," the unconverted children of existing members. By conferring partial membership rights in the once-exclusive Puritan congregations, the Half-Way Covenant weakened the distinction between the "elect" and other members of society. In effect, strict religious purity was sacrificed somewhat to the cause of wider religious participation. Interestingly, from about this time onward, women were in the majority in the Puritan congregations.

Women also played a prominent role in one of New England's most frightening religious episodes. A group of adolescent girls in Salem, Massachusetts, claimed to have been bewitched by certain older women. A hysterical "witch hunt" ensued, leading to the execution in 1692 of twenty individuals.

Primary source
Ann Putnam's Deposition
college.hmco.com/pic/kennedybrief7e

The reign of horror in Salem grew not only from the superstitions and prejudices of the age but also from the unsettled social and religious conditions of the rapidly evolving Massachusetts village. Most of the accused witches came from families associated with Salem's burgeoning market economy; their accusers came largely from the ranks of subsistence farming families in Salem's **hinterland.** The episode thus reflected the widening social stratification of New England, as well as the fear of many religious traditionalists that the Puritan heritage was being eclipsed by Yankee commercialism. The Salem witchcraft delusion marked an all-time high in the American experience of popular passions run wild.

New England soil, like New England religion, was hard and unyielding. Scratching a living from the rock-strewn land put a premium on industry and penny-pinching frugality, for which New Englanders became famous. The grudging land also left colonial New England less ethnically mixed than its southern neighbors. European immigrants were not attracted in great numbers to a site where the soil was so stony—and the sermons so sulfurous.

Yet the harsh climate and unproductive soil of New England eventually encouraged a diversified agriculture and industry. Staple products like tobacco did not flourish, as in the South. Black slavery, although attempted, could

The Massachusetts School Law of 1647 (later called "The Old Deluder Law"), stated,

"It being one chief project of the old deluder, Satan, to keep men from the knowledge of the Scriptures, as in former times by keeping them in an unknown tongue, it is therefore ordered that every township in this jurisdiction, after the Lord has increased them [in] number to fifty householders, shall then forthwith appoint one within their town to teach all such children as shall resort to him to write and read, whose wages shall be paid either by the parents or masters of such children, or by the inhabitants in general."

not exist profitably on small farms. Turning away from the land, New Englanders more and more looked to the sea for a living. Hacking timber from their dense forests, they became experts in shipbuilding and commerce. They also ceaselessly exploited the self-perpetuating codfish lode off the coast of Newfoundland—the fishy "gold mines of New England." As a reminder of the importance of fishing, a handsome replica of the "sacred cod" is proudly displayed to this day in the Massachusetts State House in Boston.

Just as the land shaped New Englanders, so they shaped the land. Native Americans of the region had left an early imprint on the earth, beating trails through the woods and periodically burning woodlands to restore leafy first-growth forests. But in contrast with Native Americans, who *used* the land but recognized no right to *own* it, the English settlers felt a virtual duty to "improve" the land by clearing woodlands for pasturage and tillage, building roads and fences, and laying out permanent settlements. The introduction of livestock also led colonists to clear ever more forests for pastureland, while the animals' voracious appetites and heavy hooves compacted the soil, speeding erosion and flooding.

The combination of Calvinism, soil, and climate in New England made for energy, purposefulness, sternness, stubbornness, self-reliance, and resourcefulness. Righteous New Englanders prided themselves on being God's chosen people. They long boasted that Boston was "the hub of the universe"—at least in spirit. A famous jingle of later days ran:

I come from the city of Boston
The home of the bean and the cod
Where the Cabots speak only to Lowells
And the Lowells speak only to God.

New England has had an incalculable impact on the rest of the nation. Ousted by their sterile soil, thousands of New Englanders scattered from Ohio to Oregon and even Hawaii. The democratic town meeting, the tidy schoolhouse, and "Yankee ingenuity," all originally fostered by the flinty fields and comfortless climate of New England, came to be claimed by all Americans as a proud national heritage. And the fabled "New England conscience," born of the steadfast Puritan faith, left a legacy of high idealism in the national character and inspired many later reformers.

The Early Settlers' Days and Ways

The cycles of the seasons and the sun set the schedules of all the earliest American colonists—men as well as women, blacks as well as whites. The overwhelming majority of colonists were farmers. They planted in the spring, tended their crops in the summer, harvested in the fall, and prepared in the winter to begin the cycle anew. They usually rose at dawn and went to bed at dusk. Chores might be performed after nightfall only if they were "worth the candle," a phrase that has persisted in American speech.

Women, slave or free, on southern plantations or northern farms, cooked, cleaned, and cared for children. Men worked the land, cut firewood, and butchered livestock as needed. Children helped with all these tasks, while picking up such schooling as they could.

Life was humble but comfortable by the standards of the time. Compared to most seventeenth-century Europeans, Americans lived in affluent abundance. Land was relatively cheap, though somewhat less available in the planter-dominated South than elsewhere. Wages for workmen were roughly three times those of their English counterparts.

"Dukes don't emigrate," the saying goes, for if people enjoy wealth and security, they are not likely to risk exposing their lives in the wilderness. Similarly, the very poorest members of a society may not possess even the modest means needed to pull up stakes and seek a fresh start in life. Accordingly, most white migrants to early colonial America came neither from the aristocracy nor from the dregs of European society—with the partial exception of the impoverished indentured servants.

Seventeenth-century society in all the colonies had a certain simple sameness to it, especially in the more egalitarian New England and middle colonies. Yet many settlers who considered themselves to be of the "better sort" tried to re-create on a

social structure *The basic pattern of the distribution of status and wealth in a society.*

blue bloods *Of noble or upper-class descent.*

modified scale the **social structure** they had known in the Old World. Resentment against such upper-class pretensions helped to spark outbursts like Bacon's Rebellion in Virginia in 1676, the uprising of Maryland's Protestants toward the end of the seventeenth century, and Leisler's Rebellion, an ill-starred and bloody insurgence that rocked New York City from 1689 to 1691.

For their part, would-be American **blue bloods** resented the pretensions of the "meaner sort" and passed laws to try to keep them in their place. Massachusetts in 1651 prohibited poorer folk from "wearing gold or silver lace," and in eighteenth-century Virginia a tailor was fined and jailed for arranging to race his horse—"a sport only for gentlemen." But these efforts to reproduce the finely stratified societies of Europe proved feeble in the early American wilderness, where equality and democracy found fertile soil—at least for white people.

Chapter Summary

Life was hard in the seventeenth-century southern colonies. Disease drastically shortened life spans in the Chesapeake region, even for the young single men who made up the majority of settlers. Families were few and fragile, with men greatly outnumbering women, who were much in demand and seldom remained single for long.

The tobacco economy first thrived using the labor of white indentured servants, who hoped to work their way up to become landowners and perhaps even become wealthy. But by the late seventeenth century, this hope was increasingly frustrated, and the discontents of the poor whites exploded in Bacon's Rebellion in Virginia.

With white labor increasingly troublesome, slaves (earlier a small fraction of the workforce) began to be imported from West Africa by the tens of thousands in the 1680s, and soon became essential to the colonial economy. Slaves in the Deep South died rapidly of disease and overwork, but those in the Chesapeake tobacco region survived longer. Their numbers eventually increased by natural reproduction, and they developed a distinctive African American way of life that combined African elements with features developed in the New World.

By contrast with the South, New England's clean water and cool air contributed to a healthy way of life, which actually *added* ten years to the average English life span. The New England way of life centered on strong families and tightly knit towns and churches, which were relatively democratic and equal by seventeenth-century standards. By the late seventeenth century, however, social and religious tensions developed in these narrow communities, as the Salem witch hysteria dramatically illustrates.

Rocky soil forced many New Englanders to turn to fishing and merchant shipping for their livelihoods. Their difficult lives and stern religion made New Englanders tough, idealistic, purposeful, and resourceful. In later years they spread these same values across much of American society.

All of seventeenth-century American society was relatively simple and almost entirely agrarian. Would-be aristocrats who tried to recreate the social hierarchies of Europe were generally frustrated.

Colonial Society on the Eve of Revolution

1700–1775

DRIVEN FROM EVERY OTHER CORNER OF THE EARTH, FREEDOM OF THOUGHT AND THE RIGHT OF PRIVATE JUDGMENT IN MATTERS OF CONSCIENCE DIRECT THEIR COURSE TO THIS HAPPY COUNTRY AS THEIR LAST ASYLUM.

SAMUEL ADAMS, 1776

Chapter Outline

The common term *thirteen original colonies* is misleading. Britain ruled thirty-two colonies in North America by 1775, including Canada, the Floridas, and various Caribbean islands. But only thirteen of them unfurled the standard of rebellion. A few of the nonrebels, such as Canada and Jamaica, were larger, wealthier, or more populous than some of the revolting thirteen. Why, then, did some British colonies eventually strike for their independence, while others did not? Part of the answer is to be found in the distinctive social, economic, and political structures of the thirteen Atlantic seaboard colonies—and in the halting, gradual appearance of a recognizably *American* way of life.

Focus Questions

1. **What were the major demographic and social structures that characterized Britain's eighteenth-century colonies, and how had these changed since the early seventeenth-century settlements?**
2. **How did the expanding economy of the colonies alter the patterns of social prestige and wealth, and introduce greater class divisions?**
3. **What were the causes of the first religious "Great Awakening" in American history, and how did it affect colonial identity, education, and politics?**
4. **What were the major features of education, culture, and daily life in the eighteenth century?**
5. **What issues and conflicts dominated colonial politics, and how did both formal institutions (legislatures and governors) and informal practices of public opinion affect those issues?**

Conquest by the Cradle

Among the distinguishing characteristics that the eventually rebellious settlements shared was lusty population growth. In 1700 they contained fewer than 300,000 souls, about 20,000 of whom were black. By 1775, 2.5 million people inhabited the thirteen colonies, of whom about half a million were black. White immigrants made up nearly 400,000 of the increased number, and black "forced immigrants" accounted for almost as many again. But most of the spurt stemmed from the remarkable natural fertility of all Americans, white and black. The youthful Americans, whose average age in 1775 was about sixteen, were doubling their numbers every twenty-five years. Unfriendly Dr. Samuel Johnson, back in Britain, growled that the Americans were multiplying like their own rattlesnakes.

This population boom had political consequences. In 1700 there were twenty Britons for each American colonist. By 1775 the British advantage in numbers had fallen to three to one—setting the stage for a momentous shift in the balance of power between the colonies and Britain.

Huguenots *French Calvinist dissenters from that country's dominant Catholicism. Eventually outlawed by King Louis XIV in 1685, many fled elsewhere, including to British North America.*

The bulk of the population was cooped up east of the Alleghenies. The most populous colonies in 1775 were Virginia, Massachusetts, Pennsylvania, North Carolina, and Maryland—in that order. Only four communities could properly be called cities: Philadelphia, including suburbs, was first with about 34,000 residents, trailed by New York, Boston, and Charleston. About 90 percent of the people lived in rural areas.

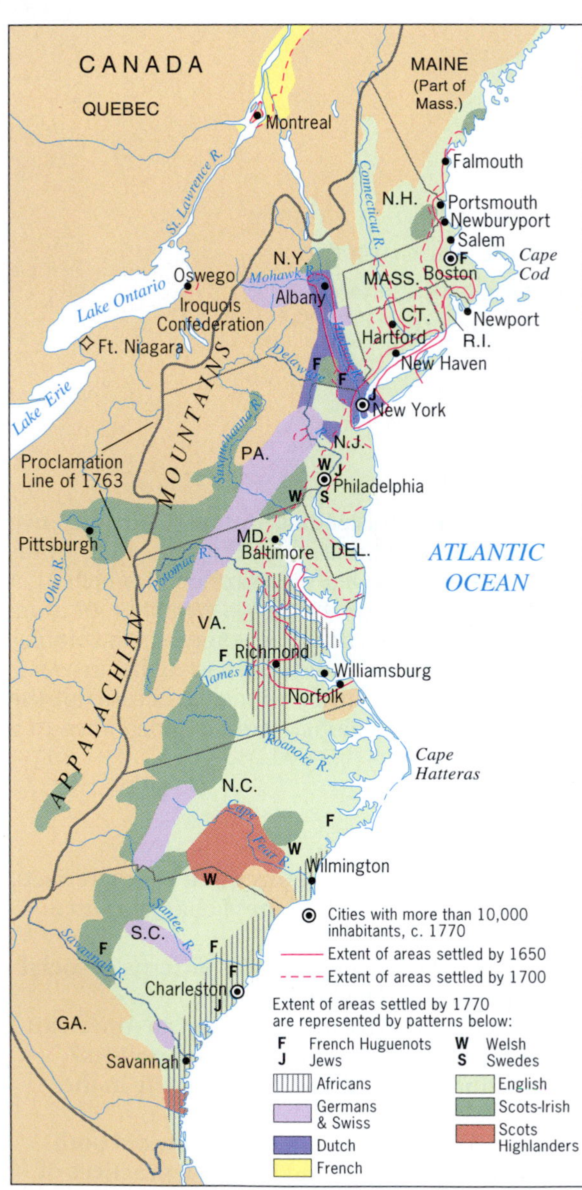

Immigrant Groups in 1775 America was already a nation of diverse ethnic groups in the colonial period. This map shows the great variety of immigrant groups, especially in Pennsylvania and New York. It also illustrates the tendency of later arrivals, particularly the Scots-Irish, to push into the backcountry. The basic ethnic makeup of many of these colonial settlements persists even today, each with distinct cultural patterns and attitudes.

A Potpourri of Peoples

Colonial America was a melting pot and had been from the outset. The population, although basically English in stock and language, was picturesquely mottled with numerous foreign groups.

Germans constituted about 6 percent of the total population, or 150,000, by 1775. Fleeing religious persecution, economic oppression, and the ravages of war, they had flocked to America in the early 1700s and had settled chiefly in Pennsylvania. They belonged to several different Protestant groups—primarily Lutheran—and thus further enhanced the religious diversity of the colony. Known popularly but erroneously as the Pennsylvania Dutch (a corruption of the German word *Deutsch,* for "German"), they totaled about one-third of the colony's population. In parts of Philadelphia, street signs were painted in both German and English. In the Pennsylvania backcountry, where many of them moved, German immigrants clung tenaciously to their language and customs.

The Scots-Irish, who in 1775 numbered about 175,000, or 7 percent of the population, were an important non-English group, although they spoke English (see "Makers of America: The Scots-Irish," p. 62). They were not Irish at all but turbulent Scots Lowlanders who had been transplanted over many decades to Northern Ireland, where they had not prospered. The Irish Catholics already there, hating Scottish Presbyterianism, resented the intruders (and still do). Early in the 1700s tens of thousands of these embittered Scots-Irish finally abandoned Ireland and came to America, chiefly to tolerant and deep-soiled Pennsylvania.

Finding the best acres already taken by Germans and Quakers, the Scots-Irish pushed out onto the Appalachian frontier, often drifting southward into the backcountry of Virginia, Maryland, and the Carolinas. There many of them illegally but defiantly squatted on the unoccupied lands and quarreled with both Indian and white owners. Pugnacious, lawless, and individualistic, the Scots-Irish brought with them the Scottish secrets of whiskey distilling and dotted the Appalachian hills and hollows with their stills. They cherished no love for the British government that had uprooted them, and many of them—including the young Andrew Jackson—eventually joined the embattled American revolutionists.

Approximately 5 percent of the colonial population consisted of other European groups, including French **Huguenots,** Welsh, Dutch, Swedes, Jews, Irish, Swiss, and Scots Highlanders. Except for the Scots Highlanders, these ethnic groups felt little loyalty to

Chronology

1693	College of William and Mary founded.
1701	Yale College founded.
1721	Smallpox inoculation introduced.
1732	First edition of Franklin's *Poor Richard's Almanack.*
1734	Jonathan Edwards begins Great Awakening.
1734-1735	Zenger free-press trial in New York.
1738	George Whitefield spreads Great Awakening.
1746	Princeton College founded.
1760	Britain vetoes South Carolina anti–slave trade measures.
1764	Brown College founded.
1766	Rutgers College founded.
1769	Dartmouth College founded.

the British crown. By far the largest single non-English group was African, accounting for nearly 20 percent of the colonial population in 1775 and heavily concentrated in the South.

The population of the thirteen colonies, though mainly Anglo-Saxon, was among the most mixed to be found anywhere in the world. The South, holding about 90 percent of the slaves, already displayed its historic black-and-white racial composition. New England, mostly staked out by the original Puritan migrants, showed the least ethnic diversity. The middle colonies, especially Pennsylvania, received the bulk of later white immigrants and boasted an astonishing variety of people. Outside of New England, about half of the population was non-English in 1775.

As these various immigrant groups mingled and intermarried, they laid the foundations for a new multicultural American national identity unlike anything known in Europe. Nor were white colonists alone in creating new societies out of diverse ethnic groups. The African slave trade long had mixed peoples from many different tribal backgrounds, giving birth to an African-*American* community far more variegated in its cultural origins than anything to be found in Africa itself. Similarly, in the New England "praying towns" where Indians were gathered to be Christianized, and in Great Lakes villages such as Detroit, home to dozens of different displaced indigenous peoples, polyglot Native American communities emerged, blurring the boundaries of individual tribal identities.

The young Frenchman Michel-Guillaume Jean de Crèvecoeur (1735–1813) wrote of the diverse population in about 1770:

"They are a mixture of English, Scotch, Irish, French, Dutch, Germans, and Swedes. From this promiscuous breed, that race now called Americans have arisen. . . . I could point out to you a family whose grandfather was an Englishman, whose wife was Dutch, whose son married a French woman, and whose present four sons have now four wives of different nations."

Interactive map
Immigration and Frontier Expansion, to 1755
college.hmco.com/pic/kennedybrief7e

The Structure of Colonial Society

In comparison to contemporary Europe, eighteenth-century America seemed like a shining land of equality and opportunity—with the notorious exception of slavery. No titled nobility dominated society from on high, and no pauperized underclass threatened it from below. Most white Americans, and even a handful of free blacks, were small farmers. The cities contained a small class of skilled artisans, as well as a few shopkeepers, tradespeople, and unskilled day laborers. The most remarkable feature of the social ladder was its openness. An ambitious colonist, even a former indentured servant, could rise from a lower rung to a higher one, a rare step in Britain.

Yet in contrast with seventeenth-century America, colonial society on the eve of the Revolution was beginning to show signs of **stratification** and barriers to **mobility** that raised worries about the "Europeanization" of America. A new class of merchant princes in New England and the middle colonies, many of whom had

stratification *The visible arrangement of society into a hierarchical pattern, with distinct social groups layered one on top of the other.*

mobility *The capacity to pass readily from one social or economic condition to another; "upward mobility" means a rise in social or economic status, while "downward mobility" is a decline in status.*

The Scots-Irish

As the British Empire spread its dominion across the seas in the seventeenth and eighteenth centuries, great masses of people poured into its ever-widening realms. Their migration unfolded in stages. They journeyed from farms to towns, from towns to great cities such as London and Bristol, and eventually from the seaports to Ireland, the Caribbean, and North America. Among these intrepid wanderers, few were more restless than the Scots-Irish, the settlers of the first American West. Never feeling at home in the British Empire, these perennial outsiders always headed for its most distant outposts. They migrated first from their native Scottish Lowlands to Northern Ireland and from there to the New World. But even in North America, the Scots-Irish remained on the periphery, ever distancing themselves from the reach of the English crown and the Church of England.

The Scottish migration from Scotland itself was driven by severe poverty. Always forced to struggle with a harsh and unyielding land, poorer Scots were oppressed further in the 1600s by merciless rent increases at the hands of the landowning lairds. Adding insult to injury, the British authorities repeatedly persecuted the Presbyterian Scots, squeezing taxes from their barren purses to support the hated Church of England.

Not surprisingly, then, some 200,000 Scots immigrated to neighboring Ireland in the 1600s. So great was the exodus that Protestant Scots eventually outnumbered Catholic natives in the several northern Irish counties that compose the province of Ulster. But soon the Scots discovered that their migration had not freed them from their ancient woes. Their Irish landlords raised rents just as ruthlessly as their Scottish lairds had done. Under such punishing pressures, waves of these already once-transplanted Scots, now known as Scots-Irish, fled again, this time to America.

Most debarked in Pennsylvania, seeking the religious tolerance and abundant land of William Penn's commonwealth. But these unquiet people did not stay put for long. They fanned out from Philadelphia into the farmlands of western Pennsylvania. Blocked temporarily by the Allegheny Mountains, they migrated south along the backbone of the Appalachian range, slowly filling the backcountry of Virginia, the Carolinas, and Georgia.

Almost every Scots-Irish community, however isolated or impermanent, maintained a Presbyterian church. Religion was the bond that yoked these otherwise fiercely independent folk. In backcountry towns, churches were erected before law courts, and clerics were pounding their pulpits before civil authorities had the chance to raise their gavels. But despite their intense faith, the Scots-Irish were not theocrats or advocates of religious rule. Their bitter struggles with the Church of England made them stubborn opponents of established religions in the United States, just as their seething resentment against the king of England ensured that they would be well represented among the Patriots in the American Revolution.

■ Georgia governor James Oglethorpe, in Scottish attire, visits Scottish settlers at New Inverness, Georgia.

made their fortunes as military suppliers in the colonial wars, roosted regally atop the social ladder. They sported imported clothing and dined at tables laid with English china and gleaming silverware. Prominent individuals came to be seated in churches and schools according to their social rank.

The plague of war also created a class of widows and orphans, who became dependent for their survival on charity. Both Philadelphia and New York built **almshouses** in the 1730s to care for the destitute. Yet the numbers of poor people remained tiny compared with the numbers in England, where about a third of the population lived in squalor.

In the New England countryside the descendants of the original settlers faced more limited prospects than had their pioneering forebears. As families grew and existing landholdings were repeatedly divided, the average size of farms shrank drastically. Younger sons as well as daughters were forced to hire out as wage laborers. By 1750 Boston contained a large number of homeless poor, who were supported by public charity and forced to wear a large red "P" on their clothing.

In the South the power of the great planters continued to be bolstered by their disproportionate ownership of slaves. Wealth was concentrated in the hands of the largest slaveowners, widening the gap between the prosperous **gentry** and the "poor whites," who were more and more likely to become **tenant farmers.** In all the colonies the ranks of the lower classes were further swelled by the continuing stream of indentured servants.

Far less fortunate than the voluntary indentured servants were the paupers and convicts involuntarily shipped to America. Altogether, about fifty thousand "jayle birds"—including robbers, rapists, and murderers—were dumped on the colonies by the London authorities. But many of the convicts were the unfortunate victims of a viciously unfair British **penal code,** and some eventually became highly respectable citizens.

Least fortunate of all, of course, were the black slaves. Oppressed and downtrodden, the slaves were America's closest approximation to Europe's volatile lower classes, and fears of black rebellion plagued the white colonists. Some colonial legislatures, notably South Carolina's in 1760, attempted to restrict or halt the importation of slaves, but British authorities vetoed all such efforts. Thomas Jefferson, himself a slaveholder, assailed the British **vetoes** in an early draft of the Declaration of Independence, but was forced to withdraw the proposed clause by a torrent of protest from southern slaveholders.

almshouses *A home for the poor, supported by charity or public funds.*

gentry *Landowners of substantial property, social standing, and leisure, but not titled nobility.*

tenant farmer(s) *One who rents rather than owns land.*

penal code *The body of criminal laws specifying offenses and prescribing punishments.*

vetoes *The executive power to prevent acts passed by the legislature from becoming law.*

apprentice(s) *A person who works under a master to acquire instruction in a trade or profession.*

Primary source
Virginia Case Involving Runaway Indentured Servants
college.hmco.com/pic/kennedybrief7e

Clergy, Physicians, and Jurists

Most honored of the professions was the Christian ministry. In 1775 the clergy wielded less influence than in the early days of Massachusetts, when piety had burned more warmly. But they still occupied a position of high prestige.

Most physicians, on the other hand, were poorly trained and not highly esteemed. Not until 1765 was the first medical school established, although European centers attracted some students. Aspiring young doctors served for a while as **apprentices** to older practitioners and were then turned loose on their "victims." Bleeding was a favorite and frequently fatal remedy; when the physician was not available, a barber was often summoned.

Epidemics were a constant nightmare. Especially dreaded was smallpox, which afflicted one out of five persons, including the heavily pock-marked George Washington. A crude form of inoculation was introduced in 1721 despite the objections of many physicians and some of the clergy, who opposed tampering with the will of God. Powdered dried toad was a favorite prescription for smallpox. Diphtheria was also a deadly killer, especially of young people. One epidemic in the 1730s took the lives of thousands.

At first the law profession was not favorably regarded. In this pioneering society of farmers and manual laborers, the parties to a dispute often presented their own cases in court. Lawyers were commonly regarded as noisy windbags or troublemaking rogues; an early Connecticut law classed them with drunkards and brothel keepers.

Primary source
Cotton Mather on the Education of His Children
college.hmco.com/pic/kennedybrief7e

Workaday America

Agriculture was the leading industry, involving about 90 percent of the people. Tobacco continued to be the staple crop in Maryland and Virginia, though wheat cultivation also spread in the Chesapeake, often on lands depleted by the excessive cultivation of tobacco. The fertile middle ("bread") colonies produced large quantities of grain, and by 1759 New York alone was exporting eighty thousand barrels of flour a year. Seemingly the farmer had only to tickle the soil with a hoe and it would laugh with a harvest. Overall, Americans probably enjoyed a higher average standard of living than the masses of any country in history up to that time.

Fishing (including whaling), though ranking in scale far below agriculture, was rewarding. Pursued in all the colonies, this harvesting of the sea was a major industry in New England, which exported smelly shiploads of dried cod to the Catholic countries of Europe. The fishing fleet also stimulated shipbuilding and served as a nursery for the seamen who manned the navy and merchant marine.

Yankee seamen were famous in many climes not only as skilled mariners but as tightfisted traders. They provisioned the Caribbean sugar islands with food and forest products. They hauled Spanish and Portuguese gold, wine, and oranges to London, to be exchanged for industrial goods, which were then sold for a juicy profit in America.

The so-called triangular trade was infamously profitable, though small in relation to total colonial commerce. A skipper would leave a New England port with a cargo of rum and sail to the Gold Coast of Africa. Bartering the fiery liquor with African chiefs for captured African slaves, he would proceed to the West Indies with his suffocating cargo sardined below deck. There he would exchange the slaves for molasses, which he would then carry to New England, where it would be distilled into rum. He would then repeat the trip, making a handsome profit on each leg of the triangle.

Manufacturing in the colonies was of only secondary importance, although there was a surprising variety of small enterprises. Huge quantities of "kill devil" rum were distilled in Rhode Island and Massachusetts, and even some of the "elect of the Lord" developed an overfondness for it. Beaver hats, iron, and clothing, spun and woven by women in the household, constituted other colonial manufactures. As in all pioneering countries, strong-backed laborers and skilled craftspeople were scarce and highly prized.

Lumbering was perhaps the most important single manufacturing activity. Countless cartloads of virgin timber were consumed by shipbuilders, who by 1770 were sending four hundred new vessels splashing into the sea each year. Colonial naval stores—such as tar, pitch, resin, and turpentine—were highly valued. Towering trees, ideal as masts for His Majesty's Navy, were marked with the king's broad arrow for future use. The luckless colonist who was caught cutting down this reserved timber was subject to a fine.

Americans held an important flank of a thriving, many-sided Atlantic economy by the dawn of the eighteenth century. Yet strains appeared in this complex network as early as the 1730s. Fast-breeding Americans demanded more and more British products—yet the slow-growing British population early reached the saturation point for absorbing imports from America. How, then, could the colonists sell the goods to make the money to buy what they wanted in Britain? The answer was obvious: by seeking foreign (non-British) markets.

Online Study Center
Interactive map
Atlantic Trade Routes
college.hmco.com/pic/kennedybrief7e

By the eve of the Revolution the bulk of Chesapeake tobacco was filling pipes in France and other European countries, though it passed through the hands of British re-exporters, who took a slice of the profits for themselves. More important was the trade with the West Indies, especially the French islands. West Indian purchases of North American timber and foodstuffs provided the crucial cash for the colonists to continue to make their own purchases in Britain. But in 1733, bowing to pressure from influential British West Indian planters, Parliament passed the Molasses Act, aimed at squelching North American trade with the French West Indies. If successful, this scheme would have struck a crippling blow to American

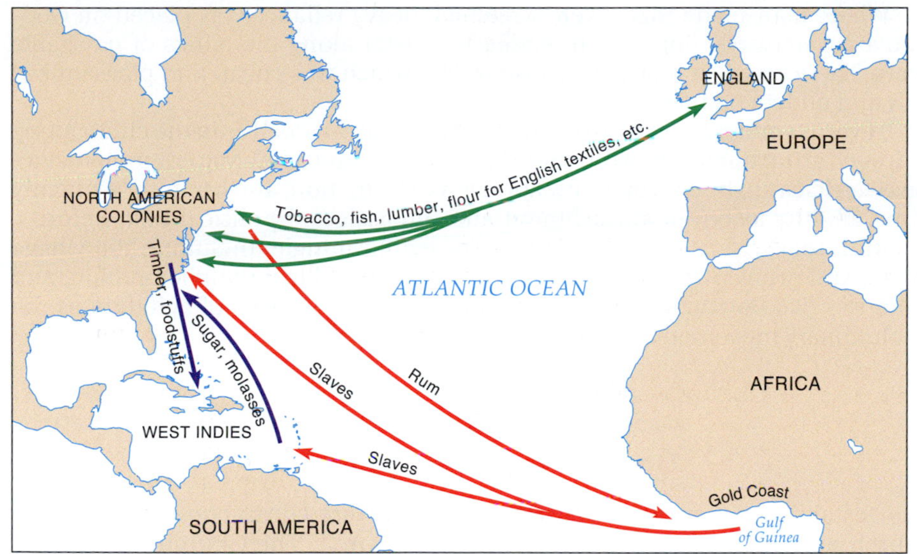

Colonial Trade Patterns, c. 1770 Future president John Adams noted about this time that "the commerce of the West Indies is a part of the American system of commerce. They can neither do without us, nor we without them. The Creator has placed us upon the globe in such a situation that we have occasion for each other."

international trade and to the colonists' standard of living. American merchants responded by bribing and smuggling their way around the law. Thus was foreshadowed the impending imperial crisis, when headstrong Americans would revolt rather than submit to the dictates of a far-off Parliament apparently bent on destroying their very livelihood.

Horsepower and Sailpower

As a sprawling and sparsely populated pioneer community, America was cursed with oppressive problems of transportation. Not until the 1700s did roads connect even the major cities. The few dirt thoroughfares that did exist were treacherously deficient, throwing up clouds of dust in summer and turning into quagmires of mud in winter. Stagecoach travelers braved additional dangers such as fallen trees, rickety bridges, carriage overturns, and runaway horses. Travel was so slow that it actually took twenty-nine days after the Fourth of July in 1776 for the news of the Declaration of Independence to reach Charleston from Philadelphia.

Estimated Religious Census, 1775

Name	Number	Chief Locale
Congregationalists	575,000	New England
Anglicans	500,000	N.Y., South
Presbyterians	410,000	Frontier
German churches (incl. Lutheran)	200,000	Pa.
Dutch Reformed	75,000	N.Y., N.J.
Quakers	40,000	Pa., N.J., Del.
Baptists	25,000	R.I., Pa., N.J., Del.
Roman Catholics	25,000	Md., Pa.
Methodists	5,000	Scattered
Jews	2,000	N.Y., R.I.
EST. TOTAL MEMBERSHIP	1,857,000	
EST. TOTAL POPULATION	2,493,000	
PERCENTAGE CHURCH MEMBERS	74%	

Where man-made roads were wretched, heavy reliance was placed on God-grooved waterways. Population tended to cluster along the banks of navigable rivers. There was also much coastwise traffic, which was cheap and pleasant but slow and undependable.

Taverns sprang up along the main routes of travel as well as in the cities. Along with such attractions as bowling alleys, pool tables, and gambling equipment, taverns were clearinghouses of information, misinformation, and rumor—frequently stimulated by alcoholic refreshment and impassioned political talk. Before a cheerful, roaring log fire all social classes would mingle, including the village loafers and drunks. Taverns were important in crystallizing public opinion, and alehouses like Boston's Green Dragon proved to be hotbeds of agitation as the revolutionary movement gathered momentum.

Dominant Denominations

Two "established," or tax-supported, churches were conspicuous in 1775: the Church of England and the Congregational Church. The Church of England, the Anglican Church, was the official faith in Georgia, North and South Carolina, Virginia, Maryland, and part of New York. British officials made vigorous attempts to impose it on additional colonies but ran into a stone wall of opposition. On the eve of the American Revolution, there was serious talk of creating a resident Anglican bishop in North America, but this scheme was also violently opposed by non-Anglicans, who feared a tightening of the royal reins. This controversy poured holy oil on the smoldering fires of rebellion.

Secure, self-satisfied, and often worldly, the Anglican Church itself fell distressingly short of its promise. So dismal was the reputation of the Anglican clergy in seventeenth-century Virginia that the College of William and Mary was founded in 1693 to train a better class of clerics.

The influential Congregational Church, the successor of the Puritans, was formally established in all the New England colonies except independent-minded Rhode Island. Presbyterianism, though closely associated with Congregationalism, was never the official church of any colony. Sometimes turning from the Bible to worldly politics, many Congregationalist and Presbyterian ministers of the gospel joined in stirring up opposition to the British crown in the 1760s and 1770s. Presbyterianism, Congregationalism, and rebellion became a neo-trinity. But most Anglican clergymen, aware of which side their tax-provided bread was buttered on, naturally supported their king.

Despite the presence of established churches, religious toleration had made enormous strides in America. Roman Catholics were still generally discriminated against, as in Britain, though the anti-papist laws were less severe and less strictly enforced. In general, people could worship—or not worship—as they pleased.

The Great Awakening

In all the colonial churches, religion was less fervid in the early eighteenth century than it had been a century earlier, when the colonies were first planted. The Puritan churches in particular sagged under the weight of two burdens: their elaborate theological doctrines and their compromising efforts to liberalize membership requirements. Churchgoers increasingly complained about the "dead dogs" who droned out tedious sermons from the pulpit. Some ministers, on the other hand, worried that their parishioners had gone soft and no longer embraced orthodox Calvinism. These twin trends toward clerical rigidity and lay indifference were sapping the spiritual vitality of many denominations.

revival *In religion, a movement of renewed enthusiasm and commitment, often accompanied by special meetings or vigorous evangelical and mission activity.*

The stage was thus set for a rousing religious **revival.** Known as the Great Awakening, it exploded in the 1730s and 1740s and swept through the colonies like a fire through prairie grass. The Awakening was first ignited in Northampton, Massachusetts, by a tall, delicate, and intellectual pastor, Jonathan Edwards. Perhaps the deepest theological mind ever nurtured in America, Edwards proclaimed with burning righteousness the need for complete dependence on God's grace. His preaching style was learned and closely reasoned, but his stark doctrines sparked a warmly sympathetic reaction among his parishioners in 1734.

Four years later, the itinerant English parson George Whitefield loosed a different style of evangelical preaching on America and touched off a conflagration of religious ardor that revolutionized the spiritual life of the colonies. A former alehouse attendant, Whitefield was a magnificent orator whose voice boomed sonorously over thousands of enthralled listeners in the open fields where he preached. Triumphantly touring the colonies, Whitefield displayed an eloquence that reduced Jonathan Edwards to tears and even caused the skeptical and thrifty Benjamin Franklin to empty his pockets into the collection plate. During Whitefield's roaring revival meetings, countless sinners professed conversion, and hundreds of the "saved" groaned, shrieked, or rolled in the snow from religious excitation. Soon, American imitators took up Whitefield's electrifying new style of preaching and shook enormous audiences with emotional appeals.

George Whitefield Preaching Americans of both genders and all races and regions were spellbound by Whitefield's fervent oratory.

Orthodox clergymen, known as "old lights," were deeply skeptical of the emotionalism and the theatrical antics of the revivalists. But "new light" ministers defended the Awakening for its role in revitalizing American religion. The Awakening left many lasting effects. Its emphasis on direct, emotive spirituality seriously undermined the older clergy, whose authority had derived from their education and erudition. The schisms that the Awakening set off in many denominations increased the numbers and competitiveness of American churches. The Awakening also encouraged a fresh wave of missionary work among the Indians and black slaves, many of whom attended open-air revivals. It also led to the founding of "new light" centers of higher learning such as Dartmouth, Brown, Rutgers, and Princeton. Perhaps most significant, the Great Awakening was the first spontaneous mass movement of the American people. By breaking down sectional boundaries and denominational lines, it contributed to the growing sense Americans had of themselves as a single people united by a common history and shared experience.

Schools and Colleges

Only slowly and painfully did American colonists break away from the English idea that education should be reserved for the aristocratic few. In Puritan New England, education was dominated by the Congregational Church, which stressed the need for Bible reading to make good Christians. Education, principally for boys, thus flourished almost from the outset in New England, which boasted an impressive number of graduates from the British universities, especially Cambridge. New Englanders, at a relatively early date, established primary and secondary schools, which varied widely in the quality of instruction and in the length of time their doors remained open each year.

Fairly adequate elementary schools were also hammering knowledge into the heads of reluctant "scholars" in the middle colonies and in the South. Some of these institutions were tax supported; others were privately operated. The South, with its white and black populations diffused over wide areas, was severely handicapped in attempting to establish an effective school system. Wealthy families leaned heavily on private tutors.

John Adams (c. 1736–1826) the future second president, wrote to his wife:

"The education of our children is never out of my mind. . . . I must study politics and war that my sons may have the liberty to study mathematics and philosophy. My sons ought to study mathematics and philosophy, geography, natural history, naval architecture, navigation, commerce, and agriculture, in order to give their children a right to study painting, poetry, music, architecture, statuary, tapestry, and porcelain."

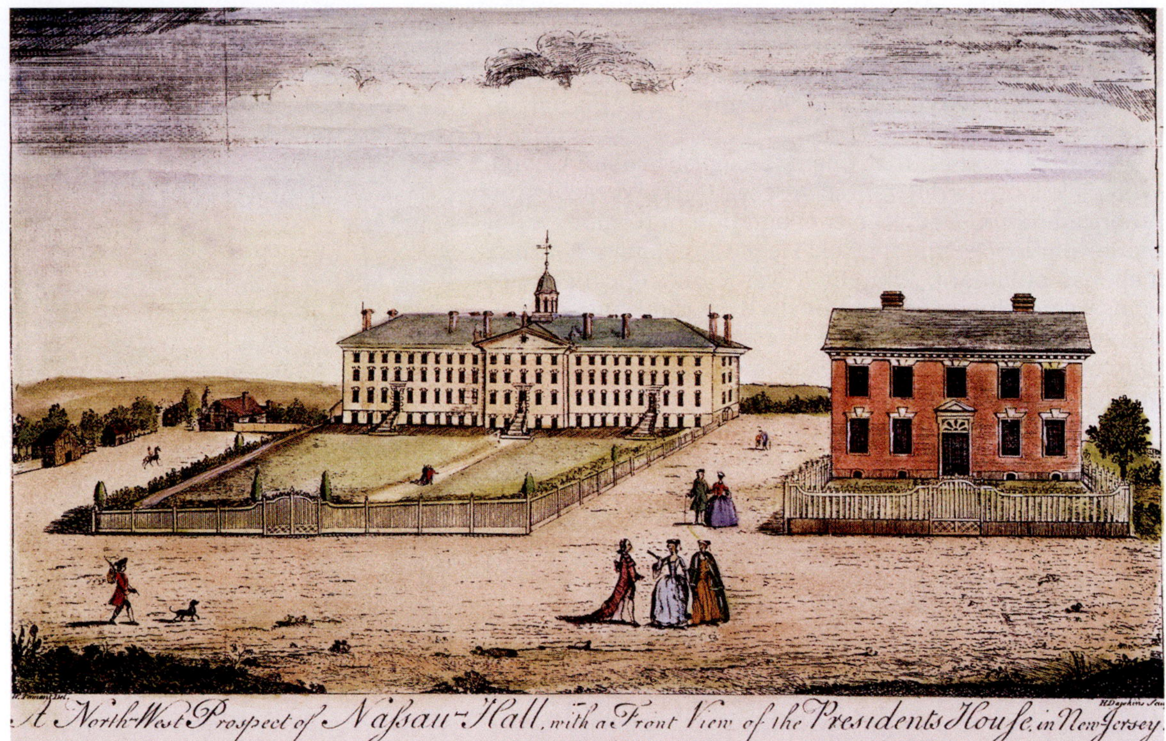

The College of New Jersey at Princeton, 1764 Later known as Princeton University, it was chartered in 1746 by the Presbyterian Synod, though open to students of all religious persuasions. The fourth college to be founded in British North America, it met in Elizabeth and Newark, New Jersey, until a gift of ten acres of land precipitated a move to Princeton in 1756. All classes were held in the large building, Nassau Hall. Here the Continental Congress met for three months during the summer of 1783, making Princeton for a short time the capital of the nation. This copper engraving, based on a drawing by one of Princeton's earliest students, was part of a series of college views that reflected colonial Americans' growing pride in institutions of higher learning.

Online Study Center

Primary source
Portrait of a Boston Merchant and His Wife
college.hmco.com/pic/kennedybrief7e

Online Study Center

Primary source
Artist in His Museum
college.hmco.com/pic/kennedybrief7e

Online Study Center

Primary source
Eighteenth-Century Home: Exterior View
college.hmco.com/pic/kennedybrief7e

Online Study Center

Primary source
Eighteenth-Century Home: Interior
college.hmco.com/pic/kennedybrief7e

The general atmosphere in the colonial schools and colleges continued grim and gloomy. Most of the emphasis was on religion and the classical languages, Latin and Greek. Instruction was poor, independent thinking was discouraged, and severe discipline was often administered with a switch cut from a birch tree. But by 1750 a distinct trend had emerged toward "live" languages and other modern subjects in the nine small colonial colleges. A significant contribution was made by Benjamin Franklin, who played a major role in launching what became the University of Pennsylvania, the first American college free from denominational control.

A Provincial Culture

When it came to art and culture, colonial Americans were still in thrall to European tastes, especially British. The simplicity of pioneering life had not yet bred many homespun patrons of the arts, nor artists either. One aspiring painter, John Trumbull of Connecticut (1756–1843), was discouraged in his youth by his father's chilling remark, "Connecticut is not Athens." Trumbull, as well as his talented artistic contemporaries Charles Willson Peale (1741–1827), Benjamin West (1738–1820), and John Copley (1738–1815), all eventually succeeded in their ambition to become famous painters. But they had to go to Britain to complete their training and find patrons to support them.

Colonial architecture, too, was largely imported from the Old World. The red-brick Georgian style, so common in the pre-Revolutionary decades, was introduced about 1720 and is best exemplified by the beauty of now-restored Williamsburg, Virginia.

Colonial literature, like art, was generally undistinguished, but a few outstanding individuals produced original and enduring work. Precocious black poet Phillis Wheatley (c. 1753–1784) was an uneducated slave girl who was brought to Boston at age eight and then taken to London when she was twenty. She overcame her disadvantages and produced polished poems that revealed the influence of Alexander Pope.

Versatile Benjamin Franklin, often called "the first civilized American," also shone as a literary light. His autobiography was his greatest literary achievement, but he was best known to his contemporaries for *Poor Richard's Almanack,* which he edited from 1732 to 1758. Emphasizing the homespun virtues of thrift, industry, and common sense, "Poor Richard" was most famous for his pithy sayings: "Plough deep while sluggards sleep"; "Fish and visitors stink in three days." *Poor Richard's* was well known in Europe and was more widely read in America than anything except the Bible. Dispensing witty advice to old and young alike, Franklin had an incalculable influence in shaping the American character.

Primary source
Poor Richard's Almanack
college.hmco.com/pic/kennedybrief7e

Franklin's scientific efforts, including his spectacular kite-flying experiments with electricity, made him the colonies' only first-rate scientist and won him numerous honors in Europe. Among the inventions produced by his practical mind were bifocal spectacles, the Franklin stove, and the lightning rod.

Pioneer Presses

Stump-grubbing Americans were generally too poor to buy quantities of books and too busy to read them. A few fine private libraries, however, like that of the Byrd family in Virginia, could be found. Bustling Benjamin Franklin established in Philadelphia the first privately supported circulating library, and by 1776 there were about fifty public libraries and collections supported by subscription.

On the eve of the Revolution there were about forty newspapers, chiefly weeklies that consisted of a single large sheet folded once. The "news," especially from overseas, often lagged many weeks behind the event, and the papers devoted much column space to somber essays. Nevertheless, newspapers proved to be a powerful agency for airing colonial grievances and rallying opposition to British control.

A celebrated legal case in 1734–1735 involved John Peter Zenger, a newspaper printer. Significantly, the case arose in New York, reflecting the tumultuous give-and-take of politics in the middle colonies, where so many different ethnic groups jostled against one another. Zenger's newspaper had assailed the corrupt royal governor. Charged with seditious libel, the accused was hauled into court, where he was defended by a former indentured servant, now a distinguished Philadelphia lawyer, Andrew Hamilton. Zenger argued that he had printed the truth, but the royal chief justice ruled that the mere fact of printing, regardless of the truth, was enough to convict. But the jury, swayed by Hamilton's eloquence, defied the bewigged judge and daringly returned a verdict of not guilty. Cheers burst from the spectators.

The Zenger decision was a banner achievement for freedom of the press. It pointed the way to the kind of open public discussion required by the diverse society that colonial New York already was and that all America was to become. Although contrary to existing law and not immediately accepted by other judges and juries, in time the ruling helped establish the doctrine that true statements about public officials could not be prosecuted as libel. Newspapers were thus eventually free to print responsible criticisms of powerful officials, though full freedom of the press was unknown during the pre-Revolutionary era.

Andrew Hamilton (c. 1676–1741) concluded his eloquent plea in the Zenger case with these words:

"The question before the court and you, gentlemen of the jury, is not of small nor private concern. It is not the cause of a poor printer, nor of New York alone, which you are now trying. No! It may, in its consequence, affect every freeman that lives under a British government on the main [land] of America. It is the best cause. It is the cause of liberty."

The Great Game of Politics

American colonists may have been backward in natural or physical science, but they were making noteworthy contributions to political science.

The thirteen colonial governments took a variety of forms. By 1775 eight of the colonies had royal governors appointed by the king. Three—Maryland, Pennsylvania, and Delaware—were under proprietors who themselves chose the governors. And two—Connecticut and Rhode Island—elected their own governors under self-governing charters.

Practically every colony utilized a two-house legislative body. The upper house, or council, was normally appointed by the crown in the royal colonies and by the proprietor in the proprietary colonies. It was chosen by the voters in the self-governing colonies. The lower house, as the popular branch, was elected by the people—or rather by those who owned enough property to qualify as voters. In several of the colonies, the backcountry settlers were seriously underrepresented, and they hated the ruling colonial clique perhaps more than they did kingly authority. Legislatures, in which the people enjoyed direct representation, voted such taxes as they deemed necessary for the expenses of colonial government. Self-taxation through representation was a precious privilege that Americans had come to cherish above most others.

Governors appointed by the king were generally able men. Some, unfortunately, were incompetent or corrupt—broken-down politicians badly in need of jobs. The worst of the group was probably impoverished Lord Cornbury, first cousin of Queen Anne, who was made governor of New York and New Jersey in 1702. He proved to be a drunkard, a spendthrift, a grafter, an embezzler, a religious bigot, and a vain fool. He was also accused (probably inaccurately) of dressing as a woman. Even the best appointees had trouble with the colonial legislatures, basically because every royal governor embodied a bothersome transatlantic authority some three thousand miles away.

The colonial assemblies found various ways to assert their authority and independence. Some of them employed the trick of withholding the governor's salary unless he yielded to their wishes. Because he was normally in need of money, the power of the purse usually forced him to terms.

Administration at the local level was also varied. County government remained the rule in the plantation South; town-meeting government predominated in New England; and a modification of the two developed in the middle colonies. In the town meeting, with its open discussion and open voting, direct democracy functioned at its best. In this unrivaled cradle of self-government, Americans learned to cherish their privileges and exercise their duties as citizens of the New World commonwealths.

Yet the ballot was by no means a birthright. Religious or property qualifications for voting, with even stiffer qualifications for officeholding, existed in all the colonies in 1775. The privileged upper classes, fearful of democratic excesses, were unwilling to grant the ballot to every "biped of the forest." Perhaps half of the adult white males were thus disfranchised. But because of the ease of acquiring land and thus satisfying property requirements, the right to vote was not beyond the reach of most industrious and enterprising colonists.

By 1775 America was not yet a true democracy—socially, economically, or politically. But it was far more democratic than Britain and the European continent. Colonial institutions were giving freer rein to the democratic ideals of tolerance, education, equality of economic opportunity, freedom of speech, freedom of the press, freedom of assembly, and representative government. And these democratic seeds, planted in rich soil, were to bring forth a lush harvest in later years.

Colonial Folkways

Everyday life in the colonies may now seem glamorous, especially as reflected in antique shops. But judged by modern standards, it was drab and tedious. For most people, the labor was heavy and constant—from "can see" to "can't see."

Basic comforts now taken for granted were lacking. Food was plentiful, though the diet could be coarse and monotonous. Churches were unheated except for charcoal foot-warmers that the women carried. During the frigid New England winters, the preaching of hellfire may not have seemed altogether unattractive. There was no running water in the houses, no plumbing, and probably not a single bathtub in all colonial America. Candles and whale-oil lamps provided faint and flickering illumination. Garbage disposal was primitive. Long-snouted hogs customarily ranged the streets to consume refuse, while buzzards, protected by law, flapped greedily over tidbits of waste.

Amusement was eagerly pursued where time and custom permitted. Militia "musters," house-raisings, quilting bees, funerals, and weddings everywhere afforded opportunities for social gatherings, which customarily involved the swilling of much strong liquor. Winter sports were common in the North, whereas the South favored hunting, horse racing, dancing, theater, card playing, and cockfighting. The agile George Washington, not surprisingly, was equally skilled at riding and dancing.

Lotteries were universally approved, even by the clergy, and were used to raise money for churches and colleges, including Harvard. Holidays were celebrated everywhere, but Christmas was frowned upon in New England as an offensive reminder of "Popery." Thanksgiving Day came to be a truly American festival, for it combined giving thanks to God with an opportunity for jollification, gorging, and guzzling.

By the mid-eighteenth century Britain's North American colonies, despite their differences, revealed some striking similarities. All were basically English in language and customs and Protestant in religion, while the widespread presence of other peoples and faiths compelled every colony to cede at least some degree of ethnic and religious toleration. Compared with contemporary Europe, the colonies all afforded unusual opportunities for economic advancement and a measure of self-government, though by no means complete democracy. British North America by 1775 looked like a patchwork quilt—each section slightly different but stitched together by common origins, common ways of life, and common beliefs in toleration, economic development, and, above all, self-rule. Fatefully, all the colonies were also separated from the seat of imperial authority by a vast ocean moat some three thousand miles wide. These simple facts of shared history, culture, and geography set the stage for the colonists' struggle to unite as an independent people.

Chapter Summary

By 1775 there were thirty-two British colonies in the Americas, but only thirteen eventually revolted to form the United States of America. These latter territories were inhabited by a rapidly expanding, youthful population of about two million whites and half a million blacks. The white population was a melting pot of diverse ethnic groups, with Germans and Scots-Irish the largest non-English contingent.

Compared with Europe, America was a land of equality and opportunity (for whites); but relative to the seventeenth-century colonies, there was a rising economic hierarchy and increasing social complexity. Ninety percent of Americans worked in agriculture. But a growing class of wealthy planters and merchants appeared at the top of the social pyramid, in contrast with slaves and "jayle birds" forcibly shipped from Britain, who formed a visible lower class. The large "middle class" of whites consisted mostly of small farmers, along with artisans and tradespeople in the few small cities.

By the early eighteenth century, the established New England Congregational church was losing religious fervor. The Great Awakening, sparked by fiery preachers like Jonathan Edwards and George Whitefield, spread a new style of emotional worship that revived religious zeal. While the Awakening led to greater religious diversity, it also created a greater sense of a shared "American" identity across the colonies. Colonial education and culture were generally undistinguished, although science and journalism displayed some vigor. Politics was everywhere an important activity, as representative colonial assemblies battled with politically appointed governors from Britain. Despite their differences, the thirteen colonies already shared something of a common "American way of life."

VARYING VIEWPOINTS

Colonial America: Communities of Conflict or Consensus?

The earliest historians of colonial society portrayed close-knit, homogeneous, and hierarchical communities. Richard Bushman in *From Puritan to Yankee* (1967) challenged that traditional view. He described colonial New England as an expanding, open society in which the colonists gradually lost the religious discipline and social structure of the founding generations. Rhys Isaac viewed the Great Awakening in the South as similar evidence of erosion in the social constraints and deference that once held colonial society together.

Some scholars dispute that a loss of common faith and morals undermined colonial communities. Christine Heyrmann in particular argued in *Commerce and Culture* (1984) that the decline of traditional mores was overstated and that religious beliefs and commercial activities coexisted throughout the late seventeenth and early eighteenth centuries. Similarly, colonial historian Jack Greene has suggested that the obsession with the decline of deference obscures the fact that colonies outside New England, like Virginia and Maryland, actually experienced a consolidation of religious and social authority throughout the seventeenth and eighteenth centuries, becoming more hierarchical and paternalistic, not less.

Since the 1970s, some historians have also attacked the traditional idea that New England was the home of American freedom and that the South spawned hierarchical, aristocratic communities. They argue that not only did the South produce many of the founders—Washington, Jefferson, and Madison—but that republican principles were actually strongest in Virginia. Some scholars, notably Edmund S. Morgan in *American Slavery, American Freedom* (1975), consider the willingness of wealthy planters to concede the equality and freedom of all white males a device to ensure racial solidarity and to mute class conflict.

Few historians still argue that the colonies offered boundless opportunities for inhabitants, white or black. Whether one accepts Morgan's arguments that "Americans bought their independence with slave labor" or those interpretations that point to the rising social conflict between whites as the salient characteristic of colonial society on the eve of the Revolution, the once-common assumption that America was a world of equality and consensus no longer reigns undisputed. Yet because one's life chances were still unquestionably better in America than in Europe, immigrants who viewed America as a land of opportunity continued to pour in.

The Duel for North America

1608–1763

A TORCH LIGHTED IN THE FORESTS OF AMERICA SET ALL EUROPE IN CONFLAGRATION.

VOLTAIRE, C. 1756

Chapter Outline

- New France
- Anglo-French Colonial Rivalries
- The French and Indian War, 1754–1763
- The Ousting of France from North America, 1763
- The Consequences of War
- Makers of America: The French

As the seventeenth century neared its sunset, a titanic struggle was shaping up for mastery of the North American continent. The contest involved three Old World nations—Britain (England),* France, and Spain—and it unavoidably swept up Native American peoples as well. From 1688 to 1763, four bitter wars convulsed Europe. All four of those conflicts were world wars. Fought on the waters and on the soil of two hemispheres, they amounted to a death struggle for domination in Europe as well as in the New World. Counting these first four clashes, nine world wars have been waged since 1688. The American people, whether as British subjects or as American citizens, proved unable to stay out of a single one of them. And one of those wars—known as the Seven Years' War in Europe and the French and Indian War in America—set the stage for America's independence.

Focus Questions

1. **What were the fundamental causes of the imperial conflict between France and Britain for control of North America?**
2. **What was the social and political character of New France, and how did it compare with Britain's North American colonies?**
3. **How were eighteenth-century political and military events in North America shaped by rivalries on the larger European stage?**
4. **Why did Britain finally win the French and Indian War, and what role did the American colonists play in the victory?**
5. **How did the British victory in the Seven Years' War ironically become one of the precipitating causes of the American Revolution?**

*After the political union of England and Scotland in 1707, the nation's official name became "Great Britain."

France Finds a Foothold in Canada

domestic *Concerning the internal affairs of a country.*

edict *A publicly announced order or law, especially one issued unilaterally by an authoritarian government, requiring immediate obedience.*

peasants *A farmer or agricultural laborer, often owing payment or services to a landlord and sometimes legally tied to the land.*

coureurs des bois *French-Canadian fur trappers; literally, "runners of the woods."*

voyageurs *French-Canadian explorers, adventurers, and traders.*

ecological (ecology) *The mutual sustaining relationships between biological organisms and their environment.*

Like England and Holland, France was a latecomer in the scramble for New World real estate, and for basically the same reasons. It was convulsed during the 1500s by foreign wars and **domestic** strife, including frightful clashes and sometimes massacres between Roman Catholics and Protestant Huguenots.

A new era dawned in 1598 when the **Edict** of Nantes, issued by the crown, granted limited toleration to French Protestants (Huguenots). Religious wars ceased, and in the new century France blossomed into the mightiest and most feared nation in Europe.

After rocky beginnings, success finally rewarded the exertions of France in the New World. In 1608, the year after the founding of Jamestown, the permanent beginnings of a vast empire were established at Quebec, a granite sentinel commanding the St. Lawrence River. The leading figure was Samuel de Champlain, an intrepid soldier and explorer whose energy and leadership fairly earned him the title "Father of New France."

Champlain entered into friendly relations—a fateful friendship—with the nearby Huron Indian tribes. At their request, he joined them in battle against their foes, the federated Iroquois tribes of the upper New York area. Two volleys from the "lightning sticks" of the whites routed the Iroquois, who left behind three dead and one wounded. France, to its sorrow, thus earned the lasting enmity of the Iroquois tribes, who thereafter hampered French penetration of the Ohio Valley, sometimes ravaging French settlements, and frequently serving as allies of the British in the prolonged struggle for supremacy on the continent.

The government of New France (Canada) finally fell under the direct control of the king after various commercial companies had faltered or failed. This royal regime was almost completely autocratic. The people elected no representative assemblies, as the English colonies did; nor did they enjoy the right of trial by jury.

The population of Catholic New France grew at a listless pace. As late as 1750 only sixty thousand or so whites inhabited New France. Landowning French **peasants,** unlike the dispossessed English tenant farmers who embarked for the British colonies, had little economic motive to move. Protestant Huguenots, who might have had a religious motive to migrate, were denied a refuge in this raw colony. The French government, in any case, favored its Caribbean island colonies, rich in sugar and rum, over the snow-cloaked wilderness of Canada.

New France Fans Out

New France did contain one valuable resource: the beaver. To adorn the heads of fashionable Europeans, French fur trappers ranged over the woods and waterways of North America in pursuit of the thick-furred beavers. These colorful ***coureurs des bois*** (runners of the woods) were also runners of risks—two-fisted drinkers, free spenders, free livers and lovers. They littered the land with scores of place names, including Baton Rouge (red stick), Terre Haute (high land), Des Moines (some monks), and Grand Teton (big breast).

Singing, paddle-swinging French **voyageurs** also recruited Indians into the fur business. But the Indians were decimated by the white man's diseases and debauched by his alcohol. Slaughtering beaver by the boatload also violated many Indian religious beliefs and sadly demonstrated the shattering effect that contact with Europeans wreaked on traditional Indian ways of life.

Pursuing the sharp-toothed beaver ever deeper into the heart of the continent, French trappers and their Indian partners covered amazing distances. They trekked in a huge arc across the Great Lakes, into present-day Saskatchewan and Manitoba, along the valleys of the Platte, the Arkansas, and the Missouri, west to the Rockies, and south to the border of Spanish Texas. In the process, they all but extinguished the beaver population in many areas, inflicting incalculable **ecological** damage.

Chronology

1598	Edict of Nantes.
1608	Champlain colonizes Quebec for France.
1682	La Salle explores Mississippi River to the Gulf of Mexico.
1689-1697	King William's War (War of the League of Augsburg).
1702-1713	Queen Anne's War (War of Spanish Succession).
1718	French found New Orleans.
1739	War of Jenkins's Ear.
1740-1748	King George's War (War of Austrian Succession).
1754	Washington battles French on frontier. Albany Congress.
1754-1763	Seven Years' War (French and Indian War).
1755	Braddock's defeat.
1757	Pitt emerges as leader of British government.
1759	Battle of Quebec.
1763	Peace of Paris. Pontiac's uprising. Proclamation of 1763.

French Catholic missionaries, notably the Jesuits, labored zealously to save the Indians for Christ and from the fur trappers. Some of the Jesuit missionaries, their efforts scorned, suffered unspeakable tortures at the hands of the Indians. But though they made few permanent converts, the Jesuits played a vital role as explorers and geographers.

Other explorers sought neither souls nor fur, but empire. To check Spanish penetration into the region around the Gulf of Mexico, ambitious Robert La Salle floated down the Mississippi in 1682 to the point where it mingles with the Gulf. Three years later he tried to return to the territory he had named "Louisiana," but he failed to find the Mississippi delta. He landed instead in Spanish Texas and in 1687 was murdered by his **mutinous** men.

Persistent French officials planted several fortified posts in what is now Mississippi and Louisiana, the most important of which was New Orleans (1718). Commanding the mouth of the Mississippi River, this **strategic** semitropical outpost controlled the trade of the huge interior valley, especially the fertile Illinois country. There the French also established forts and trading posts at Vincennes, Cahokia, and Kaskaskia.

mutinous (mutiny) *Revolt by subordinate soldiers or seamen against their commanding officers.*

strategic *Concerning the placement and planned movement of large-scale military forces so as to gain advantage, usually prior to actual engagement with the enemy.*

sallies (sally) *In warfare, very rapid military movements, usually by small units, against an enemy force or position.*

The Clash of Empires

The earliest contests among the European powers for control of North America, the War of the League of Augsburg and the War of Spanish Succession, known to the British colonists respectively as King William's War (1689–1697) and Queen Anne's War (1702–1713), mostly pitted British colonists against the French *coureurs des bois,* with both sides recruiting whatever Indian allies they could. Neither France nor Britain considered America worth the commitment of large detachments of regular troops, so the combatants in these conflicts waged a kind of guerrilla warfare. France's Indian allies ravaged with torch and tomahawk the British colonial frontiers from New York to Massachusetts. Spain, eventually allied with France, probed from its Florida base at outlying South Carolina settlements. For their part, the British colonists failed miserably in **sallies** against Quebec and Montreal but did temporarily seize the stronghold of Port Royal in Acadia (present-day Nova Scotia).

Primary source
Land Division in New Orleans Clearly Shows. . .
college.hmco.com/pic/kennedybrief7e

Chief of the Taensa Indians Receiving La Salle, March 20, 1682, by George Catlin, 1847–1848 (detail) Driven by the dream of a vast North American empire for France, La Salle spent years exploring the Great Lakes region and the valleys of the Illinois and Mississippi Rivers. This scene of his encounter with an Indian chieftain was imaginatively re-created by the nineteenth-century artist George Catlin.

In the Peace of Utrecht (1713), victorious Britain acquired French-populated Acadia and the wintry wastes of Newfoundland and Hudson Bay. These immense tracts pinched the St. Lawrence settlements of France. The British also won limited trading rights in Spanish America, but these later created much friction over smuggling. Ill feeling between Britain and Spain led to war in 1739, when the British Captain Robert Jenkins, whose ear had been sliced off by a Spanish sword, returned to London with a tale of woe on his tongue and a shriveled ear in his hand. The War of Jenkins's Ear was confined to the Caribbean Sea and to the much-buffeted buffer colony of Georgia.

This small-scale scuffle with Spain in America soon merged with the large-scale War of the Austrian Succession in Europe (called King George's War in America). Once again, France allied itself with Spain. And again operating on their own, a rustic force of New Englanders, with the help of the British fleet, captured the reputedly impregnable French fortress of Louisbourg on Cape Breton Island, which commanded the approaches to the St. Lawrence River. When the peace treaty of 1748 handed Louisbourg back to their French foe, the victorious New Englanders were outraged. The glory of their arms seemed tarnished by the wiles of Old World diplomats. Worse still, Louisbourg remained a cocked pistol pointed at the heart of the American continent. France, powerful and unappeased, still clung to its vast holdings in North America.

George Washington Inaugurates War with France

As the dogfight intensified in the New World, the Ohio Valley became the chief bone of contention between the French and British. The Ohio Country was the critical area into which the westward-pushing British would inevitably penetrate. It was the key to the continent that the French had to retain, particularly if they were going to link their Canadian holdings with those of the lower Mississippi Valley. By the mid-1700s the British colonists, painfully aware of these basic truths, were no longer so reluctant to bear the burdens of empire. Alarmed by French land-grabbing and cutthroat fur-trade competition in the Ohio Valley, they were determined to fight for their economic security and for the supremacy of their way of life in North America.

Rivalry for the lush lands of the upper Ohio Valley brought tensions to the snapping point. In 1749 a group of British colonial speculators, chiefly influential Virginians, including the Washington family, had secured shaky legal "rights" to some 500,000 acres in this region. In the same disputed wilderness, the French were in the process of erecting a chain of forts commanding the Ohio River, including Fort Duquesne on the strategic site where the Monongahela and Allegheny Rivers join to form the Ohio—the later site of Pittsburgh.

In 1754 the governor of Virginia ushered George Washington, a twenty-one-year-old surveyor and fellow Virginian, onto the stage of history. Washington was sent to the Ohio Country as a lieutenant colonel in command of about 150 Virginia militiamen. Encountering a small detachment of French troops in the forest about forty miles from Fort Duquesne, the Virginians fired the first shots of the globe-girdling new war. The French leader was killed, and his men retreated. An exultant Washington wrote: "I heard the bullets whistle, and believe me, there is something charming in the sound." It soon lost its charm.

The French promptly returned with reinforcements, who surrounded Washington's hastily constructed bastion, Fort Necessity. After a ten-hour **siege** he was forced to surrender his entire command in July 1754—ironically on the fourth of July.

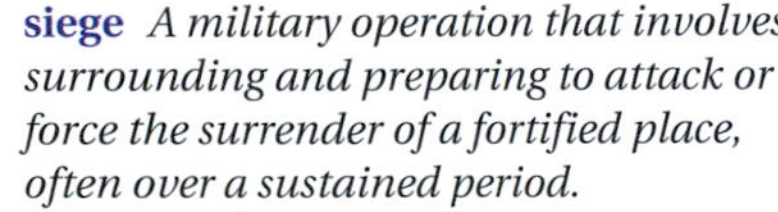

siege *A military operation that involves surrounding and preparing to attack or force the surrender of a fortified place, often over a sustained period.*

Global War and Colonial Disunity

The first three Anglo-French colonial wars had all started in Europe, but the tables were now reversed. The fourth struggle, known as the French and Indian War, began in America. Touched off by George Washington in the wilds of the Ohio Valley in 1754, it rocked along on an undeclared basis for two years and then widened into the most far-flung conflict the world had yet seen—the Seven Years' War. It was fought not only in America but in Europe, in the West Indies, in the Philippines, in Africa, and on the ocean. The Seven Years' War was a seven-seas war.

In Europe, Britain liberally subsidized Frederick the Great of Prussia to fight against his traditional enemy, France. The French wasted so much strength in this European bloodbath that they were unable to throw an adequate force into the New World. "America was conquered in Germany," declared British statesman William Pitt.

In previous colonial clashes, the Americans had revealed an astonishing lack of unity. Colonists who were nearest the shooting had responded much more generously with volunteers and money than those enjoying the safety of remoteness. Now, with musketballs already whining in the Ohio country, the crisis demanded concerted action.

In 1754 the British government summoned an intercolonial congress to Albany, New York, near the Iroquois country. Travel-weary delegates from only seven of the thirteen colonies showed up. The immediate purpose was to keep the Iroquois chiefs loyal to the British in the spreading war.

The longer-range purpose at Albany was to achieve greater colonial unity and thus bolster the common defense against France. Leading this effort was wise and witty Benjamin Franklin. Before the Albany Congress assembled, Franklin published the famous cartoon showing the separate colonies as parts of a disjointed snake above the slogan, "Join, or Die." Franklin gained the congress's unanimous approval for his well-devised but premature scheme of colonial home rule, but the individual colonies and the London regime both spurned it. To the colonists it did not seem to give enough independence; to the British officials, it seemed to give too much.

Braddock's Blundering and Its Aftermath

Led by haughty and bullheaded General Edward Braddock, the British stumbled badly in their opening clashes with the French and Indians. Braddock set out

Famous Cartoon by Benjamin Franklin
Delaware and Georgia were omitted.

regulars *Trained professional soldiers, as distinct from militia or conscripts.*

from Virginia in 1755 with a mixed force of two thousand British **regulars** and ill-disciplined colonial militiamen to capture Fort Duquesne. Experienced in European warfare, "Bulldog" Braddock displayed professional contempt for the colonial "buckskins" and their behind-the-trees method of fighting Indians.

Dragging heavy artillery through the dense forest, Braddock's expedition crept slowly to within a few miles of Fort Duquesne. There it encountered a much smaller French and Indian army. At first the enemy force was repulsed, but it quickly melted into the thickets and poured a murderous fire into the ranks of the redcoats. Braddock's energetic and fearless aide, George Washington, had two horses shot from under him and four bullets pierced his coat. Braddock himself was mortally wounded, and the entire British force was routed with appalling losses.

Inflamed by this easy victory, the Indians took to a wider warpath. The whole frontier from Pennsylvania to North Carolina, left virtually naked by Braddock's bloody defeat, felt their fury. Scalping forays occurred within eighty miles of Philadelphia, and in desperation the local authorities offered bounties for Indian scalps: $50 for a woman's and $130 for a warrior's.

The British launched a full-scale invasion of Canada in 1756, now that the undeclared war in America had at last merged into a world conflict. But they unwisely tried to attack a number of exposed wilderness posts simultaneously, instead of throwing all their strength at the key strongholds of Quebec and Montreal. Ignoring such sound strategy, the British armies experienced defeat after defeat, both in America and in Europe.

Pitt's Palms of Victory

In the hour of crisis, Britain brought forth, as it repeatedly would, a superlative leader—William Pitt. A tall and imposing figure, whose flashing eyes were set in a hawklike face, Pitt was popularly known as the "Great Commoner." He drew much of his strength from the common people, who admired him so greatly that on occasion they kissed his horses.

In 1757 Pitt became the foremost leader in the London government. He wisely decided to concentrate the war effort on the vitals of Canada—the Quebec-Montreal area. Pitt first dispatched a powerful expedition in 1758 against Louisbourg. The frowning fortress, though greatly strengthened by the French, fell after a blistering siege. Wild rejoicing swept Britain, for this was the first significant British victory of the entire war.

Primary source
Death of General Wolfe
college.hmco.com/pic/kennedybrief7e

Quebec was next on Pitt's list. For this crucial expedition he chose thirty-two-year-old James Wolfe. Though pale and sickly, Wolfe combined dash with painstaking attention to detail. In a daring move, he sent a detachment up a poorly guarded part of the rocky eminence protecting Quebec. This vanguard scaled the cliff, pulling itself upward by the bushes and showing the way for the others. In the morning the two armies faced each other on the Plains of Abraham just beyond the citadel walls, the British under Wolfe and the French under the Marquis de Montcalm. Both commanders fell fatally wounded, but the French were defeated and the city surrendered (see "Makers of America: The French," p. 80).

The Battle of Quebec in 1759 ranks as one of the most significant engagements in British and American history. When Montreal fell in 1760, the French flag had fluttered in Canada for the last time. By the peace settlement at Paris (1763), French power was thrown completely off the continent of North America, leaving behind a fertile French population that is to this day a strong minority in Canada. Britain thus emerged as the dominant power in North America, while taking its place as the leading naval power of the world.

Restless Colonists

Britain's colonists, baptized in fire, emerged with increased confidence in their military strength. They had borne the brunt of battle at first; they had fought bravely alongside the crack British regulars; and officers and men alike had gained valuable experience. In the closing days of the conflict some twenty thousand American recruits were under arms.

The French and Indian War, while bolstering colonial self-esteem, simultaneously shattered the myth of British invincibility. On Braddock's bloody field the "buckskin" militia had seen the demoralized regulars huddling helplessly together or fleeing their unseen enemy.

Ominously, friction had developed during the war between arrogant British officers and the raw colonial "boors." Displaying the professional soldier's contempt for amateurs, the British refused to recognize any American militia **commission** above the rank of captain—a demotion humiliating to "Colonel" George Washington. They also showed the usual condescension of snobs from the civilized Old Country toward the "scum" who had confessed failure by fleeing to the "outhouses of civilization." Energetic and hard-working American settlers, by contrast, believed themselves to be on the cutting edge of British civilization. They felt that they deserved credit rather than contempt for risking their lives to erect a New World empire.

commission *An official certification granting a commanding rank in the armed forces.*

British officials were further distressed by the reluctance of the colonists to support the common cause wholeheartedly. American shippers developed a treasonable but lucrative trade with the Spanish and French West Indies at the very time the British navy was trying to subdue them. Other self-centered colonists refused to provide troops and money for the conflict until Pitt reimbursed the colonies for their mounting expenditures.

The curse of intercolonial disunity, present from early days, had continued throughout the recent hostilities. It had been caused mainly by enormous distances and geographical barriers; by religious differences spanning everyone from Catholic to Quaker; by various nationalities, from German to Irish; by differing types of colonial governments; by many boundary disputes; and by the resentment that the crude backcountry settlers felt against the aristocratic bigwigs.

The Reverend Andrew Burnaby, an observant Church of England clergyman who visited the colonies in the closing months of the Seven Years' War, scoffed at any possibility of unification (1760):

". . . for fire and water are not more heterogeneous than the different colonies in North America. Nothing can exceed the jealousy and emulation which they possess in regard to each other. . . . In short . . . were they left to themselves there would soon be a civil war from one end of the continent to the other, while the Indians and Negros would . . . impatiently watch the opportunity of exterminating them all together."

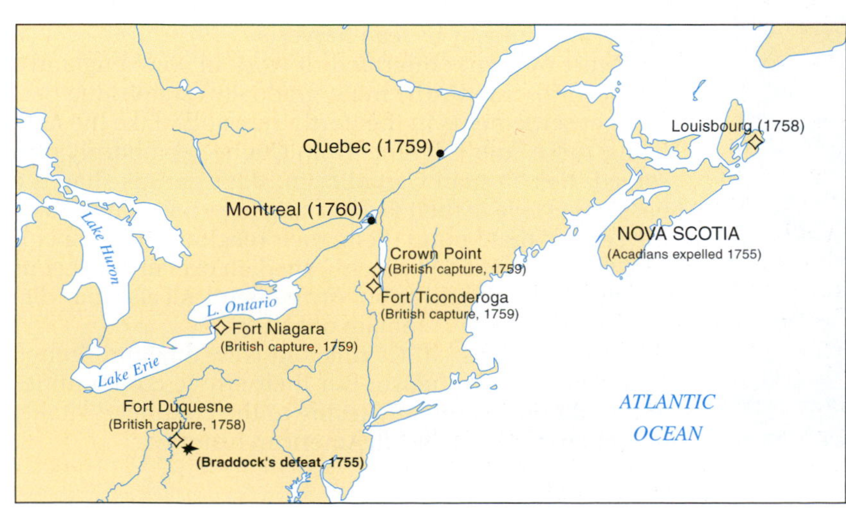

Events of 1755–1760

The French

King Louis XIV's dream of a bountiful empire in New France flickered out like a candle after the British conquered his French colonies in the eighteenth century. His former subjects in Quebec and the maritime provinces of Acadia had to suffer foreign governance in the aftermath of the French defeats in 1713 and 1763. Over the course of the next two centuries many eventually found their way to the United States.

■ **Modern-Day Quebec** A bit of the Old World in the New.

The first French to leave Canada were the Acadians, the settlers of the seaboard region that now comprises Nova Scotia, New Brunswick, Prince Edward Island, and part of Maine. In 1713 the French crown ceded this territory to the British, who demanded that the Acadians either swear allegiance to Britain or withdraw to French territory. At first doing neither, they managed to escape reprisals until Le Grand Dérangement ("The Great Displacement") in 1755, when the British expelled them from the region at bayonet point. The Acadians fled far south to the French colony of Louisiana, where they settled among the sleepy bayous, planted sugar cane and sweet potatoes, practiced Roman Catholicism, and spoke the French dialect that came to be called Cajun (a corruption of the English word *Acadian*). The Cajun settlements were tiny and secluded, many of them accessible only by small boat.

For generations these insular people were scarcely influenced by developments outside their tight-knit communities. Not until the twentieth century did Cajun parents surrender their children to public schools and submit to a state law restricting French speech. Only in the 1930s, with a bridge-building spree engineered by Governor Huey Long, was the isolation of the bayou communities broken.

In 1763, as the French settlers of Quebec fell under British rule, a second group began to leave Canada. By 1840 what had been an irregular southward trickle of Quebecois swelled to a steady stream of people who were driven away mostly by lean harvests.

Most of them emigrated to work in New England's lumberyards and textile mills, gradually establishing permanent settlements in the northern woods. Like the Acadians, these later migrants from Quebec stubbornly preserved their Roman Catholicism. Both groups shared a passionate love of their French language, believing it to be the cement that bound them, their religion, and their culture together. As one French-Canadian explained: "Let us worship in peace and in our own tongue. All else may disappear but this must remain our badge."

Today, almost all Cajuns and New England French Canadians speak English. But their ethnic communities and traditions eloquently testify to the continued vitality of French culture in North American history.

Yet unity received some encouragement during the French and Indian War. When soldiers and statesmen from widely separated colonies met around common campfires and council tables, they were often agreeably surprised to discover that they were all fellow Americans who generally spoke the same language and shared common ideals. Barriers of disunity began to melt, although a long and rugged road lay ahead before a coherent nation would emerge.

Americans: A People of Destiny

The removal of the French menace in Canada profoundly affected American attitudes. While the French hawk had been hovering in the North and West, the colonial chicks had been forced to cling close to the wings of their British mother hen. Now that the hawk was killed, they could range far afield with a new spirit of independence.

The French, humiliated by the British and saddened by the fate of Canada, consoled themselves with one wishful thought. Perhaps the loss of their American empire would one day result in Britain's loss of its American empire. In a sense the history of the United States began with the fall of Quebec and Montreal; the infant Republic was conceived on the Plains of Abraham.

The Spanish and Indian menaces were also substantially reduced. Spain was eliminated from Florida, although entrenched in Louisiana and New Orleans. As for the Indians, the Treaty of Paris dealt a harsh blow to the Creeks, Iroquois, and other interior tribes. Sensing the newly precarious position of the Indian peoples, the Ottawa chief Pontiac in 1763 led several tribes in a violent campaign to drive the British out of the Ohio Country. Pontiac's warriors seized Detroit in the spring of 1763 and eventually overran all but three British outposts west of the Appalachians.

North America Before 1754

North America After 1763 (after French losses)

Interactive map
European Claims in North America
college.hmco.com/pic/kennedybrief7e

The British retaliated swiftly and cruelly. Waging a primitive version of biological warfare, one British commander ordered blankets infected with smallpox to be distributed among the Indians. Such tactics crushed the uprising, and Pontiac's death in 1769 brought an uneasy truce to the frontier. The bloody episode convinced the British of the need to stabilize relations with the western Indians and to station regular troops along the restless frontier, a measure for which they soon asked the colonists to foot the bill.

Land-hungry American colonists were now free to burst over the dam of the Appalachian Mountains and flood out over the verdant western lands. A tiny rivulet of pioneers like Daniel Boone had already trickled into Tennessee and Kentucky. Other courageous pioneers made their preparations for the long, dangerous trek over the mountains.

Then, out of a clear sky, the London government issued its Proclamation of 1763, which flatly prohibited settlement in the area beyond the Appalachians, pending further adjustments. The truth is that this hastily drawn document was not designed to oppress the colonists at all, but to work out the Indian problem fairly and prevent another bloody eruption like Pontiac's uprising.

But countless Americans, especially land speculators, were dismayed and angered. Was not the land beyond the mountains their birthright? Had they not, in addition, bought it with their blood in the recent war? In complete defiance of the proclamation, they clogged the westward trails. In 1765 an estimated one thousand wagons rolled through the town of Salisbury, North Carolina, on their way "up west." This wholesale flouting of royal authority boded ill for the longevity of British rule in America.

The Seven Years' War caused the colonists to develop a new vision of their destiny. With the path cleared for the conquest of a continent, with their birthrate high and their energy boundless, they sensed that they were a potent people on the march. Lordly Britons, whose suddenly swollen empire had tended to produce swollen heads, were in no mood for back talk. Puffed up over their recent victories, they were already annoyed with their unruly colonial subjects. The stage was thus set for a violent family quarrel.

Chapter Summary

Like Britain, France entered late into the American colonial scramble, eventually developing an extensive though thinly settled empire based primarily on the fur trade. During much of the eighteenth century, Britain and France engaged in a bitter power struggle that frequently erupted into worldwide wars. In North America these wars constituted an extended military duel for imperial control of the continent.

The culminating phase of this struggle was inaugurated by young George Washington's venture into the sharply contested Ohio country. After early reversals in this French and Indian War (the Seven Years' War in Europe), the British under William Pitt revived their fortunes and won a decisive victory at Quebec, finally forcing the French from North America.

The American colonists had played a subordinate role in Britain's earlier imperial wars with France. But during the French and Indian War they emerged with increased confidence in their own abilities, and increased resentment of the British treatment of them as provincial inferiors. The removal of the French threat to British control of North America also decreased the colonists' reliance on Britain for their defense. The Ottawa chief Pontiac's unsuccessful uprising in 1763 convinced the British of the need to continue stationing troops in America. But the colonists saw no need for new taxes to pay for British protection, and increasingly resented Britain's authority over them.

The Road to Revolution

1763–1775

THE REVOLUTION WAS EFFECTED BEFORE THE WAR COMMENCED. THE REVOLUTION WAS IN THE MINDS AND HEARTS OF THE PEOPLE.

JOHN ADAMS, 1818

Chapter Outline

- The Merits and Menace of Mercantilism
- The Stamp Act Crisis, 1765
- The Townshend Acts, 1767
- The Boston Tea Party, 1773
- The Intolerable Acts and the Continental Congress, 1774
- Lexington, Concord, and the Gathering Clouds of War, 1775

Victory in the Seven Years' War made Britain the master of a vastly enlarged imperial domain in North America. But victory—including the subsequent need to garrison ten thousand troops along the sprawling American frontier—was painfully costly. The London government therefore struggled after 1763 to compel the American colonists to shoulder some of the financial costs of empire. This change in British colonial policy reinforced an emerging sense of American political identity and helped to precipitate the American Revolution.

The eventual conflict was by no means inevitable. Indeed, given the tightening commercial, military, and cultural bonds between the colonies and mother country since the first crude settlements a century and a half earlier, it might be considered remarkable that the Revolution happened at all. The truth is that Americans were reluctant revolutionaries. Until late in the day, they sought only to claim the "rights of Englishmen," not to separate from the mother country. But what began as a squabble about economic policies soon exposed irreconcilable differences between Americans and Britons over cherished political principles. The ensuing clash gave birth to a new nation.

Focus Questions

1. **What deeply rooted historical factors moved America toward independence from Britain?**
2. **Why did Britain seek tighter control and heavier taxation of its North American colonies after 1763, and why did these policies produce such a strong reaction from the colonists?**
3. **What were the major methods and specific events that shaped colonial resistance to taxation, and how did Britain respond to the protests?**
4. **Why did the Boston Tea Party provoke the fierce British response of the "Intolerable Acts," when earlier conflicts had been compromised or dampened down?**
5. **What advantages and disadvantages did the American "patriots" and Britain each possess as the two sides entered upon armed conflict?**

The Deep Roots of Revolution

In a broad sense, America was a revolutionary force from the day of its discovery. The New World nurtured new ideas about the nature of society, citizen, and government. In the Old World many humble folk had long lived in the shadow of graveyards that contained the bones of their ancestors for a thousand years past. Few people born into such changeless surroundings dared to question their social status. But in the American wilderness ordinary people encountered a world that was theirs to make afresh.

Two ideas in particular had taken root in the minds of the American colonists by the mid-eighteenth century: One was what historians call *republicanism.* Looking to the models of the ancient Greek and Roman republics, exponents of republicanism defined a just society as one in which all citizens willingly subordinated their private, selfish interests to the common good. The stability of society and the authority of government thus depended on the virtue of the citizenry, especially its appetite for civic involvement.

A second idea that fundamentally shaped American political thought derived from a group of British political commentators known as the "radical Whigs." Widely read by the colonists, the Whigs feared the threat to liberty posed by the arbitrary power of the monarch and his ministers, especially the "corruption" revealed by **patronage** and bribes. Whigs warned citizens to be eternally vigilant against corruption and possible conspiracies to denude them of their hard-won liberties. Together, republican and Whig ideas predisposed the American colonists to be on hair-trigger alert against any threat to their rights.

patronage *A system in which benefits, including jobs, money, or protection are granted in exchange for political support.*

mercantilism *The economic theory that all parts of an economy should be coordinated for the good of the whole state; hence, that colonial economies should be subordinated to the benefit of an imperial power.*

The circumstances of colonial life had done much to bolster those attitudes. Dukes and princes, barons and bishops were unknown in the colonies, while property ownership and political participation were relatively widespread. The Americans had also grown accustomed to running their own affairs, largely unmolested by remote officials in London. Distance weakens authority; great distance weakens authority greatly. So it came as an especially jolting shock when Britain after 1763 tried to enclose its American colonists more snugly in its grip.

Mercantilism and Colonial Grievances

Britain's empire was acquired in a "fit of absentmindedness," an old saying goes, and there is much truth in the jest. Not one of the original thirteen colonies except Georgia was formally planted by the British government. All the others were haphazardly founded by trading companies, religious groups, or land speculators.

The British authorities nevertheless embraced a theory, called "**mercantilism,**" that justified their control of the colonies. Mercantilists believed that wealth was power and that a country's economic wealth could be measured by the amount of gold or silver in its treasury. To amass gold or silver, a country needed to export more than it imported. Possessing colonies thus conferred distinct advantages, since the colonies could both supply raw materials to the mother country (thereby reducing the need for foreign imports) and provide a guaranteed market for exports.

The London government therefore looked on the American colonists more or less as tenants. They were expected to furnish raw products needed in the mother country; refrain from making finished products like cloth or beaver hats for export; buy imported manufactured goods exclusively from Britain; and not indulge in dangerous dreams of economic independence or, worse, self-government.

Primary source
William Shepherd Attempts to Collect Customs Duties
college.hmco.com/pic/kennedybrief7e

From time to time Parliament passed laws to regulate the mercantile system. The first of these, the Navigation Law of 1650, required that all commerce flowing to and from the colonies must be transported only in British (including colonial) vessels. Subsequent laws stipulated that European goods destined for America first had to be landed in Britain, where tariff duties could be collected and British middlemen would take a slice of the profits. American merchants also had to ship

Chronology

1650	First Navigation Laws to control colonial commerce.
1763	Seven Years' War (French and Indian War) ends.
1764	Sugar Act.
1765	Quartering Act. Stamp Act. Stamp Act Congress.
1766	Declaratory Act.
1767	Townshend Acts. New York legislature suspended by Parliament.
1768	British troops occupy Boston.
1770	Boston Massacre. All Townshend Acts except tea tax repealed.
1772	Committees of correspondence formed.
1773	British East India Company granted tea monopoly. Governor Hutchinson's actions provoke Boston Tea Party.
1774	"Intolerable Acts." Quebec Act. First Continental Congress. The Association boycotts British goods.
1775	Battles of Lexington and Concord.

certain "enumerated" products, notably tobacco, exclusively to Britain, even though prices might be better elsewhere.

British policy also inflicted a currency shortage on the colonies. Since the colonists bought more from Britain than they sold there, the difference had to be made up in hard cash. Every year gold and silver coins, mostly earned in illicit trade with the Spanish and French West Indies, drained out of the colonies, creating an acute money shortage. To facilitate everyday purchases, the colonists resorted to using butter, nails, pitch, and feathers for purposes of exchange.

Currency issues came to a boil when dire financial need finally forced many of the colonies to issue paper money, which swiftly **depreciated.** British merchants and creditors squawked so loudly that Parliament prohibited the colonial legislatures from printing paper currency and from passing indulgent bankruptcy laws—practices that might harm British merchants.

The British crown also reserved the right to nullify any colonial legislation that might work mischief with the mercantile system. This royal **veto** was used rather sparingly—just 469 times in connection with 8,563 laws. But the colonists nevertheless fiercely resented its very existence—another example of how principle could weigh more heavily than practice in fueling colonial grievances.

depreciated *To decrease in value, as in the decline of the purchasing power of money.*

veto *The constitutional right of a ruler or executive to block legislation passed by another unit of government.*

monopoly *The complete control of a product or sphere of economic activity by a single producer or business.*

The Merits and Menace of Mercantilism

In theory, the British mercantile system seemed thoroughly selfish and deliberately oppressive. But the truth is that until 1763 the various Navigation Laws imposed no intolerable burden, mainly because they were loosely enforced. Enterprising colonial merchants learned early to disregard or evade troublesome restrictions. Some of the first American fortunes, like that of John Hancock, were amassed by wholesale smuggling.

Americans also reaped direct benefits from the mercantile system. If the colonies existed for the benefit of the mother country, it was hardly less true that Britain existed for the benefit of the colonies. London paid liberal bounties to colonial producers of ships' parts, over the protests of British competitors. Virginia tobacco planters enjoyed a **monopoly** in the British market. The colonists also benefited from the protection of the world's mightiest navy and a strong, seasoned army of redcoats—all without a penny of cost.

But even when painted in its rosiest colors, the mercantile system burdened the colonists with annoying liabilities. Mercantilism stifled economic initiative and imposed a rankling dependency on British agents and creditors. Most grievously, many Americans simply found the mercantilist system debasing. They

■ **Paul Revere, by John Singleton Copley, c. 1768** This painting of the famed silversmith-horseman challenged convention—and reflected the new democratic spirit of the age—by portraying an artisan in working clothes. Notice how Copley has depicted the serene confidence of the master craftsman and Revere's quiet pride in his work. Photograph © 2006 Museum of Fine Arts, Boston.

felt used, kept in a state of perpetual economic adolescence, and never allowed to come of age. As Benjamin Franklin wrote in 1775:

> We have an old mother that peevish is grown;
> She snubs us like children that scarce walk alone;
> She forgets we're grown up and have sense of our own.

Revolution broke out, as Theodore Roosevelt later remarked, because Britain failed to recognize an emerging nation when it saw one.

The Stamp Tax Uproar

Victory-flushed Britain emerged from the Seven Years' War holding one of the biggest empires in the world—and also, less happily, the biggest debt, some £140 million, about half of which had been incurred defending the American colonies. To justify and service that debt, British officials now moved to redefine their relationship with their North American colonies.

Prime Minister George Grenville first aroused the resentment of the colonists in 1763 by ordering the British navy to enforce the Navigation Laws. He also secured from Parliament the so-called Sugar Act of 1764, the first law ever passed by that body for raising tax revenue in the colonies for the crown. Among various provisions, it increased the **duty** on foreign sugar imported from the West Indies. After bitter protests from the colonists, the duties were lowered substantially, and the agitation died down. But resentment was kept burning by the Quartering Act of 1765, which required certain colonies to provide food and quarters for British troops.

Then in the same year, 1765, Grenville proposed the most odious measure of all: a stamp tax, to raise revenues to support the new military force. The Stamp Act mandated the use of stamped paper or the affixing of stamps certifying payment of tax. Stamps were required on bills of sale for about fifty trade items as well as on certain types of commercial and legal documents, including playing cards, pamphlets, newspapers, diplomas, bills of lading, and marriage licenses.

Grenville regarded all these measures as reasonable and just. He was simply asking the Americans to pay their fair share of the costs for their own defense, through taxes that were already familiar in Britain. In fact, Englishmen for two generations had endured a stamp tax far heavier than that passed for the colonies.

Yet the Americans were angrily aroused at what they regarded as Grenville's fiscal aggression. The new laws did not merely pinch their pocketbooks. Far more ominously, Grenville seemed also to be striking at the local liberties they had come to assume as a matter of right. Thus some colonial assemblies defiantly refused to comply with the Quartering Act, or voted for only a fraction of the supplies that it called for.

Worst of all, Grenville's noxious legislation seemed to jeopardize the basic rights of the colonists as Englishmen. Both the Sugar Act and the Stamp Act provided for trying offenders in the hated **admiralty courts,** where juries were not allowed. The burden of proof was on the defendants, who were assumed to be guilty unless they could prove themselves innocent. Trial by jury and the precept of "innocent until proved guilty" were ancient privileges that British people everywhere, including the American colonists, held most dear.

And why was a British army needed at all in the colonies, now that the French were expelled from the continent and Pontiac's warriors crushed? Could its real purpose be to whip rebellious colonists themselves into line? Many Americans, weaned on the radical Whigs' suspicion of all authority, began to sniff the strong scent of a conspiracy to strip them of their historic liberties. They

duty (duties) *A customs tax on the export or import of goods.*

admiralty courts *In British law, special administrative courts designed to handle maritime cases without a jury.*

lashed back violently, and the Stamp Act became the target that drew their most ferocious fire.

Angry throats raised the cry, "No taxation without representation." There was some irony in the slogan, because the seaports and tidewater towns that were most wrathful against the Stamp Act had long denied full representation to their own backcountry pioneers. But now the aggravated colonists took the high ground of principle.

The Americans made a distinction between "legislation" and "taxation." They conceded the right of Parliament to legislate about matters that affected the entire empire, including the regulation of trade. But they steadfastly denied the right of Parliament, in which no Americans were seated, to impose taxes on Americans. Only their own elected colonial legislatures, the Americans insisted, could legally tax them.

Grenville dismissed these American protests as hairsplitting absurdities. The power of Parliament was supreme and undivided, he asserted, and in any case the Americans were represented in Parliament. Elaborating the theory of "**virtual representation,**" Grenville claimed that every member of Parliament represented all British subjects, even those Americans in Boston or Charleston who had never voted for a member of the London Parliament. The Americans scoffed at this notion of virtual representation.

Thus the principle of no taxation without representation was supremely important, and the colonists clung to it with tenacious consistency. When the British replied that the sovereign power of government could not be divided between "legislative" authority in London and "taxing" authority in the colonies, they forced the Americans to deny the authority of Parliament altogether and to begin to consider their own political independence. This chain of logic eventually led to revolutionary consequences.

virtual representation *The political theory that a class of persons is represented in a lawmaking body without direct vote.*

nonimportation agreements *Pledges to boycott, or decline to purchase, certain goods from abroad.*

boycotts *An organized refusal to deal with some person or organization, or to buy a product or service.*

Parliament Forced to Repeal the Stamp Act

Among colonial outcries against the hated stamp tax, the most conspicuous was the Stamp Act Congress, held in New York City in 1765. Twenty-seven distinguished delegates from nine colonies petitioned the king and Parliament to repeal the repugnant legislation. The Stamp Act Congress made little splash in America at the time, but it was one more significant step toward intercolonial unity.

Primary source
John Holt's Account of the Stamp Act Riots in New York
college.hmco.com/pic/kennedybrief7e

More effective than the congress was the widespread adoption of **nonimportation agreements** against British goods. Homespun woolen garments became fashionable, and the eating of lamb chops was discouraged so that the wool-bearing sheep would be allowed to mature. Nonimportation agreements were in fact a promising stride toward union; they spontaneously united the American people for the first time in common action.

Mobilizing in support of nonimportation gave ordinary men and women new opportunities to participate in colonial protests by signing petitions or refusing to purchase British goods. Joining consumer **boycotts,** groups of women assembled in public to hold spinning bees and make homespun cloth as a replacement for shunned British textiles. Such public defiance helped spread angry resistance throughout American colonial society.

Sometimes violence accompanied colonial protests. Crying, "Liberty, Property, and No Stamps," ardent Sons and Daughters of Liberty enforced the nonimportation agreements against violators, often with a generous coat of tar and feathers. Patriot mobs ransacked the houses of unpopular officials and hanged effigies of stamp agents on liberty poles.

Primary source
Grace Galloway Defies the Radicals in Philadelphia
college.hmco.com/pic/kennedybrief7e

Shaken by colonial commotion, the machinery for collecting the tax broke down. On that dismal day in 1765 when the new act was to go into effect, the stamp agents had all been forced to resign, and there was no one to sell the stamps. While flags flapped at half-mast, the law was openly and flagrantly defied—or rather, nullified.

Britain was hard hit. Merchants, manufacturers, and shippers suffered from the colonial nonimportation agreements, and hundreds of laborers were thrown out of work. Loud demands converged on Parliament for repeal of the Stamp Act.

Primary source
Stamp Act Protest
college.hmco.com/pic/kennedybrief7e

But many of the members could not understand why 7.5 million Britons had to pay heavy taxes to protect the colonies, whereas some 2 million colonists refused to pay for only one-third of the cost of their own defense.

After a stormy debate, Parliament in 1766 grudgingly repealed the Stamp Act. But virtually in the same breath, it provocatively passed the Declaratory Act, reaffirming Parliament's right "to bind" the colonies "in all cases whatsoever." The British government thereby drew its line in the sand. It defined the constitutional principle it would not yield: absolute and unqualified sovereignty over its North American colonies. The colonists had already drawn their own battle line by making it clear that they wanted a measure of sovereignty of their own, and would undertake drastic action to secure it. The stage was set for a continuing confrontation.

The Townshend Tea Tax and the Boston "Massacre"

Control of the British ministry was now seized by the gifted but erratic "Champagne Charley" Townshend, a man who could deliver brilliant speeches in Parliament even while drunk. Rashly promising to pluck feathers from the colonial goose with a minimum of squawking, he persuaded Parliament in 1767 to pass the Townshend Acts. The most important of these new regulations was a light import duty on glass, white lead, paper, paint, and tea. Townshend made this tax, unlike the Stamp Act, an indirect customs duty payable at American ports.

Flushed with their recent victory over the stamp tax, the colonists were in a rebellious mood. The impost on tea was especially irksome, for an estimated 1 million people drank the refreshing brew twice a day.

Primary source
Boston Gazette Describes the Boston Massacre

Primary source
Map of the Boston Massacre
Primary source
Blood Massacre Perpetrated in King Street, Boston

mulatto *A person of mixed African and European ancestry.*

The new Townshend revenues, worse yet, would be used to pay the salaries of the royal governors and judges in America. The ultrasuspicious Americans, who had beaten the royal governors into line by controlling the purse, regarded Townshend's tax as another attempt to enchain them. Their worst fears took on a greater reality when the London government, after passing the Townshend taxes, suspended the New York legislature in 1767 for failure to comply with the Quartering Act.

Nonimportation agreements, previously potent, were quickly revived against the Townshend Acts. But they proved less effective than those devised against the Stamp Act. The colonists, again enjoying prosperity, took the new tax less seriously than might have been expected, largely because it was light and indirect. They found, moreover, that they could secure smuggled tea at a cheap price, and consequently smugglers increased their activities, especially in Massachusetts.

British officials, faced with a breakdown of law and order, landed two regiments of troops in Boston in 1768. With liberty-loving colonists mercilessly taunting the often profane and drunken redcoats, a clash between citizens and soldiers was inevitable. On the evening of March 5, 1770, a crowd of some sixty townspeople, angry over the earlier death of an eleven-year old boy, began taunting and throwing snowballs at a squad of ten redcoats. Acting apparently without orders but nervous and provoked by the jeering crowd, the troops opened fire and killed or wounded eleven citizens. One of the first to die was Crispus Attucks, described by contemporaries as a "**mulatto**" and a leader of the mob. Both sides were in some degree to blame, and in the subsequent trial (in which future president John Adams served as defense attorney for the soldiers) only two redcoats were found guilty of manslaughter.

Giving new meaning to the proverbial tempest in a teapot, a group of 126 Boston women signed an agreement, or "subscription list," which announced,

"We the Daughters of those Patriots who have and now do appear for the public interest . . . do with Pleasure engage with them in denying ourselves the drinking of Foreign Tea, in hopes to frustrate a Plan that tends to deprive the whole Community of . . . all that is valuable in Life."

The Seditious Committees of Correspondence

By 1770 King George III was strenuously attempting to assert the power of the British monarchy. Earnest, industrious, stubborn, and lustful for power, he surrounded himself with cooperative yes men, notably his corpulent Tory prime minister, Lord North.

■ Two Views of the Boston Massacre, 1770 and 1856 Both of these prints of the Boston Massacre were art as well as propaganda. Paul Revere's engraving (left) began circulating within three weeks of the event in March 1770, depicting not a clash of brawlers but armed soldiers taking aim at peaceful citizens. Absent also was any evidence of the mulatto ringleader, Crispus Attucks. Revere wanted his print to convince viewers of the indisputable justice of the colonists' cause. By the mid-1850s, when the chromolithograph (right) circulated, it served a new political purpose. In the era of the abolitionist movement, freedman Crispus Attucks held center place in the scene, which portrayed his death as an American martyr in the revolutionary struggle for freedom.

The ill-timed Townshend Acts had failed to produce revenue, though they did produce near-rebellion. Net proceeds from the tax in one year were a paltry £295, and during that time the annual military costs to Britain in the colonies had mounted to £170,000. Nonimportation agreements, though feebly enforced, were pinching British manufacturers. The government of Lord North, bowing to various pressures, finally persuaded Parliament to repeal the Townshend revenue duties. But the three-pence tax on tea was retained to keep alive the principle of parliamentary taxation.

Flames of discontent in America, fanned by periodic incidents involving British officials, were further kindled by a master **propagandist** and engineer of rebellion, Samuel Adams. This cousin of John Adams was so unimpressive in appearance that his friends had to buy him a presentable suit of clothes when he left Massachusetts on intercolonial business. Zealous, tenacious, and courageous, Samuel Adams cherished a deep faith in the common people.

propaganda (propagandist) *A systematic program or particular materials designed to promote certain ideas; sometimes, but not always, the term is used negatively, implying the use of manipulative or deceptive means. (A propagandist is one who engages in such practices.)*

Samuel Adams's signal contribution was to organize in Massachusetts the local committees of correspondence. After he had formed the first one in Boston during 1772, some eighty towns in the colony speedily set up similar organizations. Their chief function was to spread the spirit of resistance by exchanging letters and thus keep alive opposition to British policy.

Intercolonial committees of correspondence were the next logical step. Virginia led the way in 1773 by creating such a body as a standing committee of the House of Burgesses. Within a short time every colony had established a central committee through which it could exchange ideas and information with other colonies. These intercolonial groups were supremely significant in stimulating and disseminating sentiment in favor of united action. They evolved directly into the first American congresses.

Tea Parties at Boston and Elsewhere

Thus far—that is, by 1773—nothing had happened to make rebellion inevitable. Nonimportation was weakening. Increasing numbers of colonists were

Ann Hulton (d. 1779?), a Loyalist, described colonial political divisions and her hopes and fears for her own future in a letter she sent to a friend in England in 1774:

"Those who are well disposed towards Government are termed Tories. They daily increase & have made some efforts to take the power out of the hands of the Patriots, but they are intimidated & overpowered by Numbers. . . . However I don't despair of seeing Peace & tranquility in America, tho' they talk very high & furious at present. They are all preparing their Arms & Ammunition & say if any of the Leaders are seized, they will make reprisals on the friends of Government."

reluctantly paying the tea tax because the legal tea was cheaper than the smuggled tea.

A new ogre entered the picture in 1773. The powerful British East India Company, overburdened with 17 million pounds of unsold tea, was facing bankruptcy. If it collapsed, the London government would lose heavily in tax revenue. The ministry therefore decided to assist the company by awarding it a complete monopoly of the American tea business. The giant corporation would now be able to sell the coveted leaves more cheaply than ever before, even with the three-pence tax tacked on. But to the determined Americans, principle remained far more important than price.

Fatefully, the British officials decided to enforce the letter of the law. Once more, the colonists rose up in wrath to defy it. Not a single one of the thousands of chests of tea shipped by the East India Company ever reached the hands of the consignees. In Philadelphia and New York, mass demonstrations forced the tea-bearing ships to return to Britain. At Annapolis, Marylanders burned both cargo and vessel, while proclaiming "Liberty and Independence or death in pursuit of it."

Only in Boston did a British official stubbornly refuse to be cowed. Massachusetts governor Thomas Hutchinson agreed that the tea tax was unjust, but believed even more strongly that the colonists had no right to flout the law. Hutchinson further inflamed the situation when he declared that "an abridgement of what are called English liberties" was necessary for the preservation of law and order in the colonies—apparently confirming the darkest conspiracy theories of the American radicals. On December 16, 1773, roughly a hundred Bostonians, disguised as Indians, boarded the docked ships, smashed open 342 chests of tea, and dumped their contents into the Atlantic. A crowd watched approvingly from the shore as Boston harbor became a vast teapot.

Reactions varied. All up and down the eastern seaboard, sympathetic colonists applauded destruction of the tea as "the hated badge of slavery." But conservatives complained that the destruction of private property violated the law and threatened anarchy. Hutchinson, disgusted with the colonies, retreated to Britain. The British authorities saw little alternative to whipping the upstart colonists into shape. Granting the Americans some measure of home rule at this stage might still have prevented rebellion, but few British politicians were willing to take that high road. The perilous path they chose instead led only to reprisals, bitterness, and escalating conflict.

■ The Boston Tea Party, December 16, 1773 Crying "Boston harbor a tea-pot this night," Sons of Liberty disguised as Indians hurled chests of tea into the sea to protest the tax on tea and to make sure that the tea's cheap price did not prove an "invincible temptation" to the people.

Parliament Passes the "Intolerable Acts"

An irate Parliament responded speedily to the Boston Tea Party with measures that brewed a revolution. By huge majorities in 1774 it passed a series of acts designed to chastise Boston in particular and Massachusetts in general.

Most drastic of all was the Boston Port Act. It closed the tea-stained harbor until damages were paid and order could be ensured. In the other "Intolerable Acts"—as they were called in America—many of the chartered rights of colonial Massachusetts were swept away. Restrictions were likewise placed on the precious town meetings. Contrary to previous practice, enforcing officials who killed colonists in the line of duty could now be sent to Britain for trial. Particularly intolerable to Bostonians was a new Quartering Act that gave local authorities the power to lodge British soldiers in private homes.

By a fateful coincidence, the "Intolerable Acts" were accompanied in 1774 by the Quebec Act. Passed at the same time, it was erroneously regarded in English-speaking America as part of the British reaction to the turbulence in Boston. Actually, the Quebec Act was a good law in bad company. For many years the British government had debated how it should administer the sixty thousand or so conquered French subjects in Canada, and it had finally framed this farsighted and statesmanlike measure. The French Canadians were guaranteed their Catholic religion. They were also permitted to retain many of their old customs and institutions, which did not include a representative assembly or trial by jury in civil cases. In addition, the old boundaries of the Province of Quebec were extended southward all the way to the Ohio River.

The Quebec Act, from the viewpoint of the French Canadians, was a shrewd and conciliatory measure. If Britain had only shown as much foresight in dealing with its English-speaking colonies, it might not have lost them.

But from the viewpoint of the American colonists as a whole, the Quebec Act was especially noxious. All the other "Intolerable Acts" slapped directly at Massachusetts, but this one had a much wider range. By sustaining unrepresentative assemblies and denials of jury trials, it seemed to set a dangerous precedent in America. It alarmed land speculators, who were distressed to see the huge trans-Allegheny area snatched from their grasp. It aroused anti-Catholics, who were shocked by the extension of Roman Catholic jurisdiction southward into a huge region once earmarked for Protestantism.

The Continental Congress and Bloodshed

Chafing over the Quebec Act and the other "Intolerable Acts," American dissenters responded to the plight of Massachusetts with acts of sympathy and solidarity. Their most memorable step was the summoning of a Continental Congress. Delegates from all of the thirteen colonies except Georgia—including Samuel Adams, George Washington, and Patrick Henry—met in Philadelphia from September 5 to October 26, 1774. A stellar role at this First Continental Congress was played by John Adams. Eloquently swaying his colleagues to a revolutionary course, he helped defeat by the narrowest of margins a proposal by moderates for a species of American home rule under British direction.

The most significant action of the Congress was the creation of The Association. Unlike previous nonimportation agreements, The Association called for a complete boycott of all British goods: nonimportation, nonexportation, and nonconsumption. Yet it is important to note that the delegates were not yet calling for independence. They sought merely to repeal the offensive legislation and return to the happy days before parliamentary taxation. Resistance had not yet ripened into open rebellion.

But the fatal drift toward war continued. Parliament rejected the First Continental Congress's petitions. In America, chickens squawked and tar kettles bubbled as violators of The Association were tarred and feathered. Muskets were gathered, men began to drill openly, and a clash seemed imminent.

In April 1775, the British commander in Boston sent a detachment of troops to nearby Lexington and Concord. They intended to seize stores of colonial gunpowder and also to bag the "rebel" ringleaders, Samuel Adams and John Hancock. At Lexington the colonial "Minute Men" refused to disperse rapidly enough, and shots were fired that killed eight Americans and wounded several more. The redcoats then pushed on to Concord, from which they were soon forced to retreat by the rough-and-ready Americans, whom Emerson immortalized:

> By the rude bridge that arched the flood,
> Their flag to April's breeze unfurled,
> Here once the embattled farmers stood,
> And fired the shot heard round the world.*

The bewildered British, fighting off murderous fire from militiamen crouched behind thick stone walls, finally regained the sanctuary of Boston. Licking their wounds, they could count about three hundred casualties, including some seventy killed. Britain now had a war on its hands.

Imperial and Colonial Strengths and Weaknesses

Aroused Americans had brashly rebelled against a mighty empire. The population odds were about three to one against the rebels—some 7.5 million Britons to 2.5 million colonists. The odds in monetary wealth and naval power overwhelmingly favored the mother country.

Britain then boasted a professional army of some fifty thousand men, as compared with the numerous but wretchedly trained American militia. King George III, in addition, hired some thirty thousand German soldiers—so-called Hessians—to bolster his army. The British also enlisted the services of about fifty thousand American Loyalists and many Indians in their cause.

Yet Britain was weaker than it seemed at first glance. British troops had to be detached to watch the smoking volcano of oppressed Ireland. Recently defeated France was bitterly awaiting an opportunity to stab Britain in the back. The London government, under stubborn George III and his pliant Tory prime minister, Lord North, was confused and inept.

Many earnest and God-fearing Britons had no desire to kill their American cousins. Many British Whigs actually believed that the battle for their own liberties was being fought in America. If George III triumphed there, they believed, his rule at home might become more tyrannical. This outspoken sympathy in Britain, though plainly a minority voice, greatly encouraged the Americans. If they continued their resistance long enough, the Whigs might come to power and deal generously with them.

Britain's army in America had to operate under endless difficulties. The generals were second-rate; the soldiers, though on the whole capable, were brutally treated. Provisions were often scarce, rancid, and wormy.

Other handicaps loomed. The redcoats had to conquer the Americans; restoring the pre-1763 status quo would be a victory for the colonists. Britain was operating some 3,000 miles from its home base, and distance often delayed military orders from London for months, so that they no longer fit the changing situation.

America's geographical expanse was enormous: roughly 1,000 by 600 miles. The united colonies had no urban nerve center like France's Paris. During the war British armies captured every city of any size, yet like a

The great conservative political theorist and champion of the American cause, Edmund Burke, made a stirring speech in Britain's House of Commons in 1775, pleading in vain for reconciliation with the colonies:

"As long as you have the wisdom to keep the sovereign authority of this country as the sanctuary of liberty . . . they will turn their faces towards you. . . . Slavery they can have anywhere; freedom they can have from none but you. This is the commodity of price, of which you have the monopoly. This is the true Act of Navigation, which binds to you the commerce of the colonies, and through them secures to you the wealth of the world. Deny them this participation of freedom, and you break that sole bond which originally made, and must still preserve, the unity of the empire."

* Ralph Waldo Emerson, Concord Hymn.

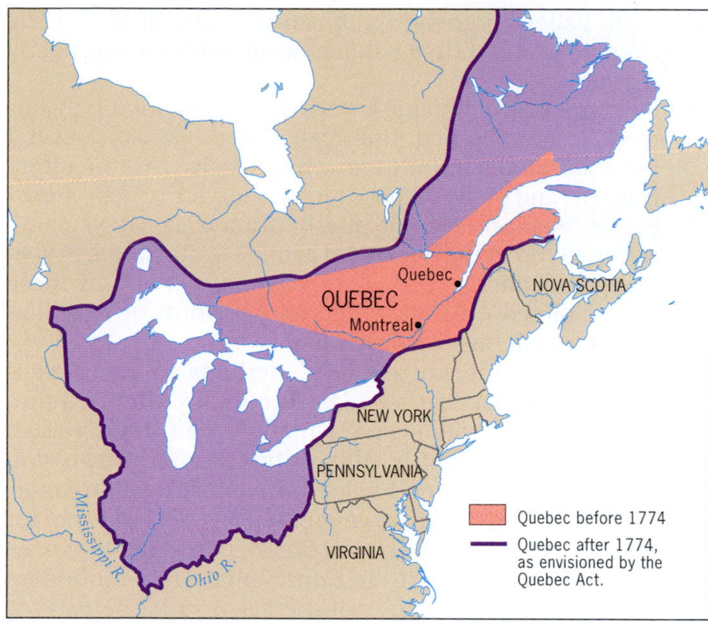

Quebec Before and After 1774 Young Alexander Hamilton voiced the fears of many colonists when he warned that the Quebec Act of 1774 would introduce "priestly tyranny" into Canada, making that country another Spain or Portugal. "Does not your blood run cold," he asked, "to think that an English Parliament should pass an act for the establishment of arbitrary power and Popery in such a country?"

boxer punching a feather pillow, they made little more than a dent in the entire country. The Americans wisely traded space for time.

The revolutionaries were also blessed with outstanding leadership. George Washington was a giant among men. Master diplomat Benjamin Franklin eventually secured open foreign aid from France. In a class by himself was Marquis de Lafayette, a wealthy young French nobleman who loved both glory and liberty. Lafayette became a major general in the colonial army at age nineteen, and the services of the teenage "French gamecock" helped secure further aid from France.

Other conditions aided the Americans. They were fighting defensively on their own terrain. In agriculture, the colonies were mainly self-sustaining, like a kind of Robinson Crusoe's island. The Americans also enjoyed the moral advantage that came from belief in a just cause.

Yet the American rebels were badly organized for war. Almost fatally lacking in unity, the new nation lurched forward uncertainly like an uncoordinated centipede. Even the Continental Congress, which directed the conflict, was hardly more than a debating society, and it grew feebler as the struggle dragged on. The disorganized colonists fought almost the entire war before adopting a written constitution—the Articles of Confederation—in 1781.

Economic difficulties were nearly insuperable. With metallic money drained away and taxation an explosive issue, the Continental Congress was forced to print "Continental" paper money in great amounts. As this currency poured from the presses, it depreciated until the expression "not worth a Continental" became current. **Inflation** of the currency inevitably skyrocketed prices, hitting the families of soldiers at the front especially hard. Debtors easily acquired handfuls of the quasi-worthless money and gleefully paid their debts "without mercy."

inflation *An increase in the supply of currency relative to the goods available, leading to a decline in the purchasing power of money and a corresponding rise in prices.*

A Thin Line of Heroes

Basic military supplies in the colonies were dangerously scanty, especially firearms. While many families and towns did own firearms, the colonists had long relied heavily on Britain for troops, armaments, and military subsidies. When the supply of British funds and war materiel evaporated, sufficient stores of gunpowder, cannons, and ships could not be found.

Other shortages bedeviled the rebels. Manufactured goods were generally in short supply in agricultural America, and clothing and shoes were appallingly scarce. The path of the Patriot fighting men was often marked by bloody snow. At

Enslaved blacks hoped that the Revolutionary crisis would make it possible for them to secure their own liberty. On the eve of the war in South Carolina, merchant Josiah Smith, Jr., noted such a rumor among the slaves:

"[Freedom] is their common Talk throughout the Province, and has occasioned impertinent behavior in many of them, insomuch that our Provincial Congress now sitting hath voted the immediate raising of Two Thousand Men Horse and food, to keep those mistaken creatures in awe."

Despite such repressive measures, slave uprisings continued to plague the southern colonies through 1775 and 1776.

frigid Valley Forge during the cruel winter of 1777–1778, twenty-eight hundred soldiers went barefoot and nearly naked.

American militiamen were numerous but highly unreliable. Able-bodied American males—perhaps several hundred thousand of them—had received rudimentary training, and many of these recruits served for short terms in the rebel armies. But poorly trained plowboys could not stand up in the open field against professional British troops advancing with bare bayonets. Many of these undisciplined warriors would, in the words of Washington, "fly from their own shadows."

A few thousand regulars—perhaps seven or eight thousand at the war's end—were finally whipped into shape by stern drillmasters. Notable among them was an organizational genius, the salty German Baron von Steuben. He spoke no English when he arrived in America, but he soon taught his men that bayonets were not for broiling beefsteaks over open fires. As they gained experience, these soldiers of the Continental Army more than held their own in battle against crack British troops.

Blacks also fought and died for the American cause. Although many states initially barred them from militia service, by war's end more than five thousand blacks, most from the northern states, had enlisted in the American armed forces. Blacks fought at Trenton, Brandywine, Saratoga, and other important battles.

African Americans also served on the British side. In November 1775 Lord Dunmore, royal governor of Virginia, issued a proclamation offering freedom to any enslaved black in Virginia who joined the British army. In time, thousands of blacks fled plantations in response to British promises of emancipation. At war's end the British kept their word, to some at least, evacuating as many as fourteen thousand "Black Loyalists" to Nova Scotia, Jamaica, and Britain itself.

Morale in the Revolutionary army was badly undermined by American profiteers. Putting profits before patriotism, these speculators sold supplies to the British and made profits of 50 to 200 percent on army garb while the American army was freezing at Valley Forge. The failures of revolutionary zeal meant that Washington never had as many as twenty thousand effective troops in one place at one time.

The brutal truth is that only a select minority of colonists attached themselves to the cause of independence with a spirit of selfless devotion. These were the dedicated souls who bore the burden of battle and the risks of defeat. Seldom have so few done so much for so many.

Chapter Summary

The American War of Independence was a military conflict fought from 1775 to 1783, but the American Revolution was a deeper transformation of thought and loyalty that began when the first settlers arrived in America and finally led to the colonies' political separation from Britain.

One source of long-term conflict was the tension between the considerable freedom and self-government the colonists enjoyed in the American wilderness and their participation in the British Empire's mercantile system. While British mercantilism actually provided economic benefits to the colonies along with certain liabilities, its limits on freedom and its patronizing goal of keeping America in a state of perpetual economic adolescence stirred growing resentment.

The short-term movement toward the War of Independence began with British attempts to impose higher taxes and tighter imperial controls after the French and Indian War. To the British these were reasonable measures, requiring the colonists simply to bear their fair share of the costs of the empire. To the colonists, however, the measures constituted attacks on fundamental rights.

Through well-orchestrated agitation and boycotts, the colonists forced repeal of the Stamp Act of 1765 as well as the Townshend Acts that replaced it, except for a symbolic tax on tea. A temporary lull in conflict between 1770 and 1773 ended with the Boston Tea Party in December 1773. This radical action was instigated by a network of Boston agitators who refused to bow to the stubborn Massachusetts governor's attempt to enforce a law that benefited primarily the British East India Company monopoly.

In response to the Tea Party, the British imposed the harsh Intolerable Acts, and coincidentally passed the Quebec Act, which roused deep fears of religious as well as political tyranny. These twin actions stirred ferocious American resistance throughout the colonies, and led directly to the calling of the First Continental Congress in September 1774 and the clash of arms at Lexington and Concord in April 1775.

As the two sides headed into war, the British enjoyed the advantages of a larger population, a professionally trained army, and much greater economic strength. American rebels had advantages of territory and leadership, but their greatest asset was the fervent commitment of that minority of Patriots who were ready to sacrifice everything for their rights.

America Secedes from the Empire

1775–1783

THESE ARE THE TIMES THAT TRY MEN'S SOULS. THE SUMMER SOLDIER AND THE SUNSHINE PATRIOT WILL, IN THIS CRISIS, SHRINK FROM THE SERVICE OF THEIR COUNTRY; BUT HE THAT STANDS IT NOW, DESERVES THE LOVE AND THANKS OF MAN AND WOMAN.

THOMAS PAINE, DECEMBER 1776

Chapter Outline

Bloodshed at Lexington and Concord in April 1775 was a clarion call to arms. About twenty thousand musket-bearing "Minute Men" swarmed around Boston, there to coop up the outnumbered British.

The Second Continental Congress met in Philadelphia the next month, on May 10, 1775; and this time the full slate of thirteen colonies was represented. The conservative element in the Congress was still strong, despite the shooting in Massachusetts. There was still no well-defined sentiment for independence—merely a desire to continue fighting in the hope that king and Parliament would consent to a redress of grievances. Congress hopefully drafted new appeals to the British people and king—appeals that were spurned. Anticipating a possible rebuff, the delegates also adopted measures to raise money and to create an army and a navy. The British and the Americans now teetered on the brink of all-out warfare.

Focus Questions

1. **How and why did Americans move in 1775–1776 from fighting only for "the rights of Englishmen" within the British Empire to declaring their independence?**
2. **What specific arguments and general political principles did Thomas Paine's *Common Sense* and Thomas Jefferson's Declaration of Independence use to promote and justify American independence?**
3. **In what ways was the Revolution a political and military "civil war" between American Patriots and American Loyalists, as well as a war for independence against Britain?**
4. **How and why did the British strategy to swiftly crush the rebellion fail, and how were Washington and his generals able to sustain the war after 1778 and take advantage of French assistance?**
5. **Why were Americans able to win not only the war but a stunning diplomatic victory in the peace settlement of 1783?**

Chronology

1775 Battles of Lexington and Concord.
Second Continental Congress.
Battle of Bunker Hill.
King George III formally proclaims colonies in rebellion.
Failed invasion of Canada.

1776 Paine's *Common Sense.*
Declaration of Independence.
Battle of Trenton.

1777 Battle of Brandywine.
Battle of Germantown.
Battle of Saratoga.

1778 Formation of French-American alliance.
Battle of Monmouth.

1778-1779 Clark's victories in the West.

1781 Battle of King's Mountain.
Battle of Cowpens.
Greene leads Carolina campaign.
French and Americans force Cornwallis to surrender at Yorktown.

1782 North's ministry collapses in Britain.

1783 Treaty of Paris.

Congress Drafts George Washington

Online Study Center

Interactive map
The First Battles in the War for Independence, 1775
college.hmco.com/pic/kennedybrief7e

Perhaps the most important single action of the Congress was to select George Washington, one of its members already in officer's uniform, to head the hastily improvised army besieging Boston. This choice was made with considerable misgivings. The tall, powerfully built, dignified Virginia planter, then forty-three, had never risen above the rank of colonel in the militia. His largest command had numbered only twelve hundred men, and that had been some twenty years earlier. Falling short of true military genius, Washington would actually lose more pitched battles than he won.

But the distinguished Virginian was gifted with outstanding powers of leadership and immense strength of character. He radiated patience, courage, self-discipline, and a sense of justice. He was a great moral force rather than a great military mind—a symbol and a rallying point. People instinctively trusted him; they sensed that when he put himself at the head of a cause, he was prepared, if necessary, to go down with the ship. He insisted on serving without pay, though he would keep a careful wartime expense account amounting to more than $100,000.

The Continental Congress initially selected Washington more for political reasons than for his leadership qualities. Americans from other sections distrusted the large New England army gathering around Boston, and prudence suggested a commander from Virginia.

Bunker Hill and Hessian Hirelings

Online Study Center

Interactive map
The War in the North, 1776–1779
college.hmco.com/pic/kennedybrief7e

The clash of arms continued on a strangely contradictory basis. On the one hand, the Americans were emphatically affirming their loyalty to the king and earnestly voicing their desire to patch up difficulties. On the other hand, they were raising armies and shooting down His Majesty's soldiers. This curious war of inconsistency was fought for fourteen long months—from April 1775 to July 1776—before the fateful plunge into independence was taken.

Gradually the tempo of warfare increased. In May 1775 a tiny American force under Ethan Allen and Benedict Arnold surprised and captured the British garrisons at Ticonderoga and Crown Point, on the scenic lakes of upper New York. A priceless store of gunpowder and artillery for the siege of Boston was thus secured.

In June 1775 the colonists seized a hill, now known as Bunker Hill (actually Breed's Hill), from which they menaced the enemy in Boston. The British blundered bloodily when they launched a frontal attack with three thousand men. Sharpshooting Americans, numbering fifteen hundred and strongly entrenched, mowed down the advancing redcoats with frightful slaughter. But the colonists' scanty store of gunpowder finally gave out, and they were forced to abandon the hill in disorder. With two more such victories, remarked the French foreign minister, the British would have no army left in America.

Following Bunker Hill, King George III slammed the door on all hope of reconciliation. In August 1775 he formally proclaimed the colonies in rebellion. The next month he widened the chasm by hiring thousands of troops from the German principality of Hesse, shocking colonists who feared the Hessians' exaggerated reputation for butchery. Actually, the Hessian hirelings turned out to be more interested in booty than in duty. Hundreds of them eventually deserted and remained in America as respected citizens.

Online Study Center
Interactive map
The War in the North
college.hmco.com/pic/kennedybrief7e

The Abortive Conquest of Canada

The unsheathed sword continued to take its toll. In October 1775 the British burned the town of Falmouth (Portland), Maine. That same autumn the rebels daringly undertook a two-pronged invasion of Canada. American leaders believed, erroneously, that the conquered French were explosively restive under the British yoke. A successful assault on Canada would add a fourteenth colony, while depriving Britain of a valuable base for striking at the colonies in revolt. But this large-scale attack, involving some two thousand American troops, contradicted the claim of the colonists that they were merely fighting defensively for a redress of grievances. Invasion northward was undisguised offensive warfare.

This bold stroke for Canada narrowly missed success. One invading column under the Irish-born General Richard Montgomery pushed up the Lake Champlain route and captured Montreal. He was joined at Quebec by the bedraggled army of General Benedict Arnold, whose men had been reduced to eating dogs and shoe leather during their grueling march through the Maine woods. An assault on Quebec, launched on the last day of 1775, was beaten off. The able Montgomery was killed; the dashing Arnold was wounded in one leg. Scattered remnants under Arnold's command retreated up the St. Lawrence River. But French Canadian leaders, who had been generously treated by the British in the Quebec Act of 1774, showed no real desire to welcome the plundering anti-Catholic invaders.

Washington at Verplanck's Point, New York, 1782, Reviewing the French Troops After the Victory at Yorktown, by John Trumbull, 1790 This noted American artist accentuated Washington's height (6 feet, 2 inches) by showing him towering over his horse. Washington so appreciated this portrait of himself that he hung it in his dining room at his home at Mount Vernon, Virginia.

Bitter fighting persisted in the colonies, though the Americans still continued to disclaim a desire for independence. In January 1776 the British set fire to the Virginia town of Norfolk. In March they were finally forced to evacuate Boston, taking with them the leading friends of the king. In the South the rebellious colonists won two victories in 1776: one in February against some fifteen hundred Loyalists at Moore's Creek Bridge in North Carolina, and the other in June against an invading British fleet in Charleston harbor.

Thomas Paine Preaches Common Sense

Why did Americans continue to deny any intention of independence? Loyalty to the empire was deeply ingrained; many

Americans continued to consider themselves part of a transatlantic community in which the mother country of Britain played a leading role; colonial unity was poor; and open rebellion was dangerous, especially against a formidable Britain. Irish rebels of that day were customarily hanged, drawn, and quartered. American rebels might have fared no better. As late as January 1776—five months before independence was declared—the king's health was being toasted by the officers of Washington's mess near Boston. "God save the king" had not yet been replaced by "God save the Congress."

Gradually the Americans were shocked into recognizing the necessity of separating from the crown. Their eyes were jolted open by harsh British acts like the burning of Falmouth and Norfolk, and especially by the hiring of the Hessians. Then in 1776 came the publication of *Common Sense,* one of the most influential pamphlets ever written. Its author was the radical Thomas Paine, once an impoverished corset-maker's apprentice, who had come over from Britain a year earlier. His tract became a whirlwind bestseller and within a few months reached the astonishing total of 120,000 copies.

Paine flatly branded the shilly-shallying of the colonists as contrary to "common sense." Nowhere in the physical universe did the smaller heavenly body control the larger one. Then why should the tiny island of Britain control the vast continent of America? As for the king, whom the Americans professed to revere, he was nothing but "the Royal Brute of Great Britain."

Paine's passionate protest was as compelling as it was eloquent and radical—even doubly radical. It called not simply for independence but for the creation of a new kind of political society, a *republic,* where power flowed from the people themselves, not from a corrupt and despotic monarch. In language laced with biblical imagery familiar to common folk, Paine argued that all government officials—governors, senators, and judges, not just representatives in a house of commons—should derive their authority from popular consent.

The colonists' experience with governance had prepared them well for Paine's summons to create a republic. Many settlers, particularly New Englanders, had practiced a kind of republicanism in their democratic town meetings and annual elections, while the popularly elected committees of correspondence during 1774 and 1775 had demonstrated the feasibility of republican government. The absence of a hereditary aristocracy and the relative equality of condition enjoyed by landowning farmers meshed well with the republican repudiation of a fixed hierarchy of power.

Most Americans considered citizen "virtue" fundamental to any successful republican government. Because political power no longer rested with the king, individuals in a republic needed to sacrifice their personal self-interest to the public good. The collective good of "the people" mattered more than the private rights and interests of individuals. Paine inspired his contemporaries to view America as fertile ground for the cultivation of such civic virtue.

In Common Sense *Thomas Paine (1737–1809) argued for the superiority of a republic over a monarchy:*

"The nearer any government approaches to a republic the less business there is for a king. It is somewhat difficult to find a proper name for the government of England. Sir William Meredith calls it a republic; but in its present state it is unworthy of the name, because the corrupt influence of the crown, by having all the places in its disposal, hath so effectively swallowed up the power, and eaten out the virtue of the house of commons (the republican part of the constitution) that the government of England is nearly as monarchical as that of France or Spain."

■ Portrait of Thomas Paine, by Auguste Millière.

Primary source
Gouverneur Morris Warns Against Democratic Revolution
college.hmco.com/pic/kennedybrief7e

Yet not all Patriots agreed with Paine's ultrademocratic approach to republicanism. Some favored a republic ruled by a "natural aristocracy" of talent. Republicanism for them meant an end to hereditary aristocracy but not an end to all social hierarchy. These more conservative republicans feared that the fervor for liberty would overwhelm the stability of the social order. They watched with trepidation as the "lower orders" of society—poorer farmers, tenants, and laboring classes in towns and cities—seemed to embrace a kind of runaway republicanism that amounted to radical "leveling." The contest to define the nature of American republicanism would noisily continue for the next hundred years.

Jefferson's "Explanation" of Independence

Members of the Philadelphia Congress, instructed by their respective colonies, gradually edged toward a clean break. On June 7, 1776, fiery Richard Henry Lee of Virginia moved that "These United Colonies are, and of right ought to be, free and independent states. . . ." After considerable debate, the motion was adopted nearly a month later, on July 2, 1776.

The passing of Lee's resolution was the formal "declaration" of independence by the American colonies, and technically this was all that was needed to cut the British tie. John Adams wrote confidently that ever thereafter July 2 would be celebrated annually with fireworks. But something more was required. An epochal rupture of this kind called for some formal explanation to "a candid world." An inspirational appeal was also needed to enlist other British colonies in the Americas, to invite assistance from foreign nations, and to rally resistance at home.

Shortly after Lee made his memorable motion on June 7, Congress appointed a committee to prepare a more formal statement of separation. The task of drafting it fell to Thomas Jefferson, a tall, freckled, sandy-haired Virginia lawyer of thirty-three. Despite his youth, he was already recognized as a brilliant writer, and he measured up splendidly to the awesome assignment. After some debate and amendment, the Declaration of Independence was formally approved by the Congress on July 4, 1776.

Jefferson's pronouncement, couched in a lofty style, was magnificent. He gave his appeal universality by invoking the "natural rights" of humankind—not just British rights. He argued persuasively that because the king had flouted these rights, the colonists were justified in cutting their connection. He then set forth a long list of the presumably tyrannous misdeeds of George III. The overdrawn bill of **indictment** included imposing taxes without consent, dispensing with trial by jury, abolishing valued laws, establishing a military **dictatorship,** maintaining standing armies in peacetime, cutting off trade, burning towns, hiring **mercenaries,** and inciting hostility among the Indians.*

indictment *A formal written accusation charging someone with a crime.*

dictatorship *A form of government characterized by absolute state power and the unlimited authority of the ruler.*

mercenaries *A professional soldier who serves in a foreign army for pay.*

The formal declaration of independence cleared the air as a thundershower does on a muggy day. Foreign aid could be solicited with greater hope of success. Those Patriots who defied the king were now rebels, not loving subjects shooting their way into reconciliation. They must all hang together, Franklin is said to have grimly remarked, or they would all hang separately. Or, in the eloquent language of the great declaration, "We mutually pledge to each other our lives, our fortunes and our sacred honor."

Patriots and Loyalists

The War of Independence, strictly speaking, was a civil war between two factions of Americans as well as a war between Americans and the British. Besides battling the British redcoats, the American rebels, called Patriots or "Whigs," fought Americans loyal to the king, called Loyalists or "Tories" (see "Makers of America: The Loyalists," p. 102).

*For an annotated text of the Declaration of Independence, see the Appendix.

Like many revolutions, the American Revolution was a minority movement. Many colonists were apathetic or **neutral,** including the Byrds of Virginia, who sat on the fence. The opposing forces contended not only against each other but also for the allegiance and support of the **civilian** population. In this struggle for the hearts and minds of the people, the Patriot militia proved far more successful than the inept British. The British military proved able to control only those areas where it could maintain a massive military presence. Elsewhere, as soon as the redcoats had marched on, the rebel militiamen appeared and took up the task of "political education"—sometimes by coercive means. Often lacking bayonets but always loaded with political zeal, the ragtag militia units convinced many colonists, even those indifferent to independence, that the British army was an unreliable friend and that they had better throw in their lot with the Patriot cause.

The American signers of the Declaration of Independence had reason to fear for their necks. In 1802, twenty-six years later, George III (1738–1820) approved this death sentence for seven Irish rebels:

". . . [You] are to be hanged by the neck, but not until you are dead; for while you are still living your bodies are to be taken down, your bowels torn out and burned before your faces, your heads then cut off, and your bodies divided each into four quarters, and your heads and quarters to be then at the King's disposal; and may the Almighty God have mercy on your souls."

Loyalists, numbering perhaps 15 percent of the American people, remained true to their king. Some fifty thousand Loyalist volunteers at one time or another bore arms for the British. They also helped the king's cause by serving as spies, by inciting the Indians, and by keeping Patriot soldiers at home to protect their families.

Many people of education and wealth, of culture and caution, remained loyal. Loyalists were more numerous among the older generation, for young people make revolutions. They also included the king's officers and other beneficiaries of the crown—people who knew which side their daily bread came from. Loyalists were most numerous where the Anglican Church was strongest, except in Virginia, where debt-burdened Anglican aristocrats flocked into the rebel camp. The king's followers were well entrenched in aristocratic New York City and Charleston, and also in Quaker Pennsylvania and New Jersey, where General Washington felt that he was fighting in "the enemy's country." Loyalists were least numerous in New England, where Presbyterianism and Congregationalism flourished, producing strong support for rebellion.

Primary source
Maryland Preacher Resists the Patriots
college.hmco.com/pic/kennedybrief7e

Before the Declaration of Independence in 1776, persecution of the Loyalists was relatively mild. But once independence was declared, Loyalists were more roughly handled. Hundreds of Loyalists were imprisoned and a few were hanged. About eighty thousand loyal supporters of George III were driven out or fled the country, and their estates were **confiscated** to finance the war. But no reign of terror comparable to that of the later French and Russian revolutions occurred. Confiscation often worked great economic hardship, but most Loyalists did not regret their stand. Ardent Loyalists had their hearts in their cause, and a major blunder of the haughty British was not to make full use of them in the fighting.

neutral *A nation or person not taking sides in a war.*

civilian *A citizen not in military service.*

confiscated *To seize private property for public use, often as a penalty.*

General Washington at Bay

Primary source
New Jersey Artisan Is Tarred and Feathered
college.hmco.com/pic/kennedybrief7e

After evacuating Boston in March 1776, the British made New York City their central base of operations. Here was a splendid seaport, centrally located, where the king could count on cooperation from the numerous Loyalists. An awe-inspiring British fleet appeared off New York in July 1776. It consisted of some five hundred ships and thirty-five thousand men—the largest armed force to be seen in America until the Civil War. General Washington, dangerously outnumbered, could muster only eighteen thousand ill-trained troops with which to meet the crack army of the invader.

Disaster befell the Americans in the summer and fall of 1776. Outgeneraled and outmaneuvered, they were routed at the Battle of Long Island, where panic seized the raw recruits. By the narrowest of margins, and thanks to a favoring wind and fog, Washington escaped to Manhattan Island. Retreating northward, he crossed the Hudson River to New Jersey and finally reached the Delaware River

The Loyalists

In late 1776 Catherine Van Cortlandt wrote to her husband, a New Jersey merchant fighting in a Loyalist brigade, about the Patriot troops who had quartered themselves in her house. "They were the most disorderly of species," she complained, "and their officers were from the dregs of the people."

Like the Van Cortlandts, many Loyalists thought of themselves as "the better sort of people." Conservative, wealthy, and well-educated, Loyalists of this breed thought a break with Britain would invite anarchy. But Loyalism was hardly confined to the well-to-do. It also appealed to many people of modest means who identified strongly with Britain or who had reason to fear a Patriot victory. They included British veterans of the Seven Years' War who had received land grants from the crown, and recent immigrants from Scotland and Ireland who had settled the backcountry of Georgia or the Carolinas. Resenting the plantation elites who ran these colonies, they filled the ranks of Tory brigades organized by the British army.

Online Study Center

Primary source
Legislative Attacks on the Loyalists
college.hmco.com/pic/kennedybrief7e

Online Study Center

Primary source
Loyalist Widow Decries the Fate of Tory Exiles in Canada
college.hmco.com/pic/kennedybrief7e

Other ethnic minorities found their own reasons to support the British. Some Dutch, German, and French religious sects believed that religious tolerance would be greater under the British than under the Americans. Encouraged by British officials, thousands of African Americans joined the Loyalist ranks in hopes that their service might bring an escape from bondage. Many of them joined black regiments that specialized in making small sorties against Patriot militia.

As the war drew to an end in 1783, the fate of black Loyalists varied enormously. Many thousands who came to Loyalism as fugitive slaves managed to find a way to freedom, especially in Nova Scotia. Other African American Loyalists suffered betrayal. British general Lord Cornwallis abandoned over four thousand former slaves in Virginia, and others found themselves sold back into slavery in the West Indies.

White Loyalists faced no threat of enslavement, but they did often suffer arrest, exile, confiscation of property, and loss of legal rights. Faced with such retribution, some eighty thousand Loyalists fled abroad, mostly to Britain or Canada. Some settled contentedly as exiles, but many, especially in Britain, had difficulty becoming accepted and lived lonely and diminished lives.

Most Loyalists, though, remained in America, despite the daunting burden of reestablishing themselves in a society that viewed them as traitors. Some succeeded remarkably, such as Hugh Gaine, a New York City printer who reopened his business and even won printing contracts from the new government. Gaine reintegrated himself into public life by siding with the Federalist call for a strong central government and a powerful executive. When New York ratified the Constitution in 1788, Gaine rode the float at the head of the city's celebration parade. He had, like many other former Loyalists, become an American.

with the British close at his heels. Tauntingly, enemy buglers sounded the fox-hunting call so familiar to Virginians of Washington's day. The Patriot cause was at low ebb when the rebel remnants fled across the river after collecting all available boats to forestall pursuit.

The wonder is that Washington's adversary, General William Howe, did not speedily crush the demoralized American forces. But Howe was no military genius, and he well remembered the horrible slaughter at Bunker Hill, where he had commanded. The country was rough, supplies were slow in coming, and Howe did not relish the rigors of winter campaigning. Washington, who was now almost counted out, stealthily recrossed the ice-clogged Delaware River. At Trenton, on December 26, 1776, he surprised and captured a thousand Hessians who were sleeping off the effects of their Christmas celebration. A week later, leaving his campfires burning as a ruse, he slipped away and inflicted another sharp defeat on a smaller British detachment at Princeton. This brilliant New Jersey campaign, crowned by these two lifesaving victories, revealed "Old Fox" Washington at his military best.

Burgoyne's Blundering Invasion

London officials adopted an intricate scheme for capturing the vital Hudson River Valley in 1777. If successful, the British would sever New England from the rest of the states and paralyze the American cause. The main invading force, under the soldier-actor-playwright General John ("Gentleman Johnny") Burgoyne, would push down the Lake Champlain route from Canada. General Howe's troops in New York would advance up the Hudson River to meet Burgoyne near Albany. A third and much smaller British force, commanded by Colonel Barry St. Leger, would come in from the west by way of Lake Ontario and the Mohawk Valley.

British planners did not reckon with General Benedict Arnold. Retreating slowly from Quebec after being repulsed there in 1775, Arnold had by heroic efforts kept his army in the field and assembled a small fleet on Lake Champlain. The British finally constructed a fleet that defeated Arnold's tiny flotilla. But by then winter was descending, and the British were forced to retire back to Canada. This delay was critical to the American cause.

Compelled to start over in the spring of 1777, General Burgoyne began his fateful invasion with seven thousand regular troops who were encumbered by a heavy baggage train and many accompanying officers' wives. Progress was painfully slow, for sweaty axmen had to chop a path through the forest, while American militiamen began to swarm like hornets on Burgoyne's flanks.

Meanwhile, astonished eyebrows rose as General Howe marched the main British army toward the rebel capital of Philadelphia at a time when it seemed obvious he should be starting up the Hudson River from New York to meet the advancing Burgoyne. As scholars now know, Howe wanted to engage and destroy Washington's army, apparently assuming he had ample time to assist Burgoyne directly should he be needed.

General Washington, keeping a wary eye on the British in New York, hastily transferred his army to the vicinity of Philadelphia. There, late in 1777, he was defeated in two pitched battles at Brandywine Creek and Germantown. Pleasure-loving General Howe then settled down comfortably in the lively capital, leaving Burgoyne to flounder through the wilds of upstate New York. Benjamin Franklin, recently sent to Paris as an **envoy,** truthfully jested that Howe had not captured Philadelphia but that Philadelphia had captured Howe. Washington finally retired to winter quarters at Valley Forge, a strong hilly position some twenty miles northwest of Philadelphia. There his frostbitten and hungry men were short of about everything except misery. This **rabble** was nevertheless whipped into a professional army by the recently arrived Prussian drillmaster, the profane but patient Baron von Steuben.

Burgoyne, meanwhile, had begun to bog down north of Albany, while a host of American militiamen, scenting the kill, hounded him on all sides. In a series of sharp engagements, the British army was trapped. Meanwhile, the Americans had driven back St. Leger's force at Oriskany, New York. Unable to advance or retreat, Burgoyne was forced to surrender his entire command at Saratoga, on October 17, 1777, to the American general Horatio Gates.

envoy *A messenger or agent sent by a government on official business.*

rabble *A mass of disorderly and crude common people.*

Primary source
Abigail Smith Adams (Mrs. John Adams)
college.hmco.com/pic/kennedybrief7e

EXAMINING THE EVIDENCE

A Revolution for Women? Abigail Adams Chides Her Husband, 1776 In the midst of the revolutionary fervor of 1776, at least one woman—Abigail Adams, wife of noted Massachusetts Patriot (and future president) John Adams—raised her voice on behalf of women. Yet she apparently raised it only in private—in this personal letter to her husband. Private documents like the correspondence and diaries of individuals both prominent and ordinary offer invaluable sources for the historian seeking to discover sentiments, opinions, and perspectives that are often difficult to discern in the official public record.

1. What does it suggest about the historical circumstances of the 1770s that Abigail Adams confined her claim for women's equality to this confidential exchange with her spouse?
2. What ideas and events inspired the arguments Adams employed?
3. Despite her privileged position and persuasive power, and despite her threat to "foment a rebellion," Abigail Adams's plea went largely unheeded in the Revolutionary era—as did comparable pleadings to extend the revolutionary principle of equality to blacks. What accounts for this limited application of the ideas of liberty and equality in the midst of a supposedly democratic revolution?

the Evils Shun it — I long to hear that you have de
-clared an independancy — and by the way in the new
Code of Laws which I suppose it will be necessary for you
to make I desire you would Remember the Ladies, &
be more generous & favourable to them than your ancestors
Do not put such unlimited power into the hands of the
Husbands. Remember all Men would be tyrants if they
could. if perticuliar care & attention is not paid to the
Laidies we are determined to foment a Rebelion, and will
not hold ourselves bound by any Laws in which we have
no voice, or Representation — That your Sex are Naturally

■ **Washington Crossing the Delaware, by Emanuel Gottlieb Leutze, 1851** On Christmas Day, 1776, George Washington set out from Pennsylvania with twenty-four hundred men to surprise the British forces, chiefly Hessians, in their quarters across the river in New Jersey. The subsequent British defeat proved to be a turning point in the Revolution, as it checked the British advance toward Philadelphia and restored American morale. Seventy-five years later, Leutze, a German-born American painter, mythologized the heroic campaign in this painting.

Saratoga ranks high among the decisive battles of both American and world history. The victory immensely revived the faltering colonial cause. Even more important, it made possible the urgently needed foreign aid from France, which in turn helped ensure American independence.

Revolutionary America and the World

France, thirsting for revenge against Britain, was eager to inflame the quarrel that had broken out in America and cripple British imperial power. The American revolutionaries badly needed help to throw off the British yoke. The stage seemed set for the embattled new nation to make its diplomatic debut by sealing an alliance with France against the common foe.

Yet just as they stood for revolutionary political ideals at home, the rebellious Americans also harbored revolutionary ideas about international affairs. They wanted to end colonialism, promote free trade and freedom of the seas, and substitute the rule of law for the ancient reliance on raw power to arbitrate the affairs of nations. The Continental Congress accordingly instructed its emissaries to France to seek no political or military alliance, but only a commercial connection. These remarkable restrictions reflected a belief among enlightened American and European thinkers of the time that history had reached a momentous turning point when military conflict would be abandoned in favor of peaceful commerce between nations. While some critics considered this dream hopelessly naïve and utopian, it infused an element of idealism into American attitudes toward international affairs that has proved stubbornly persistent.

When wily old Benjamin Franklin arrived in Paris to negotiate the treaty with France, he was determined that his very appearance should herald the diplomatic revolution the Americans hoped to achieve. Forsaking the ermined robes and

Map Skill-Builder: Understanding Military Maps

1. Examine the map carefully in relation to the text's discussion of Britain's grand strategy for crushing the rebellion quickly (pp. 101–105). Approximately where were the three British armies under Burgoyne, St. Leger, and Howe supposed to converge and trap the Americans?
2. Which one of the three British generals moved in the opposite direction he was supposed to go, and therefore failed to arrive at the appointed rendezvous?
3. Which of the three was defeated far short of the intended goal?
4. Which one got closest to the intended rendezvous point, but found himself alone and trapped by the Americans, instead of trapping them as the British plan intended?

New York–Pennsylvania Theater, 1777–1778 Distinguished members of the Continental Congress fled from Philadelphia in near-panic as the British army approached. Thomas Paine reported that at three o'clock in the morning the streets were "as full of Men, Women, and Children as on a Market Day." John Adams had anticipated that "I shall run away, I suppose, with the rest," since "we are too brittle ware, you know, to stand the dashing of balls and bombs." Adams got his chance to decamp with the others into the interior of Pennsylvania and tried to put the best face on things. "This tour," he commented, "has given me an opportunity of seeing many parts of this country which I never saw before."

fancy wigs expected in the royal court, he sported homespun garments and a simple cap of marten fur. Pompous French diplomats were shocked, but ordinary Parisians adored him as a specimen of a new democratic social order, devoid of pretense and ornament. Franklin's personal popularity was a valuable card in the diplomatic game.

Franklin also played skillfully on French fears of reconciliation between Britain and America. After the humiliation of Saratoga in 1777, the British had belatedly offered the Americans a species of home rule within the empire. To counter this, the French offered Franklin a treaty that bound both parties to wage war until the United States had fully secured its freedom and until both agreed to terms with the common enemy. In an example of practical self-interest trumping abstract idealism in the conduct of foreign affairs, the young Republic agreed to join its first entangling military alliance. The treaty with France, signed in February 1778, constituted an official recognition of America's independence and lent powerful military heft to the Patriot cause.

With France now supporting the Americans' cause, the shot fired at Lexington rapidly widened into a global conflagration. Spain entered the fray against Britain in 1779, as did Holland. Combined Spanish and French fleets outnumbered those of Britain, and on two occasions the British Isles seemed to be at the mercy of hostile warships. Catherine the Great of Russia lined up the remaining European neutrals into the "Armed Neutrality" that assumed an attitude of passive hostility toward Britain.

To Britain, now struggling for its very life, the scuffle in the New World soon became secondary. The Americans deserve credit for having kept the war going until 1778. But they did not achieve their independence until the conflict erupted into a multipower world war that was too big for Britain to handle. From 1778 to 1783, France provided the rebels with guns, money, immense amounts of equipment, about one-half of America's regular armed forces, and practically all of the new nation's naval strength.

France's entrance into the conflict forced the British to change their basic strategy in America. With powerful French fleets in American waters, Britain could no longer **blockade** the colonial coast and command the seas. To shorten their lines of supply, the British evacuated Philadelphia and escaped to New York City after the indecisive Battle of Monmouth in June 1778. Washington followed them to the New York area and hemmed them in.

blockade *The isolation of a place by hostile ships or troops.*

Blow and Counterblow

In the summer of 1780 a powerful French army of six thousand regular troops, commanded by the Comte de Rochambeau, arrived in Newport, Rhode Island. Preparations began for a Franco-American attack on New York.

Improving American morale was staggered later in 1780 when General Benedict Arnold turned traitor. A leader of undoubted dash and brilliance, he was ambitious, greedy, and unscrupulous, and he suffered from a well-grounded but petulant feeling that his valuable services were not fully appreciated. He plotted with the British to sell out the key stronghold of West Point, which commanded the Hudson River, for £6,300 and an officer's commission. By the sheerest accident the plot was detected in the nick of time, and Arnold fled to the British. "Whom can we trust now?" cried General Washington in anguish.

The British meanwhile had devised a new plan to roll up the colonies, beginning with the South, where the Loyalists were numerous. Georgia was ruthlessly overrun in 1778–1779. Charleston, South Carolina, fell in 1780. The surrender of that city to the British involved the capture of five thousand men and four hundred cannon, and was a heavier loss to the Americans, in relation to existing strength, than Burgoyne's was to the British.

Warfare now intensified in the Carolinas, where Patriots bitterly fought their Loyalist neighbors. It was not uncommon for prisoners on both sides to be butchered in cold blood after they had thrown down their arms. The tide turned later in 1780 and early in 1781, when American riflemen wiped out a British detachment at King's Mountain and then defeated a smaller force at Cowpens. In the Carolina campaign of 1781, General Nathanael Greene, a Quaker-reared tactician, distinguished himself by his strategy of delay. Standing and then retreating, he exhausted his foe, General Cornwallis, in vain pursuit. By losing battles but winning campaigns, the "Fighting Quaker" finally succeeded in clearing most of Georgia and South Carolina of British troops.

Online Study Center

Primary source
Charleston, South Carolina, Sons of Liberty
college.hmco.com/pic/kennedybrief7e

Interactive map
The War in the South, 1778–1781
college.hmco.com/pic/kennedybrief7e

Interactive map
The War in the South
college.hmco.com/pic/kennedybrief7e

The Land Frontier and the Sea Frontier

The West was ablaze during much of the war. Indian allies of George III, hoping to protect their land, were busy attacking and burning frontier settlements. They were egged on by British agents, branded as "hair buyers" because they allegedly paid bounties for American scalps. Although two nations of the Iroquois Confederacy, the Oneidas and the Tuscaroras, sided with the Americans, the Senecas, Mohawks, Cayugas, and Onondagas joined the British. They were led by Mohawk

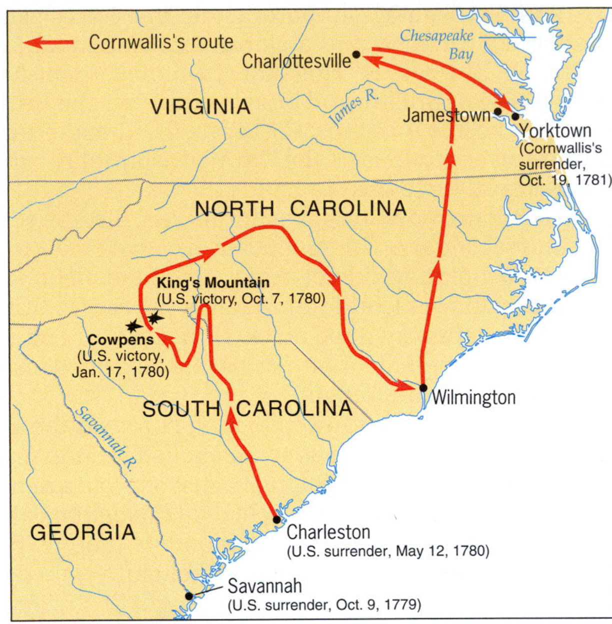

■ War in the South, 1780–1781

chief Joseph Brant, a convert to Anglicanism who believed that a victorious Britain would restrain American expansion into the West. Brant and the British ravaged large areas of back-country Pennsylvania and New York until checked by an American force in 1779.

In the wild Illinois country the British were especially vulnerable to attack, for they held only scattered posts that they had captured from the French. An audacious frontiersman, George Rogers Clark, conceived the idea of seizing these forts by surprise. In 1778–1779 he floated down the Ohio River with about 175 men and captured in quick succession Forts Kaskaskia, Cahokia, and Vincennes.

Interactive map
The Indian Confederacies
college.hmco.com/pic/kennedybrief7e

America's infant navy, commanded by daring officers like the hard-fighting young Scotsman John Paul Jones, was more successful in destroying British merchant shipping than in engaging Britain's powerful fleets. More numerous and damaging than ships of the regular American navy were swift **privateers.** Authorized by Congress, over a thousand of these privately owned armed ships preyed on enemy shipping and captured some six hundred British prizes. Although they diverted manpower from the main war effort and involved Americans in speculation and **graft,** privateers brought in urgently needed gold, harassed the enemy, and raised American morale. Unhappy British shippers and manufacturers brought increasing pressure on Parliament to end the war on honorable terms.

privateers *A private vessel temporarily authorized to capture or plunder enemy ships in wartime.*

graft *Taking advantage of one's official position to gain money or property by illegal means.*

Yorktown and the Final Curtain

One of the darkest periods of the war was 1780–1781, just before the last decisive victory. Inflation of the currency continued at full gallop, and the government was virtually bankrupt. Despair prevailed; the sense of unity withered; and mutinous sentiments infected the army.

Meanwhile, the British General Cornwallis was blundering into a trap. After futile operations in Virginia, he had fallen back to Chesapeake Bay at Yorktown to await seaborne supplies and reinforcements. He assumed Britain would continue to control the sea. But these few fateful weeks just happened to be one of the brief periods during the war when British naval superiority slipped away.

The French were now prepared to cooperate energetically in a brilliant stroke. Admiral de Grasse, operating with a powerful fleet in the West Indies, sent word to the Americans that he was free to join with them in an assault on Cornwallis at Yorktown. Quick to seize this opportunity, General Washington made a swift march of more than three hundred miles to the Chesapeake from the New York area. Accompanied by Rochambeau's French army, Washington beset the British by land, while de Grasse blockaded them by sea after beating off the British fleet. Completely cornered, Cornwallis surrendered his entire force of seven thousand men on October 19, 1781, as his band appropriately played "The World Turn'd Upside Down." The triumph was no less French than American: France provided essentially all the seapower and about half of the regular troops in the besieging army of some sixteen thousand men.

Stunned by news of the disaster, Prime Minister Lord North cried, "Oh God! It's all over! It's all over!" But it was not. George III stubbornly planned to continue the struggle, for Britain was far from being crushed. It still had fifty-four thousand troops in North America, including thirty-two thousand in the United States. Washington returned with his army to New York, there to continue keeping a vigilant eye on a British force of ten thousand men.

Fighting actually continued for more than a year after Yorktown, with Patriot-Loyalist warfare in the South especially savage. "No quarter for Tories" was the common battle cry. One of Washington's most valuable contributions was to keep the cause alive, the army in the field, and the states together during these critical months. Otherwise, a satisfactory peace treaty might never have been signed.

Baron von Steuben (1730–1794), a Prussian general who helped train the Continental Army, found the Americans to be very different from other soldiers he had known. As von Steuben explained to a fellow European,

"The genius of this nation is not in the least to be compared with that of the Prussians, Austrians, or French. You say to your soldier, 'Do this' and he doeth it; but I am obliged to say, 'This is the reason why you ought to do that,' and then he does it."

Peace at Paris

After Yorktown, many Britons were weary of war and increasingly ready to come to terms. They had suffered heavy reverses in India and in the West Indies. Lord North's Tory ministry collapsed in March 1782, and was replaced by a Whig ministry rather favorable to the Americans.

Three American peace negotiators had meanwhile gathered at Paris: the aging but astute Benjamin Franklin; the flinty John Adams, vigilant for New England interests; and the impulsive John Jay of New York, deeply suspicious of Old World intrigue. The three envoys had explicit instructions from Congress to make no separate peace and to consult with their French allies at all stages of the negotiations. But the American representatives chafed under this directive. They well knew that it had been written by a subservient Congress, with the French Foreign Office indirectly guiding the pen.

France was in a painful position. It had induced Spain to enter the war on its side, and the Spanish coveted the immense trans-Appalachian area for itself. Wanting an America that would be independent but feeble, the French therefore joined the scheme to keep the new republic cooped up east of the Appalachian Mountains.

But John Jay was unwilling to play France's game. Suspiciously alert, he perceived that the French could not satisfy the conflicting ambitions of both Americans and Spaniards. He saw signs—or thought he did—indicating that the Paris Foreign Office was about to betray America's trans-Appalachian interests to satisfy those of Spain. He therefore secretly made separate overtures to London, contrary to his instructions from Congress. The hard-pressed British, eager to entice one of their enemies from the alliance, speedily came to terms with the Americans. The final Treaty of Paris concluding the war was signed in 1783.

By terms of the treaty, the British formally recognized the independence of the United States. In addition, they granted

Benjamin Franklin (1706–1790), by Charles Willson Peale, 1789 He left school at age ten, and became a wealthy businessman, a journalist, an inventor, a scientist, a legislator, and preeminently a statesman-diplomat. He was sent to France in 1776 as the American envoy at age seventy, and he remained there until 1785, negotiating the alliance with the French and helping to negotiate the treaty of peace. His fame had preceded him, and when he discarded his wig for the fur cap of a simple "American agriculturist," he took French society by storm. French aristocratic women, with whom he was a great favorite, honored him by adopting the high coiffure à la Franklin in imitation of his cap.

generous boundaries, stretching majestically to the Mississippi on the west, to the Great Lakes on the north, and to Spanish Florida on the south. (Spain had recently captured Florida from Britain.)

The Americans, on their part, had to yield important concessions. Loyalists were not to be further persecuted, and Congress was to *recommend* to the state legislatures that confiscated Loyalist property be restored. As for the debts long owed to British creditors, the states vowed to put no lawful obstacles in the way of their collection. Unhappily for future harmony, the assurances regarding both Loyalists and debts were not carried out in the manner hoped for by London.

A New Nation Legitimized

Britain's terms were liberal almost beyond belief. The enormous trans-Appalachian area was thrown in as a virtual gift, for George Rogers Clark had captured only a small segment of it. Why the generosity? Had the United States beaten Britain to its knees?

The key to the riddle may be found in the Old World. At the time the peace terms were drafted, Britain was trying to seduce America from its French alliance, so it made the terms as alluring as possible. The shaky Whig ministry, hanging on by its fingernails for only a few months, was more friendly to the Americans than were the Tories. It was determined, by a policy of liberality, to salve recent wounds, reopen old trade channels, and prevent future wars over the coveted trans-Appalachian region. This far-visioned policy was regrettably not followed by the successors of the Whigs.

In spirit, the Americans made a separate peace—contrary to the French alliance. In fact, they did not. The Paris Foreign Office formally approved the terms of peace, though disturbed by the lone-wolf course of its American ally. France was immensely relieved by the prospect of bringing the costly conflict to an end, and of freeing itself from its embarrassing promises to the Spanish crown.

America alone gained from the world-girdling war. The British, though soon to stage a comeback, were battered and beaten. The French savored sweet revenge but plunged headlong down the slippery slope to bankruptcy and revolution. The Americans fared much better. Snatching their independence from the furnace of world conflict, they began their national career with a splendid territorial birthright and a priceless heritage of freedom. Seldom, if ever, have any people been so favored.

Chapter Summary

Even after the shooting began at Lexington and Concord in April 1775, the Second Continental Congress did not at first pursue independence. Instead, it continued to appeal to the king to respect "the rights of Englishmen." The Congress's most important action was selecting George Washington as military commander.

After further armed clashes, George III formally proclaimed the colonists in rebellion. In early 1776, Thomas Paine's *Common Sense* finally persuaded Americans to fight for independence as well as liberty. Paine and other leaders promoted the Revolution as an opportunity for self-government by the people, though more conservative republicans disliked revolutionary egalitarianism and hoped to retain a strong political hierarchy without monarchy. Jefferson's Declaration of Independence deepened the meaning of the American Revolution by proclaiming it a fight for self-evident and universal human rights applicable to all peoples everywhere.

The committed revolutionary Patriots, only a minority of the American population, had to fight a civil war with Loyalist Americans as well as the professionally trained and better-armed British army and navy. Loyalists were strongest among conservatives, city-dwellers, and Anglicans (except in Virginia). Patriots were strongest in New England and among Presbyterians and Congregationalists.

In the first phase of the war, Washington was barely able to hold off the British, who botched their grand plan to isolate New England and quash the rebellion quickly. Victory in the Battle of Saratoga brought Americans new respect and the prospect of international assistance. Partially compromising their idealistic revolutionary beliefs that traditional military alliances were wrong, Franklin and other U.S. emissaries joined an alliance with France. With active French involvement, the Revolutionary War became a world war.

American fortunes turned very sour in 1780–1781, as political and economic troubles and military stalemate again nearly led to defeat. But General Nathanael Greene's Continental Army in the South held on until Cornwallis stumbled into a French-American trap at Yorktown. Lord North's ministry collapsed in Britain, and American negotiators achieved an extremely generous settlement from the new Whig government in London.

VARYING VIEWPOINTS

Whose Revolution?

Historians once assumed that the American Revolution was just another chapter in the unfolding story of human liberty—an important way station on a divinely ordained pathway toward moral perfection in human affairs. This approach, often labeled the "Whig view of history," was best expressed in George Bancroft's ten-volume *History of the United States*, published between the 1830s and the 1870s.

In the nineteenth century, an "imperial school" of historians like Charles Andrews and Lawrence Gipson argued that the revolution was primarily a constitutional conflict within the British Empire. By the early twentieth century, both the Whig and imperial-school interpretations were sharply challenged by so-called progressive historians, who argued that neither divine destiny nor constitutional squabbles had much to do with the Revolution. Rather, progressives like Carl Becker and J. Franklin Jameson claimed the Revolution stemmed from deep-seated class tensions within American society that, once released by revolt, produced a truly transformed social order. The Revolution, therefore, was not only about "home rule" within the British Empire but about "who should rule at home" in America.

In the 1950s, the progressive historians fell out of favor as the political climate became more conservative. Historians such as Robert Brown and Edmund Morgan downplayed the role of class conflict in the Revolutionary era, but emphasized that colonists of all ranks shared a commitment to certain fundamental political principles of self-government. The unifying power of ideas was now back in fashion almost a hundred years after Bancroft.

Since the 1950s two broad interpretations have contended with each other and perpetuated the controversy over whether political ideals or economic and social realities were most responsible for the Revolution. The first, articulated most prominently by Bernard Bailyn, has emphasized inherent ideological and psychological factors. Bailyn argued that the colonists, incited by their reading of earlier English theorists, grew extraordinarily suspicious of any attempts to tighten the imperial reins. When confronted with new taxes and imperial regulations, the colonists screamed "conspiracy against liberty" and took up armed insurrection in defense of their intellectual commitment to liberty.

A second school of historians, inspired by the social movements of the turbulent 1960s and 1970s, revived the progressive interpretation of the Revolution. Gary Nash in *An Urban Crucible* (1979) and Edward Countryman in *A People in Revolution* (1981) pointed to attacks by laborers on political elites and expressions of resentment toward wealth as evidence of a society breeding revolution from within, quite aside from British provocations. The neoprogressives argue that the varying material circumstances of American participants gave the Revolution a less unified and more complex ideological underpinning than the idealistic historians had previously suggested.

More recently, scholars have taken a more transatlantic view of the Revolution's origins, asking when and how colonists shifted from identifying as "British" to viewing themselves as "American." Fred Anderson argued that the Seven Years' War helped create a sense of American identity apart from Britain, and T. H. Breen said that American nationalism emerged because the British failed to see Americans as equal imperial citizens, entitled to the same rights as Englishmen.

PART TWO

Building The New Nation

1776–1860

By 1783 Americans had won their freedom. Now they had to build their country. To be sure, they were blessed with a vast and fertile land, and they inherited from their colonial experience a proud legacy of self-rule. But history provided scant precedent for erecting a democracy on a national scale. No law of nature guaranteed that the thirteen rebellious colonies would stay glued together as a single nation, or that they would preserve, not to mention expand, their democratic way of life. New institutions had to be created, new habits of thought cultivated. Who could predict whether the American experiment in government by the people would succeed?

The ramshackle national government cobbled together under the Articles of Confederation during the Revolutionary War soon proved woefully inadequate to the task of nation building. Less than ten years after the war's conclusion, the Articles were replaced by a new constitution, but even its adoption did not end the debate over what form American democracy should take. Would the president, or the congress, or the courts be the dominant branch of government? What should be the proper division of authority between the federal government and the states? How could the rights of individuals be protected against a potentially powerful government? What economic policies would best serve the infant Republic? How should the nation defend itself against foreign foes? What principles should guide foreign policy? Was America a nation at all, or was it merely a geographic expression, destined to splinter into several bitterly quarreling sections, as had happened to so many other would-be countries?

After a shaky start under George Washington and John Adams in the 1790s, buffeted by foreign troubles and domestic crises, the new Republic passed a major test when power was peacefully transferred from the conservative Federalists to the more liberal Jeffersonians in the election of 1800. A confident President Jefferson proceeded boldly to expand the national territory with the landmark Louisiana Purchase in 1803. But before long Jefferson, and then his successor, James Madison, were embroiled in what eventually proved to be a fruitless effort to spare the United States from the ravages of the war then raging in Europe.

America was dangerously divided during the War of 1812 and suffered a humiliating defeat. But a new sense of national unity and purpose was unleashed in the land thereafter. President Monroe, presiding over this "Era of Good Feelings," proclaimed in the Monroe Doctrine of 1823 that both of the American continents were off-limits to further European intervention. The foundations of a continental-scale economy were laid, as a "transportation revolution" stitched the country together with canals and railroads and turnpikes. Settlers flooded over those new arteries into the burgeoning

West, often brusquely shouldering aside the native peoples. Immigrants, especially from Ireland and Germany, flocked to American shores. The combination of new lands and new labor fed the growth of a market economy, including the commercialization of agriculture and the beginnings of the factory system of production. Old ways of life withered as the market economy drew women as well as men, children as well as adults, blacks as well as whites, into its embrace. Ominously, the slave system grew robustly as cotton production, mostly for sale on European markets, exploded into the booming Southwest.

Meanwhile, the United States in the era of Andrew Jackson gave the world an impressive lesson in political science. Between roughly 1820 and 1840 Americans virtually invented mass democracy, creating huge political parties and enormously expanding political participation by enfranchising nearly all adult white males. Nor was the spirit of innovation confined to the political realm. A wave of reform and cultural vitality swept through many sectors of American society. Utopian experiments proliferated. Religious revivals and even new religions, like Mormonism, flourished. A national literature blossomed. Crusades were launched for temperance, prison reform, women's rights, and the abolition of slavery.

By the second quarter of the nineteenth century, the outlines of a distinctive American national character had begun to emerge. Americans were a diverse, restless people, tramping steadily westward, eagerly forging their own nascent industrial revolution, proudly exercising their democratic political rights, impatient with the old, in love with the new, testily asserting their superiority over all other peoples—and increasingly divided, in heart, in conscience, and in politics, over the single greatest blight on their record of nation making and democracy building: slavery.

What if . . . ?

- **What if the American people had failed to ratify the Constitution in 1788, and the United States had persisted as a loosely tied group of states under the Articles of Confederation? What would have been the implications for the development of political democracy, the character of the economy, the nature of foreign policy—and the fate of slavery?**

The Confederation and the Constitution

1776–1790

THIS EXAMPLE OF CHANGING THE CONSTITUTION BY ASSEMBLING THE WISE MEN OF THE STATE, INSTEAD OF ASSEMBLING ARMIES, WILL BE WORTH AS MUCH TO THE WORLD AS THE FORMER EXAMPLES WE HAVE GIVEN IT.

THOMAS JEFFERSON

Chapter Outline

- Changing Political Sentiments
- Economic Troubles
- The Articles of Confederation, 1781–1788
- The Northwest Ordinance, 1787
- Shays's Rebellion, 1786
- The Constitutional Convention, 1787
- Ratifying the Constitution, 1787–1790
- Examining the Evidence: Copley Family Portrait, c. 1776–1777
- Varying Viewpoints: The Constitution: Revolutionary or Counterrevolutionary?

The American Revolution did not usher in a radical or total change. It did not suddenly and violently overturn an entire political and social framework, as later occurred in the French and Russian revolutions. What happened was accelerated evolution rather than outright revolution.

Yet some striking changes were ushered in, affecting social customs, political institutions, and ideas about society and government and even gender roles. The exodus of some eighty thousand substantial Loyalists after the war robbed the new ship of state of conservative ballast. This weakening of the aristocratic upper crust, with all its culture and elegance, paved the way for new, Patriot elites to emerge. It also cleared the field for more egalitarian ideas to sweep across the land.

Focus Questions

1. **What were the political and social consequences of the American Revolution?**
2. **What were the primary achievements and failures of the United States under the Articles of Confederation?**
3. **What essentially motivated the drive to create a new foundation for government, and how did the Constitution written in Philadelphia reflect the Founders' central intentions?**
4. **What were the fundamental disagreements between the federalists and antifederalists, and why were the federalists successful in achieving ratification of the Constitution?**
5. **If the Constitution represented in part a "conservative" reaction to the American Revolution, how did it at the same preserve and protect the essential "radical" principles of the Revolution?**

Chronology

1774	First Continental Congress calls for abolition of slave trade.
1775	Philadelphia Quakers found world's first antislavery society.
1776	New Jersey constitution temporarily gives women the vote.
1777	Articles of Confederation adopted by Second Continental Congress.
1780	Massachusetts adopts first constitution drafted in convention and ratified by popular vote.
1781	Articles of Confederation put into effect.
1783	Military officers form Society of the Cincinnati.
1785	Land Ordinance of 1785.
1786	Virginia Statute for Religious Freedom. Shays's Rebellion. Meeting of five states to discuss revision of the Articles of Confederation.
1787	Northwest Ordinance. Constitutional Convention in Philadelphia.
1788	Ratification by nine states guarantees a new government under the Constitution.

The Pursuit of Equality

"All men are created equal," the Declaration of Independence proclaimed, and equality was everywhere the watchword. Most states reduced (but usually did not eliminate altogether) property-holding requirements for voting. Ordinary men and women demanded to be addressed as "Mr." and "Mrs."—titles once reserved for the wealthy and highborn. Most Americans ridiculed the lordly pretensions of Continental Army officers who formed an exclusive hereditary order, the Society of the Cincinnati. Social democracy was further stimulated by the growth of trade organizations for artisans and laborers.

A protracted fight for separation of church and state resulted in notable gains. The well-entrenched Congregational Church continued to be legally established in some New England states, but the Anglican Church, tainted by association with the British crown, was humbled. De-anglicized, it re-formed as the Protestant Episcopal Church and was everywhere **disestablished**. The struggle for divorce between religion and government proved fiercest in Virginia. It was prolonged to 1786, when free-thinking Thomas Jefferson and his co-reformers, including the Baptists, won a complete victory with the passage of the Virginia Statute for Religious Freedom.

The egalitarian sentiments unleashed by the war likewise challenged the institution of slavery. Philadelphia Quakers in 1775 founded the world's first antislavery society. The Continental Congress in 1774 called for the complete abolition of the slave trade, a summons to which most of the states responded positively. Several northern states went further and either abolished slavery outright or provided for the gradual **emancipation** of blacks. Even on the plantations of Virginia, a few idealistic masters freed their human **chattels**—the first frail sprouts of the later **abolitionist** movement.

But this revolution of sentiments was sadly incomplete. No states south of Pennsylvania abolished slavery, and in both North and South the law discriminated harshly against freed blacks and slaves alike. Emancipated African Americans could be barred from purchasing property, holding certain jobs, or educating their children. Laws against interracial marriage also sprang up at this time.

Why in this dawning democratic age did abolition not go further and clearly blot the evil of slavery from the fresh face of the new nation? The sorry truth is that the fledgling idealism of the Founders was sacrificed to political expediency. A fight over slavery would have fractured the fragile national unity that was so desperately needed. "Great as the evil [of slavery] is," the young Virginian James

disestablish *To separate an official state church from its connection with the government.*

emancipation *Setting free from servitude or slavery.*

chattels *An article of personal or movable property; hence a term applied to slaves, since they were considered the personal property of their owners.*

abolitionist *An advocate of the end of slavery.*

Elizabeth "Mumbet" Freeman (c. 1744–1829), by Susan Anne Livingston Ridley Sedgwick, 1811 In 1781, having overheard Revolutionary-era talk about the "rights of man," Mumbet sued her Massachusetts master for her freedom from slavery. She won her suit and lived the rest of her life as a paid domestic servant in the home of the lawyer who had pleaded her case.

Madison wrote in 1787, "a dismemberment of the union would be worse."

Likewise incomplete was the extension of the doctrine of equality to women. Some women did serve (disguised as men) in the military, and New Jersey's new constitution in 1776 even for a time enabled women to vote. But though Abigail Adams teased her husband John in 1776 that "the ladies" were determined "to foment a rebellion" of their own if they were not given political rights, most of the women in the Revolutionary era were still doing traditional women's work.

Yet women did not go untouched by revolutionary ideals. Republican ideology advanced the concept of "civic virtue"—the notion that democracy depended on the unselfish commitment of each citizen to the public good. Mothers, to whom society entrusted the education of the young, were often cited as the very models of proper republican behavior. The idea of "republican motherhood" thus took root, elevating women to a newly prestigious role as special keepers of the nation's conscience. Educational opportunities for women expanded, in the expectation that educated wives and mothers could better cultivate the virtues demanded by the Republic in their husbands, daughters, and sons. Republican women now bore crucial responsibility for the survival of the nation.

Constitution Making in the States

The Continental Congress in 1776 called on the colonies to draft new constitutions. In effect, Congress was actually asking the colonies to summon themselves into being as new states, whose sovereignty, according to the theory of republicanism, would rest on the authority of the people. In most of the states, writers of new constitutions worked tirelessly to capture on black-inked parchment the republican spirit of the age.

Massachusetts contributed one especially noteworthy innovation when it called a special convention to draft its constitution and then submitted the final draft directly to the people for **ratification.** Once adopted in 1780, the Massachusetts constitution could be changed only by another special convention. This procedure was later imitated in the drafting and ratification of the federal Constitution.

ratification *The confirmation or validation of an act (such as a constitution) by authoritative approval.*

The newly penned state constitutions enjoyed many features in common. As *written* documents, they were intended to represent a *fundamental* law, superior to the transient whims of ordinary legislation. Most of these documents included bills of rights, specifically guaranteeing long-prized liberties against later legislative encroachment. All of them deliberately created weak executive and judicial branches. A generation of quarreling with His Majesty's officials had implanted a deep distrust of despotic governors and arbitrary judges. But the legislatures, presumably the most democratic branch of government, were given sweeping powers.

The democratic character of the new state legislatures was vividly reflected in the presence of many members from the recently enfranchised poorer western districts. Their influence was powerfully felt in their several successful movements to relocate state capitals from the haughty eastern seaports into the less pretentious interior. These geographical shifts portended political shifts that deeply discomfited many more conservative Americans.

The Revolution enhanced the expectations and power of women as wives and mothers. As one "matrimonial republican" wrote in 1792,

"I object to the word 'obey' in the marriage-service because it is a general word, without limitations or definition. . . . The obedience between man and wife, I conceive, is, or ought to be mutual. . . . Marriage ought never to be considered a contract between a superior and an inferior, but a reciprocal union of interest, an implied partnership of interests, where all differences are accommodated by conference; and where the decision admits of no retrospect."

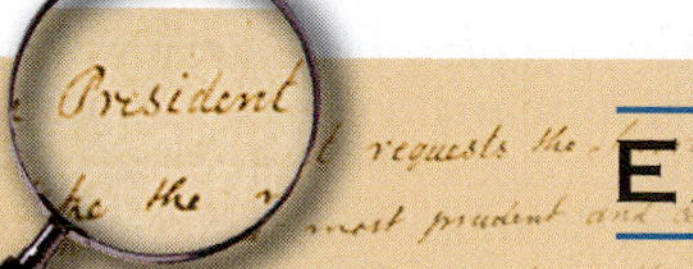

EXAMINING THE EVIDENCE

Copley Family Portrait, c. 1776–1777 A portrait painting like this one by John Singleton Copley (1738–1815) documents physical likenesses, clothing styles, and other material possessions typical of an era. But it can do more than that. In the execution of the painting itself, the preeminent portrait painter of colonial America revealed important values of his time. Copley's composition and use of light emphasized the importance of the mother in the family. Mrs. Copley is the visual center of the painting; the light falls predominantly on her, and she provides the focus of activity for the family group. Although Copley had moved to England in 1774 to avoid the disruptions of war, he had made radical friends in his hometown of Boston and surely had imbibed the sentiment of the age about "republican motherhood"—a sentiment that revered women as homemakers and mothers, the cultivators of good republican values in young citizens.

1. What prevalent eighteenth-century attitudes about gender and age might this painting reveal?
2. How does the scene visible through the opening in the rear suggest that this family is intended to be representative of an American future?
3. What attitudes toward children are revealed in the painting? What does it suggest about proper relationships among mothers, fathers, and children?

Economic Crosscurrents

Economic changes begotten by the war were likewise noteworthy, but not overwhelming. States seized control of former crown lands, and although rich **speculators** had their day, many of the large Loyalist holdings were confiscated and eventually cut up into small farms. Roger Morris's huge estate in New York, for example, was sliced into 250 parcels—thus accelerating the spread of economic democracy. The frightful excesses of the French Revolution were avoided, partly because cheap land was easily available. People do not chop off heads so readily when they can chop down trees. It is highly significant that in the United States economic democracy, broadly speaking, preceded political democracy.

speculators (speculation) *Those who buy property, goods, or financial instruments not primarily for use but in anticipation of profitable resale after a general rise in value.*

A sharp stimulus was given to manufacturing by the prewar nonimportation agreements and later by the war itself. Goods that formerly had been imported from Britain were mostly cut off, and the ingenious Yankees were forced to make their own. Ten years after the Revolution the tumbling Brandywine Creek, south of Philadelphia, was turning the waterwheels of numerous mills along an eight-mile stretch. Yet America remained overwhelmingly a nation of soil-tillers.

Economically speaking, independence had drawbacks. Much of the coveted commerce of Britain was still reserved for the loyal parts of the empire. American ships were now barred from British and British West Indian harbors. But new commercial outlets, fortunately, partially compensated for the loss of old ones. Americans could now trade freely with foreign nations, subject to local restrictions—a boon they had not enjoyed in the days of mercantilism. Enterprising Yankee shippers ventured boldly—and profitably—into the Baltic and China Seas.

Yet the general economic picture was far from rosy. War had spawned demoralizing extravagance, speculation, and profiteering, with profits for some as indecently high as 300 percent. Runaway inflation had been ruinous to many citizens, and Congress had failed in its feeble attempts to curb economic laws. While a newly rich class of profiteers was noisily conspicuous, the average citizen was probably worse off financially at the end of the shooting than before.

A Shaky Start Toward Union

What would the Americans do with the independence they had so dearly won? Prospects for erecting a lasting regime were far from bright. It is always difficult to set up a new government, doubly difficult to set up a new type of government. The picture was further clouded in America by leaders preaching "natural rights" and looking suspiciously at all persons clothed with authority. America was more a name than a nation, and unity ran little deeper than the color on the map.

Disruptive forces stalked the land. The departure of the conservative Loyalists left the political system inclined toward experimentation and innovation. Patriots had fought the war with a high degree of disunity, but they at least had concurred on allegiance to a common cause. Now even that was gone. It would have been almost a miracle if any government fashioned in all this confusion had long endured.

Online Study Center
Primary source
Socioeconomic Profile of Loyalist Claimants
college.hmco.com/pic/kennedybrief7e

Hard times, the bane of all regimes, set in shortly after the war and hit bottom in 1786. As if other troubles were not enough, British manufacturers, with dammed-up surpluses, began flooding the American market with cut-rate goods. War-baby American industries, in particular, suffered industrial colic from such ruthless competition.

Yet hopeful signs could be discerned. The thirteen sovereign states were basically alike in governmental structure and functioned under similar constitutions. Americans enjoyed a rich political inheritance, derived partly from Britain and partly from their own homegrown devices for self-government. Finally, they were blessed with political leaders of a high order in men like George Washington, James Madison, John Adams, Thomas Jefferson, and Alexander Hamilton.

Creating a Confederation

The Second Continental Congress of Revolutionary days was little more than a conference of ambassadors from the thirteen states. In nearly all respects the thirteen states were sovereign, for they coined money, raised armies and navies, and erected tariff barriers.

Shortly before declaring independence in 1776, Congress appointed a committee to draft a written constitution for the new nation. The finished product was the Articles of Confederation. Adopted by Congress in 1777, it was translated into French after the Battle of Saratoga so as to convince France that America had a genuine government in the making. The articles were not ratified by all thirteen states until 1781, less than eight months before the victory at Yorktown.

The chief apple of discord was western lands. Six of the jealous states, including Pennsylvania and Maryland, had no holdings beyond the Appalachian Mountains. Seven, notably New York and Virginia, were favored with enormous acreage on the basis of earlier sea-to-sea charter grants. The six land-hungry states argued that the more fortunate states would not have retained possession of this splendid prize if all the other states had not fought for it also. Why not turn the whole western area over to the central government?

Unanimous approval of the Articles of Confederation by the thirteen states was required, and land-starved Maryland stubbornly held out until March 1, 1781. Maryland at length gave in when New York surrendered its western claims and Virginia seemed about to do so. To sweeten the pill, Congress pledged itself to dispose of these vast areas for the "common benefit." It further agreed to carve from the new public domain not colonies but a number of "republican" states, which in time would be admitted to the Union on terms of complete equality with all the others. This extraordinary commitment faithfully reflected the anticolonial spirit

Interactive map
Western Land Claims After American Independence
college.hmco.com/pic/kennedybrief7e

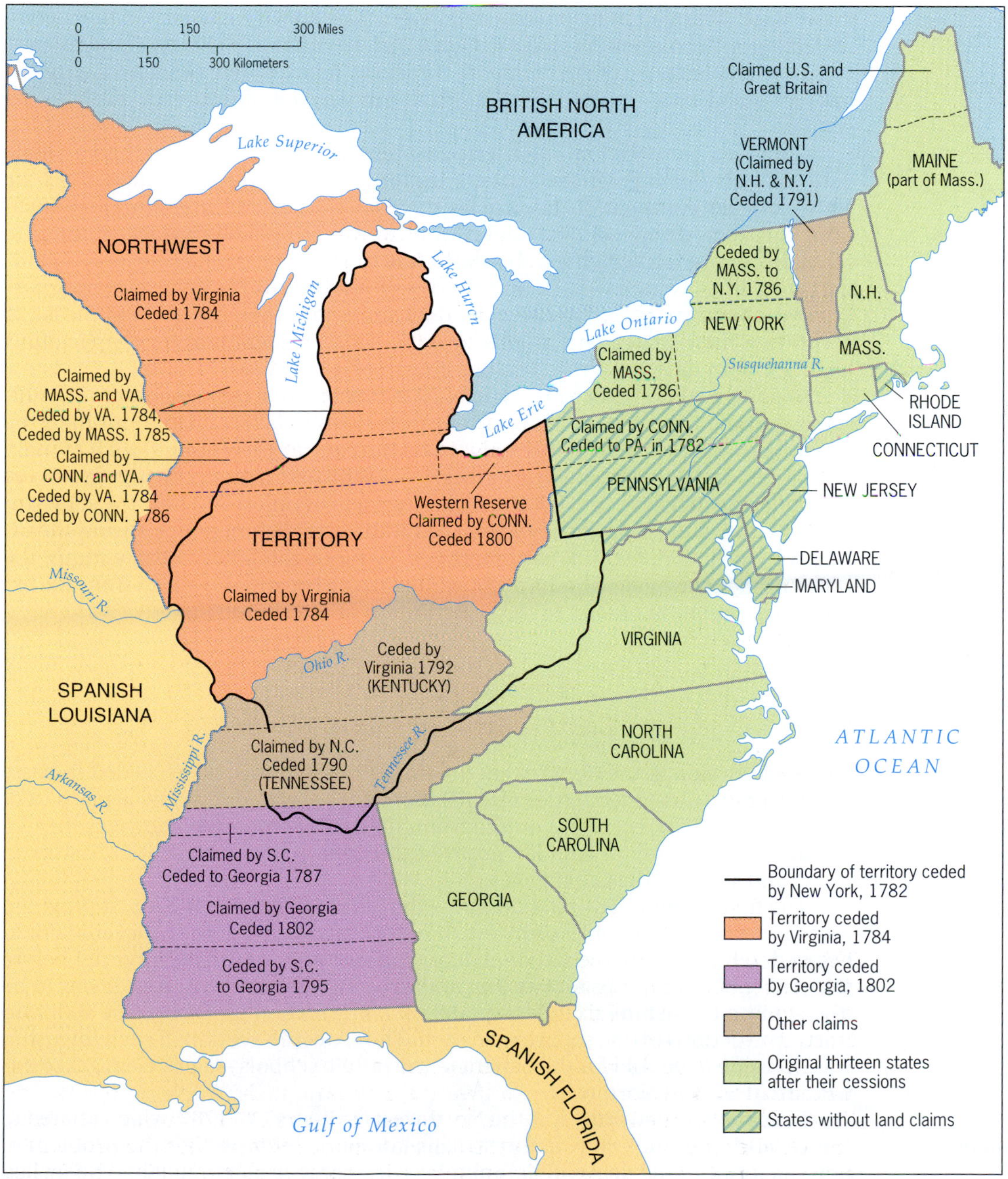

■ Western Land Cessions to the United States, 1782–1802

of the Revolution, and the pledge was later fully redeemed in the famed Northwest Ordinance of 1787.

Fertile public lands thus transferred to the central government proved to be an invaluable bond of union. The states that had thrown their heritage into the common pot had to remain in the Union if they were to reap their share of the advantages from the land sales. An army of westward-moving pioneers purchased their farms from the federal government, directly or indirectly, and they learned to look to the national capital, rather than to the state capitals—with a consequent weakening of local influence. Finally, a uniform national land policy was made possible.

The Articles of Confederation: America's First Constitution

The Articles of Confederation provided for a loose confederation or "firm league of friendship." Thirteen independent states were thus linked together for joint action in dealing with common problems, such as foreign affairs. A clumsy Congress was to be the chief agency of government. There was no executive branch—George III had left a bad taste—and the vital judicial arm was left almost exclusively to the states.

Congress, though dominant, was severely hobbled. Each state had a single vote. All bills dealing with subjects of importance required the support of nine states; any amendment of the Articles themselves required unanimous ratification. Purposely designed to be weak, Congress was crippled by its lack of power to regulate commerce, which left the states free to establish conflicting laws regarding tariffs and navigation. Lacking any power to enforce its tax-collection program, Congress set a tax quota for the individual states and then asked them please to contribute their shares on a voluntary basis. This "government by supplication" was lucky if in any year it received one-fourth of its requests.

In spite of their defects, the anemic Articles of Confederation were a significant steppingstone toward the present Constitution. They clearly outlined the general powers that were to be exercised by the central government, such as making treaties and establishing a postal service. As the first written constitution of the Republic, the Articles kept alive the flickering ideal of union and held the states together—until such time as they were ripe for the establishment of a strong constitution by peaceful, evolutionary methods. Without this intermediary jump, the states probably would never have consented to the breathtaking leap from the old boycott Association of 1774 to the Constitution of the United States.

Landmarks in Land Laws

Handcuffed though the Congress of the Confederation was, it succeeded in passing supremely farsighted pieces of legislation. These related to an immense part of the public domain recently acquired from the states commonly known as the Old Northwest. This area of land lay north of the Ohio River, east of the Mississippi River, and south of the Great Lakes.

The first of these red-letter laws was the Land Ordinance of 1785. It provided that the acreage of the Old Northwest should be sold and that the proceeds should be used to help pay off the national debt. The vast area was to be surveyed before sale and settlement, thus forestalling endless confusion and lawsuits. It was to be divided into **townships** six miles square, each of which in turn was to be split into thirty-six sections of one square mile each. The sixteenth section of each township was set aside to be sold for the benefit of the public schools—a priceless gift to education in the Old Northwest.

townships *In America, a surveyed territory six miles square; the term also refers to a unit of local government, smaller than a county, that is often based on these survey units.*

Primary source
Township and Range Map of the Old Northwest
college.hmco.com/pic/kennedybrief7e

Even more noteworthy was the Northwest Ordinance of 1787, which related to the governing of the Old Northwest. This law came to grips with the problem of how a nation should deal with its colonies—the same problem that had bedeviled the king and Parliament in London. The solution provided by the Northwest

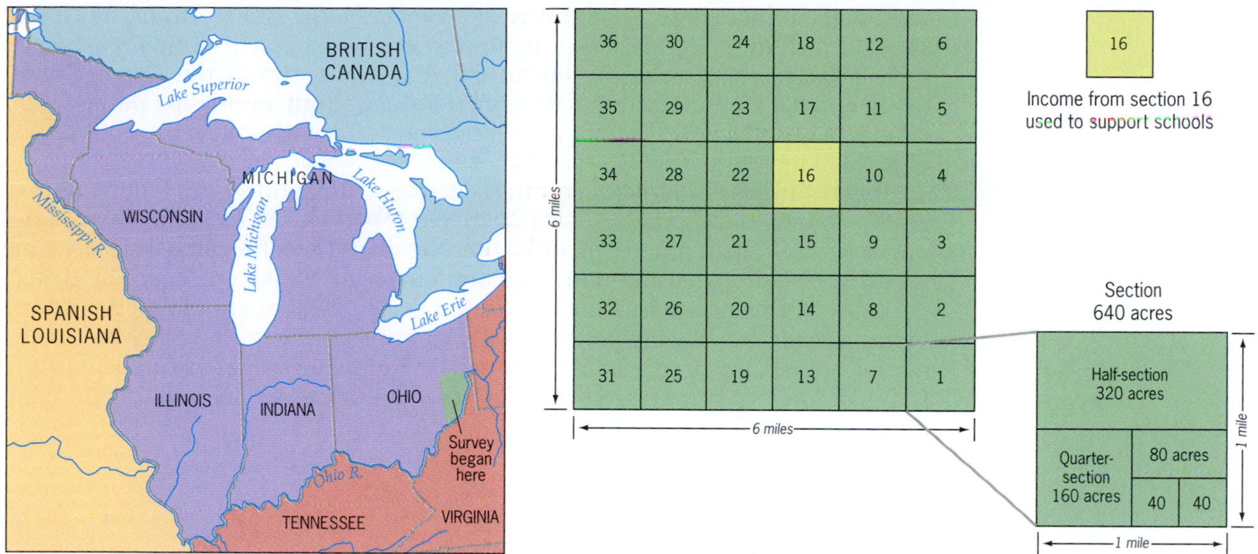

Surveying the Old Northwest Sections of a township under the Land Ordinance of 1785.

Ordinance was a judicious compromise: temporary tutelage, then permanent equality. First, there would be two evolutionary territorial stages, during which the area would be subordinate to the federal government. Then, when a **territory** could boast sixty thousand inhabitants, it might be admitted by Congress as a state, with all the privileges of the thirteen charter members. The ordinance also forbade slavery in the Old Northwest—a path-breaking step, though it exempted slaves already present.

territory *In American government, an organized political entity not yet enjoying the full and equal status of a state.*

annex *To make a smaller territory or political unit part of a larger one.*

The wisdom of Congress in handling this explosive problem deserves warm praise. If it had attempted to chain the new territories in permanent subordination, a second American Revolution almost certainly would have erupted in later years, fought this time by the West against the East. Congress thus neatly solved the seemingly insoluble problem of empire. The scheme worked so well that its basic principles were ultimately carried over from the Old Northwest to other frontier areas.

The World's Ugly Duckling

Foreign relations, especially with London, continued troubled during these anxious years of the Confederation. Britain flatly declined to send a minister to America, to make a commercial treaty, or to repeal its ancient Navigation Laws. The British Lord Sheffield argued that Britain would win back America's trade anyhow, because commerce would naturally return to old channels. The British also officially closed their profitable West Indian trade from the United States, though the Yankees still engaged in smuggling.

Along the far-flung northern frontier, scheming British agents intrigued with the disgruntled Allen brothers of Vermont and sought to **annex** that rebellious area to Britain. Redcoats continued to hold a chain of trading posts on U.S. soil, maintaining their fur trade and bolstering the Indians as a barrier against future American attacks on Canada.

Maddened by these grievances, some patriotic Americans demanded that the United States force the British into line by imposing restrictions on their imports to America. But Congress could not control commerce, and the states refused to adopt a uniform tariff policy.

Spain, though recently an enemy of Britain, was openly unfriendly to the new Republic. It controlled the mouth of the all-important Mississippi, down which the pioneers of Tennessee and Kentucky were forced to float their produce. In 1784 Spain closed the river to American commerce, threatening the

Online Study Center
Interactive map
Indian Land Cessions, 1768–1799
college.hmco.com/pic/kennedybrief7e

West with strangulation. Spain likewise claimed a large area north of the Gulf of Mexico, including Florida. From its important fort at Natchez, Spain schemed with neighboring Indians to hem in the Americans east of the Appalachians. Spain and Britain together, radiating their influence out among the powerful Indian tribes, prevented America from exercising effective control over about half of its total territory.

Even France, America's comrade-in-arms, demanded the repayment of money loaned during the war and restricted trade with its bustling West Indies ports. North African pirates, including the arrogant Dey of Algiers, were ravaging America's Mediterranean commerce and enslaving Yankee sailors. The British purchased protection for their subjects, but as an independent nation the United States was too weak to fight and too poor to bribe. John Jay, secretary for foreign affairs, hoped that these insults would at least humiliate the American people into framing a new government at home that would be strong enough to command respect abroad.

The Horrid Specter of Anarchy

Economic storm clouds continued to loom in the mid-1780s. Interest on the public debt was piling up at home, and the nation's credit was evaporating abroad. Quarreling states were levying duties on goods from their neighbors: New York, for example, taxed firewood from Connecticut and cabbages from New Jersey.

An alarming uprising, known as Shays's Rebellion, flared up in western Massachusetts in 1786 and set off widespread fear of further insurrection. Impoverished backcountry farmers, many of them Revolutionary War veterans, were losing their farms through mortgage **foreclosures** and tax delinquencies. Led by Captain Daniel Shays, a veteran of the Revolution, these desperate debtors demanded cheap paper money, lighter taxes, and a suspension of mortgage foreclosures. Hundreds of angry agitators, again seizing their muskets, attempted to enforce their demands.

foreclosures *Depriving someone of the right to redeem mortgaged property because the legal payments on the loan have not been kept up.*

Massachusetts authorities responded with drastic action. Supported partly by contributions from wealthy citizens, they raised a small army. After a few skirmishes the revolt collapsed. Daniel Shays, who believed that he was fighting anew against tyranny, was condemned to death but later pardoned.

Shays's followers were crushed—but the nightmarish memory lingered on. The outbursts of Shays and other distressed debtors struck fear in the hearts of the propertied class, who began to suspect that the Revolution had raised up a Frankenstein's monster "mobocracy." Unbridled republicanism, it seemed to many of the elite, had fed an insatiable appetite for liberty that was fast becoming license. Civic virtue was no longer sufficient to rein in self-interest and greed. It had become "undeniably evident," one skeptic sorrowfully lamented, "that some malignant disorder has seized upon our body politic." If republicanism was too shaky a ground on which to construct a new nation, a stronger central government would provide the needed foundation. How critical were conditions under the Confederation? Conservatives, anxious to safeguard their wealth and position, naturally exaggerated the seriousness of the nation's plight. They were eager to persuade their fellow citizens to amend the Articles of Confederation in favor of a muscular central government. But the poorer states' rights people pooh-poohed the talk of anarchy. Many of them were debtors who feared that a powerful federal government would force them to pay their creditors.

Social tensions reached a fever pitch during Shays's Rebellion in 1787. In an interview with a local Massachusetts paper, instigator Daniel Shays (1747–1825) explained how the debt-ridden farmers hoped to free themselves from the demands of a merchant-dominated government. The rebels would seize arms and

"march directly to Boston, plunder it, and then . . . destroy the nest of devils, who by their influence, make the Court enact what they please, burn it and lay the town of Boston in ashes."

Yet friends and critics of the Confederation agreed that it needed strengthening. Popular toasts were "Cement to the Union" and "A hoop to the barrel." The chief differences arose over how this goal should be attained and how a maximum amount of states' rights could be reconciled with a strong central government.

A Convention of "DemiGods"

Control of commerce, more than any other problem, touched off the chain reaction that led to a constitutional convention. Interstate squabbling over this issue had become so alarming by 1786 that Virginia issued a call for a convention at Annapolis, Maryland. When delegates from only five states showed up, nothing could be done about the ticklish question of commerce. A charismatic New Yorker, thirty-one-year-old Alexander Hamilton, brilliantly saved the convention from failure by engineering a call for another convention to meet the next year in Philadelphia to bolster the entire fabric of the Articles of Confederation.

Congress was reluctant to take a step that might lead to signing its own death warrant. But after six states appointed delegates anyhow, Congress belatedly issued the call for a convention "for the sole and express purpose of revising" the Articles of Confederation.

Every state chose representatives, except independent-minded Rhode Island, a stronghold of paper-moneyites. These leaders were all appointed by the state legislatures, whose members had been elected by voters who could qualify as property holders. This double distillation inevitably brought together a select group of propertied men.

A **quorum** of the fifty-five emissaries from twelve states finally convened at Philadelphia on May 25, 1787, in the imposing red-brick statehouse. The smallness of the assemblage facilitated intimate acquaintance and hence compromise. Sessions were held in complete secrecy, with armed sentinels posted at the doors. Delegates knew that they would generate heated differences, and they did not want to advertise their own dissensions or put the ammunition of harmful arguments into the mouths of the opposition.

quorum *The minimum number of persons who must be present in a group before it can conduct valid business.*

The caliber of the participants was extraordinarily high—"demigods," Jefferson called them. The crisis was such as to induce the ablest men to drop their personal pursuits and come to the aid of their country. Most of the members were lawyers, and most of them fortunately were old hands at constitution making in their own states.

George Washington, towering austere and aloof among the "demigods," was unanimously elected chairman. His enormous prestige as "the Sword of the Revolution" served to quiet overheated tempers. Benjamin Franklin, then eighty-one, added the urbanity of an elder statesman, though he was inclined to be indiscreetly talkative in his declining years. Concerned for the secrecy of their deliberations, the convention assigned chaperones to accompany Franklin to dinner parties and make sure he held his tongue. James Madison, then thirty-six and a profound student of government, made contributions so notable that he has been dubbed "the Father of the Constitution." Alexander Hamilton was present as an advocate of a super-powerful central government. His five-hour speech in behalf of his plan, though the most eloquent of the convention, left only one delegate convinced—himself.

Most of the fiery Revolutionary leaders of 1776 were absent. Thomas Jefferson, John Adams, and Thomas Paine were in Europe; Samuel Adams and John Hancock were not elected by Massachusetts. Patrick Henry, ardent champion of states' rights, was chosen as a delegate from Virginia but declined to serve, declaring that he "smelled a rat." It was perhaps well that these architects of revolution were absent. The time had come to yield the stage to leaders interested in fashioning solid political systems.

■ **Statehouse in 1778, from a drawing by Charles Willson Peale, by William L. Breton, c. 1830** Originally built in the 1730s as a meeting place for the Pennsylvania colonial assembly, this building witnessed much history: here Washington was given command of the Continental Army, the Declaration of Independence was signed, and the Constitution was hammered out. The building began to be called "Independence Hall" in the 1820s.

> *Thomas Jefferson (1743–1826), despite his high regard for the leaders at the Philadelphia convention, still was not unduly concerned about Shaysite rebellions. He wrote in November 1787,*
>
> "What country before ever existed a century and a half without a rebellion? . . . The tree of liberty must be refreshed from time to time with the blood of patriots and tyrants. It is its natural manure."

Patriots in Philadelphia

The fifty-five delegates were a conservative, well-to-do body: lawyers, merchants, shippers, land speculators, and moneylenders. Not a single spokesperson was present from the poorer debtor groups. Nineteen of the fifty-five owned slaves. They were young (the average age was about forty-two) but experienced statesmen. Above all, they were nationalists, more interested in preserving and strengthening the young Republic than in further stirring the roiling caldron of popular democracy.

The delegates hoped to crystallize the evaporating pools of revolutionary idealism into a stable political structure that would endure. They strongly desired a firm, dignified, and respected government. They believed in republicanism but sought to protect the American experiment from its weaknesses abroad and excesses at home. They aimed to clothe the central authority with genuine power, especially in controlling tariffs, so that the United States could wrest satisfactory commercial treaties from foreign nations.

anarchy *The theory that formal government is unnecessary and wrong in principle; the term is also used generally for lawlessness or antigovernmental disorder.*

bicameral, unicameral *Referring to a legislative body with two houses (bicameral) or one (unicameral).*

Other motives hovered in the Philadelphia hall. Delegates were determined to preserve the Union, forestall **anarchy,** and ensure security of life and property against dangerous uprisings by the "mobocracy." Above all, they sought to curb the unrestrained democracy rampant in the various states. The specter of the recent outburst in Massachusetts was especially alarming, and in this sense, Daniel Shays was another Founding Father. Grinding necessity extorted the Constitution from a reluctant nation. Fear occupied the fifty-sixth chair.

Hammering Out a Bundle of Compromises

Some of the travel-stained delegates, when they first reached Philadelphia, decided on a daring step. They would completely scrap the old Articles of Confederation, despite explicit instructions from Congress to *revise*. Technically, these bolder spirits were determined to overthrow the existing government of the United States by peaceful means.

A scheme proposed by populous Virginia, and known as "the large-state plan," was first pushed forward as the framework of the Constitution. Its essence was that representation in both houses of a **bicameral** Congress should be based on population—an arrangement that would naturally give the larger states an advantage. Tiny New Jersey, suspicious of brawny Virginia, countered with "the small-state plan." This provided for equal representation in a **unicameral** Congress by states, regardless of size and population.

After bitter and prolonged debate, and with the danger of complete failure looming, the "Great Compromise" of the convention was hammered out and agreed upon. The larger states were conceded representation by population in the House of Representatives (Art. I, Sec. II, para. 3; see the Appendix at the end of this book), and the smaller states were appeased by equal representation in the Senate (see Art. I, Sec. III, para. 1). Each state, no matter how poor or small, would have two senators. The big states obviously yielded more. As a sop to them, the delegates agreed that every tax bill or revenue measure must originate in the House, where population counted more heavily (see Art. I, Sec. VII, para. 1). This critical compromise broke the logjam, and from then on success seemed within reach.

> *One of the Philadelphia delegates recorded in his journal a brief episode involving Benjamin Franklin, who was asked by a woman when the convention ended,*
>
> "Well, Doctor, what have we got, a republic or a monarchy?"
>
> *The elder statesman answered,*
>
> "A republic, if you can keep it."

In a significant reversal of the arrangement most state constitutions had embodied, the new Constitution provided for a robust—though still legally restrained—executive in the presidency. The president was to have broad authority to appoint officials and judges, veto legislation, and wage war as commander in chief of the military. But Congress retained the crucial right to *declare* war—a division of responsibilities that has been an invitation to conflict between president and Congress ever since.

The Constitution as drafted was a bundle of compromises; they stand out in every section. A key compromise was the method of electing the president indirectly by the Electoral College, rather than by direct means (see Art. II, Sec. I, para. 2). While the large states would have the advantage in the first round of popular voting, the small states would gain a larger voice if no candidate got a majority of electoral votes and the election was thrown to the House of Representatives, where each state had only one vote (see Art. II, Sec. I, para. 2). Although the framers of the Constitution expected election by the House to occur frequently, it has happened just twice, in 1800 and 1824.

Sectional jealousy also intruded. Should the voteless slave of the southern states count as a person in apportioning direct taxes and representation in the House of Representatives? The South, not wishing to be deprived of influence, answered "yes." The North replied "no," arguing that slaves were not citizens. As a compromise between total representation and none at all, it was decided that a slave might count as three-fifths of a person. Hence the memorable, if arbitrary, "three-fifths compromise" (see Art. I, Sec. II, para. 3).

Most of the states wanted to shut off the African slave trade. But slaveholding South Carolina and Georgia raised vehement protests. In another compromise the convention stipulated that the slave trade might continue until the end of 1807, at which time Congress could stop the trade (see Art. I, Sec. IX, para. 1). It did so as soon as the prescribed interval had elapsed.

Safeguards for Conservatism

Heated clashes among the delegates have been overplayed. The area of agreement was actually large; otherwise the convention would have speedily disbanded. Economically, the members of the Constitutional Convention generally saw eye to

Signing of the Constitution of the United States, 1787 George Washington presided from the dais as the Constitutional Convention's president. At a table in the front row sat James Madison, later called the Father of the Constitution, who recorded the proceedings in shorthand. Daily from 10 A.M. to 3 P.M., from late May through mid-September 1787, the fifty-five delegates wrangled over ideas for a new federal government.

Strengthening the Central Government

Under Articles of Confederation	Under Federal Constitution
A loose confederation of states	A firm union of people
1 vote in Congress for each state	2 votes in Senate for each state; representation by population in House (see Art. I, Secs. II, III)
Vote of 9 states in Congress for all important measures	Simple majority vote in Congress, subject to presidential veto (see Art. I, Sec. VII, para. 2)
Laws administered loosely by committees of Congress	Laws executed by powerful president (see Art. II, Secs. II, III)
No congressional power over commerce	Congress to regulate both foreign and interstate commerce (see Art. I, Sec. VIII, para. 3)
No congressional power to levy taxes	Extensive power in Congress to levy taxes (see Art. I, Sec. VIII, para. 1)
Limited federal courts	Federal courts, capped by Supreme Court (see Art. III)
Unanimity of states for amendment	Amendment less difficult (see Art. V)
No authority to act directly upon individuals and no power to coerce states	Ample power to enforce laws by coercion of individuals and to some extent of states

eye; they demanded sound money and the protection of private property. Politically, they were in basic agreement; they favored a stronger government, with three branches and with checks and balances among them—what critics branded a "triple-headed monster." Finally, the convention was virtually unanimous in believing that manhood-suffrage democracy—government by "democratick babblers"—was something to be feared and fought.

Daniel Shays, the prime bogeyman, still frightened the conservative-minded delegates. They deliberately erected safeguards against the excesses of the "mob," and they made these barriers as strong as they dared. The awesome federal judges were to be appointed for life. The powerful president was to be elected *indirectly* by the Electoral College; the lordly senators were to be chosen *indirectly* by state legislatures (see Art. I, Sec. III, para. 1). Only in the case of one-half of one of the three great branches—the House of Representatives—were qualified (propertied) citizens permitted to choose their officials by *direct* vote (see Art. I, Sec. II, para. 1).

Yet the new charter also contained democratic elements. Above all, it stood foursquare on the two great principles of republicanism: that the only legitimate government was one based on the consent of the governed, and that the powers of the government should be limited by a written constitution. The virtue of the people, not the authority of the state, was to be the ultimate guarantor of liberty, justice, and order. "We the people," the preamble began, in a ringing affirmation of these republican doctrines.

At the end of seventeen muggy weeks—May 25 to September 17, 1787—only forty-two of the original fifty-five members remained to sign the Constitution. Three of the forty-two, refusing to do so, returned to their states to resist ratification. The remainder, adjourning to the City Tavern, celebrated the toastworthy occasion.

The Clash of Federalists and Antifederalists

The Framing Fathers early foresaw that nationwide acceptance of the Constitution would not be easy to obtain. A formidable barrier was unanimous ratification by all thirteen states, as required for amendment by the still-standing Articles of Confederation. But since absent Rhode Island was certain to veto the Constitution, the delegates boldly adopted a different scheme. They stipulated that when nine states had registered their approval through specially elected conventions, the Constitution would become the supreme law of the land in those states ratifying (see Art. VII).

This was extraordinary, even revolutionary. It was in effect an appeal over the heads of the Congress that had called the convention, and over the heads of the legislatures that had chosen its members, to the people—or those of the people who could vote. In this way the framers could claim greater popular sanction for their handiwork. A divided Congress submitted the document to the states on this basis, without recommendation of any kind.

The American people were somewhat astonished, so well had the secrets of the convention been kept. The public had expected the old Articles of Confederation to be patched up; now it was handed a startling new document in which, many thought, the precious jewel of state sovereignty was swallowed up. One of the hottest debates of American history forthwith erupted. The antifederalists, who opposed the stronger federal government, were arrayed against the federalists, who obviously favored it.

A motley crowd gathered in the antifederalist camp. Its leaders included prominent revolutionaries like Samuel Adams, Patrick Henry, and Richard Henry Lee. Their followers consisted primarily, though not exclusively, of states' rights devotees, backcountry dwellers, and one-horse farmers—in general, the poorest classes. They were joined by paper-moneyites and debtors. Many antifederalists saw in the Constitution a plot by the upper crust to steal power back from the common folk.

Silver-buckled federalists had power and influence on their side. They enjoyed the support of such commanding figures as George Washington and Benjamin Franklin. Most of them lived along the seaboard. Overall, they were wealthier than the antifederalists, better educated, and more organized. They also controlled the press. Of about a hundred newspapers published in America in the 1780s, only a dozen supported the antifederalist cause.

Antifederalists voiced vehement objections to the "gilded trap" known as the Constitution. They cried with much truth that it had been drawn up by the aristocratic elements and hence was antidemocratic. They likewise charged that the sovereignty of the states was being submerged and that the freedoms of the individual were jeopardized by the absence of a **bill of rights.** They decried the dropping of annual elections for congressional representatives, the erecting of a federal stronghold ten miles square (later the District of Columbia), the creation of a standing army, the omission of any reference to God, and the highly questionable procedure of ratifying with only two-thirds of the states.

bill of rights *A list of fundamental freedoms assumed to be central to society.*

The Great Debate in the States

Special elections, some apathetic but others hotly contested, were held in the various states for members of the ratifying conventions. The candidates—federalist or antifederalist—were elected on the basis of their pledges for or against the Constitution.

With the ink barely dry on the parchment, four small states quickly accepted the Constitution, for they had come off much better than they expected. Pennsylvania, number two on the list of ratifiers, was the first large state to act, but not until high-handed irregularities had been employed by the federalist legislature in calling a convention. These included the forcible seating of two antifederalist members, their clothes torn and their faces red with rage, in order to complete a quorum.

Massachusetts, the second most populous state, provided an acid test. If the Constitution had failed in Massachusetts, the entire movement might easily have bogged down. The Boston ratifying convention at first contained an antifederalist majority, including grudging Shaysites and the aging Samuel Adams, as suspicious of government power in 1787 as he had been in 1776. The absence of a bill of rights especially alarmed the antifederalists. But the federalists gave solemn assurances that the new Congress would add such a safeguard by amendment, and Massachusetts then ratified by the narrow margin of 187 to 168.

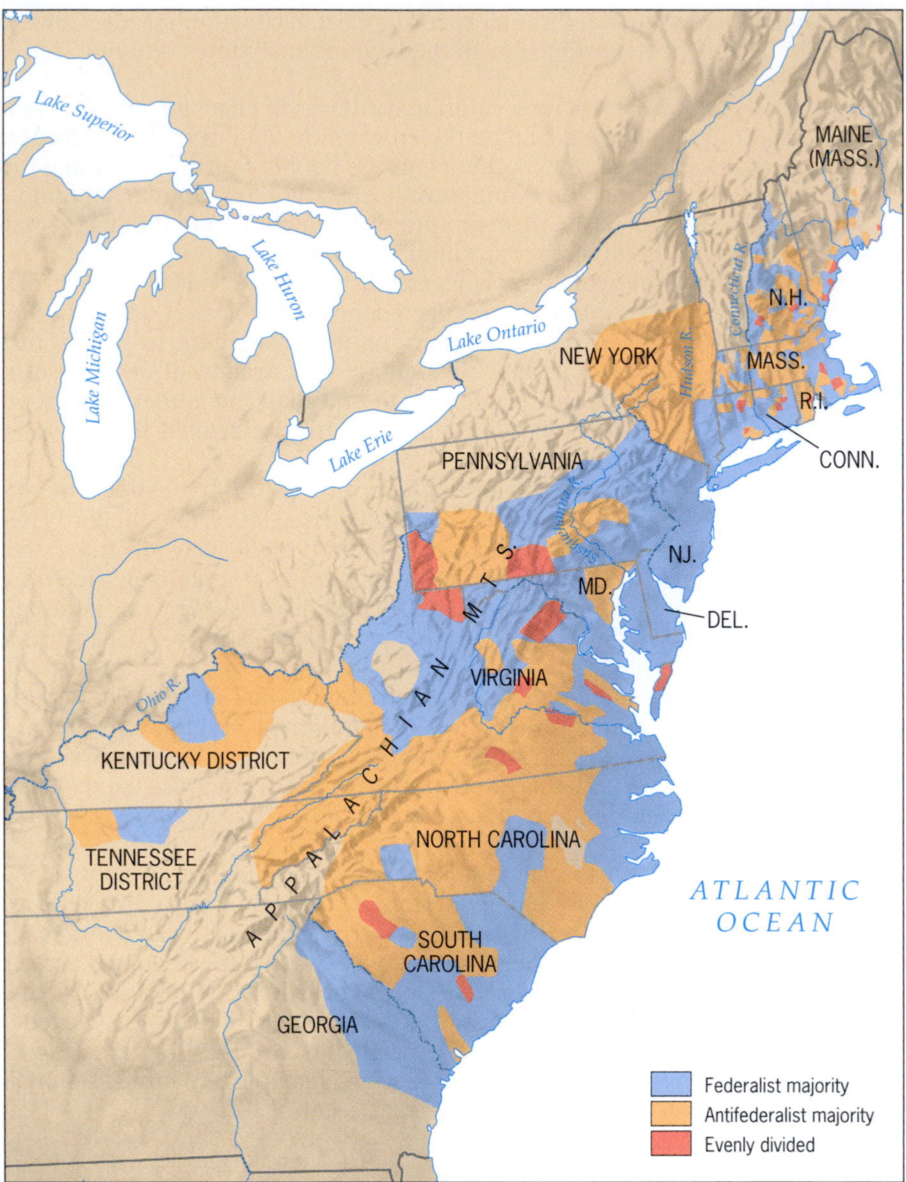

The Struggle over Ratification This mottled map shows that federalist support tended to cluster around the coastal areas, which had enjoyed profitable commerce with the outside world, including the export of grain and tobacco. Impoverished frontiersmen, suspicious of a powerful new central government under the Constitution, were generally antifederalists.

Interactive map
Federalists and Antifederalists Strongholds, 1787–1790
college.hmco.com/pic/kennedybrief7e

Three more states—Maryland, South Carolina, and New Hampshire—fell into line, though the struggle in New Hampshire was fierce. Nine states—all but Virginia, New York, North Carolina, and Rhode Island—had now taken shelter under the "new federal roof," and the document was officially adopted on June 21, 1788. But federalist rejoicing was premature so long as the four dissenters, conspicuously New York and Virginia, dug in their heels.

The Four Laggard States

Proud Virginia, the biggest and most populous state, provided fierce antifederalist opposition. There the college-bred federalist orators, for once, encountered worthy antagonists, including the fiery Patrick Henry. He professed to see in the fearsome document the death warrant of liberty. George Washington, James Madison, and John Marshall, on the federalist side, lent influential support. The new Union was going to be formed anyhow, and Virginia could not very well continue comfortably as an independent state. After exciting debate in the state convention, ratification carried, 89 to 79.

New York also experienced an uphill struggle, burdened as it was with its own heavily antifederalist state convention. Alexander Hamilton at heart favored a much stronger central government than that under debate, but he contributed his sparkling personality and persuasive eloquence to whipping up support for federalism as framed. He also joined John Jay and James Madison in penning a masterly series of articles for the New York newspapers. Though designed as propaganda, these essays remain the most penetrating commentary ever written on the Constitution and are still widely sold in book form as *The Federalist.* Probably the most famous of these is Madison's *Federalist* No. 10, which brilliantly refuted the conventional wisdom that a republic could not extend over a large territory.

New York finally yielded. Realizing that the state could not prosper apart from the Union, the convention ratified the document by the close count of 30 to 27.

Last-ditch dissent developed in only two states. A hostile convention met in North Carolina, then adjourned without taking a vote. Rhode Island did not even summon a ratifying convention, rejecting the Constitution by popular referendum. The two most ruggedly individualist centers of the colonial era—homes of the "otherwise minded"—thus ran true to form. They were to change their course, albeit unwillingly, only after the new government had been in operation for some months.

The race for ratification was close and quite bitter in some localities. No lives were lost, but riotous disturbances broke out in New York and Pennsylvania, involving bruises and bloodshed. There was much behind-the-scenes pressure on delegates who had promised their constituents to vote against the Constitution. The last four states ratified not because they wanted to but because they had to. They could not survive as lone wolves.

A Conservative Triumph

A minority had triumphed—twice. A militant minority of American radicals had engineered the military Revolution that cast off the unwritten British constitution. A militant minority of conservatives—now embracing many of the earlier radicals—had engineered the peaceful revolution that overthrew the inadequate Articles of Confederation. Eleven states, in effect, had seceded from the Confederation, leaving the two still in actually out in the cold.

Primary source
University President Denounces Conservative Coercion
college.hmco.com/pic/kennedybrief7e

A majority had not spoken. Only about one-fourth of the adult white males in the country, chiefly the propertied people, had voted for delegates to the ratifying conventions. Careful estimates indicate that if the new Constitution had been submitted to a manhood-suffrage vote, as in New York, it would have encountered much more opposition, probably defeat.

Conservatism was victorious. Safeguards had been erected against mob-rule excesses, while the republican gains of the Revolution were conserved. Radicals like Patrick Henry, who had ousted British rule, saw themselves upended in turn by American conservatives. The federalists were convinced that by setting the drifting ship of state on a steady course they could restore economic and political stability.

Yet if the architects of the Constitution were conservative, it is worth emphasizing that they conserved the principle of republican government through a redefinition of popular sovereignty. Unlike the antifederalists, who believed that the sovereignty of the people resided in a single branch of government—the legislature—the federalists contended that every branch—executive, judiciary, and legislature—effectively represented the people. By ingeniously embedding the doctrine of self-rule in a self-limiting system of checks and balances, the Constitution reconciled the potentially conflicting principles of liberty and order. It elevated the ideals of the Revolution even while setting boundaries to them. One of the distinctive—and enduring—paradoxes of American history was thus revealed: in the United States, conservatives and radicals alike have championed the heritage of republican revolution.

Chapter Summary

The American Revolution did not overturn the social order, but it did produce substantial changes in social customs, political institutions, and ideas about society and government. Among the changes were the separation of church and state in some places, the abolition of slavery in the North, written political constitutions, and a shift in political power from the eastern seaboard toward the frontier. The ideas of liberty and equality also affected many areas of society, but stopped short of promoting true equality for women or ending slavery (except where it was weakest, in the North).

The first weak national government, the Articles of Confederation, was unable to exercise real authority, although it did successfully deal with the western lands issue. The Confederation's weaknesses in handling foreign policy, commerce, and the Shays rebellion spurred the movement to alter the Articles.

Instead of revising the Articles, the young, nationalistic, and well-off delegates to the Constitutional Convention created a permanent charter for a whole new government. In a series of compromises, the convention produced a plan that provided for a vigorous central government, a strong executive, and protection for property, while still upholding republican principles and states' rights. The pro-Constitution federalists, generally representing wealthier and more commercial forces, were opposed by less sophisticated and well educated portions of the population who feared that a strong federal government would undermine their rights and their interests.

The federalists met their strongest opposition from antifederalists in Virginia and New York, but they triumphed through the use of more effective organization and argument, as well as through promises to incorporate a bill of rights into the document. By establishing the new national government, the federalists checked the Revolutionary momentum toward equality and decentralization of authority. But their "conservative" regime actually embraced the central Revolutionary values of popular republican government and liberty, making the Constitution the permanent bedrock of American political values.

VARYING VIEWPOINTS

The Constitution: Revolutionary or Counterrevolutionary?

Although the Constitution has endured over two centuries as the basis of American government, historians have differed sharply over how to interpret its origins and meaning. Early historians of the Nationalist School like John Fiske viewed the Constitution as the logical culmination of the Revolution and a crucial step in the God-given progress of Anglo-Saxon peoples.

By the early twentieth century, however, the progressive historians had turned a more critical eye to the Constitution. For historians like Carl Becker and Charles Beard, the Constitution was part of a revolutionary struggle between the lower classes (small farmers, debtors, and laborers) and the upper classes (merchants, financiers, and manufacturers). Beard's *An Economic Interpretation of the Constitution of the United States* (1913) argued that the Articles of Confederation had protected debtors and displeased wealthy elites heavily invested in trade, the public debt, and manufacturing. Reviewing the economic holdings of the Framers, Beard argued that the Constitution represented a successful attempt by conservative elites to buttress their own economic supremacy at the expense of less fortunate Americans.

Beard's economic interpretation of the Constitution held sway through the 1940s. In the 1950s, however, this analysis fell victim to "consensus" historians such as Robert Brown and Forrest McDonald, who convincingly disputed Beard's evidence and argued that the Constitution derived from an emerging consensus that the country needed a stronger central government.

Scholars since the 1950s have searched for new ways to understand the origins of the Constitution. The most influential work has been Gordon Wood's *The Creation of the American Republic* (1969). Wood reinterpreted the ratification controversy as a struggle to define the true essence of republicanism. While antifederalists feared human corruption and, consequently, a strong central government, federalists believed that a strong, balanced government would rein in selfish human instincts and channel them toward pursuit of the common good. James Madison in particular (especially in *Federalist* No. 10) developed the novel idea of an "extensive republic," a polity that would achieve stability by virtue of its great size and diversity. In this sense, Wood argued, the Constitution represented a bold experiment—fulfillment, rather than the repudiation, of the most advanced ideas of the Revolutionary era—even though it emanated from traditional elites determined to curtail dangerous disruptions to the social order.

Launching the New Ship of State

1789–1800

I SHALL ONLY SAY THAT I HOLD WITH MONTESQUIEU, THAT A GOVERNMENT MUST BE FITTED TO A NATION, AS MUCH AS A COAT TO THE INDIVIDUAL; AND, CONSEQUENTLY, THAT WHAT MAY BE GOOD AT PHILADELPHIA MAY BE BAD AT PARIS, AND RIDICULOUS AT PETERSBURG [RUSSIA].

ALEXANDER HAMILTON, 1799

Chapter Outline

- Problems of the Young Republic
- The First Presidency, 1789–1793
- The Bill of Rights, 1791
- Hamilton's Economic Policies
- The Emergence of Political Parties
- The Impact of the French Revolution
- Jay's Treaty, 1794
- President Adams Keeps the Peace
- The Alien and Sedition Acts, 1798
- The Virginia and Kentucky Resolutions, 1798–1799
- Federalists Versus Republicans

America's new ship of state did not spread its sails to the most favorable breezes. Within twelve troubled years the American people had risen up and thrown overboard both the British yoke and the Articles of Confederation. A decade of lawbreaking and constitution smashing was not the best training for government making. Americans had come to regard central authority, replacing that of George III, as a necessary evil—something to be distrusted, watched, and curbed.

The finances of the infant government were likewise precarious. The revenue had declined to a trickle, whereas the **public debt,** with interest heavily in arrears, was mountainous. Worthless paper money, both state and national, was as plentiful as metallic money was scarce. Nonetheless, the Americans were brashly trying to erect a republic on an immense scale, something that no other people had attempted and that traditional political theory deemed impossible. The eyes of a skeptical world were on the upstart United States.

Focus Questions

1. **How did George Washington's personal prestige and Alexander Hamilton's financial policies get the new federal government off to a strong beginning?**
2. **What were the policy differences between Hamilton and Thomas Jefferson within Washington's cabinet, and how did their disagreements lead to the formation of the first American political parties, the Federalists and Republicans?**
3. **How did the French Revolution and related events create conflict and polarization between Federalists and Republicans over American foreign policy, and how did President Washington maintain American neutrality?**
4. **How did the Alien and Sedition Acts reflect popular anti-French hysteria as well as Federalist political interests?**
5. **What were the underlying philosophical and political differences between Hamiltonian Federalists and Jeffersonian Republicans?**

public debt *The debt of a government or nation to individual creditors, also called the national debt.*

census *An official count of population; in the United States, the federal census occurs every ten years.*

cabinet *The body of official advisers to the head of a government; in the United States, it consists of the heads of the major executive departments.*

Interactive map
African American Population, 1790
college.hmco.com/pic/kennedy7e

Growing Pains

When the Constitution was launched in 1789, the Republic was continuing to grow at an amazing rate. Population was doubling about every twenty-five years, and the first official **census** of 1790, recorded almost 4 million people. Cities had blossomed proportionately: Philadelphia numbered 42,000; New York, 33,000; Boston, 18,000; Charleston, 16,000; and Baltimore, 13,000.

America's population was still about 90 percent rural, despite the flourishing cities. All but 5 percent of the people lived east of the Appalachian Mountains. The trans-Appalachian overflow was concentrated chiefly in Kentucky, Tennessee, and Ohio, all of which were welcomed as states within fourteen years. (Vermont had preceded them, becoming the fourteenth state in 1791.) Foreign visitors to the new Republic looked down their noses at the roughness and crudity resulting from ax-and-rifle pioneering life.

Washington for President

General Washington, the esteemed war hero, was unanimously drafted as president by the Electoral College in 1789—the only presidential nominee ever to be honored by unanimity.

His presence was imposing: 6 feet, 2 inches, 175 pounds, broad and sloping shoulders, strongly pointed chin, and pockmarks (from smallpox) on nose and cheeks. Much preferring the quiet of Mount Vernon to the turmoil of politics, he was perhaps the only president who did not in some way angle for this exalted office. Balanced rather than brilliant, he commanded his followers by strength of character rather than by the arts of the politician.

Washington's long journey from Mount Vernon to New York City, the temporary capital, was a triumphal procession. He was greeted by roaring cannon, pealing bells, flower-carpeted roads, and singing and shouting citizens. With appropriate ceremony, he solemnly and somewhat nervously took the oath of office on April 30, 1789, on a crowded balcony overlooking Wall Street.

Washington soon put his stamp on the new government by establishing the **cabinet.** The Constitution does not mention a cabinet; it merely provides that the president "may require" written opinions of the heads of the executive branch departments (see Art. II, Sec. II, para. 1). But this system proved so cumbersome that cabinet meetings gradually evolved during the Washington administration. At first only three department heads served under the president: Secretary of State Thomas Jefferson, Secretary of the Treasury Alexander Hamilton, and Secretary of War Henry Knox.

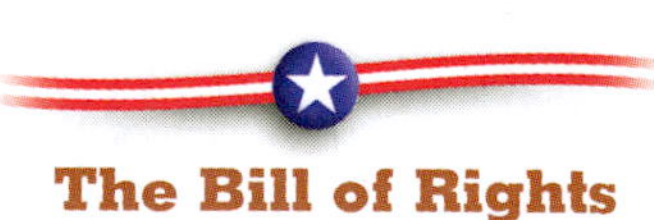

The Bill of Rights

The new nation faced some unfinished business. Many antifederalists had sharply criticized the Constitution drafted at Philadelphia for its failure to provide guarantees of individual rights such as freedom of religion and trial by jury. Many states had ratified the federal Constitution with the understanding that it would soon be amended to include such guarantees. Drawing up a bill of rights headed the list of imperatives facing the new government.

The proposed amendments were drafted and submitted to Congress by James Madison, whose intellectual and political skills were quickly making him the leading figure in the new body. Adopted by the necessary number of states in 1791, the first ten amendments to the Constitution, popularly known as the Bill of Rights, safeguard some of the most precious American principles. Among these are protections for freedom of religion, speech, and the press; the right to bear arms and to be tried by a jury; and the right to assemble and petition the government for redress of grievances. The Bill of Rights also prohibits cruel and unusual punishments and arbitrary government seizure of private property.

Chronology

1789	Constitution formally put into effect. Judiciary Act of 1789. Washington elected president. French Revolution begins.
1790	First official census.
1791	Bill of Rights adopted. Vermont becomes fourteenth state. Bank of the United States created. Excise tax passed.
1792	Washington reelected president.
1792-1793	Federalist and Democratic-Republican parties formed.
1793	Louis XVI beheaded; radical phase of French Revolution. Washington's Neutrality Proclamation. Citizen Genêt affair.
1794	Whiskey Rebellion. Battle of Fallen Timbers. Jay's Treaty with Britain.
1795	Treaty of Greenville: Indians cede Ohio. Pinckney's Treaty with Spain.
1796	Washington's Farewell Address.
1797	Adams becomes president. XYZ Affair.
1798	Alien and Sedition Acts.
1798-1799	Kentucky and Virginia resolutions.
1798-1800	Undeclared war with France.
1800	Convention of 1800: peace with France

To guard against the danger that enumerating such rights might lead to the conclusion that they were the only ones protected, Madison inserted the crucial Ninth Amendment. It declares that specifying certain rights "shall not be construed to deny or disparage others retained by the people." To reassure states' righters, he included the equally significant Tenth Amendment, which reserves all rights not explicitly delegated or prohibited by the federal Constitution "to the States respectively, or to the people." By preserving a strong central government while specifying certain protections for minority and individual liberties, Madison's amendments partially swung the federalist pendulum back in an antifederalist direction. (See Amendments I–X, in the Appendix.)

The first Congress also nailed other newly sawed governmental planks into place. It created effective federal courts under the Judiciary Act of 1789. The act organized the Supreme Court, with a chief justice and five associates, as well as federal district and **circuit courts,** and established the office of attorney general. New Yorker John Jay, Madison's collaborator on *The Federalist* papers, became the first chief justice of the United States.

circuit courts *A court that hears cases in several designated locations rather than a single place.*

fiscal *Concerning public finances—expenditures and revenues.*

Hamilton Revives the Corpse of Public Credit

The key figure in the new government was still smooth-faced Treasury Secretary Alexander Hamilton, a native of the British West Indies. Hamilton's genius was unquestioned, but critics claimed he loved his adopted country more than he loved his countrymen. Doubt about his character and his loyalty to the republican experiment always swirled about his head. Hamilton regarded himself as a kind of prime minister in Washington's cabinet, and on occasion he thrust his hands into the affairs of other departments, including that of his archrival, Secretary of State Thomas Jefferson.

A financial wizard, Hamilton set out immediately to correct the economic vexations that had crippled the Articles of Confederation. His plan was to shape the **fiscal** policies of the administration in such a way as to favor the wealthier groups. They, in turn, would gratefully lend the government monetary and political support. The new federal regime would flourish, the propertied classes would fatten, and prosperity would trickle down to the masses.

Evolution of the Cabinet

Position	Date Established	Comments
Secretary of state	1789	
Secretary of treasury	1789	
Secretary of war	1789	Loses cabinet status, 1947
Attorney general	1789	Not head of Justice Dept. until 1870
Secretary of navy	1798	Loses cabinet status, 1947
Postmaster general	1829	Loses cabinet status, 1970
Secretary of interior	1849	
Secretary of agriculture	1889	
Secretary of commerce and labor	1903	Office divided in 1913
Secretary of commerce	1913	
Secretary of labor	1913	
Secretary of defense	1947	Subordinate to this secretary, without cabinet rank, are secretaries of army, navy, and air force
Secretary of health, education, and welfare	1953	Office divided in 1979
Secretary of housing and urban development	1965	
Secretary of transportation	1966	
Secretary of energy	1977	
Secretary of health and human services	1979	
Secretary of education	1979	
Secretary of veterans affairs	1989	
Secretary of homeland security	2002	

The youthful financier's first objective was to bolster the national credit. Without public confidence in the government, Hamilton could not secure the funds with which to float his risky schemes. He therefore boldly urged Congress to "fund" the entire national debt "at par" and to assume completely the debts incurred by the states during the recent war.

"Funding at par" meant that the federal government would pay off its debts at face value, plus accumulated interest—a then-enormous total of more than $54 million. So many people believed the infant Treasury incapable of meeting those obligations that government bonds had depreciated to ten or fifteen cents on the dollar. Yet speculators held fistfuls of them, and when Congress passed Hamilton's measure in 1790, they grabbed for more. Some of them galloped into rural areas ahead of the news, buying for a song the depreciated paper holdings of farmers, war veterans, and widows.

Hamilton was willing, even eager, to have the new government shoulder additional obligations. While pushing the funding scheme, he urged Congress to assume the debts of the states, totaling some $21.5 million. The secretary made a convincing case for "**assumption**." The state debts could be regarded as a proper national obligation, for they had been incurred in the war for independence. But foremost in Hamilton's thinking was the belief that assumption would chain the states more tightly to the "federal chariot." Thus the secretary's maneuver would shift the attachment of wealthy creditors from the states to the federal government. The support of the rich for the national administration was a crucial link in Hamilton's political strategy of strengthening the central government.

assumption *The appropriation or taking on of obligations not originally one's own.*

States burdened with heavy debts, like Massachusetts, were delighted by Hamilton's proposal. States with small debts, like Virginia, were less charmed. The stage was set for some old-fashioned horse trading. Virginia did not want the state debts assumed, but it did want the forthcoming federal district*—now the District of Columbia—to be located on the Potomac River. Hamilton persuaded a reluctant Jefferson to line up enough votes in Congress for assumption. In return, Virginia would have the federal district in its backyard. The bargain was carried through in 1790.

One of the most eloquent tributes to Hamilton's apparent miracle working came from Daniel Webster (1782–1852) in the Senate (1831):

"He smote the rock of the national resources, and abundant streams of revenue gushed forth. He touched the dead corpse of public credit, and it sprung upon its feet."

Customs Duties and Excise Taxes

The new ship of state thus set sail dangerously overloaded. The national debt had swelled to $75 million owing to Hamilton's insistence on honoring the outstanding federal and state obligations alike. But Hamilton, the "Father of the National Debt," was not greatly worried. His objectives were as much political as economic. He believed that, within limits, a national debt was a "national blessing"—a kind of union adhesive. The more creditors to whom the government owed money, the more people there would be with a personal stake in the success of his ambitious enterprise.

Where was the money to come from to pay interest on this huge debt and to run the government? Hamilton's first answer was customs duties, derived from a tariff. Tariff revenues, in turn, depended on a vigorous foreign trade, another crucial link in Hamilton's overall economic strategy for the new Republic.

The first tariff law, which imposed a low tariff of about 8 percent on dutiable imports, was speedily passed by Congress in 1789. Revenue was by far the main goal, but the measure was also designed to erect a low protective wall around infant industries, which bawled noisily for more shelter than they received. Hamilton had the vision to see that the industrial revolution would soon reach America, and he argued strongly in favor of more protection for the well-to-do manufacturing groups—another vital element in his economic program. But Congress was still dominated by agricultural and commercial interests, and it voted only two slight increases in the tariff during Washington's presidency.

Hamilton, with characteristic vigor, sought additional internal revenue and in 1791 secured from Congress an **excise** tax on a few domestic items, notably whiskey. The new levy of seven cents a gallon was borne chiefly by the distillers who lived in the mountains and backcountry. Whiskey flowed so freely on the frontier that it was used for money.

excise *A tax on the manufacture, sale, or consumption of certain products.*

Hamilton Battles Jefferson for a Bank

As the capstone for his financial system, Hamilton proposed a Bank of the United States. With the Bank of England as his model, he envisioned a private institution with the government as its major stockholder. The bank would provide a convenient strongbox for surplus federal funds, stimulate business by keeping money in circulation, and print an urgently needed sound paper currency.

Jefferson, whose written opinion on this question Washington requested, argued vigorously against the bank. The Constitution, he insisted, provided no specific authorization for such a financial octopus. He was convinced that all powers not specifically granted to the central government were reserved to the states, as provided in the about-to-be-ratified Bill of Rights (see Amendment X). He therefore concluded that the states, not Congress, had the power to charter banks. Believing that the Constitution should be interpreted "literally" or "strictly," Jefferson and his states' rights disciples zealously embraced the theory of "strict construction."

Hamilton, also at Washington's request, prepared a brilliantly reasoned reply to Jefferson's arguments. He boldly invoked the clause of the Constitution that

* Authorized by the Constitution, Art. I. Sec. VIII, para. 17.

■ Alexander Hamilton (1755–1804), by John Trumbull, 1792 He was one of the youngest and most brilliant of the Founding Fathers, who might have been president but for his ultraconservatism, a scandalous adultery, and a duelist's bullet. Hamilton favored a strong central government with a weak legislature to unify the infant nation and encourage industry. His chief rival, Thomas Jefferson, who extolled states' rights as a bulwark of liberty and thought the United States should remain an agricultural society, regarded Hamilton as a monarchist plotter and never forgave him for insisting that "the British Govt. was the best in the world: and that he doubted much whether any thing short of it would do in America."

stipulates that Congress may pass any laws "necessary and proper" to carry out the powers vested in the various governmental agencies (see Art. I, Sec. VIII, para. 18). The government was explicitly empowered to collect taxes and regulate trade. In carrying out these basic functions, Hamilton argued, a national bank would be not only "proper" but "necessary." By inference or by implication—that is, by virtue of "implied powers"—Congress would be fully justified in establishing the Bank of the United States. In short, Hamilton contended for a "loose" or "broad" interpretation of the Constitution. He and his federalist followers thus evolved the theory of "loose construction" by invoking the "elastic clause" of the Constitution—a precedent for enormous federal powers.

Hamilton's financial views prevailed. Washington accepted his eloquent and realistic arguments and signed the bank measure into law. This explosive issue had been debated with much heat in Congress, where the old North-South cleavage still lurked ominously. The most enthusiastic support for the bank naturally came from the commercial and financial centers of the North; the strongest opposition arose from the agricultural South.

The Bank of the United States, as created by Congress in 1791, was chartered for twenty years. Located in Philadelphia, it was to have capital of $10 million, one-fifth of it owned by the federal government, the rest by private investors.

Mutinous Moonshiners in Pennsylvania

The Whiskey Rebellion, which flared up in southwestern Pennsylvania in 1794, sharply challenged the new national government. Hamilton's excise bore harshly on these homespun pioneer folk. They regarded it not as a tax on a luxury but as a burden on an economic necessity and a **medium of exchange.** Even preachers of the gospel were paid in "Old Monongahela rye." Defiant distillers finally erected whiskey poles, similar to the liberty poles of anti–stamp tax days in 1765, and raised the cry "Liberty and No Excise." Boldly tarring and feathering revenue officers, they brought collections to a halt.

President Washington, once a revolutionary, was alarmed by what he called these "self-created societies." With the hearty encouragement of Hamilton, he summoned the militia of several states. An army of about thirteen thousand men rallied to the colors, and two widely separated columns marched briskly forth in a gorgeous, leaf-tinted Indian summer. But when the troops reached the hills of western Pennsylvania, they found no insurrection. The "Whiskey Boys" were overawed, dispersed, or captured. Only three rebels were killed.

medium of exchange *Any item, paper or otherwise, used as money.*

The Whiskey Rebellion was minuscule, but its consequences were mighty. George Washington's government, now substantially strengthened, commanded a new respect. Yet the foes of the administration condemned its brutal display of force—for using a sledgehammer to crush a gnat.

The Emergence of Political Parties

Almost overnight, Hamilton's fiscal feats had established the government's sound credit rating. The Treasury could now borrow needed funds in the Netherlands on favorable terms.

But Hamilton's financial successes—funding, assumption, the excise, the bank, suppression of the Whiskey Rebellion—created some political liabilities. All these schemes encroached sharply on states' rights. Many Americans, dubious about the Constitution in the first place, might never have approved it if they had foreseen how the states were going to be overshadowed by the federal colossus. Now, out of resentment against Hamilton's revenue-raising and centralizing policies, an organized opposition began to build. What once was a personal feud between Hamilton and Jefferson developed into a full-blown and frequently bitter political rivalry.

Republicanism Triumphant Artists often used classical motifs to celebrate the triumph in America of republicanism—a form of government they traced back to ancient Greece and Rome.

National political parties, in the modern sense, were unknown to America when George Washington took the inaugural oath. There had been Whigs and Tories, federalists and antifederalists, but these groups were factions rather than parties. They had sprung into existence over hotly contested special issues; they had faded away when their cause had triumphed or fizzled.

The Founders at Philadelphia had not envisioned the existence of permanent political parties. Organized opposition to the government seemed tainted with disloyalty, an affront to the spirit of national unity that the glorious cause of the Revolution had inspired.

The notion of a formal party apparatus was thus a novelty in the 1790s, and when Jefferson and Madison first organized their opposition to the Hamiltonian program, they did not anticipate creating a long-lived and popular party. But as their antagonism toward Hamilton stiffened, and as the amazingly boisterous and widely read newspapers of the day spread their political message, and Hamilton's, among the people, primitive semblances of political parties emerged.

The two-party system has existed in the United States since that time. Ironically, in light of the early suspicions about the very legitimacy of parties, their competition for power has actually proved to be among the indispensable ingredients of a sound democracy. The party out of power—"the loyal opposition"—traditionally plays the invaluable role of the balance wheel on the machinery of government, ensuring that politics never drifts too far out of kilter with the wishes of the people.

The Impact of the French Revolution

When Washington's first administration ended, early in 1793, domestic controversies had already formed two political camps—Hamiltonian Federalists and Jeffersonian Democratic-Republicans. As Washington's second term began, foreign-policy issues brought the differences between them to a fever pitch.

Only a few weeks after Washington's inauguration in 1789, the curtain had risen on the first act of the French Revolution. Twenty-six years were to pass before the seething continent of Europe collapsed into a peace of exhaustion. Few non-American events have left a deeper scar on American political and social life. In a sense the French Revolution was misnamed: it was a revolution that sent tremors through much of the civilized world.

Most Americans, loving liberty and deploring despotism, cheered the early, peaceful stages of the French Revolution, involving as it did a successful attempt to impose constitutional shackles on King Louis XVI. The Revolution entered a more ominous phase in 1792, when France declared war on hostile Austria. Late that year the electrifying news reached America that French citizen armies had hurled back the invading foreigners, and that France had proclaimed itself a republic. Americans enthusiastically sang the rousing revolutionary anthem "The Marseillaise" and renamed roads "Liberty Street" and "Equality Lane."

But centuries of pent-up poison could not be purged without baleful results. The guillotine was set up, the king was beheaded in 1793, the Roman Catholic Church was attacked, and the head-rolling Reign of Terror was begun. Back in America, God-fearing Federalist aristocrats nervously fingered their tender white necks and eyed the Jeffersonian masses apprehensively. Lukewarm Federalist approval of the early Revolution turned, almost overnight, to heated talk of "blood-drinking cannibals."

despotism *Arbitrary or tyrannical rule.*

Sober-minded Jeffersonians regretted the bloodshed. But they felt, with Jefferson, that one could not expect to be carried from "**despotism** to liberty in a feather bed," and that a few thousand aristocratic heads were a cheap price to pay for human freedom.

Such approbation was shortsighted, for dire peril loomed ahead. The earlier battles of the French Revolution had not hurt America directly, but now Britain was sucked into the contagious conflict. The conflagration speedily spread to the New World, where it vividly affected the expanding young American republic.

Washington's Neutrality Proclamation

Ominously, the Franco-American alliance of 1778 was still on the books, and many Jeffersonian Democratic-Republicans favored honoring the pact. Aflame with the liberal ideals of the French Revolution, red-blooded Jeffersonians were eager to enter the conflict against Britain, the recent foe, at the side of France, the recent friend.

But levelheaded President Washington was not swayed by the clamor of the crowd. Backed by Hamilton, he believed that war had to be avoided at all costs. Accordingly, Washington boldly issued his Neutrality Proclamation in 1793, shortly after the outbreak of war between Britain and France. This epochal document not only proclaimed the government's official neutrality in the widening conflict but sternly warned American citizens to be impartial toward both armed camps. As America's first formal declaration of aloofness from Old World quarrels, Washington's Neutrality Proclamation proved to be a major prop of the spreading isolationist tradition.

The pro-French Jeffersonians were enraged by the Neutrality Proclamation; the pro-British Federalists were heartened. Debate intensified when an impetuous, thirty-year-old representative of the French republic, Citizen Edmond Genêt, landed at Charleston, South Carolina. With unrestrained zeal, he undertook to outfit privateers and otherwise take advantage of the existing Franco-American alliance. Swept away by his enthusiastic reception by the Jeffersonian Democratic-Republicans, Genêt foolishly came to believe that the Neutrality Proclamation did not reflect the true wishes of the American people. He consequently embarked on an outrageously unneutral campaign to appeal over the head of "Old Washington" to the sovereign voters, and to recruit armies to invade Spanish Florida and British Canada. The president quickly demanded Genêt's withdrawal, and the Frenchman was replaced by a less impulsive emissary.

Embroilments with Britain

President Washington's far-visioned policy of neutrality was sorely tried by the British. For ten years they had been retaining the chain of northern frontier posts on U.S. soil, all in defiance of the peace treaty of 1783. British agents openly sold firearms and firewater to the Miami Confederacy, an alliance of eight Indian nations who attacked Americans invading their lands northwest of the Ohio River. In 1790 and 1791 Little Turtle's braves defeated armies led by Generals Josiah Harmer and Arthur St. Clair, handing the United States what remains one of its worst military defeats in the history of the frontier.

American Posts Held by the British After 1783

But in 1794 General "Mad Anthony" Wayne's army routed the Miamis at the Battle of Fallen Timbers. In the Treaty of Greenville, signed in August 1795, the confederacy gave up most of the present-day states of Ohio and Indiana. In exchange the Indians received monetary compensation, the right to hunt on the lands they had ceded, and what they hoped was recognition of their sovereign status.

On the sea frontier, the British were eager to starve out the French West Indies and naturally expected the United States to defend them under the Franco-American alliance. Hard-boiled commanders of the Royal Navy, acting under instructions from London in 1793, struck savagely. They seized about three hundred American merchant ships in the West Indies, **impressed** scores of seamen into service on British vessels, and threw hundreds of others into foul dungeons. A mighty outcry arose, chiefly from Jeffersonians, that America should once again fight George III in defense of its liberties.

President Washington, in a last desperate gamble to avert war, sent Chief Justice John Jay to London in 1794. The Jeffersonians were acutely unhappy over the choice, partly because they feared that so notorious a Federalist and Anglophile would sell out his country.

impress *To force people or property into public service without choice; conscript.*

Unhappily, Jay entered the negotiations with weak cards and could win only a few concessions. The British did promise to evacuate the chain of posts on U.S. soil—a pledge that inspired little confidence, since it had been made before in Paris (to the same John Jay!) in 1783. In addition, Britain consented to pay damages for the recent seizures of American ships. But the British stopped short of pledging anything about future maritime seizures and impressments or about supplying arms to Indians.

When the Jeffersonians learned of Jay's concessions, their rage was fearful to behold. The treaty seemed like an abject surrender to Britain, as well as a betrayal of the Jeffersonian South. Jeffersonian mobs hanged, burned, and guillotined in effigy that "damn'd archtraitor, Sir John Jay." His unpopular pact, more than any other issue, vitalized the newborn Democratic-Republican party of Thomas Jefferson.

Jay's Treaty had other unforeseen consequences. Fearing that the treaty foreshadowed an Anglo-American alliance, Spain moved hastily to strike a deal with the United States. Pinckney's Treaty of 1795 with Spain granted the Americans virtually everything they demanded, including free navigation of the Mississippi and the large disputed territory north of Florida.

Exhausted after the diplomatic and partisan battles of his second term, President Washington decided to retire. His choice contributed powerfully to establishing a two-term tradition for American presidents.* In his Farewell Address to the nation in 1796, Washington strongly advised the avoidance of "permanent alliances" like the still-vexatious Franco-American treaty of 1778. Contrary to general misunderstanding, Washington did not oppose all alliances, but rather favored only "temporary alliances" for "extraordinary emergencies."

Washington's contributions as president were enormous, even though the sparkling Hamilton at times seemed to outshine him. The central government, its fiscal feet now under it, was solidly established. The West was expanding. The merchant marine was plowing the seas. Above all, Washington had kept the nation out of both overseas entanglements and foreign wars. The experimental stage had passed, and the presidential chair could now be turned over to a less impressive figure. But republics are notoriously ungrateful. When Washington left office in 1797, he was showered with the brickbats of partisan abuse, quite in contrast with the bouquets that had greeted his arrival.

* This tradition, not broken until 1940 by Franklin D. Roosevelt, was made part of the Constitution in 1951 by the Twenty-second Amendment.

Although Thomas Jefferson (1743–1826) and John Adams hardly saw eye to eye, Jefferson displayed grudging respect for Adams in a piece of private correspondence in 1787:

"He is vain, irritable, and a bad calculator of the force and probable effect of the motives which govern men. This is all the ill which can possibly be said of him. He is as disinterested as the Being who made him."

John Adams Becomes President

Who should succeed the exalted "Father of His Country"? Alexander Hamilton was the best-known Federalist leader now that Washington had bowed out. But his financial policies, some of which had fattened speculators, had made him so unpopular that he could not hope to be elected president. The Federalists were forced to turn to Washington's experienced but ungracious vice president John Adams, a rugged chip off old Plymouth Rock. The Democratic-Republicans naturally rallied behind their master organizer and leader, Thomas Jefferson.

Political passions ran feverishly high in the presidential campaign of 1796. The lofty presence of Washington had hitherto imposed some restraints on partisan attacks; now the lid was off. Cultured Federalists referred to the Jeffersonians as "fire-eating salamanders, poison-sucking toads." Federalists and Democratic-Republicans even drank their ale in separate taverns. The Jeffersonians again assailed the too-forceful crushing of the Whiskey Rebellion and, above all, the negotiation of Jay's hated treaty.

John Adams, with most of his support in New England, squeezed through by the narrow margin of 71 votes to 68 in the Electoral College. Jefferson, as runner-up, became vice president.* One of the ablest statesmen of his day, Adams at sixty-two was bald, short, and thickset ("His Rotundity"). He impressed observers as a man of stern principles who did his duty with stubborn devotion. Although learned and upright, he was a tactless and prickly intellectual aristocrat with no appeal to the masses and no desire to cultivate any. Many citizens regarded him with "respectful irritation."

The crusty New Englander suffered from other handicaps. He had stepped into Washington's shoes, which no successor could hope to fill. In addition, Adams was hated by Hamilton, who now headed the pro-war faction of the Federalist party. The famed financier even secretly plotted with certain members of the cabinet against the new president, who soon had a conspiracy rather than a cabinet on his hands. Most ominous of all, Adams inherited a violent quarrel with France—a quarrel whose gunpowder lacked only a spark.

Unofficial Fighting with France

The French were infuriated by Jay's Treaty. They condemned it as the initial step toward an American alliance with Britain, their perpetual foe. French warships, in retaliation, seized about three hundred defenseless American merchant vessels by mid-1797.

President Adams kept his head, temporarily, even though the nation was mightily aroused. Trying to reach an agreement with the French, he appointed a diplomatic commission of three men, including John Marshall, the future chief justice. When Adams's envoys reached Paris in 1797, they were secretly approached by three French go-betweens, later referred to as X, Y, and Z in the published dispatches. The French spokesmen demanded an unneutral loan of 32 million florins, plus what amounted to a bribe of $250,000, for the privilege of merely talking with Talleyrand, the French foreign minister.

These terms were intolerable. The American trio knew that bribes were standard diplomatic devices in Europe, but they gagged at paying a quarter of a million dollars for mere talk, without any assurances of a settlement. Negotiations quickly broke down.

* The possibility of such an inharmonious two-party combination in the future was removed by the Twelfth Amendment to the Constitution in 1804. (See text in the Appendix.)

War hysteria swept through the United States, catching up even President Adams. The slogan of the hour became "Millions for defense, but not one cent for tribute." Despite considerable Jeffersonian opposition in Congress, war preparations were pushed along at a feverish pace. The Navy Department was created, the three-ship navy expanded, and the United States Marine Corps re-established (it had been created in 1775 but disbanded after the Revolutionary War).

Bloodshed was confined to the sea, principally in the West Indies. In two and a half years of undeclared hostilities (1798–1800), American privateers and men-of-war of the new navy captured over eighty armed vessels flying the French colors, though several hundred Yankee merchant ships were lost to the enemy. Only a slight push, it seemed, might plunge both nations into a full-dress war.

Adams Puts Patriotism Above Party

Embattled France, its hands full in Europe, wanted no war. An outwitted Talleyrand realized that to fight the United States would add one more foe to his enemy roster. He therefore let it be known, through roundabout channels, that if the Americans would send a new minister, he would be received with proper respect.

Despite the popular acclaim that he might have enjoyed by leading the nation into a full-fledged war, Adams exploded a bombshell in early 1799 by sending to the Senate the name of a new minister to France. Hamilton and his war-hawk faction were enraged. But public opinion—Jeffersonian and reasonable Federalist alike—was favorable to one last try for peace.

America's envoys (now three) found the political skies brightening when they reached Paris early in 1800. The ambitious "Little Corporal," the Corsican Napoleon Bonaparte, had recently seized dictatorial power. He was eager to free his hands of the American squabble so that he might continue to redraw the map of Europe and perhaps create a New World empire in Louisiana. The afflictions and ambitions of the Old World were again working to America's advantage.

After a great deal of haggling, a memorable treaty known as the Convention of 1800 was signed in Paris. France agreed to annul the twenty-two-year-old

Preparation for War to Defend Commerce: The Building of the Frigate *Philadelphia* In 1803 this frigate ran onto the rocks near Tripoli harbor, and about three hundred officers and men were imprisoned by the Tripolitans. The ship was refloated for service against the Americans, but Stephen Decatur led a party of men that set it afire.

marriage of (in)convenience, but as a kind of alimony the United States agreed to pay the damage claims of American shippers. So ended the nation's only peacetime military alliance for a century and a half. Its troubled history does much to explain the traditional antipathy of the American people to foreign entanglements.

John Adams, flinty to the end, deserves immense credit for his belated push for peace, even though he was moved in part by jealousy of Hamilton. Adams not only avoided the hazards of war but unwittingly smoothed the path for the peaceful purchase of Louisiana three years later. If America had drifted into a full-blown war with France in 1800, Napoleon would not have sold Louisiana to Jefferson on any terms in 1803.

President Adams, the bubble of his popularity pricked by peace, was aware of his signal contribution to the nation. He later suggested as the epitaph for his tombstone (not used), "Here lies John Adams, who took upon himself the responsibility of peace with France in the year 1800."

The Federalist Witch Hunt

Exulting Federalists had meanwhile capitalized on the anti-French frenzy to drive through Congress in 1798 a sheaf of laws designed to muffle or minimize their Jeffersonian foes.

The first of these oppressive laws was aimed at supposedly pro-Jeffersonian "aliens." The Federalist Congress, hoping to discourage the "dregs" of Europe, erected a disheartening barrier. They raised the residence requirements for aliens who desired to become citizens from a tolerable five years to an intolerable fourteen. This drastic new law violated the traditional American policy of open-door hospitality and speedy **assimilation.**

assimilation *The merging of diverse cultures or peoples into one.*

witch-hunting *An investigation carried on with much publicity, supposedly to uncover dangerous activity but actually intended to weaken the political opposition.*

Two additional Alien Laws struck heavily at undesirable immigrants. The president was empowered to deport dangerous foreigners in time of peace and to deport or imprison them in time of hostilities. This was an arbitrary grant of executive power contrary to American tradition and to the spirit of the Constitution, even though the stringent Alien Laws were never enforced.

The "lockjaw" Sedition Act, the last measure of the harsh Federalist clampdown, was a direct slap at two priceless freedoms guaranteed in the Constitution by the Bill of Rights in the First Amendment—freedom of speech and freedom of the press. This law provided that anyone who impeded the policies of the government or falsely defamed its officials, including the president, would be liable to a heavy fine and imprisonment.

Many outspoken Jeffersonian editors were indicted under the Sedition Act. Ten were brought to trial and convicted by packed juries swayed by prejudiced Federalist judges. Among them was Vermont congressman Matthew Lyon (the "Spitting Lion"), who had earlier gained fame by spitting in the face of a Federalist and fighting on the floor of Congress.

The Sedition Act seemed to be in direct conflict with the Constitution. But the Supreme Court, dominated by Federalists, was of no mind to declare this Federalist law unconstitutional. (The law expired in March 1801.) This attempt by the Federalists to crush free speech and silence the opposition party undoubtedly made many converts for the Jeffersonians.

Yet the Alien and Sedition Acts, despite pained outcries from the Jeffersonians they muzzled, commanded widespread popular support. Anti-French hysteria played directly into the hands of **witch-hunting** conservatives. In the congressional elections of 1798–1799, the Federalists, riding a wave of popularity, scored the most sweeping victory of their entire history.

In 1800 James Callender (1758–1803) published a pamphlet that assailed the president in strong language. For blasts like the following tirade, Callender was prosecuted under the Sedition Act, fined $250, and sentenced to prison for nine months:

"The reign of Mr. Adams has, hitherto, been one continued tempest of *malignant* passions. As president, he has never opened his lips, or lifted his pen, without threatening and scolding. The grand object of his administration has been to exasperate the rage of contending parties, to caluminate and destroy every man who differs from his opinions. . . . Every person holding an office must either quit it, or think and vote exactly with Mr. Adams."

The Virginia (Madison) and Kentucky (Jefferson) Resolutions

Resentful Jeffersonians naturally refused to take the Alien and Sedition Acts lying down. Jefferson himself feared that if the Federalists managed to choke free speech and free press, they would then wipe out other precious constitutional guarantees. His own fledgling political party might even be stamped out of existence.

Fearing prosecution for sedition, Jefferson secretly penned a series of resolutions, which the Kentucky legislature approved in 1798 and 1799. His friend and fellow Virginian James Madison drafted a similar but less extreme statement, which was adopted by the Virginia legislature in 1798.

Both Jefferson and Madison stressed the compact theory—a theory popular among English political philosophers in the seventeenth and eighteenth centuries. As applied to America by the Jeffersonians, this concept meant that the thirteen sovereign states, in creating the federal government, had entered into a "**compact,**" or contract, regarding its jurisdiction. The national government was consequently the agent or creation of the states. Since water can rise no higher than its source, the individual states were the final judges of whether their agent had broken the "compact" by overstepping the authority originally granted. Invoking this logic, Jefferson's Kentucky resolutions concluded that the federal regime *had* exceeded its constitutional powers and that, with regard to the Alien and Sedition Acts, "**nullification**" was the "rightful remedy."

The Virginia and Kentucky resolutions were a brilliant formulation of the extreme states' rights view regarding the Union—indeed more sweeping in their implications than their authors had intended. They were later used by southerners to support nullification—and ultimately secession. Yet neither Jefferson nor Madison, as Founding Fathers of the Union, had any intention of breaking it up: they were groping for ways to preserve it. Their resolutions were basically campaign documents designed to crystallize opposition to the Federalist party and to unseat it in the upcoming presidential election of 1800. The only real nullification that Jefferson had in view was the nullification of Federalist abuses.

compact *An agreement or covenant between states to perform some legal act.*

nullification *In American politics, the assertion that a state may legally invalidate a federal act deemed inconsistent with its rights or sovereignty.*

Federalists Versus Democratic-Republicans

As the presidential contest of 1800 approached, the differences between Federalists and Democratic-Republicans were sharply etched. As might be expected, most federalists of the pre-Constitutional period (1787–1789) became Federalists in the 1790s. Largely welded by Hamilton into an effective group by 1793, they openly advocated rule by the "best people." "Those who own the country," remarked Federalist John Jay, "ought to govern it." With their intellectual arrogance and Tory tastes, Hamiltonians distrusted full-blown democracy as the fountain of all mischiefs and feared the "swayability" of the untutored common folk.

Hamiltonian Federalists also advocated a strong central government with the power to crush democratic excesses like Shays's Rebellion, protect the lives and estates of the wealthy, and subordinate the sovereignty-loving states. They believed the national government should support private enterprise but not interfere with it. This attitude came naturally to the seaboard merchants, manufacturers, and shippers who made up the majority of Federalist support. Farther inland, few Hamiltonians dwelled.

Leading the anti-Federalists, who eventually came to be known as Democratic-Republicans or sometimes simply Republicans, was Thomas Jefferson. Lanky and relaxed in appearance, lacking personal aggressiveness, and unable to deliver a rabble-rousing speech, he became a master political organizer through his ability to lead people rather than drive them. His strongest appeal was to the middle class and to the underprivileged—the "dirt" farmers, the laborers, the artisans, and the small shopkeepers.

Liberal-thinking Jefferson, with his aristocratic head set on a farmer's frame, was a bundle of inconsistencies. By one set of tests he should have been a

■ **Monticello, Jefferson's Self-Designed Architectural Marvel**

Federalist, for he was a Virginia aristocrat and slave-owner who lived in an imposing hilltop mansion at Monticello. A so-called traitor to his own upper class, Jefferson cherished uncommon sympathy for the common people, especially the downtrodden, the oppressed, and the persecuted. As he wrote in 1800, "I have sworn upon the altar of God eternal hostility against every form of tyranny over the mind of man."

Jeffersonian Democratic-Republicans demanded a weak central regime. They believed that the best government was one that governed least, and that the bulk of power should be retained by the states. There the people could keep a more vigilant eye on their public servants. The national debt should be paid off, and government should provide no special privileges for special classes, especially manufacturers. Agriculture, to Jefferson, was the favored branch of the economy and formed the foundation of his political thought. "Those who labor in the earth are the chosen people of God," he said. Most of his followers naturally came from the agricultural South and Southwest.

Above all, Jefferson advocated the rule of the people. But he did not propose thrusting the ballot into the hands of every adult white male. He favored government *for* the people but not by *all* the people. Since the ignorant were incapable of self-government, only people literate enough to inform themselves about citizenship should have the ballot. Universal education would have to precede universal suffrage. Jefferson had a profound faith in the reasonableness and teachableness of the masses and in their collective wisdom when taught.

Landlessness among American citizens threatened popular democracy as much as illiteracy, in Jefferson's eyes. He feared that propertyless dependents would be political pawns in the hands of their landowning superiors. How could the emergence of a landless class of voters be avoided? The answer, in part, was by slavery. A system of black slave labor ensured that southern white yeoman farmers would remain independent landowners and not be forced to labor for low wages in others' tobacco and rice fields. Jefferson thus tortuously reconciled slaveholding—his own included—with his more democratic impulses.

Yet for his time, Jefferson's confidence that white, free men could become responsible and knowledgeable citizens was open-minded. He championed freedom of speech, for without free speech and a free press, the misdeeds of tyranny could not be exposed. Although Jefferson suffered much foul abuse from editorial pens, he said that he would choose "newspapers without a government" rather than "a government without newspapers."

Differences over foreign policy defined another sharp distinction between Hamilton and Jefferson. Hamilton looked outward and eastward. He sought to build a strong national state that would assert America's commercial interests and expand foreign trade, especially with Britain. Jeffersonian Republicans, unlike "British bootlickers," were basically pro-French. They earnestly believed that it was to America's advantage to support the liberal ideals of the French Revolution rather than reactionary British Tories. Jefferson, in effect, faced inward and westward. His priorities were to strengthen democracy at home, especially in the frontier regions beyond the Appalachians, rather than to flex America's muscles abroad.

So as the young Republic's first full decade of nationhood came to a close, the Founders' hopes seemed already imperiled. Conflicts over domestic politics and foreign policy undermined the unity of the Revolutionary era and called into question the very viability of the American experiment in democracy. As the presidential election of 1800 approached, the danger loomed that the fragile and battered American ship of state would founder on the rocks of controversy. The shores of history are littered with the wreckage of nascent nations torn asunder before they could grow to stable maturity. Why should the United States expect to enjoy a happier fate?

Thomas Jefferson's vision of a republican America was peopled with virtuous farmers, not factory hands. As early as 1784, he wrote:

"While we have land to labor then, let us never wish to see our citizens occupied at a work-bench, or twirling a distaff. . . . For the general operations of manufacture, let our workshops remain in Europe. . . . The mobs of great cities add just so much to the support of pure government, as sores do to the strength of the human body."

Chapter Summary

The fledgling federal government under the new Constitution faced severe difficulties and deep skepticism about its durability, especially because traditional political theory held that large-scale republics were bound to fail. But President Washington brought credibility to the new government, while his cabinet, led by Alexander Hamilton, strengthened its political and economic foundations.

The government's first achievements were the Bill of Rights and Hamilton's financial system. Through effective leadership, Hamilton carried out his program of funding the national debt, assuming state debts, imposing customs and excise taxes, and establishing a Bank of the United States.

The bank was the most controversial part of Hamilton's program because it raised basic constitutional issues. Opposition to the bank from Jefferson and his followers reflected more fundamental political disagreements about republicanism, economics, federal power, and foreign policy. As the French Revolution evolved from moderation to radicalism, it intensified the ideological divisions between the pro-French Jeffersonians and the pro-British Hamiltonians. Their disagreements solidified into the first American political parties, the Republicans and the Federalists—a development not anticipated in the Constitution.

Washington's Neutrality Proclamation angered Republicans, who wanted America to aid Revolutionary France. Washington's policy was sorely tested by the British, who routinely violated American neutrality. In order to avoid war, Washington endorsed the conciliatory Jay's Treaty, further outraging the Jeffersonian Republicans in the United States as well as revolutionary France.

After the humiliating XYZ affair, the United States began to fight a "quasi-war" with France, but President John Adams sacrificed his political popularity and divided his party by choosing to negotiate peace.

These foreign-policy disagreements deeply embittered domestic politics: Federalists passed the repressive Alien and Sedition Acts, to which Jefferson and Madison responded with the Virginia and Kentucky resolutions, which challenged federal authority.

11

The Triumphs and Travails of the Jeffersonian Republic

1800–1812

TIMID MEN . . . PREFER THE CALM OF DESPOTISM TO THE BOISTEROUS SEA OF LIBERTY.

THOMAS JEFFERSON, 1796

Chapter Outline

- The "Revolution of 1800"
- Examining the Evidence: The Thomas Jefferson–Sally Hemings Controversy
- The Jefferson Presidency
- John Marshall and the Supreme Court
- The Louisiana Purchase, 1803
- The Embargo, 1807–1809
- Napoleon Manipulates Madison
- Battle with the Shawnees
- A Declaration of War

In the critical presidential election of 1800, the first in which Federalists and Democratic-Republicans functioned as two national political parties, John Adams and Thomas Jefferson again squared off against each other. The choice seemed clear and dramatic. Adams's Federalists waged a defensive struggle for a strong central government and public order. Their Jeffersonian opponents presented themselves as the guardians of agrarian purity, liberty, and states' rights.

The next dozen years, however, would turn what seemed like a clear-cut choice in 1800 into a messier reality, as the Jeffersonians in power were confronted with a series of opportunities and crises requiring the assertion of federal authority. As the first challengers successfully to rout a reigning party, the Republicans were also the first to learn that it is far easier to condemn from the stump than to govern consistently.

Focus Questions

1. **How did Jefferson adapt his principles and ideals to practical realities as he carried out the "Revolution of 1800"?**
2. **Why did Republicans and Federalists clash so sharply over the judiciary, and how did John Marshall perpetuate Federalist principles on the Supreme Court?**
3. **What were Jefferson's basic foreign-policy goals, and how successful was he in achieving them?**
4. **What were the causes and effects of the Louisiana Purchase?**
5. **How did America become embroiled in the turbulent crisis of the Napoleonic Wars, and why did President Madison see a new war with Britain as essential to maintaining America's republican experiment?**

Chronology

1800	Jefferson defeats Adams for presidency.
1801	Judiciary Act of 1801.
1801-1805	Naval war with Tripoli.
1802	Revised naturalization law. Judiciary Act of 1801 repealed.
1803	*Marbury* v. *Madison.* Louisiana Purchase.
1804	Jefferson reelected president.
1804-1806	Lewis and Clark expedition.
1805	Peace treaty with Tripoli.
1805-1807	Pike's explorations.
1806	Burr treason trial.
1807	*Chesapeake* affair. Embargo Act.
1809	Non-Intercourse Act replaces Embargo Act.
1810	Macon's Bill No. 2. Napoleon announces (falsely) repeal of blockade decrees. Madison reestablishes nonimportation against Britain.
1811	Battle of Tippecanoe.
1812	United States declares war on Britain.

Federalist and Republican Mudslingers

In fighting for survival, the Federalists labored under heavy handicaps. Their Alien and Sedition Acts had aroused a host of enemies, although most of these critics were dyed-in-the-wool Jeffersonians anyhow. The Hamiltonian wing of the Federalist party, robbed of its glorious war with France, split openly with President Adams, and Hamilton himself attacked the president.

Primary source
Jefferson Campaign Poster
college.hmco.com/pic/kennedybrief7e

The most damaging blow to the Federalists, however, was the refusal of Adams to give them a rousing fight with France. Their feverish war preparations had swelled the public debt and required disagreeable new taxes, including a stamp tax. After all these unpopular measures, the war scare had petered out, and the country was left with an all-dressed-up-but-no-place-to-go feeling.

Thrown on the defensive, the Federalists concentrated their fire on Jefferson himself, who became the victim of one of America's earliest "whispering campaigns." He was accused of having robbed a widow and her children of a trust fund and of having fathered numerous mulatto children by his own slave women. (Jefferson's long-rumored intimacy with his slave Sally Hemings has recently been confirmed by DNA testing; see "Examining the Evidence," p. 149.) As a liberal in religion, Jefferson had earlier incurred the wrath of the orthodox clergy, largely through his successful struggle to separate church and state in Virginia. From the New England stronghold of Federalism and Congregationalism, preachers thundered against his alleged atheism. Old ladies of Federalist families, fearing Jefferson's election, even buried their Bibles or hung them in wells.

The Jeffersonian "Revolution of 1800"

Jefferson won by a majority of 73 electoral votes to 65. In defeat, the colorless and presumably unpopular Adams polled more electoral strength than he had gained four years earlier—except for New York. The Empire State fell into the Jeffersonian basket, and with it the election, largely because Aaron Burr, a master wire-puller, turned New York to Jefferson by the narrowest of margins. The Virginian polled the bulk of his strength in the South and West, particularly in those states where universal white manhood suffrage had been adopted.

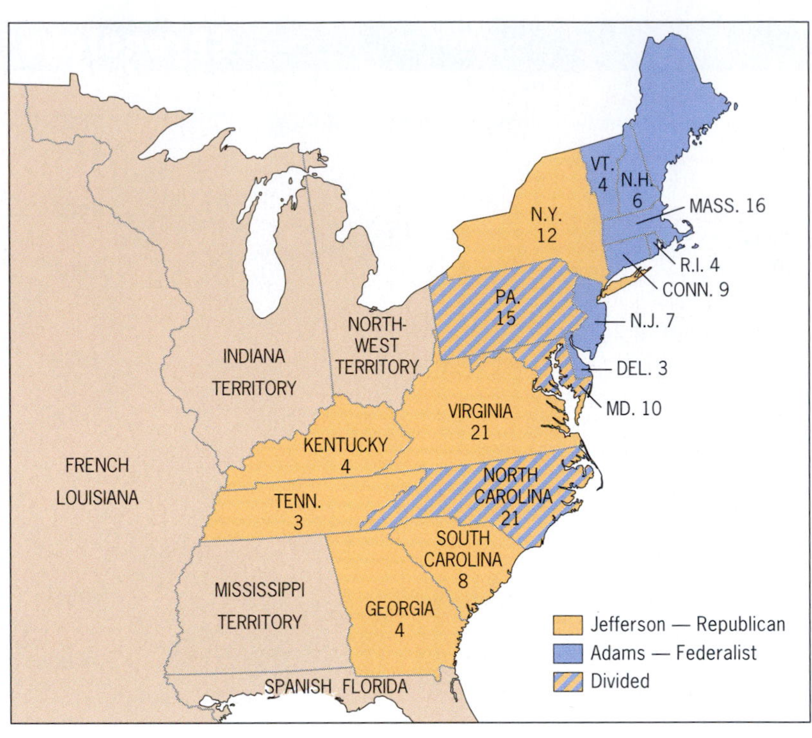

Presidential Election of 1800 (with electoral vote by state) New York was the key state in this election, and Aaron Burr helped to swing it away from the Federalists with tactics that anticipated the political machines of a later day. Federalists complained that Burr "travels every night from one meeting of Republicans to another, haranguing . . . them to the most zealous exertions. [He] can stoop so low as to visit every low tavern that may happen to be crowded with his dear fellow citizens." But Burr proved that the price was worth it. "We have beat you," Burr told kid-gloved Federalists after the election, "by superior Management."

Decisive in Jefferson's victory was the three-fifths clause of the Constitution. By counting three-fifths of the slave population for the purposes of congressional and Electoral College representations, the Constitution gave white southern voters a bonus that helped Jefferson win the White House. Northern critics fumed that Jefferson was an illegitimate embodiment of the "slave power" that southern states wielded in the Union.

Jeffersonian joy was dampened by an unexpected deadlock. Through a technicality Jefferson, the presidential candidate, and Burr, his vice-presidential running mate, received the same number of electoral votes for the presidency. Under the Constitution the tie could be broken only by the House of Representatives (see Art. II, Sec. I, para. 2). This body would be controlled for several more months by the **lame duck** Federalists, who preferred Burr to the hated Jefferson.*

lame duck *A political official during the time he or she remains in office after an electoral defeat or legal inability to seek another term, and whose power is therefore diminished.*

Voting in the House moved slowly to a climax as exhausted representatives snored in their seats. The agonizing deadlock was broken at last when a few Federalists, despairing of electing Burr and hoping for moderation from Jefferson, refrained from voting. The election then went to the rightful candidate. John Adams proved to be the last Federalist president of the United States, and his party sank slowly into political oblivion and ultimately disappeared.

Jefferson later claimed that the election of 1800 was a "revolution" comparable to that of 1776. But it was no revolution in the sense of a massive popular upheaval or an upending of the political system, for Jefferson had only narrowly squeaked through to victory. Jefferson meant that his election represented a return to what he considered the original spirit of the Revolution. In his eyes, Hamilton and Adams had betrayed the ideals of 1776 and 1787. Jefferson's mission, as he saw it, was to restore the republican experiment, to check the growth of government, and to halt the decay of virtue that had set in under Federalist rule.

No less "revolutionary" was the peaceful and orderly transfer of power on the basis of an election whose results all parties accepted. This was a remarkable achievement for a raw young nation, especially after all the partisan bitterness that had agitated the country during Adams's presidency. After a decade of division and doubt, Americans could take justifiable pride in the vigor of their experiment in democracy.

*A "lame duck" has been humorously defined as a politician whose goose has been cooked at the recent elections. The possibility of another such tie was removed by the Twelfth Amendment in 1804 (for text, see the Appendix). Before then, each elector had two votes, and the second-place finisher became the vice president.

Examining the Evidence

The Thomas Jefferson–Sally Hemings Controversy Debate over whether Thomas Jefferson had sexual relations with Sally Hemings, a slave at Monticello, began as early as 1802, when James Callender published the first accusations and Federalist newspapers gleefully broadcast them throughout the country. Two years later this print, "The Philosophic Cock," attacked Jefferson by depicting him as a rooster and Hemings as a hen. The rooster, or cock, was also a symbol of revolutionary France. Jefferson's enemies sought to discredit him for personal indiscretions as well as radical sympathies. Although he resolutely denied any affair with Hemings, a charge that at first seemed only to be a politically motivated defamation refused to go away. In the 1870s two new oral sources of evidence came to light. Madison Hemings, Sally's next-to-last child, claimed that his mother had identified Jefferson as the father of all five of her children. Soon thereafter James Parton's biography of Jefferson revealed that among Jefferson's white descendants it was said that his nephew had fathered all or most of Sally's children. In the 1950s several large publishing projects on Jefferson's life and writings uncovered new evidence and inspired renewed debate. Most convincing was Dumas Malone's calculation that Jefferson had been present at Monticello nine months prior to the birth of each of Sally's children. Speculation continued throughout the rest of the century, with little new evidence, until scientific advances made possible DNA testing of the remains of Jefferson's white and possible black descendents to establish paternity. Two centuries after James Callender first cast aspersions on Jefferson's morality, cutting-edge science helped establish the high probability that Jefferson had fathered Sally's youngest son and the likelihood that he was the father of all of her children.

1. Are there ways that historians can use unproven rumors and charges made during political campaigns—such as those leveled against Thomas Jefferson regarding Sally Hemings—to better understand a person or event, even if the accusations themselves are false or unproven? Or should such material be totally disregarded?
2. Which piece of "unscientific" historical information that existed in the nineteenth and early twentieth centuries regarding Jefferson's affair with Sally Hemings was most persuasive: the oral traditions of a liaison within both the Hemings and Jefferson families, or the recorded evidence that Jefferson had been at Monticello nine months before the birth of each of Hemings's five children? How should historians treat such material?
3. How might the scientific evidence strongly suggest that Jefferson did father Hemings's children alter historians' perceptions of Jefferson, his political opponents, and the larger issues of race relations?

> *The toleration of Thomas Jefferson (1743–1826) was reflected in his inaugural address:*
>
> "If there be any among us who would wish to dissolve this Union or to change its republican form, let them stand undisturbed as monuments of the safety with which error of opinion may be tolerated where reason is left free to combat it."

Jefferson in Casual Attire As befitted a champion of the new democracy, Jefferson typically dressed casually, shunning the sartorial pretensions affected by many Federalists.

Responsibility Breeds Moderation

"Long Tom" Jefferson was inaugurated president on March 4, 1801, in the swampy village of Washington, the crude new national capital. Tall (six feet two and a half inches), with large hands and feet, red hair ("the Red Fox"), and prominent cheekbones and chin, he was an arresting figure. Believing that the customary pomp did not befit his democratic ideals, he spurned a horse-drawn coach and strode to the Capitol from his boardinghouse.

Jefferson's inaugural address, beautifully phrased, was a classic statement of democratic principles. Seeking to allay Federalist fears of a bull-in-the-china-shop overturn, Jefferson ingratiatingly intoned, "We are all Republicans, we are all Federalists." As for foreign affairs, he pledged "honest friendship with all nations, entangling alliances with none."

With its rustic setting, Washington lent itself admirably to the simplicity and frugality of the Jeffersonian Republicans. In this respect, it contrasted sharply with the elegant atmosphere of Federalist Philadelphia, the former temporary capital.

As president, Jefferson was shockingly unconventional. He would receive callers in sloppy attire—once in a dressing gown and slippers. He started the **precedent,** unbroken until Woodrow Wilson's presidency 112 years later, of sending messages to Congress to be read by a clerk. Personal appearances, in the Federalist manner, suggested too strongly a monarchical speech from the throne.

As if compelled by an evil twin, Jefferson was forced to reverse many of the political principles he had so vigorously championed. There were in fact two Thomas Jeffersons. One was the scholarly private citizen who philosophized in his study. The other was the harassed public official, who made the disturbing discovery that bookish theories worked out differently in the noisy arena of practical politics. The open-minded Virginian was therefore consistently inconsistent; it is easy to quote one Jefferson to refute the other.

Jefferson quickly proved an able politician. He was especially effective in the informal atmosphere of a dinner party, where he would woo congressional representatives while personally pouring imported wines and serving French food. In part, Jefferson had to rely on his charm because his party was so weak-jointed. Jefferson's refusal to practice widespread patronage made it difficult for Democratic-Republicans to build a political following. Opposition to the Federalists was the chief glue holding them together, and as the Federalists faded, so did Republican unity. The era of well-developed, well-disciplined political parties still lay in the future.

At the outset, Jefferson was determined to undo the Federalist abuses begotten by the anti-French hysteria. The hated Alien and Sedition Acts had already expired. The incoming president speedily pardoned the "martyrs" serving sentences under the Sedition Act. Shortly after Congress met, the Jeffersonians enacted the new naturalization law of 1802, which reduced the requirement of fourteen years of residence to a more reasonable five years.

Jefferson actually kicked away only one substantial prop of the Hamiltonian economic system. He hated the excise tax, which bred bureaucrats and bore heavily

precedent *In law and government, a decision or action that establishes a sanctioned rule for determining similar cases in the future.*

on his farmer following, and he early persuaded Congress to repeal it. But except for excising the excise tax, Jefferson and his talented treasury secretary, Albert Gallatin, left the Hamiltonian framework essentially intact. They launched no attack on the Bank of the United States, nor did they repeal the mildly protective Federalist tariff.

Paradoxically, Jefferson's moderation thus further cemented the gains of the "Revolution of 1800." By shrewdly absorbing many major Federalist programs, Jefferson showed that a change of regime need not be disastrous for the defeated group. His restraint pointed the way toward the two-party system that was later to become a characteristic feature of American politics.

The "Dead Clutch" of the Judiciary

The "deathbed" Judiciary Act of 1801 was one of the last important laws passed by the expiring Federalist Congress. It created sixteen new federal judgeships and other judicial offices. President Adams remained at his desk until nine o'clock in the evening on his last day in office, supposedly signing the **commissions** of the Federalist "midnight judges."

This Federalist-sponsored Judiciary Act, though a long-overdue reform, aroused bitter resentment. "Packing" of these lifetime posts with anti-Jeffersonian partisans was, in Republican eyes, a brazen attempt by the ousted party to entrench itself in one of the three powerful branches of government. Jeffersonians condemned the last-minute appointees in violent language.

The newly elected Republican Congress bestirred itself to repeal the Judiciary Act of 1801 in the year after its passage. Jeffersonians thus swept sixteen benches from under their recently appointed midnight judges.

Jeffersonians likewise had their knives sharpened for the scalp of Chief Justice John Marshall, whom Adams had appointed to the Supreme Court in the dying days of his term. The strong-willed Marshall, with his rasping voice and steel-trap mind, was Thomas Jefferson's cousin. As a lifelong Federalist and fervent advocate of a powerful central government, Marshall was cordially disliked by the states' rights Jeffersonians. The Federalist party died out, but Marshall lived on, handing down Federalist decisions serenely for thirty-four years under Democratic-Republican administrations. For over three decades, the ghost of Alexander Hamilton spoke through the lanky, black-robed judge.

One of the "midnight judges" of 1801 presented John Marshall with a historic opportunity. When obscure William Marbury, whom President Adams had named a justice of the peace for the District of Columbia, learned that his commission was being shelved by the new Secretary of State James Madison, he sued for its delivery. Chief Justice John Marshall knew that his Jeffersonian rivals, entrenched in the executive branch, would hardly spring forward to enforce a **writ** to deliver the commission to his fellow Federalist Marbury. He therefore dismissed Marbury's suit, avoiding a direct showdown. But the wily Marshall snatched victory from the jaws of this judicial defeat. In explaining his ruling, Marshall said that the part of the Judiciary Act of 1789 on which Marbury tried to base his appeal was unconstitutional. The act had attempted to assign to the Supreme Court powers that the Constitution had not foreseen.

In this self-denying opinion, Marshall greatly magnified the authority of the Court—and slapped at the Jeffersonians. Until the case of *Marbury* v. *Madison* (1803), controversy had clouded the question of who had the final authority to determine the meaning of the Constitution.

commission *The official legal authorization appointing a person to an office or military position, indicating the nature of the duty, term of office, chain of command, and so on.*

writ *A formal legal document ordering or prohibiting some act.*

In his decision in Marbury *v.* Madison, *Chief Justice John Marshall (1755–1835) vigorously asserted his view that the Constitution embodied a "higher" law than ordinary legislation, and that the Court must interpret the Constitution:*

"The Constitution is either a superior paramount law, unchangeable by ordinary means, or it is on a level with ordinary legislative acts, and like other acts, is alterable when the legislature shall please to alter it.

"If the former part of the alternative be true, then a legislative act contrary to the constitution is not law; if the latter part be true, then written constitutions are absurd attempts, on the part of the people, to limit a power in its own nature illimitable. . . .

"It is emphatically the province and duty of the judicial department to say what the law is. . . .

"If, then, the courts are to regard the Constitution, and the Constitution is superior to any ordinary act of the legislature, the Constitution, and not such ordinary act, must govern the case to which they are both applicable."

Jefferson in the Kentucky resolutions (1798) had tried to assign that right to the individual states. But now his cousin on the Court had cleverly promoted the contrary principle of "judicial review"—the idea that the Supreme Court alone had the last word on the question of constitutionality. In this landmark case, Marshall inserted the keystone into the arch that supports the tremendous power of the Supreme Court in American life.*

Jefferson: A Reluctant Warrior

One of Jefferson's first actions as president was to reduce the military establishment to a mere twenty-five hundred officers and men. Jefferson's reluctance to invest in soldiers and ships was less about money than about republican ideals. He fondly hoped that America would transcend Europe's bloody wars and set an example for the world by winning friends through "peaceful coercion" rather than military force. The Republicans also distrusted standing armies as standing invitations to dictatorships. A large navy, the farm-loving Jeffersonians feared, might embroil the Republic in costly and corrupting wars far from America's shores.

But harsh realities forced Jefferson's principles to bend. Pirates of the North African Barbary States had long made a national industry of blackmailing and plundering merchant ships that ventured into the Mediterranean. Preceding Federalist administrations had been forced to buy protection. At the time of the French crisis of 1798, when Americans were shouting, "Millions for defense, but not one cent for tribute," twenty-six barrels of blackmail dollars were being shipped to Algiers.

War across the Atlantic was not part of the Jeffersonian vision—but neither was paying tribute to a pack of pirate states. The showdown came in 1801. The pasha of Tripoli, dissatisfied with his share of protection money, informally declared war on the United States by cutting down the flagstaff of the American **consulate.** A gauntlet was thus thrown squarely into the face of Jefferson—the noninterventionist, the critic of a big-ship navy, and the political foe of Federalist shippers. He reluctantly rose to the challenge by dispatching the infant navy to "the shores of Tripoli," as related in the song of the U.S. Marine Corps. After four years of intermittent fighting, Jefferson succeeded in obtaining a peace treaty with Tripoli in 1805.

consulate (consul) *A place where a government representative is stationed in a foreign country, but not the main headquarters of diplomatic representation headed by an ambassador (the embassy).*

cede *To yield or grant something, often upon request or under pressure. (Anything ceded is a cession.)*

The Louisiana Godsend

A secret pact, fraught with peril for America, was signed in 1800. Napoleon Bonaparte induced the king of Spain to **cede** to France, for attractive considerations, the immense trans-Mississippi region of Louisiana, which included the New Orleans area. Then, in 1802, the right of deposit at New Orleans, guaranteed America by the treaty of 1795, was withdrawn. Deposit (warehouse) privileges were vital to frontier farmers who floated their produce down the Mississippi to its mouth, there to await oceangoing vessels. A roar of anger rolled up the mighty river and into its tributary valleys. American pioneers talked wildly of descending on New Orleans, rifles in hand.

Thomas Jefferson was again on the griddle. Louisiana in the grip of senile Spain posed no real threat, but Louisiana in the iron fist of Napoleon, the preeminent military genius of his age, foreshadowed a dark and blood-drenched future. Hoping to quiet the clamor of the West, Jefferson moved decisively. Early in 1803 he sent James Monroe to Paris to join forces with the regular minister there, Robert R. Livingston. The two envoys were instructed to buy New Orleans and as much land to the east as they could get for a maximum of $10 million.

At this critical juncture, Napoleon suddenly abandoned his dream of a New World empire and decided to sell all Louisiana. Two developments prompted his

---

* The next invalidation of a federal law by the Supreme Court came fifty-four years late with the explosive *Dred Scott* decision (see p. 280).

change of mind. First, he had failed to reconquer the sugar-rich island of Santo Domingo, for which Louisiana was to serve as a source of foodstuffs. Infuriated ex-slaves, ably led by the gifted Toussaint L'Ouverture, had put up a stubborn resistance. Santo Domingo could not be reconquered, except perhaps at a staggering cost. Second, Bonaparte was about to end the twenty-month lull in his deadly conflict with Britain. Because the British controlled the seas, he feared that he might be forced to make them a gift of Louisiana. Rather than drive America into the arms of Britain by attempting to hold the area, he decided to sell the huge wilderness to the Americans and pocket the money for his schemes nearer home.

Events now unrolled dizzily. Suddenly, out of a clear sky, the French foreign minister asked the American minister Robert Livingston how much he would give for all Louisiana. Scarcely able to believe his ears (he was partially deaf anyhow), Livingston nervously entered upon the negotiations. After about a week of haggling, the treaties were signed on April 30, 1803, ceding Louisiana to the United States for about $15 million.

When news of the bargain reached America, Jefferson was startled. He had authorized his envoys to offer not more than $10 million for New Orleans, and as much to the east in the Floridas as they could get. Instead, they had signed three treaties that pledged $15 million for New Orleans and a vast wilderness entirely to the west—an area that would more than double the size of the United States. They had bought a wilderness to get a city.

Once again two Jeffersons wrestled with each other: the theoretical strict constructionist versus the democratic visionary. Where in his beloved Constitution was the president authorized to negotiate treaties incorporating a huge new expanse into the Union—an expanse containing tens of thousands of Indian, white, and black inhabitants? There was no such clause. Yet Jefferson also perceived that the vast domain now within his reach could form a sprawling "empire of liberty" that would ensure the health and life of America's experiment in democracy. So Jefferson shamefacedly submitted the treaties to the Senate while privately admitting that the purchase was unconstitutional.

The senators were less finicky than Jefferson. Reflecting enthusiastic public support, they registered their prompt approval of the transaction. Land-hungry Americans were not disposed to split constitutional hairs when confronted with perhaps the most magnificent real estate bargain in history—828,000 square miles at about three cents an acre.

Online Study Center

Interactive map
Louisiana Purchase and the Lewis and Clark Expedition
college.hmco.com/pic/kennedybrief7e

Exploring the Louisiana Purchase and the West
Seeking to avert friction with France by purchasing all of Louisiana, Jefferson bought trouble because of the vagueness of the boundaries. The disputants included Spain in the Floridas, Spain and later Mexico in the Southwest, and Great Britain in Canada.

Online Study Center

Primary source
President's Instructions to Meriwether Lewis, The
college.hmco.com/pic/kennedybrief7e

Online Study Center

Primary source
Sketches from the Journals
college.hmco.com/pic/kennedybrief7e

Online Study Center

Primary source
Lewis's Initial Report to the President
college.hmco.com/pic/kennedybrief7e

Jefferson's bargain with France was epochal. By scooping up Louisiana, America secured at one bloodless stroke the western half of the richest river valley in the world and further laid the foundations of a future major power. The ideal of a great agrarian republic, as envisioned by Jefferson, could now be realized in the vast "Valley of Democracy." At the same time, the transfer established a valuable precedent for acquiring foreign territories and peoples by purchase and incorporating them into the Union as full equals.

The purchase also contributed to making operational the isolationist principles of Washington's Farewell Address. With virtually the last potentially hostile European power removed from the North American continent, the United States could happily disengage from the ancient system of European power politics and rivalries.

The extent of the huge new area was more fully unveiled by a series of explorations under Jefferson's direction. In the spring of 1804, Jefferson sent Meriwether Lewis and William Clark on a voyage of discovery that took them up the Missouri River (the "Great Muddy"), across the Rockies, and down the Columbia River to the Pacific coast. Aided by the Shoshoni woman guide Sacajawea, Lewis and Clark's two-and-one-half-year expedition yielded rich scientific observations, demonstrated the viability of an overland trail to the Pacific, and bolstered American claims to Oregon. Other explorers also pushed into the uncharted West. Zebulon M. Pike explored the headwaters of the Mississippi River in 1805–1806 and the southern portion of the Louisiana territory in 1807.

secession *The withdrawal, by legal or illegal means, of one portion of a political entity from the government to which it has been bound.*

The Aaron Burr Conspiracies

In the long run, the Louisiana Purchase greatly expanded the fortunes of the United States and the power of the federal government. In the short term, the vast expanse of territory, and the feeble reach of the government obliged to control it, raised fears of **secession** and foreign intrigue.

Aaron Burr, Jefferson's first-term vice president, played no small part in provoking—and justifying—such fears. Dropped from the ticket for Jefferson's second term, Burr joined a group of Federalist extremists to plot the secession of New England and New York. Alexander Hamilton, though no friend of Jefferson, exposed and foiled this conspiracy. Incensed, Burr challenged his foe to a duel, and Hamilton reluctantly accepted. Burr killed Hamilton with a single shot. Burr's pistol blew the brightest brain out of the Federalist party and destroyed its one remaining hope of effective leadership.

His political career as dead as Hamilton's, Burr now turned his disunionist plottings to the trans-Mississippi West, where he struck up an alliance with General James Wilkinson, the unscrupulous military governor of Louisiana. Burr's schemes are still shrouded in mystery, but he and Wilkinson apparently planned to break the West away from the United States and then expand their new confederacy by invading Spanish Mexico and Florida. In the fall of 1806 Burr and his followers floated down the Mississippi to meet Wilkinson's army at Natchez, but Wilkinson betrayed Burr and fled to New Orleans. The former vice president was arrested and tried for treason, but finally acquitted. Chief Justice Marshall ruled that there was insufficient proof that Burr had committed overt acts of treason according to the Constitution (see Art. III, Sec. III). Burr then fled to Europe. His insurrectionary brashness demonstrated that purchasing a large expanse of western territory was far easier than controlling it.

■ **Meriwether Lewis** This painting portrays him as he looked on his return from the great expedition through the Louisiana Purchase and the West. Collection of The New York Historical Society, neg. 51322.

America: A Nutcrackered Neutral

Jefferson was triumphantly reelected in 1804, with 162 electoral votes to only 14 votes for his Federalist opponent. But the laurels of Jefferson's first administration soon withered under the blasts of the new storm that broke in Europe. After unloading Louisiana in 1803, Napoleon deliberately provoked a new war with Britain, an awesome conflict that raged for eleven long years. After the Battle of Trafalgar in 1805, Britain's navy controlled the seas, while Napoleon's victory in the Battle of Austerlitz made him master of the whole European continent. Like the tiger and the shark, France and Britain each reigned supreme in their chosen elements.

Unable to hurt each other directly, the two antagonists were forced to strike indirect blows. Britain ruled the waves and waived the rules. The London government, beginning in 1806, issued a series of Orders in Council that closed all ports under French control to foreign shipping, including American, unless the vessels first stopped at a British port. Napoleon struck back, ordering the seizure of all merchant ships, including American, that entered British ports. There was thus no way to trade with either nation without facing the other's guns. American vessels were, quite literally, caught between the devil and the deep blue sea.

Even more galling to American pride than the seizure of wooden ships was the seizure of flesh-and-blood American seamen. Impressment—the forcible enlistment of sailors—was a crude form of **conscription** that the British, among others, had employed for over four centuries. Clubs and stretchers (for men knocked unconscious) were standard equipment of press gangs from His Majesty's crew-hungry ships. Some six thousand bona fide U.S. citizens were impressed by the "piratical man stealers" of Britain from 1808 to 1811 alone.

conscription *Compulsory enrollment of men and women into the armed forces.*

embargo *A government order prohibiting commerce in or out of a port.*

Britain's determination was spectacularly highlighted in 1807 when a British warship, seeking deserters, fired on a U.S. frigate, the *Chesapeake,* killing three Americans and wounding eighteen. Britain was clearly in the wrong, as the London foreign office admitted. But London's contrition availed little; a roar of national wrath went up from infuriated Americans. Jefferson, the peace lover, could easily have had war if he had wanted it.

The Hated Embargo

National honor would not permit a slavish submission to British and French mistreatment. Yet a large-scale foreign war was contrary to the settled policy of the new Republic—and in addition it would be futile. The navy was weak, and the army was even weaker. A disastrous defeat would not improve America's plight.

The warring nations in Europe depended heavily on the United States for raw materials and foodstuffs. In his eager search for an alternative to war, Jefferson seized on this essential fact. He reasoned that if America voluntarily cut off its exports, the offending powers would be forced to bow, hat in hand, and agree to respect U.S. rights. Responding to the presidential lash, Congress hastily passed the Embargo Act late in 1807. This rigorous law forbade the export of all goods from the United States, whether in American or in foreign ships. More than just a compromise between submission and shooting, the **embargo** embodied Jefferson's idea of "peaceful coercion." If it worked, the embargo would vindicate the rights of neutral nations and point to a new way of conducting foreign affairs.

The American economy staggered under the effect of the embargo long before Britain or France began to bend. Forests of dead masts gradually filled once-flourishing harbors; docks that had once rumbled were deserted (except for illegal trade); and soup kitchens cared for some of the hungry unemployed. Jeffersonian Republicans probably hurt the commerce of New England, which they avowedly were trying to protect, far more than Britain and France together were doing.

Farmers of the South and West, the strongholds of Jefferson, suffered no less disastrously than New England. They were alarmed by the mounting piles of exportable cotton, grain, and tobacco. Jefferson in truth seemed to be waging war on his fellow citizens rather than on the offending foreign powers.

An enormous illicit trade mushroomed in 1808, especially along the Canadian border, where bands of armed Americans on loaded rafts overawed or overpowered federal agents. Irate citizens cynically transposed the letters of "Embargo" to read "O Grab Me," "Go Bar 'Em," and "Mobrage," while heartily cursing the "Dambargo."

Jefferson nonetheless induced Congress to pass iron-toothed enforcing legislation. It was so inquisitorial and tyrannical as to cause some Americans to think more kindly of George III, whom Jefferson had berated in the Declaration of Independence. One indignant New Hampshirite denounced the president with this ditty:

Our ships all in motion,
Once whiten'd the ocean;
They sail'd and return'd with a cargo;
Now doom'd to decay
They are fallen a prey,
To Jefferson, worms, and EMBARGO

The embargo even had the effect of reviving the moribund Federalist party. Gaining new converts, its leaders hurled their nullification of the embargo into the teeth of the "Virginia lordlings" in Washington. In 1804 the discredited Federalists had polled only 14 electoral votes out of 176; in 1808, the embargo year, the figure rose to 47 out of 175. New England seethed with talk of secession, and Jefferson later admitted that he felt the foundations of government tremble under his feet.

An alarmed Congress, yielding to the storm of public anger, finally repealed the embargo on March 1, 1809, three days before Jefferson's retirement. A half-loaf substitute was provided by the Non-Intercourse Act. This measure formally reopened trade with all the nations of the world, except the two most important, Britain and France. Though thus watered down, economic coercion continued to be the policy of the Jeffersonians from 1809 to 1812, when the nation finally plunged into war.

Why did the embargo, Jefferson's most daring act of statesmanship, collapse after fifteen dismal months? First, the president overestimated the dependence of both belligerents on America's trade. Bumper grain crops blessed the British Isles during these years, and the revolutionary Latin American republics unexpectedly threw open their ports for compensating commerce. With most of Europe under his control, Napoleon simply tightened his belt and went without American trade even as he mocked the United States by seizing American ships and cargo with the claim that he was simply helping them enforce the embargo.

More critically, perhaps, Jefferson miscalculated the unpopularity of such a self-crucifying weapon and the difficulty of enforcing it. The hated embargo was not continued long enough or tightly enough to achieve the desired results—and a leaky embargo was perhaps more costly than none at all.

Curiously enough, New England plucked a new prosperity from the ugly jaws of the embargo. With shipping tied up and imported goods scarce, the resourceful Yankees reopened old factories and erected new ones. The real foundations of modern America's industrial might were laid behind the protective wall of the embargo, followed by nonintercourse and the War of 1812. Jefferson, the avowed critic of factories, may have unwittingly done more for American manufacturing than Alexander Hamilton, industry's outspoken friend.

Madison's Gamble

Following Washington's precedent, Jefferson left the presidency after two terms, happy to escape what he called the "splendid misery" of the highest office in the land. As his successor, he strongly favored the nomination and election of his friend and fellow Virginian, the quiet, intellectual, and unassuming James Madison.

Madison took the presidential oath on March 4, 1809, as the awesome conflict in Europe was roaring to its climax. The scholarly Madison was short, thin, bald, and weak of voice. Despite a distinguished career as a legislator, he was crippled as president by factions within his party and his cabinet. Unable to dominate Congress as Jefferson had done, Madison often found himself holding the bag for risky foreign policies not of his own making.

The Non-Intercourse Act of 1809—a diluted embargo aimed solely at Britain and France—was due to expire in 1810. To Madison's dismay, Congress dismantled the embargo completely with a bargaining measure known as Macon's Bill No. 2. While reopening American trade with all the world, it dangled what

Congress hoped was an attractive lure. If either Britain or France repealed its commercial restrictions, America would restore its embargo against the nonrepealing nation. A dismayed Madison recognized that this measure emphasized America's economic weakness and left the determination of who would be America's trading partner to the potentates of London and Paris.

The crafty Napoleon saw his chance. Without actually promising to do so, he signaled in August 1810 that France might repeal its trade restrictions if Britain in turn lifted its Orders in Council. Madison knew better than to trust Napoleon, but he chose to accept the French offer as evidence of repeal, gambling that the threat of seeing the United States trade exclusively with France would lead the British to repeal their restrictions. But in fact they did not. In firm control of the seas, London saw little need to bargain. Madison's gamble had failed. He saw no choice but to reestablish the embargo against Britain alone—a decision that meant the end of American neutrality and a dangerous step toward war.

Tecumseh and the Prophet

Not all of Madison's party was reluctant to fight. The complexion of the Twelfth Congress, which met late in 1811, differed markedly from that of its predecessor. Recent elections had swept away many of the older "submission men" and replaced them with young hotheads, many from the South and West. Dubbed "war hawks" by their Federalist opponents, the newcomers were indeed on fire for a new war with the old enemy—actually two old enemies. The war hawks detested the British for their manhandling of American sailors and their Orders in Council that dammed the flow of American farm products headed for Europe. They also yearned to wipe out a renewed Indian threat to the flood of pioneer settlers then washing into the trans-Appalachian wilderness.

Two remarkable Shawnee brothers, Tecumseh and Tenskwatawa, known to non-Indians as "the Prophet," concluded that the time had come to stop this onrushing tide. They began to weld together a far-flung confederacy of all the tribes east of the Mississippi, inspiring a vibrant movement of Indian unity and cultural renewal. Their followers gave up textile clothing for traditional buckskin garments and foreswore alcohol, the better to fight a last-ditch battle with the white invaders. Rejecting whites' concept of "ownership," Tecumseh urged his supporters never to cede land to whites unless all Indians agreed.

Meanwhile, frontiersmen and their war-hawk spokesmen in Congress became convinced that British "scalp buyers" in Canada were nourishing the Indians' growing strength. In the fall of 1811 General William Henry Harrison, governor of the Indiana Territory, gathered an army and advanced on Tecumseh's headquarters at the junction of the Wabash and Tippecanoe Rivers in present-day Indiana. Tecumseh was absent, recruiting supporters in the South, but the Prophet attacked Harrison's army—foolishly, in Tecumseh's

Rivals for the presidency, and for the soul of the young Republic, Thomas Jefferson and John Adams died on the same day—the Fourth of July, 1826—fifty years to the day after both men had signed the Declaration of Independence. Adams's last words were,

"Thomas Jefferson still survives."

But he was wrong, for three hours earlier, Jefferson had drawn his last breath.

In a speech at Vincennes, Indiana Territory, Tecumseh (1768?–1813) said,

"Sell a country! Why not sell the air, the clouds, and the great sea, as well as the earth? Did not the Great Spirit make them all for the use of his children?"

Tecumseh (1768?–1813) A Shawnee Indian born in the Ohio country, he was probably the most gifted organizer and leader of his people in U.S. history. A respected warrior, he fought the tribal custom of torturing prisoners and opposed the practice of permitting any one tribe to sell land that, he believed, belonged to all Indians.

William Henry Harrison (1773–1841), Indian fighter and later president, called Tecumseh

"one of those uncommon geniuses who spring up occasionally to produce revolutions and overturn the established order of things. If it were not for the vicinity of the United States, he would perhaps be founder of an Empire that would rival in glory that of Mexico or Peru."

eyes—with a small force of Shawnees. The Shawnees were routed and their settlement burned.

The Battle of Tippecanoe made Harrison a national hero. It also discredited the Prophet and drove Tecumseh into an alliance with the British. When America's war with Britain came, Tecumseh fought fiercely for the redcoats until his death in 1813 at the Battle of the Thames. With him perished the dream of an Indian confederacy.

Mr. Madison's War

By the spring of 1812, Madison believed war with Britain to be inevitable. The British arming of hostile Indians pushed him toward this decision, as did the whoops of the war hawks in his own party who believed the only way to remove the menace of the Indians was to wipe out their Canadian base. "On to Canada, on to Canada" was the war hawks' chant. Southern expansionists, less vocal, cast a covetous eye on Florida, then held by Britain's ally Spain.

Above all, Madison turned to war to restore confidence in the republican experiment. For five years the Republicans had tried to steer a noble course between submission and battle with the warring European powers. But the only result was international derision and internal strife. Madison and the Republicans came to believe that only a vigorous assertion of American rights could demonstrate the viability of American nationhood—and of democracy as a form of government. If America could not fight to protect itself, its experiment in republicanism would be discredited in the eyes of a scoffing world.

Madison asked Congress to declare war on June 1, 1812. Congress obliged him two weeks later. The vote in the House was 79 to 49 for war, in the Senate 19 to 13. The close tally revealed deep divisions over the wisdom of fighting. The split was both sectional and partisan. Support for war came from the South and West, but also from Republicans in the populous middle states such as Pennsylvania and Virginia. Federalists in both North and South damned the conflict, but their stronghold was New England, which greeted the declaration of war with muffled bells, flags at half-mast, and public fasting.

Why should seafaring New England oppose the war for a free sea? The answer is that Federalists in the Northeast sympathized with Britain and resented the Republicans' sympathy with Napoleon, whom they regarded as the "Corsican butcher" and the "anti-Christ of the age." The Federalists also opposed the acquisition of Canada, which would only add more agrarian states and increase Jeffersonian Republican voting strength. The bitterness of New England Federalists against "Mr. Madison's War" led them to treason or near-treason. They were determined, charged one Republican versifier,

To rule the nation if they could,
But see it damned if others should.

New England gold holders probably lent more dollars to the British Exchequer than to the federal Treasury. Federalist farmers sent huge quantities of supplies and foodstuffs to Canada, enabling British armies to invade New York. New England governors stubbornly refused to permit their militias to serve outside their own states. In a sense America had to fight two enemies simultaneously, old England and New England.

Thus perilously divided, the barely United States plunged into armed conflict against Britain, then the world's most powerful empire. No sober American could have had much reasonable hope of victory, but by 1812 the Jeffersonian Republicans saw no other choice.

Chapter Summary

The ideological conflicts of the early Republic culminated in the bitter election of 1800 between Adams and Jefferson. Despite the fierce rhetoric of the campaign, Jefferson's defeat of an incumbent president in the "Revolution of 1800" demonstrated that the infant Republic could peacefully transfer power from one party to another. The election of 1800 also signaled the decline of the conservative Federalist Party, which proved unable to adjust to the democratic future of American politics.

Jefferson, as a renowned political philosopher and idealist, came to Washington determined to restore what he saw as the original American revolutionary doctrines and to implement his Republican principles of limited and frugal government, strict construction, and an antimilitarist foreign policy. But Jefferson the practical politician had to compromise many of these goals, thereby moderating the Republican-Federalist ideological conflict.

The sharpest political conflicts occurred over the judiciary, where John Marshall worked effectively to enshrine the principles of judicial review and a strong federal government. Against his original intentions, Jefferson himself also enhanced federal power by waging war against the Barbary pirates and especially by his dramatic purchase of Louisiana from Napoleon. The Louisiana Purchase was Jefferson's greatest success, increasing national unity and pointing to America's long-term future in the West. But in the short term the vast geographical expansion fostered problems like Aaron Burr's secessionist scheme to break the West away from the United States.

Nevertheless, Jefferson became increasingly entangled in the horrific European wars between Napoleonic France and Britain, as both great powers obstructed American trade and violated freedom of the seas. Jefferson attempted to avoid war through his embargo policy, which damaged the American economy and stirred bitter opposition in New England.

Jefferson's successor, James Madison, faced more British assaults on American neutrality, as well as cries from western "War Hawks" in his own party who wanted to defeat the Indians and seize Canada. Fearing for the very future of American republicanism, Madison reluctantly called for war in order to regain American national confidence. The nation went to war totally unprepared, bitterly divided, and devoid of any coherent strategy.

The Second War for Independence and the Upsurge of Nationalism

1812–1824

THE AMERICAN CONTINENTS . . . ARE HENCEFORTH NOT TO BE CONSIDERED AS SUBJECTS FOR FUTURE COLONIZATION BY ANY EUROPEAN POWERS.

JAMES MONROE, DECEMBER 2, 1823

Chapter Outline

The War of 1812 was an especially divisive and ill-fought war. There was no burning national anger, as there had been in 1807 following the *Chesapeake* outrage. The supreme lesson of the conflict was the folly of leading a divided and apathetic people into war. And yet, despite the unimpressive military outcome and the even less decisive negotiated peace, Americans came out of the war with a renewed sense of nationhood. For the next dozen years an awakened spirit of nationalism would inspire activities ranging from protecting manufacturing to building roads to defending the authority of the federal government over the states.

Focus Questions

1. **Why was the War of 1812 so politically divisive and poorly fought by the United States, and how did the course of the war reflect these problems?**
2. **Why did the War of 1812, despite its stalemated outcome, lead to an outburst of proud postwar nationalism and an "era of good feelings" in the United States?**
3. **Why did a serious conflict over slavery suddenly burst on the American scene in 1819, and how did the Missouri Compromise resolve it (at least temporarily)?**
4. **How did John Marshall's Supreme Court promote the spirit of nationalism and counter growing sectionalism through its rulings in favor of federal power?**
5. **What were the origins and essential principles of the Monroe Doctrine, and what were its short- and long-term effects in Latin America and elsewhere?**

On to Canada over Land and Lakes

On the eve of the War of 1812, the regular army was ill-trained, ill-disciplined, and widely scattered. It had to be supplemented by the even more poorly trained militia, who were sometimes distinguished by their speed of foot in leaving the battlefield. Some of the ranking generals were semisenile heirlooms from the Revolutionary War, rusting on their laurels and lacking in vigor and vision.

Chronology

1812	United States declares war on Britain. Madison reelected president.
1812-1813	American invasions of Canada fail.
1813	Battle of the Thames. Battle of Lake Erie.
1814	Battle of Plattsburgh. British burn Washington. Battle of Horseshoe Bend. Treaty of Ghent signed ending War of 1812.
1814-1815	Hartford Convention.
1815	Battle of New Orleans.
1816	Second Bank of the United States founded. Protectionist Tariff of 1816. Monroe elected president.
1817	Rush-Bagot agreement limits naval armament on Great Lakes.
1818	Treaty of 1818 with Britain.
	Jackson invades Florida.
1819	Panic of 1819. Spain cedes Florida to United States. *McCulloch* v. *Maryland*. *Dartmouth College* v. *Woodward*.
1820	Missouri Compromise. Missouri and Maine admitted to Union. Monroe reelected.
1823	Secretary of State Adams proposes Monroe Doctrine.
1825	Erie Canal completed.

The opening offensive strategy against the British in Canada was especially poorly conceived. Had the Americans captured Montreal, the center of population and transportation, everything to the west might have died, just as the leaves of a tree wither when the trunk is girdled. But instead of laying ax to the trunk, the Americans frittered away their strength in the three-pronged invasion of 1812. The trio of invading forces that set out from Detroit, Niagara, and Lake Champlain were all beaten back shortly after they crossed the Canadian border.

By contrast, the British and Canadians displayed energy from the outset. Early in the war they captured the American fort of Michilimackinac, which commanded the upper Great Lakes and the Indian-inhabited area to the south and west. Their brilliant defensive operations were led by the inspired British General Isaac Brock, assisted (in the American camp) by "General Mud" and "General Confusion."

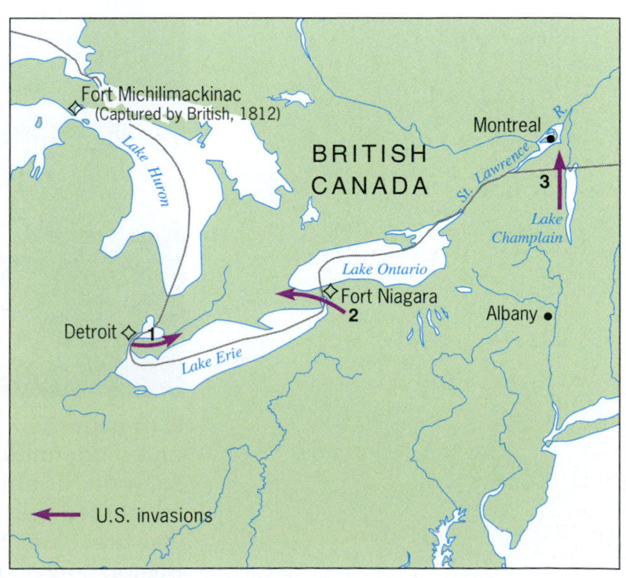

■ The Three U.S. Invasions of 1812

When several American land invasions of Canada were again hurled back in 1813, Americans looked for success on the water. Man for man and ship for ship, the American navy did better than the army. Compared to the larger British navy, American craft on the whole were more skillfully handled, had better gunners, and were manned by non–press-gang crews who were burning to avenge numerous indignities. Similarly, the American frigates, notably the *Constitution* ("Old Ironsides"), had thicker sides, heavier firepower, and larger crews, of which one sailor in six was a free black.

Control of the Great Lakes was vital, and an energetic American naval officer, Oliver Hazard Perry, managed to build a fleet of green-timbered ships on the shores of Lake Erie, manned by even greener seamen. When Perry captured a British fleet in a furious engagement on Lake Erie, he reported to his superior, "We have met the enemy and they are ours." Perry's victory and his slogan infused new life into the drooping American cause. Forced to withdraw from Detroit and Fort

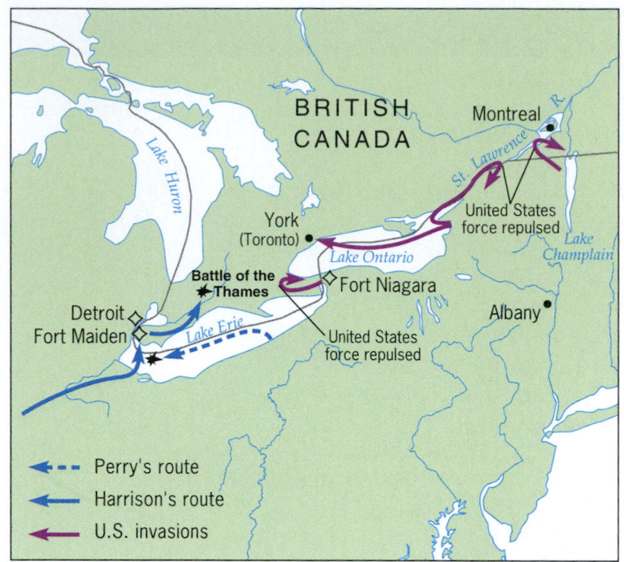

■ **Campaigns of 1813**

Malden, the retreating redcoats were overtaken by General Harrison's army and beaten at the Battle of the Thames in October 1813.

Despite these successes, the Americans by late 1814, far from invading Canada, were grimly defending their own soil against the invading British. In Europe the diversionary power of Napoleon was destroyed in mid-1814, and the dangerous despot was exiled to the Mediterranean isle of Elba. The United States, which had so brashly provoked war behind the protective skirts of Napoleon, was now left to face the music alone. Thousands of victorious veteran redcoats began to pour into Canada from Europe.

Assembling some ten thousand crack troops, the British prepared in 1814 for a crushing blow into New York, along the familiar lake-river route. In the absence of roads, the invader was forced to bring supplies over the Lake Champlain waterway. A weaker American fleet, commanded by the thirty-year-old Thomas Macdonough, challenged the British. The ensuing battle was desperately fought near Plattsburgh on September 11, 1814, on floating slaughterhouses. The American flagship at one point was in grave trouble. But Macdonough, unexpectedly turning his ship about with cables, confronted the enemy with a fresh broadside and snatched victory from the fangs of defeat.

The results of this heroic naval battle were momentous. The invading British army was forced to retreat. Macdonough thus saved at least upstate New York from conquest, New England from further disaffection, and the Union from possible dissolution. He also profoundly affected the concurrent negotiations of the Anglo-American peace treaty in Europe.

■ ***Constitution* and *Guerrière*, 1812** The *Guerrière* was heavily outweighed and outgunned, yet its British captain eagerly—and foolishly—sought combat. His ship was totally destroyed. Historian Henry Adams later concluded that this duel "raised the United States in one half hour to the rank of a first-class Power in the world." Today, the *U.S.S. Constitution,* berthed in Boston harbor, remains the oldest actively commissioned ship in the U.S. Navy.

Despite its success on the Great Lakes, the American navy could not match the powerful British fleet in the Atlantic. Its wrath aroused, the Royal Navy finally retaliated by throwing a ruinous naval blockade along America's coast and by landing raiding parties almost at will. American economic life, including fishing, was crippled. Customs revenues were choked off, and as the war continued the bankrupt Treasury was unable to meet its obligations.

Washington Burned and New Orleans Defended

A second formidable British force, numbering about four thousand, landed in the Chesapeake Bay area in August 1814. Advancing rapidly on Washington, it easily dispersed some six thousand panicky militia at Bladensburg ("the Bladensburg races"). The invaders then entered the capital and set fire to most of the public buildings, including the Capitol and the White House. But while Washington burned, the Americans at Baltimore held firm. The British fleet hammered Fort McHenry with their cannons but could not capture the city. Francis Scott Key, a detained American anxiously watching the bombardment from a British ship, was inspired to write the words of "The Star-Spangled Banner." Set to the tune of a saucy English tavern refrain, the song quickly attained popularity.

A third British blow of 1814, aimed at New Orleans, menaced the entire Mississippi Valley. Gaunt and hawk-faced Andrew Jackson, fresh from crushing the southwest Indians at the Battle of Horseshoe Bend, was placed in command. His hodgepodge force consisted of seven thousand sailors, regulars, pirates, and Frenchmen, as well as militiamen from Louisiana, Kentucky, and Tennessee. Among the defenders were two Louisiana **regiments** of free black volunteers, numbering about four hundred men. The Americans threw up their entrenchment, and in the words of a popular song:

Behind it stood our little force—
None wished it to be greater;
For ev'ry man was half a horse,
And half an alligator.

The overconfident British, numbering some eight thousand battle-seasoned veterans, blundered badly. They made the mistake of launching a frontal assault, on January 8, 1815, on the entrenched American riflemen and cannoneers. The attackers suffered the most devastating defeat of the entire war, losing over two thousand killed and wounded in half an hour, compared with seventy for the Americans. It was an astonishing victory for Jackson and his men.

News of the victory struck the country "like a clap of thunder," according to one contemporary. Andrew Jackson became a national hero, as poets and politicians lined up to sing the praises of the defenders of New Orleans. It hardly mattered when word arrived that a peace treaty had been signed at Ghent, Belgium, ending the war two weeks before the battle. The United States had fought for honor as much as material gain. The Battle of New Orleans restored that honor, at least in American eyes, and unleashed a wave of nationalism and self-confidence.

The Treaty of Ghent

Tsar Alexander I of Russia, hard-pressed by Napoleon's army and not wanting his British ally to fritter away its strength in America, proposed **mediation** between the clashing Anglo-Saxon cousins in 1812. The tsar's feeler eventually set in motion the machinery that brought five American peacemakers to the quaint Belgian city of Ghent in 1814. The bickering group was headed by early rising, puritanical John Quincy Adams, son of John Adams, who deplored the late-hour card playing of his high-living colleague Henry Clay.

regiment *A medium-sized military unit, larger than a company or battalion and smaller than a division.*

mediation *An intervention, usually with consent of the parties, to aid in voluntarily settling differences between groups or nations. (**Arbitration** involves a mandatory settlement determined by a third party.)*

In a letter to her friend Mercy Otis Warren, Abigail Adams (1744–1818) fretted that the British were taking advantage of Americans' disagreement over the War of 1812:

"We have our firesides, our comfortable habitations, our cities, our churches and our country to defend, our rights, privileges and independence to preserve. And for these are we not justly contending? Thus it appears to me. Yet I hear from our pulpits, and read from our presses, that it is an unjust, a wicked, a ruinous, and unnecessary war. . . . A house divided upon itself—and upon that foundation do our enemies build their hopes of subduing us."

armistice *A temporary stopping of warfare by mutual agreement, sometimes in preparation for an actual peace negotiation between the parties.*

Confident after their military successes, Britain's envoys made sweeping demands for a neutralized Indian buffer state in the Great Lakes region, control of the Great Lakes, and a substantial part of conquered Maine. The Americans flatly rejected these terms, and the talks appeared stalemated. But news of British reverses in upstate New York and at Baltimore, and increasing war-weariness in Britain, made London more willing to compromise. Preoccupied with the Congress of Vienna that concluded the Napoleonic wars, and eyeing still-dangerous France, the British lion resigned itself to licking its wounds.

The Treaty of Ghent, signed on Christmas Eve in 1814, was essentially an **armistice**. Both sides simply agreed to stop fighting and to restore conquered territory. No mention was made of those grievances for which America had ostensibly fought: the Indian menace, search and seizure, Orders in Council, impressment, and confiscations. With neither side able to impose its will, the treaty negotiations—like the war itself—ended as a virtual draw. Relieved Americans boasted, "Not One Inch of Territory Ceded or Lost"—a watchword that contrasted strangely with the "On to Canada" rallying cry of the war's outset.

Federalist Grievances and the Hartford Convention

Defiant New England remained a problem. It prospered during the conflict, owing largely to illicit trade with the enemy in Canada and to the absence of a British blockade until 1814. But the embittered opposition of the Federalists to the war continued unabated.

As the war dragged on, New England extremists became more vocal. The most spectacular manifestation of Federalist discontent was the ill-omened Hartford Convention. Late in 1814, when the British capture of New Orleans seemed imminent, Massachusetts issued a call for a convention at Hartford, Connecticut. Twenty-six prominent delegates from all of the New England states except Vermont met in complete secrecy for about three weeks—December 15, 1814, to January 5, 1815—to discuss their grievances and to seek redress for their wrongs. The convention's final report was actually quite moderate. It demanded financial compensation to New England for lost trade, abolition of the "three-fifths" clause of the Constitution that gave the South added representation, and a single-term limit for the presidency—a stab at the much-resented "Virginia dynasty" of presidents. These and other measures reflected Federalist fears that a once-proud New England was falling subservient to an agrarian South and West.

Three special envoys from Massachusetts brought these demands to the burned-out capital of Washington in early January 1815. The trio arrived just in time to be overwhelmed by the glorious news from New Orleans, followed by that from Ghent. As the rest of the nation congratulated itself on a glorious victory, New England's wartime complaints seemed petty at best, and treasonous at worst. Pursued by the sneers and jeers of the press, the envoys sank away into obscurity.

The Hartford resolutions, as it turned out, were the death dirge of the Federalist party. The Federalists were never again to mount a successful presidential campaign, and the party disappeared altogether in the 1820s.

Federalist doctrines of disunity, which long survived the party, blazed a fateful trail. Until 1815 there was far more talk of nullification and secession in New England than in any other section, including the South. The outright flouting of the Jeffersonian embargo and the later crippling of the war effort were the two most damaging acts of nullification in America prior to the events leading to the Civil War.

The Second War for American Independence

The War of 1812 was a small war, involving about 6,000 Americans killed or wounded. It was but a footnote to the mighty European conflagration. In 1812, when Napoleon invaded Russia with about 500,000 men, Madison tried to invade Canada with about 5,000 men. But if the American conflict was globally unimportant, its results were highly important to the United States.

Primary source
Urania White Headstone
college.hmco.com/pic/kennedybrief7e

Primary source
Rachel Weeping
college.hmco.com/pic/kennedybrief7e

The Republic had shown that it would resist, sword in hand, what it regarded as grievous wrongs. Other nations developed a new respect for America's fighting prowess. America's emissaries abroad were henceforth treated with less scorn. In a diplomatic sense, if not in a military sense, the conflict could be called the Second War for American Independence.

A new nation, moreover, was welded in the fiery furnace of armed conflict. Sectionalism, now identified with discredited New England Federalists, was given a black eye. The painful events of the war glaringly revealed, as perhaps nothing else could have done, the folly of sectional disunity. In a sense, the most conspicuous casualty of the war was the Federalist party.

War heroes emerged, especially the two Indian-fighters, Andrew Jackson and William Henry Harrison. Both of them were to become president. Left in the lurch by their British friends at Ghent, the Indians were forced to make such terms as they could. They reluctantly consented, in a series of treaties, to relinquish vast areas of forested land north of the Ohio River.

Manufacturing prospered behind the fiery wooden wall of the British blockade. In both an economic and a diplomatic sense, the War of 1812 bred greater American independence. The industries stimulated by the fighting rendered America less dependent on Europe's workshops.

Canadian patriotism and nationalism also received a powerful stimulus from the clash. Many Canadians felt betrayed by the Treaty of Ghent. They were especially aggrieved by the failure to secure an Indian buffer state or even mastery of the Great Lakes. Canadians fully expected the frustrated Yankees to return, and for a time the Americans and British engaged in a naval arms race on the Great Lakes. But in 1817 the Rush-Bagot agreement between Britain and the United States severely limited naval armament on the lakes. Better relations brought the last border fortifications down in the 1870s, with the happy result that the United States and Canada came to share the world's longest unfortified boundary—stretching 5,527 miles long.

After Napoleon's final defeat at Waterloo in 1815, Europe slumped into a peace of exhaustion. Deposed monarchs returned to battered thrones, as the Old World took the rutted road back to conservatism, illiberalism, and **reaction.** But the American people, largely unaffected by these European developments, turned their backs on the Old World and faced resolutely toward the untamed West—and toward the task of building their democracy.

reaction (reactionary) *In politics, extreme conservatism, looking to restore the political or social conditions of some earlier time.*

Nascent Nationalism

The most impressive by-product of the War of 1812 was heightened nationalism—the spirit of nation-consciousness or national oneness. America may not have fought the war as one nation, but it emerged as one nation. The changed mood even manifested itself in the birth of a distinctively national literature. Washington Irving and James Fenimore Cooper attained international recognition in the 1820s, significantly as the nation's first writers of importance to use American scenes and themes. School textbooks, often British in an earlier era, were now being written by Americans for Americans. In the world of magazines, the highly intellectual *North American Review* began publication in 1815—the year of the triumph at New Orleans. Even American painters increasingly celebrated their native landscapes on their canvases.

A fresh nationalistic spirit could be recognized in many other areas as well. The revived Bank of the United States established by Congress in 1816 reflected

View of the Capitol, by Charles Burton, 1824 This painting of the Capitol building, much smaller than it is today, reveals the rustic conditions of the early days in the nation's capital. A series of architects worked on the Capitol, following William Thornton's original design along neoclassical, or "Greek Revival," lines. After the British burned the building in 1814, Boston's Charles Bulfinch oversaw the reconstruction of the Capitol, finally completed in 1830.

nationalism in finance. A more handsome capital began to rise from the ashes of Washington. The army was expanded to ten thousand men. The navy covered itself with glory in 1815 when it administered a thorough beating to the piratical plunderers of North Africa. Stephen Decatur, naval hero of the War of 1812 and of the Barbary Coast expeditions, pungently captured the country's nationalist mood in a famous toast made on his return from the Mediterranean campaigns: "Our country, right or wrong!"

The American System

Nationalism likewise manifested itself in manufacturing. Patriotic Americans took pride in the factories that had recently mushroomed, largely as a result of the self-imposed embargoes and the war. When hostilities ended in 1815, British competitors tried to strangle the American war-baby factories in the cradle by cutting prices below cost and dumping goods on U.S. markets. In response, the infant industries bawled lustily for **protection.**

protection (protective) *In economics, the policy of stimulating or preserving domestic producers by placing barriers against imported goods, often through high tariffs.*

A nationalist Congress, out-Federalizing the old Federalists, responded by passing the path-breaking Tariff of 1816—the first tariff in American history instituted primarily for protection, not revenue. Its rates—roughly 20 to 25 percent on the value of dutiable imports—were not high enough to provide completely adequate safeguards, but the law was a bold beginning. A strongly protective trend was started that stimulated the appetites of the protected for more protection.

Nationalism was further highlighted by Henry Clay's grandiose plan for developing a profitable home market. Still radiating the nationalism of war-hawk days, Clay threw himself behind an elaborate scheme known by 1824 as the American System. This system had three main parts. The first was a strong banking system to provide easy and abundant credit. Then a high protective tariff would enable eastern manufacturing to flourish. Finally, revenues gushing from the tariff would provide funds for a network of roads and canals, especially in the burgeoning Ohio Valley. Through these new arteries of transportation would flow foodstuffs and

raw materials from the South and West to the North and East. In exchange, a stream of manufactured goods would flow in the return direction, knitting the country together economically and politically.

Persistent and eloquent demands by Henry Clay and others for **internal improvements** struck a responsive chord with the public, especially in the road-poor West. The recent attempts to invade Canada had all failed partly because of oath-provoking roads—or no roads at all.

But attempts to secure federal funding for roads and canals stumbled on Republican constitutional scruples. Congress voted in 1817 to distribute $1.5 million to the states for internal improvements. But President Madison sternly vetoed the measure as unconstitutional, forcing the individual states to undertake building programs on their own, including the Erie Canal, triumphantly completed by New York in 1825. Jeffersonian Republicans, who had gulped down Hamiltonian loose construction on other important problems, choked on the idea of direct federal support for **intrastate** internal improvements. New England also opposed federally constructed roads and canals because such outlets would further drain away population and create competing states beyond the mountains.

Boston's Columbian Centinel *was not the only newspaper to regard President Monroe's early months as the Era of Good Feelings. Washington's* National Intelligencer *observed in July 1817,*

"Never before, perhaps, since the institution of civil government, did the same harmony, the same absence of party spirit, the same national feeling, pervade a community. The result is too consoling to dispute too nicely about the cause."

raw materials *Products in their natural, unmanufactured state.*

internal improvements *The basic public works, such as roads, canals, and bridges that create the infrastructure for economic development.*

intrastate *Something existing wholly within a single state of the United States. (**Interstate** refers to movement between two or more states.)*

dynasty *A succession of rulers in the same family line; by extension, any system of predetermined succession in power.*

The So-Called Era of Good Feelings

James Monroe—six feet tall, somewhat stooped, courtly, and mild mannered—was nominated for the presidency in 1816 by the Republicans. They thus undertook to continue the so-called Virginia **dynasty** of Washington, Jefferson, and Madison. The fading Federalists ran a candidate for the last time in their checkered history, and he was crushed by 183 electoral votes to 34. The vanquished Federalist party was gasping its dying breaths, leaving the field to the triumphant Republicans and one-party rule.

In James Monroe, the man and the times auspiciously met. As the last president to wear an old-style cocked hat, he straddled two generations: the bygone age of the Founding Fathers and the emergent age of nationalism. The serene Virginian with gray-blue eyes was in intellect and personal force among the least distinguished of

Fairview Inn or Three Mile House on Old Frederick Road, by Thomas Coke Ruckle, c. 1829 This busy scene on the Frederick Road, leading westward from Baltimore, was typical as pioneers flooded into the newly secured West in the early 1800s.

the first eight presidents. But Monroe was an experienced, level-headed executive, in tune with the public in a time that required sober administration, not heroics.

President Monroe further cemented America's emerging nationalism with a goodwill tour in 1817 that took him deep into Federalist New England. The heartwarming welcome he received even in "the enemy's country" ushered in what one Boston newspaper hailed as the "Era of Good Feelings," as the Monroe administrations have commonly been called ever since.

The Era of Good Feelings, unfortunately, was something of a misnomer. Considerable tranquility and prosperity did in fact smile on the early years of Monroe, but the period was a troubled one. The acute issues of the tariff, the bank, internal improvements, and the sale of public lands were being hotly contested. Sectionalism was crystallizing, and the conflict over slavery was beginning to raise its hideous head.

The Panic of 1819 and the Curse of Hard Times

depression *In economics, a severe and very prolonged period of declining economic activity, high unemployment, and low wages and prices.*

boom *In economics, a period of sudden, spectacular expansion of business activity.*

Much of the goodness went out of the good feelings in 1819, when a paralyzing economic panic descended. It brought deflation, **depression,** bankruptcies, bank failures, unemployment, and the overcrowded pesthouses known as debtors' prisons.

This was the first national financial panic since President Washington took office. Many factors contributed to the catastrophe of 1819, but looming large was overspeculation in frontier lands. The Bank of the United States, through its western branches, had become deeply involved in this popular type of outdoor gambling.

Financial paralysis from the panic, which lasted in some degree for several years, dealt a rude setback to the nationalistic ardor. The West was especially hard hit. When the pinch came, the Bank of the United States forced the speculative ("wildcat") western banks to the wall and foreclosed mortgages on countless farms. All this was technically legal but politically unwise. In the eyes of western debtors, the nationalist Bank of the United States soon became a kind of financial devil.

The panic of 1819 also created backwashes in the political and social world. The poorer classes—the one-suspender men and their families—were severely strapped, and in their troubles was sown the seedbed of Jacksonian democracy. Hard times also directed attention to the inhumanity of imprisoning debtors. Mounting agitation against that often cruel practice bore fruit in remedial legislation in an increasing number of states.

Growing Pains of the West

The onward march to the West continued: nine frontier states had joined the original thirteen between 1791 and 1819. With an eye to preserving the North-South sectional balance, most of these commonwealths had been admitted alternately, free or slave. (See Admission of States in the Appendix.)

Why this explosive expansion? In part, it was simply a continuation of the generations-old westward movement, which had been going on since early colonial days. In addition, the siren call of cheap land—"the Ohio fever"—had a special appeal to European immigrants. With the return of peace in Europe and America, eager newcomers from abroad were beginning to stream down the gangplanks in impressive numbers. Land exhaustion in the older southern tobacco states, where the soil was "mined" rather than cultivated, likewise drove people westward. Glib speculators accepted small down payments, making it easier to buy new holdings.

The western **boom** was stimulated by additional developments. Acute economic distress during the embargo years turned many pinched faces toward the setting sun. The crushing of the Indians in the Northwest by General Harrison and in the Southwest by General Jackson pacified the frontier and opened up vast virgin tracts of land. The building of highways improved the land routes to the Ohio Valley. Noteworthy was the Cumberland Road, begun in 1811, which ran ultimately from western Maryland to Illinois. The use of the first steamboat on western waters, also in 1811, heralded a new era of upstream navigation.

But the West, despite the inflow of settlers, was still weak in population and influence. It could only make its voice heard when it formed alliances with other sections. Western pioneers' principal demands were for cheap federal land, cheap transportation, and cheap money issued by its own **"wildcat" banks** rather than the restrictive Bank of the United States. With the passage of the Land Act of 1820, which offered 80 acres at the minimum price of $1.25 an acre, the West began to make headway in achieving these goals (see "Makers of America: Settlers of the Old Northwest," p. 170).

wildcat bank *An unregulated, speculative bank that issues notes without sufficient capital to back them.*

peculiar institution *Widely used term for the institution of American black slavery.*

Slavery and Sectional Balance

Sectional tensions were stunningly revealed in 1819, when the territory of Missouri knocked on the doors of Congress seeking admission as a slave state. This fertile area contained sufficient population to warrant statehood. But the House of Representatives stymied the plans of the Missourians by passing the incendiary Tallmadge amendment. It stipulated that no more slaves should be brought into Missouri and also provided for the gradual emancipation of children born to slave parents already there. A roar of anger burst from slaveholding southerners.

Southerners saw in the Tallmadge amendment, which they eventually managed to defeat in the Senate, an ominous threat to the sectional balance. When the Constitution was adopted in 1788, the North and South were running neck and neck in wealth and population. But with every passing decade, the North was becoming wealthier and also more thickly settled—an advantage reflected in an increasing northern majority in the House of Representatives. Yet in the Senate, with eleven free states and eleven slave states, the southerners had maintained equality. They were therefore in a good position to thwart any northern effort to interfere with the expansion of slavery, and they did not want to lose this equal balance in the Senate.

The future of the slave system caused southerners profound concern. Missouri was the first state entirely west of the Mississippi River to be carved out of the Louisiana Purchase, and the Missouri emancipation amendment might set a damaging precedent for all the rest of the area. Even more disquieting was another possibility. If Congress could abolish the "**peculiar institution**" in Missouri, might it not attempt to do likewise in the older states of the South? The wounds of the Constitutional Convention of 1787 were once more ripped open.

Burning moral questions also protruded, even though the main issue was political and economic balance. A small but growing group of antislavery agitators in the North seized the occasion to raise an outcry against the evils of slavery. They were determined that the plague of human bondage should not spread farther into the untainted territories.

The Uneasy Missouri Compromise

Deadlock in Washington was at length broken in 1820 by the time-honored American solution of compromise—actually a bundle of three compromises. Courtly and gifted Henry Clay of Kentucky played a leading role as a conciliator. Congress did agree to admit Missouri as a slave state. But at the same time, free-soil Maine, which until then had been part of Massachusetts, was admitted as a separate state. The balance between North and South was thus kept at twelve states each and remained there for the next fifteen years. Although Missouri was permitted to retain slaves, all future bondage was prohibited in the remainder of the Louisiana Purchase north of the line of 36° 30′—the southern boundary of Missouri.

Primary source
Missouri Compromise, The
college.hmco.com/pic/kennedybrief7e

Neither North nor South was completely happy with this horse-trading adjustment, though they had each gained something as well as yielded something. Fortunately, the Missouri Compromise lasted thirty-four years—a vital formative period in the life of the young Republic—and during that time it preserved the

Settlers of the Old Northwest

The Old Northwest beckoned to settlers after the War of 1812. The withdrawal of the British protector weakened the Indians' grip on the territory. Then the canal and highway boom of the 1820s opened broad arteries along which the westward movement flowed.

The first wave of newcomers came mainly from Kentucky, Tennessee, and the upland regions of Virginia and the Carolinas. Most migrants were roughhewn white farmers who had been pushed from good land to bad by an expanding plantation economy. Some settlers acquired land for the first time. John Palmer, whose family left Kentucky for Illinois in 1831, recalled his father telling him "of land so cheap that we could all be landholders, where men were *equal*." Migrants from the South settled mainly in the southern portions of Ohio, Indiana, and Illinois.

Having escaped from a lowly social position in a slaveholding society, many of these new immigrants sought to prevent the spread of slavery by enacting Black Codes in their new territories that prevented blacks from following them. They wanted their own democratic communities, free of rich planters and African Americans alike.

If southern "Butternuts," as these settlers were called, dominated settlement in the 1820s, the next decade brought equally land-starved Yankees from the Northeast. Yankee settlers came especially to the northern parts of Ohio, Indiana, and Illinois. Unlike the Butternuts who wanted to quit forever the imposing framework of southern society, northerners hoped to re-create the world they had left behind.

Conflict soon emerged between Yankees and southerners. As self-sufficient farmers who did not produce for the market, southerners viewed the northern newcomers as inhospitable, greedy, and excessively ambitious. Northerners, in turn, viewed the southerners as uncivilized, a "coon dog and butcher knife tribe" with no interest in education, self-improvement, or agricultural innovation. While Yankees advocated taxes to establish public schools and fund roads and canals, southerners opposed such efforts, especially public schooling. Religion also divided settlers. Northerners typically embraced denominations like Congregationalism and Presbyterianism that supported a learned ministry. Southerners preferred the more revivalist Methodists and Baptists, and preferred humble, uneducated preacher-farmers who would, in their eyes, stay closer to the Lord and his people.

As the population swelled and the region acquired its own character, the stark contrasts between northerners and southerners started to fade. Some residents like Abraham Lincoln, with roots in Kentucky, came to adopt views more akin to those of the Yankees than the southerners. Railroads and Great Lakes shipping tied the region economically ever more tightly to the Northeast. Yankees and southerners sometimes allied as new kinds of economic, ethnic, and religious cleavages emerged.

Still, echoes of the clash between Yankees and Butternuts persisted. During the Civil War, the southern counties of Ohio, Indiana, and Illinois, where southerners had first settled, harbored sympathizers with the South and served as a key area for Confederate military infiltration into the North. Decades later these same counties became a stronghold of the Ku Klux Klan. The Old Northwest may have become firmly anchored to the economy of the Northeast, but vestiges of its early dual personality persisted.

shaky compact of the states. Yet the embittered dispute over slavery heralded the future breakup of the Union. Ever after, the morality of the South's peculiar institution was an issue that could not be swept under the rug. The Missouri Compromise only ducked the question—it did not resolve it. Sooner or later, Thomas Jefferson predicted, it will "burst on us as a tornado."

The Missouri Compromise and the concurrent panic of 1819 should have dimmed the political star of President Monroe. Certainly both unhappy events had a dampening effect on the Era of Good Feelings. But smooth-spoken James Monroe was so popular, and the Federalist opposition so weak, that he received every electoral vote in the election of 1820 except one. Unanimity remained an honor reserved for George Washington.

> *While the debate over Missouri was raging, Thomas Jefferson (1743–1826) wrote to a correspondent,*
>
> "The Missouri question . . . is the most portentous one which ever yet threatened our Union. In the gloomiest moment of the revolutionary war I never had any apprehensions equal to what I feel from this source. . . . [The] question, like a fire-bell in the night, awakened and filled me with terror. . . . [With slavery] we have a wolf by the ears, and we can neither hold him nor safely let him go."
>
> *John Quincy Adams confided to his diary,*
>
> "I take it for granted that the present question is a mere preamble—a title-page to a great, tragic volume."

John Marshall and Judicial Nationalism

The upsurging nationalism of the post-Ghent years, despite the ominous setbacks concerning slavery, was further reflected and reinforced by the Supreme Court. The high tribunal continued to be dominated by the tall, thin, and aggressive Chief Justice John Marshall. And many of Marshall's most famous decisions bolstered the power of the federal government at the expense of the states.

Interactive map
Missouri Compromise 1820–1821
college.hmco.com/pic/kennedybrief7e

A notable case in this category was *McCulloch* v. *Maryland* (1819). The suit involved an attempt by the state of Maryland to destroy a branch of the Bank of the United States by imposing a tax on its notes. John Marshall, speaking for the Court, declared the bank constitutional by invoking the Hamiltonian doctrine of implied powers (see p. 136). At the same time, he strengthened federal authority and slapped at state infringements when he denied the right of Maryland to tax the bank, with the ringing declaration that "the power to tax is the power to destroy."

Marshall's ruling in this case gave the doctrine of "loose construction" its most famous formulation. The Constitution, he said, was "intended to endure for ages to come and, consequently, to be adapted to the various crises of human affairs." Finally, he declared, "Let the end be legitimate, let it be within the scope of the Constitution, and all means which are appropriate, which are plainly adapted to

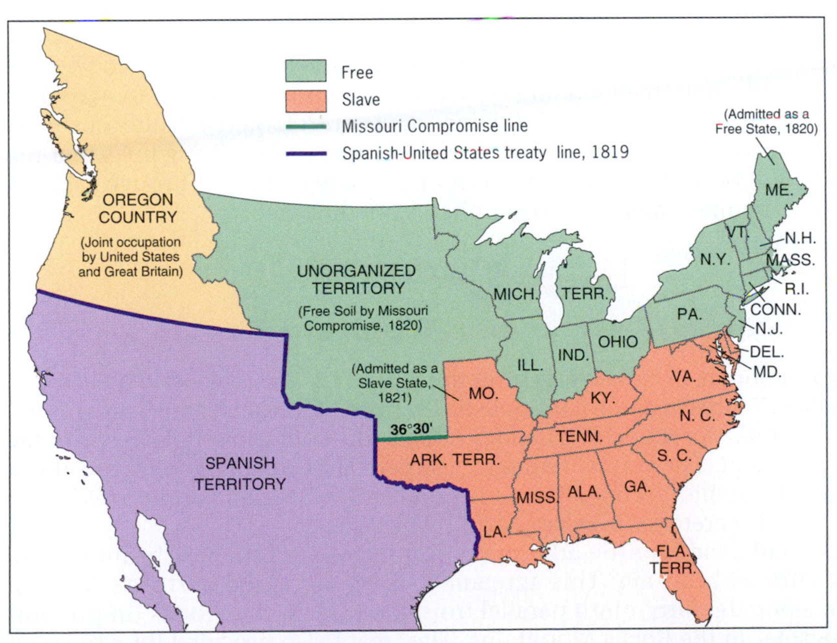

The Missouri Compromise and Slavery, 1820–1821 Note the 36° 30′ line. In the 1780s Thomas Jefferson had written of slavery in America: "Indeed I tremble for my country when I reflect that God is just; that his justice cannot sleep forever; that . . . the Almighty has no attribute which can take side with us in such a contest." Later, at the time of the Missouri Compromise, Jefferson feared that his worst forebodings were coming to pass. "I considered it at once," he said of the Missouri question, "as the knell of the Union."

■ John Marshall (1755–1835) Born in a log cabin on the Virginia frontier, he attended law lectures for just a few weeks at the College of William and Mary—his only formal education. Yet Marshall would go on to prove himself a brilliant chief justice. One admiring lawyer wrote of him, "His black eyes . . . possess an irradiating spirit, which proclaims the imperial powers of the mind that sits enthroned therein."

that end, which are not prohibited, but consist with the letter and spirit of the Constitution, are constitutional." Five years later, in the "steamboat case" of *Gibbons* v. *Ogden* (1824), Marshall again upheld federal supremacy by striking down New York's awarding of a monopoly on waterborne commerce between New Jersey and New York to a private company.

Another set of Marshall's decisions bolstered judicial barriers against democratic or **demagogic** attacks on property rights. The notorious case of *Fletcher* v. *Peck* (1810) arose when a Georgia legislature, swayed by bribery, granted 35 million acres in the Yazoo River country (present-day Mississippi) to private speculators. The next legislature, yielding to an angry public outcry, canceled the crooked transaction. But the Supreme Court, with Marshall presiding, decreed that the legislative grant was a **contract** (even though fraudulently secured) and that the Constitution forbids state laws "impairing" contracts (see Art. I, Sec. X, para. 1). The decision is perhaps most noteworthy for further protecting property rights against popular pressures. It is also one of the earliest clear assertions of the right of the Court to invalidate state laws conflicting with the federal Constitution.

A similar principle was upheld in the case of *Dartmouth College* v. *Woodward* (1819), perhaps the best-remembered of Marshall's decisions. The college had been granted a charter by King George III in 1769, but the democratic New Hampshire state legislature had seen fit to change it. Dartmouth appealed the case, employing as counsel its most distinguished alumnus, Daniel Webster, himself an ardent nationalist. The "Godlike Daniel" pulled out all the stops in his tear-inducing summary when he declaimed, "It is, sir, as I have said, a small college. And yet there are those who love it." Marshall put the states firmly in their place when he ruled that the original charter must stand. It was a contract, and the Constitution protected contracts against state encroachments. The *Dartmouth* decision had the fortunate effect of safeguarding business enterprise from domination by the states. But it had the unfortunate effect of creating a precedent that enabled chartered corporations, in later years, to escape the handcuffs of needed public control.

Marshall's decisions are felt even today. In this sense his nationalism was the most tenaciously enduring of the era. He buttressed the federal Union and helped to create a stable, nationally uniform environment for business. In an age when America was veering toward popular democratic control, Marshall almost single-handedly shaped the Constitution along conservative, centralizing lines that ran somewhat counter to the dominant spirit of the new country. Through him the conservative Hamiltonians partly triumphed from the tomb.

demagogic (demagogue) *Concerning a leader who stirs up the common people by appeals to emotion and prejudice, often for selfish or irrational ends.*

contract *In law, an agreement in which each of two or more parties binds itself to perform some act in exchange for what the other party similarly pledges to do.*

Sharing Oregon and Acquiring Florida

The robust nationalism of the years after the War of 1812 was likewise reflected in foreign policy. To this end, the nationalistic President Monroe teamed with his nationalistic secretary of state, John Quincy Adams, the cold and scholarly son of the frosty ex-president. The younger Adams, a superb statesman, happily rose above the ingrown Federalist sectionalism of his native New England and proved to be one of the great secretaries of state.

To its credit, the Monroe administration negotiated the much-underrated Treaty of 1818 with Britain. This agreement fixed the vague northern limits of Louisiana along the forty-ninth parallel from the Lake of the Woods (in present-day Minnesota) to the Rocky Mountains. The treaty also provided for a ten-year

U.S.-British Boundary Settlement, 1818 Notice that the United States gained considerable territory by securing a treaty boundary rather than the natural boundary of the Missouri River watershed. The line of 49° was extended westward to the Pacific Ocean under the Treaty of 1846 with Britain.

joint occupation of the untamed Oregon country, without a surrender of the rights or claims of either America or Britain.

To the south lay semitropical Spanish Florida, which many Americans believed geography and providence had destined to become part of the United States. Americans already claimed West Florida, where uninvited American settlers had torn down the hated Spanish flag in 1810. Congress ratified this grab in 1812, and during the War of 1812 a small American army seized the Mobile region. But the bulk of Florida remained under Spanish rule.

When an epidemic of revolutions in South America, beginning in 1816, led to the birth of several new republics there, Spain was forced to denude Florida of troops to fight the rebels. General Andrew Jackson, idol of the West and scourge of the Indians, saw opportunity in the undefended swamplands. On the pretext that hostile Seminole Indians and fugitive slaves were using Florida as a refuge, Jackson secured a commission to enter Spanish territory, punish the Indians, and recapture the runaways. But he was to respect all posts under the Spanish flag.

Early in 1818 Jackson swept across the Florida border with all the fury of an avenging angel. He hanged two Indian chiefs and executed two British subjects for assisting the Indians. He also seized the two most important Spanish forts in the area, St. Marks and Pensacola, where he deposed the Spanish governor.

Jackson had clearly exceeded his instructions from Washington. Alarmed, President Monroe consulted his cabinet. Its members were for disavowing or disciplining the overzealous Jackson—all except the lone wolf John Quincy Adams, who refused to howl with the pack. An ardent patriot and nationalist, the flinty New Englander took the offensive and demanded huge concessions from Spain.

In the mislabeled Florida Purchase Treaty of 1819, Spain ceded Florida as well as shadowy Spanish claims to Oregon, in exchange for America's abandonment of equally murky claims to Texas, soon to become part of independent Mexico. The hitherto vague western boundary of Louisiana was made to run zigzag along the Rockies to the forty-second parallel and then to turn due west to the Pacific, dividing Oregon from Spanish holdings.

The Menace of Monarchy in America

After the Napoleonic nightmare, the rethroned autocrats of Europe banded together in a kind of monarchical protective association. Determined to restore the good old days, they undertook to stamp out the democratic tendencies that had sprouted from soil they considered richly manured by the ideals of the French Revolution. The world must be made safe *from* democracy.

The crowned despots acted promptly. With complete ruthlessness, they smothered the embers of rebellion in Italy (1821) and in Spain (1823). According to the European rumor factory, they were also gazing across the Atlantic. Russia,

Austria, Prussia, and France, acting in partnership, would presumably send powerful fleets and armies to the revolted colonies of Spanish America and there restore the autocratic Spanish king to his ancestral domains.

Many Americans were alarmed. Sympathetic to democratic revolutions everywhere, they cheered when the Latin American republics rose from the ruins of monarchy. Americans feared that if the European powers intervened in the New World, the cause of republicanism would suffer irreparable harm. The physical security of the United States—the mother lode of democracy—would be endangered by the proximity of powerful and unfriendly forces.

The southward push of the Russian bear from the chilly region now known as Alaska had already publicized the menace of monarchy to North America. In 1821 the tsar of Russia issued a decree extending Russian jurisdiction over one hundred miles of the open sea down to the line of 51°, an area that embraced most of the coast of present-day British Columbia.

Britain, still Ruler of the Seas, recoiled from joining the continental European powers in crushing the newly won liberties of the Spanish-Americans. These revolutionaries had thrown open their monopoly-bound ports to outside trade, and British shippers, as well as Americans, had found the profits sweet. Accordingly, in August 1823, George Canning, the haughty British foreign secretary, approached the American minister in London to ask if the United States would join Britain in warning the European despots to keep their harsh hands off the Latin American republics? The American minister, lacking instructions, referred this fateful scheme to his superiors in Washington.

Monroe and His Doctrine

The tenacious nationalist, Secretary Adams, was hardheaded enough to be wary of Britons bearing gifts. Why should the lordly British, with the mightiest navy afloat, need America as an ally—an America that had neither naval nor military strength? Such a union, argued Adams, was undignified—like a tiny American "cockboat" sailing "in the wake of the British man-of-war."

Adams, ever alert, thought that he detected a joker in the Canning proposal. If Canning could seduce the United States into guaranteeing existing territorial arrangements in the New World, America's hands would be morally tied against its own expansion. Adams suspected—correctly—that European powers had no definite plans for invading the Americas. In any event the British navy would prevent hostile fleets from interfering with South American markets, so Adams decided it was safe for Uncle Sam to blow a defiant nationalistic blast at all Europe.

The Monroe Doctrine was born late in 1823, when the nationalistic Adams won the nationalistic Monroe over to his way of thinking. The president, in his regular annual message to Congress on December 2, 1823, incorporated a stern warning to the European powers. Its two basic features were (1) noncolonization and (2) nonintervention.

Monroe first directed his verbal volley primarily at Russia in the Northwest. He proclaimed, in effect, that the era of colonization in the Americas had ended and that henceforth the hunting season was permanently closed. What the great powers had they might keep, but neither they nor any other Old World governments could seize or otherwise acquire more.

Primary source
Monroe Doctrine
college.hmco.com/pic/kennedybrief7e

At the same time Monroe trumpeted a warning blast against foreign intervention. He was clearly concerned with regions to the south, where the fledgling Latin American republics were extremely vulnerable. Monroe bluntly directed the crowned heads of Europe to keep their hated monarchical systems out of the Western Hemisphere. For its part the United States would not intervene in the war that the Greeks were then fighting against the Turks for their independence.

Monroe's Doctrine Appraised

The ermined monarchs of Europe were angered at Monroe's doctrine. Having resented the incendiary American experiment from the beginning, they were deeply offended by Monroe's high-flown declaration—all the more so because of the gulf between America's pretentious pronouncements and its puny military strength. But though offended by the upstart Yankees, the European powers found their hands tied, and their frustration increased their annoyance. Even if they had worked out plans for invading the Americas, they would have been helpless before the booming broadsides of the British navy.

Monroe's solemn warning made little splash in the newly hatched republics to the south. Anyone could see that Uncle Sam was only secondarily concerned about his neighbors, because he was primarily concerned about defending himself against future invasion. Only a relatively few educated Latin Americans knew of the message, and they generally recognized that it was the British navy—not the paper pronouncement of James Monroe—that stood between them and a hostile Europe.

In truth, Monroe's message actually did not have very much contemporary significance. Americans applauded it and then forgot it as they turned back to such activities as felling trees and fighting Indians. Not until 1845 did President James Polk revive it, and not until midcentury did it become an important national dogma.

The Monroe Doctrine might more accurately have been called the Self-Defense Doctrine. President Monroe was concerned mainly with the security of his own country—not of Latin America. The United States has never willingly permitted a powerful foreign nation to secure a foothold near its strategic Caribbean vitals. Yet in the absence of the British navy or other allies, the strength of the Monroe Doctrine has never been greater than America's power to eject the trespasser.

The Monroe Doctrine has had a long career of ups and downs. It was never law—domestic or international. It was not, technically speaking, a pledge or an agreement. It was merely a simple statement of the policy of President Monroe. What one president says, another may unsay. And Monroe's presidential successors have ignored, revived, distorted, or expanded the original version, chiefly by adding interpretations. In 1823 the Monroe Doctrine was largely an expression of post-1812 American nationalism directed at a specific menace, and hence is a kind of period piece. But the doctrine proved to be the most famous and long-lived offspring of that nationalism. While giving vent to a spirit of patriotism, it simultaneously deepened the American illusion of isolationism. Many Americans falsely concluded, then and later, that the Republic was in fact insulated from European dangers simply because it wanted to be.

Chapter Summary

Americans began the War of 1812 with high hopes of conquering Canada and delivering a severe blow to their British tormentors. But their strategy and efforts were badly flawed, and before long British and Canadian forces had thrown the United States on the defensive. The Americans fared somewhat better in naval warfare on the Great Lakes, but by 1814 the British had burned Washington and were threatening elsewhere. The Treaty of Ghent in 1814 ended the war in a stalemate that solved none of the original issues. But largely because of Andrew Jackson's "postwar" victory in the Battle of New Orleans in 1815, Americans counted the war a success and increasingly turned away from European affairs and toward isolationism.

Despite some secessionist talk by New Englanders at the Hartford Convention, the ironic outcome of the divisive and near-disastrous war was a strong surge of American nationalism and unity. Partisan political conflict disappeared during the "Era of Good Feelings" under President Madison. A fervent new nationalism appeared in diverse areas of culture, economics, and foreign policy.

But the Era of Good Feelings was soon threatened by the economic panic of 1819, caused largely by excessive land speculation and unstable banks. An even more serious threat to national unity came from the first major sectional dispute over slavery, which was postponed but not really resolved by the Missouri Compromise of 1820.

Under Chief Justice John Marshall, the Supreme Court further enhanced its role as the major force upholding a powerful national government and conservative defense of property rights. Marshall's rulings partially checked the general movement toward states' rights and popular democracy.

Nationalism also led to a more assertive American foreign policy. Andrew Jackson's military adventures in Spanish Florida resulted in the forced purchase of that territory by the United States. American fears of European intervention in Latin America encouraged Monroe and J. Q. Adams to declare the Monroe Doctrine. The announcement had little immediate practical effect, but it carried large consequences for the future of United States foreign policy in the Americas.

The Rise of a Mass Democracy

1824–1840

IN THE FULL ENJOYMENT OF THE GIFTS OF HEAVEN AND THE FRUITS OF SUPERIOR INDUSTRY, ECONOMY, AND VIRTUE, EVERY MAN IS EQUALLY ENTITLED TO PROTECTION BY LAW; BUT WHEN THE LAWS UNDERTAKE TO ADD TO THOSE NATURAL AND JUST ADVANTAGES ARTIFICIAL DISTINCTIONS . . . AND EXCLUSIVE PRIVILEGES . . . THE HUMBLE MEMBERS OF SOCIETY—THE FARMERS, MECHANICS, AND LABORERS . . . HAVE A RIGHT TO COMPLAIN OF THE INJUSTICE OF THEIR GOVERNMENT.

ANDREW JACKSON, 1832

Chapter Outline

- The "Corrupt Bargain" of 1824
- President John Quincy Adams, 1825–1829
- The Triumph of Andrew Jackson, 1828
- The "Tariff of Abominations," 1828
- The Spoils System
- The South Carolina Nullification Crisis, 1832–1833
- Indian Removal
- Jackson's War on the Bank of the United States
- The Emergence of the Whig Party, 1836
- Martin Van Buren and the Depression of 1837
- The Texas Revolution

The so-called Era of Good Feelings was never entirely tranquil, but even the illusion of national consensus was shattered by the panic of 1819 and the Missouri Compromise of 1820. Economic distress and the slavery issue raised the political stakes in the 1820s and 1830s. Vigorous political conflict, once feared, came to be celebrated as necessary for the health of democracy. New political parties emerged. New styles of campaigning took hold. A new chapter opened in the history of American politics. The political landscape of 1824 was similar, in its broad outlines, to that of 1796. By 1840 it would be almost unrecognizable.

The **deference,** apathy, and virtually nonexistent party organizations of the Era of Good Feelings yielded to the boisterous democracy, frenzied vitality, and strong political parties of the Jacksonian era. The old suspicion of political parties as illegitimate disrupters of society's natural harmony gave way to an acceptance of the sometimes wild contentiousness of political life.

In 1828 an energetic new party, the Democrats, captured the White House. By the 1830s the Democrats faced an equally vigorous opposition party in the form of the Whigs. This two-party system institutionalized divisions that had vexed the Revolutionary generation and came to constitute an important part of the nation's checks and balances on political power.

New forms of politicking emerged in this era, as candidates used banners, badges, parades, barbecues, free drinks, and baby kissing to get out the vote. Voter turnout rose dramatically; only about one-quarter of eligible voters cast a ballot in the presidential election of 1824, but that proportion doubled in 1828, and in the election of 1840 it reached 78 percent. Everywhere people flexed their political muscles.

Focus Questions

1. **How did John Quincy Adams's victory through an alleged "corrupt bargain" in the election of 1824 set the stage for Andrew Jackson's election as the popular hero of the Democratic party in 1828 and the emergence of a new democratic politics?**
2. **How did Jackson's policies of westward expansion and Indian removal lead to the "Trail of Tears" to Oklahoma and the Seminole Wars in Florida?**

Chronology

1822	Vesey slave rebellion conspiracy in Charleston, South Carolina.
1823	Mexico opens Texas to American settlers.
1824	Lack of electoral majority for presidency throws election into the House of Representatives.
1825	House elects John Quincy Adams president.
1828	Tariff of 1828 ("Tariff of Abominations"). Jackson elected president.
1829	Indian Removal Act.
1832	"Bank War"—Jackson vetoes bill to recharter Bank of the United States. Tariff of 1832. Jackson defeats Clay for presidency. Black Hawk War.
1832-1833	South Carolina nullification crisis.
1833	Compromise Tariff of 1833. Jackson removes federal deposits from Bank of the United States.
1836	Bank of the United States expires. Specie Circular issued. Bureau of Indian Affairs established. Battle of the Alamo. Battle of San Jacinto. Texas wins independence from Mexico. Van Buren elected president.
1837	Seminole Indians defeated and most eventually removed from Florida. Panic of 1837. United States recognizes republic of Texas but refuses annexation.
1838-1839	Cherokee Indians removed on "Trail of Tears."
1840	Independent Treasury established. Harrison defeats Van Buren for presidency.

3. **How did Andrew Jackson's "war" against the Second Bank of the United States fuel popular democracy as well as the anti-Jackson Whig party?**
4. **What were the causes of the Texas revolution and independence, and why did efforts to bring Texas into the Union stir such sharp controversy?**
5. **What were the central features of America's new mass democracy and two-party system, and how were these developments reflected in the flamboyant "log cabin and hard cider" campaign of 1840?**

- William Henry Harrison's "Log Cabin" Campaign, 1840
- The Establishment of the Two-Party System
- Examining the Evidence: Satiric Bank Note, 1837
- Makers of America: Mexican or Texican?
- Varying Viewpoints: What Was Jacksonian Democracy?

The "Corrupt Bargain" of 1824

The last of the old-style elections was marked by the controversial "corrupt bargain" of 1824. The woods were full of presidential timber as James Monroe, last of the Virginia dynasty, completed his second term. Four candidates towered above the others: John Quincy Adams of Massachusetts, highly intelligent, experienced, and aloof; Henry Clay of Kentucky, the gamy and gallant "Harry of the West"; William H. Crawford of Georgia, an able though ailing giant of a man; and Andrew Jackson of Tennessee, the gaunt and gutsy hero of New Orleans.

All four rivals professed to be "Republicans." Well-organized parties had not yet emerged; their identities were so fuzzy, in fact, that John C. Calhoun appeared as the vice-presidential candidate on both the Adams and the Jackson tickets.

The results of the noisy campaign were interesting but confusing. Jackson, the war hero, clearly had the strongest personal appeal, especially in the West, where his campaign against the forces of corruption and privilege in government resonated deeply. He polled almost as many popular votes as his next two rivals combined, but he failed to win a majority of the electoral vote (see table on p. 178). In such a deadlock the House of Representatives, as directed by the Twelfth Amendment (see the Appendix), must choose among the top three candidates. Clay was thus eliminated, yet as Speaker of the House he presided over the very chamber that had to pick the winner.

deference *The yielding of opinion to the judgment of someone else; in politics, the inclination of lower social or economic classes to conform to the political views and choices of social elites.*

■ **Canvassing for a Vote, by George Caleb Bingham, 1852** This painting shows the "new politics" of the Jacksonian era. Politicians now had to take their message to the common man.

puritanical *Extremely or excessively strict in matters of morals or religion.*

The influential Clay was in a position to throw the election to the candidate of his choice. He reached the decision by the process of elimination. Crawford, recently felled by a paralytic stroke, was out of the picture. Clay hated the "military chieftain" Jackson, who in turn bitterly resented Clay's public denunciation of his Florida foray in 1818. The only candidate left was the **puritanical** Adams, with whom Clay—a free-living gambler and duelist—had never established cordial personal relations. But the two men had much in common politically: both were fervid nationalists and advocates of the American System. Shortly before the final ballot in the House, Clay met privately with Adams and assured him of his support.

Decision day came early in 1825. The House of Representatives met amid tense excitement, with sick members being carried in on stretchers. On the first ballot, thanks largely to Clay's behind-the-scenes influence, Adams was elected president. A few days later, the victor announced that Henry Clay would be the new secretary of state.

Masses of angered Jacksonians, most of them common folk, roared in protest against this "corrupt bargain." Jackson condemned Clay as the "Judas of the West," and John Randolph of Virginia declared that Clay "shines and stinks like . . . a rotten mackerel by moonlight." No positive evidence has ever been unearthed to prove that Adams and Clay entered into a formal bargain. Clay was a natural choice for secretary of state, and Adams was scrupulously honest and not given to patronage. Even if a bargain had been struck, it was not necessarily corrupt. Deals of this nature have long been the stock-in-trade of politicians. But the outcry over Adams's election showed that change was in the wind. What had once been common practice was

Primary source
Election Day at the State House
college.hmco.com/pic/kennedybrief7e

Election of 1824

Candidates	Electoral Vote	Popular Vote	Popular Percentage
Jackson	99	153,544	42.16%
Adams	84	108,740	31.89%
Crawford	41	46,618	12.95%
Clay	37	47,136	12.99%

now condemned as furtive, elitist, and subversive of democracy. The next president would not be chosen behind closed doors.

A Yankee Misfit in the White House

John Quincy Adams was a chip off the old family glacier. Short, thickset, and billiard-bald, he was even more frigidly austere than his presidential father, John Adams. Shunning people, he often went for early morning swims, sometimes stark naked, in the then-pure Potomac River. Essentially a closeted thinker rather than a politician, he was irritable, sarcastic, and tactless. Yet few individuals have ever come to the presidency with a more brilliant record in statecraft, especially in foreign affairs. He ranks as one of the most successful secretaries of state, yet one of the least successful presidents.

A man of scrupulous honor, Adams entered upon his four-year "sentence" in the White House smarting under charges of "bargain," "corruption," and "**usurpation.**" Fewer than one-third of the voters had voted for him. As the first "minority president," he would have found it difficult to win popular support even under the most favorable conditions. He possessed almost none of the arts of the politician and scorned those who did. He refused to engage in the growing practice of patronage, appointing almost none of his political supporters to office. In the dawning age of back-slapping and baby-kissing democracy, the cold fish John Quincy Adams could hardly hope for success at the polls.

usurpation *The act of seizing, occupying, or enjoying the place, power, or functions of someone without legal right.*

mudslinging *Malicious, unscrupulous attacks against an opponent.*

Adams's nationalistic views contributed to his woes in the White House. Much of the nation was turning away from post-Ghent nationalism toward states' rights and sectionalism. But Adams swam against the tide. Confirmed nationalist that he was, the new president urged Congress in his first annual message to construct a national network of roads and canals. He also renewed George Washington's proposal for a national university and went so far as to advocate federal support for an astronomical observatory.

The public reaction to these proposals was prompt and unfavorable. To many workaday Americans grubbing out stumps, astronomical observatories seemed like a scandalous waste of public funds. The South in particular bristled. If the federal government could meddle in local concerns like education and roads, it might some day try to lay its hand on the "peculiar institution" of black slavery.

Going "Whole Hog" for Jackson in 1828

The presidential campaign for Andrew Jackson had started early—on February 9, 1825, the day of John Quincy Adams's controversial election by the House—and it continued noisily for nearly four years.

Even before the election of 1828, the temporarily united Republicans of the Era of Good Feelings had split into two camps. One was the National Republicans, with Adams as their standard-bearer. The other was the Democratic-Republicans, with the fiery Jackson heading their ticket. Chanting "All hail, Old Hickory" and planting hickory poles for their hickory-tough hero, Jackson's zealots argued that the will of the people had been thwarted in 1825 by the backstairs "corrupt bargain" between Adams and Clay. The only way to right the wrong was to seat Jackson, who would then bring about "reform" by sweeping out the "dishonest" Adams gang.

Mudslinging reached new lows in 1828, and the electorate developed a taste for bare-knuckle politics. Adams would not stoop to gutter tactics, but many of his backers were less squeamish. They described Jackson's mother as a prostitute and his wife as an adulteress, and they recounted "Old Hickory's" numerous duels and brawls and his hanging of six militiamen.

Jackson men also hit below the belt. A billiard table that President Adams had purchased with his own money became, in the mouths of rabid Jacksonites, "gambling tables" in the "presidential palace." Jackson campaigners mocked Adams's large federal salaries and even accused him of having served as a pimp for the Russian tsar during his time as minister to St. Petersburg.

On voting day the electorate split on largely sectional lines. Jackson's strongest support came from the West and South. The middle Atlantic states and the Old Northwest were divided, while Adams won the backing of his own New England as well as the propertied "better elements" of the Northeast. But when the popular vote was converted to electoral votes, General Jackson's triumph could not be denied. Old Hickory had trounced Adams by an electoral count of 178 to 83. Although a considerable part of Jackson's support was lined up by **machine** politicians in eastern cities, particularly in New York and Pennsylvania, the political center of gravity clearly had shifted away from the conservative eastern seaboard toward the emerging states across the mountains.

machine *A hierarchical political organization, often controlled through patronage or spoils, where professional workers deliver large blocs of voters to preferred candidates.*

The Advent of Old Hickory Jackson

The new president cut a striking figure—tall, lean, with bushy iron-gray hair brushed high above a prominent forehead, craggy eyebrows, and blue eyes. His irritability and emaciated condition resulted in part from long-term bouts with dysentery, malaria, tuberculosis, and lead poisoning from two bullets that he carried in his body from near-fatal duels. His autobiography was written in his lined face.

Jackson's upbringing had its shortcomings. Born in the Carolinas and early orphaned, "Mischievous Andy" grew up without parental restraints. As a youth, he displayed much more interest in brawling and cockfighting than in his scanty opportunities for reading and spelling. Although he eventually learned to express himself in writing with vigor and clarity, his grammar was always rough-hewn and his spelling original. He sometimes misspelled a word two different ways in the same letter.

The youthful Carolinian shrewdly moved "up West" to Tennessee, where fighting was prized above writing. There—through native intelligence, force of personality, and powers of leadership—he became a judge and a member of Congress. Afflicted with a violent temper, he early became involved in numerous duels, stabbings, and bloody frays. His passions were so profound that on occasion he would choke into silence when he tried to speak.

The first president from the West, the first nominated in a formal party convention (in 1832), and only the second without a college education (Washington was the first), Jackson was unique. His university was adversity. He had risen from the masses but was not one of them, except insofar as he shared many of their prejudices. Essentially a frontier aristocrat, he owned many slaves, cultivated broad acres, and lived in one of the finest mansions in America—the Hermitage, near Nashville, Tennessee.

Jackson's inauguration symbolized the ascendancy of the masses. "Hickoryites" poured into Washington from far away, sleeping on hotel floors and in hallways. They were eager to see their hero take office, and perhaps to pick up a well-paying office for themselves. Nobodies mingled with notables as the White House, for the first time, was thrown open to the multitude. A milling crowd of rubbernecking clerks and shopkeepers, hobnailed artisans, and grimy laborers surged in, allegedly wrecking the china and furniture and threatening the "people's champion" with cracked ribs. Jackson was hastily spirited through a side door, and the White House miraculously emptied itself when the word was passed that huge bowls of well-spiked punch had been placed on the lawns. Such was the "inaugural brawl."

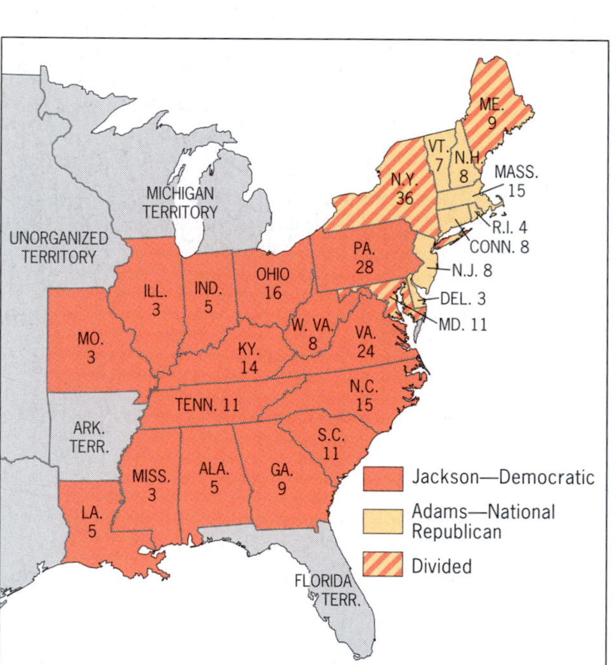

Presidential Election of 1828 (with electoral vote by state) Jackson swept the South and West, while Adams retained the old Federalist stronghold of the Northeast. Yet Jackson's inroads in the Northeast were decisive. He won twenty of New York's electoral votes and all twenty-eight of Pennsylvania's. If those votes had gone the other way, Adams would have been victorious—by a margin of one vote.

In 1824 Thomas Jefferson (1743–1826) said of Jackson,

"When I was President of the Senate he was a Senator; and he could never speak on account of the rashness of his feelings. I have seen him attempt it repeatedly, and as often choke with rage. His passions are no doubt cooler now . . . but he is a dangerous man."

To conservatives, this orgy seemed like the end of the world. "King Mob" reigned triumphant as Jacksonian vulgarity replaced Jeffersonian simplicity. Faint-hearted traditionalists shuddered, drew their blinds, and recalled with trepidation the opening scenes of the French Revolution.

Jackson Nationalizes the Spoils System

Once in power, the Democrats, famously suspicious of the federal government, demonstrated they were not above striking some bargains of their own. Under Jackson the **spoils** system—that is, rewarding political supporters with public office—was introduced into the federal government on a large scale. Its name came from Senator William Marcy's classic remark in 1832, "To the victors belong the spoils of the enemy." The system had already secured a firm hold in New York and Pennsylvania, where well-greased machines ladled out the "gravy" of office.

Andrew Jackson (1767–1845), by Thomas Sully, 1845
A self-taught and popularly elected major general of the Tennessee militia, Andrew Jackson became a major general of the U.S. Army in 1814. He was noted for his stern discipline, iron will ("Old Hickory"), and good luck.

Jackson defended the spoils system on democratic grounds. "Every man is as good as his neighbor," he declared—perhaps "equally better." As this was believed to be so, and as the routine of office was thought to be simple enough for any upstanding American to learn quickly, why encourage the development of an aristocratic, bureaucratic, officeholding class? Better to bring in new blood, Jackson argued. But the spoils system was less about qualifications than about rewarding old cronies. The questions Democrats asked each appointee were not "What can he do for the country?" but "What has he done for the party?" and "Is he loyal to Jackson?"

Scandal inevitably accompanied the new system. Men who had openly bought their posts by campaign contributions were appointed to high office. Illiterates, incompetents, and plain crooks were given positions of public trust; men on the make lusted for the spoils—rather than the toils—of office. Samuel Swartwout, despite ample warnings of his untrustworthiness, was awarded the lucrative post of collector of customs for the port of New York. Nearly nine years later he "Swartwouted out" for Britain, leaving his accounts more than a million dollars short—the first person to steal a million from the Washington government.

spoils *Public offices given as a reward for political support.*

But despite its undeniable abuses, the spoils system was an important element of the emerging two-party order, cementing as it did loyalty to party over competing claims from economic class or geographic region. The promise of patronage provided a compelling reason for Americans to pick a party and stick with it through thick and thin.

The Tricky "Tariff of Abominations"

The touchy tariff issue had been one of John Quincy Adams's biggest headaches. Now Andrew Jackson felt his predecessor's pain. In 1824 Congress had increased the general tariff significantly, but wool manufacturers bleated for still-higher barriers. Ardent Jacksonites now played a cynical political game. They promoted a high-tariff bill, expecting it to be defeated, which would give a black eye to then President Adams. To their surprise the tariff passed in 1828, and Andrew Jackson inherited the political hot potato.

Southerners, as heavy consumers of manufactured goods with little manufacturing of their own, were hostile to tariffs, particularly to this high Tariff of 1828. Hotheads branded it the "Black Tariff" and the "Tariff of Abominations." Several southern states adopted formal protests, and in South Carolina flags were lowered to half-mast.

Why did the South react so angrily to the tariff? Southerners believed, not illogically, that the "Yankee tariff" discriminated against them. Southerners who sold their cotton in an unprotected world market were forced to buy expensive manufactured goods from Yankee and middle state producers heavily protected by tariffs, and the tariff provided a convenient and plausible scapegoat for the hard times befalling the Old South.

But much deeper issues underlay the southern outcry—in particular, a growing anxiety about possible federal interference with the institution of slavery. The congressional debate on the Missouri Compromise had kindled those anxieties, and they were further fanned by an abortive slave rebellion in Charleston in 1822, led by a free black named Denmark Vesey. South Carolinians, still closely tied to the British West Indies, knew full well that slaveholding West Indians were feeling the mounting pressures of British abolitionism on the London government. American abolitionists might similarly use the power of the Washington government to suppress slavery. If so, now was the time, and the tariff was the issue, for making a strong stand against all federal encroachments on states' rights.

South Carolinians took the lead in protesting the "Tariff of Abominations." Vice President John C. Calhoun, a topflight political theorist, secretly authored a pamphlet known as the "South Carolina Exposition" that the state legislature published in 1828. (As vice president he was forced to conceal his authorship.) Going a stride beyond the Kentucky and Virginia resolutions of 1798, it bluntly and explicitly proposed that the states should nullify the tariff—that is, they should declare it null and void within their borders.

"Nullies" in South Carolina

The stage was set for a showdown. Through Jackson's first term the South Carolina nullifiers—"nullies" they were called—tried strenuously to muster the necessary two-thirds vote in the legislature, but they were blocked by a determined minority of Unionists. Congress pared away the worst "abominations" by passing the new, somewhat lower Tariff of 1832, but it was still frankly protectionist and fell far short of satisfying southern demands.

South Carolina was now nerved for drastic action. After the "nullies" won a commanding majority in the state election of 1832, the legislature called a special convention. Meeting in Columbia, the delegates solemnly declared the existing tariff null and void in South Carolina, and threatened to take their state out of the Union if Washington attempted to collect the customs duties by force.

Such tactics might have intimidated John Quincy Adams, but Andrew Jackson was the wrong president to stare down. The cantankerous general would never permit defiance or disunion. Privately threatening to invade the state and hang the nullifiers, he publicly dispatched naval and military forces to the Palmetto State and issued a ringing proclamation against nullification. Governor Robert Hayne responded with a counterproclamation, and the lines were drawn. If civil war was to be avoided, one side would have to surrender, or both would have to compromise.

Conciliatory Senator Henry Clay of Kentucky stepped forward. Although himself a supporter of tariffs, he had no desire to see his old enemy Andrew Jackson win laurels by crushing the Carolinians and returning with the scalp of John C. Calhoun. The gallant Kentuckian therefore pushed through Congress a compromise bill that would gradually reduce the Tariff of 1832 by about 10 percent over eight years, to the mildly protective level of 1816.

South Carolinians welcomed this opportunity to extricate themselves from a dangerously tight corner without loss of face. To the consternation of the Calhounites, no other southern states had sprung to their support, and an appreciable Unionist minority within South Carolina was gathering guns and nailing the Stars and Stripes to flagpoles. Faced with civil war within and invasion from without, the Columbia convention met again and repealed the ordinance of nullification.

Neither Jackson nor the "nullies" won a clear-cut victory in 1833. Clay was the true hero of the hour, hailed in Charleston and Boston alike for saving the country. Armed conflict had been avoided, but the fundamental issues had not been resolved. When next the "nullies" and the Union clashed, compromise would prove more elusive.

The Trail of Tears

Jackson's Democrats were committed to western expansion, but such expansion necessarily meant confrontation with the current inhabitants of the land. More than 125,000 Native Americans lived in the forests and prairies east of the Mississippi in the 1820s. Federal policy toward them varied. Beginning in the 1790s, the Washington government ostensibly recognized the tribes as separate nations and agreed to acquire land from them only through formal treaties. The Indians were shrewd and determined negotiators, but this availed them little when Americans routinely violated their own covenants as white settlement pushed west.

Many white Americans felt respect and admiration for the Indians and believed that the Native Americans could be assimilated into white society. Much energy was therefore devoted to Christianizing and "civilizing" the Indians. Many **denominations** sent missionaries into Indian villages, and in 1793 Congress appropriated $20,000 for Indian literacy programs and agricultural instruction.

denominations *In American religion, the branches of Christianity, organized into distinct church structures and traditions, such as Presbyterians, Baptists, Disciples of Christ, and so forth.*

Primary source
Jesuit's Interpretation of Gender Roles Among . . .
college.hmco.com/pic/kennedybrief7e

Primary source
Ball Play of the Choctaw—Ball Up
college.hmco.com/pic/kennedybrief7e

Primary source
Indian Land Cessions
college.hmco.com/pic/kennedybrief7e

Although many tribes violently resisted white encroachment, others followed the path of accommodation. The Cherokees of Georgia made especially remarkable efforts to learn white ways. They composed a written legal code and constitution, adopted a system of settled agriculture, and vigorously promoted education, using a Cherokee alphabet devised by the Indian Sequoyah. Some Cherokees became prosperous cotton planters and even turned to slaveholding. Nearly thirteen hundred black slaves toiled for their Native American masters in the Cherokee nation in the 1820s. For these efforts, the Cherokees—along with the Creeks, Choctaws, Chickasaws, and Seminoles—were numbered by the whites among the "Five Civilized Tribes."

All this embrace of "civilization" apparently was not good enough for whites. In 1828 the Georgia legislature declared the Cherokee tribal council illegal and asserted its own jurisdiction over Indian affairs and Indian lands. The Cherokees appealed this move to the Supreme Court, which thrice upheld the rights of the Indians. But President Jackson, who clearly wanted to open Indian lands to white settlement, refused to recognize the Court's decisions. In a callous jibe at the Indians' defender, Jackson reportedly snapped, "John Marshall has made his decision; now let him enforce it."*

Feeling some obligation to "this much injured race," Jackson proposed a bodily removal of the "Five Civilized Tribes" of the Southeast beyond the Mississippi. Emigration was supposed to be voluntary because it would be "cruel and unjust to compel the aborigines to abandon the graves of their fathers," Jackson declared.

Jackson's policy, passed by Congress as the Indian Removal Act of 1830, led to the forced uprooting of more than 100,000 Indians. In the ensuing decade, countless Indians died on the "Trail of Tears" to the newly established Indian Territory (present-day Oklahoma) where they were to be "permanently" free of white encroachments. The Bureau of Indian Affairs was established in 1836 to administer relations with America's original inhabitants. But as the land-hungry "palefaces" pushed rapidly west, the government's guarantees of a "permanent" Indian homeland went up in smoke.

Suspicious of white intentions from the start, the Sauk and Fox tribes of Illinois and Wisconsin, ably led by Black Hawk, resisted eviction. They were bloodily crushed in 1832 by regular troops, including Lieutenant Jefferson Davis of Mississippi, and by militia volunteers, including Captain Abraham Lincoln of Illinois. In Florida the Seminoles, under the leadership of Osceola, retreated into the swampy Everglades, and for seven years (1835–1842) waged a bitter guerrilla war that took the lives of some fifteen hundred soldiers. The American commander's treacherous seizure of Osceola under a flag of truce finally led to the Seminoles' defeat. Some Seminoles fled deeper into the Everglades, where their descendants now

---

*One hundred sixty years later, in 1992, the state of Georgia formally pardoned the two white missionaries, Samuel Austin Worcester and Elihu Butler, who had figured prominently in the decision Jackson condemned. They had been convicted of living on Cherokee lands without a license from the state of Georgia. They served sixteen months at hard labor on a chain gang and later accompanied the Cherokees on the "Trail of Tears" to Oklahoma.

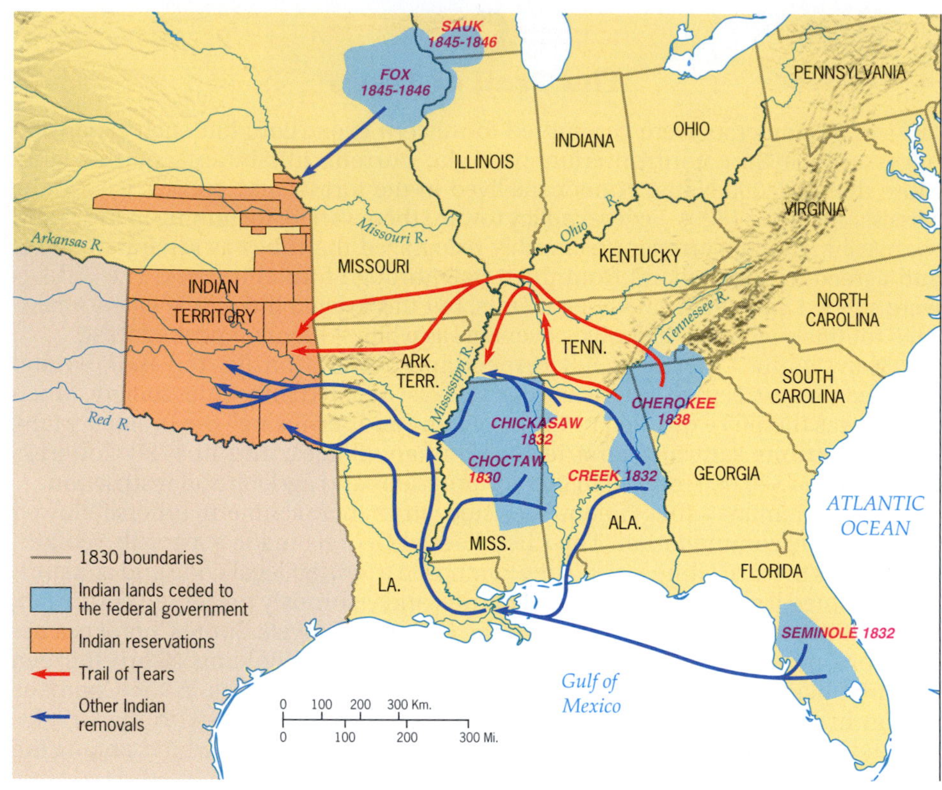

■ **Indian Removals, 1830–1846**

Online Study Center

Interactive map
Removal of Native Americans from the South, 1820–1840
college.hmco.com/pic/kennedybrief7e

Online Study Center

Primary source
Removal of the Southern Tribes to the West
college.hmco.com/pic/kennedybrief7e

live, but about four-fifths of them were moved to Oklahoma, where several thousand of the tribe survived.

The Bank War

President Jackson did not hate all banks and all businesses, but he distrusted monopolistic banking and overbig business, as did his followers. A man of virulent dislikes, he came to share the prejudices of his own West against the "moneyed monster" known as the Bank of the United States.

What made the bank a monster in Jackson's eyes? The national government minted gold and silver coins in the mid-nineteenth century but did not issue paper money. Paper notes issued by private banks in effect functioned as money, giving private bankers considerable power over the nation's economy.

No bank in America had more power than the Bank of the United States. In many ways the bank acted like a branch of government. It was the principal depository for the funds of the Washington government and controlled much of the nation's gold and silver. A source of credit and stability, the bank was an important and useful part of the nation's expanding economy.

But the Bank of the United States was a private institution, accountable not to the people but only to its elite circle of moneyed investors. Its president, the brilliant but arrogant Nicholas Biddle—dubbed "Czar Nicholas I" by his enemies—held immense power over the nation's financial affairs.

To some the bank's very existence seemed to sin against the egalitarian credo of American democracy.

One survivor of the Indians' forced march in 1838–1839 on the "Trail of Tears" to Indian Territory, farther west, remembered,

"One each day, and all are gone. Looks like maybe all dead before we get to new Indian country, but always we keep marching on. Women cry and make sad wails. Children cry, and many men cry, and all look sad when friends die, but they say nothing and just put heads down and keep on toward west. . . . She [his mother] speak no more; we bury her and go on."

The "Trail of Tears" In the fall and winter of 1838–1839, the U.S. Army forcibly removed about 15,000 Cherokees, some of them in manacles, from their ancestral homelands in the southeastern United States and marched them to Indian Territory (present-day Oklahoma). Freezing weather and inadequate food supplies led to unspeakable suffering. The escorting troops refused to slow the forced march so that the ill could recover, and some 4,000 Cherokees died on the 116-day journey.

That conviction formed the deepest source of Jackson's opposition. The bank also won no friends by foreclosing on many western farms and draining "tribute" into eastern coffers. Profit, not public service, was its first priority.

The Bank War erupted in 1832, when Daniel Webster and Henry Clay presented Congress with a bill to renew the Bank of the United States' charter. The charter was not set to expire until 1836, but Clay pushed for renewal four years early to make it an election issue in 1832. As Jackson's leading rival for the presidency, Clay, with fateful blindness, believed he had set a perfect trap for Jackson. If Jackson signed the bill he would alienate his worshipful followers, but if he vetoed it he would lose the presidency to Clay.

Clay's recharter bill slid through Congress on greased skids, but was killed by a scorching veto from Jackson. The "Old Hero" declared the monopolistic bank to be unconstitutional, ignoring the Supreme Court's earlier decision upholding its constitutionality in *McCulloch* v. *Maryland* (1819). The old general growled privately, "The Bank . . . is trying to kill me, but I will kill it." Jackson's veto message not only squashed the bank bill but vastly amplified the powers of the presidency. If the legislative and executive branches were partners in government, Jackson implied, the president was unmistakably the senior partner.

Henry Clay's political instincts continued to fail him. Delighted with the veto message's financial fallacies, but blind to its political appeal to the common people, Clay arranged to have thousands of copies printed as a campaign document. The bank issue was now thrown into the noisy arena of the presidential contest of 1832.

"Old Hickory" Wallops Clay in 1832

Clay and Jackson were the chief gladiators in the fierce electoral combat of 1832. The grizzled old general's supporters again raised hickory poles and shouted "Jackson Forever: Go the Whole Hog!" Clay's admirers called for "Freedom and Clay," while his detractors harped on his dueling, gambling, cockfighting, and fast living.

Novel features made the campaign of 1832 especially memorable. For the first time, a third party entered the field—the newborn Anti-Masonic party, which opposed the influence and fearsome secrecy of the Masonic order. Energized by the mysterious disappearance and probable murder in 1826 of a New Yorker who was threatening to expose the Masons' secret rituals, the Anti-Masonic party quickly became a potent political force throughout the middle Atlantic and New England states. The Anti-Masons appealed to Americans' democratic suspicions of secret societies, but since Jackson was a proud Mason, the anti-Masonic party was also an anti-Jackson party. The Anti-Masonic party also attracted support from many **evangelical** Protestants seeking to use political power to effect moral and religious reforms, such as prohibiting mail deliveries on Sunday.

evangelical *In American religion, those believers and groups, usually Protestant, who emphasize personal salvation, individual conversion experiences, voluntary commitment, and the authority of Scripture.*

hard money *Metal money—gold or silver—as distinguished from paper money. (The term also came to mean any reliable or secure money that maintained or increased its purchasing power over time.* ***Soft money,*** *or paper money, was assumed to inflate or lose value.)*

A further novelty of the presidential contest in 1832 was the calling of national nominating conventions (three of them) to name candidates. The Anti-Masons and National Republicans added still another innovation when they adopted formal platforms, articulating and publicizing their positions on the issues.

Henry Clay and his overconfident National Republicans sailed into the campaign with a lush $50,000 campaign chest, much of it from the Bank of the United States, and strong newspaper backing, some of it "bought" with Biddle's bank loans. Yet Jackson, idol of the masses, easily defeated the big-money Kentuckian. A Jacksonian wave again swept over the West and South, surged into Pennsylvania and New York, and even washed into rock-ribbed New England. The popular vote stood at 687,502 to 530,189 for Jackson; the electoral count a lopsided 219 to 49.

Burying Biddle's Bank

Its charter denied, the Bank of the United States was due to expire in 1836. But Jackson was not one to let the financial octopus die in peace. He was convinced that he now had a mandate from the voters for its extermination, and he feared that the slippery Biddle might try to manipulate the bank (as he did) so as to force its recharter. Jackson therefore proposed to bury the bank for good by removing all federal deposits from its vaults, thereby bleeding the bank dry and ensuring its demise.

Even the president's closest advisers opposed this vindictive and possibly unconstitutional policy. Jackson, his dander up, was forced to reshuffle his cabinet twice before he could find a secretary of the treasury who would bend to his iron will. Hoping to demonstrate the bank's importance, the desperate Biddle called in its loans in order to produce a minor financial crisis—"Biddle's Panic." But Jackson's resolution was firm. If anything, the vengeful conduct of the dying "monster" seemed to justify the earlier accusations of its adversaries.

But the death of the Bank of the United States left a financial vacuum in the American economy and kicked off a lurching cycle of booms and busts. Surplus federal funds were placed in several dozen pro-Jackson state banks, the so-called "pet banks." Without a sober central bank in control, the pet banks and smaller "wildcat" banks—fly-by-night operations that often consisted of little more than a few chairs and a suitcase full of printed notes—flooded the country with unsound paper money.

Jackson tried to rein in the runaway economy in 1836, the year Biddle's bank breathed its last. "Wildcat" currency had become so unreliable, especially in the West, that Jackson authorized the Treasury to issue a Specie Circular—a decree that required all public lands to be purchased with **"hard,"** or metallic**, money.** This drastic step slammed the brakes on the speculative boom, a neck-snapping change of direction that contributed to a financial crash in 1837.

Primary source
Jackson's Farewell Address
college.hmco.com/pic/kennedybrief7e

But by then Jackson had retired to his Nashville home, hailed as the hero of his age. His successor would have to deal with the damage.

The Birth of the Whigs

New political parties were gelling as the 1830s lengthened. As early as 1828, the Democratic-Republicans of Jackson had unashamedly adopted the once-tainted name of "Democrats." Jackson's opponents condemned him as "King Andrew I" and began to coalesce as the Whigs—a name deliberately chosen to recollect eighteenth-century British and Revolutionary American opposition to the monarchy.

The Whig party contained so many diverse elements that it was mocked at first as "an organized incompatibility." Hatred of Jackson and his "executive usurpation" was its only apparent cement in its formative days. The Whigs first emerged as an identifiable group in the Senate, where Clay, Webster, and Calhoun joined forces in 1834 in opposition to Jackson's bank policies. Thereafter, the Whigs rapidly evolved into a potent national political force by attracting other groups alienated by Jackson: supporters of Clay's American System, southern states' righters offended by Jackson's stand on nullification, the larger northern industrialists and merchants, and eventually many of the evangelical Protestants associated with the Anti-Masonic party.

Whigs thought of themselves as conservatives, yet they were progressive in their support of active government programs and reforms. Instead of boundless territorial acquisition, they called for internal improvements like canals, railroads, and telegraph lines, and they supported institutions like prisons, asylums, and public schools. The Whigs welcomed the market economy, drawing support from manufacturers in the North, planters in the South, and merchants and bankers in all sections. But they were not simply a party of wealthy fat cats, however dearly the Democrats wanted to paint them as such. By absorbing the egalitarian Anti-Masonic party, the Whigs blunted much of the Democratic appeal to the common man. Turning Jacksonian rhetoric on its head, the Whigs portrayed Jackson and his successor, Martin Van Buren, as imperious aristocrats, and the Democrats as the party of cronyism and corruption.

The Election of 1836

The smooth-tongued and keen-witted vice president, Martin Van Buren of New York, was Jackson's choice for "appointment" as his successor in 1836. Jackson was too old and ailing to consider a third term, but he was not loath to try to serve a third term through Van Buren, something of a "yes man." Leaving nothing to chance, Jackson carefully rigged the nominating convention and rammed his favorite down the throats of the delegates. Van Buren was supported by the Jacksonites without wild enthusiasm, even though he had promised "to tread generally" in the military-booted footsteps of his predecessor.

As the election neared, the still-ramshackle organization of the Whigs showed in their inability to nominate a single presidential candidate. Their long-shot strategy was instead to run several prominent "**favorite sons**" from different regions, hoping thereby to scatter the vote and throw the election into the House of Representatives. With Henry Clay elbowed aside, the leading Whig "favorite son" was heavy-jawed General William Henry Harrison, hero of the Battle of Tippecanoe (see p. 158). The fine-spun schemes of the Whigs availed nothing, however. Van Buren, the dapper "Little Magician," squirmed into office by the close popular vote of 765,483 to 735,795, but by the comfortable margin of 170 to 124 votes (for all the Whigs combined) in the Electoral College.

favorite sons *In American politics, presidential candidates nominated by their own state, primarily out of local loyalty, but not usually expected to win.*

Big Woes for the "Little Magician"

Martin Van Buren was the first president to be born under the American flag. Short and slender, bland and bald, the adroit little New Yorker has been described as "a first-class second-rate man." An accomplished strategist and spoilsman—"the wizard of Albany"—he was also a statesman of wide experience in both legislative and administrative life. Unfortunately, he fell victim to a series of misfortunes over which he had little control.

From the outset the new president labored under severe handicaps. As a machine-made candidate, he incurred the resentment of many Democrats. Jackson, the master showman, had been the dynamic type of chief executive whose administration had resounded with furious quarrels and cracked heads. Mild-mannered Martin Van Buren seemed to rattle about in the military boots of his bull-in-the-china-shop predecessor. The people felt let down. Inheriting Jackson's mantle without his popularity, Van Buren also inherited the ex-president's numerous and vengeful enemies.

Van Buren's four years overflowed with toil and trouble. A rebellion in Canada in 1837 caused ugly incidents along the border that threatened to trigger war with

Britain. Antislavery agitators in the North were in full cry, condemning among other things the prospective annexation of Texas.

Worst of all, Jackson bequeathed to Van Buren the makings of a searing depression. Much of Van Buren's energy had to be devoted to the purely negative task of battling the panic, and there were not enough rabbits in the "Little Magician's" tall silk hat. Hard times ordinarily blight the reputation of a president, and Van Buren was no exception.

Depression Doldrums and the Independent Treasury

The panic of 1837 was a symptom of the financial sickness of the times. Its basic cause was rampant speculation prompted by a mania of get-rich-quick-ism. Gamblers in western lands were doing a "land-office business" on borrowed capital, much of it in the shaky currency of "wildcat" banks. The speculative craze spread to canals, roads, railroads, and slaves.

But speculation alone did not cause the crash. Jacksonian finance, including the Bank War and the Specie Circular, gave an additional jolt to an already teetering structure. The collapse of two British banks late in 1836 caused investors to call in loans in the United States. Failures of wheat crops deepened the distress. Grain prices were forced so high that three weeks before Van Buren took the oath of office mobs in New York City stormed warehouses and broke open flour barrels.

Soon the depression's full fury burst about Van Buren's bewildered head. Hardship was acute and widespread. American banks collapsed by the hundreds, including some of the "pet banks," which carried down with them several millions in government funds. Commodity prices drooped, sales of public lands fell off, and customs revenues dried to a rivulet. Factories closed their doors, and unemployed workers milled about in the streets.

The Whigs came forward with proposals for active government remedies for the economy's ills. They called for the expansion of bank credit, higher tariffs, and subsidies for internal improvements. But Van Buren, shackled by the Jacksonian philosophy of keeping the government's paws off the economy, spurned all such ideas.

The beleaguered Van Buren tried to apply vintage Jacksonian medicine to the ailing economy through his controversial "Divorce Bill." Convinced that some of the financial fever was fed by the injection of federal funds into private banks, he championed the principle of "divorcing" the government from banking altogether. By establishing a so-called independent treasury, the government could lock its surplus money in vaults. Government funds would thus be safe, but they would also be denied to the banking system as reserves, thereby shriveling available credit resources.

Van Buren's "divorce" scheme was never highly popular. His fellow Democrats, many of whom longed for the risky but lush days of the "pet banks," supported it only lukewarmly. The Whigs condemned it because it shriveled their hopes for a revived Bank of the United States. After a prolonged struggle, the Independent Treasury Bill passed Congress in 1840. Repealed the next year by the victorious Whigs, the scheme was reenacted by the triumphant Democrats in 1846 and then continued until merged with the Federal Reserve System in the next century.

Philip Hone (1780–1851), a New York businessman, described in his diary (May 10, 1837) a phase of the financial crisis:

"The savings-bank also sustained a most grievous run yesterday. They paid 375 depositors $81,000. The press was awful; the hour for closing the bank is six o'clock, but they did not get through the paying of those who were in at that time till nine o'clock. I was there with the other trustees and witnessed the madness of the people—women nearly pressed to death, and the stoutest men could scarcely sustain themselves; but they held on as with a death's grip upon the evidences of their claims, and, exhausted as they were with the pressure, they had strength to cry 'Pay! Pay!' "

Gone to Texas

Americans, greedy for land, continued to covet the vast expanse of Texas, which the United States had abandoned to Spain when acquiring Florida in 1819. The Spanish authorities wanted to populate this virtually unpeopled area, but before they could carry through their

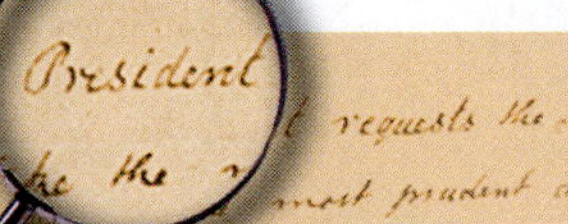

Examining the Evidence

Satiric Bank Note, 1837 Political humor can take more forms than the commonly seen caustic cartoon. Occasionally historians stumble upon other examples, such as this fake bank note. A jibe at Andrew Jackson's money policies, it appeared in New York in 1837 after Jackson's insistence on shutting down the Bank of the United States resulted in the suspension of specie payments. The clever creator of this satiric bank note for six cents left little doubt about the worthlessness of the note or Jackson's responsibility for it. The six cents payable by the "Humbug Glory Bank"—whose symbols were a donkey and a "Hickory Leaf" (for Old Hickory)—were redeemable "in mint drops or Glory at cost." The bank's cashier was "Cunning Reuben," possibly an anti-Semitic allusion to usurious Jewish bankers. Can you identify other ways in which this document takes aim at Jackson's banking policies? What symbols did the note's creator assume the public would comprehend?

1. Identify at least three *visual* images or symbols that serve to link this satirical currency with Andrew Jackson's "pet banks."
2. Point to at least three *verbal* terms or phrases that highlight the supposed fraudulency of Jacksonian banking practices.
3. What historical conclusions about the "Bank War" might you draw from the printing of this kind of "money" by Jackson's opponents? Exactly what political purpose does this form of satire serve that more straightforward argument would not?

Collection of the New York Historical Society, neg. 44812.

contemplated plans, the Mexicans won their independence. A new regime in Mexico City thereupon concluded arrangements in 1823 for granting a huge tract of land to Stephen Austin, with the understanding that he would bring into Texas three hundred American families. Immigrants were to be of the established Roman Catholic faith and upon settlement were to become properly Mexicanized.

Those two stipulations were largely ignored. Hardy Texan pioneers remained Americans at heart, resenting the trammels imposed by a "foreign" government. They were especially annoyed by the presence of Mexican soldiers, many of whom were ragged ex-convicts.

Energetic and prolific, Texan Americans numbered about thirty thousand by 1835 (see "Makers of America: Mexican or Texican?" p. 190). Most of them were law-abiding, God-fearing people, but some of them had left the "states" only one or two jumps ahead of the sheriff. "G.T.T." (Gone To Texas) became current descriptive slang. Among the adventurers were Davy Crockett, the famous rifleman and former Congressman, and James Bowie, the presumed inventor of the murderous knife that bears his name. A distinguished latecomer and leader was an ex-governor of Tennessee, Sam Houston. His life had been temporarily shattered in 1829 when his bride of a few weeks left him and he took up transient residence with the Arkansas Indians, who dubbed him "Big Drunk."

The pioneer individualists who came to Texas were not easy to push around. Friction rapidly increased between Mexicans and Texans over such issues as slavery, immigration, and local rights. Slavery was a particularly touchy topic.

Mexican or Texican?

Moses Austin, born a Connecticut Yankee in 1761, was determined to be Spanish—if that's what it took to acquire cheap land and freedom from pesky laws. In 1798 he tramped into untracked Missouri, still part of Spanish Louisiana, and pledged his allegiance to the king of Spain. In 1820, with his old Spanish passport in his saddlebag, he rode into Spanish Texas and asked for permission to establish a colony of three hundred families.

The Spanish authorities had repeatedly stamped out previous attempts at American settlement in Texas. But the governor somewhat reluctantly allowed Austin's colonists to enter the territory, hoping that they might "civilize" the land and wrest it from the Indians. Upon Moses Austin's death in 1821, the task of realizing his dream fell to his twenty-seven-year-old son, Stephen. "I bid an everlasting farewell to my native country," Stephen Austin said, and he crossed into Texas on July 15, 1821, "determined to fulfill rigidly all the duties and obligations of a Mexican citizen." (Mexico declared its independence from Spain in early 1821.) Soon he learned fluent Spanish and was signing his name as "Don Estévan F. Austin."

Austin fell just three families short of recruiting the three hundred households that his father had contracted to bring to Texas. The original settlers in the colony between the Brazos and Colorado Rivers were nevertheless dubbed "the Old Three Hundred," the Texas equivalent of New England's Mayflower Pilgrims or the "First Families of Virginia." Mostly Scots-Irish southerners from the trans-Appalachian frontier, the Old Three Hundred were cultured folk by frontier standards; all but four of them were literate. Other settlers followed, from Europe as well as America. Within ten years the "Anglos" (many of them French and German) outnumbered the Mexican residents, or *tejanos,* ten to one and soon evolved a distinctive "Texican" culture. The wide-ranging horse patrols organized to attack Indians became the Texas Rangers. Samuel Maverick, whose unbranded cattle roamed the limited prairies, left his surname as a label for rebellious loners. Jared Groce, who came from Alabama with fifty covered wagons and a hundred slaves, etched the original image of the larger-than-life big-time Texas operator.

The original Anglo-Texans brought with them the old Scots-Irish frontiersman's hostility to officialdom and authority. When the Mexican government tried to impose its will on the Anglo-Texans in the 1830s, they took up their guns. Like the American revolutionaries of the 1770s, who at first demanded only the rights of Englishmen, the Texans began by asking simply for Mexican recognition of their rights as guaranteed by the Mexican constitution of 1824. But bloodshed at the Alamo in 1836, like that at Lexington in 1775, transformed protest into rebellion.

Texas lay—and still lies—along the frontier where Hispanic and Anglo-American cultures met, mingled, and clashed. In part the Texas Revolution was a contest between those two cultures. But it was also a contest about philosophies of government, pitting liberal frontier ideals of freedom against the conservative concept of centralized control. Stephen Austin sincerely tried to "Mexicanize" himself and his followers—until the Mexican government grew too arbitrary and authoritarian. Some of those who adhered to this philosophy were not "Anglos" but *tejanos.* Seven *tejanos* died at the Alamo, and several others signed the Texas declaration of independence. Lorenzo de Zavala, an ardent Mexican liberal who had long resisted the centralizing tendencies of Mexico's dominant political party, became vice president of the Texas republic's interim government in 1836. Like the Austins, these *tejanos* and Mexicans sought in Texas an escape from overbearing governmental authority. Their role in the Texas revolution underscores the fact that it was a struggle between defenders of local rights and agents of central authority as much as it was a fight between Anglo and Mexican cultures.

Mexico emancipated its slaves in 1830 and prohibited their further importation into Texas, as well as further colonization by troublesome Americans. The Texans refused to honor this decree. They kept their slaves in bondage, and new American settlers kept bringing more slaves into Texas. The explosion finally came in 1835, when Mexican dictator Santa Anna wiped out all local rights and started to raise an army to suppress the upstart Texans.

The Lone Star Rebellion

Early in 1836 the Texans unfurled their Lone Star flag and declared their independence, naming Sam Houston as commander in chief. Santa Anna, at the head of about six thousand men, stormed ferociously into Texas. Trapping a band of nearly two hundred pugnacious Texans at the Alamo in San Antonio, he wiped them out to a man after a thirteen-day siege. A short time later a band of about four hundred surrounded and defeated American volunteers, having thrown down their arms at Goliad, were butchered as "pirates."

Slain heroes like Jim Bowie and Davy Crockett, well known in life, became legendary in death. Texan war cries—"Remember the Alamo!" "Remember Goliad!" and "Death to Santa Anna!"—swept up into the United States. Scores of vengeful Americans seized their rifles and rushed to the aid of relatives, friends, and compatriots.

General Sam Houston's small army retreated to the east, luring Santa Anna to San Jacinto, near the site of the city that now bears Houston's name. The Mexicans numbered about thirteen hundred men, the Texans about nine hundred. Suddenly, on April 21, 1836, Houston turned, wiping out the pursuing force. The captured Santa Anna was forced to sign two treaties in which he agreed to withdraw Mexican troops and to recognize the Rio Grande as the extreme southwestern boundary of Texas. When released, he repudiated the whole agreement as illegal because it was extorted under duress.

These events put the U.S. government in a sticky situation. As the Mexicans bitterly complained, the Washington government's weak enforcement of neutrality laws had permitted American men and supplies to leak across the border and

Mexican Forces Assault the Alamo The defenders fought bravely but were overwhelmed by Santa Anna's army. Among those who died defending the historic mission were Colonel William Travis, Captain James Bowie, and former congressman David Crockett.

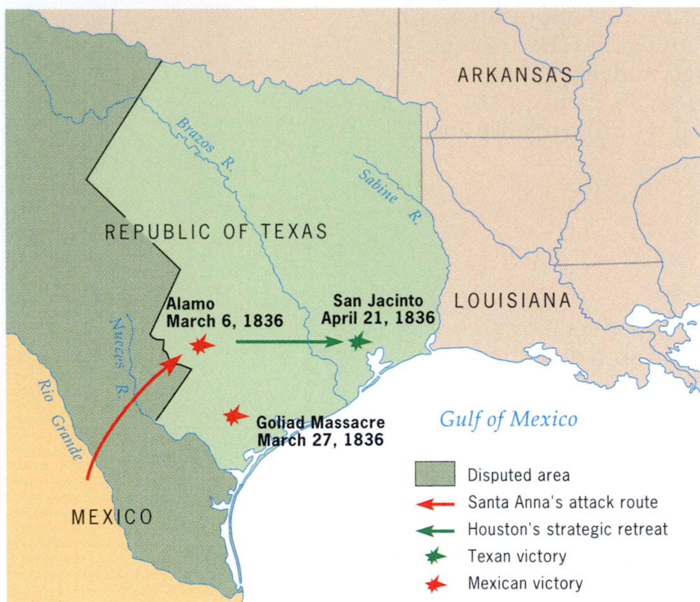

The Texas Revolution, 1835–1836 General Houston's strategy was to retreat and use defense in depth. His line of supply from the United States was shortened as Santa Anna's lengthened. The Mexicans were forced to bring up supplies by land because the Texas navy controlled the sea. This force consisted of only four small ships, but it was big enough to do the job.

aid the Texans. But American public opinion, overwhelmingly favorable to the Texans, left the federal authorities powerless to act. On the day before he left office in 1837, President Jackson extended the right hand of recognition to the Lone Star Republic, led by his old comrade-in-arms against the Indians, Sam Houston.

Many Texans wanted not just recognition of their independence, but outright union with the United States. The radiant Texan bride, officially petitioning for annexation in 1837, presented herself for marriage. But the expectant groom, Uncle Sam, was jerked back by the strong arm of the slavery issue. Antislavery crusaders in the North were opposing annexation with increasing vehemence; they contended that the whole scheme was merely a conspiracy cooked up by the southern "slavocracy" to bring new slave pens into the Union.

At first glance, the "slavery plot" charge seemed plausible. Most of the early settlers in Texas, as well as American volunteers during the revolution, had come from slaveholding states of the South and Southwest. But scholars have concluded that the settlement of Texas was merely the normal and inexorable march of the westward movement. The explanation was proximity rather than conspiracy. Yet the fact remained that many Texans were slaveholders, and admitting Texas to the Union inescapably meant enlarging American slavery.

Log Cabins and Hard Cider of 1840

Martin Van Buren was renominated by the Democrats in 1840, albeit without terrific enthusiasm. The party had no acceptable alternative to the man the Whigs called "Martin Van Ruin."

The Whigs, hungering for the spoils of office, scented victory in the breeze. Pangs of the panic were still being felt, and voters blamed their woes on the party in power. Learning from their mistake in 1836, the Whigs united behind one candidate, Ohio's William Henry Harrison. He was not their ablest statesman—that would have been Webster or Clay—but he was believed to be their ablest vote-getter.

The aging hero, nearly sixty-eight when the campaign ended, was known for his successes against Indians and the British at the Battles of Tippecanoe (1811) and the Thames (1813). Harrison's views on current issues were only vaguely known. "Old Tippecanoe" was nominated primarily because he was issueless and enemyless—a tested recipe for electoral success that still appeals today. John Tyler of Virginia, an afterthought, was selected as his vice-presidential running mate.

The Whigs, eager to avoid offense, published no official platform, hoping to sweep their hero into office with a frothy huzza-for-Harrison campaign reminiscent of Jackson's triumph in 1828. A dull-witted Democratic editor played directly into Whig hands. Stupidly insulting the West, he lampooned Harrison as an impoverished old farmer who should be content with a pension, a log cabin, and a barrel of hard cider—the poor westerner's champagne. Whigs gleefully adopted honest hard cider and the sturdy log cabin as symbols of their campaign. Harrisonites portrayed their hero as the poor "Farmer of North Bend" who had been called from his cabin and his plow to drive corrupt Jackson spoilsmen from the "presidential palace." They denounced Van Buren as a supercilious aristocrat, a simpering dandy who wore corsets and ate French food from golden plates. As a jeering Whig campaign song proclaimed,

Old Tip, he wears a homespun shirt,
He has no ruffled shirt, wirt, wirt.
But Matt, he has the golden plate,
And he's a little squirt, wirt, wirt.

William Henry Harrison Campaign in Philadelphia, 1840 The parties of Democratic incumbent Martin Van Buren and his Whig challenger, "The Hero of Tippecanoe," took their electoral rivalry into the streets of cities like Philadelphia, launching modern-style popular politics. Harrison won, but a mere month after delivering the longest inaugural address ever (two hours), he succumbed to pneumonia and died. He served the shortest term of any president (thirty-one days). One of his forty-eight grandchildren, Benjamin Harrison, became the twenty-third president of the United States.

The Whig campaign was a masterpiece of hoopla. Log cabins were dished up in every conceivable form. Bawling Whigs, stimulated by fortified cider, rolled huge balls from village to village and state to state, representing the snowballing majority for "Tippecanoe and Tyler too." In truth, Harrison was not lowborn but from one of the FFV's ("First Families of Virginia"). He was not a poverty-stricken dweller in a one-room log cabin, but rather lived in a sixteen-room mansion on a three-thousand acre estate. He did not swill down gallons of hard cider (he evidently preferred whiskey). And he did not plow his fields with his own "huge paws." But such details had not mattered when General Jackson rode to victory, and they did not matter now.

The Democrats who hurrahed Jackson into the White House in 1828 now discovered to their chagrin that whooping it up for a backwoods Westerner was a game two could play. Harrison won by the surprisingly close margin of 1,275,016 popular votes to 1,129,102, but by an overwhelming electoral margin of 234 to 60. With hardly a real issue debated, though with hard times blighting the incumbent's fortunes, Van Buren was washed out of Washington in a wave of apple juice.

Interactive map
Settled Areas of the United States, 1820, and 1840
college.hmco.com/pic/kennedybrief7e

Although campaigners in 1840 did their best to bury substantive issues beneath the ballyhoo, voters actually faced a stark choice between economic visions of how to cope with the nation's first major depression. Whigs sought to expand and stimulate the economy, while Democrats favored retrenchment and an end to high-flying banks and aggressive corporations.

Politics for the People

populist *A political program or style focused on the common people, and attacking perspectives and policies associated with the well-off, well-born, or well-educated. (The Populist party was a specific third-party organization of the 1890s.)*

divine right *The belief that government or rulers are directly established by God.*

The election of 1840 conclusively demonstrated two major changes in American politics since the Era of Good Feelings. The first was the triumph of a **populist** democratic style. Democracy had been something of a taint in the days of the lordly Federalists. But by the 1840s, aristocracy was the taint, and democracy was respectable. Politicians were forced to unbend and curry favor with the voting masses. Lucky indeed was the aspiring office seeker who could boast of birth in a log cabin. The semiliterate frontiersman Davy Crockett of Tennessee had been elected to Congress mainly on the basis of his bear-hunting prowess. Hopelessly handicapped was the candidate who appeared too well dressed, too grammatical, too high-browishly intellectual. In truth, most high political offices continued to be filled by "leading citizens," but now these wealthy and prominent men had to forsake all social pretensions and cultivate the common touch if they hoped to win elections.

Snobbish bigwigs sneered at the "coonskin Congressmen" elected by newly enfranchised "bipeds of the forest." But these critics protested in vain. The common man was moving to the center of the national political stage: the sturdy American who donned plain trousers rather than breeches, who sported a plain haircut and a coonskin cap rather than a silk top hat. Instead of the old **divine right** of kings, America was now bowing to the divine right of the people.

The Two-Party System

President Andrew Jackson advised a supporter in 1835 on how to tell the difference between Democrats and "Whigs, nullies, and blue-light federalists." In doing so, he neatly summarized the Jacksonian philosophy:

"The people ought to inquire [of political candidates]—are you opposed to a national bank; are you in favor of a strict construction of the Federal and State Constitutions; are you in favor of rotation in office; do you subscribe to the republican rule that the people are the sovereign power, the officers their agents, and that upon all national or general subjects, as well as local, they have a right to instruct their agents and representatives, and they are bound to obey or resign; in short, are they true Republicans agreeable to the true Jeffersonian creed?"

The second dramatic change resulting from the 1840 election was the formation of a vigorous and durable two-party system. The Jeffersonians of an earlier day had been so successful in absorbing the programs of their Federalist opponents that a full-blown two-party system had never truly emerged in the subsequent Era of Good Feelings. The idea had prevailed that parties of any sort smacked of conspiracy and "faction" and were injurious to the health of the body politic in a virtuous republic. By 1840 political parties had fully come of age, a lasting legacy of Andrew Jackson's tenaciousness.

Both national parties, the Democrats and the Whigs, grew out of the rich soil of Jeffersonian republicanism, and each laid claim to different aspects of the republican inheritance. Jacksonian Democrats glorified the liberty of the individual and were fiercely on guard against the inroads of "privilege" into government. Whigs trumpeted the natural harmony of society and the value of community, and were willing to use government to realize their objectives. Whigs also berated those leaders—and they considered Jackson to be one—whose appeals to self-interest fostered conflict among individuals, classes, or sections.

Democrats clung to states' rights and federal restraint in social and economic affairs as their basic doctrines. Whigs tended to favor a renewed national bank; protective tariffs; internal improvements; public schools;

and, increasingly, moral reforms such as the prohibition of liquor and eventually the abolition of slavery.

The two parties were thus separated by real differences of philosophy and policy. But they also had much in common. Both were mass-based "catchall" parties that tried deliberately to mobilize as many voters as possible for their cause. Although it is true that Democrats tended to be more humble folk and Whigs more prosperous, both parties nevertheless commanded the loyalties of all kinds of Americans, from all social classes and in all sections. The social diversity of the two parties fostered horse-trading compromises *within* each party that prevented either from assuming extreme or radical positions. By the same token, the geographical diversity of the two parties retarded the emergence of purely sectional political parties—temporarily suppressing, through compromise, the ultimately uncompromisable issue of slavery. When the two-party system began to creak in the 1850s, the Union was mortally imperiled.

Chapter Summary

Beginning in the 1820s, a powerful movement celebrating the common person and promoting the "New Democracy" transformed the earlier elitist character of American politics. The controversial election of the Yankee sophisticate John Quincy Adams in 1824 angered the followers of Andrew Jackson, who had received more popular votes.

Jackson's sweeping presidential victory in 1828 represented the political triumph of the New Democracy, including the spoils-rich political machines that thrived in the new environment. Jackson's simple, popular ideas and rough-hewn style reinforced the patronage system's growing belief that any ordinary person could hold public office. The "Tariff of Abominations" and the nullification crisis with South Carolina revealed a growing sectionalism and anxiety about slavery that challenged Jackson's fierce nationalism.

Jackson vigorously wielded the powers of the presidency against his opponents, particularly Calhoun and Clay. He made the Bank of the United States a symbol of evil financial power and killed it after a bitter political fight. Destroying the bank reinforced Jacksonians' hostility to all forms of concentrated political or financial power in the hands of elites, but also left the United States without any effective financial system. In opposition to Jackson's aggressive assertion of power and his numerous controversial policies, a new Whig party emerged to compete with the Jacksonian Democrats.

Jackson's presidency also focused on issues of westward expansion. Pressured to adopt paths of "civilization," Native Americans of the Southeast engaged in extensive agricultural and educational development. But white settlers and state governments still encroached upon the Cherokees and other tribes, and Jackson ordered the forced removal of all southeastern Indians to Oklahoma along the "Trail of Tears."

Jackson's ill-considered economic policies came home to roost under the unlucky Martin Van Buren, his handpicked successor. As the country plunged into a serious depression following the panic of 1837, Van Buren continued futile Jacksonian policies by forcing the removal of all federal funds from private banks.

In Texas, American settlers successfully rebelled against Mexico and declared their independence. Jackson recognized the Texas Republic, but because of the slavery controversy, he refused its application for annexation to the United States.

The Whigs saw these economic and political troubles as a path to the White House. But rather than campaign on issues, they used the political hoopla of the new mass democratic process to turn a western aristocrat and military hero, William Henry Harrison, into a democratic symbol of the "log cabin and hard cider." The Whig victory signaled the emergence of a new two-party system, in which the two parties' genuine philosophical differences and somewhat different constituencies proved less important than their widespread popularity and shared roots in the new American democratic spirit.

VARYING VIEWPOINTS

What Was Jacksonian Democracy?

Aristocratic, eastern-born historians of the nineteenth century damned Jackson as a backwoods barbarian and Jacksonianism as democracy run riot. In the late nineteenth and early twentieth centuries, however, another generation of historians, many of them midwesterners, rejected the elitist views of their predecessors. Frederick Jackson Turner and his disciples saw the western frontier as the fount of democratic virtue, and they hailed Jackson as a true popular hero sprung from the forests of the West to protect the people against the moneyed interests.

When Arthur M. Schlesinger, Jr., published *The Age of Jackson* in 1945, however, the debate on Jacksonianism shifted dramatically. Schlesinger cast the Jacksonian era not as a sectional conflict but as a class conflict between poor farmers, laborers, and noncapitalists on the one hand and the business community on the other.

Soon after Schlesinger's book appeared, the discussion again shifted ground and entirely new interpretations of Jacksonianism emerged. Richard Hofstadter argued in *The American Political Tradition and the Men Who Made It* (1948) that Jacksonian democracy was not a rejection of capitalism, as Schlesinger insisted, but rather the effort of aspiring entrepreneurs to serve their own interests against their entrenched, monopolistic, eastern competitors. Lee Benson contended in *The Concept of Jacksonian Democracy* (1961) that the political conflicts of the Jacksonian era were rooted not in class or region but in religious and ethnic splits within American society that led to local conflicts over cultural issues.

In the 1980s Sean Wilentz and other scholars began to resurrect some of Schlesinger's arguments about the importance of class to Jacksonianism. In *Chants Democratic* (1984), Wilentz maintained that Jacksonian politics could not be understood without reference to the changing national economy. Artisans and small producers, Wilentz argued, believed that impersonal institutions and large-scale employers threatened the very existence of a republic founded on virtuous self-sufficiency. Jackson's attack on the Bank of the United States symbolized the antagonism these individuals felt toward the emerging capitalist economy.

The scholarly cycle came full circle in Charles Sellers's *The Market Revolution: Jacksonian America, 1815–1846* (1991). In many ways this ambitious synthesis offered an updated version of Schlesinger's argument about class conflict. American democracy and free-market capitalism, Sellers suggested, were not natural twins but rather adversaries, with Jacksonians inventing mass democracy in order to hold capitalist expansion in check. Like Schlesinger's thesis, Sellers's interpretation provoked a storm of controversy. Critics like William E. Gienapp charged that Sellers suffered from a hopelessly romantic view of preindustrial society, and that no political party could prevail by appealing exclusively to rich or poor. The complex connections between capitalism and American democracy reflected in the Jacksonian era remain a lively subject for historical research and analysis.

Forging the National Economy

1790–1860

THE PROGRESS OF INVENTION IS REALLY A THREAT [TO MONARCHY]. WHENEVER I SEE A RAILROAD I LOOK FOR A REPUBLIC.

RALPH WALDO EMERSON, 1866

Chapter Outline

- The Westward Movement
- Irish and German Immigrants
- Nativism and Assimilation
- The Coming of the Factory System
- Women and the Economy
- The Ripening of Commercial Agriculture
- The Transportation Revolution
- Overseas Trade and Communication
- Examining the Evidence: The Invention of the Sewing Machine
- Makers of America: The Irish
- Makers of America: The Germans

The new nation went bounding into the nineteenth century in a burst of movement. New England Yankees, Pennsylvania farmers, and southern yeomen all pushed west in search of cheap land and prodigious opportunity, soon to be joined by vast numbers of immigrants from Europe. But not only people were in motion. Newly invented machinery quickened the cultivating of crops and the manufacturing of goods, while workers found themselves laboring under new, more demanding expectations for their pace of work. Better roads, faster steamboats, farther-reaching canals, and tentacle-stretching railroads all helped move people, raw materials, and manufactured goods from coast to hinterland and Gulf to Great Lakes by the mid-nineteenth century. The momentum gave rise to a more dynamic, market-oriented economy.

Focus Questions

1. **How did the westward migration and German and Irish immigration alter the geographical distribution and composition of the American population in the early nineteenth century?**
2. **Why was America relatively slow to embrace urbanization, industrialization, and the factory system of production?**
3. **How did Eli Whitney's system of interchangeable parts and other inventions and innovations, especially in transportation and communications, lay the foundations for the first wave of American industrialization?**
4. **How did early industrialization affect workers and alter the role of women both inside and outside the home?**
5. **What were the large-scale effects of the emerging national American market economy, including its impact on regional and social class relationships?**

Westward Movement of the Center of Population, 1790–2000 The triangles indicate the points at which a map of the United States weighted for the population of the country in a given year would balance. Note the remarkable equilibrium of the north-south pull from 1790 to about 1940, and the strong spurt west and south thereafter. The 1980 census revealed that the nation's center of population had at last moved west of the Mississippi River. The map also shows the slowing of the westward movement between 1890 and 1940—the period of heaviest immigration from Europe, which ended up mainly in East Coast cities.

The Westward Movement

The rise of Andrew Jackson, the first president from beyond the Appalachian Mountains, exemplified the inexorable westward march of the American people. The West, with its raw frontier, was the most typically American part of the nation. As Ralph Waldo Emerson wrote in 1844, "Europe stretches to the Alleghenies; America lies beyond."

The Republic was young, and so were the people—as late as 1850, half of Americans were under the age of thirty. They were also restless and energetic, seemingly always on the move, and always westward. By 1840 the "demographic center" of the American population had crossed the Alleghenies. By the eve of the Civil War, it had marched beyond the Ohio River.

Legend portrays an army of muscular axmen triumphantly carving civilization out of the western woods. But in reality life was downright grim for most pioneer families. Poorly fed, ill-clad, housed in hastily erected shanties, they were perpetual victims of disease, depression, and premature death. Above all, unbearable loneliness haunted them, especially the women, who were often cut off from human contact, even their neighbors, for days or even weeks, while confined to the cramped orbit of a dark cabin erected in a secluded clearing. Breakdowns and even madness were all too frequently the "opportunities" that the frontier offered to pioneer women.

A Pioneer Homestead in Wisconsin, c. 1847 This frontier family felled trees both to build a crude cabin and to provide fuel for cooking. After the remaining stumps were burned, the cleared fields were ready for planting. Cooking outdoors (weather permitting) spared the rough shelter from smoke and odors.

Chronology

c. 1750	Industrial Revolution begins in Britain.
1791	Samuel Slater builds first U.S. textile factory.
1793	Eli Whitney invents the cotton gin.
1798	Whitney develops interchangeable parts for muskets.
1807	Robert Fulton's first steamboat. Embargo spurs American manufacturing.
1811	Cumberland Road construction begins.
1817	Erie Canal construction begins.
1825	Erie Canal completed.
1828	First railroad in United States.
1830s	Cyrus McCormick invents mechanical mower-reaper.
1834	Anti-Catholic riot in Boston.
1837	John Deere develops steel plow.
1840	President Van Buren establishes ten-hour day for federal employees.
1842	Massachusetts declares labor unions legal in *Commonwealth* v. *Hunt.*
1844	Samuel Morse invents telegraph. Anti-Catholic riot in Philadelphia.
1845–1849	Potato famine in Ireland.
1846	Elias Howe invents sewing machine.
1848	First general incorporation laws in New York. Democratic revolutions collapse in Germany.
1849	American (or Know-Nothing party) formed.
1852	Cumberland Road completed.
1858	Cyrus Field lays first transatlantic cable.
1860	Pony Express established.
1861	First transcontinental telegraph.
1866	Permanent transatlantic cable established.

Frontier life could be tough and crude for men as well. No-holds-barred wrestling, which permitted such niceties as the biting off of noses and the gouging out of eyes, was a popular entertainment. Pioneering Americans, marooned by geography, were often ill-informed, superstitious, provincial, and fiercely individualistic. Emerson's popular lecture-essay "Self-Reliance" struck a deeply responsive chord. Popular literature of the period abounded with portraits of heroically unique, isolated figures such as James Fenimore Cooper's courageous Natty Bumppo and Herman Melville's restless Captain Ahab—just as Jacksonian politics aimed to emancipate the lone-wolf, enterprising businessperson. Yet even in this heyday of "rugged individualism," there were important exceptions. Pioneers, in tasks clearly beyond their own individual resources, would call upon neighbors for logrolling and barn raising and upon their governments for help in building internal improvements.

Shaping the Western Landscape

The westward movement also molded the physical environment. Pioneers in a hurry often exhausted the land and then pushed on, leaving behind barren and rain-gutted fields. In the Kentucky bottomlands, settlers discovered that they could burn off the native cane and plant "Kentucky bluegrass," which made ideal pasture for livestock.

The American West felt the pressure of civilization in additional ways. By the 1820s American fur trappers were setting their trap lines all over the vast Rocky Mountain region. Each summer, trappers came down from the mountains and swapped their beaver pelts for manufactured goods from the East. This trade thrived for some two decades, until the hapless beavers had all but disappeared from the region. Trade in buffalo robes also flourished. On the California coast, other traders pursued sea-otter pelts, driving the once-bountiful otters nearly to extinction. Some historians have called this aggressive and often heedless exploitation of the West's natural bounty "ecological imperialism."

Yet Americans in this period also revered nature and admired its beauty. Indeed the spirit of nationalism fed a growing belief in the uniqueness of the American wilderness. Searching for the United States' distinctive characteristics in this nation-conscious age, many observers found the wild, unspoiled land of the West to be among the young nation's defining attributes. Devotion to the pristine natural beauty of the American wilderness became in time a national mystique, inspiring literature and painting and eventually kindling a powerful conservation movement.

George Catlin, a painter and student of Native American life, was among the first Americans to advocate the preservation of nature as a deliberate national policy. Appalled at the reckless slaughter of Indians and buffalo alike, Catlin proposed the creation of a national park to preserve nature and wildlife. His idea later bore fruit with the creation of a national park system, beginning with Yellowstone Park in 1872.

The March of the Millions

Online Study Center
Primary source
Continental Expansion
college.hmco.com/pic/kennedybrief7e

As the American people moved west, they also multiplied at an amazing rate. By midcentury the population was still doubling approximately every twenty-five years, as in fertile colonial days. By 1860 the original thirteen states had more than doubled in number: thirty-three stars graced the American flag. The United States was the fourth most populous nation in the western world, exceeded only by three European countries—Russia, France, and Austria.

Urban growth continued explosively. In 1790 only two American cities could boast populations of twenty thousand or more: Philadelphia and New York. By 1860 there were forty-three, and about three hundred other places claimed over five thousand inhabitants apiece. New York was the metropolis; New Orleans, the "Queen of the South"; and Chicago, the swaggering lord of the Midwest, destined to be "hog butcher for the world."

Such overrapid urbanization unfortunately brought undesirable by-products. It intensified the problems of smelly slums, feeble street lighting, impure water, foul sewage, ravenous rats, and improper garbage disposal. Hogs poked their scavenging snouts about many city streets as late as the 1840s. Boston in 1823 pioneered with a sewage system, and New York in 1842 abandoned wells and cisterns for a piped-in water supply. The city thus unknowingly eliminated many of the breeding places of disease-carrying mosquitoes.

A continuing high birthrate accounted for most of the increase in population, but by the 1840s the tides of immigration were adding hundreds of thousands more. Before this decade, immigrants had been flowing in at the rate of about sixty thousand a year, but suddenly the influx tripled in the 1840s and then quadrupled in the 1850s. During these two feverish decades, over a million and a half Irish, and nearly as many Germans, swarmed down the gangplanks. Why did they come?

Irish and German Immigration by Decade, 1830–1900

Years	Irish	Germans
1831–1840	207,381	152,454
1841–1850	780,719	434,626
1851–1860	914,119	951,667
1861–1870	435,778	787,468
1871–1880	436,871	718,182
1881–1890	655,482	1,452,970
1891–1900	388,416	505,152
TOTAL	3,818,766	5,000,519

The immigrants came partly because Europe seemed to be running out of room. The population of the Old World more than doubled in the nineteenth century, and Europe began to generate a seething pool of apparently "surplus" people. They were displaced and footloose in their homelands before they felt the tug of the American magnet. Indeed, at least as many people moved about *within* Europe as crossed the Atlantic.

Yet America still beckoned most strongly to the struggling masses of Europe. About 35 million of the nearly 60 million emigrants who abandoned Europe in the century after 1840 headed for "the land of freedom and opportunity," where no aristocratic **caste** or state church oppressed the individual. Much-read letters sent home by immigrants—"America letters"—often described in glowing terms the richer life: low taxes, no compulsory military service, and "three meat meals a day." The introduction of transoceanic steamships also meant that the immigrants could come speedily, in a matter of ten or twelve days instead of ten or twelve weeks. On board, they were still jammed into unsanitary quarters, thus suffering an appalling death rate from infectious diseases, but the nightmare was more endurable because it was shorter.

caste *An exclusive or rigid social distinction based on birth, wealth, occupation, and so forth.*

The Emerald Isle Moves West

Ireland, already groaning under the heavy hand of British overlords, was prostrated in the mid-1840s. A terrible rot attacked the potato crop, on which the people had become dangerously dependent, and about one-fourth of them were swept away by disease and hunger. Dead bodies were found by the roadsides with grass in their mouths. All told, about 2 million perished.

Tens of thousands of destitute souls, fleeing the Land of Famine for the Land of Plenty, flocked to America in the "Black Forties." Ireland's great export has been population, and the Irish take their place beside the Africans and the Jews as a dispersed people (see "Makers of America: The Irish," pp. 202–203). These uprooted newcomers swarmed into the larger seaboard cities, such as Boston and New York, which rapidly became the largest Irish city in the world. Before many decades, more people of Irish descent lived in America than on the "ould sod" of Erin's isle.

The luckless Irish immigrants received no red-carpet treatment. They were scorned by the older American stock, especially "proper" Protestant Bostonians, who regarded the scruffy Catholic arrivals as a social menace. Barely literate "Biddies" (Bridgets) took jobs as kitchen maids. Broad-shouldered "Paddies" (Patricks) were pushed into pick-and-shovel drudgery on canals and railroads, where thousands left their bones as victims of disease and accidental explosions. It was said that an Irishman lay buried under every railroad tie. As wage-depressing competitors for jobs, the Irish were hated by native workers. "No Irish Need Apply" was a sign commonly posted at factory gates. The Irish, for similar reasons, fiercely resented the blacks, with whom they shared society's basement. Race riots between black and Irish dockworkers flared up in several port cities, and the Irish were generally cool to the abolitionist cause.

The friendless "famine Irish" were forced to fend for themselves. The Ancient Order of Hibernians, a semisecret society founded in Ireland to fight rapacious landlords, served in America as a benevolent society, aiding the downtrodden. It also helped to spawn the "Molly Maguires," a shadowy Irish miners' union that rocked the Pennsylvania coal districts in the 1860s and 1870s.

The Irish tended to remain in low-skill occupations but gradually improved their lot, usually by acquiring modest amounts of property. The education of children was cut short as families struggled to save money to

Margaret McCarthy, a recent arrival in America, captured much of the complexity of the immigrant experience in a letter she wrote from New York to her family in Ireland in 1850:

"This is a good place and a good country, but there is one thing that's ruining this place. The emigrants have not money enough to take them to the interior of the country, which obliges them to remain here in New York and the like places, which causes the less demand for labor and also the great reduction in wages. For this reason I would advise no one to come to America that would not have some money after landing here that would enable them to go west in case they would get no work to do here."

The Irish

During the wars that ravaged Europe from 1793 to 1815, Irish tenant farmers temporarily prospered by planting every available acre with wheat and potatoes to feed ravenous armies. But when peace came, wheat prices plummeted, and hard-pressed landlords, aided by British police, forced their tenants off the unprofitable land. Many displaced Irish farmers sought work in England; some went to America. Then in 1845 a blight that ravaged the potato crop sounded the final knell for the Irish peasantry. The resultant famine spread desolation throughout the island. In five years, more than a million people died. Another million sailed for America.

Most of the emigrants were under thirty-five years old. Families typically pooled money to send strong young sons to the New World, where they would earn wages to pay the fares for those who waited at home. These "famine Irish" mostly remained in the port cities of the Northeast, abandoning the farmer's life for the dingy congestion of the urban metropolis.

The disembarking Irish were poorly prepared for urban life. They found progress up the economic ladder painfully slow. Their work as domestic servants or construction laborers was dull and arduous, and mortality rates were astoundingly high. Escape from the potato famine hardly guaranteed a long life to an Irish-American; a gray-bearded Irishman was a rare sight in nineteenth-century America. For Irish-born women, opportunities were even scarcer; they worked mainly as domestic servants.

But it was their Roman Catholicism, even more than their penury or their perceived fondness for alcohol, that earned the Irish the distrust and resentment of their native-born Protestant American neighbors. The cornerstone of social and religious life for Irish immigrants was the Catholic parish. Worries about safeguarding their children's faith inspired the construction of parish schools, financed by the pennies of struggling working-class Irish parents.

If Ireland's green fields scarcely equipped her sons and daughters for the scrap and scramble of economic life in America's cities, life in the Old Country had instilled in them an aptitude for politics. Irish Catholic resistance against centuries of English-Anglican domination had instructed many Old Country Irish in the ways

■ **Outward Bound, The Quay at Dublin, 1854**
Thousands fled famine in Ireland by coming to America in the 1840s and 1850s.
Collection of the New York Historical Society, neg. 41082.

of mass politics. That political experience readied them for the boss system of the political "machines" in America's northeastern cities. Irish voters soon became a bulwark of the Democratic party, reliably supporting the party of Jefferson and Jackson in cities like New York and Boston. As Irish-Americans like New York's "Honest John" Kelly themselves became bosses, white-collar jobs in government service opened up to the Irish. They became building inspectors, aldermen, and even policemen—an astonishing irony for a people driven from their homeland by the nightsticks and bayonets of the British police.

purchase a home. But for humble Irish peasants, cruelly cast out of their homeland, property ownership counted as a grand "success."

Politics quickly attracted these gregarious Gaelic newcomers. They soon began to gain control of powerful city machines, notably New York's Tammany Hall, and reaped the patronage rewards. Before long, brogued Irishmen dominated police departments in many big cities, where they drove the "Paddy wagons" that had once carted their forebears to jail.

The German Forty-Eighters

The influx of refugees from Germany between 1830 and 1860 was hardly less spectacular than that from Ireland. During these troubled years, over a million and a half Germans stepped onto American soil (see "Makers of America: The Germans," p. 206). Most were uprooted farmers, displaced by crop failures and by other hardships, but a strong sprinkling were liberal political refugees. Saddened by the collapse of the democratic revolutions of 1848, they had decided to leave the autocratic fatherland and flee to America—the brightest hope of democracy. Germany's loss was America's gain. Zealous German liberals like the public-spirited and antislavery Carl Schurz contributed richly to the elevation of American political life.

Unlike the Irish, many of the German newcomers possessed a modest amount of material goods. Most of them pushed out to the lush lands of the Midwest, notably Wisconsin, where they settled and established model farms.

The hand of Germans in shaping American life was widely felt in other ways. Like the Irish, they formed an influential body of voters. Having fled German militarism and European wars, they came to be a bulwark of isolationist sentiment in the upper Mississippi Valley. Better educated on the whole than the stump-grubbing Americans, they warmly supported public schools, including their *Kindergarten* ("children's garden"). They likewise did much to stimulate art and music. As outspoken champions of freedom, they became relentless enemies of slavery during the fevered years before the Civil War.

Yet the Germans—often dubbed "damned Dutchmen"—were occasionally regarded with suspicion by their old-stock American neighbors. Seeking to preserve their language and culture, they sometimes settled in compact "colonies" and kept aloof from the surrounding community. Accustomed to the "Continental Sunday" and uncurbed by Puritan tradition, they made merry on the Sabbath and drank huge quantities of their favorite amber beverage, *Bier* (beer). Their Old World drinking habits, like those of the Irish newcomers, spurred advocates of temperance in the use of alcohol to redouble their reform efforts.

Flare-ups of Antiforeignism

The invasion by this so-called immigrant "rabble" in the 1840s and 1850s inflamed the prejudices of American "**nativists.**" Not only did the newcomers take jobs from "native" Americans, but most of the displaced Irishmen were Roman Catholics, as were a substantial minority of the Germans. The Church of Rome was still widely regarded by many old-line Americans as a "foreign" and "popish" church.

nativist(s) *One who advocates favoring native-(born) citizens over aliens or immigrants.*

Strong antiforeignism was reflected in the platform of the American (Know-Nothing) party in 1856:

"Americans must rule America; and to this end, native-born citizens should be selected for all state, federal, or municipal offices of government employment, in preference to naturalized citizens."

Roman Catholics were now on the move. Seeking to protect their children from Protestant indoctrination in the public schools, they began in the 1840s to construct an entirely separate Catholic educational system—an enormously expensive undertaking for a poor immigrant community, but one that revealed the strength of its religious commitment. A negligible minority during colonial days, Catholics became a powerful religious group with the enormous influx of the Irish and Germans in the 1840s and 1850s. In 1840 they had ranked fifth, behind the Baptists, Methodists, Presbyterians, and Congregationalists. By 1850, with some 1.8 million communicants, they had bounded into first place—a position they have never lost.

Older-stock Americans were alarmed by these mounting figures. They professed to believe that in due time the "alien riffraff" would "establish" the Catholic Church at the expense of Protestantism and introduce "popish idols." The noisier American "nativists" rallied for political action. In 1849 they formed the Order of the Star-Spangled Banner, which soon developed into the formidable American, or "Know-Nothing" party—a name derived from its secretiveness. "Nativists" agitated for rigid restrictions on immigration and naturalization, and for laws authorizing the deportation of alien paupers. They also promoted a lurid literature of exposure, most of it pure fiction. The authors, sometimes posing as "escaped nuns," described shocking sins they imagined the cloisters concealed, including the secret burial of babies. One of these sensational books—Maria Monk's *Awful Disclosures* (1836)—sold over 300,000 copies.

Even uglier was occasional mass violence. As early as 1834 a Catholic convent near Boston was burned by a howling mob, and in ensuing years a few scattered attacks fell upon Catholic schools and churches. The most frightful flare-up occurred during 1844 in Philadelphia, where the Irish Catholics fought back against the threats of the "nativists." The City of Brotherly Love did not quiet down until two Catholic churches had been burned and some thirteen citizens had been killed and fifty wounded in several days of fighting. These outbursts of intolerance, though infrequent and generally localized, remain an unfortunate blot on the record of America's treatment of minority groups.

Crooked Voting A bitter "nativist" cartoon charging Irish and German immigrants with "stealing" elections.

Immigrants were undeniably making America a more pluralistic society—one of the most ethnically and racially varied in the history of the world. Why, in fact, were such episodes of intolerance not even more frequent and more violent? Part of the answer lies in the robust American economy. The vigorous growth of the economy in these years ensured that immigrants could claim their share of American wealth without jeopardizing the wealth of others. Their hands and brains, in fact, helped fuel economic expansion. Immigrants and the American economy, in short, needed one another. Without the newcomers, a preponderantly agricultural United States might have been condemned to watch in envy as the Industrial Revolution swept through nineteenth-century Europe.

Interactive map
Origin and Settlement of Immigrants, 1820–1850
college.hmco.com/pic/kennedybrief7e

The March of Mechanization

A group of gifted British inventors, beginning about 1750, perfected a series of machines for the mass production of textiles. This enslavement of steam multiplied the power of human muscles some ten-thousandfold and ushered in the modern **factory** system—and with it the so-called Industrial Revolution.

factory *An establishment for the mass manufacturing of goods, including buildings and substantial machinery.*

trademark *A distinguishing symbol or word used by a manufacturer on its goods, usually registered by law to protect against imitators.*

capitalist *An individual or group who uses accumulated funds or private property to produce goods for profit in a market.*

The factory system gradually spread from Britain to other lands. It took a generation or so to reach Western Europe, and then the United States. Why was the youthful American Republic, eventually to become an industrial giant, so slow to embrace the machine?

For one thing, land was cheap in America. Land-starved descendants of land-starved peasants were not going to coop themselves up in smelly factories when they might till their own acres in God's fresh air and sunlight. Labor was therefore generally scarce, and enough nimble hands to operate the machines were hard to find—until immigrants began to pour ashore in the 1840s. Money for capital investment, moreover, was not plentiful in pioneering America. Raw materials lay undeveloped, undiscovered, or unsuspected.

If labor was scarce, consumers were not. But the young country had difficulty producing goods of high enough quality and cheap enough to compete with European products. Long-established British factories, in particular, provided cut-throat competition. Their superiority was attested by the fact that a few unscrupulous Yankee manufacturers, out to make a dishonest dollar, stamped their own products with faked English **trademarks.**

The British also enjoyed a monopoly of the textile machinery, whose secrets they were anxious to hide from foreign competitors. Parliament enacted laws forbidding the export of the machines or the emigration of mechanics able to reproduce them.

Although a number of small manufacturing enterprises existed in the early Republic, the future industrial colossus was still snoring. Not until well past the middle of the nineteenth century did the value of the output of factories exceed that of farms.

Whitney Ends the Fiber Famine

Samuel Slater has been acclaimed the "Father of the Factory System" in America, and seldom can the paternity of a movement more properly be ascribed to one person. A skilled British mechanic of twenty-one, he was attracted by bounties being offered to British workers familiar with the textile machines. After memorizing the plans for the machinery, he escaped in disguise to America, where he won the backing of Moses Brown, a Quaker **capitalist** in Rhode Island. Laboriously reconstructing the essential apparatus with the aid of a blacksmith and a carpenter, he put into operation in 1791 the first efficient American machinery for spinning cotton thread.

The ravenous mechanism was now ready, but where was the cotton fiber? Handpicking one pound of lint from three pounds of seed was a full day's work for one slave, and this process was so expensive that American-made cotton cloth was relatively rare.

Another mechanical genius, Massachusetts-born Eli Whitney, now made his mark. After graduating from Yale, he journeyed to Georgia to serve as a private

The Germans

Between 1820 and 1920, a sea of Germans lapped at America's shores and seeped into its very heartland. Their numbers surpassed those of any other immigrant group, even the prolific and often detested Irish. Yet this Germanic flood, unlike its Gaelic equivalent, stirred little panic in the hearts of native-born Americans because the Germans largely stayed to themselves, far from the madding crowds and nativist fears of northeastern cities.

These "Germans" actually hailed from many different lands, because there was no unified nation of Germany until 1871, when the ruthless and crafty Prussian Otto von Bismarck assembled the German state out of a mosaic of independent principalities, kingdoms, and duchies. Until that time, "Germans" came to America as Prussians, Bavarians, Hessians, Rhinelanders, Pomeranians, and Westphalians. They arrived at different times and for many different reasons. Some, particularly the so-called Forty-Eighters—refugees from the abortive democratic revolution of 1848—hungered for the democracy they had failed to win in Germany. Others, particularly Jews, Pietists, and Anabaptist groups like the Amish and the Mennonites, coveted religious freedom.

Typical German immigrants arrived with fatter purses than their Irish counterparts. Small landowners or independent artisans in their native countries, they did not have to settle for bottom-rung industrial employment in the grimy factories of the Northeast and instead could afford to push on to the open spaces of the West.

In Wisconsin these immigrants found a home away from home, a place with a climate, soil, and geography much like central Europe's. Milwaukee, a crude frontier town before their arrival, became the "German Athens." It boasted a German theater, German beer gardens, a German volunteer fire company, and a German-English academy. In distant Texas, German settlements like New Braunfels and Friedrichsburg flourished. These German colonies in the frontier Southwest mixed high European elegance with Texas ruggedness. When landscape architect and writer Frederick Law Olmsted toured these frontier outposts, he came across a German household where the settlers sat on "barrels for seats, to hear a Beethoven symphony on the grand piano."

These German colonizers of America's heartland also formed religious communities, none more distinctive or durable than the Amish settlements of Pennsylvania, Indiana, and Ohio. The Amish took their name from their founder and leader, the Swiss Anabaptist Jacob Amman. Like other Anabaptist groups, they shunned extravagance and reserved baptism for adults, repudiating the tradition of infant baptism. For this they were persecuted, even imprisoned, in Europe. Seeking escape from their oppression, some five hundred Amish ventured to Pennsylvania in the 1700s, followed by three thousand in the years from 1815 to 1865.

In America they formed enduring religious communities—isolated enclaves where they could shield themselves from the corruption and the conveniences of the modern world. To this day the German-speaking Amish travel in horse-drawn carriages and farm without heavy machinery. No ringing telephones punctuate the reverent tranquility of their mealtime prayer; no ornaments relieve the simplicity of their black garments. The Amish remain a stalwart, traditional religious community in a rootless, turbulent society.

"Little Germany" Cincinnati's "Over-the-Rhine" district in 1887.

tutor while preparing for the law. There he was told that the poverty of the South would be relieved if someone could only invent a workable device for separating the seed from the short-staple cotton fiber. Within ten days, in 1793, he built a crude machine called the cotton gin (short for engine), which was fifty times more effective than the handpicking process.

Few machines have ever wrought so wondrous a change. Almost overnight the raising of cotton became highly profitable, and the South was tied hand and foot to the throne of King Cotton. Human bondage had been dying out, but the insatiable demand for cotton reriveted the chains on the limbs of the downtrodden southern blacks.

South and North both prospered. Slave-driving planters cleared more acres for cotton, pushing the Cotton Kingdom westward off the depleted tidewater plains, over the Piedmont, and onto the black loam bottomlands of Alabama and Mississippi. Humming gins poured out avalanches of snowy fiber for the spindles of the Yankee machines. The American phase of the Industrial Revolution, which first blossomed in cotton textiles, was well on its way.

Factories at first flourished most actively in New England. Its stony soil made farming difficult and manufacturing attractive, and the rapid rivers provided abundant water power to turn the cogs of the machines. By 1860 more than 400 million pounds of southern cotton poured annually into the gaping maws of over a thousand mills. Factories eventually branched out into the populous areas of New York, New Jersey, and Pennsylvania. But the South, increasingly wedded to the production of cotton, developed little manufacturing because most of its capital was bound up in slaves.

Marvels in Manufacturing

America's factories spread slowly until about 1807, when there began the fateful sequence of the embargo, non-intercourse, and the War of 1812. The stoppage of European commerce drove both capital and labor from the waves onto the factory floor. Generous bounties were offered by local authorities for homegrown goods. "Buy American" and "Wear American" became popular slogans, and patriotism prompted the wearing of baggy homespun garments. President Madison donned some at his inauguration, where he was said to have been a walking argument for the better processing of native wool.

But the manufacturing boomlet broke abruptly with the peace of Ghent in 1815, as British competitors unloaded their dammed-up surpluses at ruinously low prices. Responding to pained outcries, Congress provided some relief when it passed the mildly protective Tariff of 1816—among the earliest political contests to control the shape of the economy.

As the factory system flourished, it embraced numerous other industries in addition to textiles. Prominent among them was the manufacturing of firearms, and here the wizardly Eli Whitney again appeared with an extraordinary contribution. Frustrated in his earlier efforts to monopolize the cotton gin, he turned to the mass production of muskets for the U.S. Army. Up to this time each part of a firearm had been hand-tooled, and if the trigger of one broke, the trigger of another might or might not fit. About 1798 Whitney seized upon the idea of having machines make each part, so that all the triggers, for example, would be as much alike as the successive imprints of a copperplate engraving. Journeying to Washington, he reportedly dismantled ten of his new muskets in the presence of skeptical officials, scrambled the parts together, and then quickly reassembled ten different muskets.

The principle of interchangeable parts was widely adopted by 1850, and it ultimately became the basis of modern mass-production, assembly-line methods. Ironically, the Yankee Eli Whitney, by perfecting the cotton gin, gave slavery a renewed lease on life, and thus perhaps made inevitable the Civil War. At the same time, by popularizing the principle of interchangeable parts, Whitney helped factories to flourish in the North, giving the Union a decided advantage when that showdown came.

The sewing machine, invented by Elias Howe in 1846 and perfected by Isaac Singer, gave another strong boost to industrialization. The sewing machine

Primary source
Fetridge & Co.'s Periodical Arcade
college.hmco.com/pic/kennedybrief7e

patents *The legal certification of an original invention, product, or process, guaranteeing its holder sole rights to profits from its use or reproduction for a specified period of time.*

liability *Legal responsibility for loss or damage.*

incorporation *The formation of individuals into an organized entity with legally defined privileges and responsibilities.*

labor union *An organization of workers—usually wage-earning workers—to promote the interests and welfare of its members, often by collective bargaining with employers.*

strike *An organized work stoppage by employees in order to obtain better wages, working conditions, and so on.*

became the foundation of the ready-made clothing industry, which took root about the time of the Civil War. It drove many a seamstress from the shelter of the private home to the factory where, like a human robot, she tended the clattering mechanisms.

Each momentous new invention seemed to stimulate still more imaginative inventions. For the decade ending in 1800 only 306 **patents** were registered in Washington; but the decade ending in 1860 saw the amazing total of 28,000. Yet in 1838 the clerk of the Patent Office resigned in despair, complaining that all worthwhile inventions had been discovered.

Technical advances spurred equally important changes in the form and legal status of business organizations. The principle of limited **liability** aided the concentration of capital by permitting the individual investor, in cases of legal claims or bankruptcy, to risk no more than his or her own share of the corporation's stock. Laws of "free **incorporation**," first passed in New York in 1848, meant that businessmen could create corporations without applying for individual charters from the legislature.

Samuel F. B. Morse's telegraph was among the inventions that tightened the sinews of an increasingly complex business world. A distinguished but poverty-stricken portrait painter, Morse finally secured from Congress, to the accompaniment of the usual jeers, an appropriation of $30,000 to support his experiment with "talking wires." In 1844 Morse strung a wire forty miles from Washington to Baltimore and tapped out the historic message, "What hath God wrought?" The invention brought fame and fortune to Morse, as he put distant people into almost instant communication with one another. By the eve of the Civil War, a web of singing wires spanned the continent, revolutionizing news gathering, diplomacy, and finance.

Workers and "Wage Slaves"

One ugly outgrowth of the factory system was an increasingly acute labor problem. Hitherto manufacturing had been done in the home, or in the small shop, where the master craftsman and his apprentice, rubbing elbows at the same bench, could maintain an intimate and friendly relationship. The Industrial Revolution submerged this personal association in the impersonal ownership of stuffy factories in "spindle cities." Around these, like tumors, the slumlike hovels of the "wage slaves" tended to cluster.

Primary source
Robert Owen's Alternative to Industrial Degradation
college.hmco.com/pic/kennedybrief7e

Clearly the early factory system did not shower its benefits evenly on all. While many owners grew plump, working people often wasted away at their workbenches. Hours were long, wages were low, and meals were skimpy and hastily gulped. Workers were forced to toil in unsanitary buildings that were poorly ventilated, lighted, and heated. They were forbidden by law to form **labor unions** to raise wages, for such cooperative activity was regarded as a criminal conspiracy. Not surprisingly, only twenty-four recorded **strikes** occurred before 1835.

Especially vulnerable to exploitation were child workers. In 1820 half the nation's industrial toilers were children under ten years of age. Victims of factory labor, many children were mentally blighted, emotionally starved, physically stunted, and even brutally whipped in special "whipping rooms." In Samuel Slater's mill of 1791, the first machine tenders were seven boys and two girls, all under twelve years of age.

By contrast, the lot of most adult wage workers improved markedly in the 1820s and 1830s. In the full flush of Jacksonian democracy, many of the states granted the laboring man the vote. Brandishing the ballot and strongly backing Andrew Jackson, workers pushed for the ten-hour workday, better wages and working conditions, public education for their children, and an end to the inhuman practice of imprisonment for debt.

Employers, abhorring the rise of the "rabble" in politics, fought the ten-hour day to the last ditch. But labor registered a red-letter gain in 1840 when President Van Buren established the ten-hour day for federal employees on public works. In ensuing years a number of states gradually fell into line by reducing the hours of working people.

Day laborers at last learned that their strongest weapon was to lay down their tools, even at the risk of prosecution under the law. Dozens of strikes erupted in the 1830s and 1840s, most of them for higher wages, some for the ten-hour day. The workers usually lost more strikes than they won, for the employer could resort to such tactics as importing strikebreakers—often derisively called "scabs" or "rats," and often fresh off the boat from the Old World. Labor long raised its voice against the unrestricted inpouring of wage-depressing and union-busting immigrant workers.

> *A woman worker in the Lowell mills wrote a friend in 1844:*
>
> "You wish to know minutely of our hours of labor. We go in [to the mill] at five o'clock; at seven we come out to breakfast; at half-past seven we return to our work, and stay until half-past twelve. At one, or quarter-past one four months in the year, we return to our work, and stay until seven at night. Then the evening is all our own, which is more than some laboring girls can say, who think nothing is more tedious than a factory life."

Labor's early and painful efforts at organization had netted some 300,000 trade unionists by 1830. But such encouraging gains were dashed on the rock of hard times following the severe depression of 1837. Yet toilers won a promising legal victory in 1842 when the Massachusetts Supreme Court ruled in *Commonwealth* v. *Hunt* that labor unions were not illegal conspiracies, provided that their methods were "honorable and peaceful." This enlightened decision did not legalize the strike overnight throughout the country, but it was a significant signpost of the times. Trade unions still had nearly a century to go before they could meet management on relatively even terms.

Women and the Economy

Women were also sucked into the clanging mechanism of factory production. Farm women and daughters had an important place in the pre-industrial economy, spinning yarn, weaving cloth, and making candles, soap, butter, and cheese. New factories undermined these activities, cranking out manufactured goods faster than they could be made by hand at home. Yet these same factories offered employment to the very young women whose work they were displacing. Factory jobs promised greater economic independence for women, as well as the means to buy the manufactured products of the new market economy.

"Factory girls" typically toiled six days a week, earning a pittance for dreary, ear-splitting stints of twelve or thirteen hours—"from dark to dark." The Boston Associates' textile mills at Lowell, Massachusetts, employed New England farm girls, carefully supervised on and off the job by watchful matrons who escorted them to church from their company boardinghouses.

But factory jobs of any kind were still unusual for women. Opportunities for women to be economically self-supporting were scarce and consisted mainly of nursing, domestic service, and especially teaching. The dedicated Catharine Beecher, daughter of a famous preacher and sister of Harriet Beecher Stowe, tirelessly urged women to enter the teaching profession. She eventually succeeded beyond her dreams, as men left teaching for other lines of work and school teaching became a thoroughly "feminized" occupation. By 1850 about 10 percent of white women were working for pay outside their own homes, and about 20 percent of all women had been employed at some time prior to marriage.

The vast majority of working women were single. Upon marriage, they left their paying jobs and took up their new work (without wages) as wives and mothers. In the home they were enshrined in a "cult of domesticity," a widespread cultural creed that glorified the traditional functions of the homemaker. From their pedestals, married women commanded immense moral power, and they increasingly made decisions that altered the character of the family itself.

Women's changing roles and the spreading Industrial Revolution brought some important changes in the life of the nineteenth-century home—the traditional "women's sphere." Love, not parental "arrangement," more and more frequently determined the choice of a spouse—yet parents often retained the power

Primary source
Weighing and Printing
college.hmco.com/pic/kennedybrief7e

of veto. Families thus became more closely knit and affectionate, providing the emotional refuge that made the threatening impersonality of big-city industrialism tolerable to many people.

Most striking, families grew smaller. The average household had nearly six members at the end of the eighteenth century but fewer than five members a century later. The "fertility rate," or number of births among women age fourteen to forty-five, dropped sharply among white women in the years after the Revolution and, in the course of the nineteenth century as a whole, fell by half. Birth control was still a taboo topic for polite conversation, and contraceptive technology was primitive, but clearly some form of family limitation was being practiced quietly and effectively in countless families, rural and urban alike. Women undoubtedly played a large part—perhaps the leading part—in decisions to have fewer children. This newly assertive role for women has been called "domestic feminism" because it signified the growing power and independence of women, even while they remained trapped in the "cult of domesticity."

Smaller families, in turn, meant child-centered families, since where children are fewer, parents can lavish more care on them individually. European visitors to the United States in the nineteenth century often complained about the unruly behavior of American "brats." But though American parents may have increasingly spared the rod, they did not spoil their children. What Europeans saw as permissiveness was in reality the consequence of an emerging new idea of child-rearing, in which the child's will was not to be simply broken, but shaped.

In the little republic of the family, as in the Republic at large, good citizens were raised not to be meekly obedient to authority, but to be independent individuals who could make their own decisions on the basis of internalized moral standards. Thus the outlines of the "modern" family were clear by midcentury: it was small, affectionate, and child-centered, and it provided a special arena for the talents of women. Feminists of a later day might decry the stifling atmosphere of the nineteenth-century home, but to many women of the time it seemed a big step upward from the conditions of grinding toil—often alongside men in the fields—in which their mothers had lived.

■ **The Sewing Floor of Thompson's Skirt Factory, 1859** The burgeoning textile industry provided employment for thousands of women in antebellum America—and also produced the clothes that women wore. This view of a New York City shop in 1859 illustrates the transition from hand-sewing (on the right) to machine-stitching (on the left). It also vividly illustrates the contrast between the kinds of "sewing circles" in which women had traditionally sought companionship to the impersonal mass-production line of the modern manufacturing plant. Note especially the stark exhortation on the wall: "Strive to Excel."

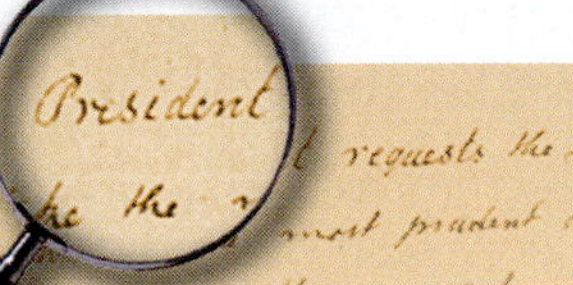

EXAMINING THE EVIDENCE

The Invention of the Sewing Machine Historians of technology examine not only the documentary evidence of plans and patents left behind by inventors, but surviving machines themselves. In 1845 Elias Howe, a twenty-six-year-old apprentice to a Boston watchmaker, invented a sewing machine that could make 250 stitches a minute, five times what the swiftest hand-sewer could do. A year later Howe received a patent for his invention, but because the hand-cranked machine could only stitch straight seams for a short distance before requiring resetting, it had limited commercial appeal. Howe took his sewing machine abroad, where he worked with British manufacturers to improve it, and then returned to America and combined his patent with those of other inventors, including Isaac M. Singer. Hundreds of thousands of sewing machines were produced beginning in the 1850s for commercial manufacturing of clothing, books, shoes, and many other products and also for home use. The sewing machine became the first widely advertised consumer product. Due to its high cost, the Singer company introduced an installment buying plan, which helped place sewing machines in most middle-class households. Why was the sewing machine able to find eager customers in commercial workshops and home sewing rooms alike? How might the sewing machine have changed other aspects of American life, such as work patterns, clothing styles, and retail selling? What other advances in technology might have been necessary for the invention of the sewing machine?

1. Examine the photo of this sewing machine, built only one year after Elias Howe invented the first such machine in 1845. What are the key components that Howe had to combine in order to improve on hand sewing? In what ways was this machine more limited than hand sewing?
2. What functional and economic differences were there between Howe-Singer machines aimed at sewing within the home and those that came to be built for factory production of the ready-made clothing industry?
3. What made the sewing machine the rare invention that was *both* a capital-intensive industrial product *and* the "first widely advertised consumer product" sold "on the installment plan"?

Western Farmers Reap a Revolution in the Fields

As smoke-belching factories altered the eastern skyline, flourishing farms were changing the face of the West. The trans-Allegheny region—especially the Ohio-Indiana-Illinois tier—was fast becoming the nation's breadbasket. Before long, it would become a granary to the world.

Pioneer farmers first hacked a clearing out of the forest and then planted their painfully furrowed fields to corn. The yellow grain was amazingly versatile. It could be fed to hogs ("corn on the hoof") or distilled into liquor ("corn in the bottle"). Both these products could be transported more easily than the bulky grain itself, and they became the early western farmer's staple market items. So many corn-fed hogs were butchered, traded, or shipped at Cincinnati that the city was known as the "Porkopolis" of the West.

Most western produce was at first floated down the Ohio-Mississippi river system to feed the booming Cotton Kingdom. Spurred on by the easy availability of the seemingly boundless acres, farmers continuously sought ways to bring more and more acres into cultivation. They were often frustrated by the thickly matted soil of the West that snagged and snapped fragile wooden plows. John Deere of Illinois in 1837 finally produced a light, steel plow that broke the stubborn soil.

Online Study Center

Primary source
McCormick's Harvesting Machines
college.hmco.com/pic/kennedybrief7e

In the 1830s Virginia-born Cyrus McCormick contributed the most wondrous contraption of all: a mechanical mower-reaper. The clattering cogs of McCormick's horse-drawn machine were to the western farmers what the cotton gin was to the southern planters. Seated on his red-chariot reaper, a single harvester could do the work of five men with sickles and scythes.

No other American invention cut so wide a swath. It made ambitious capitalists out of humble plowmen, who now scrambled for more acres on which to plant more fields of billowing wheat. Specialized cash-crop agriculture came to dominate the West, producing mounting indebtedness as farmers bought more land and more machinery to work it. With hustling farmers producing more than the South could devour, they began to dream of markets in the mushrooming eastern factory towns, or across the faraway Atlantic. But they were still largely landlocked. Commerce moved north and south on the river systems. Before it could begin to move east-west in bulk, a transportation revolution would have to occur.

Highways and Steamboats

In 1789, when the Constitution was launched, primitive methods of travel were still in use. Waterborne commerce, whether along the coast or on the rivers, was slow, uncertain, and often dangerous. Stagecoaches and wagons lurched over bone-shaking roads. Passengers would be rousted out to lay nearby fence rails across muddy stretches, and occasionally horses would drown in muddy pits while wagons sank slowly out of sight.

Cheap and efficient carriers were imperative if raw materials were to be transported to the factories, and if the finished product was to be delivered to consumers. A promising improvement came in the 1790s, when a private company completed the Lancaster **turnpike,** a broad, hard-surfaced highway that ran sixty-two miles from Philadelphia to Lancaster, Pennsylvania. The highly successful Lancaster turnpike returned dividends as high as 15 percent annually to its stockholders, attracted a rich trade to Philadelphia, and touched off the westward migration of the canvas-covered Conestoga wagons.

turnpike *A toll road.*

Westerners scored a notable triumph in 1811 when the federal government began to construct the elongated National Road, or Cumberland Road. When finally completed in 1852, after interruptions caused by the War of 1812 and states' rights shackles on internal improvements, the highway stretched 591 miles from Cumberland, Maryland, to Vandalia, Illinois.

The steamboat craze, which overlapped the turnpike craze, was touched off by an ambitious painter-engineer named Robert Fulton. In 1807 he installed a powerful steam engine in the *Clermont,* dubbed "Fulton's Folly" by a dubious public. Belching

Mississippi in Time of Peace, by Mrs. Frances Flora Bond Palmer, 1865 By the mid-nineteenth century, steamboats had made the Mississippi a bustling river highway—as it remains today.
Photograph © 2006 Museum of Fine Arts, Boston.

sparks from its single smokestack, the quaint little ship steadily churned up the Hudson River from New York City to Albany, making the run of 150 miles in 32 hours.

The success of the steamboat was sensational. People could now in large degree defy wind, wave, tide, and downstream current. Within a few years Fulton had changed all of America's navigable streams into two-way arteries, thereby doubling their carrying capacity. Hitherto keelboats had been pushed up the Mississippi, with quivering poles and raucous profanity, at less than one mile an hour—a process that was prohibitively expensive. Now the steamboats could churn rapidly against the current, ultimately attaining speeds in excess of ten miles an hour. The mighty Mississippi had finally met its master. By 1820 there were some sixty steamboats on the Mississippi and its tributaries; by 1860 about a thousand steamboats, including some luxurious river palaces, were plying the inland waters.

Canals and the Iron Horse

A canal-cutting craze paralleled the boom in turnpikes and steamboats. Blessed with the driving leadership of Governor DeWitt Clinton, New York State started the trend when it dug the Erie Canal linking the Hudson River to the Great Lakes.

Begun in 1817, the canal eventually ribboned 363 miles. On its completion in 1825, a garland-bedecked canal boat glided from Buffalo, on Lake Erie, to the Hudson River and on to New York harbor. There, with colorful ceremony, Governor Clinton emptied a cask of water from the lake to symbolize "the marriage of the waters."

The water from Clinton's keg baptized the Empire State. Mule-drawn passengers and bulky freight could now be handled with thrift and dispatch, at the dizzy speed of five miles an hour. The cost of shipping a ton of grain from Buffalo to New York City fell from $100 to $5, and the time of transit from about twenty days to six.

Ever-widening economic ripples followed the completion of the Erie Canal. The value of land along the route skyrocketed, and new cities—such as Rochester and Syracuse—blossomed. Industry in the state boomed. The new profitability of farming in

The Railroad Revolution Note the explosion of new railroad construction in the 1850s and its heavy concentration in the North.

Interactive map
Population Distribution, 1790 and 1850
college.hmco.com/pic/kennedybrief7e

the Old Northwest—notably in Ohio, Michigan, Indiana, and Illinois—attracted thousands of European immigrants to the unaxed and untaxed lands now available. Flotillas of steamships soon traversed the Great Lakes, connecting with waiting canal barges at Buffalo. Interior waterside villages like Cleveland, Detroit, and Chicago exploded into mighty cities.

The greatest single contribution to the developing continental economy initiated by the canals proved to be the railroad. It was fast, reliable, cheaper than canals to construct, and not frozen over in winter. Able to go almost anywhere, even through the Appalachian barrier, it defied terrain and weather. The first railroad appeared in the United States in 1828. By 1860, only thirty-two years later, the United States boasted thirty thousand miles of railroad track, three-fourths of it in the rapidly industrializing North.

At first the railroad faced strong opposition from vested interests, especially canal backers. Anxious to protect its investment in the Erie Canal, the New York legislature in 1833 prohibited the railroads from carrying freight—at least temporarily. Early railroads were also considered a dangerous public menace, for flying sparks could set fire to haystacks and houses, and appalling railway accidents could turn the wooden "miniature hells" into flaming funeral pyres for their riders.

Primary source
Railroad Growth
college.hmco.com/pic/kennedybrief7e

Railroad pioneers had to overcome other obstacles as well. Arrivals and departures were conjectural, and numerous differences in gauge (the distance between the rails) meant frequent changes of trains for passengers. In 1840 there were seven transfers between Philadelphia and Charleston. But gauges gradually became standardized, safety devices were adopted, and the Pullman "sleeping palace" was introduced in 1859. America at long last was being bound together with ribs of iron, later to be made of steel.

Cables, Clippers, and Pony Riders

Other forms of transportation and communication were binding together the United States and the world. A crucial step came in 1858 when Cyrus Field, called "the greatest wire puller in history," stretched a telegraph cable under the deep North Atlantic waters from Newfoundland to Ireland. Although this initial cable went dead after three weeks of public rejoicing, a heavier cable laid in 1866 permanently linked the American and European continents.

American commercial shipping fell behind in the early nineteenth century, and American naval designers made few contributions to maritime progress. A pioneer American steamer, the *Savannah,* crept across the Atlantic in 1819, but it used sail most of the time and was pursued for a day by a British captain who thought it afire.

In the 1840s and 1850s, a golden age dawned for American shipping. Yankee naval yards, notably Donald McKay's at Boston, began to send down the ways sleek new crafts called clipper ships. Long, narrow, and majestic, they glided across the sea under towering masts and clouds of canvas. In a fair breeze they could outrun any steamer. The stately clippers sacrificed cargo space for speed, and their captains made killings by hauling high-value cargoes across the oceans in record times.

But the hour of glory for the clipper was relatively brief. On the eve of the Civil War, the British had clearly won the world race for maritime ascendancy with their iron tramp steamers ("teakettles"). Although slower and less romantic than the clipper, these vessels were steadier, roomier, more reliable, and hence more profitable.

No story of rapid American communication would be complete without including the Far West. By 1858 horse-drawn overland stage coaches, immortalized in Mark Twain's *Roughing It,* were a familiar sight. Their dusty tracks stretched from the banks of the muddy Missouri River clear to California.

Even more dramatic was the Pony Express, established in 1860 to carry mail speedily the two thousand lonely miles from St. Joseph, Missouri, to Sacramento, California. Daring, lightweight riders, leaping onto wiry ponies saddled at stations approximately ten miles apart, could make the trip in an amazing ten days. These unarmed horsemen galloped on, summer or winter, day or night, through dust or snow, past Indians and bandits. The speeding postmen missed only one trip, though the whole enterprise lost money and folded after only eighteen legend-leaving months.

Just as the clippers had succumbed to steam, the Pony Express riders were unhorsed by Morse's clacking keys, which began tapping messages to California in 1861. The swift ships and fleet ponies ushered out a dying technology of wind and muscle. In the future, machines would be in the saddle.

The Transport Web Binds the Union

More than anything else, the desire of the East to tap the West stimulated the "transportation revolution." Until about 1830, the produce of the western region drained southward to the cotton belt or to the heaped-up wharves of New Orleans. The steamboat vastly aided the reverse flow of finished goods up the watery western arteries and helped bind the West and South together. But the truly revolutionary changes in commerce and communication came in the three decades before the Civil War, as canals and railroad tracks radiated out from the East, across the Appalachians, and into the blossoming heartland. The ditch-diggers and tie-layers were attempting nothing less than a conquest of nature itself. They would offset the "natural" flow of trade on the interior rivers by laying down an impressive grid of "internal improvements."

The builders succeeded beyond their wildest dreams. The Mississippi was increasingly robbed of its traffic, as goods moved eastward on chugging trains, puffing lake boats, and mule-tugged canal barges. By the 1840s Buffalo was handling more western produce than New Orleans. Between 1836 and 1860, grain shipments through Buffalo increased a staggering sixtyfold. New York City became the seaboard queen of the nation, a gigantic port through which a vast hinterland poured its wealth and to which it daily paid economic tribute.

By the eve of the Civil War, a truly continental economy had emerged. The principle of division of labor, which spelled **productivity** and profits in the factory, applied on a national scale as well. Each region now specialized in a particular type of economic activity. The South raised cotton for export to New England and Britain; the West grew grain and livestock to feed factory workers in the East and in Europe; the East made machines and textiles for the South and West.

productivity *In economics, the relative capacity to produce goods and services, measured in terms of the number of workers and machines needed to create goods in a certain length of time.*

barter *The direct exchange of goods and services for one another, without the use of cash or any medium of exchange.*

The economic pattern thus woven had fateful political and military implications. Many southerners regarded the Mississippi as a silver chain that naturally linked together the upper valley states and the Cotton Kingdom. They would become convinced, as secession approached, that some or all of these states would have to secede with them or be strangled. But they overlooked the man-made links that now bound the upper Mississippi Valley to the East in intimate commercial union. Southern rebels would have to fight not only Northern armies but the tight bonds of an interdependent continental economy. Economically, the two northerly sections were Siamese twins.

The Market Revolution

No less revolutionary than the political upheavals of the antebellum era was the "market revolution" that transformed a subsistence economy of scattered farms and tiny workshops into a national network of industry and commerce. As more and more Americans linked their economic fates to the burgeoning market economy, the self-sufficient households of colonial days were transformed. Most families had once raised all their own food, spun their own wool, and **bartered** with their neighbors for the few necessities they could not make themselves. In growing numbers, they now scattered to work for wages in the mills, or they planted just a few crops for sale at market and used the money to buy goods made by strangers in far-off factories.

As store-bought fabrics, candles, and soap replaced homemade products, a quiet revolution occurred in the household division of labor and status. Traditional women's work was rendered superfluous and devalued. The home itself, once a center of economic production in which all family members cooperated, grew into a place of refuge from the world of work, a refuge that became increasingly the special and separate sphere of women.

Revolutionary advances in manufacturing and transportation brought increased prosperity to all Americans, but they also widened the gulf between the rich and the poor. Millionaires had been rare in the early days of the Republic, but by the eve of the Civil War, several specimens of colossal financial success were strutting across the national stage. Spectacular was the case of fur-trader and real estate speculator John Jacob Astor, who left an estate of $30 million on his death in 1848.

Cities bred the greatest extremes of economic inequality. Unskilled workers, then as always, fared worst. Many of them came to make up a floating mass of "drifters," buffeted from town to town by the shifting prospects for menial jobs. These wandering workers accounted at various times for up to half the population of the brawling industrial centers. Although their numbers were large, they left little behind them but the homely fruits of their transient labor. Largely unstoried and unsung, they are among the forgotten men and women of American history.

Many myths about "social mobility" grew up over the buried memories of these unfortunate day laborers. Mobility did exist in industrializing America—but not in the proportions that legend often portrays. Rags-to-riches success stories were relatively few.

Yet America, with its dynamic society and its wide open spaces, undoubtedly provided more "opportunity" than did the contemporary countries of the Old World—which is why millions of immigrants packed their bags and headed for New World shores. Moreover, a rising tide lifts all boats, and the improvement in overall standards of living was real. Wages for unskilled workers in labor-hungry America rose about 1 percent a year from 1820 to 1860. This general prosperity helped to defuse the potential class conflict that otherwise might have exploded—and that did explode in many European countries.

Chapter Summary 

The youthful American republic expanded dramatically on the frontier in the early nineteenth century. Frontier life was often crude and hard on the pioneers, especially women.

Westward-moving pioneers often ruthlessly exploited the environment, exhausting the soil and exterminating wildlife. Yet the wild beauty of the West was also valued as a symbol of American national identity, and eventually environmentalists would create a national park system to preserve pieces of the wilderness.

Other changes altered the character of American society and its workforce. Old cities expanded, and new cities sprang up in the wilderness. Irish and German immigrants poured into the country in the 1830s and 1840s, and the Irish in particular aroused nativist hostility because of their Roman Catholic faith.

Inventions and business innovations like free incorporation laws spurred economic growth. Women and children were the most exploited early factory laborers. Male wage workers made some genuine gains in wages and hours but generally failed in unionization attempts.

The economic changes brought new roles not only for those women who worked in factories (usually only in their early years) but within the traditional sphere of the home. Families became smaller as well as more close-knit and affectionate, and women gained a larger authority within the home, exerting a kind of "domestic feminism." Families also became more child-centered, as child-rearing practices changed from authority to nurture.

The most far-reaching economic advances before the Civil War occurred in agriculture and transportation. The early railroads, despite many obstacles, gradually spread their tentacles across the country. Foreign trade remained only a small part of the American economy, but changing technology gradually created growing economic links to Europe. By the early 1860s the telegraph, railroad, and steamship had gone far toward replacing older means of travel and communication like the canals, clipper ships, stagecoach, and pony express.

The new means of transportation and distribution laid the foundations for a continental market economy. The new national economy created a pattern of sectional specialization and altered the traditional economic functions of the family. There was growing concern over the class differences spawned by industrialization, especially in the cities. But the general growth of opportunities and the increased standard of living made America a magnetic "land of opportunity" to many people at home and abroad.

The Ferment of Reform and Culture

1790–1860

WE [AMERICANS] WILL WALK ON OUR OWN FEET; WE WILL WORK WITH OUR OWN HANDS; WE WILL SPEAK OUR OWN MINDS.

RALPH WALDO EMERSON, "THE AMERICAN SCHOLAR," 1837

Chapter Outline

- Religious Revivals
- The Mormons
- Educational Advances
- The Roots of Reform
- Women's Roles and Women's Rights
- Utopian Experiments
- A National Literature
- Examining the Evidence: Dress as Reform
- Makers of America: The Oneida Community
- Varying Viewpoints: Reform: Who? What? How? And Why?

A third revolution accompanied the reformation of American politics and the transformation of the American economy in the mid-nineteenth century. This was a diffuse yet deeply felt commitment to improve the character of ordinary Americans, to make them more upstanding, God-fearing, and literate. Some high-minded souls were disillusioned by the rough-and-tumble realities of democratic politics. Others, notably women, were excluded from the political game altogether. As the young Republic grew, increasing numbers of Americans poured their considerable energies into religious revivals and reform movements.

Reform campaigns of all types flourished in sometimes bewildering abundance. There was not "a reading man" who was without some scheme for a new utopia in his "waistcoat pocket," claimed Ralph Waldo Emerson. Reformers promoted better public schools and rights for women, as well as **polygamy,** celibacy, rule by prophets, and guidance by spirits. Societies were formed against alcohol, tobacco, profanity, and the transit of mail on the Sabbath. Eventually overshadowing all other reforms was the great crusade against slavery (see pp. 242–244). Many reformers drew their crusading zeal from religion. Beginning in the late 1790s and boiling over into the early nineteenth century, the Second Great Awakening swept through America's Protestant churches, transforming the place of religion in American life and sending a generation of believers out on their mission to perfect the world.

Focus Questions

1. What were the most important changes in American religion in the early nineteenth century, and how did they lead to movements for social reform?
2. What were the most important social and educational reform movements of the period, and how successful were they?
3. How did the early women's movement react against the widespread "separate spheres" gender ideology, and what successes and failures did female reformers experience?
4. How were the early utopian experiments and ideologies related to the general religious, social, and intellectual ferment of early American democracy?
5. How did American intellectual and literary life generally reflect the spirit of American democracy, and why did some notable writers dissent from the idealistic spirit of transcendentalism and other optimistic ideologies?

polygamy *The practice of having two or more spouses at one time. (**Polygyny** refers specifically to two or more wives; **polyandry** to two or more husbands.)*

Reviving Religion

Church attendance was still a regular ritual for about three-fourths of the 23 million Americans in 1850. Alexis de Tocqueville declared that there was "no country in the world where the Christian religion retains a greater influence over the souls of men than in America." Yet the austere Calvinist rigor had long been seeping out of the nation's churches.

The rationalist ideas of the French Revolutionary era had done much to soften the older orthodoxy. Thomas Paine's widely circulated book *The Age of Reason* (1794) shockingly declared that all churches were set up "to terrorize and enslave mankind." American anticlericalism was seldom that vehement, but many of the Founders, including Jefferson and Franklin, embraced the liberal doctrines of Deism. Deists relied on reason rather than revelation, rejected the concept of original sin, and denied Christ's divinity. Yet they believed in a Supreme Being who had endowed human beings with a capacity for moral behavior

Deism helped to inspire an important spinoff from Puritanism—the Unitarian faith, which began to gather momentum in New England at the end of the eighteenth century. Unitarians held that God existed in only *one* person (hence *uni*-tarian) and not in the orthodox Trinity (God the Father, God the Son, and God the Holy Spirit). Although denying the deity of Jesus, Unitarians stressed the essential goodness of human nature, the possibility of salvation through good works, and God as a loving Father rather than a stern Creator. Embraced by many leading thinkers (including Ralph Waldo Emerson), the Unitarian movement appealed mostly to intellectuals whose rationalism and optimism contrasted sharply with the Calvinist doctrines of predestination and human depravity.

A boiling reaction against the growing liberalism in religion set in about 1800. A fresh wave of roaring revivals, beginning on the southern frontier but soon rolling even into the cities of the Northeast, sent the Second Great Awakening surging across the land. Sweeping up more people than the First Great Awakening almost a century earlier (see p. 66), the Second Awakening was one of the most momentous episodes in the history of American religion. This tidal wave of spiritual fervor left in its wake countless converted souls, shattered and reorganized churches, and numerous new sects.

The Second Great Awakening was spread to the masses on the frontier by huge "camp meetings" where as many as twenty-five thousand people would gather for an encampment of several days. Thousands of spiritually starved souls "got

■ **A Camp Meeting at Sing Sing, New York** The preacher stands with hands uplifted under the canopy at the left. A British visitor wrote in 1839 of a revival meeting, "In front of the pulpit there was a space railed off and strewn with straw, which I was told was the anxious seat, and on which sat those who were touched by their consciences."

Chronology

1770s	First Shaker communities formed.
1795	University of North Carolina founded.
1800	Second Great Awakening begins.
1819	Jefferson founds University of Virginia.
1821	Cooper publishes *The Spy,* his first successful novel. Emma Willard establishes Troy (New York) Female Seminary.
1825	New Harmony commune established.
1826	American Temperance Society founded.
1828	American Peace Society founded. Noah Webster publishes dictionary.
1830	Joseph Smith founds Mormon church. *Godey's Lady's Book* first published.
1830-1831	Finney conducts revivals in eastern cities.
1835	Lyceum movement flourishes.
1837	Emerson delivers "The American Scholar" address. Mary Lyon establishes Mount Holyoke Seminary. Oberlin College admits female students.
1841	Brook Farm commune established.
1843	Dorothea Dix petitions Massachusetts legislature on behalf of the insane.
1846-1847	Mormon migration to Utah.
1848	Seneca Falls Woman's Rights Convention held. Oneida community established.
1850	Hawthorne publishes *The Scarlet Letter.*
1851	Melville publishes *Moby Dick.* Maine passes first law prohibiting liquor.
1855	Whitman publishes *Leaves of Grass.*

religion" at these gatherings, which boosted church membership and stimulated a variety of humanitarian reforms. Responsive easterners were moved to engage in missionary work among the Indians, in Hawaii, and in Asia. Everywhere the Second Awakening encouraged an effervescent evangelicalism that bubbled up into innumerable areas of American life—including prison reform, the temperance cause, the women's movement, and the crusade to abolish slavery.

Methodists and Baptists reaped the most abundant harvest of souls from the fields fertilized by revivalism. Both sects stressed personal conversion (contrary to predestination), a relatively democratic control of church affairs, and a rousing emotionalism. As a frontier jingle ran,

> *The devil hates the Methodists*
> *Because they sing and shout the best.*

Powerful Peter Cartwright (1785–1872), was the best known of the Methodist "circuit riders," or traveling frontier preachers. This sinewy servant of the Lord ranged for a half-century from Tennessee to Illinois, calling upon sinners to repent. Bell-voiced Charles Grandison Finney, the greatest of the revival preachers, abandoned his career as a lawyer to become an evangelist after a deeply moving conversion experience as a young man. Tall and athletically built, Finney held huge crowds spellbound with the power of his oratory and the pungency of his message. He led massive revivals in Rochester and New York City in 1830 and 1831. Holding out the promise of a perfect Christian kingdom on earth, Finney denounced both alcohol and slavery. He eventually served as president of Oberlin College in Ohio, which he helped to make a hotbed of revivalist activity and abolitionism.

In his lecture "Hindrances to Revivals," delivered in the 1830s, Charles Grandison Finney (1792–1875) proposed the excommunication of drinkers and slaveholders:

"Let the churches of all denominations speak out on the subject of temperance, let them close their doors against all who have anything to do with the death-dealing abomination, and the cause of temperance is triumphant. A few years would annihilate the traffic. Just so with slavery. . . . It is a great national sin. It is a sin of the church. The churches by their silence, and by permitting slaveholders to belong to their communion, have been consenting to it. . . . The church cannot turn away from this question. It is a question for the church and for the nation to decide, and God will push it to a decision."

A key feature of the Second Great Awakening was the feminization of religion, in terms of both church membership and theology. Middle-class women were the first and most fervent enthusiasts of religious revivalism, and they were the most likely to stay within the fold when the tents were packed up and the traveling evangelist left town. Perhaps women's greater ambivalence than men about the changes wrought by the expanding market economy made them such eager converts to piety. It helped as well that evangelicals preached a gospel of female spiritual worth and offered women an active role in bringing their husbands and families back to God. That accomplished, many women turned to saving the rest of society. They formed a host of benevolent and charitable organizations and spearheaded crusades for most, if not all, of the era's ambitious reforms.

Denominational Diversity

Revivals also furthered the fragmentation of religious faiths. Western New York, where many descendants of New England Puritans had settled, was so blistered by sermonizers preaching "hellfire and damnation" that it came to be known as the "Burned-Over District." Millerites, or Adventists, who mustered several hundred thousand adherents, rose from the superheated soil of the Burned-Over District in the 1830s. The failed prophecy of their eloquent leader, William Miller, that Christ would return to earth on October 22, 1844, dampened but did not destroy the movement.

Like the First Great Awakening, the Second Great Awakening tended to widen the gaps between classes and regions. The more prosperous and conservative denominations in the East were little touched by revivalism, and Episcopalians, Presbyterians, Congregationalists, and Unitarians continued to rise mostly from the wealthier, better-educated levels of society. Methodists, Baptists, and members of the new denominations spawned by the swelling evangelistic fervor tended to come from less prosperous, less "learned" communities in the rural South and West.

Religious diversity further reflected social cleavages when the churches faced up to the slavery issue. By 1844–1845 both the southern Baptists and the southern Methodists had split with their northern brethren over human bondage. In 1857 the Presbyterians, North and South, parted company. The secession of the southern churches foreshadowed the secession of the southern states. First the churches split, then the political parties split, and then the Union split.

A Desert Zion in Utah

The smoldering spiritual embers of the Burned-Over District kindled one especially ardent flame in 1830. In that year Joseph Smith—a rugged visionary, proud of his prowess at wrestling—reported that he had received some golden plates from an angel. When deciphered, they constituted the Book of Mormon, and the Church of Jesus Christ of Latter-Day Saints (Mormons) was launched. It was a native American product, a new religion, destined to spread its influence worldwide.

After establishing a religious oligarchy, Smith ran into serious opposition from his non-Mormon neighbors, first in Ohio and then in Missouri and Illinois. His cooperative sect antagonized rank-and-file Americans, who were individualistic and dedicated to free enterprise. The Mormons aroused further antagonism by voting as a unit and by openly but understandably drilling their militia for defensive purposes. Accusations of polygamy likewise arose and increased in intensity, for Joseph Smith was reputed to have several wives.

Continuing hostility finally drove the Mormons to desperate measures. In 1844 Joseph Smith and his brother were murdered and mangled by a mob in Carthage, Illinois, and the movement seemed near collapse. The falling torch was seized by a remarkable Mormon Moses named Brigham Young. Stern and austere, in contrast to Smith's charm and affability, the barrel-chested Young quickly proved to be an aggressive leader, eloquent preacher, and gifted administrator. Determined to

The Mormon World After the murder of Joseph Smith in 1844, the Mormons abandoned their thriving settlement at Nauvoo, Illinois (which had about twenty thousand inhabitants in 1845), and set out for the valley of the Great Salt Lake, then still part of Mexico. When the Treaty of Guadalupe Hidalgo in 1848 brought the vast Utah Territory into the United States, the Mormons rapidly expanded their desert colony, which they called Deseret, especially along the "Mormon Corridor" that stretched from Salt Lake to southern California.

escape further persecution, Young in 1846–1847 led his oppressed Latter-Day Saints over vast rolling plains to Utah as they sang "Come, Come, Ye Saints."

Overcoming pioneer hardships, the Mormons soon made the desert bloom like a new Eden by means of ingenious and cooperative methods of irrigation. The crops of 1848, threatened by hordes of crickets, were saved when flocks of gulls appeared, as if by a miracle, to gulp down the invaders.

Semiarid Utah grew remarkably. By the end of 1848 some five thousand settlers had arrived, and other large bands were to follow them. Many dedicated Mormons in the 1850s actually made the 1,300-mile trek across the plains pulling two-wheeled carts.

Under the rigidly disciplined management of Brigham Young, the community became a prosperous frontier **theocracy** and cooperative commonwealth. Young married as many as twenty-seven women and begot fifty-six children.

A crisis developed when the Washington government seemed unable to control the hierarchy of Brigham Young, who had been made territorial governor in 1850. A federal army marched in 1857 against the Mormons, who harassed its lines of supply and rallied to die in their last dusty ditch. Fortunately, the quarrel was finally adjusted without serious bloodshed. The Mormons later ran afoul of the antipolygamy laws passed by Congress in 1862 and 1882, and their unique marital customs delayed statehood for Utah until 1896.

theocracy *Literally, rule by God; the term is often applied to a state where religious leaders exercise direct or indirect political authority.*

Interactive map
Major American Cities in 1830 and 1860
college.hmco.com/pic/kennedybrief7e

■ School Days Schoolteaching in the early nineteenth century was a poorly paid occupation that was often pursued by single men who were not very well educated themselves. This drawing depicts John Pounds (1766–1839), who taught school and supplemented his income by mending shoes.

Free Schools for a Free People

Tax-supported primary schools were scarce in the early years of the Republic. They had the odor of pauperism about them, since they existed chiefly to educate the children of the poor—the so-called ragged schools. Advocates of "free" public education met stiff opposition.

Between 1825 and 1850, the spread of democratic ideals and manhood suffrage for whites gradually won acceptance for the public schools, except in the slavery-cursed South. A free vote cried aloud for free education. A civilized nation that was both ignorant and free, declared Thomas Jefferson, "never was and never will be."

But most of the one-room, one-teacher "little red schoolhouses" of the time were imperfect shrines of democracy. Early free schools stayed open only a few months of the year. Schoolteachers, most of them men in this era, were often ill-trained, ill-tempered, and ill-paid. These knights of the blackboard often "boarded around" in the community, and some knew scarcely more than their older pupils. They usually taught only the "three Rs—readin', 'ritin', and 'rithmetic."

Reform was urgently needed. Into the breach stepped Horace Mann (1796–1859), a brilliant and idealistic graduate of Brown University. As secretary of the Massachusetts Board of Education, he campaigned effectively for more and better schoolhouses, longer school terms, higher pay for teachers, and an expanded curriculum. His influence radiated out to other states, and impressive improvements were chalked up. Yet education remained an expensive luxury for many communities. As late as 1860 the nation counted only about a hundred public secondary schools—and nearly a million white adult illiterates. Black slaves in the South were legally forbidden to receive instruction in reading or writing, and even free blacks, in the North as well as the South, were usually excluded from the schools.

Educational advances were aided by improved textbooks, notably those of Noah Webster (1758–1843), a Yale-educated Connecticut Yankee who was known as the "Schoolmaster of the Republic." His "reading lessons," used by millions of children in the nineteenth century, were partly designed to promote patriotism. Webster devoted twenty years to his famous dictionary, published in 1828, which helped to standardize the American language.

Equally influential was Ohioan William H. McGuffey (1800–1873), a teacher-preacher of rare power. His grade-school readers, first published in the 1830s, sold 122 million copies in the following decades. *McGuffey's Readers* hammered home lasting lessons in morality, patriotism, and idealism.

Higher Goals for Higher Learning

Higher education was likewise stirring. The religious zeal of the Second Great Awakening led to the planting of many small, denominational, liberal arts colleges, chiefly in the South and West. The first state-supported universities sprang up in the South, beginning with North Carolina in 1795. Conspicuous among the early group was the University of Virginia, founded in 1819 by Thomas Jefferson, who also designed its beautiful architecture. He dedicated the university to freedom from religious or political shackles, and modern languages and the sciences received unusual emphasis.

Women's higher education was frowned upon in the early decades of the nineteenth century. A woman's place was believed to be in the home, and training in needlecraft seemed more important than training in algebra. Prejudices prevailed that too much learning injured the feminine brain, undermined health, and rendered a young lady unfit for marriage. The teachers of Susan B. Anthony, the future feminist, refused to instruct her in long division.

Women's schools at the secondary level began to attain some respectability in the 1820s, thanks in part to the dedicated work of Emma Willard (1787–1870). In 1821 she established the Troy (New York) Female Seminary. Oberlin College in Ohio shocked traditionalists in 1837 when it opened its doors to women as well as men. (Oberlin had already created shock waves by admitting black students.) In the same year, Mary Lyon established an outstanding women's school, Mount Holyoke Seminary (later College), in South Hadley, Massachusetts.

Adults who craved more learning satisfied their thirst for knowledge at private subscription libraries or, increasingly, at tax-supported libraries. House-to-house peddlers also did a lush business in feeding the public appetite for culture. Traveling lecturers helped to carry learning to the masses through the lyceum lecture associations, which numbered about three thousand by 1835. The lyceums provided platforms for speakers in such areas as science, literature, and moral philosophy. Talented talkers like Ralph Waldo Emerson journeyed thousands of miles on the lyceum circuits, casting their pearls of civilization before appreciative audiences.

Magazines flourished in the pre–Civil War years. The *North American Review,* founded in 1815, was the long-lived leader of the intellectuals. *Godey's Lady's Book,* founded in 1830, survived until 1898 and attained the enormous circulation (for those days) of 150,000. It was devoured devotedly by millions of women, many of whom read the dog-eared copies of their relatives and friends.

An Age of Reform

As the young Republic grew, reform campaigns of all types flourished in sometimes bewildering abundance. Some of the reformers, usually touched by the fire of evangelical religion, were simply cranks, but most were intelligent, inspired idealists. The optimistic fervor of the Second Great Awakening inspired countless souls to do battle against earthly evils. These modern idealists dreamed anew the old Puritan vision of a perfected society free from cruelty, war, intoxicating drink, discrimination, and—ultimately—slavery. Women were particularly prominent in these reform crusades, especially in their own struggle for suffrage. For many middle-class women, the campaigns provided a unique opportunity to escape the confines of the home and enter the arena of public affairs.

In part the practical, activist Christianity of these reformers resulted from their desire to reaffirm traditional values as they plunged ever further into a world disrupted and transformed by the turbulent forces of a market economy. Often blissfully unaware that they were witnessing the dawn of the industrial era, they either ignored the factory workers or blamed their problems on bad habits. Reformers sometimes applied conventional virtue to refurbishing an older order—while events hurtled them headlong into the new.

Imprisonment for debt continued to be a nightmare. As late as 1830 hundreds of penniless people were languishing in filthy holes. The poorer working classes were especially hard hit by this merciless practice. But as the embattled laborer won the ballot and asserted himself, state legislators gradually abolished the debtors' prisons and softened the criminal codes. The number of capital offenses was reduced, and brutal punishments, such as whipping and branding, were slowly eliminated. A refreshing idea began taking hold that prisons should reform as well as punish—hence "reformatories," "houses of correction," and "penitentiaries" (for penance).

Sufferers from so-called insanity were still being treated with incredible cruelty. The mentally deranged were considered willfully perverse and depraved—to be treated only as beasts. A formidable New England teacher-author, Dorothea

■ Dorothea Dix (1802–1887) A tireless reformer, she worked mightily to improve the treatment of the mentally ill. At the outbreak of the Civil War, she was appointed superintendent of women nurses for the Union forces.

Dix (1802–1887) spent eight years observing these conditions at first hand and then presented her classic petition to the Massachusetts legislature in 1843. Her description of cells so foul that visitors were driven back by the stench turned legislative stomachs and hearts. Her persistent prodding resulted in improved conditions and in a gain for the concept that the demented were not willfully perverse but mentally ill.

Agitation for peace also gained momentum in the pre–Civil War years. In 1828 the American Peace Society was formed, with a ringing declaration of war on war. The American peace crusade, linked with a European counterpart, was making promising progress by midcentury, but it was set back by the bloodshed of the Crimean War in Europe and the Civil War in America.

Demon Rum: The "Old Deluder"

The ever-present drink problem also attracted dedicated reformers. Excessive drinking of hard liquor was common even among women, clergymen, and members of Congress. Weddings and funerals all too often became disgraceful brawls, and occasionally a drunken mourner would fall into the open grave with the corpse. Drunkenness also fouled the sanctity of the family, threatening the spiritual welfare—and physical safety—of women and children.

After earlier and feebler efforts, the American Temperance Society was formed at Boston in 1826. Within a few years about a thousand local groups sprang into existence. They implored drinkers to sign the temperance pledge and organized children's clubs, known as the "Cold Water Army."

The most popular anti-alcohol tract of the era was T. S. Arthur's melodramatic novel, *Ten Nights in a Barroom and What I Saw There* (1854). It described in shocking detail how a once-happy village was ruined by Sam Slade's tavern. The book was second only to Harriet Beecher Stowe's *Uncle Tom's Cabin* as a bestseller in the 1850s, and it enjoyed a highly successful run on the stage.

zealot *One who is carried away by a cause to an extreme or excessive degree.*

Early foes of Demon Drink adopted two major lines of attack. One was to stiffen the individual's will to resist the wiles of the little brown jug. The moderate reformers thus stressed temperance rather than the total elimination of intoxicants. But less patient **zealots** came to believe that temptation should be removed by legislation. Prominent among this group was Neal S. Dow of Maine, a blue-nosed reformer who, as mayor of Portland and an employer of labor, had often witnessed the debauching effect of alcohol.

Dow—the "Father of Prohibition"—sponsored the so-called Maine Law of 1851. This drastic new statute, hailed as "the law of Heaven Americanized," prohibited the manufacture and sale of intoxicating liquor. Other states in the North followed Maine's example, and by 1857 about a dozen had passed various prohibitory laws.

On the eve of the Civil War the prohibitionists had registered inspiriting gains. There was much less drinking among women than earlier in the century and probably much less per capita consumption of hard liquor.

In presenting her case to the Massachusetts legislature for more humane treatment for the mentally ill, Dorothea Dix (1802–1887) quoted from the notebook she carried with her as she traveled around the state:

"Lincoln. A woman in a cage. *Medford.* One idiotic subject chained, and one in a close stall for seventeen years. *Pepperell.* One often doubly chained, hand and foot; another violent; several peaceable now. . . . *Dedham.* The insane disadvantageously placed in the jail. In the almshouse, two females in stalls . . . ; lie in wooden bunks filled with straw; always shut up. One of these subjects is supposed curable. The overseers of the poor have declined giving her a trial at the hospital, as I was informed, on account of expense."

Women in Revolt

When the nineteenth century opened, it was still a man's world, both in America and in Europe. A wife was supposed to immerse herself in her home and subordinate herself to her husband. Like black slaves, she could not vote; like black slaves, she could be legally beaten by her overlord "with a reasonable instrument." When she married, she could not retain title to her property; it passed to her husband. Women in America were still the "submerged sex" in the early part of the century, though their position was somewhat better than that of their European cousins. French visitor Alexis de Tocqueville noted that in his native France rape was punished only lightly, whereas in America it was one of the few crimes punishable by death.

But as the decades unfolded, American women increasingly surfaced to breathe the air of freedom and self-determination. In contrast to women in colonial times, many women now avoided marriage altogether—about 10 percent of adult women remained "spinsters" at the time of the Civil War.

Gender differences were strongly emphasized in nineteenth-century America—largely because the burgeoning market economy was increasingly separating women and men into sharply distinct economic roles. Women were thought to be physically and emotionally weak, but also artistic and refined. Endowed with finely tuned moral sensibilities, they were the keepers of society's conscience, with special responsibility to teach the young how to be good citizens of the Republic. Men were considered strong but crude, always in danger of slipping into some savage or beastly way of life if not guided by the gentle hands of their loving ladies.

The home was a woman's special sphere, the centerpiece of the "cult of domesticity." Even reformers like Catharine Beecher, who urged her sisters to seek employment as teachers, endlessly celebrated the role of the good homemaker. But some women increasingly felt that the glorified sanctuary of the home was in fact a gilded cage. They yearned to tear down the bars that separated the private world of women from the public world of men.

Clamorous female reformers—most of them white and well-to-do—began to gather strength as the century neared its halfway point. Most were broad-gauge battlers; while demanding rights for women, they joined in the general reform movement of the age, fighting for temperance and the abolition of slavery. Like men, they had been touched by the evangelical spirit that offered the promise of earthly reward for human endeavor. Neither foul eggs nor foul words, when hurled by disapproving men, could halt women heartened by these doctrines.

The women's rights movement was mothered by some arresting characters. Prominent among them was Lucretia Mott, a sprightly Quaker whose ire had been aroused when she and her fellow female delegates to the London antislavery convention of 1840 were not recognized. Elizabeth Cady Stanton, a mother of seven who had insisted on leaving "obey" out of her marriage ceremony, shocked fellow feminists by going so far as to advocate suffrage for women. Quaker-reared Susan B. Anthony, a militant lecturer for women's rights, fearlessly exposed herself to rotten garbage and vulgar epithets.

Other feminists challenged the man's world. Dr. Elizabeth Blackwell, a pioneer in a previously forbidden profession for women, was the first female graduate of a medical college. Precocious Margaret Fuller edited a transcendentalist journal, *The Dial,* and took part in the struggle to bring unity and republican government to Italy. The talented Grimké sisters, Sarah and Angelina, championed antislavery. Lucy Stone retained her maiden name after marriage—hence the latter-day "Lucy Stoners," who follow her example. Amelia Bloomer revolted against the current "street-sweeping" female attire by donning a short skirt with Turkish trousers—"bloomers," they were called—amid much bawdy ridicule about "Bloomerism" and "loose habits." A jeering male rhyme of the times jabbed

Gibbey, gibbey gab
The women had a confab
And demanded the rights
To wear the tights
Gibbey, gibbey gab.

Unflinching feminists met at Seneca Falls, New York, in a memorable Woman's Rights Convention (1848). The defiant Stanton read a "Declaration of Sentiments," which in the spirit of the Declaration of Independence declared that "all men and women are created equal." One resolution formally demanded the

> *When early feminist Lucy Stone (1818–1893) married fellow abolitionist Henry B. Blackwell (1825–1909) in West Brookfield, Massachusetts, in 1855, they added the following vow to their nuptial ceremony:*
>
> "While acknowledging our mutual affection by publicly assuming the relation of husband and wife, yet in justice to ourselves and a great principle, we deem it a duty to declare that this act on our part implies no . . . promise of voluntary obedience to such of the present laws of marriage, as refuse to recognize the wife as an independent, rational being, while they confer upon the husband an injurious and unnatural superiority."

ballot for females. Amid scorn and denunciation from press and pulpit, the Seneca Falls meeting launched the modern women's rights movement.

The crusade for women's rights was eclipsed by the campaign against slavery in the decade before the Civil War. Still, any white male over twenty-one could vote, while no woman could. Yet women were being gradually admitted to colleges, and some states, beginning with Mississippi in 1839, were even permitting wives to own property after marriage.

Wilderness Utopias

Bolstered by the **utopian** spirit of the age, various reformers, ranging from the high-minded to the "lunatic fringe," set up more than forty communities of a cooperative, **communistic,** or "**communitarian**" nature. Seeking human betterment, a wealthy and idealistic Scottish textile manufacturer, Robert Owen, founded in 1825 a communal society of about a thousand people at New Harmony, Indiana. Little harmony prevailed in the colony, which, in addition to hard-working visionaries, attracted a sprinkling of radicals, work-shy theorists, and outright scoundrels. The colony sank in a morass of contradiction and confusion.

Brook Farm in Massachusetts, comprising two hundred acres of grudging soil, was started in 1841 by about twenty intellectuals committed to the philosophy of transcendentalism. They prospered reasonably well until 1846, when they lost by fire a large new communal building shortly before its completion. The whole venture in "plain living and high thinking" then collapsed in debt. The Brook Farm experiment inspired Nathaniel Hawthorne's classic novel *The Blithedale Romance* (1852), whose main character was modeled on the feminist writer Margaret Fuller.

A more radical experiment was the Oneida Colony, founded in New York in 1848. It practiced free love ("complex marriage"), birth control (through "male continence," or ***coitus reservatus***), and the **eugenic** selection of parents to produce superior offspring. This curious enterprise flourished for more than thirty years, largely because its artisans made superior steel traps and Oneida Community (silver) Plate. In 1879–1880 the group embraced monogamy and abandoned communism (see "Makers of America: The Oneida Community," p. 228).

Among the longest-lived communitarian sects were the Shakers. Led by Mother Ann Lee, they began in the 1770s to set up a score or so of religious communities. The Shakers attained a membership of about six thousand in 1840, but since their monastic customs prohibited both marriage and sexual relations, they were virtually extinct by 1940.

utopian *Referring to any place or plan that aims at an ideal social order.*

communistic *Referring to the theory or practice in which the means of production are owned by the community as a whole.*

communitarian *Referring to the belief in or practice of the superiority of community life or values over individual life, but not necessarily the common ownership of material goods.*

coitus reservatus *A form of sexual intercourse in which male ejaculation is suppressed.*

eugenic *Concerning the improvement of the human species through selective breeding or genetic control.*

Online Study Center
Primary source
Orestes Brownson Views Brook Farm as an Expression
college.hmco.com/pic/kennedybrief7e

Online Study Center
Primary source
Noyes Acknowledges the Associationist Debt to the Shakers
college.hmco.com/pic/kennedybrief7e

Online Study Center
Primary sources
John H. Noyes Discusses Free Love, as Practiced at Oneida
college.hmco.com/pic/kennedybrief7e

Artistic Achievements

The arts in practical, pioneering early America were slow to gain momentum, and even slower to achieve real distinction. Architecturally, America contributed little of note in the first half of the century. The rustic Republic, still under pressure to erect shelters in haste, was continuing to imitate European models. Public buildings and other important structures followed Greek and Roman lines, which seemed curiously out of place in a wilderness setting. A remarkable Greek revival came between 1820 and 1850. About midcentury strong interest developed in a revival of Gothic forms, with their emphasis on pointed arches and large windows.

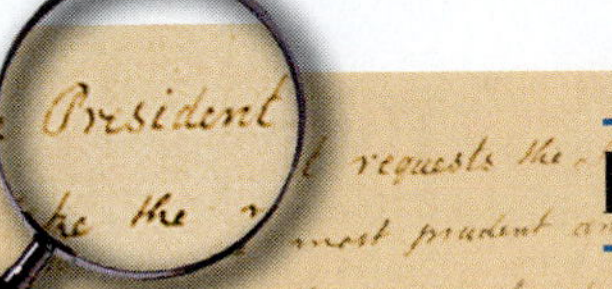

Examining the Evidence

Dress as Reform Among the many social movements that swept nineteenth-century America, dress reform emerged in the 1840s as a critique of materialism and the constraints that fashion imposed on women. Medical professionals, social reformers, and transcendentalist intellectuals all argued that corsets constricting vital organs and voluminous skirts dragging along garbage-strewn streets unfairly restricted women's mobility, prevented women from bearing healthy children, and even induced serious sickness and death. The "Bloomer costume" depicted in this illustration from *Harper's New Monthly Magazine* in 1851 included Turkish-style trousers, a jacket, and a short overskirt that came to the knees. Named after reformer Amelia Bloomer (1818–1894), who publicized the new style in her magazine, *The Lily,* the bloomer dress was first adopted by utopian communities such as the Owenites in New Harmony, Indiana, and the Oneidans in New York. Radical social critic Henry David Thoreau also advocated rational dress as a way of rejecting the artificial desires created by industrialization. But while applauded by reformers, new-style dress was viciously ridiculed by mainstream society, as this print demonstrates. Critics claimed that women blurred gender distinctions by adopting "male" attire, endangering the family and even American civilization. After only a decade, practitioners gave up wearing bloomers in public, adopting plain and simplified clothing instead. But Owenites, some Mormons, women's rights advocates, farmers, and travelers on the overland trail continued to wear bloomers in private. How did dress reform intersect with other religious and social movements of the era? Why did bloomers upset so many antebellum Americans? Have there been other historical eras when new styles of dress came to symbolize broader social change?

1. In this illustration of the "Bloomer costume" from *Harper's* (1851), what evidence is there of the hostility of the illustrator to the new and socially significant fashion? Besides the trousers, how is the supposed loss of "femininity" conveyed?
2. How does the bloomer outfit itself contrast with the more conventional mid-nineteenth-century female attire worn by the woman on the right?
3. What are the responses of the witnesses, including the children, to this innovation? How do the bloomer wearers themselves apparently respond to these attitudes?

The Oneida Community

John Humphrey Noyes (1811–1886), the founder of the Oneida Community, repudiated the old Puritan doctrines that God was vengeful and that sinful mankind was doomed to dwell in a vale of tears. Noyes believed in a benign deity, in the sweetness of human nature, and in the possibility of a perfect Christian community on earth. "The more we get acquainted with God," he declared, "the more we shall find it our special duty to be happy."

That sunny thought was shared by many early-nineteenth-century American utopians (a word derived from Greek that slyly combines the meanings of "a good place" and "no such place"). But Noyes added some wrinkles of his own. The key to happiness, he taught, was the suppression of selfishness. True Christians should possess no private property—nor should they indulge in exclusive emotional relationships, which bred jealousy, quarreling, and covetousness. Material things and sexual partners alike, Noyes preached, should be shared. Marriage should not be monogamous. Instead all members of the community should be free to love one another in "complex marriage." Noyes called his system "Bible Communism."

Tall and slender, with piercing blue eyes and reddish hair, the charismatic Noyes began voicing these ideas in his hometown of Putney, Vermont, in the 1830s. He soon attracted a group of followers who called themselves the Putney Association, a kind of extended family whose members farmed five hundred acres by day and sang and prayed together in the evenings.

The Putney Association also indulged in sexual practices that outraged the surrounding community's sense of moral propriety. Indicted for adultery in 1847, Noyes led his followers to Oneida, in the supposedly more tolerant region of New York's Burned-Over District, the following year.

The Oneidans struggled in New York until the manufacture of steel animal traps and other goods put the Community on a sound financial footing. By the 1860s Oneida was a flourishing commonwealth of some three hundred people. Men and women shared equally in all the community's tasks, from field to factory to kitchen. Children at the age of three were removed from direct parental care and raised communally until the age of thirteen or fourteen, when they took up jobs in the community's industries. They imbibed their religious doctrines with their school lessons:

> *I-spirit*
> *With me never shall stay,*
> *We-spirit*
> *Makes us happy and gay.*

Oneida's apparent success fed the utopian dreams of others, and for a time it became a great tourist attraction. Visitors from as far away as Europe came to picnic on the shady lawns, speculating on the sexual secrets that the Community guarded, while their hosts fed them strawberries and cream and entertained them with music.

But eventually the same problems that had driven Noyes and his band from Vermont began to shadow their lives at Oneida. Their New York neighbors grew increasingly horrified at the Oneidans' licentious sexual practices, including the selective breeding program by which the community matched mates and gave permission—or orders—to procreate, without regard to the niceties of matrimony.

Yielding to their neighbors' criticisms, the Oneidans gave up complex marriage in 1879. Soon other "communistic" practices withered away as well. In 1880 the Oneidans abandoned communism altogether and became a joint-stock company specializing in the manufacture of silver tableware. Led by Noyes's son Pierrepont, Oneida Community, Ltd., grew into the world's leading manufacturer of stainless steel knives, forks, and spoons, with annual sales by the 1990s of some half a billion dollars. Ironically, what grew from Noyes's religious vision was not utopia but a mighty capitalist corporation.

Talented Thomas Jefferson, architect of revolution, was probably the ablest American architect of his generation. He brought a **classical** design to his Virginia hilltop home, Monticello—perhaps the most stately mansion in the nation. The quadrangle of the University of Virginia at Charlottesville, another of Jefferson's creations, remains one of the finest examples of classical architecture in America.

Painting, like the theater, suffered from the Puritan prejudice that art was a sinful waste of time—and often obscene. When Edward Everett, the eminent Boston scholar and orator, placed a statue of Apollo in his home, he had its naked limbs draped.

Competent painters nevertheless emerged. Gilbert Stuart (1775–1828), a Rhode Islander and one of the most gifted of the early group, wielded his brush in Britain in competition with the best artists. He produced several portraits of Washington, all of them somewhat idealized and dehumanized. Charles Willson Peale (1741–1827), a Marylander, painted some sixty portraits of Washington, who patiently sat for about fourteen of them. John Trumbull (1756–1843), who had fought in the Revolutionary War, recaptured its scenes and spirit on scores of striking canvases.

During the nationalistic upsurge after the War of 1812, American painters turned increasingly from human subjects to romantic landscapes. The Hudson River School excelled in this type of art. At the same time, portrait painters gradually encountered some unwelcome competition from the invention of a crude photograph known as the daguerreotype, perfected about 1839 by a Frenchman, Louis Daguerre.

Music was slowly shaking off the restraints of colonial days, when the prim Puritans had frowned upon nonreligious singing. Rhythmic and nostalgic "darky" tunes were becoming immense hits by midcentury. Special favorites were the uniquely American minstrel shows, featuring white actors with darkened faces. The most famous black songs, ironically, came from a white Pennsylvanian, Stephen C. Foster (1826–1864). Foster made a valuable contribution to American folk music by capturing the plaintive spirit of the slaves in songs like "Old Folks at Home." An odd and pathetic figure, he finally lost both his art and his popularity and died in a charity ward after drowning his sorrows in drink.

The Blossoming of a National Literature

"Who reads an American book?" sneered a British critic in 1820. The painful truth was that the nation's rough-hewn, pioneering civilization gave little encouragement to "polite" literature. America produced praiseworthy political essays like *The Federalist,* political orations like the masterpieces of Daniel Webster, and classics like Benjamin Franklin's *Autobiography* (1818). But most reading matter before 1820 was imported or plagiarized from Britain.

A genuinely American literature received a strong boost from the wave of nationalism that followed the Revolutionary War and especially the War of 1812. By 1820 the older seaboard areas were sufficiently removed from the survival mentality of tree chopping so that literature could be supported as a profession. The Knickerbocker Group in New York blazed brilliantly across the literary heavens, enabling America for the first time to boast of a literature to match its magnificent landscapes.

Washington Irving (1783–1859), born in New York City, was the first American to win international recognition as a literary figure. Steeped in the traditions of New Netherland, he published in 1809 his *Knickerbocker's History of New York,* with its amusing caricatures of the Dutch. Irving won fame at home and abroad with his *Sketch Book* (1819–1820), which included such immortal Dutch-American tales as "Rip Van Winkle" and "The Legend of Sleepy Hollow." Europe was amazed to find at last an American with a feather in his hand, not in his hair.

The novelist James Fenimore Cooper (1789–1851) was the first American novelist, as Washington Irving was the first general writer, to gain world fame and make New World themes respectable. After an initial failure, Cooper launched his illustrious career in 1821 with his second novel *The Spy*—an absorbing tale of the American Revolution. His fame rests most enduringly on the *Leatherstocking Tales.* A deadeye rifleman named Natty Bumppo, one of nature's noblemen, meets with Indians in stirring adventures like *The Last of the Mohicans.* Some Europeans who read Cooper's novels came to think of all Americans as born with a tomahawk

Primary sources
Oneida Sisters Comment on Love and Labor
college.hmco.com/pic/kennedybrief7e

Primary source
Shaker Village at Alfred, Maine
college.hmco.com/pic/kennedybrief7e

Online Study Center

Primary source
Dwight's Reflections on the Promise and . . .
college.hmco.com/pic/kennedybrief7e

Online Study Center

Primary source
Ohio Associationist Sees Women's Activism as . . .
college.hmco.com/pic/kennedybrief7e

Online Study Center

Primary source
Lowell Offering Correspondent Describes a Shaker
college.hmco.com/pic/kennedybrief7e

Online Study Center

Interactive map
Religious and Utopian Communities, 1800–1845
college.hmco.com/pic/kennedybrief7e

classical *Concerning the culture of ancient Greece and Rome, or any artistic or cultural values presumed to be based on those enduring principles.*

in hand. Actually Cooper was exploring the viability and destiny of America's republican experiment by contrasting the values of "natural men" of the wilderness with the artificiality of modern civilization.

A third member of the Knickerbocker Group in New York was the belatedly Puritan William Cullen Bryant (1794–1878). At age sixteen he wrote the meditative and melancholy "Thanatopsis," (published in 1817), one of the first high-quality poems produced in the United States. Critics could hardly believe that it had been written on "this side of the water."

Trumpeters of Transcendentalism

A golden age in American literature dawned in the second quarter of the nineteenth century, when an amazing outburst shook New England. One of the mainsprings of this literary flowering was transcendentalism, especially around Boston, which preened itself as "the Athens of America."

mystical *Referring to the belief in the direct apprehension of God or divine mystery, without reliance on reason or human comprehension.*

nonconformist *One who refuses to follow established or conventional ideas or habits.*

The transcendentalist movement of the 1830s resulted in part from a liberalizing of the straitjacket Puritan theology. It also owed much to foreign influences, including the German romantic philosophers and the religions of Asia. The transcendentalists rejected the prevailing theory, derived from John Locke that all knowledge comes to the mind through the senses. Truth, rather, "transcends" the senses: it cannot be found by observation alone. Every person possesses an inner light that can illuminate the highest truth and put him or her in direct touch with God, or the "Oversoul."

These **mystical** doctrines of transcendentalism defied precise definition, but they underlay concrete beliefs. Foremost was a stiff-backed individualism in matters religious as well as social. Closely associated was a commitment to self-reliance, self-culture, and self-discipline. These traits naturally bred hostility to authority and to formal institutions of any kind, as well as to all conventional wisdom. Finally came exaltation of the dignity of the individual, whether black or white—the mainspring of a whole array of humanitarian reforms.

Best known of the transcendentalists was Boston-born Ralph Waldo Emerson (1803–1882). Tall, slender, and intensely blue-eyed, he mirrored serenity in his noble features. Trained as a Unitarian minister, he early forsook his pulpit and ultimately reached a wider audience by pen and platform. He was a never-failing favorite as a lyceum lecturer and for twenty years took a western tour every winter. Perhaps his most thrilling public effort was a Phi Beta Kappa address, "The American Scholar," delivered at Harvard College in 1837. This brilliant appeal was an intellectual Declaration of Independence, for it urged American writers to throw off European traditions and delve into the riches of their own backyards.

Hailed as both a poet and a philosopher, Emerson was not of the highest rank as either. He was more influential as a practical philosopher and through his fresh and vibrant essays enriched thousands of humdrum lives. Catching the individualistic mood of the Republic, he stressed self-reliance, self-improvement, optimism, and freedom. The secret of Emerson's popularity lay largely in the fact that his ideals reflected those of an expanding America. By the 1850s he was an outspoken critic of slavery, and he ardently supported the Union cause in the Civil War.

Henry David Thoreau (1817–1862) was Emerson's close associate—a poet, a mystic, a transcendentalist, and a **nonconformist.** Condemning a government that supported slavery, he refused to pay his Massachusetts poll tax and was jailed for a night.* A gifted prose writer, he is

In 1849 Henry David Thoreau (1817–1862) published "Resistance to Civil Government," (later renamed "Civil Disobedience"), asserting:

"All men recognize the right of revolution; the right to refuse allegiance to and to resist the government, when its tyranny or its inefficiency are great and endurable. But almost all say that such is not the case now. . . . I say, when a sixth of the population of a nation which has undertaken to be the refuge of liberty are slaves, and a whole country is unjustly overrun and conquered by a foreign army, and subjected to military law, I think that it is not too soon for honest men to rebel and revolutionize. What makes this duty more urgent is the fact, that the country so overrun is not our own, but ours is the invading army."

* The story (probably apocryphal) is that Emerson visited Thoreau at the jail and asked, "Why are you here?" The reply came, "Why are you not here?"

well known for *Walden: Or Life in the Woods* (1854). The book is a record of Thoreau's two years of simple existence in a hut that he built on the edge of Walden Pond, near Concord, Massachusetts. A stiff-necked individualist, he believed that he should reduce his bodily wants so as to gain time for a pursuit of truth through study and meditation. Thoreau's *Walden* and his essay *On the Duty of Civil Disobedience* exercised a strong influence in furthering idealistic thought, both in America and abroad. His writings later encouraged Mohandas Gandhi to resist British rule in India and, still later, inspired the development of American civil rights leader Martin Luther King, Jr.'s thinking about **nonviolence.**

■ Walt Whitman This portrait of the young poet appeared in the first edition of *Leaves of Grass* (1855).

Bold, brassy, and swaggering was the open-collared figure of Brooklyn's Walt Whitman (1819–1892). In his famous collection of poems, *Leaves of Grass* (1855), he gave free rein to his gushing genius with what he called a "barbaric yawp." Highly romantic, emotional, and unconventional, he dispensed with titles, stanzas, rhymes, and at times even regular meter. He handled sex with shocking frankness, and his book was banned in Boston.

Whitman's *Leaves of Grass* was at first a financial failure. The only three enthusiastic reviews that it received were written by the author himself—anonymously. But in time the once-withered *Leaves of Grass,* revived and honored, won for Whitman an enormous following in both America and Europe.

Leaves of Grass gained for Whitman the informal title "Poet Laureate of Democracy." Singing with transcendental abandon of his love for the masses, he caught the exuberant enthusiasm of an expanding America that had turned its back on the Old World:

> *All the Past we leave behind;*
> *We debouch upon a newer, mightier world, varied world;*
> *Fresh and strong the world we seize—world of labor and the march—*
> *Pioneers! O Pioneers!*

Here at last was the native art for which critics had been crying.

Two women writers whose work remains enormously popular today were also tied to the New England literary world. Louisa May Alcott (1832–1888) grew up in Concord, Massachusetts, in the bosom of transcendentalism, alongside neighbors Emerson, Thoreau, and Fuller. Her philosopher father Bronson Alcott occupied himself more devotedly to ideas than to earning a living, leaving his daughter to write *Little Women* (1868) and other books to support her mother and sisters. Not far away, in Amherst, Massachusetts, poet Emily Dickinson (1830–1886) lived as a recluse but created her own original world through precious gems of poetry. In deceptively spare language and simple rhyme schemes, she explored universal themes of nature, love, death, and immortality. Although she refused during her lifetime to publish any of her poems, when she died, nearly two thousand of them were found among her papers and eventually made their way into print.

nonviolence *The principle of resolving or engaging in conflict without resort to physical force.*

Literary Individualists and Dissenters

Not all writers in these years believed so keenly in human goodness and social progress as Whitman and the New England transcendentalists. Edgar Allan Poe (1809–1849), who spent much of his youth in Virginia, was an eccentric genius. Orphaned at an early age, cursed with ill health, and married to a child-wife of thirteen who fell fatally ill of tuberculosis, he suffered hunger, cold, poverty, and debt. Poe was a gifted lyric poet, as "The Raven" attests. If he did not invent the modern detective novel, he at least set new high standards for it in tales like "The Gold Bug." A master stylist, he also excelled in the short story, especially of the horror genre, in which he shared his nightmares with fascinated readers.

Poe was fascinated by the ghostly and ghastly, as in "The Fall of the House of Usher" and other stories; Poe reflected a dark sensibility distinctly at odds with the usually optimistic tone of American culture. Partly for this reason, Poe has perhaps been even more prized by Europeans than by Americans. His brilliant career was cut short when he was found drunk in a Baltimore gutter and shortly thereafter died.

Two other writers reflected the continuing Calvinist obsession with original sin and with the never-ending struggle between good and evil. In somber Salem, Massachusetts, Nathaniel Hawthorne (1804–1864) grew up in an atmosphere heavy with the memories of his Puritan forebears and the tragedy of his father's premature death on an ocean voyage. His masterpiece was *The Scarlet Letter* (1850), which described the Puritan practice of forcing an adulteress to wear a scarlet "A" on her clothing. In *The Marble Faun* (1860), Hawthorne dealt with a group of young American artists who witness a mysterious murder in Rome. The book explores the concepts of the omnipresence of evil and the dead hand of the past weighing upon the present.

Herman Melville (1819–1891), an orphaned and ill-educated New Yorker, went to sea as a youth and served eighteen adventuresome months on a whaler. "A whale ship was my Yale College and my Harvard," he wrote. Jumping ship in the South Seas, he lived among cannibals, from whom he **providentially** escaped uneaten. His fresh and charming tales of the South Seas were immediately popular, but his masterpiece, *Moby Dick* (1851), was not. The epic novel is a complex allegory of good and evil, told in terms of the conflict between a whaling captain, Ahab, and a giant white whale, Moby Dick. Captain Ahab, having lost a leg to the marine monster, lives only for revenge. His pursuit finally ends when Moby Dick rams and sinks his ship, leaving only one survivor. The whale's exact identity and Ahab's motives remain obscure. In the end the sea, like the terrifyingly impersonal and unknowable universe of Melville's imagination, simply rolls on.

providential *Under the care and direction of God or other benevolent natural or supernatural forces.*

Moby Dick was widely ignored at the time of its publication; people were accustomed to more straightforward and upbeat prose. A disheartened Melville continued to write unprofitably for some years, part of the time eking out a living as a customs inspector, and then died in relative obscurity and poverty. Ironically, his brooding masterpiece about the mysterious white whale had to wait until the more jaded twentieth century for readers and for proper recognition.

Portrayers of the Past

A distinguished group of American historians was emerging at the same time that other writers were winning distinction. Energetic George Bancroft (1800–1891), who as secretary of the navy helped found the Naval Academy at Annapolis in 1845, has deservedly received the title "Father of American History." He published a spirited, superpatriotic history of the United States to 1789 in six volumes (1834–1876), a work that grew out of his vast researches in dusty archives in Europe and America.

Two other historians are read with greater pleasure and profit today. William H. Prescott (1796–1859) published classic accounts of the conquest of Mexico (1843) and Peru (1847). Francis Parkman (1823–1893) penned a brilliant series of volumes beginning in 1851. In epic style he chronicled the struggle between France and Britain in colonial times for the mastery of North America.

Early American historians of prominence were almost without exception New Englanders, largely because the Boston area provided well-stocked libraries and a stimulating literary tradition. These writers numbered abolitionists among their relatives and friends and hence were disposed to view the South unsympathetically. The writing of American history suffered for generations from an antisouthern bias perpetuated by this early "made in New England" interpretation.

Chapter Summary

In early-nineteenth-century America, movements of moral and religious reform accompanied the democratization of politics and the creation of a national market economy. After a period of growing rationalism in religion, a new wave of revivals beginning about 1800 swept out of the West and effected great change not only in religious life but also in other areas of society. Existing religious groups were further fragmented, and new groups like the Mormons emerged. Women were especially prominent in these developments, becoming a major presence in the churches and discovering in reform movements an outlet for energies that were often stifled in masculinized political and economic life.

Among the first areas to benefit from the reform impulse was education. The public elementary school movement gained strength, while a few women made their way into still tradition-bound colleges. Women were also prominent in movements for improved treatment of the mentally ill, peace, temperance, and other causes. By the 1840s some women also began to agitate for their own rights, including suffrage. The movement for women's rights, closely linked to the antislavery crusade, gained adherents even while it met strong obstacles and vehement opposition.

While many reformers worked to improve society as a whole, others created utopian experiments to model their religious and social ideals. Some of these groups promoted radical sexual and economic doctrines, while others appealed to high-minded intellectuals and artists.

American culture was still quite weak in theoretical sciences and the fine arts, but a vigorous national literature blossomed after the War of 1812. In New England the literary renaissance was closely linked to the philosophy of transcendentalism promoted by Emerson and others. Many of the great American writers like Walt Whitman reflected the national spirit of utopian optimism, but a few dissenters like Hawthorne and Melville explored the darker side of life and of their own society.

VARYING VIEWPOINTS

Reform: Who? What? How? and Why?

Early chronicles of the antebellum period universally lauded the era's reformers, portraying them as idealistic, altruistic crusaders intent on improving American society. After World War II, however, some historians began to detect selfish and even conservative motives underlying the apparent benevolence of the reformers. They described reforms like temperance, asylums, prisons, and mandatory public education as efforts by anxious upper-class men and women to assert social control over the ferment of antebellum life.

The wave of reform activity in the 1960s prompted a reevaluation of the reputations of the antebellum reformers. These more recent interpretations found much to admire in the authentic religious commitments of reformers and especially in the participation of women, who sought various social improvements as an extension of their function as protectors of the home and family.

Abolitionism, for example, which had once been blamed by some historians for the Civil War, received new favorable treatment as the racial climate began to change during the 1960s. By the end of the twentieth century abolitionist men and women were revered as ideologically committed individuals dedicated not just to freeing the enslaved but to saving the soul of America.

Scholars animated by the modern feminist movement have also inspired a reconsideration of women's reform activity. Historians like Nancy Cott, Kathryn Sklar, and Mary Ryan began to look more closely at what Cott called "the bonds of womanhood" and uncover the links between women's domestic lives and their public benevolent behavior. When men behaved in immoral or illegal ways, women reformers claimed that they had the right and duty to leave the confines of their homes and actively purify society.

More recently, historians Nancy Hewitt and Lori Ginzburg have challenged the idea of a single female reform identity, pointing to class-based tensions within female ranks and detecting a shift from an early focus on moral uplift to a more class-based appeal for social control. Historians of the suffrage movement have emphasized another kind of exclusivity among women reformers—the boundaries of race. Ellen DuBois has shown that after a brief alliance with the abolitionist movement, many female suffrage reformers abandoned the cause of black liberation in order to achieve their own goal. Whatever historians may conclude about the liberating or leashing character of the early reform, it is clear that they now have to contend with the ways in which class, gender, and race divided reforms, making the plural—*reform movements*—the more accurate depiction of the impulse to "improve" that pervaded American society in the early nineteenth century.

PART THREE

Testing the New Nation

1820–1877

The Civil War of 1861 to 1865 was the awesome trial by fire of American nationhood and of the American soul. All Americans knew, said Abraham Lincoln, that slavery "was somehow the cause of this war." The war tested, in Lincoln's ringing phrase at Gettysburg, whether any nation "dedicated to the proposition that all men are created equal . . . can long endure." How did this great and bloody conflict come about? And what were its results?

American slavery was by any measure a "peculiar institution." It was rooted in both racism and economic exploitation and depended for its survival on brutal repression. Yet the American slave population was the only enslaved population in history that grew by means of its own biological reproduction—a fact that suggests to many historians that conditions under slavery in the United States were somehow less punitive than in other slave societies. Indeed, a distinctive and durable African American culture managed to flourish under slavery, further suggesting that the slave regime provided some "space" for African American cultural development. But however benignly it might be painted, slavery remained a cancer in the heart of American democracy, a moral outrage that mocked the nation's claim to be a model of social and political enlightenment. As time went on, more and more voices called more and more stridently for its abolition.

The nation lived uneasily with slavery from the outset. Thomas Jefferson was only one among many in the founding generation who felt acutely the conflict between the high principle of equality and the ugly reality of slavery. The federal government in the early Republic took several steps to check the growth of slavery. It banned slavery in the Old Northwest in 1787, prohibited the further importation of slaves after 1808, and declared in the Missouri Compromise of 1820 that the vast western territories secured in the Louisiana Purchase were forever closed to slavery north of the state of Missouri. Antislavery sentiment even abounded in the South in the immediate post-Revolutionary years. But as time progressed, and especially after Eli Whitney's invention of the cotton gin in the 1790s, the southern planter class became increasingly dependent on slave labor to wring profits from the sprawling plantations that carpeted the South. As cotton cultivation spread westward, the South's stake in slavery grew deeper, and the abolitionist outcry grew louder.

The controversy over slavery significantly intensified following the war with Mexico in the 1840s. "Mexico will poison us," predicted the philosopher Ralph Waldo Emerson, and he proved distressingly prophetic. The lands acquired from Mexico—most of the present-day American Southwest, from Texas to California—

reopened the question of extending slavery into the western territories. The decade and a half following the Mexican War—from 1846 to 1861—witnessed a series of ultimately ineffective efforts to come to grips with that question, including the ill-starred Compromise of 1850, the conflict-breeding Kansas-Nebraska Act of 1854, and the Supreme Court's inflammatory decision in the *Dred Scott* case of 1857. Ultimately, the slavery question was settled by force of arms, in the Civil War itself.

The Civil War, as Lincoln observed, was assuredly about slavery. But as Lincoln also repeatedly insisted, the war was about the viability of the Union as well and about the strength of democracy itself. Could a democratic government, built on the principle of popular consent, rightfully deny some of its citizens the same right to independence that the American revolutionaries had exercised in seceding from the British Empire in 1776? Southern rebels, calling the conflict "The War for Southern Independence," asked that question forcefully, but ultimately it, too, was answered not in the law courts or in the legislative halls but on the battlefield.

The war unarguably established the supremacy of the Union, and it ended slavery as well. But as the victorious Union set about the task of "reconstruction" after the war's end in 1865, a combination of weak northern will and residual southern power frustrated the goal of making the emancipated blacks full-fledged American citizens. The Civil War in the end brought nothing but freedom—but over time, freedom proved a powerful tool indeed.

What if . . . ?

- **What if some sort of compromise between the North and South had prevented the Civil War?**

  What might such a compromise have looked like?

  What might have been its consequences for the future of slavery, and for American nationhood?

  Was *any* such compromise politically possible—or morally defensible?

The South and the Slavery Controversy

1793–1860

IF YOU PUT A CHAIN AROUND THE NECK OF A SLAVE, THE OTHER END FASTENS ITSELF AROUND YOUR OWN.

RALPH WALDO EMERSON, 1841

Chapter Outline

- The Economy of the Cotton Kingdom
- Poor Whites and Free Blacks
- The Plantation System
- The Human Face of the "Peculiar Institution"
- The Abolitionist Crusade
- Southern and Northern Responses to Abolitionism
- Examining the Evidence: Bellegrove Plantation, Donaldsville, Louisiana, Built 1857
- Varying Viewpoints: What Was the True Nature of Slavery?

At the dawn of the Republic, slavery faced an uncertain future. Touched by Revolutionary idealism, some southern leaders, including Thomas Jefferson, were talking openly of freeing the slaves. Others predicted that the iron logic of economics would eventually expose slavery's unprofitability, speeding its demise.

But the introduction of Eli Whitney's cotton gin in 1793 scrambled all those predictions. Whitney's invention made possible the wide-scale cultivation of short-staple cotton. The white fiber rapidly became the dominant southern crop, eclipsing tobacco, rice, and sugar. The explosion of cotton cultivation created an insatiable demand for labor, chaining the slave to the gin and the planter to the slave. As the nineteenth century opened, the reinvigoration of southern slavery carried fateful implications for blacks and whites alike—and threatened the survival of the nation itself.

Focus Questions

1. **How did a small, elite planter aristocracy come to dominate the "Cotton Kingdom" of the South, and what were the strengths and weaknesses of the region's plantation-controlled economic and social system?**
2. **Why did the majority of nonslaveholding whites in the South support slavery, and what was their relationship with both the slaveholding planters and the black slaves?**
3. **What were the central features of slavery, and what was life like for African Americans under slavery (as well as for the small number of free blacks)?**
4. **What were the effects of the "peculiar institution" on blacks, whites, and the nation as a whole?**
5. **How and why did abolitionism gradually gain strength, despite the strong initial hostility of most northerners, and why did southerners respond so fiercely to the movement's very existence?**

Chronology

1793 Whitney's cotton gin transforms southern economy.

1800 Gabriel slave rebellion in Virginia.

1808 Congress outlaws slave trade.

1817 American Colonization Society formed.

1820 Missouri Compromise.

1822 Republic of Liberia established in Africa.
Vesey slave rebellion in Charleston, South Carolina.

1831 Garrison begins publishing the *Liberator*.
Nat Turner slave rebellion in Virginia.

1833 British abolish slavery in West Indies.
American Anti-Slavery Society founded.

1834 Abolitionist students expelled from Lane Theological Seminary.

1835 U.S. Post Office orders destruction of abolitionist mail.
"Broadcloth Mob" attacks Garrison.

1836 House of Representatives passes "Gag Resolution."

1837 Mob kills abolitionist Lovejoy in Alton, Illinois.

1839 Weld publishes *American Slavery As It Is.*

1845 Douglass publishes *Narrative of the Life of Frederick Douglass.*

1848 Free Soil party organized.

"Cotton Is King!"

As time passed, the Cotton Kingdom developed into a huge agricultural factory, pouring out avalanches of the fluffy fiber. Quick profits drew planters to the virgin bottomlands of the Gulf states. As long as the soil was still vigorous, the yield was bountiful, and the rewards were high. Caught up in an economic spiral, the planters bought more slaves and land to grow more cotton, so as to buy still more slaves and land.

To a large degree, the prosperity of both North and South rested on the bent backs of southern slaves. Cotton accounted for half the value of all American exports after 1840, and northern shippers reaped a large part of the profits from the cotton trade.

Cotton even held foreign nations in partial bondage. Britain's most important single manufacture in the 1850s was cotton cloth, from which about one-fifth of its population, directly or indirectly, drew their livelihood. About 75 percent of this precious supply of fiber came from the white-carpeted acres of the South.

Southern leaders were fully aware that Britain was tied to them by cotton threads, and this dependence gave them a heady sense of power. In their eyes "Cotton Was King," the gin was his throne, and the black slaves were his henchmen. If war should ever break out between North and South, northern warships would presumably cut off the outflow of cotton. Fiber-famished British factories would then close their gates, starving mobs would force the London government to break the blockade, and the South would triumph. Cotton was a powerful monarch indeed.

Primary source
Southern Cotton Production
college.hmco.com/pic/kennedybrief7e

Slaves of the Slave System

Before the Civil War the South was in some respects not so much a democracy as an **oligarchy**—or a government by the few, in this case a planter aristocracy. In 1850 only 1,733 families owned more than 100 slaves each, and this select

oligarchy *Rule by a small elite.*

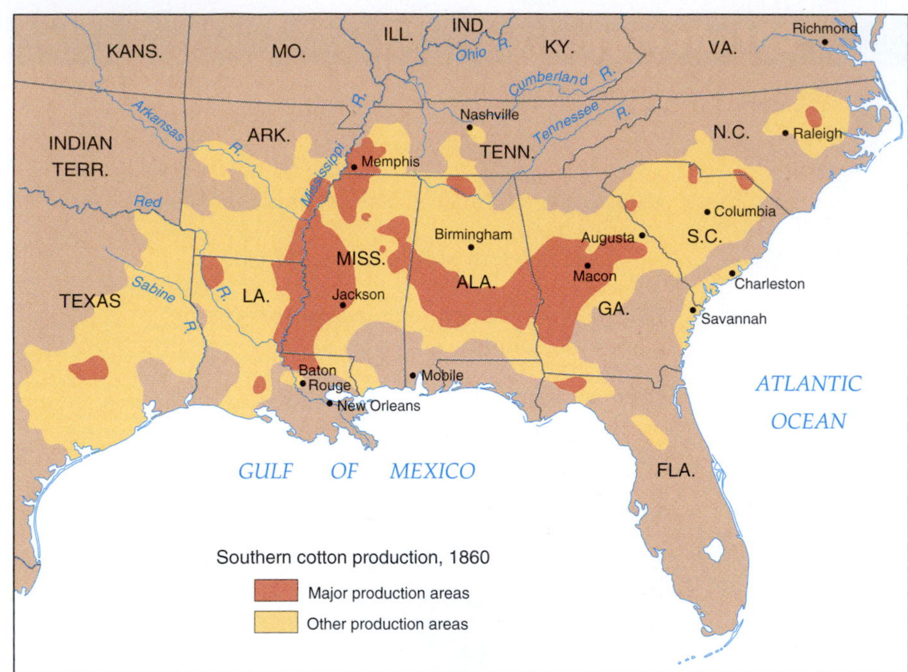

Southern Cotton Production, 1860 The concentration of cotton-growing was in the "black belt" stretching from South Carolina to Louisiana.

group provided the cream of the political and social leadership of the section and nation. Here was the mint-julep South of the tall-columned and white-painted plantation mansion—the "big house," where dwelt the "cottonocracy."

The planter aristocrats, with their blooded horses and Chippendale chairs, enjoyed the lion's share of southern wealth. They could educate their children in the finest schools, often in the North or abroad. Their money provided the leisure for study, reflection, and statecraft, as was notably true of men like John C. Calhoun (a Yale graduate) and Jefferson Davis (a West Point graduate).

The plantation system also shaped the lives of southern women. The mistress of a great plantation commanded a sizable household staff of mostly female slaves. She gave daily orders to cooks, maids, seamstresses, laundresses, and personal servants. Some mistresses showed tender regard for their bondswomen, while others treated their slaves atrociously. But virtually no slaveholding women believed in abolition, and relatively few protested when the husbands and children of their slaves were sold.

Despite the occasional benevolent relations between owners and slaves, the moonlight-and-magnolia tradition concealed much that was worrisome, distasteful, and sordid. The domination of southern society by a favored aristocracy was fundamentally undemocratic, widening the gap between rich and poor and hampering public education. Plantation agriculture was wasteful, largely because King Cotton and his money-hungry subjects despoiled the good earth. Quick profits led to excessive cultivation or "land butchery," which in turn caused a heavy leakage of population to the West and Northwest.

The economic structure of the South became increasingly monopolistic. As the land wore thin, many small farmers sold their holdings to more prosperous neighbors. The big got bigger and the small got smaller. When the Civil War finally erupted, a large percentage of southern farms had passed from the hands of the families that had originally cleared them.

Another cancer in the bosom of the South was the financial instability of the plantation system. The temptation to overspeculate in land and slaves caused many planters, including Andrew Jackson in his later years, to plunge in beyond their depth. The slaves represented a heavy investment of capital, perhaps $1,200 each in the case of "prime field hands," and they might deliberately injure themselves or run away.

Dominance by King Cotton likewise led to a dangerous dependence on a one-crop economy, whose price level was at the mercy of world conditions. The whole system discouraged the healthy diversification of agriculture and particularly of manufacturing.

Southern planters resented watching the North grow fat at their expense. They were pained by the heavy outward flow of **commissions** and interest to northern **middlemen,** bankers, agents, and shippers. True souls of the South, especially by the 1850s, deplored the fact that when they were born they were wrapped in Yankee-made

Online Study Center

Interactive map
The Legal Status of Slavery, from the Revolution to the Civil War
college.hmco.com/pic/kennedybrief7e

commissions *Fee paid to an agent in a transaction, usually as a percentage of the sale.*

middlemen *In commerce, those who stand between the original producer of goods and the retailer or consumer.*

Basil Hall (1788–1844), an Englishman, visited part of the cotton belt on a river steamer (1827–1828). Noting the preoccupation with cotton, he wrote,

"All day and almost all night long, the captain, pilot, crew, and passengers were talking of nothing else; and sometimes our ears were so wearied with the sound of cotton! cotton! cotton! that we gladly hailed a fresh inundation of company in hopes of some change—but alas! . . . 'What's cotton at?' was the first eager inquiry. 'Ten cents [a pound],' 'Oh, that will never do!' "

Slaveowning Families, 1850 More than half of all slaveholding families owned fewer than four slaves. In contrast, 2 percent of slaveowners owned more than fifty slaves each. A tiny slaveholding elite held a majority of slave property in the South. The great majority of white southerners owned no slaves at all.

swaddling clothes, spent their lives in servitude to Yankee manufacturing, and when they died they were laid in coffins made with Yankee nails and buried in graves dug with Yankee shovels. The South furnished the corpse and the hole in the ground.

The Cotton Kingdom also repelled large-scale European immigration, which added so richly to the manpower and wealth of the North. In 1860 only 4.4 percent of the southern population was foreign-born, compared with 18.7 percent for the North. The diverting of non-British immigration to the North caused the white South to become the most Anglo-Saxon section of the nation.

The White Majority

Primary source
Hermitage, Main House
college.hmco.com/pic/kennedybrief7e

Only a handful of southern whites lived in pillared mansions. Below those 1,733 families in 1850 who owned one hundred or more slaves were some 345,000 less wealthy slaveowning families, representing about 1,725,000 white persons. Over two-thirds of these families—255,268 in all—owned fewer than ten slaves each. All told, only about one-fourth of white southerners owned any slaves or belonged to a slaveowning family.

The smaller slaveowners did not own a majority of the slaves, but they made up a majority of the masters. With the striking exception that their households contained a slave or two, or perhaps an entire slave family, the small slaveowners' lifestyles resembled that of small farmers in the North more than it did that of the southern planter aristocracy. They lived in modest farmhouses and sweated beside their bondsmen in the cotton fields, laboring callous for callous just as hard as their slaves.

Beneath the slaveowners in the social pyramid was the great body of whites who owned no slaves at all. By 1860 their numbers had swelled to 6,120,825—three-quarters of all southern whites. Shouldered off the richest bottomlands by the mighty planters, they scratched a simple living from the thinner soils of the backcountry and the mountain valleys. These rednecked farmers participated in the market economy scarcely at all. As subsistence farmers, they raised corn and hogs, not cotton, and often lived

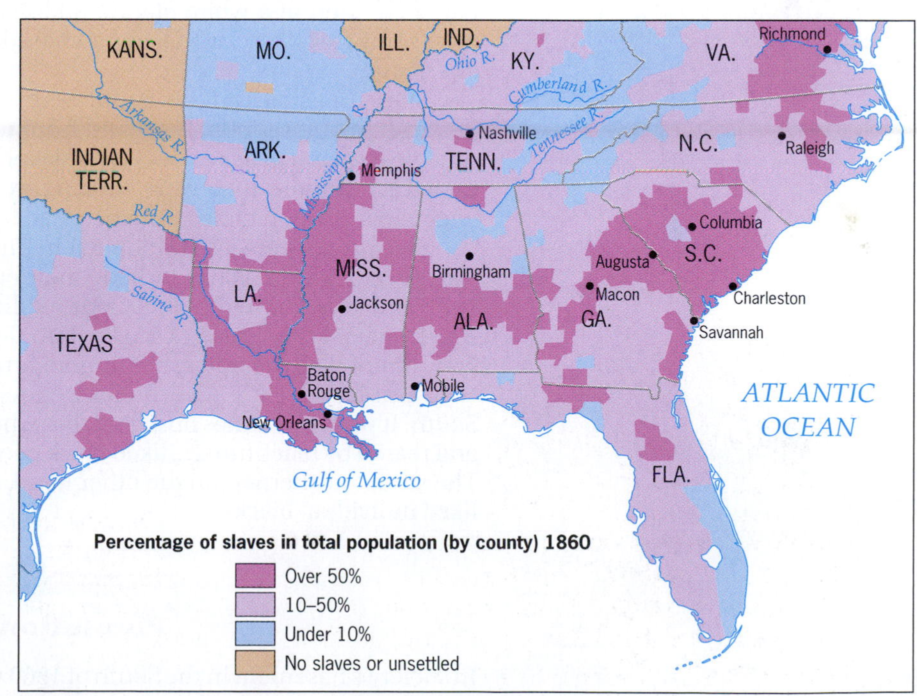

Distribution of Slaves, 1860 The philosopher Ralph Waldo Emerson, a New Englander, declared in 1856, "I do not see how a barbarous community and a civilized community can constitute a state. I think we must get rid of slavery or we must get rid of freedom."

isolated lives, punctuated by extended socializing and sermonizing at religious revival meetings. Some of the least prosperous non-slaveholding whites were scorned even by slaves as "poor white trash," "hillbillies," or "crackers."

All these whites without slaves had no direct stake in the preservation of slavery, yet they were among the stoutest defenders of the system. Why? The answer is not far to seek.

The carrot on the stick ever dangling before their eyes was the hope of buying a slave or two and of parlaying their holdings into riches—all in accord with the "American dream" of upward social mobility. They also took fierce pride in their presumed racial superiority, which would be watered down if the slaves were freed. Many of the poorer whites were hardly better off economically than the slaves, but even the most wretched whites could take perverse comfort from the knowledge that they outranked someone in status: the still more wretched African American slave. Thus did the logic of economics join with the illogic of **racism** in buttressing the slave system.

racism *Belief in the superiority of one race over another; or behavior reflecting such a belief.*

In a special category among white southerners were the mountain whites, more or less marooned in the valleys of the Appalachian range that stretched from western Virginia to northern Georgia and Alabama. As independent small farmers, hundreds of miles distant from the heart of the Cotton Kingdom and rarely if ever in sight of a slave, these mountain whites had little in common with the whites of the flatlands. Many of them, including future president Andrew Johnson of Tennessee, hated both the haughty planters and their gangs of blacks. When the Civil War came, the tough-fibered mountain men constituted a vitally important peninsula of Unionism jutting down into the secessionist southern sea. They ultimately played a significant role in crippling the Confederacy.

Free Blacks: Slaves Without Masters

Precarious in the extreme was the standing of the South's free blacks, who numbered about 250,000 by 1860. In the upper South, the free black population traced its origins to a wavelet of emancipation inspired by the idealism of Revolutionary days. In the deep South, many free blacks were mulattoes, usually the emancipated children of a white planter and his black mistress. Throughout the South were some free blacks who had purchased their freedom with earnings from labor after hours.

These free blacks in the South were a kind of "third race." They were prohibited from certain occupations and from testifying in court, and were always vulnerable to being hijacked back into slavery by unscrupulous slave traders. As free men and women, they were walking examples of what might be achieved by emancipation, and hence were detested by defenders of the slave system.

Free blacks were also unpopular in the North, where about another 250,000 of them lived. Several states forbade their entrance, most denied them the right to vote, and some barred blacks from public schools. Much of the agitation in the North against the spread of slavery into the new territories in the 1840s and 1850s grew out of race prejudice, not humanitarianism.

Antiblack feeling was in fact frequently stronger in the North than in the South. It was sometimes observed that white southerners, who were often suckled and reared by black nurses, liked black people as individuals but despised the race. The white northerner, on the other hand, often professed to like the race but disliked individual blacks.

Plantation Slavery

In society's basement in the South of 1860 were nearly 4 million black human chattels. Their numbers had quadrupled since the dawn of the century, as the booming cotton economy created a seemingly unquenchable demand for slave labor. Congress ended the legal slave trade in 1808, but the price of "black ivory" was so high in the years before the Civil War that thousands of slaves were smuggled illegally into the South. Yet the huge bulk of the increase in the slave population came not from imports but instead from natural reproduction—a fact that distinguished slavery in America from slavery in other New World societies and implied much about the tenor of the regime and the conditions of family life under slavery.

Above all, the planters regarded the slaves as investments, into which they had sunk nearly $2 billion by 1860. Slaves were the primary form of wealth in the South, and as such they were cared for as any asset is cared for by a prudent capitalist. Masters sometimes hired cheap Irish wage laborers to perform dangerous work like tunnel blasting or swamp draining, rather than risk the life of a valuable slave, worth $1,800 by 1860 (a price that had quintupled since 1800).

Slavery was profitable for the great planters, though it hobbled the economic development of the region as a whole. The profits from the cotton boom sucked ever more slaves from the upper to the lower South. Thousands of blacks from the soil-exhausted states of the Old South, especially Virginia, were "sold down the river" to the cotton frontier of the lower Mississippi Valley. By 1860 the Deep South states of South Carolina, Georgia, Florida, Mississippi, Alabama, and Louisiana each had a majority or near-majority of blacks and accounted for about half of all slaves in the South.

The forced "breeding" of slaves was not openly encouraged. But white masters all too frequently forced their attention on female slaves, fathering a sizable mulatto population, most of which remained enchained.

A Market in People Held captive in a net, a slave sits on the Congo shore, waiting to be sold and shipped.

Slave auctions were brutal sights. The open selling of human flesh under the hammer was among the most revolting aspects of slavery. On the auction block, families were separated with distressing frequency, usually for economic reasons such as **bankruptcy** or the division of "property" among heirs. The sundering of families in this fashion was perhaps slavery's greatest psychological horror. Abolitionists decried the practice, and Harriet Beecher Stowe seized on the emotional power of this theme by putting it at the heart of the plot of *Uncle Tom's Cabin.*

bankruptcy *Legally, the condition of being declared unable to meet legitimate financial obligations or debts, requiring special supervision by the courts.*

overseer *Someone who governs or directs the work of another.*

Life Under the Lash

White southerners often romanticized about the happy life of their singing, dancing, banjo-strumming "darkies." But how did the slaves actually live? There is no simple answer to this question. Conditions varied greatly from region to region, from large plantation to small farm, and from master to master. Everywhere, of course, slavery meant hard work, ignorance, and oppression. The slaves—both men and women—usually toiled from dawn to dusk in the fields, under the watchful eyes and ready whip-hand of a white **overseer** or black "driver." They had no civil or political rights, and even minimal protection from murder or unusually cruel punishment was difficult to enforce. Slaves were forbidden to testify in court, and their marriages were not legally recognized.

Primary source
Slave Perspective on Family Ties,
college.hmco.com/pic/kennedybrief7e

Floggings were common, for the whip was the substitute for the wage-incentive system and the most visible symbol of the planter's mastery. Strong-willed slaves were sometimes sent to "breakers," whose technique consisted mostly in lavish laying on of the lash. As an abolitionist song of the 1850s lamented,

To-night the bond man, Lord
Is bleeding in his chains;
And loud the falling lash is heard
On Carolina's plains!

But savage beatings made sullen laborers, and lash marks hurt resale values. There are, to be sure, sadistic monsters in any population, and the planter class

In 1852 Maria Perkins, a woman enslaved in Virginia, wrote plaintively to her husband about the disruption that the commercial traffic in slaves was visiting upon their family:

"I write you a letter to let you know of my distress my master has sold albert to a trader on Monday court day and myself and other child is for sale also and I want you to let hear from you very soon before next cort if you can I dont know when I dont want you to wait till Christmas I want you to tell Dr Hamelton and your master if either will buy me they can attend to it know and then I can go after-wards I dont want a trader to get me they asked me if I had got any person to buy me and I told them no they took me to the court houste too they never put me up a man buy the name of brady bought albert and is gone I dont know whare they say he lives in Scottesville my things is in several places some is in staunton and if I should be sold I dont know what will become of them I dont expect to meet with the luck to get that way till I am quite heart sick nothing more I am and ever will be your kind wife Maria Perkins."

contained its share. But the typical planter had too much of his own prosperity riding on the backs of his slaves to beat them bloody on a regular basis.

By 1860 most slaves were concentrated in the "black belt" of the deep South that stretched from South Carolina and Georgia into the new southwest states of Alabama, Mississippi, and Louisiana. A majority of blacks lived on larger plantations that harbored communities of twenty or more slaves. In some counties of the deep South, especially along the lower Mississippi River, blacks accounted for more than 75 percent of the population. There the family life of slaves tended to be relatively stable, and a distinctive African American culture developed. Forced separations of spouses, parents, and children were evidently more common on smaller plantations and in the upper South. Slave marriage vows sometimes proclaimed, "Until death or *distance* do you part."

With impressive resilience, blacks managed to sustain family life in slavery, and most slaves were raised in stable two-parent households. Continuity of family identity across generations was evidenced in the widespread practice of naming children for grandparents or adopting the surname not of a current master but of a forebear's master. African Americans also displayed their African cultural roots when they avoided marriage between first cousins, in contrast to the frequent intermarriage of close relatives among the ingrown planter aristocracy.

African roots were also visible in the slaves' religious practices. Though heavily Christianized by itinerant evangelists of the Second Great Awakening, blacks in slavery molded their own distinctive religious forms from a mixture of Christian and African elements. They emphasized those aspects of the Christian heritage that seemed most pertinent to their own situation—especially the captivity of the Israelites in Egypt. One of the most haunting spirituals implored,

Tell old Pharaoh,
"Let my people go."

And another lamented,

Nobody knows de trouble I've seen
Nobody knows but Jesus.

African practices also persisted in the "responsorial" style of preaching, in which the congregation frequently punctuates the minister's remarks with assents and amens—an adaptation of the give-and-take between caller and dancers in the African ringshout dance.

Primary source
Slaves Dancing the Juba
college.hmco.com/pic/kennedybrief7e

The Burdens of Bondage

Slavery was intolerably degrading to the victims. They were deprived of the dignity and sense of responsibility that come from independence and the right to make choices. Slaves were denied an education, because reading brought ideas, and ideas brought discontent. Many states passed laws forbidding their instruction, and perhaps nine-tenths of adult slaves at the beginning of the Civil War were illiterate. For all slaves—indeed for virtually all blacks, slave or free—the "American dream" of bettering one's lot through study and hard work was a cruel and empty mockery.

Not surprisingly, victims of the "peculiar institution" devised countless ways to throw sand in its gears. Slaves often slowed the pace of their labor to the barest minimum that would spare them the lash, thus fostering the myth of black "laziness" in the minds of whites. They filched food from the "big house" and pilfered other goods that had been produced by their labor. They sometimes **sabotaged** expensive equipment and occasionally even poisoned their masters' food.

The slaves also universally pined for freedom. Many took to their heels as runaways, frequently in search of a separated family member. Others rebelled, though never successfully. In 1800 an armed insurrection led by a slave named Gabriel in Richmond, Virginia, was foiled by informers, and in 1822 Denmark Vesey, a free black, led another ill-fated rebellion in Charleston. In both cases the rebels were betrayed by informers and hanged. In 1831 Nat Turner, a visionary black preacher, led an uprising that slaughtered about sixty Virginians, mostly women and children. Reprisals were swift and bloody.

The dark taint of slavery also left its mark on the whites. It fostered the brutality of the whip, the bloodhound, and the branding iron. White southerners increasingly lived in a state of imagined siege, surrounded by potentially rebellious blacks inflamed by abolitionist propaganda from the North. Their fears bolstered an intoxicating theory of biological racial superiority and turned the South into a reactionary backwater in an era of progress—one of the last bastions of slavery in the Western world. The defenders of slavery were forced to degrade themselves, along with their victims. As Booker T. Washington, a distinguished black leader and former slave, later observed, whites could not hold blacks in a ditch without getting down there with them.

Slave Nurse and Young White Master Southern whites would not allow slaves to own property or exercise civil rights, but, paradoxically, they often entrusted them with the raising of their own precious children. Many a slave "mammy" served as a surrogate mother for the offspring of the planter class.

Early Abolitionism

The inhumanity of the "peculiar institution" gradually caused antislavery societies to sprout forth. Abolitionist sentiment first stirred at the time of the Revolution, especially among Quakers. Because of the widespread loathing of blacks, some of the earliest abolitionist efforts focused on transporting blacks back to Africa. The American Colonization Society was founded for this purpose in 1817, and in 1822 the Republic of Liberia was established for former slaves on the West African coast. Most native-born African Americans had no wish to be transplanted into a strange civilization, and only some fifteen thousand were actually transported there over the next four decades. Yet the colonization idea appealed to some antislaveryites, including Abraham Lincoln, until the time of the Civil War.

sabotage *Intentional destruction or damage of goods, machines, or productive processes.*

In the 1830s the abolitionist movement took on new energy and momentum, mounting to the proportions of a crusade. American abolitionists took heart in 1833 when their British counterparts unchained the slaves in the West Indies. Most important, the religious spirit of the Second Great Awakening inflamed the hearts of many abolitionists against the sin of slavery.

Prominent among them was lanky, tousle-haired Theodore Dwight Weld, who had been evangelized by Charles Grandison Finney in the 1820s. In 1832 Weld enrolled at Lane Theological Seminary in Cincinnati, whose president was the formidable Lyman Beecher, father of novelist Harriet Beecher Stowe, reformer Catharine Beecher, and preacher-abolitionist Henry Ward Beecher. Expelled along with several other students in 1834 for organizing an eighteen-day debate on slavery, Weld and his fellow "Lane Rebels"—full of the energy and idealism of youth—fanned out across the Old Northwest preaching the antislavery gospel. Weld also assembled a potent propaganda tract, *American Slavery As It Is* (1839), which greatly influenced Harriet Beecher Stowe's *Uncle Tom's Cabin.*

Radical Abolitionism

Primary source
Down with the Abolitionists
college.hmco.com/pic/kennedybrief7e

On New Year's Day, 1831, a shattering abolitionist blast came from the bugle of William Lloyd Garrison, a mild-looking reformer of twenty-six. A spiritual child of the Second Great Awakening, Garrison published in Boston the first issue of his militantly antislavery newspaper the *Liberator.* With this mighty paper broadside, Garrison triggered a thirty-year war of words and in a sense fired one of the opening barrages of the Civil War.

Stern and uncompromising, Garrison proclaimed in strident tones that under no circumstances would he tolerate the poisonous weed of slavery:

> I will be as harsh as truth and as uncompromising as justice. . . . I am in earnest—I will not equivocate—I will not excuse—I will not retreat a single inch—and I WILL BE HEARD!

Other dedicated abolitionists rallied to Garrison's standard, and in 1833 they founded the American Anti-Slavery Society. Prominent among them was eloquent Wendell Phillips, a Boston patrician known as "abolition's golden trumpet."

Black abolitionists distinguished themselves as living monuments to the cause of African American freedom. Their ranks included David Walker, whose incendiary *Appeal to the Colored Citizens of the World* advocated a bloody end to white supremacy. Also noteworthy were Sojourner Truth, a freed black woman who fought tirelessly for black emancipation and women's rights, and Martin Delany, one of the few black leaders to take seriously the notion of black recolonization in Africa.

Sojourner Truth Also known simply as "Isabella," she held audiences spellbound with her deep, resonant voice and the religious passion with which she condemned the sin of slavery. This photo was taken about 1870.

The greatest of the black abolitionists was Frederick Douglass. Escaping from bondage in 1838 at the age of twenty-one, Douglass was "discovered" by the abolitionists in 1841 when he gave a stunning impromptu speech at an antislavery meeting in Massachusetts. Thereafter he lectured widely for the cause, despite frequent beatings and threats against his life. In 1845 he published his classic autobiography, *Narrative of the Life of Frederick Douglass.* It depicted his remarkable origins as the son of a black slave woman and a white father, his struggle to learn to read and write, and his eventual escape to the North.

Douglass was as flexibly practical as Garrison was stubbornly principled. Garrison often appeared to be more interested in his own righteousness than in the substance of the slavery evil itself. He repeatedly demanded that the "virtuous" North secede from the "wicked" South. Renouncing politics, on the Fourth of July, 1854, he publicly burned a copy of the Constitution as "a covenant with death and an agreement with hell." Douglass, on the other hand, along with other abolitionists, increasingly looked to politics to end the blight of slavery. These political abolitionists backed the antislavery Liberty party in 1840, the Free Soil party in 1848, and eventually the Republican party in the 1850s. In the end, most abolitionists, including even the pacifist Garrison himself, followed out the logic of their beliefs and supported a frightfully costly **fratricidal** war as the price of emancipation.

fratricidal *Literally, concerning the killing of brothers; the term is often applied to the killing of relatives or countrymen in feuds or civil wars. (The killing of sisters is* ***sororicide;*** *of fathers* ***patricide;*** *and of mothers* ***matricide.****)*

High-minded and courageous, the abolitionists were men and women of goodwill and various colors who faced the cruel choice that people in many ages have had thrust upon them:

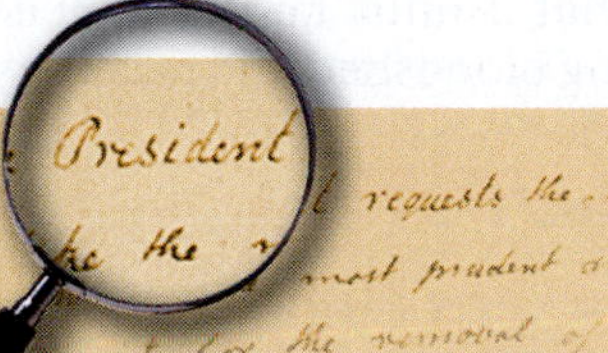

EXAMINING THE EVIDENCE

Bellegrove Plantation, Donaldsville, Louisiana, Built 1857 The sugar-growing Bellegrove Plantation—on the banks of the Mississippi River ninety-five miles north of New Orleans—was laid out on a grander scale than many southern plantations. In this rendering from an advertisement for Bellegrove's sale in 1867, the planter John Orr's home was identified as a "mansion," and quarters for his field hands proved extensive: twenty double cabins built for slaves (now for "Negroes") and a dormitory, described in the ad but not pictured here, housing 150 laborers. Because of the unhealthy work involved in cultivating sugar cane, such as constant digging of drainage canals to keep the cane from rotting in standing water, many planters hired immigrant (usually Irish) labor to keep their valuable slaves out of physical danger. The presence of a hospital between the slave cabins and the mansion indicates the very real threat to health. The layout of Bellegrove reflects the organization of production as well as the social relations on a sugar plantation. The storehouse where preserved sugar awaited shipping stood closest to the Mississippi River, the principal transportation route, whereas the sugar house, the most important building on the plantation, with its mill, boilers, and cooking vats for converting syrup into sugar, dominated the canefields. Although the "big house" and slave quarters stood in close proximity, hedges surrounding the planter's home shut out views of both sugar production and labor. Within the slave quarters, the overseer's larger house signified his superior status, while the arrangement of cabins ensured his supervision of domestic as well as work life.

1. What else does the physical layout of the plantation reveal about settlement patterns, sugar cultivation, and social relationships along the Mississippi?
2. Besides living quarters and facilities for the production and shipping of sugar, what other major supporting activities had to be carried out on a large plantation such as Bellegrove—such that separate buildings were dedicated to those functions?
3. In rough terms, what proportion of the total land of Bellegrove Plantation was given over to growing sugar cane, and what proportion to dwellings, sugar production facilities, and woodlands?

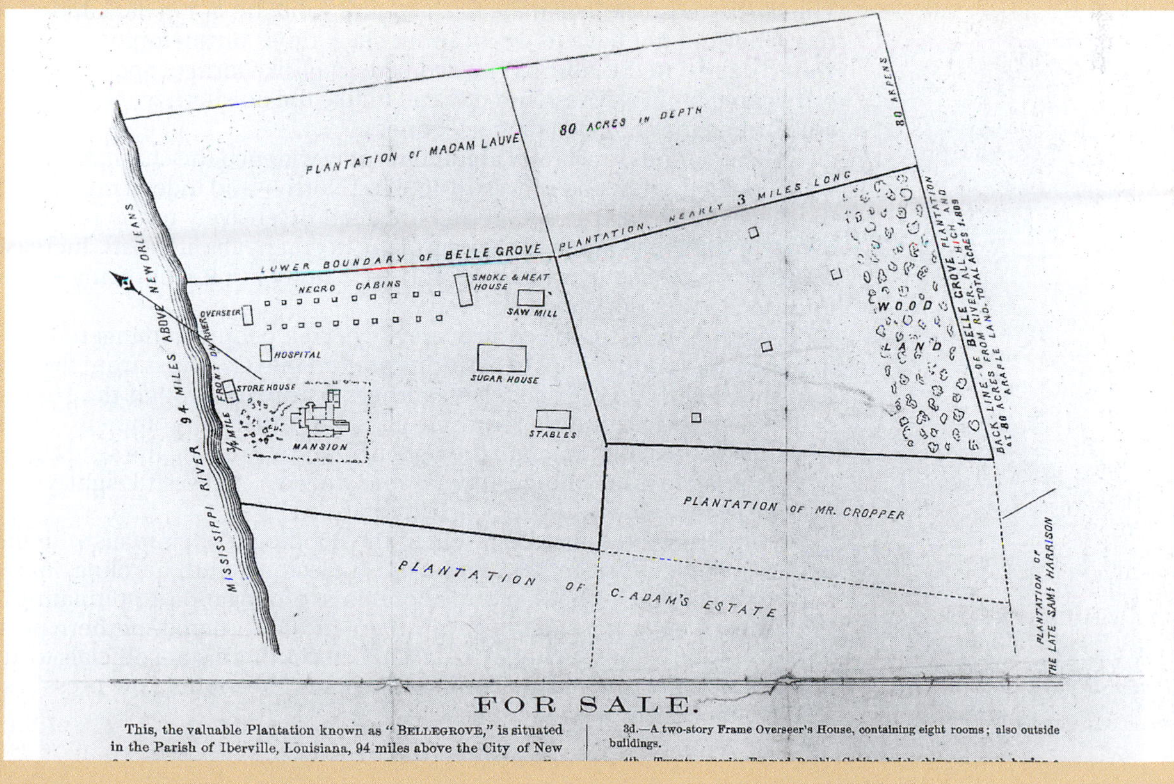

when is evil so enormous that it must be denounced, even at the risk of precipitating bloodshed and butchery?

After hearing Frederick Douglass speak in Bristol, England, in 1846, Mary A. Estlin wrote to an American abolitionist,

"[T]here is but one opinion of him. Wherever he goes he arouses sympathy in your cause and love for himself. . . . Our expectations were highly roused by his narrative, his printed speeches, and the eulogisms of the friends with whom he has been staying: but he far exceeds the picture we had formed both in outward graces, intellectual power and culture, and eloquence."*

The South Lashes Back

Antislavery sentiment was not unknown in the South up to the 1820s, but after 1830 the voice of white southern abolitionism was silenced. The Virginia legislature actually debated and eventually defeated various emancipation proposals in 1831–1832. Nat Turner's rebellion in 1831 sent a wave of hysteria sweeping over the snowy cotton fields, and planters in growing numbers slept with pistols by their pillows.

The nullification crisis of 1832 further implanted haunting fears in white southern minds, conjuring up nightmares of black incendiaries and abolitionist devils. Jailings, whippings, and lynchings now greeted rational efforts to discuss the slavery problem in the South.

Proslavery whites responded to the abolitionist groundswell by launching a massive defense of slavery as a positive good. In doing so they forgot their own section's previous doubts about the morality of the "peculiar institution." Slavery, they claimed, was supported by the authority of the Bible and the wisdom of Aristotle. It was good for the Africans, who were lifted from the "**barbarism** of the jungle" and clothed with the blessings of Christian civilization.

barbarism (barbarian) *The condition of being crude, uneducated, or uncivilized.*

Slavemasters strongly encouraged religion in the slave quarters, emphasizing those teachings that encouraged obedience. White apologists also contended that master-slave relationships really resembled those of a family. Southern whites were quick to contrast the "happy" lot of their "servants" with that of the overworked northern wage slaves, including exploited women and stunted children. The blacks mostly toiled in the fresh air and sunlight, not in dark and stuffy factories. They did not have to worry about slack times or unemployment, as did the "hired hands" of the North. Provided with a jail-like form of Social Security, slaves were cared for in sickness and old age, unlike the northern workers, who were set adrift when they outlived their usefulness.

These curious proslavery arguments only widened the chasm between a backward-looking South and a forward-looking North—and indeed much of the rest of the Western world. The southerners reacted defensively to the pressure of their own fears and the merciless nagging of the northern abolitionists. Increasingly the white South turned in upon itself and grew hotly intolerant of any embarrassing questions about the status of slavery.

Regrettably, also, the controversy over free people endangered free speech in the entire country. Piles of petitions poured into Congress from the antislavery reformers, and in 1836 sensitive southerners drove through the House the so-called Gag Resolution. It required all such antislavery appeals to be tabled without debate. This attack on the right of petition aroused the aged ex-president, Representative John Quincy Adams, who waged a successful eight-year fight for its repeal.

Southern whites likewise resented the flooding of their mails with incendiary abolitionist literature. In 1835 a mob in Charleston, South Carolina, looted the local post office and burned a pile of abolitionist propaganda. Capitulating to southern pressures, the Washington government in 1835 ordered southern postmasters to destroy abolitionist material and called on southern state officials to arrest federal postmasters who did not comply. Such was "freedom of the press" as guaranteed by the Constitution.

*From Clare Taylor, ed., British and American Abolitionists, An Episode in Transatlantic Understanding (Edinburgh University Press, 1974), p. 282.

The Abolitionist Impact in the North

Abolitionists—especially the extreme Garrisonians—were for a long time unpopular in many parts of the North. Northerners had been brought up to revere the Constitution and to regard the clauses on slavery as a lasting bargain. The ideal of Union, hammered home by the thundering eloquence of Daniel Webster and others, had taken deep root; and Garrison's wild talk of secession grated harshly on northern ears.

The North also had a heavy economic stake in Dixieland. By the late 1850s, southern planters owed northern bankers and other creditors about $300 million, and much of this immense sum would be lost—as, in fact, it later was—should the Union dissolve. New England textile mills were fed with cotton raised by the slaves, and a disrupted labor system might cut off this vital supply and bring unemployment. The Union during these critical years was partly bound together with cotton threads, tied by lords of the loom in collaboration with the so-called lords of the lash. It was not surprising that strong hostility developed in the North against the boat-rocking tactics of the radical antislaveryites.

Interactive map
Escaping from Slavery
college.hmco.com/pic/kennedybrief7e

Repeated tongue-lashings by the extreme abolitionists provoked many mob outbursts in the North, some led by respectable gentlemen. A gang of young toughs broke into abolitionist Lewis Tappan's New York house in 1834 and demolished its interior, while a crowd in the street cheered. In 1835 Garrison, with a rope tied around him, was dragged through the streets of Boston by the so-called Broadcloth Mob but escaped almost miraculously. Reverend Elijah P. Lovejoy, of Alton, Illinois, had his printing press destroyed four times. In 1837 he was killed by a mob and became "the martyr abolitionist." So unpopular were the antislavery zealots that ambitious politicians, like Abraham Lincoln, usually avoided the taint of Garrisonian abolition like the plague.

Primary source
Border Ruffians Invading Kansas
college.hmco.com/pic/kennedybrief7e

Yet by the 1850s the abolitionist outcry had made a deep dent in the northern mind. Many citizens had come to see the South as the land of the unfree and the home of a hateful institution. Few northerners were prepared to abolish slavery outright, but a growing number, including Lincoln, opposed extending it to the western territories. People of this stamp, commonly called "free-soilers," swelled their ranks as the Civil War approached.

Chapter Summary

Whitney's cotton gin made cotton production enormously profitable, and created an ever-increasing demand for slave labor. The South's dependence on cotton production tied it economically to the plantation system and racially to white supremacy. The cultural gentility and political domination of the relatively small plantation aristocracy concealed slavery's great social and economic costs for whites as well as blacks.

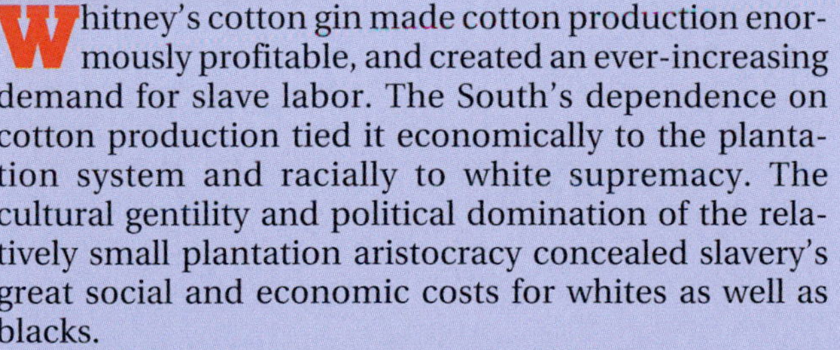

Most slaves were held by a few large planters. But most slaveowners had few slaves, and most southern whites had no slaves at all. Nevertheless, except for a few mountain whites, the majority of southern whites strongly supported slavery and racial supremacy because they cherished the hope of becoming slaveowners themselves, and because white racial identity gave them a sense of superiority to the blacks.

The treatment of the economically valuable slaves varied considerably. Within the bounds of the cruel system, slaves yearned for freedom and struggled to maintain their humanity, including family life.

The older black colonization movement was largely replaced in the 1830s by a radical Garrisonian abolitionism demanding an immediate end to slavery. Abolitionism and the Nat Turner rebellion caused a strong backlash in the South. Earlier southern criticism of slavery disappeared, and proslavery whites increasingly defended slavery as a positive good that actually benefited the slaves. In defending slavery, the South turned its back not only on many of the liberal political and social ideas gaining strength in the North, but on most of progressive Western civilization.

Most northerners were hostile to radical abolitionism as a threat to the cherished Union, and respected the Constitution's evident protection of slavery where it existed. But many also gradually came to see the South as a land of oppression, and any attempt to extend slavery as a threat to free society.

VARYING VIEWPOINTS

What Was the True Nature of Slavery?

By the early twentieth century, the predictable accounts of slavery written by partisans of the North or South had receded in favor of a romantic vision of the Old South. A scholarly version of this vision was Ulrich Bonnell Phillips's landmark study, *American Negro Slavery* (1918), which portrayed slavery as a dying, unprofitable economic institution where benevolent masters treated their slaves with kindly paternalism and racially inferior blacks submissively accepted the system that enslaved them.

Later in the twentieth century historians challenged many of these views. Economic historians have decisively refuted Phillips's claim that slavery was unprofitable by showing that it was a viable, profitable, expanding system. Beginning in the late 1950s, historians came increasingly to emphasize the harshness of the slave system. One study, Stanley Elkins's *Slavery* (1959), went so far as to compare the "peculiar institution" to the Nazi concentration camps of World War II.

More recently, scholars such as Eugene Genovese have contended that slavery did indeed embrace a strange form of paternalism, one reflecting not slaveholders' benevolence but their need to control and coax work out of their reluctant and often recalcitrant "investments." Furthermore, within this paternalist system, black slaves were able to make reciprocal demands of their white owners and to protect a "cultural space" of their own in which family and religion particularly could flourish.

The revised conceptions of the master-slave relationship also spilled over into the debate about slave personality. Kenneth Stampp rejected Stanley Elkins's view that slaves were "infantilized" like concentration camp inmates, and stressed the frequency and variety of slave resistance. In another perspective, Lawrence Levine imaginatively argued in *Black Culture and Black Consciousness* (1977) that the Sambo character was an act, an image that slaves used to confound their masters without incurring punishment. More recently, historians have attempted to avoid the polarity of repression versus autonomy. The challenge before historians today is to capture the vibrancy of slave culture and its legacy for African American society after emancipation, without diminishing the brutality of life under the southern slave regime.

A new sensitivity to gender, spurred by the growing field of women's history, has also expanded the horizons of slavery studies. Historians such as Elizabeth Fox-Genovese, Jacqueline Jones, and Catherine Clinton have focused on the ways in which slavery differed for men and women, both slaves and slaveholders. Enslaved black women, for example, had the unique task of negotiating an identity out of their dual responsibilities as plantation laborer, even sometimes caretaker of white women and children, and anchor of the black family. By tracing the interconnectedness of race and gender in the American South, these historians have also shown how slavery shaped conceptions of masculinity and femininity within southern society, further distinguishing its culture from that of the North.

Scholarship on slavery continues to grow. The newest work by Philip D. Morgan and Ira Berlin has drawn attention to how both the institution of slavery and the experience of the enslaved changed over time. Slavery adapted to particular geographic and environmental factors, and also changed from one generation to the next. As southern slaveholders responded to new social and economic conditions, they gradually altered the legal status of slaves, outlawing manumission in many places and rendering freedom for the enslaved increasingly difficult to attain.

Manifest Destiny and Its Legacy

1841–1848

OUR MANIFEST DESTINY [IS] TO OVERSPREAD THE CONTINENT ALLOTTED BY PROVIDENCE FOR THE FREE DEVELOPMENT OF OUR YEARLY MULTIPLYING MILLIONS.

JOHN L. O'SULLIVAN, 1845*

Chapter Outline

- "Tyler Too" Becomes President, 1841
- The Annexation of Texas, 1845
- Oregon and California
- James K. Polk, The "Dark Horse" of 1844
- War with Mexico, 1846–1848
- Makers of America: The Californios

Territorial expansion dominated American diplomacy and politics in the 1840s. Settlers swarming into the still-disputed Oregon country aggravated relations with Britain, which had staked its own claims in the Pacific Northwest. The clamor to annex Texas to the Union provoked bitter tension with Mexico, which continued to regard Texas as a Mexican province in revolt. And when Americans began casting covetous eyes on Mexico's northernmost province, the great prize of California, open warfare erupted between the United States and its southern neighbor. Victory over Mexico added vast new domains to the United States, but it also raised thorny questions about the status of slavery in the newly acquired territories—questions that would be answered in blood in the Civil War of the 1860s.

Focus Questions

1. What was "Manifest Destiny," and why did it inspire a burst of American expansionism in the 1840s?
2. Why did American expansionist efforts provoke increasing tensions with Britain over Oregon and other issues, as well as increasing domestic conflict over the possible annexation of Texas?
3. How did the issues of Oregon and Texas become central to the election of 1844, and why was Polk's victory taken to be a mandate for Manifest Destiny?
4. How did the issues of California and the Texas boundary lead to war with Mexico, and how did the American victory lead to the territorial acquisition of the entire Southwest?
5. What were the consequences of the Mexican War? In particular, why did it reignite the slavery question?

* This is the earliest known use of the term *Manifest Destiny.*

The Accession of "Tyler Too"

A horde of office-hungry hard-ciderites descended on Washington in 1841, bewildering newly elected President William Henry Harrison. The real leaders of the Whig party regarded "Old Tippecano" as little more than an impressive figurehead. Daniel Webster, as secretary of state, and Henry Clay, the uncrowned king of the Whigs and their ablest spokesman in the Senate, would grasp the helm.

Unluckily for Clay and Webster, their schemes soon hit a fatal snag. Before the new term had fairly started, Harrison contracted pneumonia and died after only four weeks in the White House—by far the shortest administration in American history.

The "Tyler too" part of the Whig ticket, hitherto only a rhyme, now claimed the spotlight. With blue eyes, classical features, and a high forehead, John Tyler was a Virginia gentleman of the old school—gracious and kindly, yet stubbornly attached to principle. He had earlier resigned from the Senate, quite unnecessarily, rather than accept distasteful instructions from the Virginia legislature. Still a lone wolf, he had forsaken the Jacksonian Democratic fold for that of the Whigs, largely because he could not stomach the dictatorial tactics of Jackson.

Tyler's enemies accused him of being a Democrat in Whig clothing. But the Whig party, like the Democratic party, was something of a catchall, and the accidental president simply belonged to the minority wing, which embraced a number of Jeffersonian states' righters. Tyler had in fact been put on the ticket partly to attract the vote of this fringe group, many of whom were influential southern gentry.

It was true, however, that on virtually every major issue the obstinate Virginian was at odds with the majority of his Whig party, which was pro-bank, pro–protective tariff, and pro–internal improvements. "Tyler too" rhymed with "Tippecanoe," but there the harmony ended. As events turned out, President Harrison, the Whig, served for only 4 weeks, whereas Tyler, the ex-Democrat who was still largely a Democrat at heart, served for 204 weeks.

John Tyler: A President Without a Party

After their hard-won, hard-cider victory, the Whigs brought their not-so-secret **platform** out of Clay's waistcoat pocket. To the surprise of no one, it outlined a strongly nationalistic program.

platform *The campaign document stating a party's or candidate's position on the issues, and upon which they "stand" for election.*

caucus *An unofficial organization or consultation of like-minded people to plan a political course or advance their cause, often within some larger body.*

Financial reform came first. The Whig Congress hastened to pass a law ending the independent treasury system, and President Tyler, disarmingly agreeable, signed it. Clay next drove through Congress a bill to establish a new Bank of the United States.

Tyler's hostility to a centralized bank was notorious, and Clay—the "Great Compromiser"—would have done well to conciliate him. But the Kentuckian, robbed repeatedly of the presidency by lesser men, was in an imperious mood and riding for a fall. When the bank bill reached the presidential desk, Tyler flatly vetoed it on both practical and constitutional grounds. A drunken mob gathered late at night near the White House and shouted insultingly, "Huzza for Clay!" "A Bank! A Bank!" "Down with the Veto!"

Whig extremists, seething with indignation, condemned Tyler as "His Accidency" and as an "Executive Ass." To the delight of Democrats, the stiff-necked Virginian was formally expelled from his party by a **caucus** of Whig congressmen, and a serious attempt to impeach him was broached in the House of Representatives. His entire cabinet resigned in a body, except Secretary of State Webster, who was in the midst of delicate negotiations with Britain.

The proposed Whig tariff also felt the prick of the president's well-inked pen. Tyler vetoed a tariff bill that included a scheme for distributing to the states revenues from the sale of public land. But he reluctantly signed the revised Clay-sponsored Tariff of 1842, which pushed rates back down to the moderately protective level of 1832, about 32 percent.

Chronology

1841	Harrison dies after four weeks in office. Tyler assumes presidency.
1842	Aroostook War over Maine boundary. Webster-Ashburton Treaty.
1844	Polk defeats Clay in "Manifest Destiny" election.
1845	United States annexes Texas.
1846	United States settles Oregon dispute with Britain.
1846	United States and Mexico clash over Texas boundary.
1846	Kearny takes Santa Fe. Frémont conquers California. Wilmot Proviso passes House of Representatives.
1846–1848	Mexican War.
1847	Battle of Buena Vista. Scott takes Mexico City.
1848	Treaty of Guadalupe Hidalgo.

Tensions With Britain

Hatred of Britain during the nineteenth century periodically came to a head and had to be lanced by treaty settlement or by war. The poison festered ominously in the late 1830s, especially because of private American involvement in an unsuccessful Canadian rebellion in 1837. When an American steamer, the *Caroline*, attempted to deliver supplies to Canadian insurgents, British troops sank the ship in the Niagara River, killing one American.

Anglo-American controversy then exploded in the early 1840s over the disputed Maine boundary. Hoping to bypass the icebound St. Lawrence River, the British planned to build a road westward from the seaport of Halifax to Quebec. But the proposed route ran through territory claimed by Maine under the treaty of 1783. Tough-knuckled lumberjacks from both Maine and Canada commenced fighting in the disputed **no-man's-land** of the tall-timbered Aroostook River valley. When both sides summoned the local militias, the small-scale lumberjack clash, dubbed the "Aroostook War," threatened to widen into a full-dress shooting war.

no-man's-land *A territory to which neither of two disputing parties has clear claim and where they may meet as combatants.*

As the crisis deepened in 1842, the London Foreign Office sent to Washington a conciliatory diplomat, Lord Ashburton, who had married a wealthy American woman. He speedily established cordial relations with Secretary of State Webster. After protracted and nerve-wracking negotiations in the heat of a Washington summer, the two statesmen finally agreed to compromise on the Maine boundary. On the basis of a rough, split-the-difference arrangement, the Americans retained some 7,000 square miles of the 12,000 square miles of wilderness in dispute. The British got less land but won the desired Halifax-Quebec route.

An overlooked bonus sneaked by in small print of the same treaty: the British, in adjusting the U.S.-Canadian boundary farther west, surrendered 6,500 square miles. The area was later found to contain the priceless Mesabi iron range of Minnesota.

Old Glory Adds the Lone Star of Texas

During the uncertain eight years since 1836, Texas had led a precarious existence. Mexico, refusing to recognize Texas's independence, regarded the Lone Star Republic as a province in revolt, to be reconquered in the future. Mexican

protectorate *The relation of a strong nation to a weak one under its control and protection.*

colossus *Anything of extraordinary size and power; therefore, in international affairs, a major or hegemonic great power.*

mandate *In politics, the belief that an official has been issued a clear charge by the electorate to pursue some particular policy goal.*

resolution *In government, a formal statement of policy or judgment by a legislature, but requiring no legal statute.*

intrigue *A plot or scheme formed by secret, underhanded means.*

officials loudly threatened war if the American eagle should ever gather the fledgling republic under its protective wings.

Confronted with such perils, Texas was driven to open negotiations with Britain and France in the hope of securing the defensive shield of a **protectorate**. In 1839 and 1840 the Texans concluded treaties with France, Holland, and Belgium.

Britain was intensely interested in an independent Texas. Such a republic would check the southward surge of the American **colossus**, whose bulging biceps posed a constant threat to nearby British possessions in the New World. Clashes between a puppet Texas and the Yankees would create a smoke-screen diversion behind which foreign powers could move into the Americas and challenge the insolent Monroe Doctrine. French schemers likewise hoped that an independent Texas would result in the fragmentation and militarization of America.

British abolitionists were also busily intriguing in Texas, hoping that gaining freedom for blacks there would inflame the nearby slaves of the South. In addition, British merchants regarded Texas as a potentially important free-trade area—an offset to the tariff-walled United States. British textile manufacturers believed that an independent Texas, with its vast cotton-producing plains, would relieve British looms of their dependence on American fiber—a supply that might be cut off by embargo or war.

Partly because of the fears aroused by these British and French schemers, Texas became a leading issue in the presidential campaign of 1844. The proexpansion Democrats under James K. Polk finally triumphed over the Whigs under Henry Clay, the hardy perennial candidate. Lame duck President Tyler thereupon promptly interpreted the narrow Democratic victory as a "**mandate**" to acquire Texas.

Eager to crown his troubled administration with this splendid prize, Tyler quickly shepherded Texas into the fold. Many "conscience Whigs" feared that Texas in the Union would be red meat to nourish the lusty "slave power." Aware of their opposition, Tyler despaired of securing the needed two-thirds vote for a treaty in the Senate. He therefore arranged for annexation by a joint **resolution**. This solution required only a simple majority in both houses of Congress. After a spirited debate, the resolution passed early in 1845, and Texas was formally invited to become the twenty-eighth star on the American flag.

Mexico angrily charged that the Americans had despoiled it of Texas. Yet realistic observers could see that the Mexicans would not be able to reconquer their lost province. By 1845 the Lone Star Republic had become a danger spot, inviting foreign **intrigue** that menaced the American people. The continued existence of Texas as an independent nation threatened to involve the United States in a series of ruinous wars, both in America and in Europe.

What other power would have spurned the imperial domain of Texas? The bride was so near, so rich, so fair, so willing. Whatever the peculiar circumstances of the Texas Revolution, the United States can hardly be accused of unseemly haste in achieving annexation. Nine long years were surely a decent wait between the beginning of the courtship and the consummation of the marriage.

Interactive map
Texas Revolution
college.hmco.com/pic/kennedybrief7e

Oregon Fever Populates Oregon

The Oregon Country was an enormous wilderness. It sprawled magnificently west of the Rockies to the Pacific Ocean, and north of California to the line of 54°40′—the present southern tip of the Alaska panhandle. All or substantial parts of this immense area were claimed at one time or another by four nations: Spain, Russia, Britain, and the United States.

Two claimants dropped out of the scramble. Spain, though the first to raise its banner in Oregon, bartered away its claims to the United States in the Florida Treaty of 1819. Russia retreated to the line of 54°40′ by the treaties of 1824 and 1825 with America and Britain. These two remaining rivals now had the field to themselves.

British claims to Oregon were strong—at least to that portion north of the Columbia River. They were based squarely on prior discovery and exploration, on treaty rights, and on actual occupation. The most important colonizing agency was the far-flung Hudson's Bay Company, which was trading profitably with the Indians of the Pacific Northwest for furs.

> *In winning Oregon, the Americans had great faith in their procreative powers. Boasted one congressman in 1846,*
>
> "Our people are spreading out with the aid of the American multiplication table. Go to the West and see a young man with his mate of eighteen; after the lapse of thirty years, visit him again, and instead of two, you will find twenty-two. That is what I call the American multiplication table."

Americans, for their part, could also point to exploration and occupation. Captain Robert Gray in 1792 had stumbled upon the majestic Columbia River, which he named after his ship; and the famed Lewis and Clark expedition of 1804–1806 had ranged overland through the Oregon Country to the Pacific. This shaky American toehold was ultimately strengthened by the presence of missionaries and other settlers, a sprinkling of whom reached the grassy Willamette River valley, south of the Columbia, in the 1830s. These men and women of God, in saving the souls of the Indians, were also instrumental in saving the soil of Oregon for the United States. They stimulated interest in a faraway domain that Americans had earlier assumed would not be settled for centuries.

Scattered American and British pioneers in Oregon continued to live peacefully side by side. At the time of negotiating the Treaty of 1818 (see pp. 172–173), the United States had sought to divide the vast domain at the forty-ninth **parallel**. But the British, who regarded the Columbia River as the St. Lawrence of the West, were unwilling to yield this vital artery. A scheme for peaceful "joint occupation" was thereupon adopted, pending future settlement.

parallel *In geography, the imaginary lines parallel to the earth's equator, marking latitude. (There are 360 degrees of latitude on the globe.)*

dark horse *In politics, a candidate with little apparent support who unexpectedly wins a nomination or election.*

The handful of Americans in the Willamette Valley was suddenly multiplied in the early 1840s, when "Oregon fever" seized hundreds of restless pioneers. In increasing numbers, their creaking covered wagons jolted over the two-thousand-mile Oregon Trail as the human rivulet widened into a stream. By 1846 about five thousand Americans, some of them tough ruffians, had settled south of the Columbia River.

The British, in the face of this rising torrent of humanity, could muster only seven hundred or so subjects north of the Columbia. Losing out lopsidedly in the population race, they were beginning to see the wisdom of arriving at a peaceful settlement before being engulfed by their neighbors.

A curious fact is that only a relatively small segment of the Oregon Country was in actual controversy by 1845. The area in dispute consisted of the rough quadrangle between the Columbia River on the south and east, the forty-ninth parallel on the north, and the Pacific Ocean on the west—most of the present state of Washington (see the map on p. 253). Britain had repeatedly offered the line of the Columbia; America had repeatedly offered the forty-ninth parallel. The whole fateful issue was now tossed into the presidential election of 1844, where it was largely overshadowed by the question of annexing Texas.

A Mandate (?) for Manifest Destiny

The two major parties nominated their presidential standard-bearers in May 1844. Ambitious but often-frustrated Henry Clay, easily the most popular man in the country, was enthusiastically chosen by the Whigs at Baltimore. The Democrats, meeting there later, nominated James K. Polk of Tennessee, America's first "**dark horse**," or "surprise," presidential candidate.

Polk may have been a dark horse, but he was hardly an unknown or decrepit nag. Speaker of the House of Representatives for four years and governor of Tennessee for two terms, Polk was a determined, industrious, ruthless, and intelligent public servant. Whigs attempted to jeer him into oblivion with the taunt, "Who is James K. Polk?" They soon found out.

The campaign of 1844 was in part an expression of the mighty emotional upsurge known as "Manifest Destiny."

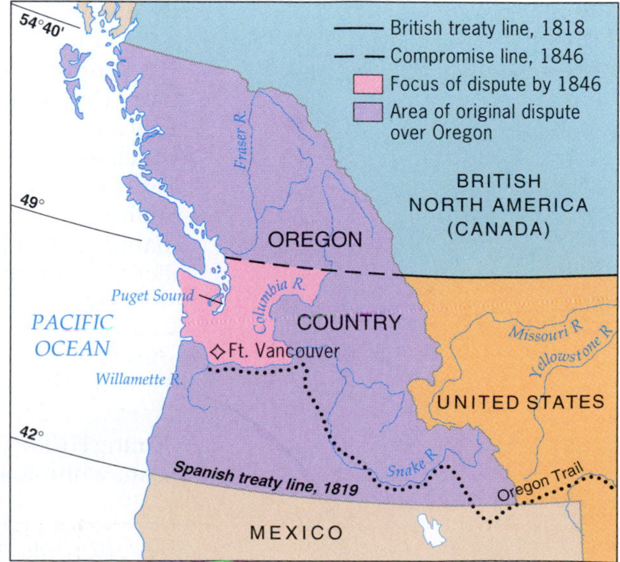

The Oregon Controversy, 1846

■ **Westward the Course of Empire Takes Its Way** This romantic tribute to the spirit of Manifest Destiny was commissioned by Congress in 1860 and may still be seen in the Capitol.

Countless citizens in the 1840s and 1850s, feeling a sense of mission, believed that Almighty God had "manifestly" destined the American people for a hemispheric career. They would irresistibly spread their uplifting and ennobling democratic institutions over at least the entire North American continent, and possibly over South America as well. Land greed and ideals—"empire" and "liberty"—were thus conveniently conjoined.

Expansionist Democrats were strongly swayed by the intoxicating spell of Manifest Destiny. They came out flat-footedly in their platform for the "Re-annexation of Texas"* and the "Reoccupation of Oregon," all the way to 54°40′. The Whigs countered with such slogans as "Polk, Slavery, and Texas, or Clay, Union, and Liberty."

On the crucial issue of Texas, the acrobatic Clay tried to ride two horses at once. The "Great Compromiser" compromised away the presidency when he wrote letters saying that while he personally favored annexing slave-holding Texas (an appeal to the South), he also favored postponement (an appeal to the North). By straddling the issue this way, Clay alienated ardent antislaveryites.

In the stretch drive, "Dark Horse" Polk nipped Henry Clay at the wire, 170 to 105 votes in the Electoral College and 1,338,464 to 1,300,097 in the popular column. Clay would have won if he had not lost New York by a scant 5,000 votes. There the tiny antislavery Liberty party absorbed nearly 16,000 votes, many of which would otherwise have gone to the unlucky Kentuckian. Ironically, the anti-Texas Liberty party, by helping to elect the pro-Texas Polk, hastened the annexation of Texas. The victorious Democrats proclaimed that they had received a mandate from the voters to take Texas, and three days before leaving office President Tyler signed the joint resolution of annexation.

Polk the Purposeful

"Young Hickory" Polk, unlike "Old Hickory" Jackson, was not an impressive figure. Lean, white-haired, gray-eyed, and stern-faced, he took life seriously and drove

* The United States had given up its claims to Texas in the Florida Purchase Treaty with Spain in 1819 (see p. 173). The slogan "fifty-four forty or fight" was evidently not coined until two years later, in 1846.

himself mercilessly into a premature grave. His burdens were increased by an unwillingness to delegate authority. Methodical and hard-working but not brilliant, he was shrewd, narrow-minded, and persistent. "What he went for he fetched," wrote a contemporary. Purposeful in the highest degree, he developed a positive four-point program and with remarkable success achieved it completely in less than four years.

Polk's first goal was a lower tariff. Robert J. Walker, his secretary of the Treasury, lobbied through Congress a tariff bill that reduced the average rates of the Tariff of 1842 from about 32 percent to 25 percent. The Walker Tariff of 1846 proved to be an excellent revenue producer.

A second objective of Polk was restoration of the independent treasury, unceremoniously dropped by the Whigs in 1841. Pro-bank Whigs in Congress raised a storm of opposition, but victory at last rewarded the president's efforts in 1846.

The third and fourth points on Polk's "must list" were the settlement of the Oregon dispute and the acquisition of California.

"Reoccupation" of the "whole" of Oregon had been promised northern Democrats in the campaign of 1844. But southern Democrats, once they had annexed Texas, rapidly cooled off. Polk, himself a southerner, had no intention of insisting on the 54°40′ pledge of his own platform. He again proposed the compromise line of 49°, but the British minister in Washington brusquely spurned this olive branch.

Fortunately for peace, British anti-expansionists ("Little Englanders") were now persuaded that the Columbia River after all was not the St. Lawrence of the West. Early in 1846 the British came around and themselves proposed the line of 49°. The senators speedily accepted the offer and approved the subsequent treaty, despite a few diehard shouts of "Fifty-four forty forever!"

Satisfaction with the Oregon settlement among Americans was not unanimous. The northwestern states, hotbeds of Manifest Destiny and "fifty-four forty-ism," joined the antislavery forces in condemning what they regarded as a base betrayal by the South. Why *all* of Texas and not *all* of Oregon? Because, retorted the expansionist Senator Thomas Hart Benton of Missouri, "Great Britain is powerful and Mexico is weak."

So Polk, despite all the campaign bluster, got neither "fifty-four forty" nor a fight. But he did get something that in the long run was better: a reasonable compromise without a rifle being raised.

Misunderstandings with Mexico

Faraway California was Polk's final objective. He and other disciples of Manifest Destiny had long coveted its verdant valleys and especially the spacious bay of San Francisco. This splendid harbor was widely regarded as America's future gateway to the Pacific Ocean.

The population of California in 1845 was curiously mixed. It consisted of perhaps thirteen thousand sun-blessed Spanish Mexicans and as many as seventy-five thousand dispirited Indians. There were fewer than a thousand "foreigners," mostly Americans, some of whom had "left their consciences" behind them as they rounded Cape Horn. Given time, these transplanted Yankees might bring California into the Union by "playing the Texas game."

Polk was eager to buy California from Mexico, but relations with Mexico City were dangerously embittered. One point of friction was some $3 million in claims against Mexico for damages to American citizens and their property. The most serious bone of contention was Texas. After threatening war if the United States acquired the Lone Star Republic, the Mexican government completely severed diplomatic relations following annexation.

Deadlock with Mexico over Texas was further tightened by a question of boundaries. During the long era of Spanish occupation of Mexico, the southwestern boundary of Texas had been the Nueces River. But the expansive Texans, on rather far-fetched grounds, were claiming the more southerly Rio Grande instead. Polk, for his part, felt a strong obligation to defend Texas in its claim, once it was annexed.

deadlock *To completely block or stop action as a consequence of the mutual pressure of equal and opposed forces.*

The Mexicans were far less concerned about this boundary quibble than the United States. In their eyes all of Texas was still theirs, although temporarily in revolt, and a dispute over the two rivers seemed pointless. Yet Polk was careful to keep American troops out of virtually all of the explosive no-man's-land between the Nueces and the Rio Grande, as long as there was any real prospect of peaceful adjustment.

The golden prize of California continued to cause Polk much anxiety. Disquieting rumors (now known to have been ill-founded) were circulating that Britain was about to buy or seize California—a grab that Americans could not tolerate under the Monroe Doctrine. In a last desperate throw of the dice, Polk dispatched John Slidell to Mexico City as minister late in 1845. The new envoy, among other alternatives, was instructed to offer a maximum of $25 million for California and territory to the east. But the proud Mexican people would not even permit Slidell to present his "insulting" proposition.

American Blood on American (?) Soil

A frustrated Polk was now prepared to force a showdown. On January 13, 1846, he ordered four thousand men, under General Zachary Taylor, to march from the Nueces River to the Rio Grande, provocatively near Mexican forces. Polk's presidential diary reveals that he expected at any moment to hear of a clash. When none occurred after an anxious wait, he informed his cabinet on May 9, 1846, that he proposed to ask Congress to declare war on the basis of (1) unpaid claims and (2) Slidell's rejection. These, at best, were rather flimsy pretexts. Two cabinet members spoke up and said that they would feel better satisfied if Mexican troops should fire first.

That very evening news of bloodshed arrived. On April 25, 1846, Mexican troops had crossed the Rio Grande and attacked General Taylor's command, with a loss of sixteen Americans killed or wounded.

Polk, further aroused, sent a vigorous war message to Congress. He declared that despite "all our efforts" to avoid a clash, hostilities had been forced upon the country by the shedding of "American blood upon the American soil." A patriotic Congress overwhelmingly voted for war, and enthusiastic volunteers cried, "Ho for the Halls of the Montezumas!" and "Mexico or Death!" Inflamed by the war fever, even antislavery Whig bastions joined with the rest of the nation, though they later condemned "Jimmy Polk's war." As James Russell Lowell of Massachusetts lamented,

Massachusetts, God forgive her,
She's akneelin' with the rest.

In his message to Congress, Polk was making history—not writing it. If he had been a historian, he would have explained that American blood had been shed on soil that the Mexicans had good reason to regard as their own. A gangling, rough-featured Whig congressman from Illinois, one Abraham Lincoln, introduced certain resolutions that requested information as to the precise "spot" on American soil where American blood had been shed. He pushed his "spot" resolutions with such persistence that he came to be known as the "spotty Lincoln" who could die of "spotted fever." More extreme antislavery agitators branded the president a liar—"Polk the Mendacious."

> *On June 1, 1860, less than a year before he became president, Abraham Lincoln (1809–1865) wrote,*
>
> "The act of sending an armed force among the Mexicans was unnecessary, inasmuch as Mexico was in no way molesting or menacing the United States or the people thereof; and . . . it was unconstitutional, because the power of levying war is vested in Congress, and not in the President."

Did Polk provoke war? California was an imperative point in his program, and Mexico would not sell it at any price. The only way to get it was to use force or wait for an internal American revolt. But in 1846, patience had ceased to be a virtue as far as Polk was concerned. Bent on grasping California by fair means or foul, he pushed the quarrel to a bloody showdown.

Both sides, in fact, were spoiling for a fight. Feisty Americans, especially southwestern expansionists, were eager to teach the Mexicans a lesson. The Mexicans, in turn, were burning to humiliate the "Bullies of the North." Possessing a considerable standing army, they boasted of invading the United States, freeing the black slaves, and lassoing whole regiments of Americans. They were hoping that the quarrel with Britain over Oregon would blossom into a full-dress war, as it came near doing, and further pin down the hated *yanquis*. Fired by indignation, Mexicans and Americans each believed the other was the aggressor.

The Mastering of Mexico

Polk wanted California—not war. But when war came, he hoped to fight it on a limited scale and then pull out when he had captured the prize. The conflict would not be so simple. The dethroned and devious Mexican dictator Santa Anna, then exiled in Cuba, returned to Mexico and proceeded to rally his countrymen to a desperate defense of their soil.

Primary source
Texas Revolution, The
college.hmco.com/pic/kennedybrief7e

American operations in the Southwest and in California were completely successful. In 1846 General Stephen W. Kearny led a detachment of seventeen hundred troops over the famous Santa Fe Trail from Fort Leavenworth to Santa Fe. This sun-baked outpost, with its drowsy plazas, was easily captured. But before Kearny could reach California, the fertile province was won. When war broke out, Captain John C. Frémont, the dashing explorer, just "happened" to be there with several dozen well-armed men. In helping to overthrow Mexican rule in 1846, he collaborated with American naval officers and with the local Americans, who had hoisted the banner of the short-lived California Bear Flag Republic.

General Zachary Taylor meanwhile had been spearheading the main thrust. Known as "Old Rough and Ready" because of his iron constitution and unsoldierly appearance—he sometimes wore a Mexican straw hat—he fought his way across the Rio Grande into Mexico. After several gratifying victories, he reached Buena Vista. There, on February 22–23, 1847, his weakened force of five thousand men was attacked by some twenty thousand march-weary troops under Santa Anna. The Mexicans were finally repulsed with extreme difficulty, and overnight Zachary Taylor became the "Hero of Buena Vista."

Sound American strategy now called for a crushing blow at the enemy's vitals—Mexico City. Though a good leader, General Taylor could not decisively win the war in the semideserts of northern Mexico. The command of the main expedition, which pushed inland from the coastal city of Vera Cruz early in 1847, was entrusted to General Winfield Scott. A handsome giant of a man, Scott had emerged as a hero from the War of 1812 and later earned the nickname "Old Fuss and Feathers" because of his resplendent uniforms and strict discipline. Scott succeeded in battling a more numerous enemy through mountainous terrain up to Mexico City by September 1847 in one of the most brilliant campaigns in American military annals. He proved to be the most distinguished general produced by his country between 1783 and 1861.

Primary source
General Scott's Triumph
college.hmco.com/pic/kennedybrief7e

Fighting Mexico for Peace

Polk was anxious to end the shooting as soon as he could secure his territorial goals. Accordingly, he sent along with Scott's invading army a State Department official, Nicholas P. Trist. Grasping a fleeting opportunity to negotiate, Trist signed the Treaty of Guadalupe Hidalgo on February 2, 1848, and forwarded it to Washington.

Interactive map
The Mexican War
college.hmco.com/pic/kennedybrief7e

The terms of the treaty were breathtaking. They confirmed the American title to Texas and yielded the enormous area stretching northward to Oregon and west to the ocean, embracing coveted California. This total expanse, including Texas, was about one-half of Mexico. The United States agreed to pay $15 million for the land and to assume the claims of its citizens against Mexico in the amount of $3,250,000 (see "Makers of America: The Californios," pp. 260–261).

Primary source
Southwest and the Mexican War
college.hmco.com/pic/kennedybrief7e

Polk quickly submitted the treaty to the Senate. Speed was imperative. The antislavery Whigs in Congress—dubbed "Mexican Whigs" or "conscience Whigs"—

■ Major Campaigns of the Mexican War

were denouncing this "damnable war" with increasing heat. Having secured control of the House in 1847, they were even threatening to vote down supplies for the armies in the field. If they had done so, Scott probably would have been forced to retreat, and the fruits of victory might have been tossed away.

Another peril impended. A swelling group of expansionists, intoxicated by Manifest Destiny, was clamoring for the United States to take all of Mexico. If America had seized it, the nation would have been saddled with a vexatious problem. Farseeing southerners like Calhoun, alarmed by the mounting anger of antislavery agitators, realized that the South would do well not to be too greedy. The treaty was finally approved by the Senate, 38 to 14. Oddly enough, it was condemned both by those opponents who wanted all of Mexico and by opponents who wanted none of it.

Profit and Loss in Mexico

As wars go, the Mexican War was a small one. It cost some thirteen thousand American lives, most of them taken by disease. But the fruits of the fighting were enormous.

America's total expanse, already vast, was increased by about one-third (counting Texas)—an addition even greater than that of the Louisiana Purchase. A sharp stimulus was given to the spirit of Manifest Destiny for, as the proverb has it, the appetite comes with eating.

The Mexican War proved to be the blood-spattered schoolroom of the Civil War. The campaigns provided priceless field experience for most of the officers destined to become leading generals in the forthcoming conflict, including Captain Robert E. Lee and Lieutenant Ulysses S. Grant. The Military Academy at West Point, founded in 1802, fully justified its existence through the well-trained officers. Useful also was the navy, which did valuable work in throwing a crippling blockade around Mexican ports. The Marine Corps, in existence since 1798, won new laurels and to this day sings, in its stirring hymn, about the Halls of Montezuma.

The army waged war without defeat and without a major blunder, despite formidable obstacles and a half-dozen or so achingly long marches. Chagrined British critics, as well as other foreign skeptics, reluctantly revised upward their estimate of Yankee military prowess. Opposing armies, moreover, emerged with increased respect for each other. The Mexicans, though poorly led, fought heroically. At Chapultepec, near Mexico City, the teenage lads of the military academy there (*los niños*) perished to a man.

Early in 1848 the New York Evening Post *demanded,*

"Now we ask, whether any man can coolly contemplate the idea of recalling our troops from the [Mexican] territory we at present occupy . . . and . . . resign this beautiful country to the custody of the ignorant cowards and profligate ruffians who have ruled it for the last twenty-five years? Why, humanity cries out against it. Civilization and Christianity protest against this reflux of the tide of barbarism and anarchy."

Such was one phase of Manifest Destiny.

War News from Mexico, by Richard Caton Woodville The newfangled telegraph kept the nation closely informed of events in far-off Mexico.

The Californios

When the United States acquired the Mexican Cession in 1848, it took in a vast land that stretched from the arid desert Southwest to the fruited valleys and port cities of California. There, at the conclusion of the Mexican War, dwelled some thirteen thousand Californios—descendants of the Spanish and Mexican conquerors who had once ruled California.

The Spanish had first arrived in California in 1769, extending their New World empire and outracing Russian traders to bountiful San Francisco Bay. Father Junipero Serra, an enterprising Franciscan friar, soon established twenty-one missions along the coast. Indians in the iron grip of the missions were encouraged to adopt Christianity and often forced to toil endlessly as farmers and herders, in the process suffering disease and degradation. These frequently maltreated mission Indians occupied the lowest rungs on the ladder of Spanish colonial society.

Upon the loftiest rungs perched the Californios. Pioneers from the Mexican heartland of New Spain, they had trailed Serra to California, claiming land and civil offices in their new home. Yet even the proud Californios had deferred to the all-powerful Franciscan missionaries until Mexico threw off the Spanish colonial yoke in 1826 and transferred power from the missions to secular (that is, governmental) authorities.

Online Study Center

Primary source
Richard Henry Dana Looks at California
college.hmco.com/pic/kennedybrief7e

■ California Indians Dancing at the Mission in San José, by Sykes, 1806

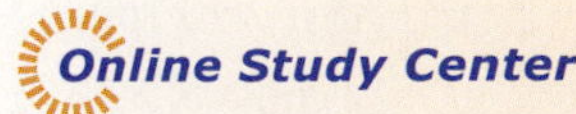

Primary source
Spanish Missions and Presidios in California
college.hmco.com/pic/kennedybrief7e

This "secularization" program attacked and eroded the immense power of the Franciscans, who had confidently commanded their rich fiefdoms and resisted even minor efforts to reform their harsh treatment of the Indians. But during the 1830s much of their land and many of their assets were confiscated by the Californios. Vast *ranchos* (ranches) formed, and from those citadels the Californios ruled until the Mexican War.

The Californios' glory faded in the wake of the American victory. Overwhelmed by the inrush of Anglo golddiggers after the discovery at Sutter's Fort in 1848, the Californios saw their recently acquired lands and political power slip through their fingers. When the Civil War broke out in 1861, so harshly did the word *Yankee* ring in their ears that many Californios supported the South.

By 1870 the Californios' brief ascendancy had utterly vanished—a short and sad tale of riches to rags in the face of the Anglo onslaught. Half a century later, beginning in 1910, hundreds of thousands of young Mexicans would flock into California and the Southwest. They would enter a region liberally endowed with Spanish architecture and artifacts, bearing the names of Spanish missions and Californio ranchos. But they would find it a land dominated by Anglos, a place far different from that which their Californio ancestors had settled so hopefully in earlier days.

Long-memoried Mexicans have never forgotten that their northern enemy tore away about half of their country. The argument that they were lucky not to lose all of it, and that they had been paid something for their land, has scarcely lessened their bitterness. The war also marked an ugly turning point in the relations between the United States and Latin America as a whole. Hitherto, Uncle Sam had been regarded with some friendliness. Henceforth, he was increasingly feared as the "Colossus of the North." Suspicious neighbors to the south condemned him as a greedy and untrustworthy bully, who might next despoil them of their soil.

Most ominous of all, the war rearoused the snarling dog of the slavery issue, and the beast did not stop yelping until drowned in the blood of the Civil War. Abolitionists assailed the Mexican conflict as one provoked by the southern "slavocracy" for its own evil purposes.

Quarreling over slavery extension also erupted on the floors of Congress. In 1846, shortly after the shooting started, Polk requested an appropriation of $2 million with which to buy a peace. Representative David Wilmot of Pennsylvania, fearful of the southern "slavocracy," introduced a fateful amendment. It stipulated that slavery should never exist in any of the territory wrested from Mexico.

The disruptive Wilmot amendment twice passed the House but not the Senate. Southern members, unwilling to be robbed of prospective slave states, fought the restriction tooth and nail. Antislavery men, in Congress and out, battled no less bitterly for the exclusion of slaves. The "Wilmot Proviso" never became law, but it soon came to symbolize the burning issue of slavery in the territories.

In a broad sense, the opening shots of the Mexican War were the opening shots of the Civil War. President Polk left the nation the splendid physical heritage of California and the Southwest but also the ugly moral heritage of an embittered slavery dispute. "Mexico will poison us," said the philosopher Ralph Waldo Emerson. Mexicans could later take some satisfaction in knowing that the territory wrenched from them had proved to be a venomous apple of discord that could well be called Santa Anna's revenge.

Chapter Summary

As Tyler assumed the presidency after Harrison's early death, the United States became engaged in a series of sharp disputes with Britain. A conflict over the Maine boundary was resolved, but British involvement in Texas revived the movement to annex the Lone Star Republic to the United States.

The Texas and Oregon questions became embroiled in the hotly contested 1844 campaign, as the Democrats nominated and elected the militantly expansionist Polk. After Texas was added to the Union, Polk pursued an aggressive policy of expansion. He successfully acquired part of the disputed Oregon country from Britain. Unable to obtain Mexican California peaceably, Polk led the nation into war with an equally belligerent Mexico in 1846.

American forces quickly conquered California and New Mexico. Winfield Scott's and Zachary Taylor's invasion of Mexico was also successful, and the United States obtained large new territories in the peace treaty.

Besides adding California, New Mexico, and Utah to American territory, the Mexican War trained a new generation of military leaders and aroused long-term Latin American resentment of the United States. But its most important consequence was to force the slavery controversy to the center of national politics, as first indicated by the Wilmot Proviso proposing to ban slavery from the newly acquired territories.

Renewing the Sectional Struggle

1848–1854

SECESSION! PEACEABLE SECESSION! SIR, YOUR EYES AND MINE ARE NEVER DESTINED TO SEE THAT MIRACLE.

DANIEL WEBSTER, 1850

Chapter Outline

- "Popular Sovereignty"
- The Compromise of 1850
- The Inflammatory Fugitive Slave Law
- President Pierce and Expansion, 1853–1857
- Senator Douglas and the Kansas-Nebraska Act, 1854

The year 1848, highlighted by a rash of revolutions in Europe, was filled with unrest in America. The Treaty of Guadalupe Hidalgo had officially ended the war with Mexico but initiated a new and perilous round of political warfare in the United States. The vanquished Mexicans had been forced to relinquish an enormous tract of real estate, including Texas, California, and all the area between. The acquisition of this huge domain raised anew the burning issue of extending slavery into the territories. Northern antislaveryites had rallied behind the Wilmot Proviso, which flatly prohibited slavery in any territory acquired in the Mexican War. Southern senators had blocked the passage of the proviso, but the issue did not die. Ominously, debate over slavery in the area of the Mexican Cession threatened to disrupt the ranks of both Whigs and Democrats and to split national politics along North-South sectional lines.

Focus Questions

1. **What were the major terms of the Compromise of 1850, and how did they try to defuse the furious controversies over the territories acquired from Mexico in 1848?**
2. **How successful was the Compromise of 1850?**
3. **Why did the Whig party disintegrate and then disappear?**
4. **How and why did the Democratic Pierce administration, as well as private American adventurers, pursue overseas schemes designed to expand slavery?**
5. **What was the content and purpose of Douglas's Kansas-Nebraska Act, and why did it stir the sectional controversy to new heights?**

The Popular Sovereignty Panacea

Each of the two great political parties was a vital bond of national unity, for each enjoyed powerful support in both North and South. If they should be replaced by two purely sectional groupings, the Union would be in peril. To politicians, the wisest strategy seemed to be to sit on the lid of the slavery issue and ignore the boiling beneath. Even so, the cover bobbed up and down ominously in response

Primary source
Mexican News
college.hmco.com/pic/kennedybrief7e

self-determination *In politics, the right of a people to assert its own national identity or form of government without outside influence.*

to the agitation of zealous northern abolitionists and impassioned southern "fire-eaters."

President Polk, broken in health, did not seek a second term. The Democratic National Convention in Baltimore turned to aging General Lewis Cass, an experienced but pompous senator whose enemies dubbed him "General Gass." The Democratic platform, in line with the lid-sitting strategy, was silent on the burning issue of slavery in the territories. But Cass himself was well-known as the reputed father of "popular sovereignty," the doctrine that the people of a territory, under the principles of the Constitution, should themselves determine the status of slavery.

Popular sovereignty had a persuasive appeal. The public liked it because it accorded with the democratic tradition of **self-determination**. Politicians liked it because it seemed a comfortable compromise between the abolitionist bid for a ban on slavery in the territories and southern demands that Congress protect slavery in the territories. Popular sovereignty tossed the slavery problem into the laps of the people in the various territories. Advocates of the principle thus hoped to dissolve the most stubborn national issue of the day into a series of local issues. Yet popular sovereignty had one fatal defect: it might serve to spread the blight of slavery.

Meeting in Philadelphia, the Whigs turned away from the controversial Henry Clay and nominated the frank General Zachary Taylor, the Hero of Buena Vista, who had never held civil office or even voted for president. As usual, the Whigs pussyfooted in their platform. Eager to win at any cost, they dodged all troublesome issues and extolled the homespun virtues of their candidate. Taylor had not committed himself on the issue of slavery extension, but as a wealthy Louisiana sugar planter he owned scores of slaves.

Aroused by the conspiracy of silence in the Democratic and Whig platforms, ardent antislavery northerners organized the Free Soil party. They came out foursquare for the Wilmot Proviso and against slavery in the territories. The new party nominated former President Martin Van Buren as its candidate, and went into the campaign shouting "Free soil, free speech, free labor, and free men."

These freedoms provided the bedrock of its principles, but the new party assembled a strange assortment of new fellows in the same political bed. It contained a large element of "conscience Whigs," heavily influenced by the abolitionist crusade, who condemned slavery on moral grounds. But it also harbored many northerners who condemned slavery not so much for enslaving blacks as for destroying the chances of free white workers to rise up from wage-earning dependence to the esteemed status of self-employment. Free-Soilers argued that only with free soil in the West could a traditional American commitment to upward mobility continue to flourish. To avoid ruinous competition with unpaid labor, they believed that slavery—and African Americans—should be kept out of the West. As the first widely inclusive party organized around the issue of slavery and confined to a single section, the Free Soil party foreshadowed the emergence of the Republican party six years later.

With the slavery issue officially shoved under the rug by the two major parties, politicians on both sides opened fire on personalities. The amateurish Taylor had to be carefully watched, lest his indiscreet pen puncture the reputation won by his sword. Taylor's wartime popularity pulled him through. He harvested 1,360,967 popular and 163 electoral votes, compared with Cass's 1,222,342 popular and 127 electoral votes. Free-Soiler Van Buren, although winning no state, polled 291,263 votes and apparently diverted enough Democratic strength from Cass in the crucial state of New York to throw the election to Taylor.

Sectional Balance and the Underground Railroad

The South of 1850 was relatively well off. It had seated in the White House the war hero Zachary Taylor, a Virginia-born, slaveowning planter from Louisiana. It boasted a majority in the cabinet and on the Supreme Court. If outnumbered in the House, the South had equality in the Senate, where it could at least neutralize

Chronology

1848	Treaty of Guadalupe Hidalgo ends Mexican War. Taylor defeats Cass and Van Buren for presidency.
1849	California gold rush. Fillmore assumes presidency after Taylor's death. Compromise of 1850, including Fugitive Slave Law. Clayton-Bulwer Treaty with Britain.
1852	Pierce defeats Scott for presidency.
1853	Gadsden Purchase from Mexico.
1854	Commodore Perry "opens" Japan. "Ostend Manifesto" proposes seizure of Cuba. Kansas-Nebraska Act. Republican party organized.
1856	William Walker becomes president of Nicaragua and legalizes slavery.

northern maneuvers. Its cotton fields were expanding, and cotton prices were profitably high. Few sane people, North or South, believed that slavery was seriously threatened where it already existed below the Mason-Dixon line. The fifteen slave states could easily veto any proposed constitutional amendment.

Yet the South was deeply worried, as it had been for several decades, by the ever-tipping political balance. There were then fifteen slave states and fifteen free states. But the discovery of gold in California immediately after the Mexican War drew tens of thousands of forty-niners to the area. Soon the newcomers were clamoring for the direct admission of California to the Union. California's admission as a free state would destroy the delicate equilibrium in the Senate, perhaps forever. With agitation already developing in the territories of New Mexico and Utah for admission to the Union as nonslave states, the fate of California might well establish a precedent for the rest of the Mexican Cession territory.

Texas nursed an additional grievance of its own. It claimed a huge area east of the upper Rio Grande and north to the forty-second parallel, about half the territory of present-day New Mexico. The federal government was proposing to detach this prize, while hot-blooded Texans were threatening to descend on Santa Fe and seize what they regarded as rightfully theirs. The explosive quarrel foreshadowed shooting.

Many southerners were also angered by the nagging agitation in the North for the abolition of slavery in the District of Columbia. They looked with alarm on the prospect of a ten-mile-square oasis of free soil thrust between slaveholding Maryland and slaveholding Virginia.

Even more disagreeable to the South was the loss of runaway slaves, many of whom were assisted north by the Underground Railroad. This virtual freedom train consisted of an informal chain of "stations" (antislavery homes), through which scores of "passengers" (runaway slaves) were spirited by "conductors" (usually white and black abolitionists) from the slave states to the free-soil **sanctuary** of Canada.

The most amazing of these "conductors" was a runaway slave from Maryland, fearless Harriet Tubman. During nineteen forays into the South, she rescued more than three hundred slaves, including her aged parents, and deservedly earned the title "Moses." Lively imaginations later exaggerated the role of the Underground Railroad, but its importance was undisputed.

By 1850 southerners were demanding a new and more stringent **fugitive**-slave law. The old one, passed by Congress in 1793, had proved inadequate to cope with runaways, especially since unfriendly state authorities failed to cooperate.

Estimates indicate that the South in 1850 was losing perhaps 1,000 runaways a year out of its total of some 4 million slaves. In fact, more blacks probably gained their freedom by self-purchase or voluntary emancipation than ever escaped. But the principle weighed heavily with the slavemasters. "Although the loss of property is felt," said a southern senator, "the loss of honor is felt more."

Primary source
Levi Coffin Remembers the Underground Railroad
college.hmco.com/pic/kennedybrief7e

Primary source
Runaway Slave Advertisements
college.hmco.com/pic/kennedybrief7e

sanctuary *A place of refuge or protection, where people are safe from punishment by the law.*

fugitive *A person who flees from danger or prosecution.*

■ **Harriet Tubman, Premier Assistant of Runaway Slaves** John Brown called her "General Tubman" for her effective work in helping slaves escape to Canada on the Underground Railroad. During the Civil War, she served as a Union spy behind Confederate lines. Herself illiterate, she worked after the war to bring education to the freed slaves in North Carolina.

Twilight of the Senatorial Giants

Southern fears were such that Congress was confronted with catastrophe in 1850. Free-soil California was banging on the door for admission. "Fire-eaters" in the South were voicing ominous threats of secession. The failure of Congress to act could easily mean the failure of the United States as a country. The crisis brought into the congressional forum the most distinguished assemblage of statesmen since the Constitutional Convention of 1787—the Old Guard of the dying generation and the young gladiators of the new. That "immortal trio"—Clay, Calhoun, and Webster—appeared together for the last time on the public stage.

Henry Clay, now seventy-three years of age, played a crucial role by proposing a series of compromises. He was ably seconded by thirty-seven-year-old Senator Stephen A. Douglas of Illinois, the "Little Giant" (five feet four inches), whose role was less spectacular but even more important. Clay persuasively urged both North and South to make concessions.

Senator John C. Calhoun, then sixty-eight and dying of tuberculosis, championed the South in his last formal speech. Too weak to deliver it himself, he sat bundled up in the Senate chamber, his eyes glowing within a stern face, while a younger colleague read his fateful words. Rejecting Clay's proposed concessions, Calhoun's impassioned plea was to leave slavery alone, return runaway slaves, give the South its rights as a minority, and restore the political balance. Calhoun died in 1850, before the debate was over, murmuring the sad words, "The South! The South! God knows what will become of her!"

Daniel Webster, sixty-eight years old and also ailing, next took the Senate spotlight to uphold Clay's compromise measures in his own last great speech. Webster urged all reasonable concessions to the South, including a new fugitive-slave law with teeth. Because climate and **topography** would prevent the spread of cotton production to the Mexican Cession territory, Webster argued, it was unnecessary to legislate on slavery there.* Webster's famed speech of the Seventh of March, 1850, was his finest effort. It visibly strengthened Union sentiment and especially pleased northern banking and commercial centers, which stood to lose millions of dollars by secession. But the Free-Soilers and abolitionists, who had

topography *The precise surface features and details of a place—for example, rivers, canyons, hills—in relation to one another.*

Compromise of 1850

Concessions to the North	Concessions to the South
California admitted as a free state	The remainder of the Mexican Cession area to be formed into the territories of New Mexico and Utah, without restriction on slavery, hence open to popular sovereignty
Territory disputed by Texas and New Mexico to be surrendered to New Mexico	Texas to receive $10 million from the federal government as compensation
Abolition of the domestic slave trade (but not slavery) in the District of Columbia	A more stringent fugitive-slave law, going beyond that of 1793

* Webster was wrong here; within one hundred years California had become one of the great cotton-producing states of the Union.

assumed Webster was one of them, upbraided him as a traitor.

The stormy congressional debate of 1850 was not finished, for the Young Guard from the North were yet to have their say. Led by wiry freshman Senator William Seward of New York, this new generation of antislavery leaders was more interested in purifying the Union than in patching and preserving it. Seward unequivocally opposed further concessions to the South. Seward argued earnestly that Christian legislators must obey God's moral law as well as man's mundane law, and therefore appealed to a "higher law" than the Constitution to exclude slavery from the territories.

As the great debate in Congress ran its heated course, deadlock seemed certain. Blunt old President Taylor seemed bent on vetoing any compromise passed by Congress. In response to threats of Texas to seize Santa Fe, the crusty soldier-president seemed ready to lead an army into Texas in person and hang all the "damned traitors." If troops had marched, the South probably would have rallied to the defense of Texas, and the Civil War might have erupted in 1850.

Ralph Waldo Emerson, the philosopher and moderate abolitionist, was outraged by Webster's support of concessions to the South in the Fugitive Slave Act. In February 1851 he wrote in his Journal,

"I opened a paper to-day in which he [Webster] pounds on the old strings [of liberty] in a letter to the Washington Birthday feasters at New York. 'Liberty! liberty!' Pho! Let Mr. Webster, for decency's sake, shut his lips once and forever on this word. The word *liberty* in the mouth of Mr. Webster sounds like the word *love* in the mouth of a courtesan."

Breaking the Congressional Logjam

At the height of the controversy in 1850, President Taylor unknowingly helped the cause of concession by dying suddenly. The portly and colorless Vice President Millard Fillmore took the reins. As presiding officer of the Senate, he had been impressed with the arguments for conciliation, and he gladly signed the series of compromise measures that passed Congress after seven long months of stormy debate.

The struggle to get these measures accepted by the country was hardly less heated than in Congress. In the northern states, "Union savers" like Senators Clay, Webster, and Douglas orated on behalf of the compromise. The ailing Clay himself delivered more than seventy speeches, as a powerful sentiment for acceptance gradually crystallized in the North. It was strengthened by a growing feeling of goodwill and an upsurge of prosperity enriched by California gold.

But the southern "fire-eaters" were still violently opposed to concessions. In June 1850 the assemblage of southern extremists met in Nashville, Tennessee, to condemn the compromise. Meeting again in November, the convention proved to be a dud. By that time southern opinion had reluctantly accepted the verdict of Congress.

Like the calm after a storm, a second Era of Good Feelings dawned. Peace-loving people, both North and South, were determined that the compromises should finally bury the explosive issue of slavery. But this placid period proved all too brief.

Balancing the Compromise Scales

Who got the better deal in the Compromise of 1850? The answer is clearly the North. California, as a free state, tipped the Senate balance permanently against the South. The territories of New Mexico and Utah were open to slavery on the basis of popular sovereignty. But the iron law of nature—the "highest law" of all—had loaded the dice in favor of free soil. Southerners urgently needed more slave territory to restore the "sacred balance." If they could not carve new states out of the recent conquests from Mexico, where else could they get them? The Caribbean was one answer.

Even the apparent gains of the South rang hollow. Disgruntled Texas was to be paid $10 million toward discharging its indebtedness, but in the long run this was a

A Ride for Liberty, by Eastman Johnson In this famous painting, Johnson, a New England artist, brilliantly evokes the anxiety of fleeing slaves.

modest sum. The immense area in dispute had been torn from the side of slaveholding Texas and was almost certain to be free. The South had halted the drive toward abolition in the District of Columbia, at least temporarily, by permitting the outlawing of the slave *trade* in the federal district. But even this move was an entering wedge toward complete emancipation in the nation's capital.

Most alarming of all, the drastic new Fugitive Slave Law of 1850—"the Bloodhound Bill"—stirred up a storm of opposition in the North. The fleeing slaves could not testify on their own behalf, and they were denied a jury trial. These harsh practices threatened to create dangerous precedents for white Americans. Freedom-loving northerners who aided the slave to escape were liable to heavy fines and jail sentences. They might even be ordered to join the slave-catchers, and this possibility rubbed salt into old sores.

So abhorrent was this "Man-Stealing Law" that it touched off an explosive chain reaction in the North. Many shocked moderates, hitherto passive, were driven into the swelling ranks of the antislaveryites.

The Underground Railroad stepped up its timetable, and infuriated northern mobs rescued slaves from their pursuers. Massachusetts, in a move toward nullification suggestive of South Carolina in 1832, made it a penal offense for any state official to enforce the new federal statute. Other states passed "personal liberty laws," which denied local jails to federal officials and otherwise hampered enforcement. The abolitionists rent the heavens with their protests against the man-stealing statute. A meeting presided over by William Lloyd Garrison in 1851 declared, "We execrate it, we spit upon it, we trample it under our feet."

Primary source
Compromise of 1850, The
college.hmco.com/pic/kennedybrief7e

Beyond question, the Fugitive Slave Law was an appalling blunder on the part of the South. No single irritant of the 1850s was more persistently galling to both sides, and none did more to awaken in the North a spirit of antagonism against the South. The southerners in turn were embittered because the northerners would not in good faith execute the law—the one real and immediate southern "gain" from the Great Compromise. Slave-catchers, with some success, redoubled their efforts.

Should the shooting showdown have come in 1850? From the standpoint of the secessionists, yes; from the standpoint of the Unionists, no. Time was fighting for the North. With every passing decade, this huge section was forging further ahead in population and wealth—in crops, factories, foundries, ships, and railroads.

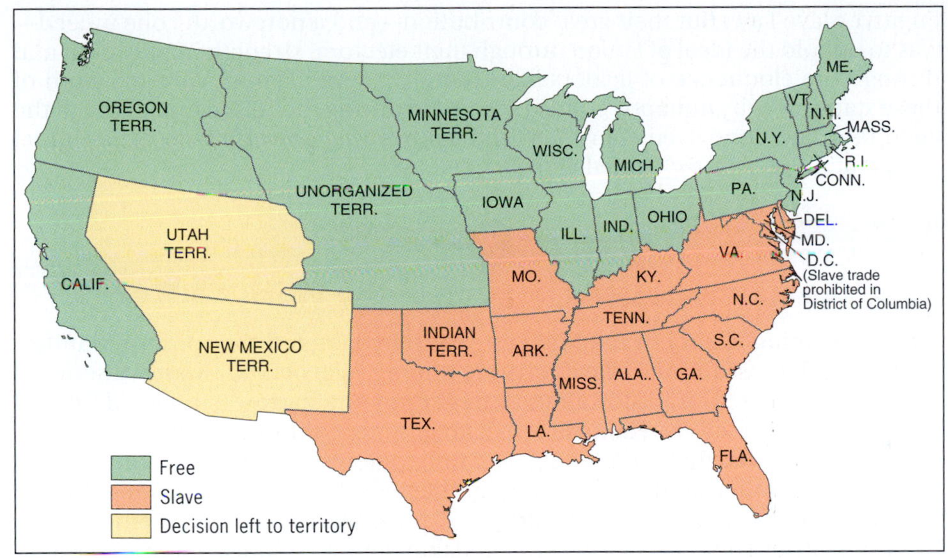

Slavery After the Compromise of 1850 Regarding the Fugitive Slave Act provisions of the Compromise of 1850, Ralph Waldo Emerson declared (May 1851) at Concord, Massachusetts, "The act of Congress . . . is a law which every one of you will break on the earliest occasion—a law which no man can obey, or abet the obeying, without loss of self-respect and forfeiture of the name of gentleman." Privately he wrote in his *Journal,* "This filthy enactment was made in the nineteenth century, by people who could read and write. I will not obey it, by God."

Delay also added immensely to the moral strength of the North—to its will to fight for the Union. In 1850 thousands of northern moderates were unwilling to pin the South to the rest of the nation with bayonets. But the inflammatory events of the 1850s did much to bolster the Yankee will to resist secession, whatever the cost. This one feverish decade gave the North time to accumulate the material and moral strength that provided the margin of victory. Thus the Compromise of 1850, from one point of view, won the Civil War for the Union.

Defeat and Doom for the Whigs

Meeting in Baltimore, the deadlocked Democratic convention of 1852 finally stampeded to the second "dark horse" candidate in American history, Franklin Pierce, an unrenowned New Hampshire lawyer-politician. Weak and indecisive, Pierce was called the "Fainting General" by his opponents because a painful groin injury had caused him to fall off a horse during the Mexican War. As a prosouthern northerner, Pierce was acceptable to the slavery wing of the Democratic party. His platform emphatically endorsed the Compromise of 1850, Fugitive Slave Law and all.

The Whigs, also convening in Baltimore, might logically have nominated figures associated with the Compromise of 1850, such as President Fillmore or Senator Webster. But having won in the past only with military heroes, they turned to another, "Old Fuss and Feathers," Winfield Scott. Although Scott was the ablest American general of his generation as well as an impressive statesman, his haughty personality repelled the masses. Democrats ridiculed Scott's pomposity and cried exultantly, "We Polked 'em in '44; we'll Pierce 'em in '52."

Luckily for the Democrats, the Whig party was hopelessly split. Antislavery Whigs of the North swallowed Scott as their nominee but deplored his platform, which endorsed the hated Fugitive Slave Law. Southern Whigs, who doubted Scott's loyalty to the Compromise of 1850 and especially to the Fugitive Slave Law, accepted the platform but spat on the candidate. In the end the politically inexperienced Scott was stabbed in the back by his fellow Whigs, notably in the South. The Free Soil candidate, New Hampshire Senator John P. Hale, also siphoned off northern Whig votes that might have gone to Scott. The pliant Pierce won in a landslide, 254 electoral votes to 42, although the popular vote was closer, 1,601,117 to 1,385,453.

The election of 1852 was fraught with frightening significance, though it seemed tame at the time. It marked the effective end of the disorganized Whig party and, within a few years, its complete death. The Whigs' demise augured the eclipse of *national* parties and the worrisome rise of purely *sectional* political alignments. The Whigs were governed at times by the crassest opportunism, and they won only two presidential elections in their colorful career (1840, 1848), both with war heroes. They finally choked to death trying to swallow the distasteful

Fugitive Slave Law. But their great contribution—and a noteworthy one indeed—was to uphold the ideal of Union through their electoral strength in the South and through the eloquence of leaders like Henry Clay and Daniel Webster. Both of these statesmen, by unhappy coincidence, died during the 1852 campaign. But the good they had done lived after them and contributed powerfully to the eventual preservation of a *united* United States.

The Expansionist Legacy of the Mexican War

The intoxicating victory in the Mexican War reinvigorated the spirit of Manifest Destiny and a lust for new slave territory among "slavocrats." Many Americans were also looking for transportation routes across the narrow isthmus of Central America, through either Panama or Nicaragua, to California's new gold fields. Whoever controlled that route would hold imperial sway over all maritime nations, including the United States. A sharp conflict between the United States and Britain, which had been encroaching on Nicaragua's "Mosquito Coast," was avoided by the Clayton-Bulwer Treaty of 1850. It stipulated that neither America nor Britain would fortify or seek exclusive control over any future **isthmian** waterway (later rescinded by the Hay-Pauncefote Treaty of 1901; see p. 270).

isthmus (isthmian) *A narrow strip of land connecting two larger bodies of land.*

filibustering (filibuster) *Adventurers who conduct a private war against a foreign country. (In a different meaning, the term also refers to deliberately prolonged speechmaking in order to block legislation.)*

cloak-and-dagger *Concerning the activities of spies or undercover agents, especially involving elaborate deceptions.*

manifesto *A proclamation or document aggressively asserting a controversial position or advocating a daring course of action.*

Southerner "slavocrats" cast especially covetous eyes southward in the 1850s. They lusted for new slave territory after the Compromise of 1850 seemingly closed most of the Mexican Cession to the "peculiar institution." In 1856 a Texan proposed a toast "to the Southern republic bounded on the north by the Mason and Dixon line and on the South by the Isthmus of Tehuantepec [southern Mexico], including Cuba and all the lands on our Southern shore."

Nicaragua beckoned beguilingly. A brazen American adventurer, William Walker, tried repeatedly to grab control of this Central American country in the 1850s. Backed by an armed force recruited largely in the South, he installed himself as president in July 1856 and promptly legalized slavery. One southern newspaper proclaimed to the planter aristocracy that Walker—the "gray-eyed man of destiny"—"now offers Nicaragua to you and your slaves." But a coalition of Central American nations formed an alliance to overthrow him. President Pierce withdrew diplomatic recognition, and the gray-eyed man's destiny was to crumple before a Honduran firing squad in 1860.

Sugar-rich Cuba, lying just off the nation's southern doorstep, was also an enticing prospect for annexation. This remnant of Spain's once-mighty New World empire, with its large population of enslaved blacks, might be carved into several states, restoring the political balance in the Senate. President Polk had considered offering Spain $100 million for Cuba, but the proud Spaniards replied that they would sooner see the island sunk into the sea than in the hands of the hated Yankees.

Some southern adventurers now undertook to shake the tree of Manifest Destiny. During 1850–1851, two "**filibustering**" expeditions, each numbering several hundred armed men, descended on Cuba. Both feeble efforts were repelled, and fifty of the invaders were summarily shot or strangled.

When Spanish officials in Cuba rashly seized an American steamer in 1854, southern-dominated President Pierce decided that now was the time to provoke a war with Spain and seize Cuba. An incredible **cloak-and-dagger** episode followed. Pierce's secretary of state instructed the American ministers to Spain, Britain, and France to meet in Ostend, Belgium, and draw up a plan to acquire Cuba. Their top-secret dispatch, known as the "Ostend **Manifesto**," urged the administration to offer $120 million for Cuba. If Spain refused to sell, the United States would "be justified in wresting" the island from the Spanish.

When the secret Ostend Manifesto leaked out, Northern free-soilers rose up in wrath against the "manifesto of brigands." The red-faced Pierce administration hurriedly dropped its reckless schemes for Cuba. The slavery issue thus checked territorial expansion in the 1850s.

Besides Latin America, another arena of American international assertiveness in the 1850s was in the Pacific and East Asia. The acquisition of California and Oregon had made the United States a Pacific power—or would-be power. In 1842 Britain gained free access to so-called treaty ports in China as well as outright control of the island of Hong Kong. To secure comparable concessions for the United States, President Tyler in 1844 dispatched dashing Massachusetts diplomat Caleb Cushing, along with four warships, to the southern Chinese port of Macao. In July 1844 Cushing signed the Treaty of Wanghia with China. It secured the United States equal trading rights with other nations and the principle of "extraterritoriality" that provided for trying accused Americans in American, not Chinese, courts. American trade with China flourished, and thousands of American missionaries soon arrived through the treaty ports to convert the "heathen Chinese."

Success in China inspired a still more consequential mission to pry open the bamboo gates of Japan, which had been closed to outsiders for centuries. In 1852 President Millard Fillmore dispatched to Japan a fleet of four awesome, smoke-belching warships, commanded by Commodore Matthew C. Perry, to Edo (later Tokyo) Bay. Perry returned in February 1854 with an even larger force of seven men-of-war, and with a combination of bluster and grace, persuaded the Japanese to sign the landmark Treaty of Kanagawa on March 31, 1854. It provided for proper treatment of shipwrecked sailors, American coaling rights in Japan, and the establishment of consular relations. This commercial toe in the door cracked Japan's two-century shell of isolation open, and began to propel the Land of the Rising Sun headlong into the modern world.

The first platform of the newly born (antislavery) Republican party in 1856 lashed out at the Ostend Manifesto, with its transparent suggestion that Cuba be seized. The plank read,

"Resolved, That the highwayman's plea, that 'might makes right,' embodied in the Ostend Circular, was in every respect unworthy of American diplomacy, and would bring shame and dishonor upon any Government or people that gave it their sanction."

Pacific Railroad Promoters and the Gadsden Purchase

Acute transportation problems were another legacy of the Mexican War. The newly acquired prizes of California and Oregon might just as well have been islands some eight thousand miles west of the nation's capital. The sea routes to and from the Isthmus of Panama, to say nothing of those around South America, were too long. Covered-wagon travel past bleaching animal bones was possible, but slow and dangerous. A popular song recalled the formidable trek.

They swam the wide rivers and crossed the tall peaks,
And camped on the prairie for weeks upon weeks.
Starvation and cholera and hard work and slaughter,
They reached California spite of hell and high water.

Feasible land transportation was imperative—or the newly won possessions on the Pacific Coast might break away. Camels were even imported from the Near East as an attempted answer, but mule-driving Americans did not adjust to the temperamental beasts. A transcontinental railroad was clearly the only real solution to the problem.

Should its terminus be in the North or in the South? The favored section would reap rich rewards in wealth, population, and influence. The South, losing the economic race with the North, was eager to extend a railroad through adjacent southwestern territory all the way to California.

Another chunk of Mexico now seemed desirable, because the best railway route across the Southwest ran slightly south of the Mexican border. Secretary of War Jefferson Davis therefore appointed a South Carolina railroad man, James Gadsden, as minister to Mexico. He negotiated a treaty in 1853 that ceded to the United States the Gadsden Purchase area for $10 million. The transaction aroused northern criticism, but the Senate approved the pact.

Southerners now argued that because their proposed rail line ran through the state of Texas and the organized New Mexico Territory, the southern route should be built first. Northern railroad **boosters** quickly replied that if organized territory was the test, then Nebraska, site of the proposed northern route, should also be organized. But southerners in Congress greeted all schemes for organizing Nebraska with apathy or hostility. Why should the South help create new free-soil states and thus cut its own throat by facilitating a northern railroad?

booster *One who promotes a person or enterprise, especially in a highly enthusiastic way.*

■ **Gadsden Purchase, 1853** The purchase made possible a southern rail route to the West Coast. But the Southern Pacific railroad (whose route is shown here) was not built until 1882, after the Civil War.

Douglas's Kansas-Nebraska Scheme

At this point in 1854, Senator Stephen A. Douglas of Illinois delivered a counterstroke to offset the Gadsden thrust for southern expansion westward. A squat, bull-necked, and heavy-chested figure, the "Little Giant" radiated the energy and breezy optimism of the self-made man. An ardent booster for the West, he longed to break the North-South deadlock over westward expansion and stretch a line of settlements across the continent. He also had invested heavily in Chicago real estate and in railway stock and was eager to have the Windy City become the eastern terminus of the proposed Pacific railroad. He would thus endear himself to the voters of Illinois, benefit his section, and enrich his own purse.

A veritable "steam engine in breeches," Douglas threw himself behind a legislative scheme that would enlist the support of a reluctant South. The proposed Territory of Nebraska would be carved into two territories, Kansas and Nebraska. Their status regarding slavery would be settled by popular sovereignty—a democratic concept to which Douglas and his western constituents were deeply attached. Kansas, which lay due west of slaveholding Missouri, would presumably choose to

Interactive map
The Kansas-Nebraska Act, 1854
college.hmco.com/pic/kennedybrief7e

■ **Kansas and Nebraska, 1854** The route of the future Union Pacific Railroad (completed in 1869) is shown. Notice the Missouri Compromise line of 36°30° (1820).

become a slave state. But Nebraska, lying west of free-soil Iowa, would presumably become a free state.

Douglas's Kansas-Nebraska scheme flatly contradicted the Missouri Compromise of 1820, which had forbidden slavery in the proposed Nebraska Territory north of the sacred 36°309 line. The only way to open the region to popular sovereignty was to repeal the ancient compact outright. This bold step Douglas was prepared to take, even at the risk of shattering the uneasy **truce** patched together by the Compromise of 1850.

Many southerners, who had not conceived of Kansas as slave soil, rose to the bait. Here was a chance to gain one more slave state. The pliable President Pierce, under the thumb of southern advisers, threw his full weight behind the Kansas-Nebraska Bill.

But the Missouri Compromise, now thirty-four years old, could not be brushed aside lightly. Whatever Congress passes it can repeal, but by this time the North had come to regard the sectional pact as almost as sacred as the Constitution itself. Free-soil members of Congress struck back with a vengeance. They met their match in the violently gesticulating Douglas, who was the ablest rough-and-tumble debater of his generation. Employing twisted logic and oratorical fireworks, he rammed the bill through Congress with strong support from many southerners. So heated were political passions that bloodshed was barely averted. Some members carried a concealed revolver or a bowie knife—or both.

Douglas's motives in prodding anew the snarling dog of slavery have long puzzled historians. His personal interests have already been mentioned. In addition, his foes accused him of angling for the presidency in 1856. Yet his admirers have argued in his defense that if he had not championed the ill-omened bill, someone else would have.

The truth seems to be that Douglas acted somewhat impulsively and recklessly. His heart did not bleed over the issue of slavery, and he declared repeatedly that he did not care whether it was voted up or down in the territories. What he failed to perceive was that hundreds of thousands of his fellow citizens in the North *did* feel deeply on this moral issue. They regarded the repeal of the Missouri Compromise as an intolerable breach of faith, and they would henceforth resist to the last trench all future southern demands for slave territory.

Genuine leaders, like skillful chess players, must foresee the possible effects of their moves. Douglas predicted a "hell of a storm," but he grossly underestimated its proportions. His critics in the North, branding him a "Judas" and a "traitor," greeted his name with frenzied boos, hisses, and "three groans for Doug." But he still enjoyed a high degree of popularity among his following in the Democratic party, especially in Illinois, a stronghold of popular sovereignty.

Stephen A. Douglas (1813–1861) Despite having stirred up sectional bitterness, Douglas was so devoted to the Union that he warmly supported his rival, Lincoln, when war broke out. He attended the inauguration and reportedly held Lincoln's stovepipe hat while the president spoke.

truce *A temporary suspension of warfare by agreement of the hostile parties.*

Congress Legislates a Civil War

The Kansas-Nebraska Act—curtain raiser to a terrible drama—was one of the most momentous measures ever to pass Congress. By one way of reckoning, it greased the slippery slope to civil war.

Antislavery northerners were angered by what they condemned as an act of bad faith by the "Nebrascals" and their "Nebrascality." All future compromise with the South would be immeasurably more difficult, and without compromise there was bound to be conflict.

Henceforth the Fugitive Slave Law of 1850, previously enforced in the North only halfheartedly, was a dead letter. The Kansas-Nebraska Act wrecked two compromises: that of 1820, which it repealed specifically, and that of

Massachusetts senator Charles Sumner (1811–1874) described the Kansas-Nebraska Bill as "at once the worst and the best Bill on which Congress ever acted." It was the worst because it represented a victory for the slave power in the short run. But it was the best, he said prophetically, because it

"annuls all past compromises with slavery, and makes all future compromises impossible. Thus it puts freedom and slavery face to face, and bids them grapple. Who can doubt the result?"

Primary source
Kansas-Nebraska Act, The
college.hmco.com/pic/kennedybrief7e

1850, which northern opinion repealed indirectly. Emerson wrote, "The Fugitive [Slave] Law did much to unglue the eyes of men, and now the Nebraska Bill leaves us staring."

Northern abolitionists and southern "fire-eaters" alike saw less and less they could live with. The growing legion of antislaveryites gained numerous recruits, who resented the grasping move by the "slavocracy" for Kansas. The southerners, in turn, became inflamed when the free-soilers attempted to control Kansas, contrary to the presumed "deal."

The proud Democrats—a party now over half a century old—were shattered by the Kansas-Nebraska Act. They did elect a president in 1856, but he was the last one they were to boost into the White House for twenty-eight long years.

Undoubtedly the most durable offspring of the Kansas-Nebraska blunder was the new Republican party. It sprang up spontaneously in the Midwest, notably in Wisconsin and Michigan, as a mighty moral protest against the gains of slavery. Gathering together dissatisfied elements, it soon included disgruntled Whigs (among them Abraham Lincoln), Democrats, Free-Soilers, Know-Nothings, and other foes of the Kansas-Nebraska Act. The hodgepodge party spread eastward with the swiftness of a prairie fire and with the zeal of a religious crusade. Unheard of and unheralded at the beginning of 1854, it elected a Republican Speaker of the House of Representatives within two years. Never really a third-party movement, it erupted with such force as to become almost overnight the second major political party—and a purely sectional one at that.

At long last the dreaded sectional rift had appeared. The new Republican party would not be allowed south of the Mason-Dixon line. Countless southerners subscribed wholeheartedly to the sentiment that it was "a nigger stealing, stinking, putrid, abolition party." The Union was in dire peril.

Chapter Summary

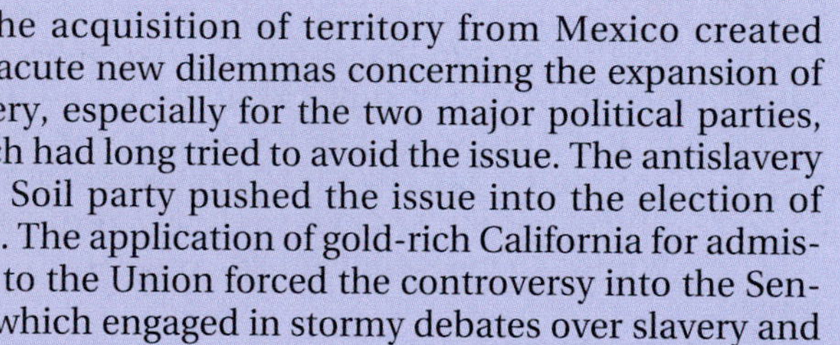

The acquisition of territory from Mexico created acute new dilemmas concerning the expansion of slavery, especially for the two major political parties, which had long tried to avoid the issue. The antislavery Free Soil party pushed the issue into the election of 1848. The application of gold-rich California for admission to the Union forced the controversy into the Senate, which engaged in stormy debates over slavery and the Union.

After the timely death of President Taylor, who had blocked a settlement, Congress resolved the crisis by passing the delicate Compromise of 1850. The compromise eased sectional tension for the moment, although the Fugitive Slave Law aroused opposition in the North.

As the sectionally divided Whig party died, the Democratic Pierce administration became the tool of proslavery expansionists. Attempts at further expansion into Nicaragua, Cuba, and the Gadsden Purchase showed the increasing assertiveness of proslavery expansionists, who stirred strong resistance in the North.

For complex and somewhat mysterious reasons that included the desire for a northern railroad route, Senator Stephen Douglas rammed the Kansas Nebraska Act through Congress in 1854. By repealing the Missouri Compromise and making new territory subject to "popular sovereignty" on slavery, this act aroused the fury of the North, sparked the rise of the Republican party, and set the stage for the Civil War.

Drifting Toward Disunion

1854–1861

A HOUSE DIVIDED AGAINST ITSELF CANNOT STAND.

I BELIEVE THIS GOVERNMENT CANNOT ENDURE PERMANENTLY HALF SLAVE AND HALF FREE.

ABRAHAM LINCOLN, 1858

Chapter Outline

- *Uncle Tom's Cabin* and the Spread of Abolitionist Sentiment in the North
- The Contest for Kansas
- The Election of James Buchanan, 1856
- The *Dred Scott* Case, 1857
- The Lincoln-Douglas Debates, 1858
- John Brown's Raid on Harpers Ferry, 1859
- Lincoln and Republican Victory, 1860
- Secession
- Examining the Evidence: Harriet Beecher Stowe, *Uncle Tom's Cabin*
- Varying Viewpoints: The Civil War: Repressible or Irrepressible?

The slavery question continued to churn the cauldron of controversy throughout the 1850s. As moral temperatures rose, prospects for a peaceful political solution to the slavery issue simply evaporated. Kansas Territory erupted in violence between proslavery and antislavery factions in 1855. Two years later the Supreme Court's *Dred Scott* decision invalidated the Missouri Compromise of 1820, which had imposed a shaky lid on the slavery problem for more than a generation. Attitudes on both sides progressively hardened. When in 1860 the newly formed Republican party nominated for president Abraham Lincoln, an outspoken opponent of the further expansion of slavery, the stage was set for all-out civil war.

Focus Questions

1. **What were the major crises in the 1850s that led from the Kansas-Nebraska Act to secession, and how did each work to tear apart the Union and create the climate for the Civil War?**
2. **How and why did "bleeding Kansas" become a small-scale dress rehearsal for the Civil War?**
3. **How did the new Republican party emerge as a powerful new voice against the expansion of slavery, and what enabled Abraham Lincoln to emerge from obscurity to become its most effective leader and presidential nominee?**
4. **What were the central issues in the campaign of 1860, and how did the Democratic party's divisions as well as Republican unity lead to Lincoln's victory?**
5. **Why did the lower South secede immediately after Lincoln's victory, and why did last-ditch efforts like the Crittenden Compromise fail to prevent Civil War?**

Stowe and Helper: Literary Incendiaries

Sectional tensions were further strained in 1852, and later, by an inky phenomenon. Harriet Beecher Stowe, a wisp of a woman and the mother of a half-dozen children, published her heart-rending novel *Uncle Tom's Cabin.* Dismayed by the passage of the Fugitive Slave Law, she was determined to awaken the North to the wickedness of slavery by laying bare its terrible inhumanity, especially the cruel splitting of families. Her wildly popular book relied on powerful imagery and touching pathos. "God wrote it," she explained in later years—a reminder that the deeper sources of her antislavery sentiments lay in the evangelical religious crusades of the Second Great Awakening.

Online Study Center
Primary source
Southern Critique of *Uncle Tom's Cabin,* A
college.hmco.com/pic/kennedybrief7e

The success of the novel at home and abroad was sensational. Several hundred thousand copies were published in the first year, and the totals soon ran into the millions as the tale was translated into more than a score of languages. It was also put on the stage in "Tom shows" for lengthy runs. No other novel in American history—perhaps in all history—can be compared with it as a political force. To millions of people it made slavery appear almost as evil as it really was.

When Mrs. Stowe was introduced to President Lincoln in 1862, he reportedly remarked, "So you're the little woman who wrote the book that made this great war." The truth is that *Uncle Tom's Cabin* did help start the Civil War—and win it.

Online Study Center
Primary source
***Uncle Tom's Cabin* at the Theater**
college.hmco.com/pic/kennedybrief7e

Uncle Tom, endearing and enduring, left a profound impression on the North. Thousands of readers swore that henceforth they would have nothing to do with the enforcement of the Fugitive Slave Law. The tale was devoured by millions of impressionable youths in the 1850s—some of whom later became the Boys in Blue who volunteered to fight the Civil War through to its grim finale. The memory of a beaten and dying Uncle Tom helped sustain them in their determination to wipe out the plague of slavery.

Harriet Beecher Stowe (1811–1896), Daguerreotype by Southworth and Hawes Stowe was a remarkable woman whose pen helped to change the course of history.

Another trouble-brewing book appeared in 1857, five years after the debut of *Uncle Tom.* Titled *The Impending Crisis of the South,* it was written by Hinton R. Helper, a nonaristocratic white from North Carolina. Hating both slavery and blacks, he attempted to prove by an array of statistics that indirectly the non-slaveholding whites were the ones who suffered most from the millstone of slavery. Helper's book, with its "dirty allusions," was banned in the South and fed to the flames at book-burning parties. But in the North thousands of copies, many in condensed form, were distributed as campaign literature by the Republicans.

The North-South Contest for Kansas

The rolling plains of Kansas had meanwhile been providing an example of the worst possible workings of popular sovereignty. Newcomers who ventured into Kansas were a motley lot. Most of the northerners were just ordinary westward-moving pioneers. But a small part of the inflow was financed by groups of northern abolitionists or free-soilers, especially the New England Emigrant Aid Company, which sent about two thousand people to the troubled area to forestall the South. Shouting "Ho for Kansas!" many of them carried the deadly new breech-loading Sharps rifles, nicknamed "Beecher's Bibles" after the Reverend Henry Ward Beecher (Harriet Beecher Stowe's brother), who had helped raise

Chronology

1852 Harriet Beecher Stowe publishes *Uncle Tom's Cabin.*

1854 Kansas-Nebraska Act.
Republican party forms.

1856 Buchanan defeats Frémont and Fillmore for presidency.
Sumner beaten by Brooks in Senate chamber.
Brown's Pottawatomie massacre.

1856-1860 Civil war in "bleeding Kansas."

1857 *Dred Scott* decision.
Lecompton Constitution rejected.

1857 Panic of 1857.
Hinton R. Helper publishes *The Impending Crisis of the South.*

1858 Lincoln-Douglas debates.

1859 Brown raids Harpers Ferry.

1860 Lincoln wins four-way race for presidency.
South Carolina secedes from the Union.
Crittenden Compromise fails.

1861 Seven seceding states form Confederate States of America.

money for their purchase. Many of the Kansas-bound pioneers sang Whittier's marching song (1854):

We cross the prairie as of old
The pilgrims crossed the sea,
To make the West, as they the East,
The homestead of the free!

Southern spokesmen, now more than ordinarily touchy, raised furious cries of betrayal. They had supported the Kansas-Nebraska scheme of Douglas with the unspoken understanding that Kansas would become slave and Nebraska free. The northern "Nebrascals" were now apparently out to "abolitionize" *both* Kansas and Nebraska.

A few southern hotheads, quick to respond in kind, attempted to "assist" small groups of well-armed slaveowners to Kansas. But despite such efforts slavery never took hold in Kansas. The census of 1860 found only 2 slaves among 107,000 souls in all Kansas Territory, and only 15 in Nebraska. Nevertheless, crisis conditions in Kansas rapidly worsened. When the day came in 1855 to elect members of the first territorial legislature, proslavery "border ruffians" poured in from Missouri to vote early and often. The slavery supporters triumphed and then set up their own **puppet government** at Shawnee Mission. The free-soilers, unable to stomach this fraudulent conspiracy, established an extralegal regime of their own in Topeka. The confused Kansans thus had their choice between two governments—one based on fraud, the other on illegality. Tensions reached the breaking point in 1856 when a gang of proslavery raiders shot up and burned a part of the free-soil town of Lawrence. This outrage was but the prelude to a bloodier tragedy.

puppet government *A government set up and controlled by outside forces.*

In the closing scenes of Harriet Beecher Stowe's novel, Uncle Tom's brutal master, Simon Legree, orders the $1,200 slave savagely beaten (to death) by two fellow slaves. Through tears and blood, Tom exclaims,

"No! no! no! my soul an't yours, Mas'r! You haven't bought it,—ye can't buy it! It's been bought and paid for, by one that is able to keep it,—no matter, no matter, you can't harm me!" "I can't," said Legree, with a sneer; "we'll see,—we'll see! Here, Sambo, Quimbo, give this dog such a breakin' in as he won't get over, this month!"

Kansas in Convulsion

The fanatical figure of John Brown now stalked upon the Kansas battlefield. Spare, gray-bearded, and iron-willed,

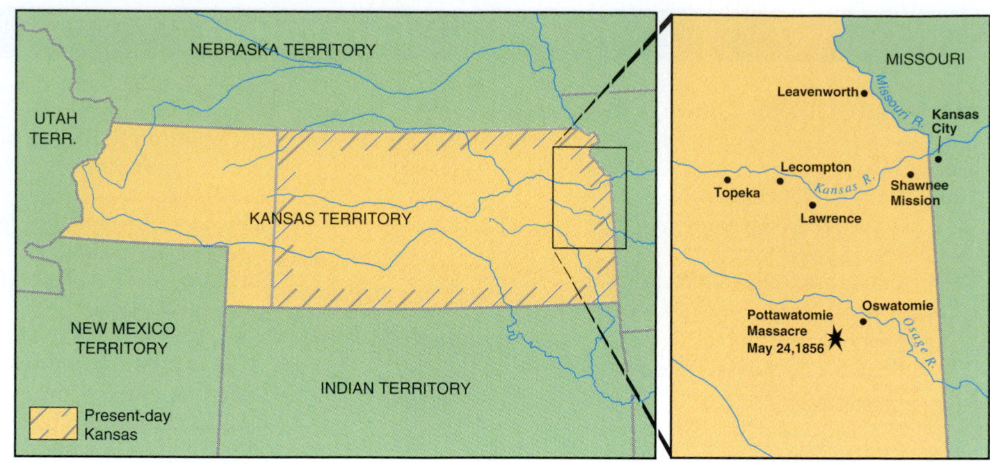

Bleeding Kansas, 1854–1860 "Enter every election district in Kansas . . . and vote at the point of a bowie knife or revolver," one proslavery agitator exhorted a Missouri crowd. Proslavery Missouri senator David Atchison declared that "there are 1,100 men coming over from Platte County to vote, and if that ain't enough we can send 5,000—enough to kill every Goddamned abolitionist in the Territory."

he was obsessively dedicated to the abolitionist cause. The power of his glittering gray eyes was such, so he claimed, that his stare could force a dog or cat to slink out of a room. Brooding over the recent attack on Lawrence, "Old Brown" of Osawatomie led a band of his followers to Pottawatomie Creek, in May 1856. There they literally hacked to pieces five surprised men, presumed to be proslaveryites. This fiendish butchery brought vicious retaliation from proslavery forces. Civil war in Kansas thus flared forth in 1856 and continued intermittently until it merged with the large-scale Civil War of 1861–1865.

The proslavery forces intensified the conflict in 1857 when they attempted to bring Kansas into the Union under a tricky document known as the Lecompton Constitution. Although the majority of Kansans were free-soilers, the vote on the proposed constitution was arranged so that it was impossible to prohibit all black bondage and still obtain statehood. With infuriated free-soilers boycotting the election, the proslaveryites approved the constitution with slavery late in 1857.

Preston Brooks Caning Charles Sumner, 1856 Cartoonist John Magee of Philadelphia depicted Brooks's beating of Sumner in the Senate as a display of southern ruthlessness in defending slavery, ironically captioned "southern chivalry."

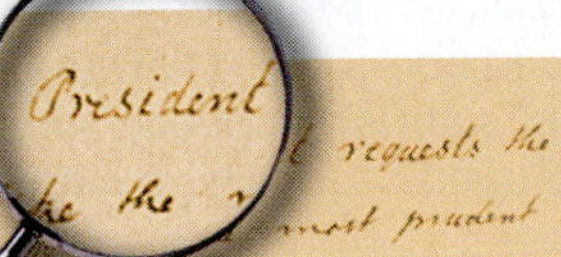

EXAMINING THE EVIDENCE

As works of fiction, novels pose tricky problems to historians, whose principal objective is to get the factual record straight. Works of the imagination are notoriously unreliable as descriptions of reality, and only rarely is it known with any degree of certainty what a reader might have felt when confronting a particular fictional passage or theme. Yet a novel like Harriet Beecher Stowe's *Uncle Tom's Cabin* had such an unarguably large impact on the American (and worldwide) debate over slavery that historians have inevitably looked to it for evidence of the mid-nineteenth-century ideas and attitudes to which Stowe appealed. The passage quoted here is especially rich in such evidence—and even offers an explanation for the logic of the novel's title. Stowe cleverly aimed to mobilize not simply her readers' sense of injustice, but also their sentiments, on behalf of the antislavery cause.

> The February morning looked gray and drizzling through the window of Uncle Tom's cabin. It looked on downcast faces, the images of mournful hearts. The little table stood out before the fire, covered with an ironing-cloth; a coarse but clean shirt or two, fresh from the iron, hung on the back of a chair by the fire, and Aunt Chloe had another spread out before her on the table. Carefully she rubbed and ironed every fold and every hem, with the most scrupulous exactness, every now and then raising her hand to her face to wipe off the tears that were coursing down her cheeks.
>
> Tom sat by, with his Testament open his knee, and his head leaning upon his hand;—but neither spoke. It was yet early, and the children lay all asleep together in their little rude trundle-bed.
>
> Tom, who had, to the full, the gentle, domestic heart, which, woe for them! has been a peculiar characteristic of his unhappy race, got up and walked silently to look at his children.
>
> "It's the last time," he said.

1. What sentimental values does the *cabin* represent, and why is it so central to Stowe's novel?
2. What is the nature of the threat to those values?
3. How does Stowe convey the importance of both religion and family for her slave characters, and why might these elements particularly appeal to the novel's middle-class readers?

The new president, James Buchanan, was just as much under southern influence as President Pierce had been, and he threw the weight of his administration behind the notorious Lecompton Constitution. But Senator Douglas, who had championed true popular sovereignty, would have none of this semipopular fraudulency. Deliberately tossing away his strong support in the South for the presidency, he fought courageously to submit the entire Lecompton Constitution to a fair popular vote. The free-soil voters thereupon snowed it under at the polls. Kansas remained a territory until 1861, when the southern secessionists left Congress.

President Buchanan, by antagonizing the numerous Douglas Democrats in the North, hopelessly divided the once-powerful Democratic party. Until then, it had been the only remaining national party, for the Whigs were dead and the Republicans were sectional. With the disruption of the Democrats came the snapping of one of the last important strands in the rope that was barely binding the Union together.

"Bully" Brooks and His Bludgeon

"Bleeding Kansas" also spattered blood on the floor of the Senate in 1856. The abolitionist Senator Charles Sumner of Massachusetts, a tall and imposing figure, delivered a blistering speech titled "The Crime Against Kansas," in which he viciously condemned proslavery men as "hirelings picked from the drunken spew and vomit of an uneasy civilization." The speech also insulted white-haired Senator Andrew Butler of South Carolina.

Hot-tempered South Carolina Congressman Preston S. Brooks, Butler's distant cousin, took vengeance into his own hands. On May 22, 1856, he approached Sumner, then sitting at his Senate desk, and pounded the orator with an eleven-ounce cane until it broke. The victim fell bleeding and unconscious to the floor, suffering serious injuries to his head and nervous system.

Bleeding Sumner thus joined bleeding Kansas as a hotly divisive political issue. South Carolina triumphantly reelected Brooks to Congress, and Massachusetts defiantly did the same for Sumner, even though the battered abolitionist was unable to take his seat for over three years. Meanwhile, Sumner's abusive speech sold by the thousands in the North, while southern admirers deluged Brooks with canes to replace the one he had broken over Sumner's head.

The Sumner-Brooks clash and the ensuing reactions revealed how dangerously inflamed passions were becoming, North and South. It was ominous that the cultured Sumner should have used the language of a barroom bully and that the gentlemanly Brooks should have employed the tactics and tools of a thug. Emotion was displacing thought. The blows rained on Sumner's head were, broadly speaking, among the first blows of the Civil War.

"Old Buck" Versus "The Pathfinder"

With bullets whining in Kansas, the Democrats met in Cincinnati to nominate their presidential standard-bearer of 1856. Both weak-kneed President Pierce and dynamic Senator Douglas were too indelibly tainted by the Kansas-Nebraska Act, so the delegates finally turned to a well-to-do Pennsylvania lawyer and diplomat, James Buchanan, who had been serving as minister to London during the recent Kansas-Nebraska uproar. Although his "Kansasless" neutrality made him acceptable to the party, "Old Buck" Buchanan was mediocre, irresolute, and confused.

The fast-growing Republican party, in their enthusiastic convention in Philadelphia, passed over "Higher Law" Senator William Seward, their most conspicuous leader, and instead chose John C. Frémont, a dashing but erratic explorer-soldier-surveyor. Republicans hoped that the so-called "Pathfinder of the West" would blaze them a path to the White House. Vigorously condemning the extension of slavery into the territories, Republicans sang,

Arise, arise ye brave!
And let our war-cry be
Free speech, free press, free soil, free men,
Fré-mont and victory!

An ugly dose of antiforeignism was injected into the campaign, even though slavery extension loomed largest. The recent influx of immigrants from Ireland and Germany had alarmed the old-stock Protestant nativists who had organized the American or Know-Nothing party. Antiforeign and anti-Catholic, these superpatriots nominated former President Millard Fillmore as their candidate, and campaigned under the slogan, "Americans Must Rule America." With remnants of the dying Whig party also endorsing Fillmore, the Know-Nothings cut into Republican party strength.

The bland Buchanan, although polling less than a majority of the popular vote, won handily. His tally in the Electoral College was 174 to 114 for Frémont, with Fillmore garnering 8. The popular vote was 1,832,955 for Buchanan to 1,339,932 for Frémont, with 871,731 for Fillmore.

Democrats had carried the hapless "Old Buck" into office, but the Republicans could rightfully claim a "victorious defeat" in 1856. The new party—a mere two-year-old toddler—had made an astonishing showing against the well-oiled Democratic machine. John Greenleaf Whittier exulted:

Then sound again the bugles,
Call the muster-roll anew;
If months have well-nigh won the field,
What may not four years do?

That question cast a long shadow forward, as politicians, North and South, peered anxiously toward 1860.

The Dred Scott Bombshell

The *Dred Scott* decision, handed down by the Supreme Court on March 6, 1857, abruptly ended the two-day presidential honeymoon of the unlucky bachelor, James Buchanan. Basically, the case was simple. Dred Scott, a black slave, had lived with his master for five years in free-state Illinois and Wisconsin Territory. Backed by interested abolitionists, he sued for freedom on the basis of his long residence on free soil.

Spiritual overtones developed in the Frémont campaign, especially over slavery. The Independent, *a prominent religious journal, saw in Frémont's nomination "the good hand of God." As election day neared, it declared,*

"Fellow-Christians! Remember it is for Christ, for the nation, and for the world that you vote at this election! Vote as you pray! Pray as you vote!"

The Supreme Court proceeded to turn a simple legal case into a complex political issue. It ruled, not surprisingly, that Dred Scott was a black slave and not a citizen, and hence could not sue in federal courts.* The tribunal could then have thrown out the case on these technical grounds alone. But a majority decided to go further, under the leadership of emaciated Chief Justice Roger Taney from the slave state of Maryland.

Taney's sweeping judgment on the larger question of slavery rocked the free-soilers back on their heels. Speaking for a majority of the Court, Taney decreed that because a slave was private property, he or she could be taken into *any* territory and legally held there in slavery. The reasoning was that the Fifth Amendment clearly forbade Congress to deprive people of their property without due process of law. The Court, to be consistent, went further. The Missouri Compromise of 1820, banning slavery north of 36°30′, had been repealed three years earlier by the Kansas-Nebraska Act, but its spirit was still venerated in the North. Now the Court ruled that the Missouri Compromise had been unconstitutional all along: Congress had no power to ban slavery from the territories, regardless even of what the territorial legislatures might want.

Southerners were delighted with this unexpected victory. Champions of popular sovereignty, including Senator Douglas and most northern Democrats, were aghast. Another lethal wedge was thus driven between the northern and southern wings of the once-united Democratic party.

Foes of slavery extension, especially the Republicans, were infuriated by the *Dred Scott* setback. Because a majority of the Supreme Court justices were southerners, Republicans insisted that the ruling was merely an opinion, not a decision, and no more binding than the views of a "southern debating society." Southerners in turn wondered how much longer they could remain joined to a section that refused to honor the Supreme Court, to say nothing of the constitutional compact that had established it.

The Financial Crash of 1857

Bitterness caused by the *Dred Scott* decision was deepened by hard times, which dampened a period of feverish prosperity. Late in 1857, a financial panic burst about Buchanan's harassed head. The storm was not so bad economically as the panic of 1837, but psychologically it was probably the worst of the nineteenth century.

The North, including its grain growers, was hardest hit by the sharp economic downturn. The South, enjoying favorable cotton prices abroad, rode out the storm with flying colors. Panic conditions seemed further proof that cotton was king, and that its economic kingdom was stronger than that of the North. This fatal delusion helped drive the overconfident southerners closer to a shooting showdown.

---

* This part of the ruling, denying blacks their citizenship, seriously menaced the precarious position of the south's quarter-million free blacks.

public domain *Land or other property belonging to the whole nation, controlled by the federal government.*

Financial distress in the North, especially in agriculture, gave a new vigor to the demand for free farms of 160 acres from the **public domain**. Overcoming the objections of both eastern industrialists and southern slaveholders, Congress in 1860 finally passed a homestead act that made public lands available at the nominal sum of twenty-five cents an acre. But it was stabbed to death by the veto pen of Buchanan, near whose elbow sat leading southern sympathizers.

The panic of 1857 also created a clamor for higher tariff rates. The Tariff of 1857 had lowered duties to about 20 percent, but hardly had the revised rates been placed on the books when financial misery descended like a black pall. Northern manufacturers noisily blamed their misfortunes on the low tariff and clamored for increased protection. Thus the panic of 1857 gave the Republicans two surefire economic issues for 1860: protection for the unprotected and farms for the farmless.

An Illinois Rail-Splitter Emerges

The Illinois senatorial election of 1858 now claimed the national spotlight. Senator Douglas's term was about to expire, and the Republicans decided to run against him a rustic Springfield lawyer, one Abraham Lincoln. The Republican candidate—6 feet, 4 inches in height and 180 pounds in weight—presented an awkward but arresting figure. Lincoln's legs, arms, and neck were grotesquely long; his head was crowned by coarse, black, and unruly hair; and his face was sad, sunken, and weather-beaten.

Primary source
Railsplitter, The
college.hmco.com/pic/kennedybrief7e

Lincoln was no silver-spoon child of the elite. Born in 1809 in a Kentucky log cabin to impoverished parents, he attended a frontier school for not more than a year; being an avid reader, he was mainly self-educated. All his life he said "git," "thar," and "heered." Although narrow-chested and somewhat stoop-shouldered, he shone in his frontier community as a wrestler and weight lifter, and spent some time, among other pioneering pursuits, as a splitter of logs for fence rails. A superb teller of earthy and amusing stories, he would sometimes plunge into protracted periods of melancholy.

bandwagon *In politics, a movement or candidacy that gains rapid momentum because of people's purported desire to join a successful cause.*

Lincoln's private and professional lives had not been especially noteworthy. He married "above himself" socially, into the influential Todd family of Kentucky. After reading a little law, he gradually emerged as one of the dozen or so better-known trial lawyers in Illinois, although still accustomed to carrying important papers in his stovepipe hat. He was widely referred to as "Honest Abe," partly because he would refuse cases that he had to suspend his conscience to defend.

The rise of Lincoln as a political figure was less than rocketlike. After making his mark in the Illinois legislature as a Whig politician of the logrolling variety, he served one undistinguished term in Congress, 1847–1849. Until 1854, when he was forty-five years of age, he had done nothing to establish a claim to statesmanship. But the passage of the Kansas-Nebraska Act in that year lighted within him unexpected fires. After mounting the Republican **bandwagon**, he emerged as one of the foremost politicians and orators of the Northwest. At the Philadelphia convention of 1856, where Frémont was nominated, Lincoln actually received 110 votes for the vice-presidential nomination.

Lincoln expressed his views on the relation of the black and white races in 1858, in his first debate with Stephen A. Douglas:

"I, as well as Judge Douglas, am in favor of the race to which I belong, having the superior position. I have never said anything to the contrary, but I hold that notwithstanding all this, there is no reason in the world why the negro is not entitled to all the natural rights enumerated in the Declaration of Independence, the right to life, liberty, and the pursuit of happiness. I hold that he is as much entitled to those rights as the white man. I agree with Judge Douglas he is not my equal in many respects—certainly not in color, perhaps not in moral or intellectual endowment. But in the right to eat the bread, without leave of anybody else, which his own hand earns, he is my equal and the equal of Judge Douglas, and the equal of every living man."

The Great Debate: Lincoln Versus Douglas

Lincoln, as Republican nominee for the Senate seat, boldly challenged Douglas to a series of joint debates. This was a rash act because the stumpy senator was probably the nation's most devastating debater. Douglas promptly accepted Lincoln's challenge, and seven meetings were arranged from August to October 1858.

The most famous debate came at Freeport, Illinois, where Lincoln nearly impaled his opponent on the horns of a dilemma. Suppose, he queried, the people of a territory should vote slavery down? The Supreme Court in the *Dred Scott* decision had decreed that they could not. Who would prevail, the Court or the people?

Douglas's reply, which came to be known as the "Freeport Doctrine," was that no matter how the Supreme Court ruled, slavery would stay down if the people voted it down. Laws to protect slavery would have to be passed by the territorial legislatures. These would not be forthcoming in the absence of popular approval, and black bondage would soon disappear.

The upshot was that Douglas defeated Lincoln for the Senate seat. The "Little Giant's" loyalty to popular sovereignty, which still had a powerful appeal in Illinois, probably was decisive. But Douglas, in winning Illinois, hurt his chances of winning the presidency, while further splitting his **splintering** Democratic party. After his opposition to the Lecompton Constitution for Kansas, and his further defiance of the Supreme Court at Freeport, southern Democrats were determined to break up the party (and the Union) rather than accept him. For his part, Lincoln lost the election but shambled into the national limelight as a leading northern spokesman and potential Republican nominee for president. The Lincoln-Douglas debate platform thus proved to be one of the preliminary battlefields of the Civil War.

splintering *Concerning the small political groups left after a larger group has divided or broken apart.*

John Brown: Murderer or Martyr?

The gaunt, grim figure of John Brown of bleeding Kansas infamy now appeared again in an even more terrible way. His fanatical scheme was to invade the South secretly with a handful of followers, call upon the slaves to rise, furnish them with arms, and establish a kind of black free state as a sanctuary. Brown secured several thousand dollars for firearms from northern abolitionists and finally arrived in hilly western Virginia with some twenty men. He seized the federal arsenal at scenic Harpers Ferry in October 1859, incidentally killing seven innocent people, including a free black, and injuring ten or so more. But the slaves failed to rise, and the wounded Brown and the remnants of his tiny band were quickly captured by U.S. Marines under the command of Lieutenant Colonel Robert E. Lee. "Old Brown" was convicted of murder and treason after a hasty but legal trial.

But Brown—"God's angry man"—was given every opportunity to pose and to enjoy martyrdom. He was clever enough to see that he was worth much more to the abolitionist cause dangling from a rope than in any other way. His demeanor during the trial was dignified and courageous, and he marched up the scaffold steps without flinching. So the hangman's trap was sprung, and Brown plunged not into oblivion but into world fame. A memorable marching song of the impending Civil War ran,

> *John Brown's body lies a-mould'ring in the grave,*
> *His soul is marching on.*

Last Moments of John Brown, by Thomas Hovenden Sentenced to be hanged, John Brown wrote to his brother, "I am quite cheerful in view of my approaching end, being fully persuaded that I am worth inconceivably more to hang than for any other purpose. . . . I count it all joy. 'I have fought the good fight,' and have, as I trust, 'finished my course.' " This painting of Brown going to his execution may have been inspired by the journalist Horace Greeley, who was not present but wrote that "a black woman with a little child stood by the door. He stopped for a moment, and stooping, kissed the child." That scene never took place, as Brown was escorted from the jail only by a detachment of soldiers. But this painting has become famous as a kind of allegorical expression of the pathos of Brown's martyrdom for the abolitionist cause.

Upon hearing of John Brown's execution, escaped slave and abolitionist Harriet Tubman (c. 1820–1913) paid him the highest tribute for his self-sacrifice:

"I've been studying, and studying upon it, and its clar to me, it wasn't John Brown that died on that gallows. When I think how he gave up his life for our people, and how he never flinched, but was so brave to the end; its clar to me it wasn't mortal man, it was God in him."

Not all opponents of slavery, however, shared Tubman's reverence for Brown. Republican presidential candidate Abraham Lincoln dismissed Brown as deluded:

"[The Brown] affair, in its philosophy, corresponds with the many attempts, related in history, at the assassination of kings and emperors. An enthusiast broods over the oppression of a people till he fancies himself commissioned by Heaven to liberate them. He ventures the attempt, which ends in little else than his own execution."

The effects of Harpers Ferry were calamitous. In the eyes of the South, already embittered, "Osawatomie Brown" was a wholesale murderer and an apostle of treason. Many southerners asked how they could possibly remain in the Union while a "murderous gang of abolitionists" were financing armed bands to "Brown" them. Moderate northerners, including Republican leaders, openly deplored this mad exploit. But the South naturally concluded that the violent abolitionist view was shared by the entire North, dominated by "Brown-loving" Republicans.

Abolitionists and other ardent free-soilers were infuriated by Brown's execution. On the day of his hanging, free-soil centers in the North tolled bells, fired guns, lowered flags, and held rallies. Some spoke of "Saint John" Brown, and Ralph Waldo Emerson compared the new **martyr**-hero with Jesus. The gallows became a cross. E. C. Steman wrote,

And Old Brown,
Osawatomie Brown,
May trouble you more than ever
when you've nailed his coffin down!

The ghost of the martyred Brown would not be laid to rest.

Democrats Divide and Republicans Rise

Online Study Center
Primary source
Election of 1860
college.hmco.com/pic/kennedybrief7e

martyr *One who is tortured or killed for adherence to a belief.*

border state *The northernmost slave states contested by North and South; during the Civil War the four border states (Maryland, Delaware, Kentucky, and Missouri) remained within the Union, though they contained many Confederate sympathizers and volunteers.*

Beyond question the presidential election of 1860 was the most fateful in American history. Deeply divided, the Democrats met in Charleston, South Carolina. Northern Democrats looked to Douglas as the leading candidate of their party, but southern "fire-eaters" regarded him as a traitor. After a bitter platform fight, delegates from most of the cotton states walked out of the convention. When the remainder could not scrape together the necessary two-thirds vote for Douglas, the entire body dissolved. The southerners' departure from the Democratic convention was the first tragic act of secession. Departure became habit forming.

The Democrats tried again in Baltimore. With northern Douglas Democrats firmly in the saddle, the cotton-state delegates again took a walk, and the rest of the convention enthusiastically nominated their hero. Angered southern Democrats promptly organized a rival convention in Baltimore and selected as their nominee the stern-jawed vice president, John C. Breckinridge, from the **border state** of Kentucky. The platform favored the extension of slavery into the territories and the annexation of slave-populated Cuba.

A middle-of-the-road group, fearing for the Union, hastily organized the Constitutional Union party. It consisted mainly of former Whigs and Know-Nothings. This "gathering of graybeards" met in Baltimore and nominated John Bell of Tennessee for the presidency on a platform of "the Union, the Constitution, and the enforcement of the law."

Elated Republicans, scenting victory in the breeze as their opponents split hopelessly, gathered in Chicago in a huge boxlike wooden structure called the Wigwam. William H. Seward was by far the best known of the contenders, but Seward's radical utterances, including his "irrepressible conflict" speech at Rochester in 1858,* had ruined his prospects. Lincoln, the favorite son of Illinois,

* Seward had referred to an "irrepressible conflict" between slavery and freedom, though not necessarily a bloody one.

was a stronger candidate because he had made fewer enemies than Seward. Overtaking Seward on the third ballot, he was nominated amid scenes of the wildest excitement.

The Republican platform had a seductive appeal for almost every important nonsouthern group: for the free-soilers, the nonextension of slavery; for northern manufacturers, a protective tariff; for immigrants, no abridgement of rights; and for farmers, free homesteads from the public domain.

Southern secessionists promptly served notice that the election of the "baboon" Lincoln would split the Union. In fact, "Honest Abe," though hating slavery, was no outright abolitionist. He campaigned quietly and issued no new statements in response to these threats. The most active opposition to southern extremism came from the "Little Giant" Douglas, who waged a vigorous speaking campaign, even in the South, and threatened to put the rope with his own hands around the neck of the first secessionist.

The returns, breathlessly awaited, proclaimed a sweeping victory for Lincoln (see the table and map, p. **000**).

The Electoral Upheaval of 1860

Awkward "Abe" Lincoln had run a curious race. To a greater degree than any other holder of the nation's highest office (except John Quincy Adams), he was a minority president. Sixty percent of the voters preferred some other candidate. He was also a sectional president, for in ten southern states, where he was not allowed on the ballot, he polled no popular votes. The election of 1860 was virtually two elections: one between Lincoln and Douglas in the North, the other between Bell and Breckinridge in the South. South Carolinians rejoiced over Lincoln's victory; they now had their excuse to secede. In winning the North the "rail-splitter" had split off the South.

Primary source
Preserving the Union
college.hmco.com/pic/kennedybrief7e

Douglas, though scraping together only twelve electoral votes, made an impressive showing. He drew important strength from all sections and ranked a fairly close second in the popular-vote column. In fact, the Douglas Democrats and the Breckinridge Democrats together amassed 366,484 more popular votes than did Lincoln. But contrary to myth, Lincoln's electoral vote victory did not occur because his opponents were divided. Even if all the Democrats and Constitutional Unionists had united behind Douglas, Lincoln would have carried the populous northern states and therefore would still have won the electoral vote 169 to 134 instead of 180 to 123.

Significantly, the verdict of the ballot box did not indicate a strong sentiment for secession. Breckinridge, while favoring the extension of slavery, was no disunionist. Although the candidate of the "fire-eaters," he polled fewer votes in the slave states than Douglas and Bell combined. Despite its electoral defeat, the South was not badly off. Southerners still controlled the Supreme Court, both houses of Congress, and more than enough states to block any attempt to end slavery by constitutional amendment.

The Secessionist Exodus

Primary source
Louisiana Newspapers Respond to Lincoln's Victory
college.hmco.com/pic/kennedybrief7e

But a tragic chain reaction of secession now began to erupt. South Carolina had threatened to go out if the "Illinois baboon" were elected, and in December 1860 a special convention called by the legislature carried out the threat by voting unanimously to secede. During the next six weeks, six other states of the Lower South followed the leader over the precipice: Alabama, Mississippi, Florida, Georgia, Louisiana, and Texas. Four more were to join them later, bringing the total to eleven.

With the eyes of destiny upon them, the seven seceders, formally meeting in Montgomery, Alabama, in February 1861, created a government known as

Election of 1860

Candidate	Popular Vote	Percentage of Popular Vote	Electoral Vote
Lincoln	1,865,593	39.79%	180 (every vote of the free states except for 3 of New Jersey's 7 votes)
Douglas	1,382,713	29.40	12 (only Missouri and 3 of New Jersey's 7 votes)
Breckinridge	848,356	18.20	72 (all the cotton states)
Bell	592,906	12.61	39 (Virginia, Kentucky, Tennessee)

Presidential Election of 1860 (with electoral vote by state) A surprising fact is that Lincoln, often rated among the greatest presidents, ranks near the bottom in percentage of popular votes. In all eleven states that seceded, he received only a scattering of one state's votes—about 1.5 percent in Virginia.

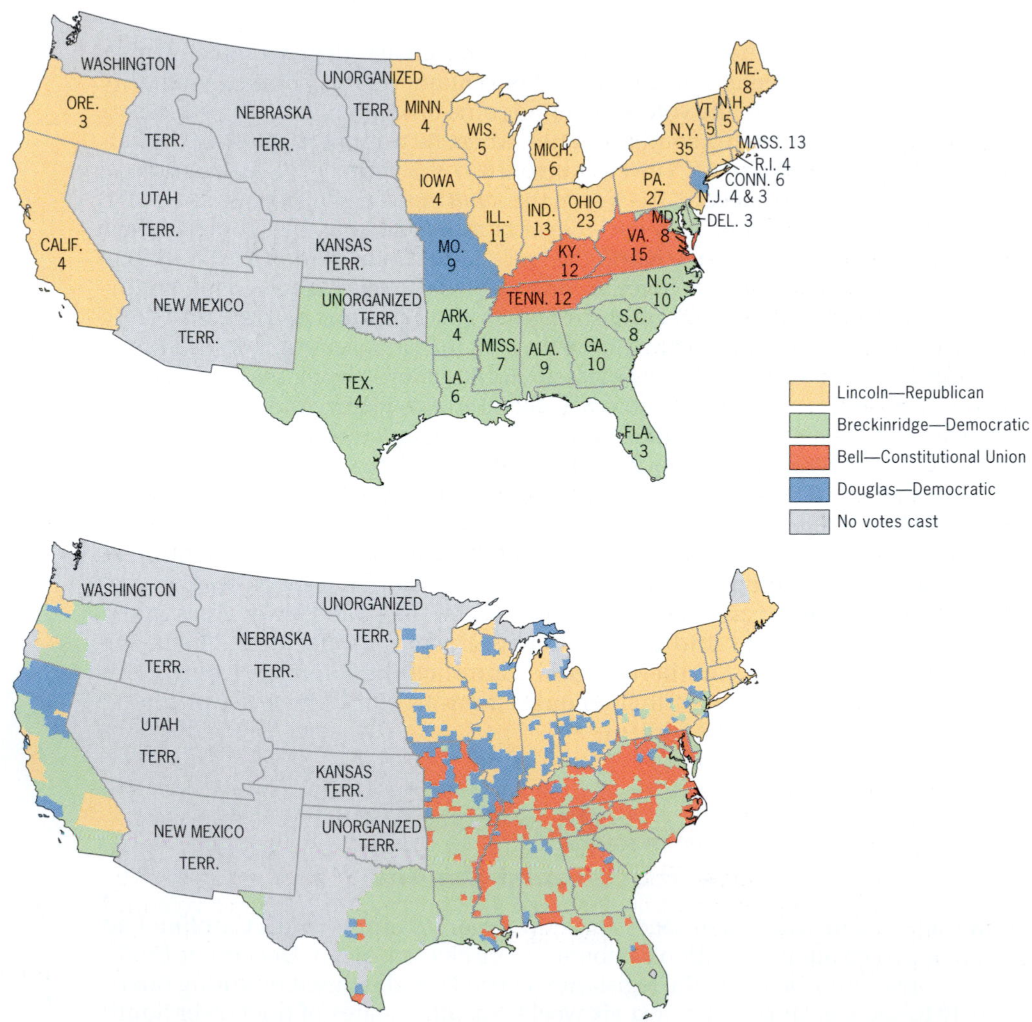

Presidential Election of 1860 (showing popular vote by county) The vote by county for Lincoln was virtually all cast in the North. The northern Democrat, Douglas, was also nearly shut out in the South, which divided its votes between Breckenridge and Bell.

the Confederate States of America. As their president they chose Jefferson Davis, a dignified and austere former secretary of war and recent U.S. senator from Mississippi.

The crisis, already critical enough, was deepened by the "lame duck" interlude. Lincoln, although elected president in November 1860, could not take office until four months later, March 4, 1861. During this period of protracted uncertainty, when Lincoln was still a private citizen in Illinois, seven of the eleven deserting states pull out of the Union.

Meanwhile, the aging incumbent President Buchanan chose to wring his hands rather than secessionist necks. Surrounded by prosouthern advisers, Buchanan found constitutional and practical justifications for inaction. One important reason why he did not resort to force was that the tiny standing army of fifteen thousand men was widely scattered, fighting Indians in the West. Public opinion in the North, at that time, was far from willing to unsheathe the sword. Fighting would shatter all prospects of adjustment, and until the guns began to boom, there was still a flickering hope of reconciliation rather than a contested divorce. The weakness lay not so much in Buchanan as in the Constitution and in the Union itself. Ironically, when Lincoln became president in March, he essentially continued Buchanan's wait-and-see policy.

A Failed Compromise and Secession

Impending bloodshed spurred final and frantic attempts at compromise, most notably by Senator James Henry Crittenden of Kentucky. Crittenden proposed several constitutional amendments designed to appease the South. Slavery in the territories was to be prohibited north of 36°30′, but south of that line it was to be given federal protection in all territories existing or "hereafter to be acquired" (such as Cuba). Future states, north or south of 36°30′, could come into the Union with or without slavery, as they should choose. In short, the slavery supporters were to be guaranteed full rights in the southern territories, as long as they were territories, regardless of the wishes of the majority under popular sovereignty. Federal protection in a territory south of 36°30′ might conceivably, though improbably, turn the entire area permanently to slavery.

Lincoln flatly rejected the Crittenden scheme, which offered some slight prospect of success, and all hope of compromise evaporated. He had been elected on a platform that opposed the extension of slavery, and he felt that as a matter of principle he could not afford to yield, even though gains for slavery in the territories might be only temporary. Larger gains might come later in Cuba and Latin America. Crittenden's proposal, said Lincoln, "would amount to a perpetual covenant of war against every people, tribe, and state owning a foot of land between here and Tierra del Fuego."

Secessionists who parted company with their sister states left for a number of avowed reasons, mostly relating in some way to slavery. They were alarmed by the inexorable tipping of the political balance against them—"the despotic majority of numbers." The "crime" of the North, observed James Russell Lowell, was the census returns. Southerners were also dismayed by the triumph of the new sectional Republican party, which seemed to threaten their rights as a slaveholding minority. They were weary of free-soil criticism, abolitionist nagging, and northern interference, ranging from the Underground Railroad to John Brown's raid. "All we ask is to be let alone," declared President Jefferson Davis in an early message to his congress.

* The lame duck period was shortened to ten weeks in 1933 by the Twentieth Amendment (see the Appendix).

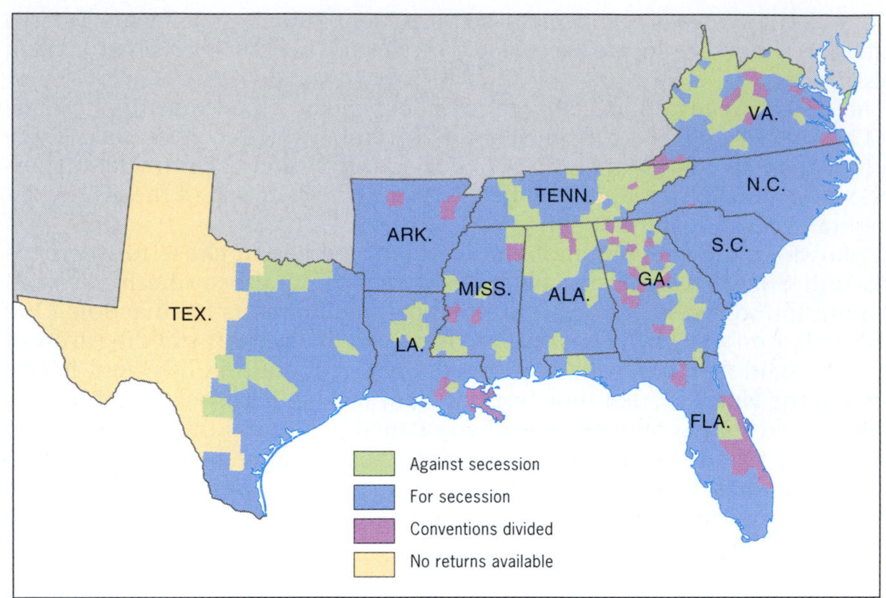

Southern Opposition to Secession, 1860–1861 (showing vote by county) This county vote shows the opposition of the antiplanter, antislavery mountain whites in the Appalachian region. There was also considerable resistance to secession in Texas, where Governor Sam Houston, who led the Unionists, was deposed by secessionist hotheads.

Many southerners supported secession because they felt sure that their departure would be unopposed, despite "Yankee yawp" to the contrary. They were confident that the clodhopping and cod fishing Yankee would not or could not fight. They also believed that northern manufacturers and bankers, so heavily dependent on southern cotton and markets, would not dare to cut their own economic throats with their own unionist swords.

vassalage *The service and homage given by a feudal subordinate to an overlord; by extension, any similar arrangement between political figures or entities.*

Southern leaders regarded secession as a golden opportunity to cast aside their generations of "**vassalage**" to the North. An independent Dixieland could develop its own banking and shipping, trade directly with Europe, and forever rid itself of the threat of high tariffs. For decades this fundamental friction had pitted the manufacturing North against the agricultural South.

The principles of self-determination—of the Declaration of Independence—seemed to many southerners to apply perfectly to them. Few, if any, of the seceders felt that they were doing anything wrong or immoral. The thirteen original states had voluntarily entered the Union and now seven—ultimately eleven—southern states were voluntarily withdrawing from it.

Historical parallels ran even deeper. In 1776 thirteen American colonies, led by the rebel George Washington, had seceded from the British Empire by throwing off the yoke of King George III. In 1860–1861 eleven American states, led by the rebel Jefferson Davis, were seceding from the Union by throwing off the yoke of "King" Abraham Lincoln. With that burden gone, the South was confident that it could work out its own peculiar destiny more quietly, happily, and prosperously.

Chapter Summary

The 1850s were punctuated by a series of increasingly violent incidents and confrontations that deepened sectional hostility, until it broke out in the Civil War.

Harriet Beecher Stowe's *Uncle Tom's Cabin* fanned northern antislavery feeling. In Kansas, Douglas's "popular sovereignty" scheme proved a disaster, as proslavery and antislavery forces fought a bloody little preview of the Civil War. Prosouthern President Buchanan's support of the proslavery Lecompton Constitution alienated moderate northern Democrats like Douglas. Congressman Brooks's beating of Senator Sumner aroused passions in both sections.

The 1856 election signaled the rise of the sectionally based Republican party. The *Dred Scott* case delighted the South, while northern Republicans pledged defiance. The Lincoln-Douglas debates of 1858 made Lincoln a national Republican leader and deepened the controversy over slavery. The fanatical abolitionist John Brown's raid on Harpers Ferry made him a heroic martyr in the North but caused outraged southerners to fear a slave uprising.

In the campaign of 1860, the Democratic party split along sectional lines. Lincoln won the resulting four-way election with support only from the North. Seven southern states quickly seceded and organized the Confederate States of America.

As southerners enthusiastically cast off their ties to the hated North, lame-duck President Buchanan proved unable to act. The last-minute Crittenden Compromise effort failed because of Lincoln's conviction that it would allow slavery to expand into Latin America.

VARYING VIEWPOINTS

The Civil War: Repressible or Irrepressible?

Few topics have generated as much controversy among American historians as the causes of the Civil War. Interpretations of the great conflict have naturally differed according to section and have been charged with both emotional and moral fervor. Yet despite long and keen interest in the origins of the conflict, the causes of the Civil War remain as passionately debated today as they were a century ago.

The so-called Nationalist School of the late nineteenth century, typified by James Ford Rhodes, claimed that slavery caused the Civil War and credited the conflict with ending "the peculiar institution" and preserving the Union. But in the early twentieth century, progressive historians like Charles and Mary Beard argued that the war was not fought over slavery per se, but rather was a deeply rooted economic struggle between an industrial North and an agricultural South. Anointing the Civil War "the Second American Revolution," the Beards claimed that the war transferred the dominant class power in America from the southern plantation aristocracy to the rising class of northern industrialists.

Shaken by the disappointing results of World War I, a new wave of historians argued that the Civil War, too, had actually been a big mistake. James G. Randall and Avery Craven asserted that the war had been a "repressible conflict," and they attributed the bloody confrontation to overzealous reformers and blundering political leaders.

Following the Second World War, however, a neonationalist view, echoing the earlier views of Rhodes, began depicting the Civil War as an unavoidable conflict between two societies, one slave and one free. For Allan Nevins and David M. Potter, irreconcilable differences in morality, politics, culture, social values, and economic systems increasingly eroded the ties between the sections and inexorably set the United States on the road to Civil War.

Eric Foner and Eugene Genovese have emphasized each section's nearly paranoid fear that the survival of its way of life was threatened by the expansion of the other section. In *Free Soil, Free Labor, Free Men* (1970), Foner emphasized that most northerners detested slavery not because it enslaved blacks but because its rapid extension threatened the position of free white laborers. Genovese has argued that the South, convinced that its labor system was superior to the northern factory system, saw northern designs to destroy their way of life lurking at every turn.

More recently, historians of the "Ethnocultural School," especially Michael Holt, have offered a different analysis of how the collapse of the two established political parties caused the Civil War. They note that the two great political parties had earlier muted sectional differences over slavery by focusing on issues such as the tariff, banking, and internal improvements. According to this argument, it was the temporary *consensus* on almost all national issues *other than* slavery that enabled the slavery issue to rise to the fore. Slavery fueled the rise of purely regional parties that saw their political opponents as threats to their way of life, even to the life of the Republic itself.

Girding for War: The North and the South

1861–1865

I CONSIDER THE CENTRAL IDEA PERVADING THIS STRUGGLE IS THE NECESSITY THAT IS UPON US, OF PROVING THAT POPULAR GOVERNMENT IS NOT AN ABSURDITY. WE MUST SETTLE THIS QUESTION NOW, WHETHER IN A FREE GOVERNMENT THE MINORITY HAVE THE RIGHT TO BREAK UP THE GOVERNMENT WHENEVER THEY CHOOSE. IF WE FAIL IT WILL GO FAR TO PROVE THE INCAPABILITY OF THE PEOPLE TO GOVERN THEMSELVES.

ABRAHAM LINCOLN, MAY 7, 1861

Chapter Outline

- The Attack on Fort Sumter, April 1861
- The Crucial Border States
- The Balance of Forces
- Diplomacy and the Threat of European Intervention
- Lincoln and Civil Liberties
- Men in Uniform
- Wartime Finance and Economy
- Women and the War
- The Fate of the South

Abraham Lincoln solemnly took the presidential oath of office on March 4, 1861, after having slipped into Washington at night, partially disguised to thwart assassins. He thus became president not of the *United* States of America, but of the dis-United States of America. Seven had already departed; eight more teetered on the edge. The girders of the unfinished Capitol dome loomed nakedly in the background, as if to symbolize the imperfect state of the Union. Before the nation was restored—and the slaves freed at last—the American people would endure four years of anguish and bloodshed, and Lincoln would face tortuous trials of leadership such as have been visited upon few presidents.

Focus Questions

1. **Why did the South fire the first shots of the Civil War? How did that assault and Lincoln's call for troops galvanize both sides for war and lead to the secession of four more Southern states?**
2. **What were the strengths and weaknesses of both sides as they went to war, and why were the Border States so critical to the balance of forces?**
3. **Why was the issue of British or French recognition of the Confederacy so central to the diplomacy of both sides?**
4. **How did Lincoln and Davis each mobilize their nation's forces and shape the moral and political character of the struggle?**
5. **What were the economic and social consequences of the war for both sides, including its effects on the roles of women?**

Chronology

1861	Confederate government formed. Lincoln takes office (March 4). Fort Sumter fired upon (April 12). Four upper South states secede (April–June). Morrill Tariff Act passed. *Trent* affair. Lincoln suspends writ of habeas corpus.
1862	Confederacy enacts conscription. Homestead Act.
1862–1864	*Alabama* raids Northern shipping.
1863	Union enacts conscription. New York City draft riots. National Banking System established.
1863–1864	Napoleon III installs Archduke Maximilian as emperor of Mexico.
1864	*Alabama* sunk by Union warship.

The Menace of Secession

Lincoln's inaugural address was firm yet conciliatory: there would be no conflict unless the South provoked it. Secession, the president declared, was wholly impractical because, "physically speaking, we cannot separate."

Here Lincoln put his finger on a profound geographical truth. The North and South were bound inseparably together. If they had been divided by the Pyrenees Mountains or the Danube River, a sectional divorce might have been more feasible. But the Appalachian Mountains and the mighty Mississippi River both ran the wrong way.

Uncontested secession would create new controversies. What share of the national debt should the South be forced to take with it? What portion of the jointly held federal territories, if any, should the Confederate states be allotted—areas so largely won with Southern blood? How would the fugitive-slave issue be resolved? The Underground Railroad would certainly redouble its activity, and it would have to transport its passengers only across the Ohio River, not all the way to Canada. Was it conceivable that all such problems could have been solved without ugly armed clashes?

A *united* United States had hitherto been the paramount republic in the Western Hemisphere. If this powerful democracy broke into two hostile nations, the European nations would be delighted. They could gleefully transplant to America their ancient concept of the **balance of power**. Playing the no-less-ancient game of divide and conquer, they could incite one snarling fragment of the dis–United States against the other. The colonies of the European powers in the New World, notably those of Britain, would thus be made safer against the rapacious Yankees. And European imperialists, with no unified republic to stand across their path, could more easily defy the Monroe Doctrine and seize territory in the Americas.

balance of power *The distribution of political or military strength among several nations so that no one of them becomes too strong or dangerous.*

Secretary of State William H. Seward (1801–1872) entertained the dangerous idea that if the North picked a fight with one or more European nations, the South would once more rally around the flag. On April Fools' Day, 1861, he submitted to Lincoln a memorandum:

"I would demand explanations from Spain and France, categorically, at once. I would seek explanations from Great Britain and Russia. . . . And, if satisfactory explanations are not received from Spain and France . . . would convene Congress and declare war against them." *Lincoln quietly but firmly quashed Seward's scheme.*

South Carolina Assails Fort Sumter

The issue of the divided Union came to a head over the matter of federal forts in the South. As the seceding states left, they seized the United States' arsenals, mints, and other public property within their borders. When Lincoln took office, only two significant forts in the South still flew the Stars and Stripes. The more important of the pair was square-walled Fort Sumter, in Charleston harbor, with fewer than a hundred men.

Ominously, the choices presented to Lincoln by Fort Sumter were all bad. This stronghold had provisions that would last only a few weeks—until the middle of April 1861. If no supplies were forthcoming, its commander would have to surrender without firing a shot. Lincoln, quite understandably, did not feel that such a weak-kneed course squared with his obligation to protect federal property. But if he sent reinforcements, the South Carolinians would undoubtedly fight back; they could not tolerate a federal fort blocking the mouth of their most important Atlantic seaport.

After agonizing indecision, Lincoln adopted a middle-of-the-road solution. He notified the South Carolinians that an expedition would be sent to *provision* the garrison, though not to *reinforce* it. But to Southern eyes "provision" still spelled "reinforcement."

A Union naval force started on its way to Fort Sumter—a move that the South regarded as an act of aggression. On April 12, 1861, the cannon of the Carolinians opened fire on the fort, while crowds in Charleston applauded and waved handkerchiefs. After a thirty-four-hour bombardment, the dazed garrison surrendered.

The shelling of the fort electrified the North, which at once responded with cries of "Remember Fort Sumter!" and "Save the Union!" Hitherto, countless Northerners had been saying that if the Southern states wanted to go, they should not be pinned to the rest of the nation with bayonets. "Wayward sisters, depart in peace" was a common sentiment. But the assault on Fort Sumter provoked the North to a fighting pitch: the fort was lost, but the Union was saved.

Lincoln had turned a tactical defeat into a strategic victory. Southerners had wantonly fired upon the glorious Stars and Stripes, and honor demanded an armed response. Lincoln promptly (April 15) issued a call to the states for seventy-five thousand militiamen, and volunteers sprang to the colors in such enthusiastic numbers that many were turned away. On April 19 and 27, the president proclaimed a leaky blockade of Southern seaports.

The call for troops, in turn, aroused the South much as the attack on Fort Sumter had aroused the North. Lincoln was now waging war—from the Southern view an aggressive war—on the Confederacy. Virginia, Arkansas, and Tennessee, all of which had earlier voted down secession, reluctantly joined their embattled sister states, as did North Carolina. Thus the seven states became eleven as the "submissionists" and "Union shriekers" were overcome. Richmond, Virginia, replaced Montgomery, Alabama, as the Confederate capital—too near Washington for strategic comfort on either side.

Brothers' Blood and Border Blood

The only slave states left were the crucial Border States. This group consisted of Missouri, Kentucky, Maryland, Delaware, and later West Virginia—the "mountain white" area that somewhat illegally uprooted itself from Virginia in mid-1861. If the North had fired the first shot, some or all of these doubtful states probably would have seceded, and the South might well have succeeded. The border group actually contained a white population more than half that of the entire Confederacy. Lincoln reportedly said that he *hoped* to have God on his side but he *had* to have Kentucky.

In dealing with the Border States, President Lincoln did not rely solely on moral suasion but successfully used methods of dubious legality. In Maryland he declared **martial law** where needed and sent in troops because this state threatened to cut off Washington from the North. Lincoln also deployed Union soldiers in western Virginia and notably in Missouri, where they fought beside Unionists in a local civil war within the larger Civil War.

martial law *The imposition of military rule above or in place of civil authority during times of war and emergency.*

Any official statement of the North's war aims was profoundly influenced by the teetering Border States. At the very outset, Lincoln was obliged to declare publicly that he was not fighting to free the blacks. An antislavery declaration would no doubt

Lincoln wrote to the antislavery editor Horace Greeley in August 1862, even as he was about to announce the Emancipation Proclamation,

"If I could save the Union without freeing any slave, I would do it; and if I could save it by freeing all the slaves, I would do it; and if I could do it by freeing some and leaving others alone, I would also do that."

have driven the Border States into the welcoming arms of the South. An antislavery war was also extremely unpopular in the so-called Butternut region of southern Ohio, Indiana, and Illinois, originally settled largely by racially prejudiced Southerners (see "Makers of America: Settlers of the Old Northwest," p. 170). Lincoln insisted repeatedly—even though undercutting his high moral ground—that his paramount purpose was to save the Union at all costs. Thus the war began not as one between slave soil and free soil, but one for the Union—with slaveholders on both sides and many proslavery sympathizers in the North.

Slavery also colored the character of the war in the West. In Indian Territory (present-day Oklahoma), most of the Five Civilized Tribes—the Cherokees, Creeks, Choctaws, Chickasaws, and Seminoles—sided with the Confederacy. Some of these Indians, notably the Cherokees, owned slaves and thus felt themselves to be making common cause with the slaveowning South. The Confederate government invited the Native Americans to send delegates to the Confederate congress, and they in return supplied troops to the Confederate army. A rival faction of Cherokees and most of the Plains Indians, however, sided with the Union.

Unhappily, the conflict between "Billy Yank" and "Johnny Reb" was a brothers' war. There were many Northern volunteers from the Southern states, and many Southern volunteers from the Northern states. The "mountain whites" of the South sent north some 50,000 men, and the loyal slave states contributed some 300,000 soldiers to the Union. In many a family of the Border States, one brother rode north to fight with the Blue, another south to fight with the Gray. Senator Crittenden of Kentucky, who fathered the abortive Crittenden Compromise, fathered two sons: one became a general in the Union army, the other a general in the Confederate army.

The Balance of Forces

Online Study Center

Primary source
Enlisted Man Describes Life in a Confederate Prison Camp
college.hmco.com/pic/kennedybrief7e

When war broke out, the South seemed to have great advantages. The Confederacy could fight defensively behind interior lines. The North had to invade the vast territory of the Confederacy, conquer it, and drag it bodily back into the Union. In fact, the South did not have to win the war in order to win its independence. If it merely fought the invaders to a draw and stood firm, Confederate independence would be won. Fighting on their own soil for self-determination and preservation of their way of life, Southerners at first enjoyed an advantage in morale as well.

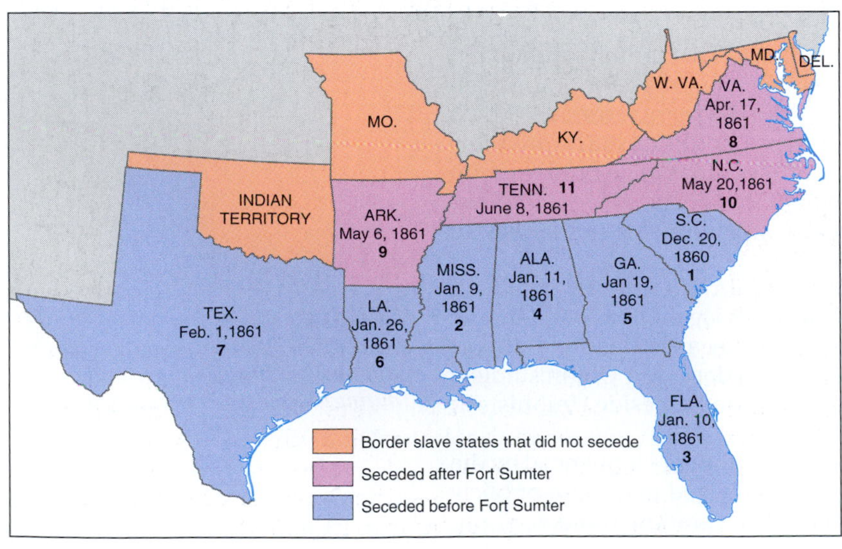

Seceding States (with dates and order of secession) Notice the long interval—nearly six months—between the secession of South Carolina, the first state to go, and that of Tennessee, the last state to leave the Union. These six months were a time of terrible trial for moderate Southerners. When a Georgia statesman pleaded for restraint and negotiations with Washington, he was rebuffed with the cry, "Throw the bloody spear into this den of incendiaries!"

Militarily, the South from the opening volleys of the war had the most talented officers. Most conspicuous among a dozen or so first-rate commanders was gray-haired General Robert E. Lee, whose knightly bearing and chivalric sense of honor embodied the Southern ideal. Lincoln had unofficially offered him command of the Northern armies, but when Virginia seceded Lee felt honor-bound to go with his native state. Lee's chief lieutenant for much of the war was black-bearded Thomas J. ("Stonewall") Jackson, a gifted tactical theorist and a master of speed and deception.

Besides their brilliant leaders, ordinary Southerners were also bred to fight. Accustomed to managing horses and bearing arms from boyhood, they made excellent cavalrymen and foot soldiers. Their high-pitched "rebel yell" ("yeeeahhh") was designed to strike terror into the hearts of fuzz-chinned Yankee recruits.

As one immense farm, the South seemed to be handicapped by the scarcity of its factories. Yet by seizing federal weapons, running Union blockades, and developing their own ironworks, Southerners managed to obtain sufficient weaponry. "Yankee ingenuity" was not confined to Yankees.

Nevertheless, as the war dragged on, grave shortages of shoes, uniforms, and blankets afflicted the South. Even with immense stores of food on Southern farms,

■ **The Technology of War** One of the new machines of destruction that made the Civil War the first mechanized war, this eight-and-a-half ton federal mortar sat on a railroad flatcar in Petersburg, Virginia, ready to hurl two-hundred-pound missiles as far as two and a half miles. This powerful artillery piece rode on the tracks of a captured Southern railroad—itself another artifact of modern technology that figured heavily in the war. Of the 31,256 miles of railroad track in the United States in 1861, less than 30 percent, or 9,283 miles, were in the Confederate states, soon reduced by Union capture and destruction to 6,000 miles. The Confederate government's failure to understand the military importance of railroads contributed substantially to its defeat.

Primary source
Union Soldier's Opinion of the War, A
college.hmco.com/pic/kennedybrief7e

Immigration to United States, 1860–1866

Year	Total	Britain	Ireland	Germany	All Others
1860	153,640	29,737	48,637	54,491	20,775
1861	91,918	19,675	23,797	31,661	16,785
1862	91,985	24,639	23,351	27,529	16,466
1863	176,282	66,882	55,916	33,162	20,322
1864	193,418	53,428	63,523	57,276	19,191
1865*	248,120	82,465	29,772	83,424	52,459
1866	**318,568**	**94,924**	**36,690**	**115,892**	**71,062**

*Only the first three months of 1865 were war months.

civilians and soldiers often went hungry because of supply problems. "Forward, men! They have cheese in their haversacks," cried one Southern officer as he attacked the Yankees. Much of the hunger was caused by a breakdown of the South's rickety transportation system, especially where the railroad tracks were cut or destroyed by the Yankee invaders.

The economy was the greatest Southern weakness; it was the North's greatest strength. The North was not only a huge farm but a sprawling factory as well. Yankees boasted about three-fourths of the nation's wealth, including three-fourths of the thirty thousand miles of the railroads.

The North also controlled the sea. With its vastly superior navy, it established a blockade that, though a sieve at first, soon choked off Southern supplies and eventually shattered Southern morale. Its sea power also enabled the North to exchange huge quantities of grain for munitions and supplies from Europe, thus adding the output from the factories of Europe to its own.

The Union also enjoyed a much larger reserve of manpower. The loyal states had a population of some 22 million; the seceding states had 9 million people, including about 3.5 million slaves. Adding to the North's overwhelming supply of soldiery were immigrants from Europe, who continued to pour into the North even during the war (see the table on p. 296). Over 800,000 newcomers arrived between 1861 and 1865, most of them British, Irish, and German. Large numbers of them were induced to enlist in the Union armies. Altogether about one-fifth of the Union forces were foreign-born, and in some units military commands were given in four different languages.

Whether immigrant or native, ordinary Northern boys were much less prepared than their Southern counterparts for military life. Yet the Northern "clodhoppers" and "shopkeepers" eventually adjusted themselves to soldiering and became known for their discipline and determination.

The North was much less fortunate in its higher commanders. Lincoln was forced to use a costly trial-and-error method to sort out effective leaders from the many incompetent political officers, until he finally uncovered a general, Ulysses Simpson Grant, who was determined to slog his way to victory at whatever cost to life and limb.

In the long run, as the Northern strengths were brought to bear, they outweighed those of the South. But when the war began, the chances for Southern independence were unusually favorable—certainly better than the prospects for success of the thirteen colonies in 1776. The turn of a few events could easily have produced a different outcome.

The might-have-beens are fascinating. *If* the Border States had seceded, or *if* the uncertain states of the upper Mississippi Valley had turned against the Union, or *if* a wave of Northern defeatism had demanded an armistice, or *if* Britain and/or France had broken the naval blockade, the South might well have won. All of these possibilities almost became realities, but none of them actually occurred, and lacking their impetus, the South could not win.

Dethroning King Cotton

Successful revolutions, including the American Revolution of 1776, have generally succeeded because of foreign intervention. The South counted on it, did not get it, and lost. Of all the Confederacy's potential assets, none counted more weightily than the prospect of assistance from abroad. Europe's ruling classes, which had long abhorred the incendiary example of American democracy, were openly sympathetic to the semifeudal, aristocratic South.

In contrast, the masses of working people in Britain, and to some extent in France, were pulling and praying for the North. Many of them had read *Uncle Tom's Cabin*, and they sensed that the war—though at the outset officially fought only over the question of union—might extinguish slavery if the North emerged victorious. The hostility of British common folk to any official intervention on behalf of the South had a sobering effect on the British government. Yet the fact remained that British textile mills depended on the American South for 75 percent of their cotton supplies. Humanitarian sympathies aside, Southerners counted on hard economic need to bring Britain to their aid. Why did King Cotton fail them?

He failed in part because he had been so lavishly productive in the immediate prewar years of 1857–1860. When the shooting started in 1861, British manufacturers had on hand enormous surpluses of cotton piled up in their warehouses. The real pinch did not come until about a year and a half later, when thousands of hungry operatives were thrown out of work. But by this time Lincoln had announced his slave-emancipation policy, and the "wage slaves" of Britain were not going to demand a war to defend the slaveowners of the South.

The direct effects of the "cotton famine" in Britain were relieved in several ways. As Union armies penetrated the South, they captured or bought considerable supplies of cotton and shipped them to Britain; the Confederates also ran a limited quantity through the blockade. In addition, the cotton growers of Egypt and India, responding to high prices, increased their output. Finally, booming war industries in Britain, which supplied both the North and the South, relieved unemployment.

King Wheat and King Corn—the monarchs of Northern agriculture—proved to be more potent potentates than King Cotton. Blessed with ideal weather and the efficient harvesting of McCormick's mechanical reaper, the North produced bountiful crops during the war years. The grain was purchased by Britain, which suffered a series of bad harvests in the same period. If the British had broken the blockade to gain cotton, they would have provoked the North to war and would have lost this precious granary.

Foreign Flare-ups

America's diplomatic front has seldom been so critical as during the Civil War. The South never wholly abandoned its dream of foreign intervention, and Europe's rulers schemed to take advantage of America's distress.

The first major crisis with Britain came over the *Trent* affair, late in 1861. A Union warship cruising on the high seas north of Cuba stopped a British mail steamer, the *Trent*, and forcibly removed two Confederate diplomats bound for Europe.

Britons were outraged: upstart Yankees could not so boldly offend the Mistress of the Seas. War preparations buzzed, and red-coated troops embarked for Canada with bands blaring "I Wish I Was in Dixie." The London Foreign Office prepared an **ultimatum** demanding surrender of the prisoners and an apology. But luckily, slow communications gave passions on both sides a chance to cool. Lincoln came to see the *Trent* prisoners as "white elephants" and reluctantly released them.

ultimatum *A final proposal or demand, as by one nation to another, that if rejected, will likely lead to war.*

Another major crisis in Anglo-American relations arose over the unneutral building in Britain of Confederate commerce-raiders, notably the *Alabama*. These

loopholed *Characterized by small exceptions or conditions that enable escape from the general rule or principle.*

squadron *A special unit of warships assigned to a particular naval task.*

vessels were not warships within the meaning of **loopholed** British law because they left their shipyards unarmed and picked up their guns elsewhere. The *Alabama* escaped in 1862 to the Portuguese Azores and there took on weapons and a crew from two British ships that followed it.

The *Alabama* lighted the skies from Europe to East Asia with the burning hulks of Yankee merchantmen. All told, this "British pirate" captured over sixty vessels. Competing British shippers were delighted, while an angered North had to divert naval strength from its blockade for wild-goose chases. The *Alabama* was finally sunk by a Union cruiser off the coast of France in 1864.

A final Anglo-American crisis was touched off in 1863 by the Laird rams—two Confederate warships being constructed in Great Britain. Designed to destroy the wooden ships of the Union navy with their iron rams and large-caliber guns, they were far more dangerous than the swift and lightly armed *Alabama*. If delivered to the South, they probably would have sunk the blockading **squadrons** and then brought Northern cities under their fire. In retaliation, the North doubtless would have invaded Canada, and a full-dress war with Britain would have erupted. But America's minister to Britain, Charles Francis Adams, took a hard line, warning that "this is war" if the rams were released. At the last minute the London government relented and bought the two ships for the Royal Navy. Everyone seemed satisfied—except the disappointed Confederates.

Emperor Napoleon III of France, taking advantage of America's preoccupation with its own internal problems, dispatched a French army to occupy Mexico City in 1863. The following year he installed on the ruins of the crushed republic his puppet, the Austrian Archduke Maximilian, as emperor of Mexico. Sending the army and enthroning Maximilian were both flagrant violations of the Monroe Doctrine. Napoleon was gambling that the Union would collapse and thus America would be too weak to enforce its hands-off policy in the Western Hemisphere.

The North, as long as it was convulsed by war, pursued a walk-on-eggs policy toward France. But when the shooting stopped in 1865, Secretary of State Seward, speaking with the authority of nearly a million war-tempered bayonets, prepared to march south. Napoleon realized that his costly gamble was doomed. He reluctantly took French leave of his ill-starred puppet in 1867, and Maximilian soon crumpled ingloriously before a Mexican firing squad.

President Davis Versus President Lincoln

The Confederate government, like King Cotton, harbored fatal weaknesses. Its constitution, borrowing liberally from that of the Union, contained one deadly defect. Created by secession, it could not logically deny future secession to its constituent states. Jefferson Davis, while making his bow to states' rights, had in view a well-knit central government. But determined states' rights supporters fought him bitterly to the end. The Richmond regime encountered difficulty even in persuading certain state troops to serve outside their own borders.

Sharp-featured President Davis—tense, humorless, legalistic, and stubborn—was repeatedly in hot water. Although an eloquent orator and an able administrator, he at no time enjoyed real personal popularity and was often at loggerheads with his congress. At times there was serious talk of impeachment. Unlike Lincoln, Davis was somewhat imperious and inclined to defy rather than lead public opinion. Suffering acutely from neuralgia and other nervous disorders (including a tic), he overworked himself with the details of both civil government and military operations. No one could doubt his courage, sincerity, integrity, and devotion to the South, but the task proved beyond his powers.

Lincoln also had his troubles, but on the whole they were less prostrating. The North enjoyed the prestige of a long-established government, financially stable and fully recognized both at home and abroad. Lincoln, the inexperienced prairie politician, proved superior to the more experienced but less flexible Davis. Able to relax with droll stories at critical times, "Old Abe" grew as the war dragged on.

Primary source
Allen Pinkerton and Others at Antietam
college.hmco.com/pic/kennedybrief7e

Tactful, quiet, patient, yet firm, he developed a genius for interpreting and leading a fickle public opinion. Holding aloft the banner of Union with inspiring utterances, he revealed charitableness toward the South and forbearance toward backbiting colleagues. "Did [Secretary of War Edwin] Stanton say I was a damned fool?" he reportedly replied to a talebearer. "Then I dare say I must be one, for Stanton is generally right and he always says what he means."

One of "Honest Abe" Lincoln's greatest challenges was to preserve the Union while upholding America's Constitutionally protected freedoms in wartime. He reluctantly concluded that if he did not abridge some civil liberties in order to quell the rebellion, there might not be a Constitution of a *united* United States to mend.

Congress was not in session when war broke out, so Lincoln proclaimed a blockade and increased the size of the federal army—something that only Congress can do under the Constitution (see Art. I, Sec. VIII, para. 12). He also advanced federal funds to private citizens without authorization, and suspended the precious writ of habeas corpus, so that anti-Unionists might be summarily arrested. These questionable acts led critics to call him a "Simple Susan Tyrant." But Lincoln believed that his ironhanded authority would be lifted once the Union was preserved. He pointedly remarked in 1863 that a man suffering from a "temporary illness" would not persist in taking bitter medicines for "the remainder of his healthful life."

Volunteers and Draftees: North and South

Ravenous, the gods of war demanded men—lots of men. Northern armies were at first manned solely by volunteers, with each state assigned a **quota** based on population. But in 1863, after volunteering had slackened off, Congress passed a federal conscription law for the first time on a nationwide scale in the United States. The provisions were grossly unfair to the poor. Rich boys, including young John D. Rockefeller, could hire substitutes to go in their places or purchase exemption outright by paying $300.

quota *The proportion or share of a larger number of things that a smaller group is assigned to contribute.*

The draft was especially damned in the Democratic strongholds of the North, notably in New York City. A frightful riot broke out in 1863, touched off largely by underprivileged and antiblack Irish Americans who shouted "Down with Lincoln!" and "Down with the draft!" For several days the city was at the mercy of a burning, drunken, pillaging mob. Scores of lives were lost, and the victims included many lynched blacks. Elsewhere in the North, conscription met with resentment and an occasional minor riot.

More than 90 percent of the Union troops were volunteers, since social and patriotic pressures to enlist were strong. As able-bodied men became scarcer, generous bounties for enlistment were offered by federal, state, and local authorities. With money flowing so freely, an unsavory crew of "bounty brokers" and "substitute brokers" sprang up at home and abroad. They combed the poorhouses of the British Isles and western Europe, and many an Irishman or German was befuddled with whiskey and induced to enlist.

Like the North, the South at first relied mainly on volunteers. But since the Confederacy was much less populous, it scraped the bottom of its manpower barrel much more quickly. The Richmond regime, robbing both "cradle and grave" (ages seventeen to fifty), was forced to resort to conscription as early as April 1862, nearly a year earlier than the Union.

Confederate draft regulations also worked serious injustices. As in the North, a rich man could hire a substitute or purchase exemption. Slave owners or overseers with twenty slaves might also claim exemption. These special privileges, later modified, made for bad feelings among the less prosperous, many of whom complained that this was "a rich man's war and a poor man's fight." No large-scale draft riots broke out in the South, as in New York City. But Confederate conscription agents often found it prudent to avoid areas inhabited by sharp shooting mountain whites, who were branded "Tories," "traitors," and "Yankee lovers."

The Dollar Goes to War

Blessed with the lion's share of the wealth, the North rode through the financial breakers much more smoothly than the South. Excise taxes on tobacco and alcohol were substantially increased by Congress. An income tax was levied for the first time in the nation's experience.

Customs receipts likewise proved to be important revenue-raisers. Early in 1861, after enough antiprotection Southern members had seceded, Congress passed the Morrill Tariff Act. It increased the existing duties some 5 to 10 percent, but these modest rates were soon pushed sharply upward by the necessities of war. The increases were designed partly to raise additional revenue and partly to provide more protection for the prosperous manufacturers who were being plucked by the new internal taxes. A protective tariff thus became identified with the Republican party, as American industrialists, mostly Republicans, waxed fat on these welcome benefits.

greenback *United States paper currency, especially that printed before the establishment of the Federal Reserve System.*

bond *In finance, an interest-bearing certificate issued by a government or business that guarantees repayment to the purchaser on a specified date at a predetermined rate of interest.*

The Washington Treasury also issued **greenback** paper money totaling nearly $450 million at face value. This printing-press currency was inadequately supported by gold, and hence its value was determined by the nation's credit. Greenbacks thus fluctuated with the fortunes of Union arms and at one low point were worth only 39 cents on the gold dollar.

Borrowing far outstripped both greenbacks and taxes as a money raiser. The federal Treasury netted $2,621,916,786 through the sale of **bonds**, which bore interest and were payable at a later date. A financial landmark of the war was the National Banking System, authorized by Congress in 1863. Launched partly as a stimulant to the sale of government bonds, it was also designed to establish a standard bank-note currency. (The country was then flooded with depreciated "rag money" issued by unreliable bankers.) Banks that joined the National Banking System could buy government bonds and issue sound paper money backed by them. The war-born National Banking Act thus turned out to be the first significant step taken toward a unified banking network since 1836, when the "monster" Bank of the United States was killed by Andrew Jackson. Spawned by the war, this new system continued to function for fifty years, until replaced by the Federal Reserve System in 1913.

The impoverished South was beset by different financial woes. Customs duties were choked off as the coils of the Union blockade tightened. Large issues of Confederate bonds were sold at home and abroad, amounting to nearly $400 million. The Richmond regime also increased taxes sharply and imposed a 10 percent levy on farm produce. But in general, the states' rights Southerners were immovably opposed to heavy direct taxation by the central authority: only about 1 percent of the total income was raised this way.

As revenue began to dry up, the Confederate government was forced to print blueback paper money with complete abandon. "Runaway inflation" occurred as Southern presses continued to grind out the poorly backed treasury notes, totaling in all more than $1 billion. The Confederate paper dollar finally sank to the point where it was worth only 1.6 cents when Lee surrendered. Overall, the war inflicted a 9,000 percent inflation rate on the Confederacy, contrasted with 80 percent for the Union.

A contemporary (October 22, 1863) Richmond diary portrays the ruinous effects of inflation:

"A poor woman yesterday applied to a merchant in Carey Street to purchase a barrel of flour. The price he demanded was $70. 'My God!' exclaimed she, 'how can I pay such prices? I have seven children; what shall I do?' 'I don't know, madam,' said he coolly, 'unless you eat your children.' "

"The North's Economic Boom

Wartime prosperity in the North was little short of miraculous. New factories, sheltered by the friendly umbrella of the new protective tariffs, mushroomed forth. Soaring prices, resulting from inflation, unfortunately pinched the laborers and white-collar workers to some extent, but manufacturers and businesspeople raked in "the fortunes of war." The Civil War bred a millionaire class for the first time in American history.

Primary source
Zouave Soldier
college.hmco.com/pic/kennedybrief7e

Yankee "sharpness" appeared at its worst during the war. Dishonest agents, putting profits above patriotism, palmed off aged and blind horses on government purchasers. Unscrupulous Northern manufacturers supplied shoes with cardboard soles and fast-disintegrating uniforms of reprocessed or "shoddy" wool, rather than virgin wool. Hence the reproachful term "shoddy millionaires" was doubly fair.

Newly invented laborsaving machinery enabled the North to expand economically, even though the cream of its manpower was being drained off to the fighting front. The sewing machine wrought wonders in fabricating uniforms and military footwear. Clattering mechanical reapers, which numbered about 250,000 by 1865, proved hardly less potent than thundering guns. They not only released tens of thousands of farm boys for the army but fed them their field rations.

Other industries were humming. The discovery of petroleum gushers in 1859 had led to a rush of "Fifty-Niners" to Pennsylvania. The result was the birth of a new industry, with its "petroleum plutocracy" and "coal oil Johnnies." Pioneers continued to push westward during the war, altogether an estimated 300,000 people. Major magnets were free gold nuggets and free lands under the Homestead Act of 1862.

Primary source
Women and the Attack on Slavery
college.hmco.com/pic/kennedybrief7e

The Civil War was a woman's war, too. The protracted conflict opened new opportunities for women. When men departed in uniform, women often took their jobs. In Washington, D.C., five hundred women clerks ("government girls") became government workers, with over one hundred in the Treasury Department alone. The booming military demand for shoes and clothing, combined with technological marvels like the sewing machine, likewise drew countless women into industrial employment. Before the war, one industrial worker in four had been female; during the war, the ratio rose to one in three.

Other women on both sides stepped up to the fighting front—or close behind it. More than four hundred women accompanied husbands and sweethearts into battle by posing as male soldiers. Other women took on dangerous spy missions. One woman was executed for smuggling gold to the Confederacy. Dr. Elizabeth Blackwell, America's first female physician, helped organize the U.S. Sanitary Commission to assist Union armies in the field. The commission trained nurses, collected medical supplies, and equipped hospitals. Commission work helped many women to acquire the organizational skills and the self-confidence that would propel the women's movement forward after the war. Heroically energetic Clara Barton and dedicated Dorothea Dix, superintendent of nurses for the Union army, helped transform nursing from a lowly service into a respected profession—and in the process opened up another major sphere of employment for women in the postwar era. Equally renowned in the South was Sally Tompkins, who ran a Richmond infirmary for wounded Confederate soldiers and was awarded the rank of captain by Confederate president Jefferson Davis. Still other women, North as well as South, organized bazaars and fairs that raised millions of dollars for the relief of widows, orphans, and disabled soldiers.

A Crushed Cotton Kingdom

The South fought to the point of exhaustion. The suffocation caused by the blockade, together with the destruction wrought by invaders, took a terrible toll. Possessing 30 percent of the national wealth in 1860, the South claimed only 12 percent in 1870. Transportation collapsed. The South was even driven to the economic cannibalism of pulling up rails from the less-used lines to repair the main lines. Window weights were melted down into bullets; gourds replaced dishes; pins became so scarce that they were loaned with reluctance.

To the brutal end, the South mustered remarkable resourcefulness and spirit. Women buoyed up their menfolk, many of whom had seen enough of war at first hand to be heartily sick of it. A number of women proposed that they cut off their

■ Booth at the Sanitary Fair in Chicago, 1863 The Chicago Sanitary Fair was the first of many such fairs throughout the nation to raise funds for soldier relief efforts. Mainly organized by women, the fair sold captured Confederate flags, battle relics, handicrafts like these potholders (right), and donated items, including President Lincoln's original draft of the Emancipation Proclamation (which garnered $3,000 in auction). When the fair closed, the Chicago headquarters of the U.S. Sanitary Commission had raised $100,000, and its female managers had gained organizational experience that many would put to work in the postwar movement for women's rights.

Online Study Center
Primary source
Women's War, The
college.hmco.com/pic/kennedybrief7e

long hair and sell it abroad to support the cause. Self-sacrificing Southern women took pride in denying themselves the silks and satins of their Northern sisters.

The chorus of a song, "The Southern Girl," touched a cheerful note:

So hurrah! hurrah! For Southern Rights,
Hurrah!
Hurrah! for the homespun dress the Southern
ladies wear.

At war's end, the Northern Captains of Industry had conquered the Southern Lords of the Manor. A crippled South left the capitalistic North free to work its own way, with high tariffs and other benefits. The manufacturing moguls of the North, ushering in the full-fledged Industrial Revolution, were headed for increased dominance over American economic and political life. Hitherto the agrarian "slavocracy" of the South had partially checked the rising plutocracy of the North. Now cotton capitalism lost out to industrial capitalism. The South of 1865 was to be rich in little but amputees, war heroes, ruins, and memories.

Chapter Summary

South Carolina's firing on Fort Sumter aroused the North for war. Lincoln's call for troops to suppress the rebellion drove four upper South states into the Confederacy. Lincoln used an effective combination of political persuasion and force to keep the deeply divided Border States in the Union.

The Confederacy enjoyed initial advantages of upper-class European support, military leadership, and a defensive position on its own soil. The North enjoyed the advantages of lower-class European support, industrial and population resources, and political leadership.

The British upper classes sympathized with the South and abetted Confederate naval efforts, while France's Emperor Napoleon III took advantage of the war to intervene in Mexico. But effective diplomacy and Union military success prevented foreign recognition and further assistance for the Confederacy.

Lincoln's political leadership proved effective in mobilizing the North for war, despite political opposition and resistance to his infringement on civil liberties. The North eventually mobilized its larger troop resources for war and ultimately turned to an unpopular and unfair draft system.

Northern economic and financial strengths enabled it to gain an advantage over the less-industrialized South. The changes in society opened new opportunities for women, who had contributed significantly to the war effort in both the North and South. Since most of the war was waged on Southern soil, the South was left devastated by the war.

The Furnace of Civil War

1861–1865

MY PARAMOUNT OBJECT IN THIS STRUGGLE IS TO SAVE THE UNION, AND IS NOT EITHER TO SAVE OR TO DESTROY SLAVERY.

ABRAHAM LINCOLN, 1862

Chapter Outline

- Bull Run Ends the "Ninety-Day War"
- The Peninsula Campaign
- The Union Wages Total War
- The Battle of Antietam
- The Emancipation Proclamation, 1863
- Black Soldiers
- Confederate High Tide at Gettysburg
- Politics in Wartime
- Appomattox, 1865
- The Assassination of Lincoln, April 1865
- The Legacy of War
- Examining the Evidence: Abraham Lincoln's Gettysburg Address
- Varying Viewpoints: What Were the Consequences of the Civil War?

When President Lincoln issued his call to the states for seventy-five thousand militiamen on April 15, 1861, he envisioned them serving for only ninety days. Reaffirming his limited war aims, he declared that he had "no purpose, directly or indirectly, to interfere with slavery in the States where it exists." With a swift flourish of federal force, he hoped to show the folly of secession and rapidly return the rebellious states to the Union. But the war was to be neither brief nor limited. When the guns fell silent four years later, hundreds of thousands of soldiers on both sides lay dead, slavery was ended forever, and the nation faced the challenge of reintegrating the defeated but still recalcitrant South into the Union.

Focus Questions

1. **Why did the Northern defeats in the First Battle of Bull Run and the Peninsula Campaign transform the Civil War from a limited struggle for the Union to a total war against slavery?**
2. **What was the significance of the Battles of Antietam, Vicksburg, and Gettysburg as key turning points of the Civil War?**
3. **What were the strengths and limits of the Emancipation Proclamation, and what role did African Americans play in the Union army and navy?**
4. **What were Lincoln's central political problems with the Copperheads and Peace Democrats, and how did he successfully outmaneuver them to win reelection in 1864?**
5. **How did Sherman's "March to the Sea" and Grant's 1864–1865 campaign in Virginia finally complete the Union's grand military strategy and force Lee's surrender?**

Bull Run Ends the "Ninety-Day War"

Northern newspapers, at first sharing Lincoln's expectation of quick victory, raised the cry "On to Richmond!" In this yeasty atmosphere, a Union army of some thirty thousand men drilled near Washington in the summer of 1861. It was ill prepared for battle, but the press and the public clamored for action. Lincoln eventually concluded that an attack on a smaller Confederate force at Bull Run

Chronology

1861	First Battle of Bull Run.
1862	Grant takes Forts Henry and Donelson. Battle of Shiloh. McClellan's Peninsula Campaign. Seven Days' Battles. Second Battle of Bull Run. Naval battle of the *Merrimack* (the *Virginia*) and the *Monitor*. Battle of Antietam. Preliminary Emancipation Proclamation. Battle of Fredericksburg. Northern army seizes New Orleans.
1863	Final Emancipation Proclamation. Battle of Chancellorsville. Battle of Gettysburg. Fall of Vicksburg. Fall of Port Hudson.
1864	Sherman's march through Georgia. Grant's Wilderness Campaign. Battle of Cold Harbor. Lincoln defeats McClellan for presidency.
1865	Lee surrenders to Grant at Appomattox. Lincoln assassinated. Thirteenth Amendment ratified.

(Manassas Junction), some thirty miles southwest of Washington, might be worth a try. If successful, it would demonstrate the superiority of Union arms. It might even lead to the capture of the Confederate capital at Richmond, one hundred miles to the south. If Richmond fell, secession would be thoroughly discredited, and the Union could be restored without damage to the economic and social system of the South.

Raw Yankee recruits swaggered out of Washington toward Bull Run on July 21, 1861, as if they were headed for a sporting event. Congressmen and spectators trailed along with their lunch baskets to witness the fun. At first the battle went well for the Yankees. But "Stonewall" Jackson's gray-clad warriors stood like a stone wall (here he won his nickname), and Confederate reinforcements arrived unexpectedly. Panic seized the green Union troops, many of whom fled in shameful confusion. The Confederates, themselves too exhausted or disorganized to pursue, feasted on captured lunches.

The "military picnic" at Bull Run, though not decisive militarily, had significant psychological and political consequences. Victory was worse than defeat for the South because it inflated an already dangerous overconfidence. Many of the Southern soldiers promptly deserted, feeling that the war was now surely over. Southern enlistments fell off sharply, and preparations for a protracted conflict slackened. Defeat was better than victory for the Union, because it dispelled all illusions of a one-punch war and caused the Northerners to buckle down to the staggering task at hand. It also set the stage for a war that would be waged not merely for the cause of Union but also, eventually, for the abolitionist ideal of emancipation.

Primary source
War in the East, The (early phase)
college.hmco.com/pic/kennedybrief7e

"Tardy George" McClellan and the Peninsula Campaign

Primary source
War in the East, The (middle phase)
college.hmco.com/pic/kennedybrief7e

Northern hopes brightened later in 1861, when General George B. McClellan was given command of the Army of the Potomac, as the major Union force near Washington was now called. Red-haired and red-mustached, strong and stocky, McClellan ("Young Napoleon") was a brilliant, thirty-four-year-old West Pointer who had seen plenty of fighting in the Mexican War.

Interactive map
The War in the East, 1861–1862
college.hmco.com/pic/kennedy/brief7e

Cocky George McClellan embodied a curious mixture of virtues and defects. He was a superb organizer and drillmaster, and he injected splendid **morale** into the Army of the Potomac. Hating to sacrifice his troops, he was idolized by his men, who affectionately called him "Little Mac." But he was a perfectionist who seems not to have realized that an army is never ready to the last button and that wars cannot be won without running some risks. He consistently but erroneously believed that the

morale *The condition of courage, confidence, and willingness to endure hardship.*

Preparing for Battle These troops of the 69th New York State Militia, a largely Irish regiment, were photographed attending Sunday morning Mass in May 1861, just weeks before the Battle of Bull Run. Because the regiment was camped near Washington, D.C., women were able to visit.

enemy outnumbered him, partly because his **intelligence** reports from the head of Pinkerton's Detective Agency were unreliable. He was overcautious—Lincoln once accused him of having "the slows"—and he addressed the president in an arrogant tone that a less forgiving person than Lincoln would never have tolerated. Privately the general referred to his chief as a "baboon."

After threatening to "borrow" the army if it was not going to be used, Lincoln finally issued firm orders to move. A reluctant McClellan at last decided on a waterborne approach to Richmond. Moving up the narrow peninsula formed by the James and York Rivers, McClellan warily inched toward the Confederate capital in the spring of 1862 with about 100,000 men in what was called the Peninsula Campaign. After taking a month to capture historic Yorktown, which bristled with imitation wooden cannon, he finally came within sight of the spires of Richmond. Aided by "Jeb" Stuart's Confederate cavalry, General Robert E. Lee suddenly launched a devastating counterattack—the Seven Days' Battles—June 26–July 2, 1862. The Confederates slowly drove McClellan back to the sea. The Union forces abandoned the Peninsula Campaign as a costly failure, and Lincoln temporarily removed McClellan as commander of the Army of the Potomac.

Lee had achieved a brilliant, if bloody, triumph. Yet the ironies of his accomplishment are striking. If McClellan had succeeded in taking Richmond and ending the war in mid-1862, the Union would probably have been restored with minimal disruption, and slavery would have survived, at least for a time. By his successful defense of Richmond and defeat of McClellan, Lee had in effect ensured that the war would endure until slavery was uprooted and the Old South thoroughly destroyed. Lincoln himself now declared that the rebels "cannot experiment for ten years trying to destroy the government and if they fail still come back into the Union unhurt." He began to draft an emancipation **proclamation**.

intelligence *In military affairs or diplomacy, specific information about an adversary's forces, deployments, production, and so on.*

proclamation *An official announcement or publicly declared order.*

Union strategy now turned toward total war. As finally developed, the Northern military plan had six components: first, slowly suffocate the South by blockading its coasts; second, liberate the slaves and hence undermine the economic foundations of the Old South; third, cut the Confederacy in half by seizing control of its Mississippi River backbone; fourth, chop the Confederacy to pieces by sending troops from Tennessee through Georgia and then the Carolinas; fifth, decapitate it by capturing its capital at Richmond; and sixth (this was Ulysses Grant's idea, especially), try everywhere to engage the enemy's main strength and grind it into submission.

Abraham Lincoln (1809–1865) treated the demands of George McClellan for reinforcements and his excuses for inaction with infinite patience. One exception came when the general complained that his horses were tired. On October 24, 1862, Lincoln wrote,

"I have just read your dispatch about sore-tongued and fatigued horses. Will you pardon me for asking what the horses of your army have done since the battle of Antietam that fatigues anything?"

The War at Sea

The blockade started leakily; it was not clamped down all at once but extended by degrees. Blockading was simplified by concentrating on the principal ports and inlets, where dock facilities were available for loading bulky bales of cotton. The blockade was further strengthened when Britain recognized it as binding and warned its shippers that they ignored it at their peril.

Blockade-running was risky but profitable, as the growing scarcity of Southern goods drove prices skyward. A leading rendezvous for successful runners was the West Indies port of Nassau, in the British Bahamas, where at one time thirty-five of the speedy ships rode at anchor. But the lush days of blockade-running finally passed as Union squadrons gradually pinched off the leading Southern ports from New Orleans to Charleston.

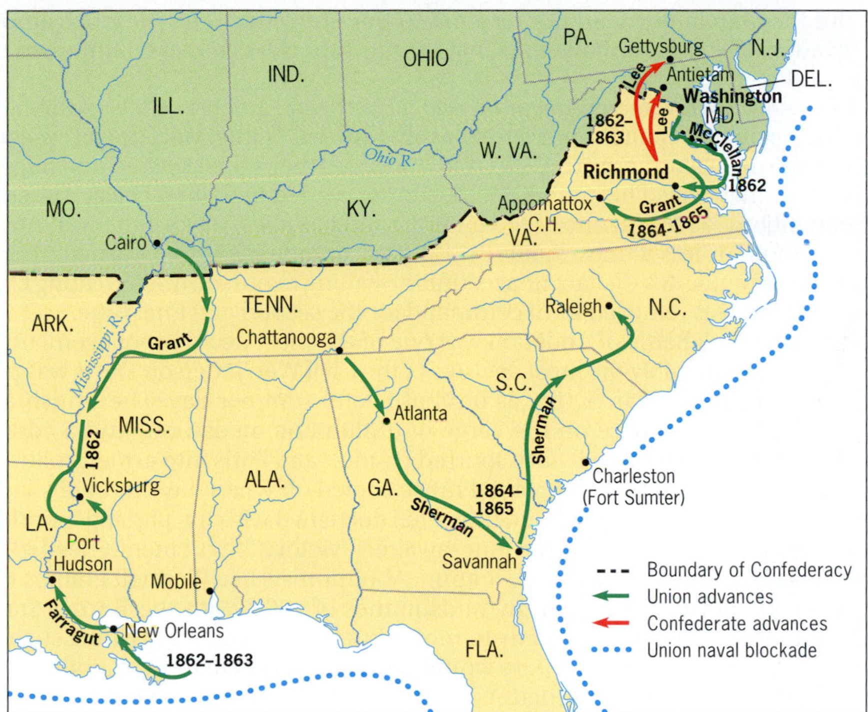

Main Thrusts, 1861–1865 Northern strategists at first believed that the rebellion could be snuffed out quickly by a swift, crushing blow. But the stiffness of Southern resistance to the Union's early probes, and the North's inability to strike with sufficient speed and severity, revealed that the conflict would be a war of attrition, long and bloody.

Online Study Center

Interactive map
The Anaconda Plan and the Battle of Antietam
college.hmco.com/pic/kennedy/brief7e

The most alarming Confederate threat to the blockade came in 1862. Resourceful Southerners raised and reconditioned a former wooden United States warship, the *Merrimack*, and plated its sides with old iron railroad rails. Renamed the *Virginia*, this clumsy but powerful monster easily destroyed two wooden ships of the Union navy in the Virginia waters of Chesapeake Bay; it also threatened the entire Yankee blockading fleet.

A tiny Union ironclad, the *Monitor*, built in about one hundred days, arrived on the scene in the nick of time. For four hours, on March 9, 1862, the little "Yankee cheesebox on a raft" fought the wheezy *Merrimack* to a standstill. Britain and France had already built several powerful ironclads, but the first battle test of these new craft heralded the doom of wooden warships.

The Pivotal Point: Antietam

Robert E. Lee, having broken the back of McClellan's assault on Richmond, next moved northward. Emboldened by a victory at the Second Battle of Bull Run (August 29–30, 1862), Lee daringly thrust into Maryland. He hoped to strike a blow that would not only encourage foreign intervention but also seduce the still wavering Border State and its sisters from the Union. The Confederate troops sang lustily,

Thou wilt not cower in the dust,
Maryland! my Maryland!
Thy gleaming sword shall never rust,
Maryland! my Maryland!

A Confederate soldier assigned to burial detail after the Seven Days' Battles (1862) wrote,

"The sights and smells that assailed us were simply indescribable . . . corpses swollen to twice their original size, some of them actually burst asunder with the pressure of foul gasses. . . . The odors were so nauseating and so deadly that in a short time we all sickened and were lying with our mouths close to the ground, most of us vomiting profusely."

But the Marylanders did not respond to the siren song. The presence among the invaders of so many blanketless, hatless, and shoeless soldiers dampened the state's ardor.

Events finally converged toward a critical battle at Antietam Creek, Maryland. Lincoln, yielding to popular pressure, hastily restored "Little Mac" to active command of the main Northern army. His soldiers tossed their caps skyward and hugged his horse as they hailed his return. McClellan succeeded in halting Lee at Antietam on September 17, 1862, in one of the bitterest and bloodiest days of the war. Antietam was more or less a draw militarily. But Lee, finding his thrust parried, retired across the Potomac. McClellan, unaccountably failing to pursue the retreating Confederate army, was removed from command for the second and final time.

Primary source
Confederate Offensive in the West, The
college.hmco.com/pic/kennedybrief7e

The landmark Battle of Antietam was one of the most decisive engagements of world history—probably the most decisive of the Civil War. Jefferson Davis was perhaps never again so near victory as on that fateful summer day. The British and French governments were on the verge of diplomatic mediation, and a certain Washington rebuff might well have spurred London and Paris into armed collusion with Richmond. But both Britain and France cooled off when the Union displayed unexpected power at Antietam, and their chill deepened with the passing months.

Bloody Antietam was also the long-awaited "victory" that Lincoln needed for launching his Emancipation Proclamation. Abolitionists like Wendell Phillips had long been clamoring for action. By midsummer of 1862, with the Border States safely in the fold, Lincoln was ready to move. But he believed that issuing such an edict on the heels of military failure would seem like an act of desperation.

Antietam served as the needed emancipation springboard. The halting of Lee's offensive was just enough of a victory to justify Lincoln's issuing, on September 23, 1862, the preliminary Emancipation Proclamation. This hope-giving document announced that on January 1, 1863, the president would issue a final proclamation. On the scheduled date he fully redeemed his promise, and the Civil War became a moral crusade and what Lincoln called a "remorseless revolutionary struggle." After January 1, 1863, Lincoln said, "The character of the war will be changed. It will be one of subjugation. . . . The [old] South is to be destroyed and replaced by new propositions and ideas."

A Proclamation Without Emancipation

Lincoln's Emancipation Proclamation of 1863 declared "forever free" the slaves in those Confederate states still in rebellion. Bondsmen in the loyal Border States were not affected, nor were those in specific conquered areas in the South—all told, about 800,000. The tone of the document was dull and legalistic. But if Lincoln stopped short of a clarion call for a holy war to achieve freedom, he pointedly concluded his historic document by declaring that the Proclamation was an "act of justice" and calling for "the considerate judgment of mankind and the gracious favor of Almighty God."

The presidential pen did not formally strike the shackles from a single slave. Where Lincoln could presumably free the slaves—that is, in the loyal Border States—he refused to do so, lest he spur disunion. Where he could not—that is, in the Confederate states—he tried to. In short, where he *could* he would not, and where he *would* he could not. Thus the Emancipation Proclamation was stronger on proclamation than emancipation.

Yet much unofficial do-it-yourself liberation did take place. Thousands of jubilant slaves, learning of the proclamation, flocked to the invading Union armies, stripping already rundown plantations of their work force. In this sense the Emancipation Proclamation was heralded by the drumbeat of running feet. The slaves' presence in Union army camps helped put emancipation atop Lincoln's agenda and strengthened the moral cause of the Union at home and abroad. At the same time Lincoln's proclamation clearly foreshadowed the ultimate doom of slavery. This was legally achieved by actions of the individual states and by their ratification of the Thirteenth Amendment (see the Appendix) in 1865. The Emancipation Proclamation also fundamentally changed the nature of the war because it effectively removed any chance of a negotiated settlement. Both sides now knew that the war would be a fight to the finish.

Public reactions to the long-awaited proclamation of 1863 were varied. "God bless Abraham Lincoln," exulted the antislavery editor Horace Greeley in his *New York Tribune*. But many ardent abolitionists complained that Lincoln had not gone far enough. On the other hand, formidable numbers of Northerners, especially in the "Butternut" regions of the Old Northwest and the Border States, felt that he had gone too far. A Democratic rhymester quipped,

> *Honest old Abe, when the war first began,*
> *Denied abolition was part of his plan;*
> *Honest old Abe has since made a decree,*
> *The war must go on till the slaves are all free.*
> *As both can't be honest, will someone tell how,*
> *If honest Abe then, is he honest Abe now?*

The Killing Fields of Antietam These Confederate corpses testify to the awful slaughter of the battle. The twelve-hour fight at Antietam Creek ranks as the bloodiest single day of the war, with more than ten thousand Confederate casualties and even more on the Union side. "At last the battle ended," one historian wrote, "smoke heavy in the air, the twilight quivering with the anguished cries of thousands of wounded men."

Opposition mounted in the North against supporting an "abolition war." Many Boys in Blue, especially from the Border States, had volunteered to fight for the Union, not against slavery. Desertions increased sharply. The crucial congressional elections in the autumn of 1862 went heavily against the administration, particularly in New York, Pennsylvania, and Ohio. Democrats even carried Lincoln's Illinois, although they did not secure control of Congress.

The Emancipation Proclamation caused an outcry to rise from the South that "Lincoln the fiend" was trying to stir up the "hellish passions" of a slave insurrection. Many European aristocrats sympathized with the Southern protests. But the Old World working classes, especially in Britain, reacted otherwise. They sensed that the proclamation spelled the ultimate doom of slavery, and many laborers became more determined than ever to oppose intervention. Gradually the diplomatic position of the Union improved.

The North now had much the stronger moral cause. In addition to preserving the Union, it had committed itself to freeing the slaves. The moral position of the South was correspondingly diminished.

Blacks Battle Bondage

As Lincoln moved to emancipate the slaves, he also took steps to enlist blacks in the armed forces. Although some African Americans had served in the Revolution and the War of 1812, the regular army contained no blacks at the war's outset, and the War Department refused to accept those free Northern blacks who tried to volunteer. (The Union navy, however, enrolled many blacks, mainly as cooks, stewards, and firemen.)

But as manpower ran low and emancipation was proclaimed, black enlistees were accepted, sometimes over ferocious protests from Northern as well as Southern whites. By war's end some 180,000 blacks served in the Union armies, most of them from the slave states, but many from the free-soil North. Blacks accounted for about 10 percent of the total enlistments in the Union forces, on land and sea, and included two black Massachusetts regiments raised largely through the efforts of ex-slave Frederick Douglass.

Black fighting men unquestionably had their hearts in the war against slavery that the Civil War had become after Lincoln proclaimed emancipation. Participating in about five hundred engagements, they received twenty-two Congressional Medals of Honor—the highest military award.

Abraham Lincoln defended his policies toward blacks in an open letter to Democrats on August 26, 1863:

"You say you will not fight to free negroes. Some of them seem willing to fight for you; but, no matter. Fight you, then, exclusively to save the Union. I issued the proclamation on purpose to aid you in saving the Union."

Their casualties were extremely heavy; more than thirty-eight thousand died, whether from battle, sickness, or reprisals from vengeful masters. Many, when captured, were put to death as slaves in revolt. In one notorious case, several black soldiers were massacred after they had formally surrendered at Fort Pillow, Tennessee. Thereafter vengeful black units cried "Remember Fort Pillow!" as they swung into battle and vowed to take no prisoners.

For reasons of pride, prejudice, and principle, the Confederacy could not bring itself to enlist slaves until a month before the war ended. Meanwhile tens of thousands were impressed into building fortifications, supplying armies, and other war-connected activities. Slaves, moreover, were "the stomach of the Confederacy," for they kept the farms going while the white men fought.

In many ways the actions of Southern slaves hamstrung the Confederate war effort and subverted the institution of slavery. Fear of slave insurrection required many eligible young white men to serve as Confederate "home guards" far from the fighting front. Everyday forms of slave resistance and defiance increased, diminishing productivity and undermining discipline. As Union armies approached, escaping slaves served as spies, guides, and scouts. By war's end nearly half a million slaves took the ultimate risk of revolting "with their feet," abandoning their plantations. Although they stopped short of violent uprising, slaves contributed powerfully to the collapse of slavery and the disintegration of the antebellum Southern way of life.

Lee's Last Lunge at Gettysburg

After Antietam, Lincoln replaced McClellan as commander of the Army of the Potomac with General A. E. Burnside, whose ornate side-whiskers came to be known as "burnsides" or "sideburns." Protesting his unfitness for this responsibility, Burnside proved it when he launched a rash frontal attack on Lee's strong position at Fredericksburg, Virginia, on December 13, 1862. A chicken could not have lived in the line of fire, remarked one Confederate officer. More than ten thousand Northern soldiers were killed or wounded in "Burnside's Slaughter Pen."

A new slaughter pen was prepared when General Burnside yielded his command to "Fighting Joe" Hooker, an aggressive but headstrong officer. At Chancel-

A Bit of War History: Contraband, Recruit, Veteran, by Thomas Waterman Wood, 1865–1866 This painting dramatically commemorates the contributions and sacrifices of the 180,000 African Americans who served in the Union army during the Civil War.

EXAMINING THE EVIDENCE

Abraham Lincoln's Gettysburg Address

Political speeches are unfortunately all too often composed of claptrap, platitudes, and just plain bunk—and they are frequently written by someone other than the person delivering them. But Abraham Lincoln's address at the dedication of the cemetery at Gettysburg battlefield on November 19, 1863, has long been recognized as a masterpiece of political oratory and as a foundational document of the American political system, as weighty a statement of the national purpose as the Declaration of Independence (which it deliberately echoes in its statement that all men are created equal) or even the Constitution itself. In just 272 simple but eloquent words that Lincoln himself indisputably wrote, he summarized the case for American nationhood.

Four score and seven years ago our fathers brought forth, upon this continent, a new nation, conceived in Liberty, and dedicated to the proposition that all men are created equal.

Now we are engaged in a great civil war, testing whether that nation, or any nation, so conceived, and so dedicated, can long endure. We are met here on a great battle field of that war. We have come to dedicate a portion of it as a final resting place for those who here gave their lives, that that nation might live. It is altogether fitting and proper that we should do this.

But in a larger sense we can not dedicate— we can not consecrate— we can not hallow this ground. The brave men, living and dead, who struggled here, have consecrated it far above our poor power to add or detract. The world will little note, nor long remember, what we say here, but can never forget what they did here. It is for us, the living, rather to be dedicated here to the unfinished work which they have, thus far, so nobly carried on. It is rather for us to be here dedicated to the great task remaining before us— that from these honored dead we take increased devotion to that cause for which they here gave the last full measure of devotion— that we here highly resolve that these dead shall not have died in vain; that this nation shall have a new birth of freedom, and that this government of the people, by the people, for the people, shall not perish from the earth.

we here highly resolve that these dead shall not have died in vain; that this nation shall have a new birth of freedom, and that this government of the people, by the people, for the people, shall not perish from the earth.

1. What did Lincoln believe was at stake in the Civil War? (Conspicuously, he made no direct mention of slavery in this address.) Another speech that Lincoln gave in 1861 offers some clues. He said, "I have often inquired of myself what great principle or idea it was that kept this [nation] together. It was not the mere separation of the colonies from the motherland, but that sentiment in the Declaration of Independence which gave liberty not alone to the people of this country, but hope to the world, for all future time."
2. Using the text of the Gettysburg Address, consider: how does Lincoln use language and images of parent and child, conception, rebirth, and sacrifice to present the American nation as a living entity?
3. In Lincoln's view, how does the dead soldiers' "last full measure of devotion" hallow the cause of liberty and Union, and create new obligations for "we the living"?

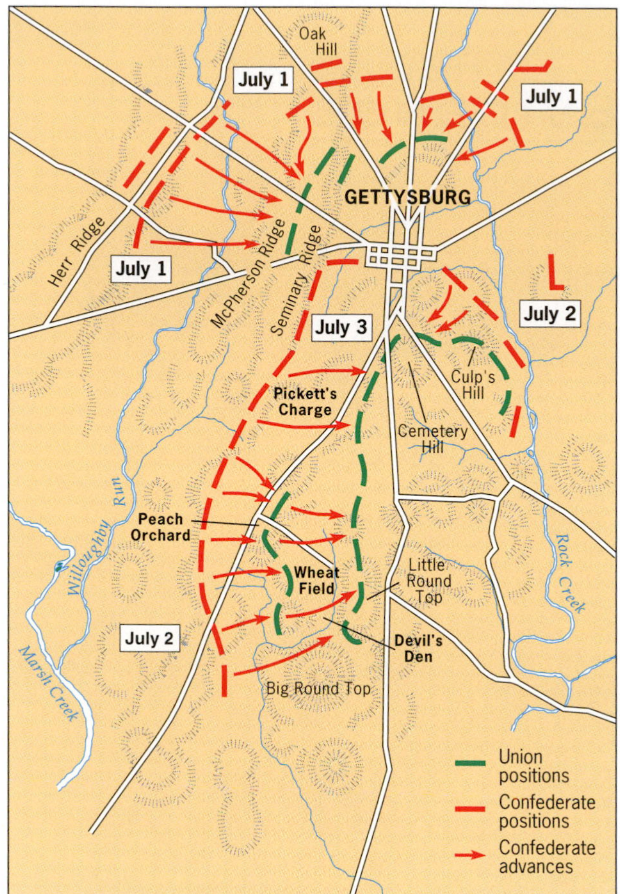

The Battle of Gettysburg, 1863 With the failure of Pickett's charge, the fate of the Confederacy was sealed—though the Civil War dragged on for almost two more bloody years.

lorsville, Virginia, on May 2–4, 1863, Lee daringly divided his numerically inferior force and sent "Stonewall" Jackson to attack the Union **flank**. The strategy worked. Hooker, temporarily dazed by a near-hit from a cannonball, was badly beaten but not crushed. This victory was probably Lee's most brilliant, but it was dearly bought. Jackson was mistakenly shot by his own men in the gathering dusk and died a few days later. "I have lost my right arm," lamented Lee. Southern folklore relates how Jackson outflanked the angels while galloping into Heaven.

Lee now prepared to follow up his brilliant victory by invading the North again, this time through Pennsylvania. A decisive blow would add strength to the noisy peace prodders in the North and would also encourage foreign intervention—still a Southern hope. Quite by accident, the Northern army, now under the scholarly and unspectacular General George G. Meade, took its stand on the rolling hills near quiet little Gettysburg, Pennsylvania. There his 92,000 men in blue locked horns in furious combat with Lee's 76,000 gray-clad warriors. The battle seesawed across the rolling green slopes for three agonizing days, July 1–3, 1863, and the outcome was in doubt until the very end. The failure of General George Pickett's magnificent but futile charge finally broke the back of the Confederate attack—and broke the heart of the Confederate cause.

Pickett's charge has been called the "high tide of the Confederacy." It defined both the northernmost point reached by any significant Southern force and the last real chance for the Confederates to win the war. After Gettysburg, Lincoln spurned Southern efforts to reach a negotiated peace settlement between the parties. From now on the Southern cause was doomed. Yet the men of Dixie fought for nearly two years longer, through sweat, blood, and weariness of spirit.

Later in that dreary autumn of 1863, with the graves still fresh, Lincoln journeyed to Gettysburg to dedicate the cemetery. He read a two-minute address, following a two-hour speech by the orator of the day. Lincoln's noble remarks were branded by the *London Times* as "ludicrous" and by Democratic editors as "dishwatery" and "silly." The address attracted relatively little attention at the time, but the president was speaking for the ages.

Online Study Center

Interactive map
The War in the East, 1863
college.hmco.com/pic/kennedy/brief7e

Primary source
Battle of Gettysburg
college.hmco.com/pic/kennedybrief7e

flank *The side of an army, where it is vulnerable to attack.*

court-martial *A military court or a trial held in such a court under military law.*

The War in the West

Events in the western theater of the war at last provided Lincoln with an able general who did not have to be shelved after every reverse. Ulysses S. Grant had been a mediocre student at West Point, although he did do well in mathematics and horsemanship. After fighting creditably in the Mexican War, he was stationed at isolated frontier posts, where boredom and loneliness drove him to drink. Resigning from the army to avoid a **court-martial** for drunkenness, he failed at various business ventures, and when war came he was working in his father's leather store in Illinois for $50 a month.

Grant did not cut much of a figure. The shy and silent shopkeeper was short, stooped, awkward, stubble-bearded, and sloppy in dress. He managed with some difficulty to secure a colonelcy in the volunteers. From then on his military experience—combined with his boldness, resourcefulness, and doggedness—catapulted him on a meteoric rise.

Grant's first signal success came in the northern Tennessee theater. After heavy fighting, he captured Fort Henry and Fort Donelson on the Tennessee and Cumberland Rivers in February 1862. When the Confederate commander at Fort Donelson asked for terms, Grant bluntly demanded "an unconditional and immediate surrender."

Grant's triumph in Tennessee was crucial. It not only riveted Kentucky more securely to the Union but also opened the gateway to the strategically important region of Tennessee, and eventually to Georgia and the heart of Dixie. Grant next attempted to exploit his victory by capturing the junction of the main Confederate north-south and east-west railroads in the Mississippi Valley at Corinth, Mississippi. But a Confederate force foiled his plans in the gory Battle of Shiloh, just over the Tennessee border from Corinth, on April 6–7, 1862. The impressive Confederate showing at Shiloh confirmed that there would be no quick end to the war in the West.

Lincoln resisted all demands for the removal of "Unconditional Surrender" Grant, insisting, "I can't spare this man; he fights." When talebearers later told Lincoln that Grant drank too much, the president allegedly replied, "Find me the brand, and I'll send a barrel to each of my other generals."

Other Union thrusts were in the making. In the spring of 1862, a flotilla commanded by David G. Farragut joined with a Northern army to strike the South a staggering blow by seizing New Orleans. With Union gunboats both ascending and descending the Mississippi, the eastern part of the Confederacy was left with a jeopardized back door. Through this narrowing entrance, between Vicksburg and Port Hudson, flowed herds of vitally needed cattle and other provisions from Louisiana and Texas. The fortress of Vicksburg, located on a hairpin turn of the Mississippi, was the South's sentinel protecting the lifeline to the western sources of supply.

In command of the Union forces attacking Vicksburg, General Grant displayed rare skill and daring in the teeth of grave difficulties. The siege of Vicksburg was his best-fought campaign of the war. The beleaguered city at length surrendered, on July 4, 1863, with the **garrison** reduced to eating mules and rats. Five days later came the fall of Port Hudson, the last Southern bastion on the Mississippi. The spinal cord of the Confederacy was now severed, and, in Lincoln's quaint phrase, the Father of Waters at last flowed "unvexed to the sea."

The Union's victory at Vicksburg (July 4, 1863) came the day after the Confederate defeat at Gettysburg. The political significance of these back-to-back military successes was monumental. Reopening the Mississippi helped to quell strong peace agitation in southern Ohio, Indiana, and Illinois. Confederate control of the Mississippi had cut off that region's usual trade routes down the Ohio-Mississippi River system to New Orleans, thus adding economic pain to that border section's already shaky support for the "abolition war." The twin victories also conclusively tipped the diplomatic scales in favor of the North, as Britain stopped delivery of the Laird rams to the Confederates and as France killed a deal for the sale of six naval vessels to the Richmond government. By the end of 1863 all Confederate hopes for foreign help were irretrievably lost.

Primary source
War in the West, The
college.hmco.com/pic/kennedybrief7e

garrison *A military fortress, or the troops stationed at such a fortress, usually designed for defense or occupation of a territory.*

Sherman Scorches Georgia

General Grant, the victor of Vicksburg, was now transferred to the east Tennessee theater, where Confederates had driven Union forces from the battlefield of Chickamauga into the city of Chattanooga. Grant won a series of desperate engagements in November 1863 in the vicinity of besieged Chattanooga, including Missionary Ridge and Lookout Mountain ("the Battle Above the Clouds"). Chattanooga was liberated, the state was cleared of Confederates, and the way was thus opened for an invasion of Georgia. Grant was rewarded by being made general in chief. Georgia's conquest was entrusted to General William Tecumseh Sherman. Red-haired and red-bearded, grim-faced and ruthless, he captured Atlanta in September 1864 and burned the city in November of that year. He then daringly left his supply base, lived off the country for some 250 miles, and emerged at Savannah on the sea.

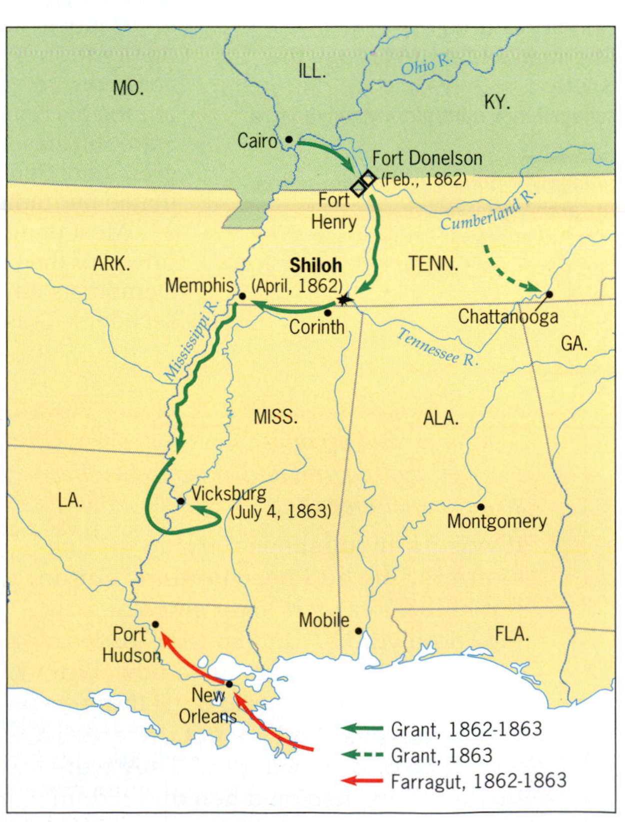

■ **The Mississippi River and Tennessee, 1862–1863**

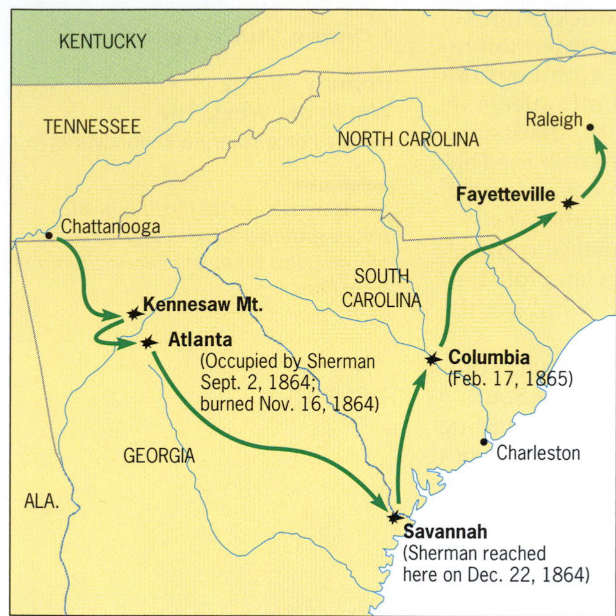

■ **Sherman's March, 1864–1865**

Sherman's hated "Blue Bellies," sixty thousand strong, cut a sixty-mile-wide swath of destruction through Georgia. They burned buildings, leaving only the blackened chimneys ("Sherman's Sentinels"). They tore up railroad rails, heated them red-hot, and twisted them into "iron doughnuts" and "Sherman's hairpins." They bayoneted family portraits and ran off with valuable "souvenirs." "War . . . is all hell," admitted Sherman later, and he proved it by his efforts to "make Georgia howl." His major purposes were to destroy supplies destined for the Confederate army and to weaken the morale of the men at the front by waging war on their homes.

Sherman was a pioneer practitioner of total war. His success in "Shermanizing" the South was attested by increasing numbers of Confederate desertions. Although effective, his methods were unquestionably brutal. At times the discipline of his army broke down, as roving riffraff (Sherman's "bummers") engaged in an orgy of **pillaging**. "Sherman the Brute" was universally damned in the South.

After seizing Savannah as a Christmas present for Lincoln, Sherman's army veered north into South Carolina, where the destruction was even more vicious. Many Union soldiers believed that this state, the "hell-hole of secession," had wantonly provoked the war. The capital city, Columbia, was put to the torch. Crunching northward, Sherman's conquering army had rolled deep into North Carolina by the time the war ended.

Interactive map
Sherman's Campaign in the South
college.hmco.com/pic/kennedy/brief7e

Primary source
Sherman's March Through the South
college.hmco.com/pic/kennedybrief7e

pillaging *Plundering, looting, destroying property by violence.*

The Politics of War

Presidential elections come by the calendar and not by the crisis. The election of 1864 fell most inopportunely in the midst of war.

Political infighting in the North added greatly to Lincoln's cup of woe. Factions within his own party, distrusting his ability or doubting his commitment to abolition, sought to tie his hands or even remove him from office. Conspicuous among his critics was a group led by the overambitious secretary of the Treasury, Salmon Chase. Especially burdensome to Lincoln was the creation of the Congressional Committee on the Conduct of the War, formed in late 1861. It was dominated by "radical" Republicans who pressed Lincoln zealously on emancipation.

Most dangerous of all to the Union cause were the Northern Democrats. Deprived of the talent that had departed with the Southern wing of the party, those Democrats remaining in the North were left with the taint of association with the seceders. Tragedy befell the Democrats—and the Union—when their gifted leader, Stephen A. Douglas, died of typhoid fever seven weeks after the war began. Unshakably devoted to the Union, he probably could have kept much of his following on the path of loyalty.

Lacking a leader, the Democrats divided. A large group of "War Democrats" patriotically supported the Lincoln administration, but tens of thousands of "Peace Democrats" did not. At the extreme were the so-called Copperheads, named for the poisonous snake that strikes without a warning rattle. Copperheads openly obstructed the war through attacks against the draft, against Lincoln, and especially, after 1863, against emancipation. They denounced the president as the "Illinois Ape" and condemned the "Nigger War." They commanded considerable political strength in the southern parts of Ohio, Indiana, and Illinois.

Notorious among the Copperheads was a sometime congressman from Ohio, Clement L. Vallandigham. This tempestuous character possessed brilliant oratorical gifts

A letter picked up on a dead Confederate in North Carolina and addressed to his "deer sister" concluded that

it was "dam fulishness" trying to "lick shurmin." He had been getting "nuthin but hell & lots uv it" ever since he saw the "dam yanks," and he was "tirde uv it." He would head for home now, but his old horse was "plaid out." If the "dam yankees" had not got there yet, it would be a "dam wunder." They were thicker than "lise on a hen and a dam site ornerier."

and unusual talents for stirring up trouble. A Southern partisan, he publicly demanded an end to the "wicked and cruel" war. In 1863 he was convicted and sentenced to prison by a **military tribunal** for treasonable utterances. Lincoln decided that if Vallandigham liked the Confederates so much, he ought to be banished to their lines. This was done. But Vallandigham was not so easily silenced. Making his way to Canada, he ran for the governorship of Ohio on foreign soil and polled a substantial but insufficient vote.

military tribunal *A special military court or commission charged with trying cases outside ordinary civilian or military courts.*

running mate *In American politics, the candidate for the lesser of two offices when they are decided together—for example, the U.S. vice presidency.*

The Election of 1864

As the election of 1864 approached, Lincoln's precarious authority depended on his retaining Republican support while spiking the threat from the Peace Democrats and the Copperheads. Fearing defeat, the Republican party executed a clever maneuver. Joining with the War Democrats, it proclaimed itself to be the Union party. Thus the Republican party passed temporarily out of existence.

Lincoln's renomination at first encountered surprisingly strong opposition. Hostile factions whipped up considerable agitation to shelve him in favor of Secretary of the Treasury Chase. Lincoln was accused of lacking force, of not having won the war, and of having shocked many sensitive souls by his ill-timed and earthy jokes. But the "ditch Lincoln" move collapsed, and he was nominated by the Union party without serious dissent.

Lincoln's **running mate** was ex-tailor Andrew Johnson, a loyal War Democrat from Tennessee who had been a small slaveowner when the conflict began. He was placed on the Union party ticket to "sew up" the election by attracting War Democrats and voters in the Border States and, sadly, with no proper regard for the possibility that Lincoln might die in office.

Embattled Democrats—regulars and Copperheads—nominated the deposed and overcautious war hero, General McClellan. The Copperheads managed to force into the Democratic platform a plank denouncing the prosecution of the war as a failure. But McClellan, who could not otherwise have faced his old comrades-in-arms, repudiated this defeatist declaration.

The campaign was noisy and nasty. Lincoln's reelection was at first gravely in doubt. The war was going badly, and Lincoln himself gave way to despondency, fearing that political defeat was imminent. But the atmosphere of gloom was changed electrically, as balloting day neared, by a succession of Northern victories. Admiral Farragut captured Mobile, Alabama, after defiantly shouting the now famous order, "Damn the torpedoes! Go ahead." General Sherman seized Atlanta. General ("Little Phil") Sheridan laid waste the verdant Shenandoah Valley of Virginia so thoroughly that in his words, "a crow could not fly over it without carrying his rations with him."

The president pulled through, but nothing more than necessary was left to chance. At election time many Northern soldiers were furloughed home to support Lincoln at the polls. Other Northern soldiers cast their ballots at the front.

Bolstered by the "bayonet vote," Lincoln vanquished General McClellan by 212 electoral votes to 21, losing only Kentucky, Delaware, and New Jersey. But "Little Mac" ran a much closer race than the electoral count indicates. He netted a healthy 45 percent of the popular vote, 1,803,787 to Lincoln's 2,206,938, piling up much support in the Old Northwest, in New York, and also in his native state of Pennsylvania (see the map).

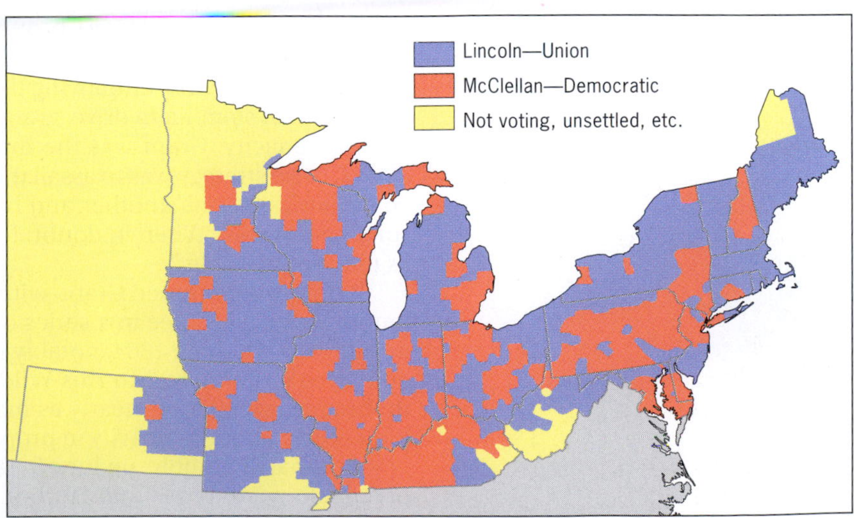

■ **Presidential Election of 1864 (showing popular vote by county)** Lincoln also carried California, Oregon, and Nevada, but there was a considerable McClellan vote in each. Note McClellan's strength in the Border States and in the southern tier of Ohio, Indiana, and Illinois—the so-called "Butternut" region.

General Ulysses S. Grant and General Robert E. Lee Trained at West Point, Grant (left) proved to be a better general than a president. Oddly, he hated the sight of blood and recoiled from rare beef. Lee (right), a gentlemanly general in an ungentlemanly business, remarked when the Union troops were bloodily repulsed at Fredericksburg, "It is well that war is so terrible, or we should get too fond of it."

One of the most crushing defeats suffered by the South was the defeat of the Northern Democrats in 1864. The removal of Lincoln was the last ghost of a hope for a Confederate victory, and Southern soldiers would wishfully shout, "Hurrah for McClellan!" When Lincoln triumphed, desertions from the sinking Southern ship increased sharply.

Grant Outlasts Lee

After Gettysburg, Grant was brought in from the West over Meade, who was blamed for failing to pursue the defeated but always dangerous Lee. Lincoln needed a general who, employing the superior resources of the North, would have the intestinal stamina to drive straight ahead, regardless of casualties. A soldier of bulldog tenacity, Grant was the man for this meat-grinder type of warfare. His overall basic strategy was to assail the enemy's armies simultaneously, so that they could not assist one another and hence could be destroyed piecemeal. His personal motto was "When in doubt, fight." Lincoln urged him "to chew and choke, as much as possible."

A grimly determined Grant, with more than 100,000 men, struck toward Richmond. He engaged Lee in a series of furious battles in the Wilderness of Virginia during May and June 1864, notably in the leaden hurricane of the "Bloody Angle" and "Hell's Half Acre." In this Wilderness Campaign Grant suffered about fifty thousand casualties, or nearly as many men as Lee had commanded at the start. But Lee lost about as heavily in proportion.

In a ghastly gamble, on June 3, 1864, Grant ordered a frontal assault on the impregnable position of Cold Harbor. Union soldiers advanced to almost certain death with papers pinned on their backs bearing their names and addresses. In a few minutes, about seven thousand men were killed or wounded.

Public opinion in the North was appalled by this "blood and guts" fighting, and critics assailed "Grant the Butcher." But Grant's reputation was undeserved, while Lee's was overrated. Lee's rate of loss (one casualty for every five soldiers) was the highest of any general in the war. By contrast, Grant lost one in ten. It was

Lee, not Grant, who turned the eastern campaign into a war of attrition fought in the trenches. Lee's new defensive posture in turn forced Grant into some brutal arithmetic. Grant could trade two men for one and still beat the enemy to his knees. "I propose to fight it out on this line," he wrote, "if it takes all summer." It did—and it also took all autumn, all winter, and a part of the spring.

Online Study Center

Primary source
Wounded Escaping from the Burning Woods of the Wilderness
college.hmco.com/pic/kennedybrief7e

Online Study Center

Interactive map
Grant's Campaign Against Lee
college.hmco.com/pic/kennedy/brief7e

In February 1865 the Confederates, tasting the bitter dregs of defeat, tried desperately to negotiate for peace between the "two countries." But Lincoln could accept nothing short of Union and emancipation, and the Southerners could accept nothing short of independence. So the tribulation wore on—amid smoke and agony—to its terrible climax.

The end came with dramatic suddenness. Rapidly advancing Northern troops captured Richmond and then cornered Lee at Appomattox Courthouse in Virginia, in April 1865. Grant—stubble-bearded and informally dressed—met with Lee on the ninth, Palm Sunday, and granted generous terms of surrender. Among other concessions, the hungry Confederates were allowed to keep their own horses for spring plowing.

Tattered Southern veterans—"Lee's Ragamuffins"—wept as they took leave of their beloved commander. The elated Union soldiers cheered, but they were silenced by Grant's stern admonition, "The war is over; the rebels are our countrymen again."

Lincoln traveled to conquered Richmond and sat in Jefferson Davis's evacuated office just forty hours after the Confederate president had left it. As he walked the blasted streets of the city, crowds of freed slaves gathered to see and touch "Father Abraham." One black man fell to his knees before the Emancipator, who said to him, "Don't kneel to me. This is not right. You must kneel to God only, and thank Him for the liberty you will enjoy hereafter." Sadly, as many freed slaves would discover, the hereafter of their full liberty was a long time coming.

The Martyrdom of Lincoln

On the night of April 14, 1865 (Good Friday), only five days after Lee's surrender, Ford's Theater in Washington witnessed its most sensational drama. A half-crazed, fanatically pro-Southern actor, John Wilkes Booth, slipped behind Lincoln as he sat in his box and shot him in the head. After lying unconscious all night, the Great Emancipator died the following morning. "Now he belongs to the ages," remarked the once-critical Secretary of War Edwin Stanton.

Lincoln expired in the arms of victory at the very pinnacle of his fame. From the standpoint of his reputation, his death could not have been better timed if he had hired the assassin. A large number of his countrymen had not suspected his greatness, and many others had even doubted his ability. But his dramatic death helped to erase the memory of his shortcomings and caused his nobler qualities to stand out in clearer relief.

The full impact of Lincoln's death was not at once apparent to the South. Hundreds of bedraggled ex-Confederate soldiers cheered, as did some Southern civilians and Northern Copperheads, when they learned of the assassination. But as time wore on, increasing numbers of Southerners perceived that Lincoln's death was a calamity for them. Belatedly they recognized that his kindliness and moderation would have been the most effective shields between them and vindictive treatment by the victors. The assassination unfortunately increased the bitterness of the North, partly because of the fantastic rumor that Jefferson Davis had plotted it.

A few historians have argued that if the rail-splitter had lived, he would have suffered Andrew Johnson's fate of being impeached by the embittered members of his own party who demanded harshness, not forbearance, toward the South. Lincoln no doubt would have clashed with Congress. But the surefooted and experienced Lincoln could hardly have blundered into the same quicksands that engulfed Johnson. Lincoln was a victorious president, and there is no arguing with victory. In addition to his powers of leadership refined in the war crucible, Lincoln possessed in full measure tact, sweet reasonableness, and an uncommon amount of common sense. Andrew Johnson, hot-tempered and impetuous, lacked all of

New York Mourns Lincoln's Death, April 25, 1865 Lincoln's body traveled by train to lie in state in fourteen cities before arriving at his final resting place of Springfield, Illinois. In New York City, 160,000 mourners accompanied the hearse as the funeral procession slowly made its way down Broadway. Scalpers sold choice window seats for four dollars and up. Blacks were barred from participating, until the mayor changed his mind at the last minute—but only if they marched at the rear. This souvenir stereo view, bringing the scene to three-dimensional life when seen through the popular device of a hand-held stereopticon, allowed many more Americans to observe the funeral than could be there in person.

these priceless qualities. Ford's Theater, with its tragic murder of Lincoln, set the stage for the wrenching ordeal of Reconstruction.

The Aftermath of the Nightmare

The Civil War took a grisly toll in gore, about as much as all of America's subsequent wars combined. Over 600,000 men died in action or of disease, and in all over a million were killed or seriously wounded. To its lasting hurt, the nation lost the cream of its young manhood and potential leadership.

Direct monetary costs of the conflict totaled about $15 billion. But this colossal figure does not include continuing expenses, such as pensions and interest on the national debt. The intangible costs—dislocations, wasted energies, lowered ethics, blasted lives, bitter memories, and burning hates—cannot be calculated.

The greatest constitutional decision of the century, in a sense, was written in blood and handed down at Appomattox Courthouse, near which Lee surrendered. The extreme states' righters were crushed. The national government, tested in the fiery furnace of war, emerged unbroken. Nullification and secession, those twin nightmares of previous decades, were laid to rest.

Beyond doubt the Civil War—the nightmare of the Republic—was the supreme test of American democracy. It finally answered the question, in the words of Lincoln at Gettysburg, whether a nation dedicated to such principles "can long endure." The preservation of democratic ideals, though not an officially announced war aim, was subconsciously one of the major objectives of the North.

Victory for Union arms also provided inspiration to the champions of democracy and liberalism the world over. The great English Reform Bill of 1867, under which Britain became a true political democracy, was passed two years after the

Primary source
Appomattox Court House
college.hmco.com/pic/kennedybrief7e

Civil War ended. American democracy had proved itself, and its success was an additional argument used by the disfranchised British masses in securing similar blessings for themselves.

The "Lost Cause" of the South was lost, but few Americans today would argue that the end result was not for the best. The shameful cancer of slavery was sliced away by the sword, and African Americans were at last in a position to claim their rights to life, liberty, and the pursuit of happiness. The nation was again united politically, though for many generations it was still divided spiritually by the passions of the war. Grave dangers were averted by a Union victory, including the indefinite prolongation of the "peculiar institution," the unleashing of the "slave power" on weak Caribbean neighbors, and the transformation of the area from Panama to Hudson's Bay into an armed camp, with several hostile states constantly snarling and sniping at one another. America still had a long way to go to make the promises of freedom a reality for all its citizens, black and white. But emancipation laid the necessary groundwork, and a united and democratic United States was free to fulfill its destiny as the dominant republic of the hemisphere—and eventually of the world.

Chapter Summary

The Union defeats at Bull Run and the Peninsula Campaign ended Northern complacency about a quick victory, and also prevented a quick return of the South to the Union with slavery intact. George McClellan and other early Union generals proved unable to defeat the tactically brilliant Confederate armies under Lee. The Union naval blockade put a slow but devastating economic noose around the South.

The political and diplomatic dimensions of the war quickly became critical. In order to retain the border states, Lincoln first de-emphasized any intention to destroy slavery. But the Battle of Antietam in 1862 enabled Lincoln to prevent foreign intervention and turn the struggle into a total war against slavery. Blacks and abolitionists joined enthusiastically in a war for emancipation, but white resentment in part of the North created political problems for Lincoln.

The Union first gained military success in the West, succeeding at Vicksburg in cutting the Confederacy in half. Lee's failed invasion of the North ended at Gettysburg, and completely turned the military tide against the South. Southern resistance remained strong, with the hope that political defeatist ("Copperheads") would force a negotiated peace settlement. But the Union victories at Atlanta and Mobile assured Lincoln's success in the election of 1864 and ended the last Confederate hopes. The war ended the issues of disunion and slavery, but at a tremendous cost to both North and South.

VARYING VIEWPOINTS

What Were the Consequences of the Civil War?

With the end of the Civil War in 1865, the United States was permanently altered despite the reunification of the Union and the Confederacy. Slavery was officially banned, secession was a dead issue, and industrial growth surged forward. With the Union's victory, power rested firmly with the North, and it would orchestrate the future development of the country.

According to historian Eric Foner, the war redrew the economic and political map of the country. For example, the first twelve amendments to the Constitution, ratified before the war, had all served to limit government power. In contrast, the Thirteenth Amendment, which abolished slavery, and the revolutionary Fourteenth Amendment, which conferred citizenship on and guaranteed civil rights to all those born in the United States, marked unprecedented expansions of federal power.

Historian James M. McPherson has noted still other ways in which the Civil War extended the authority of the central government. It expanded federal powers of taxation, conscripted soldiers, developed a National Banking System and printed currency, bolstered federal courts, and established the first federal social welfare agency—the Freedmen's Bureau—to aid former slaves.

Some scholars have disputed whether the Civil War marked an absolute watershed in American history. They correctly note that racial inequality scandalously persisted after the Civil War despite the supposed protections extended by federal civil rights legislation. Others have argued that the industrial growth of the post–Civil War era had its real roots in the Jacksonian era. Regional differences between North and South endured, moreover, even down to the present day.

Yet the argument that the Civil War launched a modern America remains convincing. The lives of Americans, white and black, North and South, were transformed by the war experience. Industry entered a period of unprecedented growth. The emergence of new, national legal and governmental institutions marked the birth of the modern American state. All considered, it is hard to deny that the end of the Civil War brought one chapter of the nation's history to a close while opening another.

22

The Ordeal of Reconstruction

1865–1877

WITH MALICE TOWARD NONE, WITH CHARITY FOR ALL, WITH FIRMNESS IN THE RIGHT AS GOD GIVES US TO SEE THE RIGHT, LET US STRIVE ON TO FINISH THE WORK WE ARE IN, TO BIND UP THE NATION'S WOUNDS, TO CARE FOR HIM WHO SHALL HAVE BORNE THE BATTLE AND FOR HIS WIDOW AND ORPHAN, TO DO ALL WHICH MAY ACHIEVE AND CHERISH A JUST AND LASTING PEACE AMONG OURSELVES AND WITH ALL NATIONS.

ABRAHAM LINCOLN, SECOND INAUGURAL ADDRESS, MARCH 4, 1865

Chapter Outline

The battle was done, the buglers silent. Bone-weary and bloodied, the American people, North and South, now faced the staggering challenges of peace. Four questions loomed large. How would the South, physically devastated by war and socially revolutionized by emancipation, be rebuilt? How would the liberated blacks fare as free men and women? How would the Southern states be reintegrated into the Union? And who would direct the process of Reconstruction—the Southern states themselves, the president, or Congress?

Focus Questions

1. **What were the major problems facing the South and the nation after the Civil War?**
2. **How did African Americans and whites, Southern and Northern, respond to the end of slavery and conduct race relations under new conditions of freedom?**
3. **How did Andrew Johnson's blunders enable the Radical Republicans to gain control of Reconstruction policy?**
4. **What were the actual effects of congressional Reconstruction in the South, and how did militant white opposition and growing northern apathy eventually bring an end to Reconstruction in the Compromise of 1877?**
5. **What were the primary successes and failures of Reconstruction, and what legacy did it leave for later generations of Americans?**

The Problems of Peace

Other questions also clamored for answers. What should be done with the captured Confederate ringleaders? All Confederate officials were subject to charges of treason, and during the war a popular Northern song had been "Hang Jeff Davis to a Sour Apple Tree." Davis was clapped into prison for two years, but no **treason** trials were ever held. President Andrew Johnson pardoned all "rebel" leaders as a sort of Christmas present in 1868. Congress removed their **civil disabilities** thirty years later.

treason *The crime of betrayal of one's country, involving some overt act violating an oath of allegiance or providing illegal aid to a foreign state. In the United States, treason is the only crime specified in the Constitution.*

civil disabilities *Legally imposed restrictions of a person's civil rights or liberties.*

Online Study Center

Primary source
Ruins in Charleston, South Carolina
college.hmco.com/pic/kennedybrief7e

Online Study Center

Primary source
Ruins of the Arsenal at Richmond
college.hmco.com/pic/kennedybrief7e

Online Study Center

Primary source
Ruins of Atlanta
college.hmco.com/pic/kennedybrief7e

Online Study Center

Primary source
Ruins of Petersburg Railroad Bridge
college.hmco.com/pic/kennedybrief7e

Dismal indeed was the picture presented by the war-wracked South when the rattle of musketry faded. Not only had an age perished, but a civilization had collapsed, in both its economic and its social structure. The moonlight-and-magnolia Old South, largely imaginary in any case, had forever gone with the wind.

Handsome cities of yesteryear, such as Charleston and Richmond, were rubble-strewn and weed-choked. An Atlantan returned to his once-fair hometown and remarked, "Hell has laid her egg, and right here it hatched." Economic life had creaked to a halt. Banks and businesses had locked their doors, ruined by runaway inflation. Factories were smokeless, silent, dismantled. The transportation system had broken down completely. Efforts to untwist the rails corkscrewed by Sherman's soldiers proved bumpily unsatisfactory.

Agriculture—the economic lifeblood of the South—was almost hopelessly crippled. Once-white cotton fields yielded a lush harvest of nothing but green weeds. The slave-labor system had collapsed, seed was scarce, and livestock had been driven off by plundering Yankees. Pathetic instances were reported of men hitching themselves to plows, while women and children gripped the handles.

The princely planter aristocrats were humbled by the war—at least temporarily. Reduced to proud poverty, they faced charred and gutted mansions, lost investments, and almost worthless land. Their investment of more than $2 billion in slaves, their primary form of wealth, had evaporated with emancipation.

Beaten but unbent, many high-spirited white Southerners remained dangerously defiant. They cursed the "damn yankees" and spoke of "your government" in Washington instead of "our government." Conscious of no crime, these former Confederates continued to believe that their view of secession was correct and that the "lost cause" was still a just war. One popular anti-Union song ran,

I'm glad I fought agin her, I only wish we'd won,
And I ain't axed any pardon for anything I've done.

Such attitudes boded ill for the prospects of painlessly binding up the Republic's wounds.

Freedmen Define Freedom

Confusion abounded in the still-smoldering South about the precise meaning of "freedom" for blacks. Emancipation took effect haltingly and unevenly in different parts of the conquered Confederacy. As Union armies marched in and out of various localities, many blacks found themselves emancipated and re-enslaved. A North Carolina slave estimated that he had celebrated freedom about twelve times. In some regions planters stubbornly protested that slavery was legal until state legislatures or the Supreme Court might act. For many slaves the shackles of bondage were not struck off in a single mighty blow; long-suffering blacks often had to pry off their chains link by link.

Richmond Devastated Charleston, Atlanta, and other Southern cities looked much the same, resembling bombed-out Berlin and Dresden in 1945.

The variety of responses to emancipation, by whites as well as blacks, illustrated the sometimes startling complexity of the master-slave relationship. Loyalty to the plantation master prompted some slaves to resist the liberating Union armies, while other slaves' pent-up bitterness burst violently forth on the day of liberation. In one instance, a group of Virginia slaves laid twenty lashes on the back of their former master—a painful dose of his own favorite medicine.

Prodded by the bayonets of Yankee armies of occupation, all

Chronology

1863	Lincoln announces "10 percent" Reconstruction plan.
1864	Lincoln vetoes Wade-Davis Bill.
1865	Lincoln assassinated. Johnson issues Reconstruction proclamation. Congress refuses to seat Southern congressmen. Freedmen's Bureau established. Southern states pass Black Codes.
1866	Congress passes Civil Rights Bill over Johnson's veto. Congress passes Fourteenth Amendment. Johnson-backed candidates lose congressional election. *Ex parte Milligan* case. Ku Klux Klan founded.
1867	Reconstruction Act. Tenure of Office Act. United States purchases Alaska from Russia.
1868	Johnson impeached and acquitted. Johnson pardons Confederate leaders.
1870	Fifteenth Amendment ratified.
1870-1871	Force Acts.
1872	Freedmen's Bureau ended.
1877	Reconstruction ends.

masters were eventually forced to recognize their slaves' permanent freedom. The once-commanding planter would assemble his former human chattels in front of the porch of the "big house" and announce their liberty. Though some blacks initially responded to news of their emancipation with suspicion and uncertainty, they soon celebrated their newfound freedom. Many took new names in place of the ones given by their masters and demanded that whites formally address them as "Mr." or "Mrs."

Primary source
Black Recollections of Freedom's Impact
college.hmco.com/pic/kennedybrief7e

Primary source
Black Recollections of Freedom's Impact
college.hmco.com/pic/kennedybrief7e

Tens of thousands of emancipated blacks took to the roads, some to test their freedom, others to search for long-lost spouses, parents, and children. Emancipation thus strengthened the black family, and many newly freed men and women formalized "slave marriages" for personal and pragmatic reasons, including the desire to make their children legal heirs.

Whole communities sometimes moved together in search of opportunity. From 1878 to 1880, some twenty-five thousand blacks from Louisiana, Texas, and Mississippi surged in a mass exodus to Kansas.

The church became the focus of black community life in the years following emancipation. As slaves, blacks had worshiped alongside whites, but now they formed their own churches pastored by their own ministers. Black churches grew robustly. The 150,000-member black Baptist Church of 1850 reached 500,000 by 1870, while the African Methodist Episcopal Church quadrupled in size from 100,000 to 400,000 in the first decade after emancipation. These churches formed the bedrock of black community life, and they soon gave rise to other benevolent, fraternal, and **mutual aid societies.** All these organizations helped blacks protect their newly won freedom.

Emancipation also meant education for many blacks. Learning to read and write had been a privilege generally denied to them under slavery. Freedmen wasted no time establishing societies for self-improvement, which undertook to raise funds to purchase land, build schoolhouses, and hire teachers. With qualified black teachers in short supply, they turned for help to Northern white women sent by the American Missionary Association and to the federal government.

Houston H. Holloway, age twenty at the time of his emancipation, recalled his feelings upon hearing of his freedom:

"I felt like a bird out of a cage. Amen. Amen. Amen. I could hardly ask to feel any better than I did that day. . . . The week passed off in a blaze of glory."

The reunion of long-lost relatives also inspired joy; one Union officer wrote home,

"Men are taking their wives and children, families which had been for a long time broken up are united and oh! such happiness. I am glad I am here."

mutual aid societies *Nonprofit organizations designed to provide their members with financial and social benefits, often including medical aid, life insurance, funeral costs, and disaster relief.*

The Freedmen's Bureau

Online Study Center
Primary source
Black Testimony on the Aftermath of Enslavement
college.hmco.com/pic/kennedybrief7e

Abolitionists had long preached that slavery was a degrading institution. Now the emancipators were faced with the brutal reality that the former slaves were overwhelmingly unskilled, unlettered, without property or money, and with scant knowledge of how to survive as free people. To cope with this problem throughout the conquered South, Congress created the Freedmen's Bureau on March 3, 1865.

confiscation *Legal government seizure of private property without compensation.*

On paper at least, the bureau was intended to be a kind of primitive welfare agency. It was to provide food, clothing, and education both to freedmen and to white refugees. It was also authorized to distribute up to forty acres of abandoned or **confiscated** land to black settlers. Headed by General O. O. Howard, who later founded and served as president of Howard University in Washington, D.C., the bureau achieved its greatest successes in education. It taught an estimated 200,000 blacks how to read. Many former slaves had a passion for learning, partly because they wanted to close the gap between themselves and the whites and partly because they longed to read the Word of God.

Online Study Center
Primary source
Southern Skepticism of the Freedmen's Bureau
college.hmco.com/pic/kennedybrief7e

But in other areas the bureau's accomplishments were meager—or even mischievous. Little confiscated Confederate land actually passed into black hands. Instead local administrators often collaborated with planters in expelling blacks from towns and cajoling them into signing labor contracts to work for their former masters. Still, the white South resented the bureau as a meddlesome federal interloper that threatened to upset white racial dominance. President Andrew Johnson, who shared the white supremacist views of most white Southerners, repeatedly tried to kill it, and it expired in 1872.

■ **Educating Young Freedmen and Women, 1870s** Freed slaves in the South regarded schooling as the key to improving their children's lives and the fulfillment of a long-sought right that had been denied blacks in slavery. These well-dressed school children are lined up outside their rural, one-room schoolhouse alongside their teachers, both black and white.

EXAMINING THE EVIDENCE

Letter from a Freedman to His Old Master, 1865

What was it like to experience the transition from slavery to freedom? Four million southern blacks faced this exhilarating and formidable prospect with the end of the war. For historians, recovering the African American perspective on emancipation is challenging. Unlike their white masters, freed blacks left few written records. But one former slave captured in a letter to his "Old Master" (whose surname he bore) the heroic determination of many blacks to build new independent and dignified lives for themselves and their families.

During the war Jourdon Anderson escaped slavery in Tennessee with his wife and two daughters. After relocating to the relative safety of Ohio, he received a communication from his former owner asking him to return. In his bold reply, reportedly "dictated by the old servant" himself, Anderson expressed his family's new expectations for life as free people and an uneasiness about his former master's intentions. He made reference to his "comfortable home," his daughters' schooling, the church that he and his wife were free to attend regularly, and the peace of mind that came with knowing that "my girls [would not be] brought to shame by the violence and wickedness of their young masters." To test the white man's sincerity, Anderson and his wife asked for the astronomical figure of $11,680 in back wages from decades as slaves. He closed by reiterating that "the great desire of my life is to give my children an education and have them form virtuous habits." This rare letter demonstrates that many black correspondents may have been illiterate, but they were hardly inarticulate. And they asserted themselves as parents, workers, and citizens not only from the distance of a former free state like Ohio but also deep within the former slave states of the South.

1. Was the tone of Anderson's letter (and postscript) serious, sarcastic, or tongue-in-cheek? What specific phrases support your answer?
2. How did the eventual accomplishments of Reconstruction correspond with the initial expectations of people like Anderson and his former owner?
3. What does this letter reveal about the complicated relationships between freedmen and their former masters? Is the relationship a "personal" one, or was it entirely dominated by Jourdan Anderson's having been held by Colonel P.H. Anderson as "property"?

Letter from a Freedman to his Old Master.

The following is a genuine document. It was *dictated* by the old servant, and contains his ideas and forms of expression. [Cincinnati Commercial.

DAYTON, Ohio, August 7, 1865.

To my Old Master, Col. P. H. ANDERSON, *Big Spring, Tennessee.*

SIR: I got your letter and was glad to find that you had not forgotten Jordan, and that you wanted me to come back and live with you again, promising to do better for me than anybody else can. I have often felt uneasy about you. I thought the Yankees would have hung you long before this for harboring Rebs. they found at your hourse. I suppose they never heard about your going to Col. Martin's to kill the Union soldier that was left by his company in their stable. Although you shot at me twice before I left you, I did not want to hear of your being hurt, and am glad you are still living. It would do me good to go back to the dear old home again and see Miss Mary and Miss Martha and Allen, Esther, Green and Lee. Give my love to them all, and tell them I hope we will meet in the better world, if not in this. I would have gone back to see you all when I was working in the Nashville Hospital, but one of the neighbors told me Henry intended to shoot me if he ever got a chance.

I want to know particularly what the good chance is you propose to give me. I am doing tolerably well here; I get $25 a month, with victuals and clothing; have a comfortable home for Mandy (the folks here call her Mrs. Anderson), and the children, Milly Jane and Grundy, go to school and are learning well; the teacher says Grundy has a head for a preacher. They go to Sunday-School, and Mandy and me attend church

As to my freedom, which you say I can have, there is nothing to be gained on that score, as I got my free-papers in 1864 from the Provost-Marshal-General of the Department at Nashville. Mandy says she would be afraid to go back without some proof that you are sincerely disposed to treat us justly and kindly—and we have concluded to test your sincerity by asking you to send us our wages for the time we served you. This will make us forget and forgive old sores, and rely on your justice and friendship in the future. I served you faithfully for thirty-two years, and Mandy twenty years, at $25 a month for me, and $2 a week for Mandy. Our earnings would amount to $11,680. Add to this the interest for the time our wages has been kept back and deduct what you paid for our clothing and three doctor's visits to me, and pulling a tooth for Mandy, and the balance will show what we are in justice entitled to. Please send the money by Adams Express, in care of V. Winters, esq., Dayton, Ohio. If you fail to pay us for faithful labors in the past we can have little faith in your promises in the future.

P. S.—Say howdy to George Carter, and thank him for taking the pistol from you when you were shooting at me.

Women from the North enthusiastically embraced the opportunity to go south and teach in Freedmen's Bureau schools for emancipated blacks. One volunteer explained her motives:

"I thought I must do something, not having money at my command, what could I do but give myself to the work. . . . I would go to them, and give them my life if necessary."

Johnson: The Tailor President

Few presidents have ever been faced with a more perplexing sea of troubles than that confronting Andrew Johnson. What manner of man was this dark-eyed, black-haired Tennessean, now chief executive by virtue of the bullet that killed Lincoln?

No citizen, not even Lincoln, ever reached the White House from humbler beginnings. Born to impoverished parents in North Carolina and orphaned early, Johnson never attended school but was apprenticed to a tailor at age ten. Ambitious to get ahead, he taught himself to read, and later his wife taught him to write and do simple arithmetic. Like many another self-made man, he was inclined to overpraise his maker.

Johnson early became active in politics in Tennessee, where he had moved when seventeen years old. He shone as an impassioned champion of the poor whites against the planter aristocrats, and as a two-fisted stump speaker before angry and heckling crowds. Elected to Congress, he attracted much favorable attention in the North when he refused to secede with his own state. After Tennessee was partially liberated by Union armies, he was appointed war governor of the state.

Political exigency next thrust Johnson into the vice presidency. Lincoln's Union party in 1864 needed to attract support from the War Democrats and other pro-Southern elements, and Johnson, a Democrat, seemed to be the ideal man.

"Old Andy" Johnson was no doubt a man of parts—unpolished parts. He was intelligent, able, forceful, and steadfastly devoted to duty and to the Constitution. Yet the man who had raised himself from the tailor's bench to the president's chair was a misfit. A Southerner who did not understand the North, a Tennessean who had earned the distrust of the South, a Democrat who had never been accepted by the Republicans, a president who had not been elected to the office, he was not at home in a Republican White House. Hotheaded, contentious, and stubborn, he was the wrong man in the wrong place at the wrong time. A Reconstruction policy devised by the angels might well have failed in his tactless hands.

Presidential Reconstruction

Even before the shooting war had ended, the political war over Reconstruction had begun. Abraham Lincoln believed that the Southern states had never legally withdrawn from the Union. Their formal restoration to the Union would therefore be relatively simple. Accordingly, Lincoln in 1863 proclaimed his "10 percent" Reconstruction plan. It decreed that a state could be reintegrated into the Union when 10 percent of its voters in the presidential election of 1860 had taken an oath of allegiance to the United States and pledged to abide by emancipation. The next step would be formal erection of a state government. Lincoln would then recognize the purified regime.

Lincoln's proclamation provoked a sharp reaction in Congress, where Republicans feared the restoration of the planter aristocracy to power and the possible re-enslavement of blacks. Republicans therefore rammed through Congress in 1864 the Wade-Davis Bill. The bill required that 50 percent of a state's voters take the oath of allegiance and demanded stronger safeguards for emancipation than Lincoln's as the price of readmission. Republicans were outraged when Lincoln "**pocket-vetoed**" this bill by refusing to sign it after Congress had adjourned.

pocket veto *The presidential act of blocking a Congressionally passed law not by direct veto but by simply refusing to sign it at the end of a session. (A president can pocket-veto a bill within ten days of a session's end or after.)*

The controversy surrounding the Wade-Davis Bill had revealed deep differences between the president and Congress. Unlike Lincoln, many in Congress insisted that the seceders had indeed left the Union—had "committed suicide" as republican states—and had therefore forfeited all their rights. They could be readmitted only as "conquered provinces" on such conditions as Congress should decree.

The episode further revealed differences among two emerging Republican factions, moderates and radicals. The majority moderate group tended to agree with Lincoln that the seceded states should be restored to the Union as simply and swiftly as reasonable—though on Congress's terms, not the president's. The minority radical group believed that before the South could be restored, its social structure should be uprooted, the haughty planters punished, and the newly emancipated blacks protected by federal power.

After President Lincoln's assassination in April 1865, some radicals hoped that spiteful Andy Johnson, who shared their hatred for the planter aristocracy, would also share their desire to reconstruct the South with a rod of iron. But Johnson soon disillusioned them. He quickly recognized several of Lincoln's 10 percent governments, and on May 29, 1865, he issued his own Reconstruction proclamation. It disfranchised certain leading Confederates and called for special state conventions, which were required to repeal secession, repudiate all Confederate debts, and ratify the slave-freeing Thirteenth Amendment.

Johnson, savoring his dominance over the high-toned aristocrats who now begged his favor, granted pardons in abundance. Bolstered by the political resurrection of the planter elite, the recently rebellious states moved rapidly in the second half of 1865 to organize governments. But as the pattern of the new governments became clear, Republicans of all stripes grew furious.

The Baleful Black Codes

Among the first acts of the new Southern regimes sanctioned by Johnson was the passage of the iron-toothed Black Codes. These laws were designed to regulate the affairs of the emancipated blacks, much as the slave statutes had done in pre–Civil War days. The Black Codes aimed, first of all, to ensure a stable and subservient labor force. Dire penalties were therefore imposed by the codes on blacks who "jumped" their labor contracts, which usually committed them to work for the same employer for one year, and generally at pittance wages.

Primary source
Louisiana Black Code
college.hmco.com/pic/kennedybrief7e

The codes also sought to restore as nearly as possible the pre-emancipation system of race relations. Freedom was legally recognized, as were some other privileges, such as the right to marry. But all the codes forbade a black to serve on a jury or vote, and some even barred blacks from renting or leasing land.

These oppressive laws mocked the ideal of freedom, so recently purchased by buckets of blood. The Black Codes imposed terrible burdens on the unfettered blacks, struggling against mistreatment and poverty to make their way as free people. Thousands of impoverished former slaves slipped into virtual **peonage** as **sharecropper** farmers, as did many landless whites.

peonage *A system in which debtors are held in servitude, to labor for their creditors.*

sharecropper *An agricultural system in which a tenant receives land, tools, and seed on credit and pledges in return a share of the crop to the creditor.*

The Black Codes made an ugly impression in the North. If the former slaves were being re-enslaved, people asked one another, had not the Boys in Blue spilled their blood in vain? Had the North really won the war?

Congressional Reconstruction

These questions grew more insistent when the congressional delegations from the newly reconstituted Southern states presented themselves in the Capitol in December 1865. To the shock and disgust of the Republicans, many former Confederate leaders were on hand to claim their seats.

The appearance of these ex-rebels was a natural but costly blunder. Voters of the South, seeking able representatives, had turned instinctively to their experienced statesmen. But most of the Southern leaders were tainted by active association with the "lost cause." Among them were four former Confederate generals, five colonels, and various members of the Richmond cabinet and Congress. Worst of all, there was the shrimpy but brainy Alexander Stephens, ex–vice president of the Confederacy, still under indictment for treason.

The presence of these "whitewashed rebels" infuriated the Republicans in Congress. The war had been fought to restore the Union, but not on these kinds of terms. Most Republicans balked at giving up the political advantage they had enjoyed while the South had been "out" from 1861 to 1865. They had passed much legislation that favored the North, such as the Morrill Act, the Pacific Railroad Act, and the Homestead Act. On the first day of the congressional session, December 4, 1865, they banged shut the door in the face of the newly elected Southern delegations.

Looking to the future, the Republicans were alarmed to realize that a restored South would be stronger than ever in national politics. Before the war a black slave had counted as three-fifths of a person in apportioning congressional representation. But now, owing to full counting of free blacks, the eleven rebel states were entitled to twelve more votes in Congress, and twelve more presidential electoral votes, than they had previously enjoyed. Again, angry voices in the North raised the cry, Who won the war?

Republicans had good reason to fear that ultimately they might be elbowed aside. Southerners might join hands with Democrats in the North and win control of Congress or maybe even the White House. If that happened, they could perpetuate the Black Codes, virtually re-enslaving the blacks. They could dismantle the economic program of the Republican party and possibly even repudiate the national debt. President Johnson thus deeply disturbed the congressional Republicans when he announced on December 6, 1865, that the recently rebellious states had satisfied his conditions and that in his view the Union was now restored.

Johnson Clashes with Congress

A clash between president and Congress was now inevitable. It exploded into the open in February 1866, when the president vetoed a bill (later repassed) extending the life of the controversial Freedmen's Bureau.

Aroused, the Republicans swiftly struck back. In March 1866 they passed the Civil Rights Bill, which conferred on blacks the privileges of American citizenship and struck at the Black Codes. President Johnson resolutely vetoed this forward-looking measure, but in April congressmen steamrollered it over his veto—something they repeatedly did henceforth. The hapless president, dubbed "Andy Veto," had his presidential wings clipped short, as Congress increasingly assumed the dominant role in running the government.

The Republicans now undertook to rivet the principles of the Civil Rights Bill into the Constitution as the Fourteenth Amendment. The proposed amendment, as approved by Congress and sent to the states in June 1866, was sweeping. It (1) conferred civil rights, including citizenship but excluding the franchise, on the freedmen; (2) reduced proportionately the representation of a state in Congress and in the Electoral College if it denied blacks the ballot; (3) disqualified from federal and state office former Confederates who as federal officeholders had once sworn to "support the Constitution of the United States"; and (4) guaranteed the federal debt, while repudiating all Confederate debts. (See the text of the Fourteenth Amendment in the Appendix.)

The radical faction was disappointed that the Fourteenth Amendment did not grant the right to vote, but all Republicans agreed that no state should be welcomed back into the Union fold without first ratifying the Fourteenth Amendment. Yet President Johnson advised the Southern states to reject it, and all of the "sinful eleven," except Tennessee, defiantly spurned the amendment.

Swinging 'Round the Circle with Johnson

As 1866 lengthened, the battle grew between Congress and the president. Now the issue was whether Reconstruction was to be carried on with or without the Fourteenth Amendment. The Republicans would settle for nothing less.

The crucial congressional elections of 1866—more crucial than some presidential elections—were fast approaching. Johnson was naturally eager to escape from the clutch of Congress by securing a majority favorable to his soft-on-the-South policy. Invited to dedicate a Chicago monument to Stephen A. Douglas, he undertook to speak at various cities en route in support of his views.

Johnson's famous "swing 'round the circle," beginning in the late summer of 1866, was a seriocomedy of errors. The president delivered a series of "give 'em hell" speeches, in which he accused the radicals in Congress of having planned large-scale antiblack riots and murder in the South. As he spoke, hecklers hurled insults at him. Reverting to his stump-speaking days in Tennessee, he shouted back angry retorts, amid cries of "You be damned!" and "Don't get mad, Andy!" The dignity of his high office sank to a new low.

As a vote-getter, Johnson was highly successful—for the opposition. His inept speechmaking heightened the cry to "Stand by Congress" against the "Tailor of the Potomac." When the ballots were counted, the Republicans had rolled up more than a two-thirds majority in both houses of Congress.

Republican Reconstruction

The Republicans now had a veto-proof Congress and virtually unlimited control of Reconstruction policy. But moderates and radicals still disagreed over the best course to pursue in the South.

The radicals were led in the Senate by the courtly and principled idealist Charles Sumner, and in the House by crusty and vindictive Pennsylvania Congressman Thaddeus Stevens. Both tirelessly labored not only for black freedom but for racial equality. Still opposed to rapid restoration of the Southern states, the radicals wanted to keep them out as long as possible and apply federal power to bring about a drastic social and economic transformation in the South.

Primary source
Union as It Was, The
college.hmco.com/pic/kennedybrief7e

But moderate Republicans, more attuned to time-honored Republican principles of states' rights and self-government, preferred policies that restrained the states from abridging citizens' rights, rather than policies that directly involved the federal government in individual lives. The actual policies adopted by Congress showed the influence of both these schools of thought, though the moderates, as the majority faction, had the upper hand. And one thing both groups had come to agree on by 1867 was the necessity to enfranchise black voters, even if it took federal troops to do it.

Against a backdrop of vicious and bloody race riots that had erupted in several Southern cities, Congress passed the Reconstruction Act on March 2, 1867. This drastic legislation divided the South into five military districts, each commanded by a Union general and policed by blue-clad soldiers, about twenty thousand all told.

Congress additionally laid down stringent requirements for the readmission of the seceded states. The wayward states were required to ratify the Fourteenth Amendment, giving the former slaves their rights as citizens, and to guarantee in their state constitutions full suffrage for their former adult male slaves. Yet the act, reflecting moderate sentiment, stopped short of giving the freedmen land or education at federal expense. The overriding purpose of the moderates was to create an electorate in Southern states that would vote those states back into the Union on acceptable terms and thus free the federal government from direct responsibility for the protection of black rights. As later events would demonstrate, this approach proved woefully inadequate to the cause of justice for the blacks.

The radical Republicans still worried that once the unrepentant states were readmitted, they would amend their constitutions to withdraw the ballot from the blacks. They therefore sought the ironclad safeguard of incorporating black suffrage in the federal Constitution. This goal was finally achieved by the Fifteenth Amendment, passed by Congress in 1869 and ratified by the required number of states in 1870 (see the Appendix).

Military Reconstruction of the South not only usurped certain functions of the president as commander in chief but set up a martial regime of dubious legality. The Supreme Court had already ruled, in the case *Ex parte Milligan* (1866), that military tribunals could not try civilians,

The prominent suffragist and abolitionist Susan B. Anthony (1820–1906) was outraged over the proposed exclusion of women from the Fourteenth Amendment. In a conversation with her former male allies Wendell Phillips and Theodore Tilton, she reportedly held out her arm and declared,

"Look at this, all of you. And hear me swear that I will cut off this right arm of mine before I will ever work for or demand the ballot for the negro and not the woman."

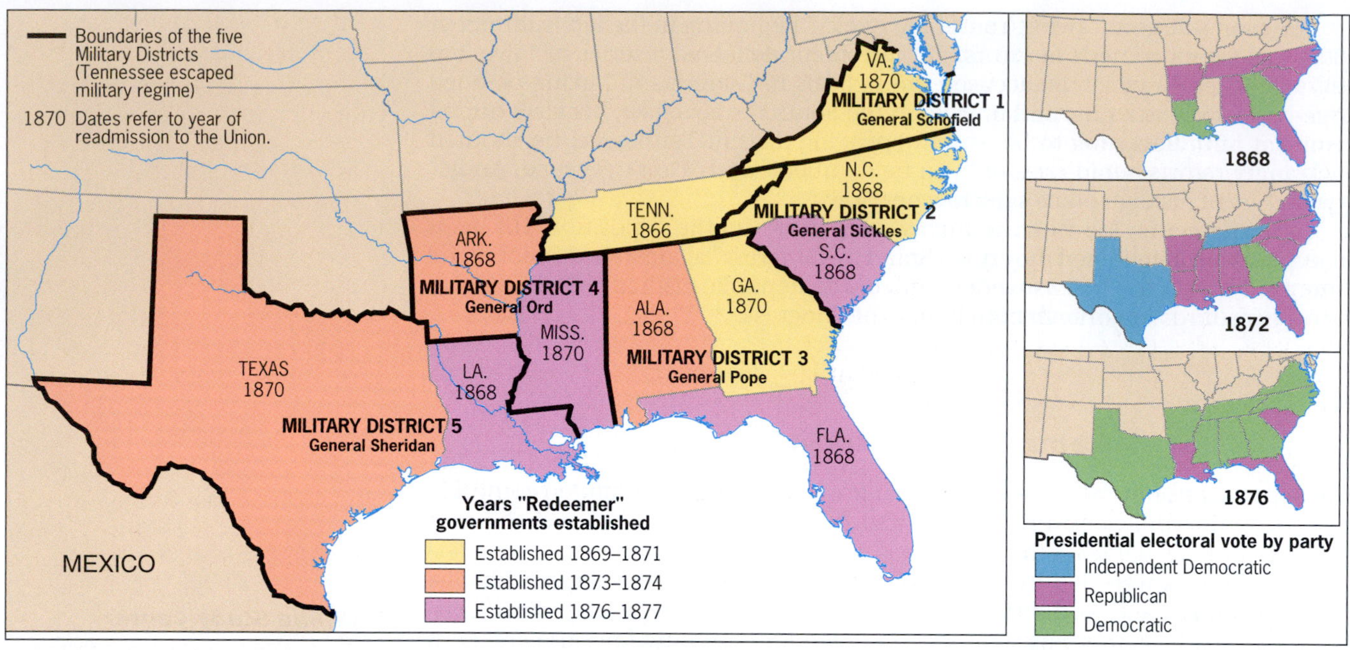

Military Reconstruction, 1867 (five districts and commanding generals) For many white Southerners, military Reconstruction amounted to turning the knife in the wound of defeat. An often-repeated story of later years had a Southerner remark, "I was sixteen years old before I discovered that damnyankee was two words."

Interactive map
The Reconstruction
college/hmco.com/pic/kennedybrief7e

even during wartime, in areas where the civil courts were open. Peacetime military rule seemed starkly contrary to the spirit of the Constitution, but for the time being the Supreme Court avoided offending the Republican Congress.

Prodded into line by federal bayonets, the Southern states got on with the task of constitution making. By 1870 all of them had reorganized their governments and had been accorded full rights. The hated "bluebellies" remained until the new regimes—usually called "radical" regimes—appeared to be firmly entrenched. Yet when the federal troops finally left a state, its government swiftly passed into the hands of white "Redeemer" regimes, which were inevitably Democratic. Finally, in 1877, the last federal muskets were removed from state politics, and the "solid" Democratic South congealed.

The passage of the three Reconstruction-era Amendments—the Thirteenth, Fourteenth, and Fifteenth—delighted former abolitionists but deeply disappointed advocates of women's rights. Women had played a prominent part in the prewar abolitionist movement, and in the eyes of many women the struggle for black freedom and the crusade for women's rights were one and the same. Now, feminist leaders reeled with shock when the Fourteenth Amendment, which defined equal national citizenship, for the first time inserted the word *male* into the Constitution in referring to a citizen's right to vote. When the Fifteenth Amendment proposed to prohibit denial of the vote on the basis of "race, color, or previous condition of servitude," women's rights leaders Susan B. Anthony and Elizabeth Cady Stanton wanted the word *sex* added to the list. They lost this battle, too. Fifty years would pass before the Constitution granted women the right to vote.

The Realities of Radical Reconstruction in the South

scalawag *A white Southerner who supported Republican Reconstruction after the Civil War.*

carpetbagger *A Northerner who moved to the South after the Civil War; hence, any politician who relocates for political advantage.*

Blacks now had freedom, of a sort. By 1867 Republican hesitation over black voting had given way to a hard determination to enfranchise the former slaves wholesale and immediately, while thousands of white Southerners were being denied the right to vote. By glaring contrast, most of the Northern states, before ratification of the Fifteenth Amendment in 1870, withheld the ballot from their tiny black minorities. White Southerners naturally concluded that the Republicans were hypocritical in insisting that blacks in the South be allowed to vote.

Having gained their right to suffrage, Southern black men seized the initiative and began to organize politically. Their primary vehicle became the Union League, originally a pro-Union organization based in the North. Assisted by Northern blacks, freedmen turned the League into a network of political clubs that educated members in their civic duties and campaigned for Republican candidates. The League's mission soon expanded to include building black churches and schools, representing black grievances before local employers and governments, and recruiting militias to protect black communities from white retaliation.

Though African American women did not obtain the right to vote, they too assumed new political roles. Black women faithfully attended the parades and rallies common in black communities during the early years of Reconstruction and helped assemble mass meetings in the newly constructed black churches. They even showed up at the constitutional conventions held throughout the South in 1867, monitoring the proceedings and participating in informal votes outside the convention halls.

But black men elected as delegates to the state constitutional conventions held the greater political authority. They formed the backbone of the black political community. At the conventions, they sat down with whites to hammer out new state constitutions, which most importantly provided for universal male suffrage.

The sight of former slaves holding office deeply offended their onetime masters, who lashed out with fury at the freedmen's white allies, labeling them "**scalawags**" and "**carpetbaggers.**" The so-called scalawags were Southerners, often former Unionists and Whigs, whom former Confederates wildly accused of plundering the treasuries of the Southern radical governments. The carpetbaggers were supposedly sleazy Northerners who had packed all their worldly goods into a carpetbag suitcase at war's end and had come South to seek personal power and profit. In fact, most were former Union soldiers and Northern businessmen and professionals who wanted to play a role in modernizing the "New South."

How well did the radical regimes rule? White southerners regularly portrayed the "Black Reconstruction" governments as run by ignorant and corrupt former slaves. Black voters did make up a majority of the electorate in five states, but only in South Carolina did blacks predominate in the lower house of the legislature. Many of the newly elected black legislators were literate and able; more than a few came from the ranks of the prewar free blacks who had acquired considerable education. More than a dozen black congressmen and two black United States senators, Hiram Revels and Blanche K. Bruce, both of Mississippi, did creditable work in the national capital.

In some radical regimes, there was truth to the charges of graft and corruption. This was especially true in South Carolina and Louisiana, where conscienceless promoters and other pocket-padders used politically inexperienced blacks as cat's-paws. The worst "black-and-white" legislatures purchased as "legislative supplies" such "stationery" as hams, perfumes, suspenders, bonnets, corsets, champagne, and a coffin. Yet this sort of corruption was no more outrageous than the scams and felonies being perpetrated in the North at the same time, especially in Boss Tweed's New York.

The radical legislatures also passed much desirable legislation. For the first time in Southern history, steps were taken toward establishing adequate public schools. Tax systems were streamlined; public works were launched; and property rights were guaranteed to women. Many of these reforms were so welcome that they were retained by the all-white "Redeemer" governments that later returned to power.

The Ku Klux Klan

Deeply embittered, some Southern whites resorted to savage measures against "radical" rule. Many whites resented the success and ability of black legislators as much as they resented alleged "corruption." A number of secret organizations mushroomed forth, the most notorious of which was the "Invisible Empire of the South," or Ku Klux Klan, founded in Tennessee in 1866. Besheeted nightriders, their horses' hoofs muffled, would pound and hammer on blacks' cabin doors or

Map Skill-Builder:
Understanding Political Maps

On page 330, the map of military Reconstruction, along with the three sidebar maps on the vote in three presidential elections, provides a wealth of political information on the relationship between the rise and decline of radical Reconstruction in the South. To understand this political information requires examining all *four* maps to look for patterns and correlations.

1. In the election of 1868, which *three* former Confederate states had not yet been readmitted to the Union, and therefore cast no electoral votes for president?
2. In 1872—the peak of radical Reconstruction—*two* states that had already been "redeemed" by conservative whites (color-coded yellow on the main Military Reconstruction map) nevertheless *still* voted Republican (Grant) in the election of 1872—suggesting the continuing strength of the radicals. Which were they?
3. By the election of 1876, radical Reconstruction had declined, and all but four southern states had been "redeemed." Three of those were the only southern states to vote Republican (Hayes) that year, but even one state still under radical rule voted Democratic. Which state was it?
4. Only *one* southern state voted consistently Democratic throughout Reconstruction, even when it was under radical rule, suggesting the weakness of Reconstruction there. Which was it? Recalling Civil War military events, what might explain the especially deep hostility to Republicans in that state?

Primary source
Mr. Solid South
college.hmco.com/pic/kennedybrief7e

terror (terrorist) *Using violence or the threat of violence in order to create intense fear and attempt to promote some political policy or objectives.*

use other tactics to frighten them. Those stubborn souls who persisted in their "upstart" ways were flogged, mutilated, or even murdered. In one Louisiana parish in 1868, whites in two days killed or wounded two hundred victims; a pile of twenty-five bodies was found half-buried in the woods. Such atrocious **terror** tactics proved partially effective in keeping many blacks from the polls.

Congress, outraged by this night-riding lawlessness, passed the harsh Force Acts of 1870 and 1871. Federal troops were able to stamp out much of the "lash law," but by this time the Invisible Empire had already done its work of intimidation. The Klan remained a refuge for numerous scoundrels and cutthroats who hid under its sheets, often continuing to operate under the guise of "dancing societies," "missionary clubs," and "rifle clubs."

White resistance undermined attempts to empower the blacks politically. The white South for many decades openly flouted the Fourteenth and Fifteenth Amendments. Wholesale disfranchisement of the blacks, starting conspicuously about 1890, was achieved by intimidation, fraud, and trickery. Among various underhanded schemes were the literacy tests, unfairly administered by whites to the advantage of illiterate whites. In the eyes of white Southerners, the goal of white supremacy fully justified these dishonorable devices.

Impeachment and Acquittal for Johnson

Radicals meanwhile had been sharpening their hatchets for President Johnson. Not content with curbing his authority, they decided to remove him altogether by constitutional processes.*

As an initial step, Congress in 1867 passed the Tenure of Office Act—as usual over Johnson's veto. Contrary to precedent, the new law required the president to secure the consent of the Senate before he could remove his cabinet members, including the secretary of war, Edwin M. Stanton, a holdover from the Lincoln administration. Although outwardly loyal to Johnson, Stanton was secretly serving as a spy and informer for the radicals.

Johnson provided the radicals with a pretext to begin impeachment proceedings when he abruptly dismissed Stanton early in 1868. The House of Representatives immediately voted 126 to 47 to impeach Andrew Johnson for "high crimes and misdemeanors," as required by the Constitution, charging him with various violations of the Tenure of Office Act. Two additional articles related to Johnson's verbal assaults on the Congress, involving "disgrace, ridicule, hatred, contempt, and reproach."

With evident zeal the radical-led Senate now sat as a court to try Johnson on the dubious impeachment charges. The House conducted the prosecution. The trial aroused intense public interest and, because only one thousand tickets for seats were printed, proved to be the biggest show of 1868. Johnson kept his dignity and maintained a discreet silence. His battery of attorneys argued that the president had fired Stanton merely to put a test case before the Supreme Court. The House prosecutors, including oily-tongued Benjamin F. Butler and embittered Thaddeus Stevens, had a harder time building a compelling case for impeachment.

On May 16, 1868, the day for voting in the Senate, the tension was electric, and heavy breathing could be heard in the galleries. By a margin of only one vote, the radicals failed to muster the two-thirds majority for Johnson's removal. Seven independent-minded Republican senators, courageously putting country above party, voted "not guilty."

Diehard radicals were infuriated. "The Country is going to the Devil!" cried the crippled Stevens as he was carried from the hall. But the nation, though violently aroused, accepted the verdict with a good temper that did credit to its political maturity.

The nation thus narrowly avoided a bad precedent that would have gravely weakened one of the three branches of the federal government. Johnson was

*For impeachment, see Art. I, Sec. II, para.5; Art. I, Sec. III, paras. 6, 7; Art. II, Sec. IV, in the Appendix.

clearly guilty of bad speeches, bad judgment, and bad temper, but not of "high crimes and misdemeanors." From the standpoint of the radicals, his greatest crime had been to stand inflexibly in their path.

The Purchase of Alaska

Johnson's administration, though largely reduced to a figurehead, achieved its most enduring success in the field of foreign relations. The Russians by 1867 were in a mood to sell the vast and chilly expanse of land now known as Alaska. The region had been ruthlessly "furred out" and was a growing economic liability to them. The Russians were therefore eager to unload their "frozen asset" on the Americans. They preferred the United States to any other purchaser primarily because they wanted to strengthen further the Republic as a barrier against their ancient enemy, Britain.

Freedmen Voting, Richmond, Virginia, 1871 The exercise of democratic rights by former slaves constituted a political and social revolution in the South, and was bitterly resented by whites.

In 1867 Secretary of State William Seward, an ardent expansionist, signed a treaty with Russia that transferred Alaska to the United States for the bargain price of $7.2 million. But Seward's enthusiasm for these frigid wastes was not shared by his ignorant or uninformed countrymen, who jeered at "Seward's Folly," "Seward's Icebox," and "Walrussia."

Then why did Congress and the American public sanction the purchase? For one thing Russia, alone among the great powers, had been conspicuously friendly to the North during the recent Civil War. Americans did not feel that they could offend their good friend the tsar by hurling his walrus-covered icebergs back into his face. Besides, the territory was rumored to be still teeming with furs, fish, and gold, and it might yet "pan out" profitably—as it later did with natural resources that included oil and gas.

The Heritage of Reconstruction

Many white Southerners regarded Reconstruction as a more grievous wound than the war itself. It left a festering scar that would take generations to heal. They resented the upending of their social and racial system, the political empowerment of blacks, and the insult of federal intervention in their local affairs. Yet given the explosiveness of the issues that had caused the war, and the bitterness of the fighting, the wonder is that Reconstruction was not far harsher than it was. Northern policymakers groped for the right policies, influenced as much by Southern responses to defeat and emancipation as by any specific plans of their own.

The Republicans acted from a mixture of idealism and political expediency. They wanted both to protect the freed slaves and to promote the fortunes of the Republican party. In the end their efforts backfired badly. Reconstruction conferred only fleeting benefits on the blacks, and it virtually extinguished the Republican party in the South for nearly one hundred years.

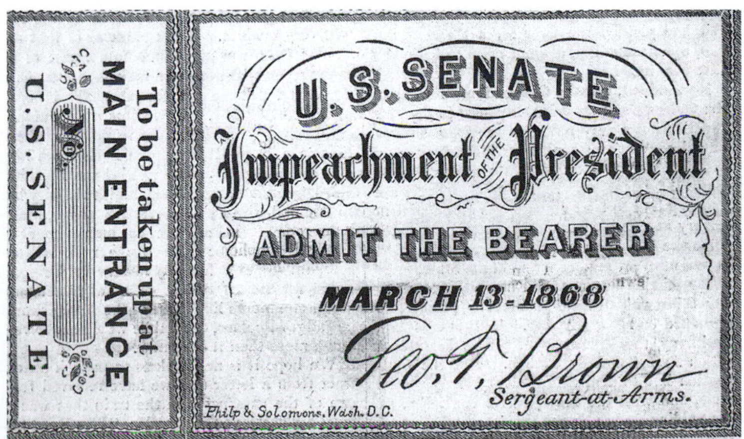

U.S. SENATE
No.
To be taken up at
MAIN ENTRANCE

U.S. SENATE
Impeachment of the President
ADMIT THE BEARER
MARCH 13-1868
Geo. T. Brown
Sergeant-at-Arms.
Philp & Solomons. Wash. D.C.

Impeachment Drama The impeachment proceedings against President Andrew Johnson, among the most severe constitutional crises in the Republic's history, were high political theater, and tickets were in sharp demand.

The remarkable ex-slave Frederick Douglass (1817?–1895) wrote in 1882,

"Though slavery was abolished, the wrongs of my people were not ended. Though they were not slaves, they were not yet quite free. No man can be truly free whose liberty is dependent upon the thought, feeling, and action of others, and who has himself no means in his own hands for guarding, protecting, defending, and maintaining that liberty. Yet the Negro after his emancipation was precisely in this state of destitution. . . . He was free from the individual master, but the slave of society. He had neither money, property, nor friends. He was free from the old plantation, but he had nothing but the dusty road under his feet. He was free from the old quarter that once gave him shelter, but a slave to the rains of summer and the frosts of winter. He was, in a word, literally turned loose, naked, hungry, and destitute, to the open sky."

Moderate Republicans never fully appreciated the extensive effort necessary to make the freed slaves completely independent citizens, nor the lengths to which Southern whites would go to preserve their system of racial dominance. Had Thaddeus Stevens's radical program of drastic economic reforms and heftier protection of political rights been enacted, things might well have been different. But deep-seated racism, ingrained American resistance to tampering with property rights, and rigid loyalty to the principle of local self-government, combined with spreading indifference in the North to the plight of blacks, formed too formidable an obstacle. Despite good intentions by Republicans, the Old South was in many ways more resurrected than reconstructed.

Chapter Summary

With the Civil War over, the nation faced the difficult problems of rebuilding the South, assisting the freed slaves, reintegrating the Southern states into the Union, and deciding who would direct the Reconstruction process.

The South was economically devastated and socially revolutionized by emancipation. As slaveowners reluctantly confronted the end of slave labor, blacks took their first steps in freedom. Black churches and freedmen's schools helped the former slaves begin to shape their own destiny.

The new President Andrew Johnson was politically inept and personally contentious. His attempt to implement a moderate plan of Reconstruction, along the lines originally suggested by Lincoln, fell victim to Southern whites' severe treatment of blacks and his own political blunders.

Republicans imposed harsh military Reconstruction on the South after their gains in the 1866 congressional elections. The Southern states reentered the Union with new radical governments, which rested partly on the newly enfranchised blacks, but also had support from some sectors of Southern society These governments were sometimes corrupt, but they also implemented important reforms, especially in education. For a time, acting from a mixture of idealism and political expediency, Republicans tried seriously to build a new Republican party in the South to guarantee black rights. But the divisions between moderate and radical Republicans meant that Reconstruction's aims were often limited and confused, despite successful passage of the important Fourteenth and Fifteenth Amendments guaranteeing black civil and voting rights.

Embittered whites hated the radical governments and mobilized reactionary terrorist organizations like the Ku Klux Klan to restore white supremacy. The radical Republican House of Representatives impeached Johnson, but the Senate failed narrowly to convict him. In the end, the inadequate Reconstruction policy, which never really addressed the deep economic and social legacy of slavery and the Civil War, failed disastrously and created as much or more bitterness than the war itself.

VARYING VIEWPOINTS

How Radical Was Reconstruction?

Few topics have triggered as much intellectual warfare as the "dark and bloody ground" of Reconstruction. The period provoked questions—sectional, racial, and constitutional—about which people felt deeply and remain deeply divided even today. Scholarly argument goes back conspicuously to a Columbia University historian, William A. Dunning, who wrote about Reconstruction as a kind of national disgrace, foisted on a prostrate region by vindictive and self-seeking radical Republican politicians.

In the 1920s, widespread suspicion that the Civil War itself had been a tragic and unnecessary blunder shifted attention to Northern politicians. Scholars like Howard Beale argued that the radical Republicans had masked a ruthless desire to exploit Southern resources and expand Republican power in the South behind a false "front" of concern for the freed slaves.

Although ignored by his contemporaries, the scholar and founder of the National Association for the Advancement of Colored People, W. E. B. Du Bois, wrote a sympathetic history of Reconstruction in 1935 that became the basis of historians' interpretations ever since. Following World War II, Kenneth Stampp and others, influenced by the modern civil rights movement, built on Du Bois's argument and claimed that Reconstruction had been a noble though ultimately failed attempt to extend American principles of equity and justice. By the early 1970s, this view had become orthodoxy, and it generally holds sway today. Yet some scholars, such as Michael Benedict and Leon Litwack, disillusioned with the inability to achieve full racial justice in the 1960s and 1970s, claimed to discover that Reconstruction was never really very radical, and argued that the Freedmen's Bureau and other agencies had merely allowed white planters to maintain local political and economic control.

More recently, Eric Foner has powerfully reasserted the argument that Reconstruction was a truly radical and noble attempt to establish an interracial democracy. Drawing on the work of Du Bois, Foner has emphasized that Reconstruction allowed blacks to form political organizations and churches and to establish some measure of economic independence. Many of the benefits of Reconstruction were erased by white Southerners during the Gilded Age, but in the twentieth century, constitutional principles and organizations developed during Reconstruction provided the foundation for the modern civil rights movement—which some have called the Second Reconstruction.

Steven Hahn's *A Nation Under Our Feet: Black Political Struggles in the Rural South from Slavery to the Great Migration* (2003) is the latest contribution to the literature on Reconstruction. Hahn emphasizes the assertiveness and ingenuity of African Americans in creating new political opportunities for themselves after emancipation.

APPENDIX

SUGGESTED READINGS

CHAPTER 1

PRIMARY SOURCE DOCUMENTS

Various English editions of Hernán Cortés's correspondence from Mexico are available, including *Five Letters, 1519–1526* (1929), trans. by J. Bayard Morris.* An important source from a *conquistador*'s perspective is Bernal Diaz del Castillo, *Historia Verdadera de la Conquista de la Nueva España,* selections of which have been recently translated into English in *The Discovery and Conquest of Mexico, 1517–1521,* edited by Genaro Garcia (1996). Bartolomé de Las Casas, *Thirty Very Judicial Propositions** (1552), and Juan Ginés de Sepúlveda, *The Second Democrates** (1547), reflect the Spanish *conquistadores'* efforts to understand the native peoples of the New World. See also Las Casas's *The Destruction of the Indies* (1542). *The Broken Spears: The Aztec Account of the Conquest of Mexico,** edited by Miguel León-Portilla (1962), is an anthology of texts compiled from indigenous sources. Olaudah Equiano, *Equiano's Travels** (1789), is a fascinating account by an African in the New World in the eighteenth century.

SECONDARY SOURCES

Brian M. Fagan reviews the evidence concerning the earliest humans to arrive in the Americas in *The Great Journey: The Peopling of Ancient America* (1987). Archaeologist Tom Dillehay revises estimates of settlement of the New World in *The Settlement of the Americas: A New Prehistory* (2000), which presents exciting new archaeological evidence. Alice Beck Keyhoe gives an engaging account of American Indian nations during the fifteen thousand years before Columbus in *America Before the European Invasions* (2002). For more on the pre-Columbian history of the Americas, see Norman Hammond, *Ancient Maya Civilization* (1982); Brian M. Fagan, *Kingdoms of Gold, Kingdoms of Jade: The Americas Before Columbus* (1991); and Stuart J. Fiedel, *Prehistory of the Americas* (1992). For a terrific study in cross-cultural perceptions between Columbus and Indians, see Tzvetan Todorov, *The Conquest of America* (1984). Immanuel Wallerstein, *The Modern World System: Capitalist Agriculture and the Origins of the European World in the Sixteenth Century* (1974), provides a theoretical overview of European colonization's international economic background. Early African history is sketched in J. D. Fage, *A History of West Africa* (1969), and John Thornton discusses Africa's role in the world economy in *Africa and Africans in the Making of the Atlantic World, 1400–1800* (1992). A fascinating brief synthesis of early European contact with the Americas is J. H. Elliott, *The Old World and the New, 1492–1650* (1970). For a comparative study, see Anthony Pagen, *Lords of All Worlds: Ideologies of Empire in Spain, Britain, and France* (1995). Alfred W. Crosby, Jr., discusses *The Columbian Exchange: Biological and Cultural Consequences of 1492* (1972). See the same author's *Ecological Imperialism: The Biological Expansion of Europe, 900–1900* (1986). A marvelously illustrated volume portraying the impact of America on the European imagination is Hugh Honour, *The New Golden Land* (1975). See also Kirkpatrick Sale, *The Conquest of Paradise: Christopher Columbus and the Columbian Legacy* (1990), and Herman J. Viola and Carolyn Margolis, *Seeds of Change: Five Hundred Years Since Columbus* (1991). D. W. Meinig presents a geographical overview of immigration in *The Shaping of America: A Geographical Perspective on 500 Years of History: Atlantic America, 1492–1800* (1986). Patricia Seed compares different forms of European conquest in *Ceremonies of Possession* (1995). For an engaging and comprehensive study of New World Iberian colonies from the preconquest period to the early nineteenth century, see Mark A. Burkholder and Lyman L. Johnson, *Colonial Latin America* (2000). Various aspects of the Spanish and Portuguese conquests of America are described in Charles Gibson, *Spain in America* (1966), and L. McAlister, *Spain and Portugal in the New World, 1492–1700* (1984). William H. Prescott, *History of the Conquest of Mexico* (1843) and *History of the Conquest of Peru* (1847) are two fascinating narrative histories of the nineteenth century. Nathan Wachtel presents the Indians' view of the Spanish conquest in *The Vision of the Vanquished* (1977). The spread of Spanish America northward is traced in Edward H. Spicer, *Cycles of Conquest: The Impact of Spain, Mexico, and the United States on the Indians of the Southwest, 1533–1960* (1962); Andrew L. Knaut, *The Pueblo Revolt of 1680: Conquest and Resistance in Seventeenth-Century New Mexico* (1997); Ramon A. Gutierrez, *When Jesus Came, the Corn Mothers Went Away* (1991); and David J. Weber's masterful synthesis, *The Spanish Frontier in North America* (1992).

CHAPTER 2

PRIMARY SOURCE DOCUMENTS

Richard Hakluyt, *Divers Voyages Touching the Discovery of America and the Islands Adjacent,* edited by J. W. Jones (1850), supplied the rationale for the establishment of English colonies in North America. John Smith, "Generall Historie of Virginia," in *Travels and Works of Captain John Smith,** edited by Edward Arber (1910), is an account by the amazing, vain man who steered Jamestown through its precarious first few years.

SECONDARY SOURCES

England's involvement in overseas settlement in the sixteenth century is described in David B. Quinn, *England and the Discovery of America, 1481–1620* (1974). In *The Elizabethans and the Irish* (1966), Quinn details the role of Ireland in the origins of Elizabethan colonization. The international economic background to colonization is sketched in Ralph Davis, *The Rise of the Atlantic Economies* (1973), and in Kenneth R. Andrews, *Trade, Plunder, and Settlement: Maritime Enterprise and the Genesis of the British Empire, 1480–1630* (1984). The immediate English backdrop is colorfully presented in Peter Laslett, *The World We Have Lost* (1965), and in Carl Bridenbaugh, *Vexed and Troubled Englishmen, 1590–1642* (1968). James Lang, *Conquest and Commerce: Spain and England in the Americas* (1975), is a comparative chronicle of colonial rivalries; Jack P. Greene, *Pursuits of Happiness: The Social Development of Early Modern British Colonies and the Formation of American Culture* (1988), compares the process of English colonization in different regions of North America and the Caribbean. Contact between Indian and European cultures is handled in Colin G. Calloway, *New Worlds for All: Indians, Europeans, and the Remaking of America* (1997), and James

*An asterisk indicates that the document, or an excerpt from it, can be found in David M. Kennedy and Thomas A. Bailey, eds., *The American Spirit: United States History as Seen by Contemporaries,* 11th ed. (Boston: Houghton Mifflin, 2006)

Axtell, *The Invasion Within: The Contest of Cultures in Colonial America* (1985). James Merrell, *The Indians' New World* (1989), which describes the wrenching experiences of the Catawba Indians, is the best ethnohistorical account of a single tribe for the early period. See also Daniel K. Richter, *The Ordeal of the Longhouse: The Peoples of the Iroquois League in the Era of European Colonization* (1992), and Richard White, *The Middle Ground: Indians, Empires, and Republics in the Great Lakes Region, 1650–1815* (1991). The Chesapeake region has continued to receive attention, especially in Paul G. E. Clemens, *The Atlantic Economy and Colonial Maryland's Eastern Shore* (1980); Lois Green Carr et al., eds., *Colonial Chesapeake Society* (1988); Lois Green Carr et al., *Robert Cole's World: Agriculture and Society in Early Maryland* (1991); Philip D. Morgan, *Slave Counterpoint: Black Culture in the Eighteenth-Century Chesapeake and Lowcountry* (1998); and James Horn, *Adapting to a New World: English Society in the Seventeenth-Century Chesapeake* (1994). Richard Dunn, *Sugar and Slaves: The Rise of the Planter Class in the English West Indies, 1624–1713* (1972), describes South Carolina society's West Indian roots. The most comprehensive account of the various colonial economies is contained in John J. McCusker and Russell R. Menard, *The Economy of British North America, 1607–1789* (1985). The role of slavery in early colonial society is examined perceptively in Edmund S. Morgan, *American Slavery, American Freedom* (1975). For a unique and important study of the role gender played in shaping racial ideologies in colonial Virginia, see Kathleen Brown, *Good Wives, Nasty Wenches, and Anxious Patriarchs* (1996). See also Peter Wood's account of South Carolina, *Black Majority* (1974), and Ira Berlin's overview, *Many Thousands Gone: The First Two Centuries of Slavery in North America* (1998). Gary Nash analyzes relations among Indians, European colonists, and blacks in *Red, White, and Black: The Peoples of Early America* (1974), as do Daniel H. Usner, Jr., in *Indians, Settlers, and Slaves in a Frontier Exchange Economy: The Lower Mississippi Valley Before 1783* (1992), and Timothy Silver in *A New Face on the Countryside: Indians, Colonists, and Slaves in South Atlantic Forests, 1500–1800* (1990). Daniel K. Richter examines European colonists through the eyes of Native Americans in *Facing East from Indian Country: A Native History of Early America* (2003).

CHAPTER 3

Primary Source Documents

John Winthrop, "A Model of Christian Charity" (1630), in *The American Primer,* edited Daniel Boorstin, outlines the goals of the Puritan errand into the wilderness. Winthrop's "Speech on Liberty"* (1645), in his *History of New England* (1853), established the colony's fundamental political principles. William Bradford, *Of Plymouth Plantation,** edited by Samuel E. Morison (1952), is a rich contemporary account.

Secondary Sources

New England has received more scholarly attention than any other colonial region. Harry Stout, *The New England Soul: Preaching and Culture in Colonial New England* (1986), is a comprehensive account. A brilliant and complex intellectual history is Perry Miller, *The New England Mind* (2 vols., 1939, 1953), a work that has long been a landmark for other scholars. Sacvan Bercovitch traces the heritage of the New England temperament in *The Puritan Origins of the American Self* (1975). Also see David Jaffe, *People of the Wachusett: Greater New England in History and Memory* (1999). Other interpretations of Puritanism include Charles Hambrick-Stowe, *The Practice of Piety* (1982), and Andrew Delbanco, *The Puritan Ordeal* (1989). David Hall, *Worlds of Wonder, Days of Judgment: Popular Religious Belief in Early New England* (1989), describes the relation between high Puritan doctrine and lay belief and practice. Jon Butler, *Awash in a Sea of Faith: Christianizing the American People* (1990), is comprehensive. John T. Ellis pays special attention to religious issues in *Catholics in Colonial America* (1965), as does Edmund S. Morgan in *Roger Williams: The Church and State* (1967). On other religious minorities, see Carla Gardina Pestana, *Quakers and Baptists in Colonial Massachusetts* (1991). For analyses of Puritan-Indian relations, see Francis Jennings, *The Invasion of America* (1975), and Neal Salisbury, *Manitou and Providence* (1982). For a fascinating account of some settlers' assimilation into Indian society, see John Demos, *The Unredeemed Captive: A Family Story from Early America* (1994). David S. Lovejoy discusses the impact of England's Glorious Revolution on the colonies in *The Glorious Revolution in America* (1975). Areas outside New England are dealt with in Gary Nash, *Quakers and Politics: Pennsylvania, 1681–1726* (1971); Patricia Bonomi, *A Factious People: Politics and Society in Colonial New York* (1971); Richard and Mary Dunn, eds., *The World of William Penn* (1986); Oliver A. Rink, *Holland on the Hudson: An Economic and Social History of Dutch New York* (1986); and Joyce D. Goodfriend, *Before the Melting Pot: Society and Culture in Colonial New York City, 1664–1730* (1992). The essays in Michael Zuckerman, ed., *Friends and Neighbors: Group Life in America's First Plural Society* (1982), argue that the middle colonies provide the best early model for America as a whole. Timothy H. Breen, *Puritans and Adventurers* (1980), draws contrasts between Virginia and New England.

CHAPTER 4

Primary Source Documents

The first slave laws of Virginia are collected in Warren M. Billings, ed., *The Old Dominion in the Seventeenth Century** (1975), as are first-hand accounts of Bacon's Rebellion. See also George L. Burr, ed., *Narratives of the Witchcraft Cases, 1648–1706** (1914).

Secondary Sources

On life and labor in the Chesapeake, consult Thad W. Tate and David L. Ammerman, eds., *The Chesapeake in the Seventeenth Century* (1979). Further probing economic conflicts and their role in the introduction of slavery is Timothy H. Breen and Stephen Innes, *Myne Owne Ground: Race and Freedom on Virginia's Eastern Shore, 1640–1676* (1980). Gloria Main chronicles *The Tobacco Colony: Life in Early Maryland, 1650–1719* (1982). Darrett B. Rutman and Anita H. Rutman examine Virginia in *A Place in Time: Middlesex County, Virginia 1650–1750* (1984). Daniel Blake Smith looks *Inside the Great House: Planter Family Life in Eighteenth-Century Chesapeake Society* (1980). Kenneth A. Lockridge analyzes the life of one of Virginia's most celebrated residents in *The Diary and Life of William Byrd II of Virginia, 1674–1744* (1987). Winthrop Jordan's fascinating *White over Black: American Attitudes Toward the Negro, 1550–1812* (1968) discusses the evolution of racial thought. Rhys Isaac's masterful *The Transformation of Virginia 1740–1790* (1999) explores the tumultuous role of religious and political conflicts in shaping colonial Virginia. Life in New England's towns and homes is scrutinized in John Demos, *A Little Commonwealth: Family Life in Plymouth Colony* (1970); Philip Greven, *Four Generations: Population, Land, and Family in Colonial Andover, Massachusetts* (1970); Kenneth Lockridge, *New England Town: Dedham* (1970); Christine Heyrman, *Commerce and Culture: The Maritime Communities of Colonial Massachusetts, 1690–1750* (1984); and Daniel Vickers, *Farmers and Fishermen: Two Centuries of Work in Essex County, Massachusetts, 1630–1850* (1994). For a less idealized portrait of early New England, see John F. Martin, *Profits in the Wilderness: Entrepreneurship and the Founding of New England Towns in the Seventeenth Century* (1991); Margret Ellen Newell, *From Dependency to Independence: Economic Revolution in Colonial New England* (1998); and Stephen Innes, *Creating the Com-*

monwealth: The Economic Culture of Puritan New England (1995). For more on the role of gender in seventeenth-century society, see Laurel T. Ulrich, *Good Wives: Image and Reality in the Lives of Women in Northern New England, 1650–1750* (1982); Marylynn Salmon, *Women and the Law of Property in Early America* (1986); Mary Beth Norton, *Founding Mothers and Fathers* (1996); Cornelia Hughes Dayton, *Women Before the Bar: Gender, Law, and Society in Connecticut, 1639–1789* (1995); Lisa Wilson, *Ye Heart of a Man: The Domestic Life of Men in Colonial New England* (1999); and Philip Greven, *The Protestant Temperament* (1977), which analyzes child-rearing practices. Edmund S. Morgan describes the crisis that beset the original Puritans when their children displayed a lesser degree of religiosity in *Visible Saints* (1963). David Grayson Allen emphasizes the persistence of English customs in *In English Ways: The Movement of Societies and the Transferral of English Local Law and Custom to Massachusetts Bay in the Seventeenth Century* (1981). See also David Cressy, *Coming Over: Migration and Communication Between England and New England in the Seventeenth Century* (1987), and David Hackett Fischer, *Albion's Seed: Four British Folkways in America* (1989). Witchcraft is the subject of Paul Boyer and Stephen Nissenbaum's *Salem Possessed* (1974), John Demos's *Entertaining Satan* (1982), and Carol F. Karlsen's *The Devil in the Shape of a Woman: Witchcraft in Colonial New England* (1987). Mary Beth Norton's recent reinterpretation of the Salem witchcraft trials, *In the Devil's Snare: The Salem Witchcraft Crisis of 1692* (2002), emphasizes New England's experience of frontier conflict in King William's War. See also Richard Godbeer, *The Devil's Dominion: Magic and Religion in Early New England* (1992), and Peter Charles Hoffer, *The Devil's Disciples: Makers of the Salem Witchcraft Trials* (1996). A sweeping survey that emphasizes the diversity of cultures already present in seventeenth-century America is E. Brooks Holifield, *Era of Persuasion: American Thought and Culture, 1521–1680* (1989). The relationship of Indians and New England whites to their environment is the subject of William Cronon's intriguing *Changes in the Land* (1983). David Konig, *Law and Society in Puritan Massachusetts: Essex County, 1629–1692* (1979), considers the role of law in mitigating social tensions.

CHAPTER 5

Primary Source Documents

Noting the ethnic diversity of colonial American society, Michel-Guillaume Jean de Crèvecoeur, *Letters from an American Farmer** (1904), and Benjamin Franklin, "Observations on the Increase of Mankind,"* in Jared Sparks, ed., *The Works of Benjamin Franklin* (1840), respectively celebrate and express unease at that diversity. Franklin's entertaining *Autobiography** (1868) is an indispensable guide to the values and preoccupations of his time. It includes an account of George Whitefield's visit to Philadelphia during the Great Awakening.

Secondary Sources

Social history is painted with broad strokes in James Henretta, *The Evolution of American Society, 1700–1815* (1973), and Jack Greene, *Pursuits of Happiness* (1988). Population trends are detailed in Robert V. Wells, *The Population of the British Colonies in America before 1776* (1975). Philip D. Curtin studies black slaves and white indentured servants in *The African Slave Trade: A Census* (1969). For pioneering work in historical demography, see Russell Menard's *Migrants, Servants and Slaves: Unfree Labor in Colonial British America* (2001), and Sharon V. Salinger, *"To Serve Well and Faithfully": Labor and Indentured Servants in Pennsylvania, 1682–1800* (1987). Bernard Bailyn captures the human face of migration and settlement on the eve of the Revolution in his masterful *Voyagers to the West* (1986). Several works detail the experiences of the very diverse groups who came to America during this period. The lives of convicts relocated to the United States are explored in A. Roger Ekirch, *Bound for America: The Transportation of British Convicts to the Colonies, 1718–1775* (1987); British immigrants in Bernard Bailyn, *The Peopling of British North America* (1986); Scottish immigrants in Alan L. Karras, *Sojourners in the Sun: Scottish Migrants in Jamaica and the Chesapeake, 1740–1800* (1992); German immigrants in Marianne S. Wokek, *Trade in Strangers: The Beginnings of Mass Migration to North America* (1999); and colonial immigration in general in Ida Altman and James Horn, eds., *"To Make America": European Emigration in the Early Modern Period* (1991). Large-scale economic patterns are traced in John J. McCusker and Russell R. Menard, *The Economy of British America, 1607–1789* (1991), and Alice H. Jones, *The Wealth of a Nation to Be: The American Colonies on the Eve of the Revolution* (1980). The complex interactions between whites and blacks are documented in Mechal Sobel, *The World They Made Together: Black and White Values in Eighteenth-Century Virginia* (1987), and William D. Piersen, *Black Yankees: The Development of an Afro-American Subculture in Eighteenth-Century New England* (1988). The toiling classes are probed in Gerald W. Mullin, *Flight and Rebellion: Slave Resistance in Eighteenth-Century Virginia* (1972); Gary B. Nash, *The Urban Crucible: Social Change, Political Consciousness and the Origins of the American Revolution* (1979); Allen Kulikoff, *Tobacco and Slaves: The Development of Southern Cultures in the Chesapeake, 1680–1800* (1986); Robert Orwell, *Masters, Slaves, and Subjects: The Culture of Power in the South Carolina Low Country* (1998); and Marcus Rediker, *Between the Devil and the Deep Blue Sea: Merchant Seamen, Pirates, and the Anglo-American Maritime World, 1700–1750* (1987). Nash links social conflict to the Great Awakening, as does Richard L. Bushman, *From Puritan to Yankee: Character and Social Order in Connecticut, 1690–1765* (1967). Patricia Bonomi also emphasizes religious conflict as a promoter of Revolutionary ideology in *Under the Cope of Heaven: Religion, Society, and Politics in Colonial America* (1986), as do the essayists in Ronald Hoffman and Peter J. Albert, eds., *Religion in a Revolutionary Age* (1994). Alan Heimert first explored the significance of the Great Awakening in *Religion and the American Mind* (1966); his interpretation has been revised by Jon Butler in *Awash in a Sea of Faith* (1992). Jon Butler has also written a cultural history of the development of American identity in the late eighteenth century in *Becoming America: The Revolution Before 1776* (2000). Other important works on religion include David S. Lovejoy, *Religious Enthusiasm in the New World: Heresy to Revolution* (1985), and Susan Juster, *Disorderly Women: Sexual Politics and Evangelicalism in Revolutionary New England* (1994). Cultural history is imaginatively presented in Howard M. Jones, *O Strange New World: American Culture in the Formative Years* (1964). Henry May's *The Enlightenment in America* is comprehensive (1976). The sometimes heroic dedication to education is portrayed by Lawrence Cremin, *American Education: The Colonial Experience, 1607–1783* (1970), and the general social implications of the early educational system are studied in James Axtell, *The School upon a Hill* (1974). Colonial politics are interpreted in a most suggestive way in Bernard Bailyn, *The Origins of American Politics* (1965). More fine-grained local studies are John Gilman Kolp, *Gentlemen and Freeholders: Electoral Politics in Colonial Virginia* (1998); Richard L. Bushman, *King and People in Provincial Massachusetts* (1985); Robert Zemsky, *Merchants, Farmers and River Gods: An Essay on Eighteenth-Century American Politics* (1971); Jackson Turner Main, *Society and Economy in Colonial Connecticut* (1985); Patricia Bonomi, *A Factious People: Politics and Society in Colonial New York* (1971); James T. Lemon, *The Best Poor Man's Country* (1972), which deals with Pennsylvania; and Daniel Blake Smith, *Inside the Great House: Planter Family Life in Eighteenth-Century Chesapeake Society* (1980). Timothy Breen examines the ways in which the increasing indebtedness of the Virginia planters changed their behavior in *Tobacco Culture: The Mentality of the Great Tidewater Planters on the Eve of Revolution* (1985).

CHAPTER 6

Primary Source Documents

"The Albany Plan of the Union" was the first great statement of colonial unity; "The Proclamation of 1763" forbade settlement west of the Appalachians. Both are collected in Henry Steele Commager, *Documents of American History.* Adolph B. Benson, ed., *The America of 1750; Petar Kalm's Travels in North America* (1937),* records the observations of a visiting Swedish naturalist with a keen eye for the behavior of humans.

Secondary Sources

A cutting-edge study of the major themes in Atlantic history is presented in David Armitage, ed., *The British Atlantic World, 1500–1800* (2002). For an analysis of Britain's concept of empire, also see Armitage's *Ideological Origins of the British Empire* (2000) and David Hancock, *Citizens of the World: London Merchants and the Integration of the British Atlantic Community* (1995). Further efforts to analyze the colonial empire are James Henretta, *"Salutary Neglect": Colonial Administration under the Duke of Newcastle* (1972); Michael Kammen's especially interesting *Empire and Interest* (1970); and John Brewer, *The Sinews of Power: War, Money and the English State, 1688–1783* (1989). The empire as seen through British eyes is captured in Paul David Nelson, *William Tryon and the Course of Empire: A Life in British Imperial Service* (1990). The French colonial effort is described in George M. Wrong, *The Rise and Fall of New France* (2 vols., 1928). William John Eccles presents a vivid study of French exploration and settlement in North America and the West Indies in *The French in North America, 1500–1783* (1998). Calvin Martin, *Keepers of the Game* (1978), offers a provocative interpretation of the fur trade and its impact on Indian societies. Other works on the role of Indians in larger imperial struggles include Armstrong Starkey, *European and Native American Warfare, 1615–1815* (1998); Francis Jennings, *Empire of Fortune: Crowns, Colonies and Tribes in the Seven Years War in America* (1988); Gregory Evans Dowd, *A Spirited Resistance: The North American Indian Struggle for Unity, 1745–1815* (1992); and Richard White, *The Middle Ground: Indians, Empires, and Republics in the Great Lakes Region, 1650–1815* (1991). The wars for empire in the eighteenth century are vividly narrated by Fred Anderson in *Crucible of War: The Seven Years' War and the Fate of Empire in British North America, 1754–1766* (2001). Anderson's *A People's Army: Massachusetts Soldiers and Society in the Seven Years' War* (1984) discusses the experience of colonial soldiers in forging resistance to Britain. Alan Rogers, *Empire and Liberty: American Resistance to the British Authority, 1755–1763* (1974), investigates American participation in the Seven Years' War, as does Douglas E. Leach, *Roots of Conflict: British Armed Forces and Colonial Americans, 1677–1763* (1986). Classic accounts are Francis Parkman's several volumes, condensed in *The Battle for North America,* edited by John Tebbel (1948), and *The Parkman Reader,* edited by Samuel E. Morison (1955).

CHAPTER 7

Primary Source Documents

Adam Smith, *An Inquiry into the Nature and Causes of the Wealth of Nations** (1776), is a penetrating analysis of British mercantilism. An intriguing Loyalist account of the Revolution, since reprinted, is Peter Oliver, *Origin and Progress of the American Rebellion* (1781). Patrick Henry, "Speech Before the Virginia House of Burgesses Against the Stamp Act"* (1765), was an influential statement of colonial opposition to British policy, as was John Dickinson's response to the Townshend Acts, *Letters from a Farmer in Pennsylvania* (1768). Revolutionary writings may also be found in Bernard Bailyn, ed., *Pamphlets of the American Revolution, 1750–1776* (1965). For contemporary accounts of the beginning of hostilities, see Peter Force, ed., *American Archives,* 4th series, vol. 2* (1839). For visual sources from the period, consult the edition compiled by Donald H. Cresswell, *The American Revolution in Drawings and Prints* (1975).

Secondary Sources

The Revolution is interpreted as a divinely ordained event in George Bancroft's *History of the United States of America* (1852). Edmund S. Morgan, *The Birth of the Republic, 1763–1789* (1959), is a brief account of the Revolutionary era. It stresses the happy coincidence of the revolutionaries' principles and their interests, as do Daniel Boorstin, *The Genius of American Politics* (1953), and Robert E. Brown, *Middle-Class Democracy and the Revolution in Massachusetts, 1691–1780* (1955). Lawrence Gipson, *The Coming of the Revolution, 1763–1775* (1954), summarizes his fifteen-volume masterwork. A more recent effort at a general synthesis is Robert Middlekauff, *The Glorious Cause: The American Revolution, 1763–1789* (1982). Robert R. Palmer, *The Age of the Democratic Revolution: A Political History of Europe and America, 1760–1800* (2 vols., 1959, 1964), places American events in the larger context of Western history. Two enlightening collections of essays are Jack P. Greene, ed., *The Reinterpretation of the American Revolution, 1763–1789* (1968), and Alfred F. Young, ed., *The American Revolution* (1976), which generally represents a "New Left" revisionist view, a perspective also found in Edward A. Countryman, *The American Revolution* (1987). A recent work that reinforces revisionist themes is Gary Nash, *The Unknown American Revolution: The Unruly Birth of Democracy and the Struggle to Create America* (2005). For an examination of ordinary people's experience in the Revolution, see Ray Raphael, *A People's History of the American Revolution* (2001). An interesting effort to blend British and American perspectives is Ian R. Christie and Benjamin W. Labaree, *Empire or Independence, 1760–1776* (1976). The sources of American dissatisfaction with the British imperial system can be traced in Carl Ubbelohde, *The American Colonies in the British Empire, 1607–1763* (1968), and Thomas C. Barrow, *Trade and Empire: The British Customs Service in Colonial America* (1967). Oliver M. Dickerson, *The Navigation Acts and the American Revolution* (1951), concludes that the navigation system did not put undue burdens on the colonies. Bernhard Knollenberg examines the effects of the British tightening of the imperial system in the 1760s in *Origin of the American Revolution, 1759–1766* (1960), as does Michael Kammen in *Empire and Interest* (1970). John Shy imaginatively explores an important aspect of the imperial system's effect on America in *Toward Lexington: The Role of the British Army in the Coming of the American Revolution* (1965). A perceptive short account of the American reaction to British initiatives is Edmund S. Morgan and Helen M. Morgan, *The Stamp Act Crisis* (1953). Benjamin W. Labaree discusses another instance of American reaction in *The Boston Tea Party* (1964). Pauline Maier focuses on the crucial role of the "mob" in *From Resistance to Revolution: Colonial Radicals and the Development of American Opposition to Britain, 1765–1776* (1972). The British side is told in Peter D. G. Thomas, *British Politics and the Stamp Act Crisis* (1975), *The Townshend Duties Crisis* (1987), and *Tea Party to Independence* (1991). Bernard Bailyn's seminal *Ideological Origins of the American Revolution* (1967) stresses the importance of ideas in pushing the Revolution forward, as well as the colonists' fears of a conspiracy against their liberties. John Philip Reid emphasizes legal ideas in *Constitutional History of the American Revolution: The Authority of Rights* (1987), as does Jerrilyn Greene Marston in *King and Congress: The Transfer of Political Legitimacy, 1774–1776* (1987). Useful local studies of American resistance are Richard D. Brown, *Revolutionary Politics in Massachusetts* (1970); Woody Holton, *Forced Founders: Indians, Debtors, Slaves, and the Making of the American Revolution in Virginia* (1999). Richard Ryerson, *The Revolution Is Now Begun: The Radical Committees of Philadelphia, 1765–1776* (1978); Joseph S. Tiedmann, *Reluctant Revolutionaries: New York City and the Road to Independence, 1763–1776* (1997); and David Hackett Fischer, *Paul*

Revere's Ride (1994). On the meaning of the Revolution for African Americans, see Sylvia R. Frey, *Water from the Rock: Black Resistance in a Revolutionary Age* (1991). Ordinary artisans' involvement in Revolutionary events is the subject of Alfred F. Young's *The Shoemaker and the Tea Party* (1999). Helpful biographies of key Revolutionary figures include Richard Beeman, *Patrick Henry* (1974); Merrill D. Peterson, *Thomas Jefferson and the New Nation* (1970); Dumas Malone, *Jefferson and His Time* (5 vols., 1948–1974); C. Bradley Thompson, *John Adams and the Spirit of Liberty* (1998); and Pauline Maier, *The Old Revolutionaries: Political Lives in the Age of Samuel Adams* (1980). Imaginative cultural history is found in Robert A. Gross, *The Minutemen and Their World* (1976). Edward A. Countryman emphasizes class conflict in *A People in Revolution: The American Revolution and Political Society in New York, 1760–1790* (1981). A psychological approach to the problem of the Revolutionary generation's assault on established authority is taken in Jay Fliegelman, *Prodigals and Pilgrims: The American Revolution Against Patriarchal Authority, 1750–1800* (1982).

CHAPTER 8

Primary Source Documents

Thomas Paine's fiery *Common Sense** (1776) is the manifesto of the Revolution. "The Declaration of Independence"* (1776) is one of the foundations of American political theory. For eyewitness accounts of the war, see John C. Dann, *The Revolution Remembered* (1980). See also the "Treaty of Peace with Great Britain" (1783), in Henry Steele Commager, *Documents of American History.*

Secondary Sources

The war is sketched in Don Higginbotham's excellent military history, *The War of American Independence: Military Attitudes, Policies, and Practice, 1763–1789* (1971). On the implications of the Revolutionary conflict, see John Shy, *A People Numerous and Armed: Reflections on the Military Struggle for American Independence* (1976); E. Wayne Carp, *To Starve the Army at Pleasure: Continental Army Administration and American Political Culture, 1775–1783* (1984); Charles Royster, *A Revolutionary People at War: The Continental Army and the American Character* (1980); Mark V. Kwasny, *Washington's Partisan War, 1775–1783* (1996); and Ronald Hoffman et al., eds., *An Uncivil War: The Southern Backcountry During the American Revolution* (1985). The conflict is considered in its European setting in Piers Mackesy, *The War for America, 1775–1783* (1964). Carl Becker's classic *The Declaration of Independence* (1922) is masterful; on the same subject, see also Garry Wills, *Inventing America: Jefferson's Declaration of Independence* (1980), and Pauline Maier, *American Scripture: The Making of the Declaration of Independence* (1997). The role of the Loyalists is treated in Robert M. Calhoon, *The Loyalists in Revolutionary America* (1973); Mary Beth Norton, *The British-Americans: The Loyalist Exiles in England* (1972); John E. Ferling, *The Loyalist Mind: Joseph Galloway and the American Revolution* (1977); Robert M. Calhoon, *Loyalists and Community in North America* (1994); Janice Potter-MacKinnon, *While the Women Only Wept: Loyalist Refugee Women* (1993); and Bernard Bailyn's unusually sensitive biography of the governor of colonial Massachusetts, *The Ordeal of Thomas Hutchinson* (1974). General treatments of an often-neglected subject are Benjamin Quarles, *The Negro in the American Revolution* (1961); Ronald Hoffman and Ira Berlin, eds., *Slavery and Freedom in the Age of the American Revolution* (1983); and Sylvia R. Frey, *Water from the Rock: Black Resistance in a Revolutionary Age* (1991). See also Duncan J. MacLeod, *Slavery, Race and the American Revolution* (1974), and David B. Davis, *The Problem of Slavery in the Age of Revolution, 1770–1823* (1975), an able, gracefully written book. International implications are developed in James H. Hutson, *John Adams and the Diplomacy of the American Revolution* (1980), and Jonathan R. Dull, *A Diplomatic History of the American Revolution* (1985). Attention to the social history of the Revolution has been largely inspired by John F. Jameson's seminal *The American Revolution Considered as a Social Movement* (1926). Jackson T. Main, *The Social Structure of Revolutionary America* (1969), takes the exploration further along the same lines, with conclusions somewhat at variance with Jameson's. Local studies of this issue include Alan Taylor, *Liberty Men and Great Proprietors: The Revolutionary Settlement on the Maine Frontier, 1760–1820* (1990); Steven Rosswurm, *Arms, Country, and Class: The Philadelphia Militia and the "Lower Sort" During the American Revolution* (1987); and Billy G. Smith, *The "Lower Sort": Philadelphia's Laboring People, 1750–1800* (1990). For information on the role of Indians in the Revolution, see Barbara Graymont, *The Iroquois in the American Revolution* (1972); Isabel T. Kelsay, *Joseph Brant, 1743–1807: Man of Two Worlds* (1984); and Colin G. Calloway, *The American Revolution in Indian Country* (1995). Thomas Doerflinger describes economic change during the Revolution in *A Vigorous Spirit of Enterprise: Merchants and Economic Development in Revolutionary Philadelphia* (1986). Interesting biographies are Samuel E. Morison's swashbuckling *John Paul Jones* (1959); Eric Foner, *Tom Paine and Revolutionary America* (1976); and James T. Flexner, *George Washington in the American Revolution, 1775–1783* (1968). British troubles are laid bare in William B. Willcox, *Portrait of a General: Sir Henry Clinton in the War of Independence* (1964). Women are the subject of Linda K. Kerber, *Women of the Republic: Intellect and Ideology in Revolutionary America* (1980); Mary Beth Norton, *Liberty's Daughters: The Revolutionary Experience of American Women* (1980); and Joy Day Buel and Richard Buel, Jr., *The Way of Duty: A Woman and Her Family in Revolutionary America* (1984). Michael Kammen brilliantly evokes the ways that the Revolution has been enshrined in the national memory in *A Season of Youth: The American Revolution and the Historical Imagination* (1978).

CHAPTER 9

Primary Source Documents

A comparison of the text of the Articles of Confederation (1781), in Henry Steele Commager, *Documents of American History,* with the Constitution* makes an intriguing study. See also Madison, Hamilton, and Jay's explanations of the Constitution in *The Federalist* papers, especially *Federalist* No. 10.* Additional primary sources may be found in Bernard Bailyn, ed., *The Debate on the Constitution: Federalist and Antifederalist Speechs, Articles, and Letters During the Struggle over Ratification* (1993). For visual sources from the period, consult *The American Revolution in Drawings and Prints* (1975), a volume compiled by Donald H. Cresswell.

Secondary Sources

John Fiske, in *The Critical Period of American History* (1888), portrayed America under the Articles of Confederation as a crisis-ridden country. His view is sharply qualified by Merrill Jensen in *The New Nation* (1950). Jack N. Rakove's *The Beginnings of National Politics* (1979) offers a history of the Continental Congress that substantially revises Jensen's work. Especially informative is Gordon S. Wood's massive and brilliant study of the entire period, *The Creation of the American Republic, 1776–1787* (1969), and his equally compelling work, *The Radicalism of the American Revolution* (1991), which documents the relative egalitarianism that swept revolutionary society during and after the war. For a similar argument that relies on the material culture of the era, see Richard Bushman, *The Refinement of America: Persons, Houses, Cities* (1992). See also Richard B. Morris, *The Forging of the Union, 1781–1787* (1987). For the intellectual foundations of the political economy, see Cathy Matson and Peter Onuf, *A Union of Interests: Political and Economic Thought in Revolutionary America* (1990). An influential transatlantic perspective on the roots of American republicanism is J. G. A. Pocock, *The Machi-*

avellian Moment: Florentine Political Thought and the Atlantic Republican Tradition (1975). Edmund S. Morgan also looks at both Britain and America in *Inventing the People: The Rise of Popular Sovereignty in England and America* (1988). On the state constitutions, see Jackson T. Main, *The Sovereign States, 1775–1783* (1973), and Willi P. Adams, *The First American Constitutions* (1980). Peter S. Onuf carefully examines the Northwest Ordinance in *Statehood and Union: A History of the Northwest Ordinance* (1987). On the Constitutional Convention, see Richard Bernstein's superb synthesis of current scholarship, *Are We to Be a Nation? The Making of the Constitution* (1987). Bernstein's work was one of a host of useful studies inspired by the bicentennial of the drafting of the Constitution. Others include Ruth Bloch, *Visionary Republic: Millennial Themes in American Thought, 1756–1800* (1986); Richard Beeman et al., eds., *Beyond Confederation: Origins of the Constitution and American National Identity* (1987); Leonard Levy, *Original Intent and the Framers' Constitution* (1988); and Jack N. Rakove, *Original Meanings: Politics and Ideas in the Making of the Constitution* (1996). For a more general interpretation of the Constitution's role in American society, see Michael G. Kammen, *A Machine That Would Go of Itself* (1986). Thornton Anderson, *Creating the Constitution* (1993), and Robert A. Rutland, *The Ordeal of the Constitution* (1966), describe the ratification struggle. Charles A. Beard caused a stir with the class-based analysis he offered in *An Economic Interpretation of the Constitution of the United States* (1913). It is seriously weakened by two blistering attacks: Robert E. Brown, *Charles Beard and the Constitution* (1956), and Forrest McDonald, *We the People: The Economic Origins of the Constitution* (1958). See also McDonald's *E Pluribus Unum: The Formation of the American Republic, 1776–1790* (1965). Jackson T. Main, *The Anti-Federalists* (1961), partially rehabilitates Beard. Gary Nash's *Race and Revolution* (1990) offers a perceptive study of controversies over race and slavery in the making of the Constitution, as do the contributors to John P. Kaminski, ed., *A Necessary Evil? Slavery and the Debate over the Constitution* (1995). David Szatmary is perceptive on *Shays' Rebellion* (1980), as are the contributors to Robert Gross, ed., *In Debt to Shays* (1993). On similar episodes of agrarian radicalism, see Alan Taylor, *Liberty Men and Great Proprietors: The Revolutionary Settlement on the Maine Frontier, 1760–1820* (1990). Charles R. Kesler has edited a collection of essays on *The Federalist* papers entitled *Saving the Revolution: The Federalist Papers and the American Founding* (1987). Also see Morton White, *Philosophy, The Federalist, and the Constitution* (1987). A concise summary of the original federalist-antifederalist debate is Herbert J. Storing, *What the Anti-Federalists Were For* (1981). Relevant biographical studies of merit are Richard Brookhiser, *Alexander Hamilton, American* (1999), and Jack Rakove, *James Madison and the Creation of the American Republic* (2002). For an engaging study of the political negotiations and infighting among several members of the founding generations, see Joseph Ellis, *Founding Brothers: the Revolutionary Generation* (2001).

CHAPTER 10

Primary Source Documents

"The Report on Manufactures" (in Daniel Boorstin, ed., *American Primer*), the last of Alexander Hamilton's messages to Congress, presented the case for the development of American industry. Thomas Jefferson expounded his views in *Notes on the State of Virginia* (1784). For further study of the Hamiltonian-Jeffersonian debate, see Harold C. Syrett, ed. *The Papers of Alexander Hamilton* (27 vols., 1961–1987), and Julian Boyd et al., eds., *The Papers of Thomas Jefferson* (30 vols., 1950–2003). Important salvos in the battle between national power and state sovereignty, and between Federalists and Jeffersonians, were the Virginia* and Kentucky resolutions (1798) and the reply of Rhode Island* (1799). Washington's Farewell Address* (1796) established the foundation for American attitudes about party politics and foreign policy. See also Benjamin Franklin Bache's stinging editorial on Washington's retirement, *Philadelphia Aurora** (1797).

Secondary Sources

Perceptive introductions are provided in James Roger Sharp's succinct *American Politics in the Early Republic: The New Nation in Crisis* (1993) and Stanley Elkins and Eric McKitrick's comprehensive work, *The Age of Federalism: The Early American Republic, 1788–1800* (1993). On administration, see Ronald Hoffman, *Launching the "Extended Republic": The Federalist Era* (1996). On the economy, see Paul Gilje, *Wages of Independence: Capitalism in the Early American Republic* (1997). Innovative work on political culture in the early national period can be found in James Sharp, *American Politics in the Early Republic* (1993), and Joanne Freeman, *Affairs of Honor* (2001). On the Bill of Rights, see Bernard Schwartz, *The Great Rights of Mankind: A History of the American Bill of Rights* (1991), and Patrick L. Conley and John P. Kaminski, eds., *The Bill of Rights and the States: The Colonial and Revolutionary Origins of American Liberties* (1992). On the use of party politics, see Richard Hofstadter's thoughtful *The Idea of a Party System* (1969); Richard Buel, Jr., *Securing the Revolution: Ideology in American Politics, 1789–1815* (1972); John Zvesper, *Political Philosophy and Rhetoric: A Study of the Origins of American Party Politics* (1977); John F. Hoadley, *Origins of American Political Parties, 1789–1803* (1986); and Lance Banning, ed., *After the Constitution: Party Conflict in the New Republic* (1989). Other interpretations of that subject, stressing the ideology of republicanism, are Drew McCoy, *The Elusive Republic: Political Economy in Jeffersonian America* (1980), and Lance Banning, *The Jeffersonian Persuasion* (1978). Charles G. Steffens examines the political beliefs of workers in *The Mechanics of Baltimore: Workers and Politics in the Age of Revolution, 1763–1812* (1984), as do Michael Merrill and Sean Wilentz in their introduction to the edited volume *The Key of Liberty: The Life and Democratic Writings of William Manning, "A Laborer," 1747–1814* (1992). For a trenchant analysis of Jeffersonianism, see Joyce Appleby, *Capitalism and a New Social Order: The Republican Vision* (1984), whose analysis emphasizes the role of liberalism in American political thought, a point previously made by Louis Hartz in *The Liberal Tradition in America* (1955). Also illuminating is Gerald Stourzh, *Alexander Hamilton and the Idea of Republican Government* (1970). Thomas P. Slaughter focuses on *The Whiskey Rebellion: Frontier Epilogue to the American Revolution* (1986). A comprehensive biography is James T. Flexner, *George Washington and the New Nation, 1783–1793* (1969). An engaging account is Joseph Ellis, *His Excellency: George Washington* (2004). Consult also Forrest McDonald, *The Presidency of George Washington* (1974), and Garry Wills, *Cincinnatus: George Washington and the Enlightenment* (1984). Of special interest is Richard H. Kohn, *Eagle and Sword: The Federalists and the Creation of the Military Establishment in America, 1783–1802* (1975). On aspects of foreign policy, see Alexander De Conde, *Entangling Alliance* (1958); Gilbert Lycan, *Alexander Hamilton and American Foreign Policy* (1970); Jerald Combs, *The Jay Treaty* (1970); Lawrence S. Kaplan, *Colonies into Nation: American Diplomacy, 1763–1801* (1972); and Daniel G. Lang, *Foreign Policy in the Early Republic: The Law of Nations and the Balance of Power* (1985). For the view from across the Atlantic, see Charles R. Ritcheson, *Aftermath of Revolution: British Policy Toward the United States, 1783–1795* (1969). On Adams, consult Page Smith, *John Adams* (2 vols., 1962), and Stephen G. Kurtz, *The Presidency of John Adams* (1957). James M. Smith, *Freedom's Fetters* (1956), treats the Alien and Sedition Acts, as does Leonard Levy in *Legacy of Suppression* (1960).

CHAPTER 11

Primary Source Documents

Thomas Jefferson's "First Inaugural Address" (1801), in Henry Steele Commager, *Documents of American History,* echoed the themes of Washington's Farewell Address and set the tone for his presidency. Reuben G. Thwaites, ed., *Original Journals of the Lewis and Clark Ex-*

*pedition** (1904), chronicles the explorers' adventures. For the political flavor of the age, see the debate over the Embargo Act* (1807); for constitutional history, read the decision of John Marshall in *Marbury* v. *Madison** (1803). See James Madison, "War Message"* (1812), in James D. Richardson, ed., *Messages and Papers of the Presidents,* vol. 1 (1896), and the protest of thirty-four Federalist congressmen, *Annals of Congress,** 12th Cong., 1st sess., 2219–2221 (1812). John Marshall's decision in *McCulloch* v. *Maryland,** 4 Wheaton 316 (1819), is a leading statement of the era's surging nationalism.

Secondary Sources

A monument of American historical writing is Henry Adams, *History of the United States During the Administrations of Jefferson and Madison* (9 vols., 1889–1891), available in a one-volume abridgement edited by Ernest Samuels. Especially fascinating are Adams's prologue and epilogue on the United States in 1800 and 1817. A brief introduction is given in Marshall Smelser, *The Democratic Republic, 1801–1815* (1968). For a succinct study of Marshall's life and legal thought, see Jean Edward Smith, *John Marshall: Definer of a Nation* (1996). A helpful analysis of challenges faced by the judiciary is Richard E. Ellis, *The Jeffersonian Crisis: Courts and Politics in the New Republic* (1971). For a broad understanding of legal developments in this period, see Lawrence Friedman, *A History of American Law* (1973); Morton J. Horwitz, *The Transformation of American Law, 1780–1860* (1977); and Alfred H. Kelly, Winfred A. Harbison, and Herman Belz, *The American Constitution: Its Origins and Development* (6th ed., 1983). On the Supreme Court, see R. Kent Newmyer, *The Supreme Court Under Marshall and Taney* (1986), and G. Edward White, *The Marshall Court and Cultural Change, 1815–1835* (1988). Politics are treated in a broad, imaginative context in James S. Young, *The Washington Community, 1800–1829* (1966). For the important role women played in early America's political society, see Catherine Allgor, *Parlor Politics* (2000). See also Robert M. Johnstone, Jr., *Jefferson and the Presidency* (1979), and the Joyce Appleby, Lance Banning, and Drew McCoy volumes cited in Chapter 10. Other works include Joseph Ellis, *American Sphinx: The Character of Thomas Jefferson* (1997), and Robert B. Tucker and David Hendrickson, *Empire of Liberty: The Statecraft of Thomas Jefferson* (1990). Noble E. Cunningham, Jr., *In Pursuit of Reason: The Life of Thomas Jefferson* (1987), is a short biography. The standard scholarly biography is Merrill D. Peterson, *Thomas Jefferson and the New Nation* (1970). Peterson has also scrutinized *The Jefferson Image in the American Mind* (1960). Forrest McDonald is highly critical of his subject in *The Presidency of Thomas Jefferson* (1976). Leonard Levy debunks Jefferson's liberalism in *Jefferson and Civil Liberties* (1963); Anthony Wallace examines Jefferson's racial ideas and his policies toward Native Americans in *Jefferson and the Indians* (1999); and Garry Wills does the same for black slaves in *Negro President: Thomas Jefferson and the Slave Power* (2003). See also Reginald Horsman, *Expansion and American Indian Policy, 1783–1812* (1967), and Gregory Evans Dowd, *A Spirited Resistance: The North American Indian Struggle for Unity, 1745–1815* (1992). Donald Jackson, *Thomas Jefferson and the Stony Mountain: Exploring the West from Monticello* (1981), captures Jefferson's fascination with the West. See also Stephen E. Ambrose's spirited biography of Meriwether Lewis, *Undaunted Courage* (1996). An engaging and recent study of the origins and diplomacy of the Louisiana Purchase is Jon Kukla's *A Wilderness so Immense* (2003). The embargo is treated in Burton Spivak, *Jefferson's English Crisis: Commerce, Embargo and the Republican Revolution* (1979). See also Doron S. Ben-Atar, *The Origins of Jeffersonian Commercial Policy and Diplomacy* (1993). Daniel Boorstin vividly evokes the intellectual climate of the age in *The Lost World of Thomas Jefferson* (1948). Irving Brant looks at *James Madison, Secretary of State* (1953), and F. E. Ewing examines Jefferson's powerful Treasury secretary in *America's Forgotten Statesman: Albert Gallatin* (1959). An important work that sets the War of 1812 in a broad context of early American history is J. C. A. Stagg, *Mr. Madison's War: Politics, Diplomacy and Warfare in the Early American Republic* (1983). Also see Steven Watts, *The Republic Reborn: War and the Making of Liberal America, 1790–1820* (1987), and Donald R. Hickey, *The War of 1812: A Forgotten Conflict* (1989). On the causes of the war, Julius W. Pratt, *Expansionists of 1812* (1925), stresses western pressures; Bradford Perkins, *Prologue to War: England and the United States, 1805–1812* (1961), and Reginald Horsman, *The Causes of the War of 1812* (1962), discuss free seas; and Roger H. Brown, *The Republic in Peril, 1812* (1964), emphasizes the need for saving the republican form of government.

CHAPTER 12

Primary Source Documents

Timothy Dwight offers a participant's view of the opposition to the War of 1812 in *The History of the Hartford Convention** (1833). Charles F. Adams, ed., *Memoirs of John Quincy Adams** (1875), offers a behind-the-scenes portrait of the creation of the Monroe Doctrine. See also the text of Monroe's public statement in James D. Richardson, ed., *Messages and Papers of the Presidents,** vol. 2 (1896). "The Missouri Compromise" (1819–1820), in Henry Steele Commager, *Documents of American History,* reveals the dangerous sectional animosities underlying such national pride.

Secondary Sources

On the War of 1812, see the books by J. C. A. Stagg, Steven Watts, and Donald R. Hickey cited in Chapter 11. Lester D. Langley, *The Americans in the Age of Revolution, 1750–1850* (1996), takes a comparative approach to the history of the Western Hemisphere. On Indian affairs and westward expansion, see Dorothy Jones, *License for Empire: Colonialism by Treaty in Early America* (1982), and the works of R. David Edmunds, *The Shawnee Prophet* (1983) and *Tecumseh and the Quest for Indian Leadership* (1984). The relevant volumes of Henry Adams's nine-volume *History of the United States* (1889–1891) still contain magnificent reading, both on the war and on the peace. Federalist reaction to Republican foreign policy is vividly etched in David H. Fisher, *The Revolution of American Conservatism* (1965), and James M. Banner, *To the Hartford Convention: The Federalists and the Origins of Party Politics in Massachusetts* (1970). Consult also James H. Broussard, *The Southern Federalists, 1800–1816* (1979). Irving Brant argues that James Madison was a strong president in *James Madison: Commander in Chief, 1812–1836* (1961). More recent treatments of Madison include Robert A. Rutland, *James Madison: The Founding Father* (1987); Drew R. McCoy, *The Last of the Fathers: James Madison and the Republican Legacy* (1989); and Jack N. Rakove, *James Madison and the Creation of the American Republic* (1990). Other useful biographical studies are Robert Remini, *Henry Clay: Statesman for the Union* (1991), and David Heidler, *Old Hickory's War: Andrew Jackson and the Quest for Empire* (2003). An excellent introduction to nationalism is George Dangerfield, *The Awakening of American Nationalism, 1815–1828* (1965). See also Robert H. Wiebe's ambitious *Opening of American Society: From the Adoption of the Constitution to the Eve of Disunion* (1984). Arand Otto Mayr and Robert C. Post, eds., detail *Yankee Enterprise: The Rise of the American System of Manufactures* (1981). Glover Moore, *The Missouri Controversy, 1819–1821* (1953), and Charles S. Sydnor, *The Development of Southern Sectionalism, 1819–1848* (1948), place the Missouri Compromise in a broader context. On the Monroe Doctrine, the classic text is Dexter Perkins, *A History of the Monroe Doctrine* (1955). James E. Lewis, *The American Union and the Problem of Neighborhood* (1998), places the Monroe Doctrine in a new interpretive context. Ernest R. May ties the doctrine to domestic politics, especially the impending election of 1824, in *The Making of the Monroe Doctrine* (1975). See also Harry Ammon, *James Monroe: The Quest for National Identity* (1971), as well as James Lewis, *John Quincy Adams: Policymaker for the Union* (2001).

CHAPTER 13

Primary Source Documents

Davy Crockett, *Exploits and Adventures in Texas** (1836), is a lively description of the democratic political order of Jacksonian America. James Fenimore Cooper's *The American Democrat** (1838) offers an incisive commentary on the era's politics, while C. W. Janson, *The Stranger in America, 1793–1806** (1807), exposes the seamier aspects of American egalitarianism. A still-powerful classic treatise on the Jacksonian period is Alexis de Tocqueville, *Democracy in America* (1835, 1840). On the Bank War, see Andrew Jackson, "Veto Message"* (July 10, 1832), in James D. Richardson, ed., *Messages and Papers of the Presidents,* vol. 2 (1896); *The Nullification Era: A Documentary Record,* edited by William W. Freehling; and Daniel Webster's "Speech on Jackson's Veto of the U.S. Bank Bill" (1832), in Richard Hofstadter, ed., *Great Issues in American History.* On the "Tariff of Abominations" and its implications, see the "Webster-Hayne Debate"* (1830). *The Diary of Philip Hone, 1828–1851* (1927) presents the everyday reflections of a Whig mayor of New York.

Secondary Sources

Overviews of Jacksonian politics include Arthur M. Schlesinger, Jr., *The Age of Jackson* (1945); Harry L. Watson, *Liberty and Power: The Politics of Jacksonian America* (1990); and Charles Sellers, *The Market Revolution: Jacksonian America, 1815–1846* (1991). A sweeping narrative of early American politics that puts Jacksonian democracy at its center is Sean Wilentz, *The Rise of American Democracy: Jefferson to Lincoln* (2005). For a more temporally focused approach that still uses a broad lens, see Louis P. Masur, *1831: Year of Eclipse.* Edward Pessen, *Jacksonian America: Society, Personality, and Politics* (rev. ed., 1978), is a good general introduction that sharply disputes Tocqueville's findings. See also Frederick Jackson Turner, *The Frontier in American History* (1920), which casts Jackson as an exemplar of the democratic spirit of the frontier. Marvin Meyers, *The Jacksonian Persuasion* (1957), and John William Ward, *Andrew Jackson: Symbol for an Age* (1955), examine the broader cultural significance of "Old Hickory" and his supporters. Lee Benson, *The Concept of Jacksonian Democracy: New York as a Test Case* (1961), attacks Schlesinger's emphasis on eastern labor's support for Jackson. For a general overview of political participation, see Glenn C. Altschuler and Stuart M. Blumin, *Rude Republic: Americans and Their Politics in the Nineteenth Century* (2001). On the evolution of mass-based political parties, see Lawrence Kohl, *The Politics of Individualism: Parties and the American Character in the Jacksonian Era* (1989); Richard P. McCormick, *The Second American Party System* (1966); and two books by Ronald P. Formisano, *The Birth of Mass Political Parties: Michigan, 1827–1861* (1971) and *The Transformation of Political Culture: Massachusetts Parties, 1790s–1840s* (1983). See also Amy Bridges, *A City in the Republic: Antebellum New York and the Origins of Machine Politics* (1984), and Richard L. McCormick's general survey of party politics from Jackson into the twentieth century, *The Party Period and Public Policy: American Politics from the Age of Jackson to the Progressive Era* (1986). Four works that consider Jacksonian politics in the South are William J. Cooper, *The South and the Politics of Slavery, 1828–1856* (1978); J. Mills Thornton III, *Politics and Power in a Slave Society: Alabama, 1800–1860* (1978); William W. Freehling, *The Road to Disunion: Secessionists at Bay, 1776–1854* (1990); and Harry L. Watson, *Jacksonian Politics and Community Conflict: The Emergence of the Second American Party System in Cumberland County, North Carolina* (1981), which discusses the opponents of Jackson. Robert V. Remini has a three-volume biography of Jackson; *Andrew Jackson and the Course of American Freedom* (1981) and *Andrew Jackson and the Course of American Democracy* (1984) cover the presidential years. Remini also has a fine biography of Clay, *Henry Clay: Statesman for the Union* (1991). A masterful analysis of the period's most celebrated statesmen is Merrill D. Peterson, *The Great Triumvirate: Webster, Clay, and Calhoun* (1987). On Van Buren, see John Niven, *Martin Van Buren: The Romantic Age of American Politics* (1983). Incisive analysis can be found in Richard Hofstadter's essay on Jackson in *The American Political Tradition and the Men Who Made It* (1948). See also Daniel Feller, *The Jacksonian Promise 1815–1840* (1995). On nullification, see Richard E. Ellis, *The Union at Risk: Jacksonian Democracy, States' Rights and the Nullification Crisis* (1987). An impressive study of the nullification crisis with a regionally specific focus is William W. Freehling's *Prelude to Civil War: The Nullification Controversy in South Carolina, 1816–1836* (1966). On Calhoun, see Gerald M. Capers, *John C. Calhoun, Opportunist* (1960), and John Niven, *John C. Calhoun and the Price of Union* (1988). Jacksonians are charged with ignorance and hypocrisy in Bray Hammond, *Banks and Politics in America from the Revolution to the Civil War* (1957). John McFaul looks at the broader picture in *The Politics of Jacksonian Finance* (1972), and Robert V. Remini focuses on political questions in *Andrew Jackson and the Bank War* (1967). For an insightful and imaginative personal biography of Jackson, see Andrew Burstein, *The Passions of Andrew Jackson* (2003). Jackson's Indian policies are scrutinized in Ronald N. Satz, *American Indian Policy in the Jacksonian Era* (1975). See also Michael D. Green, *The Politics of Indian Removal* (1982), and Anthony Wallace, *The Long, Bitter Trail: Andrew Jackson and the Indians* (1993). For studies of the so-called Five Civilized Tribes, see Charles Hudson, *The Southeastern Indians* (1976), and William G. McLaughlin, *Cherokee Renascence in the New Republic* (1986). Daniel W. Howe provides a stimulating analysis of Jackson's opponents in *The Political Culture of the American Whigs* (1980). For an illuminating and comprehensive study of the Whig party, see Michael F. Holt, *The Rise and Fall of the American Whig Party* (1999). Attempts to connect politics with the economic changes of the era include Charles Sellers's provocative synthesis, *The Market Revolution: Jacksonian America, 1815–1846* (1991), and Melvyn Stokes and Stephen Conway, eds., *The Market Revolution in America* (1996).

CHAPTER 14

Primary Source Documents

Seth Luther, *An Address to the Working-Men of New England** (1833), is the eloquent appeal of an uneducated working-class labor reformer. On the transportation revolution, see John H. B. Latrobe, *The First Steamboat Voyage on the Western Waters** (1871), and Mark Twain's classic *Life on the Mississippi** (1883). Lemuel Shaw's decision of 1842 in *Commonwealth* v. *Hunt,* 4 Metc. III (in Henry Steele Commager, *Documents of American History*) is regarded as the "Magna Carta of American labor organization." Ralph Waldo Emerson's address "The Young American," printed in *The Dial* (April 1844), expresses his enthusiasm for a new era of technological advancement. Thomas Dublin has edited *Farm to Factory: Women's Letters, 1830–1860* (rev. ed., 1993), and Charles Dickens's *American Notes* (1842) offers a European perspective on American urbanization and growth.

Secondary Sources

On immigration, see Maldwyn Jones, *American Immigration* (1960); John Bodnar, *The Transplanted: A History of Immigrants in Urban America* (1985); Hasia Diner, *Erin's Daughters in America* (1983); and Kerby A. Miller, *Emigrants and Exiles: Ireland and the Irish Exodus to North America* (1985). Bruce Levine, *The Spirit of 1848: German Immigrants, Labor Conflict, and the Coming of the Civil War* (1992), discusses German refugees and their new place in America. Solid introductions are George R. Taylor, *The Transportation Revolution, 1815–1860* (1951); Clarence H. Danhoff, *Change in Agriculture: The Northern United States, 1820–1870* (1969); and Douglas C. North, *Economic Growth in the United States, 1790–1860* (1961). See also North's *Growth and Welfare in the American Past* (rev. ed., 1974). The events of the period are placed in a larger context of economic history in Stuart Bruchey, *The Roots of American Economic Growth, 1607–1861* (1965), and Albert W. Niemi, *U.S. Economic History: A Survey of the Major Issues* (1975). On government and private sponsorship of new technologies and infrastructure, see John Lauritz Larson, *Internal Improvement: National Public Works and the Promise of Popular Government in the Early United States* (2001). Thomas C. Cochran, *Frontiers of Change: Early Industrialism in America* (1981), treats industrialization as culturally inspired change. Two fascinating case studies of the coming of industrialism are Alan Dawley, *Class and Community: The Industrial Revolution in Lynn* (1977), and Anthony F. C. Wallace, *Rockdale: The Growth of an American Village in the Early Industrial Revolution* (1978). The laboring classes are chronicled in Bruce Laurie, *Artisans into Workers: Labor in Nineteenth-Century America* (1989). Consult also Herbert Gutman's pathbreaking *Work, Culture, and Society in Industrializing America* (1976); Sean Wilentz's insightful *Chants Democratic: New York City and the Rise of the American Working Class, 1788–1850* (1984); David A. Zonderman's *Aspirations and Anxieties: New England Workers and the Mechanized Factory System, 1815–1850* (1992); and David R. Roediger's *The Wages of Whiteness: Race and the Making of the American Working Class* (1991). The experiences of women workers are the focus of Thomas Dublin, *Women at Work: The Transformation of Work and Community in Lowell, Massachusetts, 1826–1860* (1979), and Christine Stansell, *City of Women: Sex and Class in New York, 1780–1860* (1986). Mary Blewett puts the gender identities of both men and women at the center of *Men, Women, and Work: Class, Gender, and Protest in the New England Shoe Industry, 1780–1910* (1988). On the introduction of technology, see David H. Hounshell, *From the American System to Mass Production, 1800–1932: The Development of Manufacturing Technology in the United States* (1984), and David F. Hawke, *Nuts and Bolts of the Past: A History of American Technology, 1776–1860* (1988). Ideological aspects of this process are described in John F. Kasson, *Civilizing the Machine: Technology and Republican Values in America, 1776–1900* (1976), and David Nye, *Consuming Power: A Social History of American Energies* (1998). For a fascinating study of how industrialization shaped daily routine and time, see Michael O'Malley, *Keeping Watch: A History of American Time* (1996). The canal era is comprehensively described in Carter Goodrich, *Government Promotion of American Canals and Railroads, 1800–1890* (1960), and Ronald E. Shaw, *Canals for a Nation: The Canal Era in the United States, 1790–1860* (1990). On the Erie Canal, see Carol Sheriff, *The Artificial River* (1996). On railroads, consult Robert Fogel, *Railroads and American Economic Growth* (1964), which presents the startling thesis that the iron horse in fact did little to promote growth. For a different view, see Albert Fishlow, *American Railroads and the Transformation of the Ante-Bellum Economy* (1965), and James A. Ward, *Railroads and the Character of America, 1820–1887* (1986). The organization and management of railroad corporations is treated in Alfred D. Chandler, Jr., *The Visible Hand: The Managerial Revolution in American Business* (1977). The legal foundation of the market revolution is discussed in Morton Horwitz, *The Transformation of American Law, 1780–1860* (1977). Steven Hahn and Jonathan Prude, eds., *The Countryside in the Age of Capitalist Transformation: Essays in the Social History of Rural America* (1985), is a provocative look at the impact of the transportation and industrial revolutions on the countryside. See also Christopher Clark, *The Roots of Rural Capitalism: Western Massachusetts, 1780–1860* (1990), and Alan Kulikoff, *The Agrarian Origins of American Capitalism* (1992). On urbanization, see Allan R. Pred, *Urban Growth and the Circulation of Information: The United States System of Cities, 1790–1840* (1973), and Elizabeth Blackmar, *Manhattan for Rent, 1785–1850* (1989).

CHAPTER 15

Primary Source Documents

Alexis de Tocqueville, *Democracy in America** (1835, 1840), has stood for over a century and a half as the classic analysis of the American character. Joseph Smith, *The Pearl of Great Price** (1929), contains an account of the Mormon leader's religious visions, which capture the religious restiveness of the age. William H. McGuffey, *Fifth Eclectic Reader* (1879), was a popular school text. On the women's movement, see the "Seneca Falls Manifesto"* (1848), which laid the foundations of the feminist movement. Catharine Beecher and Harriet Beecher Stowe, *The American Woman's Home** (1869), discusses the role of women. Stowe's classic novel, *Uncle Tom's Cabin* (1852), offers an emotional appeal against slavery and a fascinating portrait of slavery, religion, and family life in antebellum America.

Secondary Sources

A magisterial synthesis is Daniel Boorstin, *The Americans: The National Experience* (1965). Satisfying detail is found in two Russell B. Nye books: *The Cultural Life of the New Nation, 1776–1830* (1960) and *Society and Culture in America, 1830–1860* (1974). Alexis de Tocqueville's classic account of life in the young Republic is brilliantly analyzed by James R. Schlieffer in *The Making of Tocqueville's "Democracy in America"* (1980). On the rise of the middle class, see Karen Halttunen, *Confidence Men and Painted Women* (1982); Richard L. Bushman, *The Refinement of America: Persons, Houses, Cities* (1992); and Stuart M. Blumin, *The Emergence of the Middle Class* (1989). Sydney E. Ahlstrom, *Religious History of the American People* (1972), is sweeping. On revivalism, see Nathan O. Hatch, *The Democratization of American Christianity* (1989), and Paul Johnson, *A Shopkeeper's Millennium: Society and Revivals in Rochester, New York, 1815–1837* (1978), which links revivals to economic change. Bushman describes the origins of Mormonism in *Joseph Smith and the Beginnings of Mormonism* (1984), and provides insights into Smith's extraordinary life in *Rough Stone Rolling: Joseph Smith* (2005). Leonard J. Arrington analyzes Joseph Smith's successor in *Brigham Young: American Moses* (1984). On the Shakers, see Stephen J. Stein, *The Shaker Experience in America* (1992). On reform broadly, see Ronald Walters, *American Reformers, 1815–1860* (1978), and Robert Abzug, *Cosmos Crumbling: American Reform and the Religious Imagination* (1994). For particular movements, consult David Rothman, *The Discovery of the Asylum* (1971); Gerald Grob, *Mental Institutions in America: Social Policy to 1875* (1973); and David Gallagher, *Voice for the Mad: The Life of Dorothea Dix* (1995). On the development of hospitals, see Charles Rosenberg, *The Care of Strangers: The Rise of America's Hospital System* (1987). On juvenile delinquency, see Joseph Hawes, *Children in Urban Society* (1971). On prohibition, see Ian Tyrrell, *Sobering Up: From Temperance to Prohibition in Antebellum America* (1979), and William Rorabaugh, *The Alcoholic Republic* (1979). On education, see Lawrence A. Cremin, *American Education: The National Experience, 1789–1860* (1980), and Carl F. Kaestle and Maris A. Vinovskis, *Education and Social Change in Nineteenth-Century Massachusetts* (1980). An alternative interpretation of the rise of public education can be found in Michael Katz, *The Irony of Early School Reform* (1968), and Samuel Bowles and Herbert Gintis, *Schooling in Capitalist America* (1976). Vinovskis offers a critique of these authors in *The Origins of Public High Schools: A Reexamination of the Beverly High School Controversy* (1985). A recent study of one Utopian community is Spencer Klaw, *Without Sin: The Life and Death of the Oneida Community* (1993). Women's history for this period is explored in a number of studies, including Carroll Smith-Rosenberg, *Religion and the Rise of the American City* (1971); Nancy Cott, *The Bonds of Womanhood: "Woman's Sphere" in New England: 1780–1835* (1977); Ellen Carol DuBois, *Feminism and Suffrage* (1978); Ruth Bordin, *Women and Temperance* (1981); Estelle B.

Freedman, *Their Sisters' Keepers: Women's Prison Reform in America, 1830–1930* (1981); Barbara Epstein, *The Politics of Domesticity* (1981); Nancy Hewitt, *Women's Activism and Social Change: Rochester, New York, 1822–1872* (1984); Lori D. Ginzberg, *Women and the Work of Benevolence* (1990); and Ann Douglas, *The Feminization of American Culture* (1977). Family history is covered in Steven Mintz and Susan Kellogg, *Domestic Revolutions: A Social History of American Family Life* (1988); Jeanne Boydston, *Home and Work: Housework, Wages, and the Ideology of Labor in the Early Republic* (1990); Joseph F. Kett, *Rites of Passage: Adolescence in America* (1976); Lewis Perry, *Childhood, Marriage, and Reform: Henry Clarke Wright, 1797–1870* (1980); Carl N. Degler, *At Odds: Women and the Family in America from the Revolution to the Present* (1980); and Mary P. Ryan, *Cradle of the Middle Class: The Family in Oneida County, New York* (1981). See also Kathryn Kish Sklar, *Catharine Beecher: A Study in Domesticity* (1973). Suzanne Lebsock, *The Free Women of Petersburg* (1984), discusses these issues in a southern context. For the relationship of nature to the emerging American culture, see Henry Nash Smith, *Virgin Land: The American West as Symbol and Myth* (1950); Leo Marx, *The Machine in the Garden: Technology and the Pastoral Ideal in America* (1964); and Barbara Novak, *Nature and Culture: American Landscape and Painting, 1825–1875* (1980). Studies with a cultural focus include Joseph Ellis, *After the Revolution: Profiles of Early American Culture* (1979), and Anne Rose, *Voices of the Marketplace: American Thought and Culture, 1830–1860* (1995). See also Lawrence Buell, *New England Literary Culture: From Revolution Through Renaissance* (1986), and Kenneth Cmiel, *Democratic Eloquence: The Fight over Popular Speech in Nineteenth-Century America* (1990). Edward L. Widmer, *Young America: The Flowering of Democracy in New York City* (1999), explores the literary-political nexus at the heart of Gotham culture in the 1840s. On three critically important transcendentalist figures, see Charles Capper, *Margaret Fuller: An American Romantic Life* (1992), and Robert D. Richardson's excellent volumes, *Emerson: The Mind on Fire* (1995) and *Thoreau: A Life of the Mind* (1986). Perry Miller, *The Raven and the Whale: The War of Words and Wits in the Era of Poe and Melville* (1956), remains a classic account of the New York literati in the age of the "American Renaissance."

CHAPTER 16

Primary Source Documents

Two influential abolitionist documents are Theodore Dwight Weld, *American Slavery As It Is** (1839), and the inaugural editorial of William Lloyd Garrison in *The Liberator** (1831). Roy P. Basler, ed., *The Collected Works of Abraham Lincoln* (1933), contains the Great Emancipator's assessment of abolitionism in 1854. For southern perspectives, see James Henry Hammond's famous "Cotton Is King" speech, *Congressional Globe*, 36th Cong., 1st sess., 961 (March 3, 1858).* Frederick Law Olmsted, *The Cotton Kingdom* (1861), chronicles the future landscape architect's observations while traveling through the South in the 1850s. Famous firsthand accounts of slavery include Frederick Douglass, *Narrative of the Life of Frederick Douglass* (1845), and Harriet Jacobs, *Incidents in the Life of a Slave Girl* (1861). John W. Blassingame, ed., *Slave Testimony* (1977), also offers a rich collection of slave narratives.

Secondary Sources

A good introduction to southern history is Clement Eaton, *A History of the Old South: The Emergence of a Reluctant Nation* (1975). For a discussion of the intellectual's place in a southern agrarian society, see Drew Gilpin Faust, *A Sacred Circle: The Dilemma of the Intellectual in the Old South, 1840–1860* (1977). Always incisive is C. Vann Woodward, *The Burden of Southern History* (1960). On white politics and society, see Bruce Collins, *White Society in the Antebellum South* (1985); Bertram Wyatt-Brown, *Honor and Violence in the Old South* (1986); and Drew Gilpin Faust's perceptive biography, *James Henry Hammond and the Old South: A Design for Mastery* (1982). Nonslaveholding whites are documented in Frank L. Owsley, *Plain Folk of the Old South* (1949), and Stephanie McCurry, *Masters of Small Worlds: Yeoman Households, Gender Relations, and the Political Culture of the Antebellum South Carolina Low Country* (1995). Important interpretations of the "peculiar institution" include Eugene Genovese, *Roll, Jordan, Roll: The World the Slaves Made* (1974); Barbara Jeanne Fields, *Slavery and Freedom on the Middle Ground: Maryland During the Nineteenth Century* (1985); Gavin Wright, *The Political Economy of the Cotton South* (1978); and Eugene Genovese and Elizabeth Fox-Genovese, *Fruits of Merchant Capital* (1983). Genovese and Fox-Genovese present a dense account of the slaveholders' culture and religion in *The Mind of the Master Class: History and Faith in the Southern Slaveholders' Worldview* (2005). James Oakes has questioned many of Eugene Genovese's interpretations in *The Ruling Race: A History of American Slaveholders* (1982) and *Slavery and Freedom: An Interpretation of the Old South* (1990). Catherine Clinton examines *The Plantation Mistress* (1982); Elizabeth Fox-Genovese discusses southern women more generally in *Within the Plantation Household: Black and White Women of the Old South* (1988). See also Deborah Gray White, *Ar'n't I a Woman? Female Slaves in the Plantation South* (1985); Melton Alonza McLaurin, *Celia, a Slave* (1991); and Brenda E. Stevenson, *Life in Black and White: Family and Community in the Slave South* (1996). There is a rich and varied literature on slavery and African Americans; a good place to start is John Hope Franklin, *From Slavery to Freedom* (8th ed., 2000), and Peter J. Parish, *Slavery: History and Historians* (1989). The modern debate on slavery began with Ulrich B. Phillips's apologia *American Negro Slavery* (1918); a darker view of the same subject is found in Kenneth M. Stampp, *The Peculiar Institution* (1956). Consult also Stanley Elkins's controversial essay, *Slavery* (2nd ed., 1968), which also has interesting observations on the abolitionists. Considerable furor surrounded the publication of Robert Fogel and Stanley Engerman's *Time on the Cross: The Economics of American Slavery* (2 vols., 1974). For contrasting views and rebuttals, see John W. Blassingame, *The Slave Community* (rev. ed., 1979); Herbert Gutman, *The Black Family in Slavery and Freedom, 1750–1925* (1976); Paul David, *Reckoning with Slavery* (1976); Lawrence Levine, *Black Culture and Black Consciousness: Afro-American Folk Thought from Slavery to Freedom* (1977); Albert J. Raboteau, *Slave Religion: The "Invisible Institution" in the Antebellum South* (1978); and Sterling Stuckey, *Slave Culture: Nationalist Theory and the Foundations of Black America* (1987). Vincent Harding, *There Is a River: The Black Struggle for Freedom in America* (1981), discusses slave resistance and revolt, a subject handled rather differently in Peter Kolchin's fascinating comparative study, *Unfree Labor: American Slavery and Russian Serfdom* (1987). John Hope Franklin, *Runaway Slaves: Rebels on the Plantation* (1999), analyzes the motivations and consequences of slaves who escaped from their owners' farms and plantations. Manisha Sinha, *The Counterrevolution of Slavery: Politics and Ideology in Antebellum South Carolina* (2000), is an important new study that links political radicalism with the practice of slavery. Another political history of the South is Lacy K. Ford, Jr., *The Origins of Southern Radicalism: The South Carolina Upcountry, 1800–1860* (1988), which tells the story of this Unionist stronghold. A study that compares the development of race relations in South Africa and the United States is George M. Frederickson, *White Supremacy: A Comparative Study in American and South African History* (1981). Ira Berlin examines how the institution of slavery developed in discrete chronological stages in *Many Thousands Gone: The First Two Centuries of Slavery in North America* (1998) and tells the story of free blacks in *Slaves Without Masters* (1975), which should be supplemented by Michael P. Johnson and James L. Roark, *Black Masters: A Free Family of Color in the Old South* (1984). See also Harry Reed, *Platform for Change: The Foundation of the Northern Free Black Community, 1775–1865* (1994), for the situation of blacks outside the South. For an important study of interracial families in the antebellum South, see Joshua Rothman, *Notorious in the Neighborhood: Sex and Families Across the Color Line in Virginia, 1787–1861* (2003). On the experience of the antebellum slave trade, see Walter Johnson, *Soul by Soul: Life Inside the Antebellum Slave Market* (2001). Valuable community studies include Charles Joyner, *Down by the Riverside: A South Carolina Slave Community* (1984); Suzanne Lebsock, *The Free Women of Petersburg: Status and Culture in a Southern Town, 1784–1860* (1984); and Orville Vernon Burton, *In My Father's House Are Many Mansions: Family and Community in Edgefield, South Carolina* (1985). David B. Davis provides indispensable background to the history of abolitionism in *The Problem of Slavery in Western Culture* (1966) and *The Problem of Slavery in the Age of Revolution* (1975), as does Thomas Bender, ed., in *The Antislavery Debate* (1992). The best brief history of the abolitionists is James B. Stewart, *Holy Warriors* (1976). Ronald E. Walters emphasizes the constraints that American culture placed on abolitionists in *The Antislavery Appeal: American Abolitionism After 1830* (1976). Aileen Kraditor is favorably disposed toward William Lloyd Garrison in *Means and Ends in American Abolitionism: Garrison and His Critics* (1967). See also Julie Roy Jeffrey, *The Great Silent Army of Abolitionism: Ordinary Women in the Antislavery Movement* (1998). For provocative appraisals, see Lewis Perry and Michael Fellman, eds., *Antislavery Reconsidered: New Perspectives on the Abolitionists* (1979). Benjamin Quarles examines *Black Abolitionists* (1969), as do Jane H. Pease and William H. Pease in *They Who Would Be Free: Blacks Search for Freedom, 1830–1861* (1974), and Shirley J. Yee in *Black Women Abolitionists: A Study in Activism, 1828–1860* (1992). Sojourner Truth is the subject of Nell Irvin Painter, *Sojourner Truth: A Life, a Symbol* (1996). The most prominent black abolitionist is portrayed in Waldo E. Martin, Jr., *The Mind of Frederick Douglass* (1984), and William S. McFeely, *Frederick Douglass* (1990).

CHAPTER 17

Primary Source Documents

Trader Josiah Gregg describes the Santa Fe trade in his 1845 book, *Commerce of the Prairies,* edited by Max L. Moorehead (1954), and historian Francis Parkman's classic *The California and Oregon Trail* (1849) draws a fascinating picture of the Pacific Coast. Colorful reminiscences of the pioneers are collected in Dale Morgan, ed., *Overland in 1846: Diaries and Letters of the California-Oregon Trail** (1963), and Sandra Myres, *Ho for California! Women's Overland Diaries from the Huntington Library* (1980). Stella M. Drumm, ed., *Down the Santa Fe Trail and into Mexico, 1846–1847,* is a fascinating firsthand account of New Mexico during the Mexican War written by the daughter of a prominent trader (1975). The outbreak and conduct of the war also come alive in Allan Nevins, ed., *Polk: The Diary of a President, 1845–1849* (1929).

Secondary Sources

Frederick Merk, *Manifest Destiny and Mission in American History* (1963), is a good introduction. For more recent explanations of American motivations during the imperialistic decade of the 1840s, see Thomas R. Hietala, *Manifest Design: Anxious Aggrandizement in Late Jacksonian America* (1985); Robert E. May, *Manifest Destiny's Underworld: Filibustering in Antebellum America* (2002); and Sam W. Haynes and Christopher Morris, eds., *Manifest Destiny and Empire: American Antebellum Expansionism* (1997). For explorations of the role racial thought played in Manifest Destiny, see Reginald Horsman, *Race and Manifest Destiny: The Origins of American Racial Anglo-Saxonism* (1981); the early chapters of Richard D. White, *"It's Your Misfortune and None of My Own": A History of the American West* (1992); and Michael A. Morrison, *Slavery and the American West: The Eclipse of Manifest Destiny* (1997). Norman A. Graebner, *Empire on the Pacific* (1955), discusses Polk's drive to acquire California, and Theodore J. Karamanski, *Fur Trade and Exploration: Opening the Far Northwest, 1821–1852* (1983), gives a vivid depiction of the Pacific region (1983). The definitive account of the American Southwest before U.S. invasion is David Weber's *The Mexican Frontier, 1821–1846* (1982), which traces the gradual drift of the region away from Mexican control. David M. Pletcher's *The Diplomacy of the Annexation of Texas, Oregon, and the Mexican War* (1973) is a thorough, balanced account of annexation and the coming of the war. On the conflict with Mexico, see Richard Bruce Winders, *Crisis in the Southwest: The United States, Mexico, and the Struggle over Texas* (2002); James McCaffrey, *Army of Manifest Destiny: The American Soldier in the Mexican War* (1992); and Paul Foos, *A Short, Offhand Killing Affair: Soldiers and Social Conflict During the U.S.-Mexican War* (2002). The perspectives of Mexicans are analyzed in Josefina Zoraida Vázquez, *The United States and Mexico* (1985); Gene M. Brack, *Mexico Views Manifest Destiny, 1821–1846* (1976); and Iris Engstrand et al., *Culture y Cultura: Consequences of the U.S.-Mexican War, 1846–1848* (1998). John H. Schroeder analyzes an important aspect of the conflict in *Mr. Polk's War: American Opposition and Dissent, 1846–1848* (1973). Richard Francaviglia et al., eds., *Dueling Eagles: Reinterpreting the U.S.-Mexican War 1846–1848* (2000), compiles the most recent scholarly perspectives. The second volume of Charles Sellers's excellent three-volume biography of James K. Polk focuses on the years 1843 to 1846 (1966); Paul H. Bergeron scrutinizes Polk's administration in *The Presidency of James K. Polk* (1987); and William Dusinberre explores the influence of Polk's life as a slaveowner on his public policies in *Slavemaster President: The Double Career of James K. Polk* (2003). Robert W. Johannsen uses the war to investigate American culture in *To the Halls of the Montezumas: The Mexican War in the American Imagination* (1985). John Mack Faragher provides an in-depth look at the westward migration of one community in *Sugar Creek: Life on the Illinois Prairie* (1986). Linda S. Hudson, *Mistress of Manifest Destiny: A Biography of Jane McManus Storm Cazneau, 1807–1878* (2001), chronicles the life of a woman who propagandized for westward expansion. Gregg Cantrell, *Stephen F. Austin, Empresario of Texas* (1999), is a biography of the key figure in Anglo-American colonization in Texas. For an insightful look at the cultural exchange brought about by the gold rush, see Susan Lee Johnson, *Roaring Camp: The Social World of the California Gold Rush* (2001). Three works that explore the experiences of women in the West are Julie Roy Jeffrey, *Frontier Women* (1979); Glenda Riley, *The Female Frontier* (1988); and Susan Armitage and Elizabeth Jameson, eds., *The Women's West* (1987).

CHAPTER 18

Primary Source Documents

The *Congressional Globe* for 1850 contains the dramatic orations of a dying generation of American statesmen on the Compromise of 1850. See the speeches by Webster,* Calhoun,* and Clay in Richard Hofstadter, ed., *Great Issues in American History.* The debate on the Kansas-Nebraska Bill can be found in the 1854 volume of the same source, which includes addresses by Stephen A. Douglas* and his opponent, Salmon P. Chase.*

Secondary Sources

Earlier interpretations of the sectional crisis include Charles A. and Mary R. Beard, *The Rise of American Civilization* (1927); Avery Craven, *The Repressible Conflict, 1830–1861* (1939); and Allan Nevins, *The Ordeal of the Union* (1947). A compelling account of the events of the 1850s is David M. Potter's masterful *The Impending Crisis, 1848–1861* (1976). A concise summary of the events leading to the war is also available in the opening chapters of James M. McPherson, *Battle Cry of Freedom: The Civil War Era* (1988). Comprehensive treatments may be found in David H. Donald, Jean H. Baker, and Michael

F. Holt, *The Civil War and Reconstruction* (rev. ed., 2001); William J. Cooper, *The South and the Politics of Slavery* (1978); Kenneth Stampp, ed., *The Imperiled Union: Essays on the Background of the Civil War* (1980); Richard H. Sewell, *A House Divided: Sectionalism and Civil War, 1848–1860* (1988); and William Freehling, *Road to Disunion: Secessionists at Bay, 1776–1854* (1990). The standard work is Holman Hamilton, *Prologue to Conflict: The Crisis and Compromise of 1850* (1964). See also Mark J. Stegmaier, *Texas, New Mexico, and the Compromise of 1850: Boundary Dispute and Sectional Crisis* (1996). On the southern view of events, see Kenneth S. Greenberg, *Masters and Statesmen: The Political Culture of American Slavery* (1985), and Eugene Genovese, *The World the Slaveholders Made* (1969). The emergence of the Republican party after 1854 can be studied in Eric Foner's brilliant discussion of ideology, *Free Soil, Free Labor, Free Men* (1970), and William Gienapp, *The Origins of the Republican Party, 1852–1856* (1987). Also see Michael Holt, *Forging a Majority: The Formation of the Republican Party in Pittsburgh* (1969); Paul Kleppner, *The Third Electoral System, 1853–1892: Parties, Voters, and Political Cultures* (1979); Bruce Levine, *Half Slave and Half Free: The Roots of the Civil War* (1992); and Frederick J. Blue, *The Free Soilers: Third Party Politics, 1848–1854* (1973). On the Know-Nothing party, see Tyler Anbinder, *Nativism and Slavery: The Northern Know-Nothings and the Politics of the 1850s* (1992). Holt has developed his views in *The Political Crisis of the 1850s* (1978), an unusually provocative book. Party politics are treated in two books by Joel H. Silbey, *The Shrine of Party: Congressional Voting Behavior, 1841–1852* (1967) and his unorthodox *Partisan Imperative: The Dynamics of American Politics Before the Civil War* (1985). Richard H. Sewell, *Ballots for Freedom: Antislavery Politics in the United States, 1837–1860* (1976), is a standard work. A biographical approach is taken in Merrill Peterson, *The Great Triumvirate: Webster, Clay, and Calhoun* (1987). Robert Trennert examines the impact of westward migration and the gold rush on U.S. Indian policy in *Alternative to Extinction: Federal Indian Policy and the Beginnings of the Reservation System, 1846–1851* (1975).

CHAPTER 19

Primary Source Documents

Harriet Beecher Stowe, *Uncle Tom's Cabin** (1852), and Hinton R. Helper, *The Impending Crisis of the South** (1857), are vivid and important. The Lincoln-Douglas debates* (1858) frame the issues of the 1850s and remain classics of American oratory. William W. Freehling and Craig M. Simpson, eds., *Secession Debated: Georgia's Showdown in 1860* (1992), features a dramatic debate between Unionist Alexander Stephens and secessionist Robert Toombs.

Secondary Sources

For comprehensive treatments of events leading up to the Civil War, refer to Chapter 18 for the titles by David M. Potter, James M. McPherson, William J. Cooper, Kenneth Stampp, Richard H. Sewell, Allan Nevins, and David H. Donald, Jean H. Baker, and Michael F. Holt. Gabor S. Boritt, ed., *Why the Civil War Came* (1996), is an informative compilation of articles on the causes of the war. Leonard L. Richards, *The Slave Power: The Free North and Southern Domination, 1780–1860* (2000), and Ward M. McAfee, ed., *The Slaveholding Republic* (2001), give interpretations on the coming of the war. David H. Donald, *Charles Sumner and the Coming of the Civil War* (1960), is an outstanding biography. A more recent biography is Frederick J. Blue, *Charles Sumner and the Conscience of the North* (1994). On the literary attack on slavery, see Thomas F. Gossett, *Uncle Tom's Cabin and American Culture* (1985). Nicole Etcheson, *Bleeding Kansas: Contested Liberty in the Civil War Era* (2004), tells the story of the first frontier war over slavery expansion. On the Buchanan administration, see Kenneth M. Stampp, *America in 1857: A Nation on the Brink* (1990), and Michael J. Birkner, ed., *James Buchanan and the Political Crisis of the 1850s* (1996). On the Lincoln-Douglas debates, see Harry V. Jaffa, *Crisis of the House Divided* (1959). Don E. Fehrenbacher brilliantly and thoroughly dissects *The Dred Scott Case* (1978). The final moments before fighting began are scrutinized in David M. Potter, *Lincoln and His Party in the Secession Crisis* (1942). The Southern side of the question appears in Steven A. Channing, *Crisis of Fear: Secession of South Carolina* (1970), and William L. Barney, *The Secessionist Impulse: Alabama and Mississippi* (1974). On Southern Unionists' role in beginning the war, see Daniel W. Crofts, *Reluctant Confederates: Upper South Unionists in the Secession Crisis* (1989). Jean H. Baker, *Affairs of Party: The Political Culture of Northern Democrats in the Mid-Nineteenth Century* (1983), and Robert W. Johannsen, *Stephen A. Douglas* (1973), present matters from the Democratic perspective. See also J. Mills Thornton III, *Power and Politics in a Slave Society: Alabama 1820–1860* (1978), and Marc W. Kruman, *Parties and Politics in North Carolina, 1836–1865* (1983). Stephen B. Oates paints a vivid portrait of John Brown in *To Purge This Land with Blood* (1970), as Joan Hedrick does of Harriet Beecher Stowe in *Harriet Beecher Stowe: A Life* (1994). For a broader view, see Paul Finkelman, *And His Soul Goes Marching On: Responses to John Brown and the Harpers Ferry Raid* (1995).

CHAPTER 20

Primary Source Documents

The Constitution of the Confederacy (1861) makes an interesting contrast to the U.S. Constitution. Two diaries that describe life behind Confederate lines are those of John B. Jones, published as Earl S. Miers, ed., *A Rebel War Clerk's Diary** (1958), and C. Vann Woodward, ed., *Mary Chesnut's Civil War* (1981). A comprehensive collection of primary sources about every aspect of the war can be found in William Gienapp, ed., *The Civil War and Reconstruction: A Documentary Collection* (2001). It contains Lincoln's Gettysburg Address* (1863), which poetically proclaims the president's highest war aims.

Secondary Sources

Two extensive biographies of Abraham Lincoln are Stephen B. Oates, *With Malice Toward None: The Life of Abraham Lincoln* (1977), and William Gienapp, *Abraham Lincoln and Civil War America* (2002). See also Garry Wills, *Lincoln at Gettysburg: The Words That Remade America* (1992), David H. Donald, *Lincoln* (1995), and Allen Guelzo, *Abraham Lincoln: Redeemer President*. On Mary Todd Lincoln, see Jean H. Baker, *Mary Todd Lincoln: A Biography* (1987). In *Jefferson Davis, American* (2000), William J. Cooper provides a counterpoint to the rich literature on the life of Lincoln. Home-front politics are treated in James A. Rawley, *The Politics of Union* (1974), and Joel Silbey, *A Respectable Minority: The Democratic Party in the Civil War Era* (1977). See also Eric Foner, *Politics and Ideology in the Age of the Civil War* (1980). Mark Neely has written several books on Civil War politics, including *Southern Rights: Political Prisoners and the Myth of Confederate Constitutionalism* (1999) and *The Union Divided: Party Conflict in the Civil War North* (2002). George C. Rable's *The Confederate Republic* (1994) is a comprehensive study of politics in the Confederacy. Lincoln's problems are analyzed in LaWanda Cox, *Lincoln and Black Freedom* (1981). See also Hans L. Trefousse, *The Radical Republicans: Lincoln's Vanguard for Racial Justice* (1969). Eugene C. Murdoch analyzes the military draft in the North in *One Million Men* (1971). Iver Bernstein treats *The New York City Draft Riots* (1990). Gerald F. Linderman examines the motivations of soldiers in *Embattled Courage: The Experience of Combat in the Civil War* (1987). Mary E. Massey presents the interesting story of women in the Civil War in *Bonnet Brigades* (1966). That topic also figures in Elizabeth D. Leonard, *Yankee Women: Gender Battles in the Civil War* (1994). See also the essays in Catherine Clinton and Nina Silber, eds., *Divided Houses: Gender and the Civil War* (1992), and Drew Gilpin Faust, *Mothers of Invention: Women of the Slaveholding South in the Amer-*

ican Civil War (1996). William Freehling, *The South vs. The South: How Anti-Confederate Southerners Shaped the Course of the Civil War* (2001), argues that Southern social divisions contributed to the Union victory. For more on the Confederacy, see Emory M. Thomas, *The Confederate Nation, 1861–1865* (1979), and Drew Gilpin Faust, *The Creation of Confederate Nationalism* (1988). Economic matters are handled in Ralph L. Andreano, ed., *The Economic Impact of the American Civil War* (1962); David T. Gilchrist and W. David Lewis, eds., *Economic Change in the Civil War Era* (1965); and Heather Cox Richardson, *The Greatest Nation of the Earth: Republican Economic Policies During the Civil War* (1997). Two useful anthologies are David H. Donald, ed., *Why the North Won the Civil War* (1960), and Robert P. Swierenga, ed., *Beyond the Civil War Synthesis: Political Essays on the Civil War Era* (1975). Richard E. Beringer et al. present a different viewpoint in *Why the South Lost the Civil War* (1986). The war's literary legacy is keenly analyzed in Edmund Wilson's classic *Patriotic Gore* (1962) and in Daniel Aaron's *The Unwritten War: American Writers and the Civil War* (1973). On the religious impact of the war, see Randall M. Miller et al., *Religion and the American Civil War* (1998). David W. Blight, *Race and Reunion: The Civil War in American Memory* (2001), is a study of how Americans have remembered their bloodiest conflict.

CHAPTER 21

Primary Source Documents

Abraham Lincoln's 1862 reply to Horace Greeley's "Prayer of Twenty Millions"* (*Collected Works of Abraham Lincoln,* edited by Roy P. Basler, 1953) is an early statement of the president's war aims. See also, in the same collection, the Emancipation Proclamation (1863). Reminiscences of the military struggle include Eliza Andrews, *The War-Time Journal of a Georgia Girl** (1908) and *Memoirs of General William T. Sherman** (1887). Also of interest is Stephen Crane's classic war novel, *The Red Badge of Courage* (1895).

Secondary Sources

A compelling single-volume account of the war is James M. McPherson, *Battle Cry of Freedom: The Civil War Era* (1988). Geoffrey C. Ward's *The Civil War* (1990) is beautifully illustrated, and James G. Randall, *Lincoln the President* (4 vols., 1945–1955), provides a wealth of rich detail. Other capable one-volume studies include Peter J. Parish, *The American Civil War* (1975), and Phillip S. Paludan, *"A People's Contest": The Union and the Civil War, 1861–1865* (1988). See also the multivolume study by Shelby Foote, *The Civil War* (3 vols., 1958–1974), and Allan Nevins's monumental *Ordeal of the Union* (8 vols., 1947–1971). Bruce Catton has a series of a dozen or so readable books on aspects of the Civil War, including *A Stillness at Appomattox* (1953) and *This Hallowed Ground* (1956). Herman Hattaway and Archer Jones discuss *How the North Won* (1983). For a fascinating essays on the legacy of the Civil War, see Alice Fahs and Joan Waugh, eds., *The Memory of the Civil War in American Culture* (2004). On the home front, see Reid Mitchell, *The Vacant Chair: The Northern Soldier Leaves Home* (1993); William Blair, *Virginia's Private War: Feeding Body and Soul in the Confederacy, 1861–1865* (1998); and David Williams, *Rich Man's War: Class, Caste, and Confederate Defeat in the Lower Chattahoochee Valley* (1998). On the "modern" character of the war, see Charles B. Royster, *The Destructive War: William Tecumseh Sherman, Stonewall Jackson, and the Americans* (1991). David P. Crook, *The North, the South, and the Powers* (1974), discusses the relationship of the combatants to England. James M. McPherson, *Abraham Lincoln and the Second American Revolution* (1991), posits a fateful clash between competing ways of life in North and South. Bell I. Wiley's descriptions of common soldiers, *The Life of Johnny Reb* (1943) and *The Life of Billy Yank* (1952), are classics. See also Benjamin Quarles, *The Negro in the Civil War* (1953), and James M. McPherson's collection of documents, *The Negro's Civil War* (1965). More recent accounts of the black experience include Ira Berlin et al., *Freedom: A Documentary History of Emancipation, 1861–1867,* Series 2: *The Black Military Experience* (1982), and Joseph Glatthaar, *Forged in Battle: The Civil War Alliance of Black Soldiers and White Officers* (1990). Emancipation is treated in Louis Gerteis, *From Contraband to Freedmen; Federal Policy Toward Southern Blacks, 1861–1865* (1973); Herman Belz, *Emancipation and Equal Rights: Politics and Constitutionalism During the Civil War Reconstruction* (1978); Willie Lee Rose, *Rehearsal for Reconstruction: The Port Royal Experiment* (1964); LaWanda Cox, *Lincoln and Black Freedom* (1981); and Leon Litwack's powerful *Been in the Storm So Long* (1979). On the abolitionists' role in securing emancipation, see James M. McPherson, *The Struggle for Equality* (1964), and David W. Blight, *Frederick Douglass' Civil War: Keeping Faith in Jubilee* (1989). The Southern response is discussed in Robert Durden, *The Gray and the Black: The Confederate Debate on Emancipation* (1973). The two leading Civil War generals are masterfully treated in Douglas S. Freeman, *R. E. Lee* (4 vols., 1934–1935), and William S. McFeely, *Grant* (1981). On the legal end to slavery in America, consult Michael Vorenberg, *Final Freedom: The Civil War, the Abolition of Slavery, and the Thirteenth Amendment* (2001).

CHAPTER 22

Primary Source Documents

Booker T. Washington's classic autobiography, *Up from Slavery** (1901), records one freedman's experiences. Contemporary comments on Reconstruction include the laments of editor Edwin L. Godkin, *The Nation** (December 7, 1871), and Frederick Douglass, *Life and Times of Frederick Douglass** (1882), as well as the debates in the *Congressional Globe** (1867–1868) between radicals such as Thaddeus Stevens and moderates such as Lyman Trumbull.

Secondary Sources

Eric Foner, *Reconstruction: America's Unfinished Revolution, 1863–1877* (1988), is a superb synthesis of current scholarship. Overall accounts may be found in David H. Donald, Jean H. Baker, and Michael F. Holt, *The Civil War and Reconstruction* (rev. ed., 2001), and James M. McPherson, *Ordeal by Fire: The Civil War and Reconstruction* (1981), perhaps the best brief introduction. Lincoln's early efforts at Reconstruction are handled in Peyton McCrary, *Abraham Lincoln and Reconstruction* (1978), and Herman Belz, *Emancipation and Equal Rights* (1978). Willie Lee Rose engagingly describes *Rehearsal for Reconstruction: The Port Royal Experiment* (1964). Dan Carter, *When the War Was Over: The Failure of Self-Reconstruction in the South, 1865–1867* (1985), and Eric L. McKitrick, *Andrew Johnson and Reconstruction: Principle and Prejudice, 1865–1866* (1963), chart the first years of the period. Sympathetic to the radical Republicans are James M. McPherson, *The Struggle for Equality* (1964), and Hans L. Trefousse, *The Radical Republicans* (1969). See also David Montgomery, *Beyond Equality: Labor and the Radical Republicans, 1862–1872* (1967). Siding with the radicals in the impeachment fight are Michael L. Benedict, *The Impeachment and Trial of Andrew Johnson* (1973), and Hans L. Trefousse, *Impeachment of a President* (1975). Steven Hahn exhaustively examines the post–Civil War genesis of African American political traditions in *A Nation Under Our Feet* (2003). Conditions in the South are analyzed in W. E. B. Du Bois's controversial classic *Black Reconstruction* (1935) and Leon F. Litwack's brilliantly evocative *Been in the Storm So Long* (1979), a revealing study of the initial responses, by both blacks and whites, to emancipation. An excellent account of the southern economy after the war is Gavin Wright, *Old South, New South: Revolutions in the Southern Economy Since the Civil War* (1986). It can be usefully supplemented by Roger Ransom and Richard L. Sutch, *One Kind of Freedom: The Economic Consequences of Emancipation* (1977). Julie Saville, *The Work of Reconstruction* (1994), highlights the efforts of newly freed slaves to shape the economic arrangements of the postwar

South. See also James Roark, *Masters Without Slaves: Southern Planters in the Civil War and Reconstruction* (1977), and Lawrence Powell, *New Masters: Northern Planters During the Civil War and Reconstruction* (1980). Barbara Fields looks at the border state of Maryland in *Slavery and Freedom on the Middle Ground* (1985). William McFeely offers an excellent biography of *Frederick Douglass* (1991). Dewey W. Grantham, *Life and Death of the Solid South* (1988); Edward L. Ayers, *The Promise of the New South: Life After Reconstruction* (1992); Dwight Billings, *Planters and the Making of a "New South": Class, Politics and Development in North Carolina, 1865–1900* (1979); and Jonathan M. Wiener, *Social Origins of the New South: Alabama, 1860–1885* (1978), elucidate the political economy of the postbellum South. Joel Williamson offers a psychological portrait of race relations in *The Crucible of Race: Black-White Relations in the American South Since Emancipation* (1984). Consult also Thomas Holt, *Black over White: Negro Political Leadership in South Carolina During Reconstruction* (1977), and Martha Hodes, *White Women, Black Men: Illicit Sex in the Nineteenth-Century South* (1997). C. Vann Woodward, *The Strange Career of Jim Crow* (rev. ed., 1974), is a classic study of the origins of segregation. His views have drawn criticism in Harold O. Rabinowitz, *Race Relations in the Urban South, 1865–1890* (rev. ed., 1996). See also Rabinowitz's *Southern Black Leaders of the Reconstruction Era* (1982). The Freedmen's Bureau has been the subject of several studies, including Claude Oubré, *Forty Acres and a Mule: The Freedmen's Bureau and Black Land Ownership* (1978), and Donald Nieman, *To Set the Law in Motion: The Freedmen's Bureau and the Legal Rights of Blacks, 1865–1868* (1979). Nell Irvin Painter follows African Americans who chose to leave the South altogether in *Exodusters: Black Migration to Kansas After Reconstruction* (1976). Special studies of value are William P. Vaughn, *Schools for All* (1974); William C. Gillette, *The Right to Vote: Politics and the Passage of the 15th Amendment* (1965); Stanley I. Kutler, *Judicial Power and Reconstruction Politics* (1968); and Harold M. Hyman, *A More Perfect Union: The Impact of the Civil War and Reconstruction on the Constitution* (1973). Richard N. Current rehabilitates the maligned carpetbaggers in *Those Terrible Carpetbaggers* (1988). Provocative scholarship is presented in Kenneth M. Stampp and Leon Litwack, eds., *Reconstruction: An Anthology of Revisionist Writings* (1969), and Robert P. Swierenga, ed., *Beyond the Civil War Synthesis* (1975). J. Morgan Kousser and James M. McPherson, eds., *Region, Race, and Reconstruction: Essays in Honor of C. Vann Woodward* (1982), contains some intriguing essays. Eric Foner looks at emancipation in a comparative perspective in *Nothing but Freedom* (1983). A comprehensive study of the climax of this troubled period is William Gillette, *Retreat from Reconstruction, 1869–1879* (1979). Also see Michael Perman, *The Road to Redemption: Southern Politics, 1869–1879* (1984). David W. Blight's highly acclaimed *Race and Reunion: The Civil War in American Memory* (2001) details the postbellum battle to determine the way Americans remembered the war

Declaration of Independence

In Congress, July 4, 1776

The Unanimous Declaration of the Thirteen United States of America

[Bracketed material in color has been inserted by the authors. For adoption background see pp. 145–146.]

When, in the course of human events, it becomes necessary for one people to dissolve the political bonds which have connected them with another, and to assume, among the powers of the earth, the separate and equal station to which the laws of nature and of nature's God entitle them, a decent respect to the opinions of mankind requires that they should declare the causes which impel them to the separation.

We hold these truths to be self-evident: That all men are created equal; that they are endowed by their Creator with certain unalienable rights; that among these are life, liberty, and the pursuit of happiness; that, to secure these rights, governments are instituted among men, deriving their just powers from the consent of the governed; that whenever any form of government becomes destructive of these ends, it is the right of the people to alter or to abolish it, and to institute new government, laying its foundation on such principles, and organizing its powers in such form, as to them shall seem most likely to effect their safety and happiness. Prudence, indeed, will dictate that governments long established should not be changed for light and transient causes; and accordingly all experience hath shown that mankind are more disposed to suffer, while evils are sufferable, than to right themselves by abolishing the forms to which they are accustomed. But when a long train of abuses and usurpations, pursuing invariably the same object, evinces a design to reduce them under absolute despotism, it is their right, it is their duty, to throw off such government, and to provide new guards for their future security. Such has been the patient sufferance of these colonies; and such is now the necessity which constrains them to alter their former systems of government. The history of the present King of Great Britain is a history of repeated injuries and usurpations, all having in direct object the establishment of an absolute tyranny over these states. To prove this, let facts be submitted to a candid world.

He has refused his assent to laws, the most wholesome and necessary for the public good. [See royal veto, p. 124.]

He has forbidden his governors to pass laws of immediate and pressing importance, unless suspended in their operation till his assent should be obtained; and, when so suspended, he has utterly neglected to attend to them.

He has refused to pass other laws for the accommodation of large districts of people [by establishing new countries], unless those people would relinquish the right of representation in the legislature, a right inestimable to them, and formidable to tyrants only.

He has called together legislative bodies at places unusual, uncomfortable, and distant from the depository of their public records, for the sole purpose of fatiguing them into compliance with his measures. [e.g., removal of Massachusetts Assembly to Salem, 1774.]

He has dissolved representative houses repeatedly, for opposing, with manly firmness, his invasions on the rights of the people. [e.g., Virginia Assembly, 1765.]

He has refused for a long time, after such dissolutions, to cause others to be elected; whereby the legislative powers, incapable of annihilation, have returned to the people at large for their exercise; the state remaining, in the mean time, exposed to all the dangers of invasions from without and convulsions within.

He has endeavored to prevent the population [populating] of these states; for that purpose obstructing the laws for naturalization of foreigners; refusing to pass others to encourage their migration hither, and raising the conditions of new appropriations of lands. [e.g., Proclamation of 1763, p. 121.]

He has obstructed the administration of justice, by refusing his assent to laws for establishing judiciary powers.

He has made judges dependent on his will alone, for the tenure of their offices, and the amount and payment of their salaries. [See Townshend Acts, p. 129.]

He has erected a multitude of new offices, and sent hither swarms of officers to harass our people and eat out their substance. [See enforcement of Navigation Laws, p. 131.]

He has kept among us, in times of peace, standing armies, without the consent of our legislatures. [See pp. 126, 130.]

He has affected to render the military independent of, and superior to, the civil power.

He has combined with others to subject us to a jurisdiction foreign to our constitution, and unacknowledged by our laws, giving his assent to their acts of pretended legislation:

For quartering large bodies of armed troops among us [See Boston Massacre, p. 129];

For protecting them, by a mock trial, from punishment for any murders which they should commit on the inhabitants of these states [See 1774 Acts, pp. 132–133];

For cutting off our trade with all parts of the world [See Boston Port Act, p. 132];

For imposing taxes on us without our consent [See Stamp Act, pp. 125–126];

For depriving us, in many cases, of the benefits of trial by jury;

For transporting us beyond seas, to be tried for pretended offenses;

For abolishing the free system of English laws in a neighboring province [Quebec], establishing therein an arbitrary government, and enlarging its boundaries, so as to render it at once an example and fit instrument for introducing the same absolute rule into these colonies [Quebec Act, p. 133];

For taking away our charters, abolishing our most valuable laws, and altering fundamentally the forms of our governments [e.g., in Massachusetts, p. 133];

For suspending our own legislatures, and declaring themselves invested with power to legislate for us in all cases whatsoever [See Stamp Act repeal, p. 127.]

He has abdicated government here, by declaring us out of his protection and waging war against us. [Proclamation, pp. 141–142.]

He has plundered our seas, ravaged our coasts, burned our towns, and destroyed the lives of our people. [e.g., the burning of Falmouth (Portland), p. 142.]

He is at this time transporting large armies of foreign mercenaries [Hessians, p. 142] to complete the works of death, desolation, and tyranny already begun with circumstances of cruelty and perfidy scarcely paralleled in the most barbarous ages, and totally unworthy the head of a civilized nation.

He has constrained our fellow-citizens, taken captive on the high seas [by impressment], to bear arms against their country, to become the executioners of their friends and brethren, or to fall themselves by their hands.

He has excited domestic insurrection among us [i.e., among slaves], and has endeavored to bring on the inhabitants of our frontiers the merciless Indian savages, whose known rule of warfare is an undistinguished destruction of all ages, sexes, and conditions.

In every stage of these oppressions we have petitioned for redress in the most humble terms; our repeated petitions have been answered only by repeated injury. [e.g., pp. 140–143.] A prince, whose character is thus marked by every act which may define a tyrant, is unfit to be the ruler of a free people.

Nor have we been wanting in our attentions to our British brethren. We have warned them, from time to time, of attempts by their legislature to extend an unwarrantable jurisdiction over us. We have reminded them of the circumstances of our emigration and settlement here. We have appealed to their native justice and magnanimity; and we have conjured them, by the ties of our common kindred, to disavow these usurpations, which would inevitably interrupt our connections and correspondence. They, too, have been deaf to the voice of justice and of consanguinity [blood relationship]. We must, therefore, acquiesce in the necessity which denounces [announces] our separation, and hold them, as we hold the rest of mankind, enemies in war, in peace friends.

We, therefore, the representatives of the United States of America, in General Congress assembled, appealing to the Supreme Judge of the world for the rectitude of our intentions, do, in the name and by the authority of the good people of these colonies, solemnly publish and declare, That these United Colonies are, and of right ought to be, FREE AND INDEPENDENT STATES; that they are absolved from all allegiance to the British crown, and that all political connection between them and the state of Great Britain is, and ought to be, totally dissolved; and that, as free and independent states, they have full power to levy war, conclude peace, contract alliances, establish commerce, and do all other acts and things which independent states may of right do. And for the support of this declaration, with a firm reliance on the protection of Divine Providence, we mutually pledge to each other our lives, our fortunes, and our sacred honor.

[Signed by] JOHN HANCOCK [President]
[and fifty-five others]

Constitution of the United States of America

[Boldface headings and bracketed explanatory matter and marginal comments (both in color) have been inserted for the reader's convenience. Passages that are no longer operative are printed in italic type.]

PREAMBLE

We the people of the United States, in order to form a more perfect union, establish justice, insure domestic tranquility, provide for the common defense, promote the general welfare, and secure the blessings of liberty to ourselves and our posterity, do ordain and establish this CONSTITUTION for the United States of America.

Article I. Legislative Department

SECTION I. Congress

Legislative power vested in a two-house Congress. All legislative powers herein granted shall be vested in a Congress of the United States, which shall consist of a Senate and a House of Representatives.

SECTION II. House of Representatives

1. The people elect representatives biennially. The House of Representatives shall be composed of members chosen every second year by the people of the several States, and the electors [voters] in each State shall have the qualifications requisite for electors of the most numerous branch of the State Legislature.

2. Who may be representatives. No person shall be a Representative who shall not have attained the age of twenty-five years, and been seven years a citizen of the United States, and who shall not, when elected, be an inhabitant of that State in which he shall be chosen.

See 1787 compromise, p. 179.

See 1787 compromise, p. 180.

3. Representation in the House based on population; census. Representatives and direct taxes[1] shall be apportioned among the several States which may be included within this Union, according to their respective numbers, *which shall be determined by adding to the whole number of free persons, including those bound to service for a term of years* [apprentices and indentured servants], *and excluding Indians not taxed, three-fifths of all other persons* [slaves].[2] The actual enumeration [census] shall be made within three years after the first meeting of the Congress of the United States, and within every subsequent term of ten years, in such manner as they shall by law direct. The number of Representatives shall not exceed one for every thirty thousand, but each State shall have at least one Representative; *and until such enumeration shall be made, the State of New Hampshire shall be entitled to choose three, Massachusetts eight, Rhode Island and Providence Plantations one, Connecticut five, New York six, New Jersey four, Pennsylvania eight, Delaware one, Maryland six, Virginia ten, North Carolina five, South Carolina five, and Georgia three.*

---

[1]Modified in 1913 by the Sixteenth Amendment re income taxes (see p. 683).

[2]The word *slave* appears nowhere in the original, unamended Constitution. The three-fifths rule ceased to be in force when the Thirteenth Amendment was adopted in 1865 (see p. 72 and amendments below).

4. Vacancies in the House are filled by election. When vacancies happen in the representation from any State, the Executive authority [governor] therefore shall issue writs of election [call a special election] to fill such vacancies.

See Chase and Johnson trials, pp. 219, 496–497; Nixon trial preliminaries, pp. 949–950; and discussion of Clinton's impeachment, pp. 996–997.

5. The House selects its Speaker; has sole power to vote impeachment charges (i.e., indictments). The House of Representatives shall choose their Speaker and other officers; and shall have the sole power of impeachment.

SECTION III. Senate

1. Senators represent the states. The Senate of the United States shall be composed of two Senators from each State, *chosen by the legislature thereof,*[1] for six Years; and each Senator shall have one vote.

2. One-third of senators chosen every two years; vacancies. *Immediately after they shall be assembled in consequence of the first election, they shall be divided as equally as may be into three classes. The seats of the Senators of the first class shall be vacated at the expiration of the second year, of the second class at the expiration of the fourth year, and of the third class at the expiration of the sixth year,* so that one-third may be chosen every second year; *and if vacancies happen by resignation or otherwise, during the recess of the legislature of any State, the Executive* [governor] *thereof may make temporary appointments until the next meeting of the legislature, which shall then fill such vacancies.*[2]

3. Who may be senators. No person shall be a Senator who shall not have attained to the age of thirty years, and been nine years a citizen of the United States, and who shall not, when elected, be an inhabitant of that State for which he shall be chosen.

4. The vice president presides over the Senate. The Vice President of the United States shall be President of the Senate, but shall have no vote, unless they be equally divided [tied].

5. The Senate chooses its other officers. The Senate shall choose their other officers, and also a President *pro tempore,* in the absence of the Vice President, or when he shall exercise the office of the President of the United States.

See Chase and Johnson trials, pp. 219, 496–497; and discussion of Clinton's impeachment, pp. 996–997.

6. The Senate has sole power to try impeachments. The Senate shall have the sole power to try all impeachments. When sitting for that purpose, they shall be on oath or affirmation. When the President of the United States is tried, the Chief Justice shall preside[3]: and no person shall be convicted without the concurrence of two-thirds of the members present.

7. Penalties for impeachment conviction. Judgment in cases of impeachment shall not extend further than to removal from office, and disqualification to hold and enjoy any office of honor, trust or profit under the United States: but the party convicted shall nevertheless be liable and subject to indictment, trial, judgment and punishment, according to law.

SECTION IV. Election and Meetings of Congress

1. Regulation of elections. The times, places and manner of holding elections for Senators and Representatives shall be prescribed in each State by the legislature thereof; but the Congress may at any time by law make or alter such regulations, except as to the places of choosing Senators.

2. Congress must meet once a year. The Congress shall assemble at least once in every year, and such meeting *shall be on the first Monday in December, unless they shall by law appoint a different day.*[4]

---

[1]Repealed in favor of popular election in 1913 by the Seventeenth Amendment.

[2]Changed in 1913 by the Seventeenth Amendment.

[3]The vice president, as next in line, would be an interested party.

[4]Changed in 1933 to January 3 by the Twentieth Amendment (see p. 792 and below).

SECTION V. Organization and Rules of the Houses

1. Each house may reject members; quorums. Each house shall be the judge of the elections, returns and qualifications of its own members, and a majority of each shall constitute a quorum to do business; but a smaller number may adjourn from day to day, and may be authorized to compel the attendance of absent members, in such manner, and under such penalties, as each house may provide.

See "Bully" Brooks case, pp. 414–415.

2. Each house makes its own rules. Each house may determine the rules of its proceedings, punish its members for disorderly behavior, and with the concurrence of two-thirds, expel a member.

3. Each house must keep and publish a record of its proceedings. Each house shall keep a journal of its proceedings, and from time to time publish the same, excepting such parts as may in their judgment require secrecy; and the yeas and nays of the members of either house on any question shall, at the desire of one-fifth of those present, be entered on the journal.

4. Both houses must agree on adjournment. Neither house, during the session of Congress, shall, without the consent of the other, adjourn for more than three days, nor to any other place than that in which the two houses shall be sitting.

SECTION VI. Privileges of and Prohibitions upon Congressmen

1. Congressional salaries; immunities. The Senators and Representatives shall receive a compensation for their services, to be ascertained by law and paid out of the treasury of the United States. They shall in all cases except treason, felony and breach of the peace, be privileged from arrest during their attendance at the session of their respective houses, and in going to and returning from the same; and for any speech or debate in either house, they shall not be questioned in any other place [i.e., they shall be immune from libel suits].

2. A congressman may not hold any other federal civil office. No Senator or Representative shall, during the time for which he was elected, be appointed to any civil office under the authority of the United States, which shall have been created, or the emoluments whereof shall have been increased, during such time; and no person holding any office under the United States shall be a member of either house during his continuance in office.

SECTION VII. Method of Making Laws

See 1787 compromise, p. 179.

1. Money bills must originate in the House. All bills for raising revenue shall originate in the House of Representatives; but the Senate may propose or concur with amendments as on other bills.

Nixon, more than any predecessors, "impounded" billions of dollars voted by Congress for specific purposes, because he disapproved of them. The courts generally failed to sustain him, and his impeachment foes regarded wholesale impoundment as a violation of his oath to "faithfully execute" the laws.

2. The president's veto power; Congress may override. Every bill which shall have passed the House of Representatives and the Senate, shall, before it become a law, be presented to the President of the United States; if he approve he shall sign it, but if not he shall return it with his objections to that house in which it shall have originated, who shall enter the objections at large on their journal, and proceed to reconsider it. If after such reconsideration two-thirds of that house shall agree to pass the bill, it shall be sent, together with the objections, to the other house, by which it shall likewise be reconsidered, and, if approved by two-thirds of that house, it shall become a law. But in all such cases the votes of both houses shall be determined by yeas and nays, and the names of the persons voting for and against the bill shall be entered on the journal of each house respectively. If any bill shall not be returned by the President within ten days (Sundays excepted) after it shall have been presented to him, the same shall be a law, in like manner as if he had signed it, unless the Congress by their adjournment prevent its return, in which case it shall not be a law [this is the so-called pocket veto].

3. All measures requiring the agreement of both houses go to president for approval. Every order, resolution, or vote to which the concurrence of the Senate and House of Representatives may be necessary (except on a question of adjournment) shall be presented to the President of the United States; and before the same shall take effect, shall be approved by him, or being disapproved by him, shall be repassed by two-thirds of the Senate and House of Representatives, according to the rules and limitations prescribed in the case of a bill.

Section VIII. Powers Granted to Congress

Congress has certain enumerated powers:

1. It may lay and collect taxes. The Congress shall have power to lay and collect taxes, duties, imposts, and excises, to pay the debts and provide for the common defense and general welfare of the United States; but all duties, imposts and excises shall be uniform throughout the United States;

2. It may borrow money. To borrow money on the credit of the United States;

3. It may regulate foreign and interstate trade. To regulate commerce with foreign nations, and among the several States, and with the Indian tribes;

For 1798 naturalization see p. 205.

4. It may pass naturalization and bankruptcy laws. To establish an uniform rule of naturalization, and uniform laws on the subject of bankruptcies throughout the United States;

5. It may coin money. To coin money, regulate the value thereof, and of foreign coin, and fix the standard of weights and measures;

6. It may punish counterfeiters. To provide for the punishment of counterfeiting the securities and current coin of the United States;

7. It may establish a postal service. To establish post offices and post roads;

8. It may issue patents and copyrights. To promote the progress of science and useful arts by securing for limited times to authors and inventors the exclusive right to their respective writings and discoveries;

9. It may establish inferior courts. To constitute tribunals inferior to the Supreme Court;

See Judiciary Act of 1789, p. 193.

10. It may punish crimes committed on the high seas. To define and punish piracies and felonies committed on the high seas [i.e., outside the three-mile limit] and offenses against the law of nations [international law];

11. It may declare war; authorize privateers. To declare war,[1] grant letters of marque and reprisal,[2] and make rules concerning captures on land and water;

12. It may maintain an army. To raise and support armies, but no appropriation of money to that use shall be for a longer term than two years;[3]

13. It may maintain a navy. To provide and maintain a navy;

14. It may regulate the army and navy. To make rules for the government and regulation of the land and naval forces;

15. It may call out the state militia. To provide for calling forth the militia to execute the laws of the Union, suppress insurrections, and repel invasions;

See Whiskey Rebellion, p. 196.

16. It shares with the states control of militia. To provide for organizing, arming, and disciplining the militia, and for governing such part of them as may be employed in the service of the United States, reserving to the States respectively the appointment of the officers, and the authority of training the militia according to the discipline prescribed by Congress;

---

[1]Note that presidents, though they can provoke war (see the case of Polk, p. 382) or wage it after it is declared, cannot declare it.

[2]Papers issued private citizens in wartime authorizing them to capture enemy ships.

[3]A reflection of fear of standing armies earlier expressed in the Declaration of Independence.

17. It makes laws for the District of Columbia and other federal areas. To exercise exclusive legislation in all cases whatsoever, over such district (not exceeding ten miles square) as may, by cession of particular States, and the acceptance of Congress, become the seat of government of the United States,[1] and to exercise like authority over all places purchased by the consent of the legislature of the State, in which the same shall be, for the erection of forts, magazines, arsenals, dock-yards, and other needful buildings;—and

Congress has certain implied powers:

This is the famous "elastic clause"; See p. 195.

18. It may make laws necessary for carrying out the enumerated powers. To make all laws which shall be necessary and proper for carrying into execution the foregoing powers, and all other powers vested by this Constitution in the government of the United States, or in any department or officer thereof.

Section IX. Powers Denied to the Federal Government

See 1787 slave compromise, p. 181.

1. Congressional control of slave trade postponed until 1808. *The migration or importation of such persons as any of the States now existing shall think proper to admit shall not be prohibited by the Congress prior to the year 1808; but a tax or duty may be imposed on such importation, not exceeding $10 for each person.*

See Lincoln's unlawful suspension, p. 447.

2. The writ of habeas corpus[2] may be suspended only in cases of rebellion or invasion. The privilege of the writ of habeas corpus shall not be suspended, unless when in cases of rebellion or invasion the public safety may require it.

3. Attainders[3] and ex post facto laws[4] forbidden. No bill of attainder or ex post facto law shall be passed.

4. Direct taxes must be apportioned according to population. No capitation [head or poll tax] or other direct, tax shall be laid, unless in proportion to the census or enumeration herein before directed to be taken.[5]

5. Export taxes forbidden. No tax or duty shall be laid on articles exported from any State.

6. Congress must not discriminate among states in regulating commerce. No preference shall be given by any regulation of commerce or revenue to the ports of one State over those of another; nor shall vessels bound to, or from, one State, be obliged to enter, clear, or pay duties in another.

See Lincoln's unlawful infraction, p. 447.

7. Public money may not be spent without congressional appropriation; accounting. No money shall be drawn from the treasury, but in consequence of appropriations made by law; and a regular statement and account of the receipts and expenditures of all public money shall be published from time to time.

8. Titles of nobility prohibited; foreign gifts. No title of nobility shall be granted by the United States; and no person holding office of profit or trust under them, shall, without the consent of Congress, accept of any present, emolument, office, or title, of any kind whatever, from any king, prince, or foreign state.

---

[1]The District of Columbia, ten miles square, was established in 1791 with a cession from Virginia (see p. 194).

[2]A writ of habeas corpus is a document that enables a person under arrest to obtain an immediate examination in court to ascertain whether he or she is being legally held.

[3]A bill of attainder is a special legislative act condemning and punishing an individual without a judicial trial.

[4]An ex post facto law is one that fixes punishments for acts committed before the law was passed.

[5]Modified in 1913 by the Sixteenth Amendment (see p. 691 and amendments below).

SECTION X. Powers Denied to the States

Absolute prohibitions on the states:

On contracts see Fletcher *v.* Peck, *p. 249.*

1. The states are forbidden to do certain things. No State shall enter into any treaty, alliance, or confederation; grant letters of marque and reprisal [i.e., authorize privateers]; coin money; emit bills of credit [issue paper money]; make anything but gold and silver coin a [legal] tender in payment of debts; pass any bill of attainder,[1] ex post facto,[1] or law impairing the obligation of contracts, or grant any title of nobility.

Conditional prohibitions on the states:

Cf. Confederation chaos, pp. 172–173.

2. The states may not levy duties without the consent of Congress. No State shall, without the consent of Congress, lay any imposts or duties on imports or exports, except what may be absolutely necessary for executing its inspection laws: and the net produce of all duties and imposts, laid by any State on imports or exports, shall be for the use of the treasury of the United States; and all such laws shall be subject to the revision and control of the Congress.

3. Certain other federal powers are forbidden the states except with the consent of Congress. No State shall, without the consent of Congress, lay any duty of tonnage [i.e., duty on ship tonnage], keep [nonmilitia] troops or ships of war in time of peace, enter into any agreement or compact with another State, or with a foreign power, or engage in war, unless actually invaded, or in such imminent danger as will not admit of delay.

Article II. Executive Department

SECTION I. President and Vice President

1. The president is the chief executive; term of office. The executive power shall be vested in a President of the United States of America. He shall hold his office during the term of four years,[2] and, together with the Vice President, chosen for the same term, be elected as follows:

See 1787 compromise, pp. 180–181.

See 1876 Oregon case, p. 510.

2. The president is chosen by electors. Each State shall appoint, in such manner as the legislature thereof may direct, a number of electors, equal to the whole number of Senators and Representatives to which the State may be entitled in the Congress; but no Senator or Representative, or person holding an office of trust or profit under the United States, shall be appointed an elector.

See Burr-Jefferson disputed election of 1800, p. 214.

A majority of the electoral votes needed to elect a president. *The electors shall meet in their respective States, and vote by ballot for two persons, of whom one at least shall not be an inhabitant of the same State with themselves. And they shall make a list of all the persons voted for, and of the number of votes for each; which list they shall sign and certify, and transmit sealed to the seat of government of the United States, directed to the President of the Senate. The President of the Senate shall, in the presence of the Senate and House of Representatives, open all the certificates, and the votes shall be counted. The person having the greatest number of votes shall be the President, if such number be a majority of the whole number of electors appointed; and if there be more than one who have such majority, and have an equal number of votes, then the House of Representatives shall immediately choose by ballot one of them for President; and if no person have a majority, then from the five highest on the list the said house shall in like manner choose the President. But in choosing the President the votes shall be taken by States, the representation from each State*

---

[1]For definitions see footnotes 3 and 4 on preceding page.

[2]No reference to reelection; for anti–third term Twenty-second Amendment, see below.

having one vote; a quorum for this purpose shall consist of a member or members from two-thirds of the States, and a majority of all the States shall be necessary to a choice. In every case, after the choice of the President, the person having the greatest number of votes of the electors shall be the Vice President. But if there should remain two or more who have equal votes, the Senate shall choose from them by ballot the Vice President.[1]

See Jefferson as vice president in 1796, p. 202.

3. Congress decides time of meeting of Electoral College. The Congress may determine the time of choosing the electors and the day on which they shall give their votes; which day shall be the same throughout the United States.

To provide for foreign-born people, like Alexander Hamilton, born in the British West Indies.

4. Who may be president. No person except a natural-born citizen, *or a citizen of the United States at the time of the adoption of this Constitution,* shall be eligible to the office of President; neither shall any person be eligible to that office who shall not have attained to the age of thirty-five years, and been fourteen years a resident within the United States [i.e., a legal resident].

Modified by Twentieth and Twenty-fifth Amendments below.

5. Replacements for president. In case of the removal of the President from office or of his death, resignation, or inability to discharge the powers and duties of said office, the same shall devolve on the Vice President, and the Congress may by law provide for the case of removal, death, resignation, or inability, both of the President and Vice President, declaring what officer shall then act as President, and such officer shall act accordingly, until the disability be removed, or a President shall be elected.

6. The president's salary. The President shall, at stated times, receive for his services a compensation, which shall neither be increased or diminished during the period for which he shall have been elected, and he shall not receive within that period any other emolument from the United States, or any of them.

7. The president's oath of office. Before he enter on the execution of his office, he shall take the following oath or affirmation:—"I do solemnly swear (or affirm) that I will faithfully execute the office of the President of the United States, and will to the best of my ability preserve, protect and defend the Constitution of the United States."

SECTION II. Powers of the President

See cabinet evolution, p. 192.

1. The president has important military and civil powers. The President shall be commander in chief of the army and navy of the United States, and of the militia of the several States, when called into the actual service of the United States; he may require the opinion, in writing, of the principal officer in each of the executive departments, upon any subject relating to the duties of their respective offices, and he shall have power to grant reprieves and pardons for offenses against the United States, except in cases of impeachment.[2]

For president's removal power, see p. 496.

2. The president may negotiate treaties and nominate federal officials. He shall have power, by and with the advice and consent of the Senate, to make treaties, provided two-thirds of the Senators present concur; and he shall nominate, and by and with the advice and consent of the Senate, shall appoint ambassadors, other public ministers and consuls, judges of the Supreme Court, and all other officers of the United States, whose appointments are not herein otherwise provided for, and which shall be established by law: but the Congress may by law vest the appointment of such inferior officers, as they think proper, in the President alone, in the courts of law, or in the heads of departments.

3. The president may fill vacancies during Senate recess. The President shall have power to fill up all vacancies that may happen during the recess of the Senate, by granting commissions which shall expire at the end of their next session.

---

[1]Repealed in 1804 by the Twelfth Amendment (for text see below).

[2]To prevent the president's pardoning himself or his close associates, as was feared in the case of Richard Nixon. See p. 952.

SECTION III. Other Powers and Duties of the President

For president's personal appearances, see p. 683.

Messages; extra sessions; receiving ambassadors; execution of the laws. He shall from time to time give to the Congress information of the state of the Union, and recommend to their consideration such measures as he shall judge necessary and expedient; he may, on extraordinary occasions, convene both houses, or either of them, and in case of disagreement between them, with respect to the time of adjournment, he may adjourn them to such time as he shall think proper; he shall receive ambassadors and other public ministers; he shall take care that the laws be faithfully executed, and shall commission all the officers of the United States.

SECTION IV. Impeachment

See discussion of Presidents Johnson, pp. 496–497; Nixon, pp. 949–950; and Clinton, pp. 996–997.

Civil officers may be removed by impeachment. The President, Vice President and all civil officers[1] of the United States shall be removed from office on impeachment for, and on conviction of, treason, bribery, and other high crimes and misdemeanors.

Article III. Judicial Department

SECTION I. The Federal Courts

See Judiciary Act of 1789, p. 193.

The judicial power belongs to the federal courts. The judicial power of the United States shall be vested in one Supreme Court, and in such inferior courts as the Congress may from time to time ordain and establish. The judges, both of the Supreme and inferior courts, shall hold their offices during good behavior, and shall, at stated times, receive for their services a compensation which shall not be diminished[2] during their continuance in office.

SECTION II. Jurisdiction of Federal Courts

1. Kinds of cases that may be heard. The judicial power shall extend to all cases, in law and equity, arising under this Constitution, the laws of the United States, and treaties made, or which shall be made, under their authority;—to all cases affecting ambassadors, other public ministers and consuls;—to all cases of admiralty and maritime jurisdiction;—to controversies to which the United States shall be a party;—to controversies between two or more States;—*between a State and citizens of another State*[3];—between citizens of different States;—between citizens of the same State claiming lands under grants of different States, and between a State, or the citizens thereof, and foreign states, citizens or subjects.

2. Jurisdiction of the Supreme Court. In all cases affecting ambassadors, other public ministers and consuls, and those in which a State shall be a party, the Supreme Court shall have original jurisdiction.[4] In all the other cases before mentioned, the Supreme Court shall have appellate jurisdiction,[5] both as to law and fact, with such exceptions, and under such regulations, as the Congress shall make.

3. Trial for federal crime is by jury. The trial of all crimes, except in cases of impeachment, shall be by jury; and such trial shall be held in the State where the said crimes shall have been committed; but when not committed within any State, the trial shall be at such place or places as the Congress may by law have directed.

---

[1]i.e., all federal executive and judicial officers, but not members of Congress or military personnel.

[2]In 1978, in a case involving federal judges, the Supreme Court ruled that diminution of salaries by inflation was irrelevant.

[3]The Eleventh Amendment (see below) restricts this to suits by a state against citizens of another state.

[4]i.e., such cases must originate in the Supreme Court.

[5]i.e., it hears other cases only when they are appealed to it from a lower federal court or a state court.

Section III. **Treason**

See Burr trial, p. 225.

1. Treason defined. Treason against the United States shall consist only in levying war against them, or in adhering to their enemies, giving them aid and comfort. No person shall be convicted of treason unless on the testimony of two witnesses to the same overt act, or on confession in open court.

2. Congress fixes punishment for treason. The Congress shall have power to declare the punishment of treason, but no attainder of treason shall work corruption of blood, or forfeiture except during the life of the person attained.[1]

Article IV. Relations of the States to One Another

Section I. Credit to Acts, Records, and Court Proceedings

Each state must respect the public acts of the others. Full faith and credit shall be given in each State to the public acts, records, and judicial proceedings of every other State.[2] And the Congress may by general laws prescribe the manner in which such acts, records, and proceedings shall be proved [attested], and the effect thereof.

Section II. Duties of States to States

1. Citizenship in one state is valid in all. The citizens of each State shall be entitled to all privileges and immunities of citizens in the several States.

This stipulation is sometimes openly flouted. In 1978 Governor Jerry Brown of California, acting on humanitarian grounds, refused to surrender to South Dakota an American Indian, Dennis Banks, who was charged with murder in an armed uprising.

2. Fugitives from justice must be surrendered by the state to which they have fled. A person charged in any State with treason, felony, or other crime, who shall flee from justice, and be found in another State, shall on demand of the executive authority [governor] of the State from which he fled, be delivered up, to be removed to the State having jurisdiction of the crime.

Basis of fugitive-slave laws; see pp. 399–400.

3. Slaves and apprentices must be returned. *No person held to service or labor in one State, under the laws thereof, escaping into another, shall, in consequence of any law or regulation therein, be discharged from such service or labor, but shall be delivered up on claim of the party to whom such service or labor may be due.*[3]

Section III. New States and Territories

e.g., Maine (1820); see p. 247.

1. Congress may admit new states. New States may be admitted by the Congress into this Union; but no new State shall be formed or erected within the jurisdiction of any other State; nor any State be formed by the junction of two or more States, or parts of States, without the consent of the legislatures of the States concerned as well as of the Congress.[4]

2. Congress regulates federal territory and property. The Congress shall have power to dispose of and make all needful rules and regulations respecting the territory or other property belonging to the United States; and nothing in this Constitution shall be so construed as to prejudice any claims of the United States, or of any particular State.

Section IV. Protection to the States

See Cleveland and the Pullman strike, p. 617.

United States guarantees to states representative government and protection against invasion and rebellion. The United States shall guarantee to every State in this Union a

---

[1] i.e., punishment only for the offender; none for his or her heirs.

[2] e.g., a marriage in one is valid in all.

[3] Invalidated in 1865 by the Thirteenth Amendment (for text see below).

[4] Loyal West Virginia was formed by Lincoln in 1862 from seceded Virginia. This act was of dubious constitutionality and was justified in part by the wartime powers of the president. See pp. 436–437.

republican form of government, and shall protect each of them against invasion; and on application of the legislature, or of the executive [governor] (when the legislature cannot be convened), against domestic violence.

Article V. *The Process of Amendment*

The Constitution may be amended in four ways. The Congress, whenever two-thirds of both houses shall deem it necessary, shall propose amendments to this Constitution, or, on the application of the legislature of two-thirds of the several States, shall call a convention for proposing amendments, which, in either case, shall be valid to all intents and purposes, as part of this Constitution, when ratified by the legislatures of three-fourths of the several States, or by conventions in three-fourths thereof, as the one or the other mode of ratification may be proposed by the Congress; provided *that no amendments which may be made prior to the year one thousand eight hundred and eight shall in any manner affect the first and fourth clauses in the ninth section of the first article;*[1] and that no State, without its consent, shall be deprived of its equal suffrage in the Senate.

Article VI. *General Provisions*

This pledge honored by Hamilton, pp. 193–194.

1. The debts of the Confederation are taken over. All debts contracted and engagements entered into, before the adoption of this Constitution, shall be as valid against the United States under this Constitution, as under the Confederation.

2. The Constitution, federal laws, and treaties are the supreme law of the land. This Constitution, and the laws of the United States which shall be made in pursuance thereof; and all treaties made, or which shall be made, under the authority of the United States, shall be the supreme law of the land; and the judges in every State shall be bound thereby, anything in the Constitution or laws of any State to the contrary notwithstanding.

3. Federal and state officers bound by oath to support the Constitution. The Senators and Representatives before mentioned, and the members of the several State legislatures, and all executive and judicial officers, both of the United States and of the several States, shall be bound by oath or affirmation to support this Constitution; but no religious test shall ever be required as a qualification to any office or public trust under the United States.

Article VII. *Ratification of the Constitution*

See 1787 irregularity, pp. 181–183.

The Constitution effective when ratified by conventions in nine states. The ratification of the conventions of nine States shall be sufficient for the establishment of this Constitution between the States so ratifying the same.

Done in Convention by the unanimous consent of the States present, the seventeenth day of September in the year of our Lord one thousand seven hundred and eighty-seven and of the Independence of the United States of America the twelfth. In witness whereof we have hereunto subscribed our names.

[Signed by]

G° Washington

Presidt and Deputy from Virginia

[and thirty-eight others]

---

[1]This clause, regarding slave trade and direct taxes, became inoperative in 1808

AMENDMENTS TO THE CONSTITUTION

Amendment I. Religious and Political Freedom

For background of Bill of Rights, see pp. 192–193.

Congress must not interfere with freedom of religion, speech or press, assembly, and petition. Congress shall make no law respecting an establishment of religion,[1] or prohibiting the free exercise thereof; or abridging the freedom of speech, or of the press; or the right of the people peaceably to assemble, and to petition the government for a redress of grievances.

Amendment II. Right to Bear Arms

The people may bear arms. A well-regulated militia being necessary to the security of a free State, the right of the people to keep and bear arms [i.e., for military purposes] shall not be infringed.[2]

Amendment III. Quartering of Troops

See Declaration of Independence and British quartering above.

Soldiers may not be arbitrarily quartered on the people. No soldier shall, in time of peace, be quartered in any house without the consent of the owner, nor in time of war, but in a manner to be prescribed by law.

Amendment IV. Searches and Seizures

A reflection of colonial grievances against the crown.

Unreasonable searches are forbidden. The right of the people to be secure in their persons, houses, papers, and effects, against unreasonable searches and seizures, shall not be violated, and no [search] warrants shall issue but upon probable cause, supported by oath or affirmation, and particularly describing the place to be searched, and the persons or things to be seized.

Amendment V. Right to Life, Liberty, and Property

When witnesses refuse to answer questions in court, they routinely "take the Fifth Amendment."

The individual is guaranteed certain rights when on trial and the right to life, liberty, and property. No person shall be held to answer for a capital, or otherwise infamous crime, unless on a presentment [formal charge] or indictment of a grand jury, except in cases arising in the naval forces, or in the militia, when in actual service in time of war or public danger; nor shall any person be subject for the same offense to be twice put in jeopardy of life or limb; nor shall be compelled in any criminal case to be a witness against himself, nor be deprived of life, liberty, or property, without due process of law; nor shall private property be taken for public use [i.e., by eminent domain] without just compensation.

Amendment VI. Protection in Criminal Trials

See Declaration of Independence above.

An accused person has important rights. In all criminal prosecutions, the accused shall enjoy the right to a speedy and public trial, by an impartial jury of the State and district

---

[1]In 1787 "an establishment of religion" referred to an "established church," or one supported by all taxpayers, whether members or not. But the courts have often acted under this article to keep religion, including prayers, out of the public schools.

[2]The courts, with "militia" in mind, have consistently held that the "right" to bear arms is a limited one.

wherein the crime shall have been committed, which district shall have been previously ascertained by law, and to be informed of the nature and cause of the accusation; to be confronted with the witnesses against him; to have compulsory process [subpoena] for obtaining witnesses in his favor, and to have the assistance of counsel for his defense.

Amendment VII. *Suits at Common Law*

The rules of common law are recognized. In suits at common law, where the value in controversy shall exceed twenty dollars, the right of trial by jury shall be preserved, and no fact tried by a jury shall be otherwise re-examined in any court of the United States, than according to the rules of the common law.

Amendment VIII. *Bail and Punishments*

Excessive fines and unusual punishments are forbidden. Excessive bail shall not be required, nor excessive fines imposed, nor cruel and unusual punishment inflicted.

Amendment IX. *Concerning Rights Not Enumerated*

The Ninth and Tenth Amendments were bulwarks of southern states' rights before the Civil War.

The people retain rights not here enumerated. The enumeration in the Constitution, of certain rights, shall not be construed to deny or disparage others retained by the people.

Amendment X. *Powers Reserved to the States and to the People*

A concession to states' rights, *p. 194.*

Powers not delegated to the federal government are reserved to the states and the people. The powers not delegated to the United States by the Constitution, nor prohibited by it to the States, are reserved to the States respectively, or to the people.

Amendment XI. *Suits Against a State*

The federal courts have no authority in suits by citizens against a state. The judicial power of the United States shall not be construed to extend to any suit in law or equity, commenced or prosecuted against one of the United States by citizens of another State, or by citizens or subjects of any foreign state. [Adopted 1798.]

Amendment XII. *Election of President and Vice President*

Forestalls repetition of 1800 electoral dispute, *p. 214.*

See 1876 disputed election. pp. 510–511.

See 1824 election, pp. 256–258.

1. Changes in manner of electing president and vice president; procedure when no presidential candidate receives electoral majority. The electors shall meet in their respective States, and vote by ballot for President and Vice President, one of whom, at least, shall not be an inhabitant of the same state with themselves; they shall name in their ballots the person voted for as President, and in distinct ballots the person voted for as Vice President, and they shall make distinct lists of all persons voted for as President, and of all persons voted for as Vice President, and of the number of votes for each, which lists they shall sign and certify, and transmit sealed to the seat of government of the United States, directed to the President of the Senate;—the President of the Senate shall, in the presence of the Senate and House of Representatives, open all the certificates and the votes shall be counted;—the person having the greatest number of votes for President shall be the President, if such number be a majority of the whole number of electors appointed; and if no person have such majority, then from the persons having the highest numbers not exceeding three on the list of those voted for as President, the House of Representatives shall choose immediately, by ballot, the President. But in choosing the President, the votes shall be taken by States, the representation from each State having one vote; a quorum for this purpose shall consist of a member or members from two-thirds of the States, and a majority of all the States shall be necessary to a choice. And if the House of Representatives shall not choose a President whenever the right of choice shall devolve upon them, before *the fourth day of March*[1] next following, then the Vice President shall act as President, as in the case of the death or other constitutional disability of the President.

2. Procedure when no vice presidential candidate receives electoral majority. The person having the greatest number of votes as Vice President, shall be the Vice President, if such number be a majority of the whole number of electors appointed; and if no person have a majority, then from the two highest numbers on the list the Senate shall choose the Vice President; a quorum for the purpose shall consist of two-thirds of the whole number of Senators, and a majority of the whole number shall be necessary to a choice. But no person constitutionally ineligible to the office of President shall be eligible to that of Vice President of the United States. [Adopted 1804.]

Amendment XIII. Slavery Prohibited

For background see pp. 460–462.

Slavery forbidden. 1. Neither slavery[2] nor involuntary servitude, except as a punishment for crime whereof the party shall have been duly convicted, shall exist within the United States, or any place subject to their jurisdiction.

2. Congress shall have power to enforce this article by appropriate legislation. [Adopted 1865.]

Amendment XIV. Civil Rights for Ex-slaves,[3] etc.

For background see pp. 488–489.

For corporations as "persons," see pp. 543–544.

1. Ex-slaves made citizens; U.S. citizenship primary. All persons born or naturalized in the United States, and subject to the jurisdiction thereof, are citizens of the United States and of the State wherein they reside. No State shall make or enforce any law which shall abridge the privileges or immunities of citizens of the United States; nor shall any State deprive any person of life, liberty, or property, without due process of law; nor deny to any person within its jurisdiction the equal protection of the laws.

Abolishes three-fifths rule for slaves, Art. I., Sec. II, para. 3.

2. When a state denies citizens the vote, its representation shall be reduced. Representatives shall be apportioned among the several States according to their respective numbers, counting the whole number of persons in each State, excluding Indians not taxed. But when the right to vote at any election for the choice of Electors for President and Vice President of the United States, Representatives in Congress, the executive and judicial officers of a State, or the members of the legislature thereof, is denied to any of the male inhabitants of such State, being twenty-one years of age and citizens of the United States, or in any way abridged, except for participation in rebellion, or other crime, the basis of representation therein shall be reduced in the proportion which the number of such make citizens shall bear to the whole number of male citizens twenty-one years of age in such State.[4]

Leading ex-Confederates denied office. *See p. 489.*

3. Certain persons who have been in rebellion are ineligible for federal and state office. No person shall be a Senator or Representative in Congress, or Elector of President and Vice President, or hold any office, civil or military, under the United States, or under any State, who, having previously taken an oath, as a member of Congress, or as an officer

---

[1]Changed to January 20 by the Twentieth Amendment (for text see below).

[2]The only explicit mention of slavery in the Constitution.

[3]Occasionally an offender is prosecuted under the Thirteenth Amendment for keeping an employee or other person under conditions approximating slavery.

[4]The provisions concerning "male" inhabitants were modified by the Nineteenth Amendment, which enfranchised women. The legal voting age was changed from twenty-one to eighteen by the Twenty-sixth Amendment.

of the United States, or as a member of any State legislature, or as an executive or judicial officer of any State, to support the Constitution of the United States, shall have engaged in insurrection or rebellion against the same, or given aid or comfort to the enemies thereof. But Congress may, by a vote of two-thirds of each house, remove such disability.

The ex-Confederates were thus forced to repudiate their debts and pay pensions to their own veterans, plus taxes for the pensions of Union veterans, their conquerors.

4. Debts incurred in aid of rebellion are void. The validity of the public debt of the United States, authorizing by law, including debts incurred for payment of pensions and bounties for services in suppressing insurrection or rebellion, shall not be questioned. But neither the United States nor any State shall assume or pay any debt or obligation incurred in aid of insurrection or rebellion against the United States, or any claim for the loss or emancipation of any slave; but all such debts, obligations, and claims shall be held illegal and void.

5. Enforcement. The Congress shall have power to enforce, by appropriate legislation, the provisions of this article. [Adopted 1868.]

Amendment XV. *Suffrage for Blacks*

For background see p. 492.

Black males are made voters. 1. The right of the citizens of the United States to vote shall not be denied or abridged by the United States or by any State on account of race, color, or previous condition of servitude.

2. The Congress shall have power to enforce this article by appropriate legislation. [Adopted 1870.]

Amendment XVI. *Income Taxes*

For background see p. 683.

Congress has power to lay and collect income taxes. The Congress shall have power to lay and collect taxes on incomes, from whatever source derived, without apportionment among the several States, and without regard to any census or enumeration. [Adopted 1913.]

Amendment XVII. *Direct Election of Senators*

Senators shall be elected by popular vote. 1. The Senate of the United States shall be composed of two Senators from each State, elected by the people thereof, for six years; and each Senator shall have one vote. The electors in each State shall have the qualifications requisite for electors of [voters for] the most numerous branch of the State legislatures.

2. When vacancies happen in the representation of any State in the Senate, the executive authority of such State shall issue writs of election to fill such vacancies: Provided, that the Legislature of any State may empower the executive thereof to make temporary appointments until the people fill the vacancies by election as the Legislature may direct.

3. This amendment shall not be so construed as to affect the election or term of any Senator chosen before it becomes valid as part of the Constitution. [Adopted 1913.]

Amendment XVIII. *National Prohibition*

For background see p. 725.

The sale or manufacture of intoxicating liquors is forbidden. 1. *After one year from the ratification of this article the manufacture, sale, or transportation of intoxicating liquors within, the importation thereof into, or the exportation thereof from the United States and all territory subject to the jurisdiction thereof, for beverage purposes, is hereby prohibited.*

2. *The Congress and the several States shall have concurrent power to enforce this article by appropriate legislation.*

3. *This article shall be inoperative unless it shall have been ratified as an amendment to the Constitution by the legislatures of the several States, as provided by the Constitution,* *within seven years from the date of the submission thereof to the States by the Congress.* [Adopted 1919; repealed 1933 by Twenty-first Amendment.]

Amendment XIX. Woman Suffrage

For background see pp. 702–703.

Women guaranteed the right to vote. **1.** The right of citizens of the United States to vote shall not be denied or abridged by the United States or by any State on account of sex.

2. Congress shall have power to enforce this article by appropriate legislation. [Adopted 1920.]

Amendment XX. Presidential and Congressional Terms

Shortens lame duck periods by modifying Art. I, Sec. IV, para. 2.

1. Presidential, vice presidential, and congressional terms of office begin in January. The terms of the President and Vice President shall end at noon on the 20th day of January, and the terms of Senators and Representatives at noon on the 3d day of January, of the years in which such terms would have ended if this article had not been ratified; and the terms of their successors shall then begin.

2. New meeting date for Congress. The Congress shall assemble at least once in every year, and such meeting shall begin at noon on the 3d day of January, unless they shall by law appoint a different day.

3. Emergency presidential and vice presidential succession. If, at the time fixed for the beginning of the term of the President, the President-elect shall have died, the Vice President–elect shall become President. If a President shall not have been chosen before the time fixed for the beginning of his term, or if the President-elect shall have failed to qualify, then the Vice President–elect shall act as President until a President shall have qualified; and the Congress may by law provide for the case wherein neither a President-elect nor a Vice President–elect shall have qualified, declaring who shall then act as President, or the manner in which one who is to act shall be selected, and such persons shall act accordingly until a President or Vice President shall have qualified.

4. The Congress may by law provide for the case of the death of any of the persons from whom the House of Representatives may choose a President whenever the right of choice shall have devolved upon them, and for the case of the death of any of the persons from whom the Senate may choose a Vice President whenever the right of choice shall have devolved upon them.

5. Sections 1 and 2 shall take effect on the 15th day of October following the ratification of this article.

6. This article shall be inoperative unless it shall have been ratified as an amendment to the Constitution by the Legislatures of three-fourths of the several States within seven years from the date of its submission. [Adopted 1993.]

Amendment XXI. Prohibition Repealed

For background see pp. 782–783.

1. Eighteenth Amendment repealed. The eighteenth article of amendment to the Constitution of the United States is hereby repealed.

2. Local laws honored. The transportation or importation into any State, Territory, or Possession of the United States for delivery or use therein of intoxicating liquors, in violation of the laws thereof, is hereby prohibited.

3. This article shall be inoperative unless it shall have been ratified as an amendment to the Constitution by conventions in the several States, as provided in the Constitution, within seven years from the date of the submission thereof to the States by the Congress. [Adopted 1933.]

Amendment XXII. *Anti–Third Term Amendment*

Sometimes referred to as the anti–Franklin Roosevelt amendment.

1. Presidential term is limited. No person shall be elected to the office of President more than twice, and no person who has held the office of President, or acted as President, for more than two years of a term to which some other person was elected President shall be elected to the office of President more than once. But this article shall not apply to any person holding the office of President when this article was proposed by the Congress [i.e., Truman], and shall not prevent any person who may be holding the office of President, during the term within which this article becomes operative [i.e., Truman] from holding the office of President or acting as President during the remainder of such term.

2. This article shall be inoperative unless it shall have been ratified as an amendment to the Constitution by the legislatures of three-fourths of the several States within seven years from the date of its submission to the States by the Congress. [Adopted 1951.]

Amendment XXIII. *District of Columbia Vote*

Designed to give the District of Columbia three electoral votes and to quiet the century-old cry of "No taxation without representation." Yet the District of Columbia still has only one nonvoting member of Congress.

1. Presidential electors for the District of Columbia. The District, constituting the seat of government of the United States, shall appoint in such manner as the Congress shall direct:

A number of electors of President and Vice President equal to the whole number of Senators and Representatives in Congress to which the District would be entitled if it were a State, but in no event more than the least populous State; they shall be in addition to those appointed by the States, but they shall be considered for the purposes of the election of President and Vice President, to be electors appointed by a State; and they shall meet in the District and perform such duties as provided by the twelfth article of amendment.

2. Enforcement. The Congress shall have the power to enforce this article by appropriate legislation. [Adopted 1961.]

Amendment XXIV. *Poll Tax*

Designed to end discrimination against poor people, including southern blacks who were often denied the vote through inability to pay poll taxes. See p. 924.

1. Payment of poll tax or other taxes not to be prerequisite for voting in federal elections. The right of citizens of the United States to vote in any primary or other election for President or Vice President, for electors for President or Vice President, or for Senator or Representative in Congress, shall not be denied or abridged by the United States or any State by reason of failure to pay any poll tax or other tax.

2. Enforcement. The Congress shall have the power to enforce this article by appropriate legislation. [Adopted 1964.]

Amendment XXV. *Presidential Succession and Disability*

1. Vice president to become president. In case of the removal of the President from office or of his death or resignation, the Vice President shall become President.[1]

Gerald Ford was the first "appointed president." See pp. 949, 952.

2. Successor to vice president provided. Whenever there is a vacancy in the office of the Vice President, the President shall nominate a Vice President who shall take office upon confirmation by a majority vote of both Houses of Congress.

[1]The original Constitution (Art. II, Sec. I, para. 5) was vague on this point, stipulating that "the powers and duties" of the president, but not necessarily the title, should "devolve" on the vice president. President Tyler, the first "accidental president," assumed not only the powers and duties but the title as well.

3. Vice president to serve for disabled president. Whenever the President transmits to the President pro tempore of the Senate and the Speaker of the House of Representatives his written declaration that he is unable to discharge the powers and duties of his office, and until he transmits to them a written declaration to the contrary, such powers and duties shall be discharged by the Vice President as Acting President.

4. Procedure for disqualifying or requalifying president. Whenever the Vice President and a majority of either the principal officers of the executive departments or of such other body as Congress may by law provide, transmit to the President pro tempore of the Senate and the Speaker of the House of Representatives their written declaration that the President is unable to discharge the powers and duties of his office, the Vice President shall immediately assume the powers and duties of the office as Acting President.

Thereafter, when the President transmits to the President pro tempore of the Senate and the Speaker of the House of Representatives his written declaration that no inability exists, he shall resume the powers and duties of his office unless the Vice President and a majority of either the principal officers of the executive department[s] or of such other body as Congress may by law provide, transmit within four days to the President pro tempore of the Senate and the Speaker of the House of Representatives their written declaration that the President is unable to discharge the powers and duties of his office. Thereupon Congress shall decide the issue, assembling within forty-eight hours for that purpose if not in session. If the Congress, within twenty-one days after receipt of the latter written declaration, or, if Congress is not in session, within twenty-one days after Congress is required to assemble, determines by two-thirds vote of both Houses that the President is unable to discharge the powers and duties of his office, the Vice President shall continue to discharge the same as Acting President; otherwise, the President shall resume the powers and duties of his office. [Adopted 1967.]

Amendment XXVI. Lowering Voting Age

A response to the current revolt of youth. *See p. 942.*

1. Ballot for eighteen-year-olds. The right of citizens of the United States, who are eighteen years of age or older, to vote shall not be denied or abridged by the United States or any state on account of age.

2. Enforcement. The Congress shall have the power to enforce this article by appropriate legislation. [Adopted 1971.]

Amendment XXVII. Restricting Congressional Pay Raises

Reflects anti-incumbent sentiment of early 1990s. First proposed by James Madison in 1789; took 203 years to be ratified.

Congress not allowed to increase its current pay. No law varying the compensation for the services of the Senators and Representatives shall take effect, until an election of Representatives shall have intervened. [Adopted 1992.]

PHOTOGRAPH CREDITS

Chapter 1
p. 7, Library and Archives Canada / Maps, Plans and Charts Collection / NMC 93764; **p. 8,** Ansel Adams © by the Trustees of the Ansel Adams Publishing Rights Trust / Corbis; **p. 10,** Painting by Lloyd K. Townsend, Photo by Art Grossman; **p. 14,** © Bettmann / Corbis; **p. 16** Library of Congress; **p. 17,** © Bettmann / Corbis.

Chapter 2
p. 20, National Portrait Gallery, London; **p.23,** National Portrait Gallery / Smithsonian Institution, Washington, D.C. / Art Resource, New York; **p.28,** Phil Degginger / Bruce Coleman USA Photo Library.

Chapter 3
p. 33, Judith Cantz / Stock, Boston; **p. 37,** Mike Mazzaschi / Stock, Boston; **p. 39,** © British Library Board, All Rights Reserved, shelfmark 121.35; **p. 41,** from the collection of Gilcrease Museum, Tulsa, Oklahoma; **p. 43,** Copyright of Christie's Images, Ltd., 2000.

Chapter 4
p. 49, The Colonial Williamsburg Foundation, Williamsburg, Virginia; **p. 51,** The Library of Congress; **p. 52,** Courtesy of the Historical Society of Pennsylvania Collection, Atwater Kent Museum of Philadelphia; **p. 53,** Abby Aldrich Rockefeller Folk Art Collection, Colonial Williamsburg Foundation, Williamsburg, Virginia; **p. 55,** Worcester Art Museum, Worcester, Massachusetts, Gift of Mr. and Mrs. Albert W. Rice.

Chapter 5
p. 62, The Granger Collection; **p. 67,** Private Collection / Bridgeman Art Library, Ltd.; **p. 68,** The Granger Collection.

Chapter 6
p. 76, Image © Board of Trustees, National Gallery of Art, Washington, Paul Mellon Collection; **p. 78,** The Granger Collection; **p. 80,** © Richard T. Nowitz / Corbis.

Chapter 7
p. 86, Gift of Joseph W., William B., and Edward H.R. Revere, Courtesy of the Museum of Fine Arts, Boston; **p. 89 (left)** Library of Congress; **p. 89 (right),** Courtesy of the American Antiquarian Society; **p. 90,** The Granger Collection.

Chapter 8
p. 98, The Henry Francis du Pont Winterthur Museum; **p. 99,** The Granger Collection; **p. 104,** Courtesy of the Massachusetts Historical Society; **p.105,** The Metropolitan Museum of Art, Gift of John S. Kennedy, 1897, Photograph © 1992 The Metropolitan Museum of Art, New York; **p. 109,** Courtesy of the Historical Society of Pennsylvania Collection, Atwater Kent Museum of Philadelphia.

Chapter 9
p. 116, Courtesy of the Massachusetts Historical Society; **p.117,** National Gallery of Art, Washington, Andrew W. Mellon Fund; **p.123,** Courtesy of the Historical Society of Pennsylvania Collection; **p. 125,** Fraunces Tavern ® Museum, New York City.

Chapter 10
p. 136, Credit Suisse Collection of Americana, New York City; **p. 137,** Henry Francis du Pont Winterthur Museum; **p.141,** Prints Collection, The New York Public Library, Astor, Lenox, and Tilden Foundations; **p.144,** Virginia Chamber of Commerce, photo by D'adamo.

Chapter 11
p. 149, Courtesy, American Antiquarian Society; **p. 150,** © Bettmann / Corbis; **p. 154,** Collection of The New-York Historical Society, neg. 51322; **p. 157,** AP-Wide World Photos.

Chapter 12
p. 162, © Bettmann / Corbis; **p. 166,** The Metropolitan Museum of Art, Joseph Pulitzer Bequest, 1942; **p. 167,** Maryland Historical Society; **p. 172,** Collection of the Supreme Court of the United States.

Chapter 13
p. 178, Nelson-Atkins Museum of Art, Kansas City, Missouri (Purchase: Nelson Trust); **p. 181,** Image © Board of Trustees, National Gallery of Art, Washington, D.C., Andrew W. Mellon Fund; **p. 185,** The Granger Collection; **p. 189,** Collection of The New-York Historical Society, neg. 44812; **p. 191,** Texas State Library and Archives Commission; **p. 193,** Franklin Delano Library, Hyde Park, New York.

Chapter 14
p. 198, The Granger Collection; **p. 202,** Collection of The New-York Historical Society, neg. 41082; **p. 204,** The Granger Collection; **p. 206,** Cincinnati Museum Center - Cincinnati Historical Society Library; **p. 210,** The Granger Collection; **p. 211,** National Museum of American History, Division of Work and Industry, Smithsonian Institution, Washington, D.C.; **p. 213,** Museum of Fine Arts, Boston, Gift of Maxim Karolik for the M. and M. Karolik Collection of American Watercolors and Drawings, 1800-1895.

Chapter 15
p. 218, The Library of Congress; **p. 222,** Smithsonian Institution, Division of Cultural History, Washington, D.C.; **p. 224,** © Houghton Library, Harvard University; **p. 227,** © Bettmann / Corbis; **p. 231,** Berg Collection, The New York Public Library, Astor, Lenox and Tilden Foundations.

Chapter 16
p. 241, Musee de l'Homme, Paris / Art Resource, New York; **p. 243,** Missouri Historical Society, St. Louis; **p. 244,** National Portrait Gallery, Smithsonian Institution, Washington, D.C. / Art Resource, New York; **p. 245,** Historic New Orleans Collection, accession no. 1970.13.1.

Chapter 17
p. 254, Smithsonian American Art Museum, Washington, D.C. / Art Resource, New York; **p. 259,** Private Collection, photo Courtesy Masco Corporation; **p. 260,** Courtesy of The Bancroft Library, University of California, Berkeley.

Chapter 18
p. 266, The Granger Collection; **p. 268,** Brooklyn Museum of Art, 40.59a, Gift of Gwendolyn O. L. Conkling; **p. 273,** National Portrait Gallery, Smithsonian Institution, Washington, D.C. / Art Resource, New York.

Chapter 19
p.276, The Metropolitan Museum of Art, Gift of I.N. Phelps Stokes, Edward S. Hawes, and Marion Augusta Hawes, 1937 (37.14.00); **p. 278,** Print Collection, Miriam and Ira D. Wallach Division of Art, Prints and Photographs, The New York Public Library, Astor, Lenox and Tilden Foundations; **p. 283,** The Metropolitan Museum of Art. Gift of M. and M. Carl Stoeckel, 1897.

Chapter 20
p. 295, National Archives; **p. 302, (left)** Chicago History Museum, negative ICHi-15123; **p. 302, (right)** Decorative and Industrial Arts Department, Chicago History Museum, negative G1969.1737.

Chapter 21
p. 306, Library of Congress; **p. 309,** The Library of Congress; **p. 310,** three panels, *A Bit of War History: Contraband, Recruit, and Veteran*, The Metropolitan Museum of Art, Gift of Charles Stewart Smith, 1884; **p. 311,** John Hays Papers, Manuscript Division, the Library of Congress; **p. 316, (left)** The Granger Collection; **p.316, (right)** National Archives; **p. 318,** © Bettmann / Corbis.

Chapter 22
p. 322, The Library of Congress; **p. 324,** Tuskegee University Library; **p. 325,** *New-York Tribune*, Tuesday, August 22, 1865; **p.333, (top)** The Granger Collection; **p.333, (bottom)** The Granger Collection.

INDEX

49°N
WASHINGTON
1889
Columbia R.
OREGON COUNTRY
(By Agreement
with Britain, 1846)
OREGON
1859
IDAHO
1890
42°N
MONTANA
1889
Missouri R.
NORTH DAKOT
1889
SOUTH DAKOT
1889
WYOMING
1890
NEBRASKA
1867
LOUISIA
PURCHA
(From France,
PACIFIC
OCEAN
Great
Salt
Lake
NEVADA
1864
UTAH
1896
MEXICAN CESSION
(1848)
CALIFORNIA
1850
Colorado R.
COLORADO
1876
KANS
186
ARIZONA
1912
OKLA
NEW MEXICO
1912
TEXAS
(Independent Republic,
Annexed 1845)
GADSDEN PURCHASE
(From Mexico, 1853)
Rio Grande
TEXAS
1845
Nueces R.
PACIFIC OCEAN
HAWAII
1959
HAWAII
(Annexed 1898)
0 50 100 Miles
0 50 100 Kilometers
RUSSIA
ALASKA
1959
CANADA
ALASKA PURCHASE
(From Russia, 1867)
PACIFIC
OCEAN
MEXICO
0 200 400 Miles
0 200 400 Kilometers

Territorial Growth of the United States

with Dates of States' Admission to the Union

GREENLAND
(DENMARK)
ICELAN
ALASKA
(U.S.)
CANADA
UNITED STATES
MEXICO
Azores
Bermuda
ATLANTIC OCEAN
PACIFIC OCEAN
Midway Is.
Hawaiian Is.
BAHAMAS
CUBA
DOMINICAN REP.
Virgin Is.
JAMAICA
HAITI
BELIZE
HONDURAS
Puerto Rico
ST. KITTS AND NEVIS
ANTIGUA AND BARBUDA
DOMINICA
BARBADOS
ST. LUCIA
GRENADA
ST. VINCENT AND
THE GRENADINES
GUATEMALA
EL SALVADOR
NICARAGUA
COSTA RICA
PANAMA
TRINIDAD AND TOBAGO
VENEZUELA
GUYANA
FR. GUIANA
COLOMBIA
SURINAM
ECUADOR
Galapagos Is.
PERU
BRAZIL
BOLIVIA
PARAGUAY
CHILE
URUGUAY
ARGENTINA
Falkland Is.
Easter Is.
WESTERN
SAMOA
TONGA
WESTERN
SAHARA
(MOROCCO)
CAPE
VERDE
SENEGAL
GAMBIA
GUINEA-BISSAU
SIERRA
LEONE
LIBERIA
Equator
80°N
60°N
40°N
20°N
0°
20°S
40°S
60°S
80°S
160°W
140°W
120°W
100°W
80°W
60°W
40°W
20°W

RUSSIA
FINLAND
SWEDEN
ESTONIA
LATVIA
LITHUANIA
BELARUS
POLAND
UKRAINE
MOLDOVA
CZ.
SLK.
AUS.
HUNG.
SLN.
CR.
ROMANIA
B. H.
SE.
BULGARIA
ITALY
MO.
MAC.
ALBANIA
GREECE
GEORGIA
TURKEY
ARMENIA
CYPRUS
MALTA
TUNISIA
LEBANON
ISRAEL
SYRIA
IRAQ
AZERBAIJAN
IRAN
JORDAN
KUWAIT
BAHRAIN
QATAR
SAUDI ARABIA
UNITED ARAB EMIRATES
OMAN
YEMEN
KAZAKHSTAN
UZBEKISTAN
TURKMENISTAN
KYRGYZSTAN
TAJIKISTAN
AFGHANISTAN
PAKISTAN
MONGOLIA
PEOPLE'S REPUBLIC OF CHINA
N. KOREA
S. KOREA
JAPAN
PACIFIC OCEAN
NEPAL
BHUTAN
BANGLADESH
INDIA
MYANMAR (BURMA)
LAOS
TAIWAN
THAILAND
VIETNAM
CAMBODIA (KAMPUCHEA)
PHILIPPINES
SRI LANKA
MALDIVES
BRUNEI DARUSSALAM
MALAYSIA
SINGAPORE
INDONESIA
EAST TIMOR
PALAU
PAPUA NEW GUINEA
Mariana Islands
Guam
Wake I.
MARSHALL ISLANDS
Caroline Islands
KIRIBATI
NAURU
SOLOMON IS.
TUVALU
VANUATU
FIJI
New Caledonia
LIBYA
EGYPT
CHAD
SUDAN
ERITREA
DJIBOUTI
ETHIOPIA
SOMALIA
CENTRAL AFRICAN REP.
CAMEROON
GABON
UGANDA
KENYA
RWANDA
DEM. REP. OF CONGO
BURUNDI
TANZANIA
SEYCHELLES
INDIAN OCEAN
COMOROS
ANGOLA
ZAMBIA
MALAWI
MADAGASCAR
NAMIBIA
ZIMBABWE
MAURITIUS
BOTSWANA
MOZAMBIQUE
SWAZILAND
SOUTH AFRICA
LESOTHO
AUSTRALIA
NEW ZEALAND
20°E
40°E
60°E
80°E
100°E
120°E
140°E
160°E
ABBREVIATIONS
AUS. AUSTRIA
BEL. BELGIUM
B. H. BOSNIA AND HERZEGOVINA
CR. CROATIA
CZ. CZECH REPUBLIC
DEN. DENMARK
HUNG. HUNGARY
LUX. LUXEMBOURG
MAC. FORMER YUGOSLAV REPUBLIC OF MACEDONIA
MO. MONTENEGRO
NETH. NETHERLANDS
SE. SERBIA
SLK. SLOVAKIA
SLN. SLOVENIA
SWITZ. SWITZERLAND